Personality

Personality

Fourth Edition

Seymour Feshbach

Bernard Weiner
University of California, Los Angeles

Arthur Bohart
California State University, Dominguez Hills

D. C. Heath and Company
Lexington, Massachusetts   Toronto

Address editorial correspondence to:
D. C. Heath and Company
125 Spring Street
Lexington, MA 02173

Acquisitions Editor: James Miller
Production Editor: Celena Sun
Designer: Judith Miller
Production Coordinator: Richard Tonachel
Permissions Editor: Margaret Roll

Published simultaneously in Canada.

Printed in the United States of America.

International Standard Book Number: 0-669-35442-2

Library of Congress Catalog Number: 94-73553

10 9 8 7 6 5 4 3 2 1

To Norma
　　　—S. F.

To Janna and Miira
　　　—B. W.

To Maura and Karen
　　　—A. B.

Preface

In a sense we are all personality psychologists. We are making an inference about the genetics of personality when we say, "She has her father's personality." We are judging child-rearing practices when we note, "They're good parents." We are noticing the stability of personality characteristics when we complain, "He's always been stubborn!" We also hold our own "theories" of personality with "laws" like "Thin people are introverted" and "Red hair indicates an impulsive personality." Thus the study of personality is part of our everyday lives, and good students of the subject are better able to adapt to the demands of living in a complex society. As a result, the study of personality is extremely popular at colleges and universities.

Personality is intended for an undergraduate audience at two- and four-year colleges and universities. Because we have avoided unnecessary jargon, an extensive background in psychology is not a prerequisite for the use of this book. We have tried to produce a readable text that is easily understood at the college level. However, respecting most students' intelligence and ability, we have not written "down" to them.

The Fourth Edition of *Personality* improves upon the Third Edition. One significant change is the inclusion of a new chapter on the development of identity. Another is expanded coverage of cultural issues that pertain to the study and conception of personality. As the United States becomes an increasingly multicultural society, it is imperative that psychology begin to examine its own hidden cultural assumptions and to take a broader look at human behavior. We hope we have taken a beginning step in that direction in this edition.

In addition, the Fourth Edition includes new material on the role of genetics in personality, new developments in psychoanalytic theory, the "big five" personality trait concept, and change and continuity in personality over the life span. Because the two chapters in the Third Edition on perceived freedom and control and achievement motivation appeared to have some continuity in terms of content, we have attempted to merge these two chapters in the current edition. We hope to provide a broad, integrative look at how individuals perceive the causes of their own behavior and how that influences many aspects of personal functioning.

We have moved the section on the structure of personality so that it now follows the section on personality theories. This move was requested by some reviewers, who felt that the topics of personality assessment and traits should be covered earlier in the course rather than later.

Finally, there are many other additions to various chapters, which update the text and keep it contemporary. In short, we believe the book presents an up-to-date and balanced view of the individual and includes discussion of many topics currently under investigation. The opportunity to revise the text allowed us to correct shortcomings and take into consideration the comments of many students who have used the book.

Most personality textbooks fall into one of two categories. The majority present in detail many of the theories that have been devised to account for human personality. These texts discuss between ten and twenty-five theories, introducing readers to all of the concepts and ideas of each theorist in turn. In contrast, the second type of text is narrowly focused, advocating a particular point of view and fitting the many phenomena of personality into a specific perspective. Such textbooks are often written by proponents of learning theory approaches, with their special allegiance to behavior modification or social learning, or by humanists, with their great concern for the self and subjective experience. In our opinion, both approaches are unsatisfactory, because they neglect many facets of the field of personality. The study of personality includes many subtopics, as well as theories, and no single theoretical approach can adequately account for the vast array of observations in the field.

Unlike these two approaches, *Personality* takes up many subtopics and discusses the views of the major theorists concerning them. This approach allows us to compare various viewpoints on different facets of the field of personality, while avoiding advocating any single theory as "correct" or aligning ourselves with any particular school of thought. Our organization also encourages students to think critically and to contrast each theorist's views with those of the others, thus deepening students' understanding and setting the stage for class discussions or papers on the various issues.

Personality has been guided by certain assumptions, as well as by judgments about what a personality textbook should include. Our approach begins with the assumption that there are various interrelated subparts of the field of personality, including theories of personality (Part II), personality assessment (Part III); personality development (Part IV), and personality dynamics (Part V). In addition, the person is a product of both genetic dispositions and the physical and social environment (Part I). Second, we feel that it is necessary to be eclectic rather than to advocate a particular point of view. However, we do accept the idea that there are enduring personality dispositions, or traits, and we contend that the person and the environment are always interacting and contributing to behavior. Third, we feel it essential to present a text based on the experimental findings — that is, a text guided by scientific method and grounded on empirical evidence. Finally, given the myriad of topics available for discussion, we have chosen those that are both central to the field and intrinsically interesting to students. Thus, we have devoted special attention to such areas as self-concept, dreams, hypnosis, love, aggression, achievement strivings, and personal responsibility. In *Personality,* by means of a thorough analysis of these and other topics, we hope to add to the reader's knowledge by conveying up-to-date facts and theories, as well as dispelling some of the false beliefs held by untrained people. We believe that we have achieved our goals — that *Personality* is inclusive, eclectic, empirical, and challenging—and that at times we have provided a new perspective on the various subtopics of the field of personality.

We have tried to make our text comprehensive. But although the book is of an average length for a semester course, some professors may choose not to assign every chapter. Because of the structure, we believe our book lends itself to different ways of organizing a course in personality. For instance, professors who may prefer to emphasize the development and structure of personality could assign chapters 1 and 2 on genetics and environment, the theories chapters, the structure chapters, and the development chapters, and ignore the chapters on dynamics and complex personality processes. Other teachers, who are more interested in the dynamics and structure of personality, might assign the theories chapters, the structure chapters, and the dynamics and complex personality processes chapters, omitting the development chapters. Instructors whose primary interest lies in the theories could focus on the theories, assigning selected sections of other chapters that are relevant to topics in the theories chapters. For instance, part or all of the chapter on consciousness, and part of the chapter on the dynamics of behavior might be used to supplement the chapters on psychoanalysis. The chapter on phenomenological theories could be supplemented with the chapter on perceived control and achievement motivation, and with the chapter on the self. These two chapters could also be used to supplement the chapter on learning theory approaches, particularly with regard to social learning and cognitive behavioral approaches.

Professors who are either empirically-oriented or who want to focus on what is contemporary in the field might wish to skip the theory chapters and focus on the rest of the chapters in the book, all of which tend to be relatively more empirical. Professors who are more interested in personality processes than in personality structure might wish to emphasize the chapters on dynamics and on complex personality processes, and perhaps de-emphasize the chapters on traits and assessment. In sum, there are many ways that this book can be creatively used.

To aid in the learning process, we have included a number of teaching aids in the text itself. Interesting anecdotes are highlighted and examined in detail. Each chapter is followed by a point-by-point summary that provides a ready overview of the material in that chapter. Thought Questions relate the material in the chapter to the student's everyday experiences. In addition to these in-text aids, the book is accompanied by an *Instructor's Guide*, which contains over 1,000 multiple-choice and essay-type test items.

We are grateful to those who reviewed the manuscript for this edition: Sylvia Santos, California State University, Dominguez Hills; Hal Arkowitz, University of Arizona; Etzel Cardena, Uniformed Services University of the Health Sciences; Paul M. Fromson, Elon College; Stella D. Garcia, University of Texas, San Antonio; Bill C. Henry, Colby College; Anita E. Kelly, University of Notre Dame; Carolyn C. Morf, University of Utah; Robert W. Newby, Tarleton State University; Michael F. Shaughnessy, Eastern New Mexico University; T. Gale Thompson, Bethany College; Bill Thornton, University of Southern Maine; and Paul H. Wright, University of North Dakota. We also want to thank Virginia Harrelson, Lilian Gonzales, and Lorraine Woods for their assistance in tracking down relevant articles.

S.F.
B.W.
A.B.

Contents

INTRODUCTION

Definition of *Personality*

The field of personality is enormously complex and diverse. As a student taking this class you may be interested in questions such as What is my personality — what are my fundamental characteristics? How changeable is my personality? How did I acquire my personality? How is my personality organized? What factors determine my behavior — my motives, my self, my traits, my thoughts, my emotions? How do all those factors interact and interrelate? How can I understand others' personality? Are all aspects of my personality conscious, or are some parts determined by unconscious forces — how well can I know myself? What role do my emotions play in my personality and my behavior? Why are some people more able than others to handle stress and conflict? Are humans basically aggressive, or basically loving?

As you can see, the field of personality addresses the most basic questions of what it means to be a functioning human being. Therefore, it is difficult to define *personality,* and different writers have emphasized different aspects. For the person on the street, personality most fundamentally refers to what is distinctive about an individual. People describe themselves and their friends in terms of what is distinctive about them: he is shy, quiet, and sensitive; she is outgoing, friendly, and open to different experiences. In addition, people often use the term *personality* to refer to someone who is not only distinctive but interesting in a positive way. Thus they might say that someone "has a lot of personality," meaning that the person stands out in charm, colorfulness, or interesting characteristics. When people say that someone has "no personality," they mean that there is little about the person that is distinctive, interesting, or colorful.

For some psychologists, *personality* is largely defined in terms of individual differences, that is, in terms of the enduring characteristics that differ from person to person. Thus, for many, personality is typically equated with personality traits. However, as we discuss in Chapter 13, personality can also be considered to include one's motives, thoughts, emotions, beliefs, and values. Further, one's personality may depend on how all these things are organized.

In this text, we adopt a broader view of personality than one that focuses on individual differences. For us, the field of personality consists of the study of all

1

the issues and topics we have mentioned, and how they inter-relate. In essence, it deals with the study of all the factors that play a role in how an individual's overall functioning is organized.

The study of personality intersects with other aspects of psychology. Just as how we perceive and learn is relevant to our overall functioning, so is our genetic endowment. Our overall functioning is also influenced by social and cultural variables. What distinguishes the study of personality from the study of social and cultural psychology is that we focus on how those many variables influence the functioning of the individual. How our personalities develop is also a topic of relevance, and, therefore, the field of personality intersects with that of developmental psychology. Finally, how personality functioning can go awry is an important part of personality. Therefore, the field of personality overlaps with the fields of abnormal and clinical psychology as well.

In sum, for us, personality refers to (1) the relatively enduring behavior patterns that distinguish individuals from one another, (2) the overall organization and structure of individuals' behavior patterns, and (3) the patterns of interactions between this organization and both external factors — such as cultural, environmental, and social variables — and internal factors — such as motivations, emotions, and thoughts.

The Field of Personality and the Structure of This Textbook

Because of its great complexity and diversity, the field of personality presents a great challenge to both the student and the psychologist. Many individuals associate this field of study with grand theorists, such as Sigmund Freud and Carl Jung, who postulated comprehensive schemes that attempted to explain phenomena as far ranging as war, neurosis, and dream symbolism. But the formulation of a general theory of personality is just one aspect of a vast mosaic. Other personality psychologists focus on less ambitious, and more attainable, goals. A number of personality psychologists have been concerned with the structure of personality — identifying basic traits, such as introversion or the need for achievement, and ascertaining how they can be best assessed. Others have examined how these characteristics come into existence — that is, the genetic and experiential determinants of personality development. Still other personality psychologists are interested in personality dynamics, or how personality structures interact with the environment to generate behavior. Issues such as stress, conflict, and frustration are part of the study of the dynamics of personality.

The four main divisions in the study of personality — theory, structure, development, and dynamics — are not completely separate. For example, Freud's general theory includes a discussion of personality structure (such as the "anal" character), how such a trait might develop (conflict with parents during the period of toilet training), and its effects on later behavior (the tendency to hoard money or to be compulsively clean). Nevertheless, the four major areas within personality do have somewhat separate histories and did not develop simultaneously. They therefore provide the organizing framework for this book.

In the ensuing chapters we examine contemporary theoretical and empirical efforts that address the viability of a general theory of personality; traits, their measurement, and development; and the manner in which these traits influence an individual's actions in particular environments.

We are sympathetic to many theoretical positions and types of empirical investigations because of the enormous complexity of the problems with which they attempt to deal. Thus, our discussion of personality research and theories will be from the perspective of psychologists who are not limited to one particular theory but draw upon a number of them. In our framework, the individual both acts and reacts, has unique aspirations and fantasies, and is conscious of the future as well as the past and the present. We will consider personal behavior within a broad social-cultural context, for one must be sensitive to the powerful effects that the values of the culture, the family, and the larger society exert on behavior. Individuals are social beings, functioning in particular cultural settings. At the same time, one must have some appreciation of the role of genetics and evolution in human behavior. We are also biological creatures shaped by evolution.

Psychology cannot yet provide the answers to many of the difficult questions regarding personality. The relatively objective and systematic study of personality is still in its infancy, less than seven decades old. Our scientific tools are still quite limited. We have no magical procedures that will reveal the inner depths of our minds. For ethical reasons, we cannot and should not freely experiment with infants, raising them under carefully controlled, laboratory conditions. We do not have the power to alter culture, socioeconomic structures, and other significant features of the human environment that play an important role in personality. Nor do we have the power to alter the human body. For these reasons, we cannot reach the precision of measurement and experimental control in the study of human behavior that characterizes research in physics and chemistry.

Nevertheless, much can be learned by examining personality from an empirical, scientific perspective. At the very least, adoption of a scientific approach enables one to think about personality issues in a more analytic, discriminating manner. There are a great many, often conflicting, current assertions regarding personality. For example, "One's basic personality is formed in the first two years of life" versus "We are constantly changing and growing"; "Personality changes as the situation changes" versus "We are who we are, regardless of context"; "Sex and aggression are the basic human drives" versus "The basic human goal is self-actualization." Research provides us with the data to discriminate between valid and unfounded assertions, between assertions that have yet to be tested and those that are probably not testable.

We also apply a scientific approach to the examination of theories of personality. Because personality theories typically attempt to account for different aspects of human behavior, it is often difficult to call one "better" than another. But one must also be critical when evaluating the relevant evidence and the logic of each theory. We are able to use common scientific criteria to evaluate and compare theories. These criteria include the breadth and comprehensiveness of the theory (how much of the data on personality is explained); the testability of the theory; its degree of empirical support; and its heuristic or generative value.

Chapter Topics

Our view of personality dictates the organization of this text. The two most basic aspects that influence the development and functioning of personality are biological and genetic factors, and environmental and sociocultural factors. In Part 1 we consider these two basic influences. In Part 2 we turn to a consideration of the three major groups of theories that have influenced how we think about the functioning of the whole person: psychodynamic theories, behavioral and social learning theories, and phenomenological theories. In Part 3 we examine the basic structure of personality and consider the issue of traits. We also consider the tests and procedures used to assess personality. In Part 4 we consider developmental aspects of personality, including the development of the self and identity. In Parts 5 and 6 we consider a variety of specific topics related to personality functioning: the dynamics of conflict, emotion and stress, consciousness, perceived control and achievement motivation, and love and hate.

That various sections of the book overlap and are interrelated will be evident. For example, in our discussion of personality development in Chapter 13, we must return to issues raised in Chapter 1 regarding the roles of nature and nurture in shaping the person. And in Chapter 14, which addresses conflict and frustration, we must return to issues raised by the broader personality theorists, as examined in Chapters 3–6. Although we must break the whole into parts to present details, we trust our approach will be clear to our readers; that is, we do perceive the field of personality as an integrated whole.

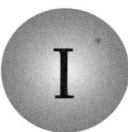

INNATE AND ENVIRONMENTAL DETERMINANTS OF PERSONALITY

A key question for personality psychologists is: "Are we what we are because of nature or because of nurture?" When the question is phrased in this manner, neither answer can be correct, for the answers are not mutually exclusive. There clearly are both inborn and social-cultural influences on the individual. Genetics and environment — nature *and* nurture — regulate and guide each person.

In Chapter 1 we examine some of the innate determinants of personality and behavior. We observe that, as products of a long evolutionary history, human beings are predisposed to certain patterns of behavior. In addition, specific genetic blueprints provide the foundation for personality and behavior.

But it is evident that individuals' personalities are greatly influenced by the contexts that surround them and by the experiences they have had. Individuals brought up in different cultures or social classes behave differently. If one wants to predict what an individual is doing or thinking at a given time, some of the best predictors are the point in history when the individual was born and where he or she is living. In Chapter 2 we examine some of these social and cultural influences as well as other kinds of environmental influences.

Culture not only influences individuals; it also influences psychological theories themselves. There is increasing reason to believe that the "grand theories" of Western psychology reflect certain biases about the nature of people that characterize Western culture. In Chapter 2 we also consider the effects of Western cultural biases on personality theories.

Chapters 1 and 2 do not attempt to give complete accounts of the genetics of personality or the social determinants of action; full courses are devoted to these topics. Rather, we introduce the context of the person: an individual with unique predispositions who is nevertheless modifiable and shaped by surroundings.

1 Genetic Determinants of Personality

Charles Darwin introduced the controversial conclusion that the human species is the product of a long period of evolution in *The Origin of Species* and *The Descent of Man*. His arguments had an enormous influence on the field of personality. First, his theory of evolution assumed scientific determinism—that is, the theory assumed that the most complex aspects of behavior in all species are subject to scientific and rational analysis and are not due to accident or divine intervention. This principle was accepted by psychologists in their study of both nonhuman and human behavior. Second, Darwin focused attention on the function or adaptive value of biological structures and behavior. Psychologists have been guided by this viewpoint as they search for the usefulness of a particular pattern of action. Still another implication of Darwin's work for the study of human personality is the importance of species differences and of individual differences within species. These issues are addressed in this chapter.

Darwin proposed a simple yet powerful theory to explain the process of evolution that linked the development of species with the concept of inheritance —the transmission of characteristics from one generation to another. He stated: "Any variation, however slight and from whatever cause proceeding, if it be in any degree of profitability to an individual . . . will tend to the preservation of that individual, and will generally be inherited by its offspring. The offspring, also, will thus have a better chance of surviving" (1869, p. 61). Because the "variations" are transmitted from generation to generation, Darwin provided a clue for the role of heredity in social evolution.

In this chapter we examine some of the genetic determinants of personality structure and behavior. Although biochemicals and hormones, brain mechanisms, and other biological factors influence personality, we focus here on the topic of genetics because of the vast research in this area and because it well illustrates the role of biological givens in behavior.

It is helpful to frame a genetic approach to personality within the context of evolutionary theory. Among the questions we discuss in this chapter are: What limitations do inherited characteristics place on learning? Do humans have instincts, or innate urges and unlearned patterns of behavior? What are the tenets of the emerging field of sociobiology? Are there universal facial expressions or behaviors that are exhibited across cultures? And can it be demonstrated scientifically that personality characteristics and behavioral problems are in part genetically influenced? We will present evidence that the answers are yes and that a complete theory of personality must consider innate factors.

THE NATURE/NURTURE CONTROVERSY

Limitations on Learning

The notion that personality structure and human behavior might be partially determined by genetically rooted factors has met with some opposition (see McClearn, 1962). First, many psychologists believe that the possible influence of inborn characteristics or propensities is overcome by humans' vast learning capacities and social experiences. This viewpoint was carried to its extreme by John B. Watson, founder of the behaviorist movement in the United States. Watson argued that a human being is a "blank slate" (*tabula rasa*) at birth.

> Give me a dozen healthy infants, well-formed, and my own specified world to bring them up in and I'll guarantee to take any one at random and train him to become any type of specialist I might select — doctor, lawyer, artist, merchant-chief and, yes, even beggar-man and thief, regardless of his talents, penchants, tendencies, abilities, vocations, and race of his ancestors. (1930, p. 104)

However, a great deal of research evidence casts doubt on Watson's conception. Primarily because of ethical constraints, this research has been conducted with nonhumans rather than with human subjects. Although one must be cautious in extrapolating or generalizing the findings to humans, the human-nonhuman continuity and the fact that humans are also biological creatures with an evolutionary history suggest that the findings do tell us something about human personality and behavior.

Teaching Nonhumans Tricks. B. F. Skinner and his followers have demonstrated that behavior can be modified through the use of reward; that is, prior responses can be increased in strength through reinforcement. It is possible to train animals like rats and pigeons to engage in such apparently bizarre behaviors as playing ping-pong by rewarding responses that approximate the behavior that one wishes to produce, until finally the experimenter-designated "correct" response is emitted. This procedure is called *shaping*.

Encouraged by these demonstrations, Breland and Breland (1961) tried to teach behavioral "tricks" to animals for commercial appearances at circuses and on television. However, many of their attempts failed. For example, the Brelands tried to teach pigs to deposit wooden coins in a piggy bank. Once the pigs associated the coins with their food reward, however, it became increasingly difficult to make them deposit the coins. Instead, they would drop and root with their new-found "money."

The Brelands suggested that the learned response (deposit) conflicted with an instinctive tendency. They labeled this process *instinctive drift*. That is, the organism was "carried" from the learned response back to the instinctive response. Thus, for example, the rooting response, which the pig instinctively employs in the process of obtaining food, replaced the banking behavior because the coins became associated with food reward. Similarly, the Brelands found it impossible to teach chicks to play baseball; the chicks chased the ball instead of performing the "correct," learned response of circling the bases. Such a search-and-follow tactic is how chicks typically find food, is instrumental in their survival, and thus conflicts with antagonistic performances. On the basis of these observations, the Brelands wrote a book amusingly entitled *The Misbehavior of Organisms,* to contrast their findings with those reported in Skinner's *The Behavior of Organisms.* The Brelands' experiences clearly demonstrate that innate factors set limits on what behaviors can be learned and performed.

Taste Aversions.   Research has also shown that not all stimuli are capable of serving as cues for animals to engage in certain responses. For example, if a rat is given saccharin-flavored water prior to a shock, that taste will not serve as a signal that shock is forthcoming. However, the saccharin can be an effective signal to learn an induced food poisoning. That is, rats will learn to avoid the saccharin water if drinking it is followed by illness, but not if it is followed by shock. On the other hand, lights and sounds are cues that *can* be learned to signal shock; rats will avoid or escape from situations in which such cues are followed by shock (Garcia and Koelling, 1966). These relationships are consistent with evolutionary demands. There is a natural connection between eating and nausea, but not between visual cues and food-related distress.

In sum, it is evident that biological factors play important roles in determining what can and cannot be learned. The simple belief that virtually any response can be learned, as espoused by Watson and perhaps Skinner, clearly is not correct. Although this research has used nonhuman subjects, the postulation of a genetic continuity between humans and nonhumans suggests that this principle also applies in the case of human behavior.

The Role of Genetics

In contrast with those who focus on learning as the primary component in behavior are those who assert that humans follow some preestablished blueprint enacted at the moment of conception. Clearly, if personality and behavior are shaped by learning and experience, then humans are subject to change, for new habits, attitudes, and modes of action can be taught. But if the cause of action is perceived as a fixed and immutable inborn characteristic, it is easy to reach the pessimistic (and erroneous) conclusion that change cannot be accomplished. This reasoning has discouraged the acceptance of genetic principles.

Still another factor that has discouraged the acceptance of heredity as an influence on personality is the American credo that "all people are created equal." Acceptance of genetic postulates carries the danger of an elitist position asserting that people are created unequal and therefore deserve to remain unequal. Elitists might contend, for example, that because males are *born* more independent and competitive, they should serve in important occupational roles, while women, because they are *born* more dependent and cooperative, should remain in the home, caring for the family. This conviction, even if the genetic assumption were true, ignores the importance of learning and socialization, so highly stressed by Watson and others, and overlooks the great biological variation that is exhibited within such groups as males and females. (Of course, in this instance there is no evidence supporting these presumed male-female genetic differences, although there are some differences in the brains of sexes in some nonhuman animal species). Indeed, racists are often interested in examining differences (along racial lines) and believe these differences to be genetically determined. However, it is an error to believe that all racists are hereditarians and that therefore all hereditarians are racists. Yet this illogical jump is often made, disposing one to dismiss the role of heredity in studying human characteristics (see Dixon & Johnson, 1980).

A further corruption of the genetic position has been exhibited by extremists advocating eugenics, or the improvement of the human race by the application of the laws of heredity. In Nazi Germany, for example, eugenicists argued for the extinction of certain individuals and groups in order to produce a more perfect species.

But in spite of learning theorists' arguments and the dangers inherent in applying the principles of heredity, there is increasing evidence for genetic influence on a wide range of aspects of personality and behavior. Our commonsense observations that "like begets like" and the vague notion that behavior is due to "human nature" do contain some degree of truth. Behavior is a product of both nature and nurture, i.e, what one brings into the world and how this is influenced by experience. Learning and experience are central explanations of human action, but genetic roots cannot be disregarded. This position is more and more evident in the field of personality. As Plomin (1989) states: "Increasing acceptance of hereditary influence on individual differences in development represents one of the most remarkable changes in the field of psychology that has occurred during the decade since 1979 . . . ." (p. 105).

The passion and political overtones surrounding the nature/nurture controversy make it especially important to think clearly about these issues. In assessing the implications of the studies presented in this chapter, a distinction must be made between scientific and social significance. It is of scientific importance to demonstrate the presence or absence of genetic determinants of such behaviors as dominance, sociability, alcoholism, criminality, and mental disorders. However, it may be that environmental factors are far more important. Moreover, behaviors that have strong genetic determinants still can be modified through learning and experience. For example, phenylketonuria (PKU), a genetic mental deficiency, can be prevented by an environmental factor (early dietary manipulation). This deficiency also is interesting from a genetic viewpoint in that it is virtually unknown among Jews. (On the other hand, Tay-Sachs disease, a lethal central nervous system disorder, is especially prevalent in the Jewish population.)

At the same time, the fact that personality or behavior can be modified through learning does not negate the significance of genetic or biological variables. Watson may have been able to train a child with a genetic tendency toward introversion to become an outgoing, successful salesperson. However, the training may have been more difficult and extensive than it would have been with a child disposed toward extroversion. One would also want to know whether there were any negative side effects of training, whether the individual enjoyed being a salesperson, and so on.

In sum, the relation between genetics and personality is complex, and as students, scientists, and citizens, we need to think sensibly about it. We want to be able to analyze the meaning of such statements as "Mothers have innate mothering instincts" and "Humans have an innate aggressive drive" and to recognize that an assertion like "War is due to the human instinct for aggression" is nonsense.

ALL HUMANS ARE ALIKE

The Question of Instincts

Instincts are often regarded as genetic givens. An *instinct* or, more appropriately, instinctive behavior can refer to either (1) an unlearned, fixed pattern of activity found in all members of a species, such as nest building in birds and web spinning by spiders; or (2) a specific motivational tendency that is inferred from overt behavior. An instinct in this second sense is a potential toward action and is considered an unlearned "want" or "urge" built into the structure of the organism. It is imperative that "must" find expression, although it does not have to be recognized by the organism. Although the ends, or goals, of instincts (urges) are presumed to be fixed, the means of expression can be quite diverse. For example, Freud suggested that aggressive instincts can be satisfied through war, antisocial behavior, or self-destructive acts.

Genotype Versus Phenotype.   The notion that an aggressive urge can be satisfied by a variety of behaviors calls attention to an important distinction between genotype and phenotype. In genetics, *phenotype* refers to the surface manifestation of a characteristic; *genotype,* to the underlying genetic structure. Even when an individual possesses a certain genotype, it may be manifested in vastly different ways on the surface depending on the environment and experience. A good example is height. While this is genetically determined to some extent, nutrition (an environmental factor) also plays a major role in how tall an individual actually will be.

In psychology, individuals who have the genotype for a certain personality trait will not necessarily display that trait in the same fashion. Experiences will shape how that trait is displayed in behavior. It is possible that irritability has a genetic component. Yet some individuals may learn to express anger in prosocial ways and become crusaders for justice; others may express it in antisocial, destructive ways; and still others may turn anger against themselves in self-destructive acts. In this chapter *genotype* refers to the underlying genetic makeup of the individual, while phenotype is an observed behavior or characteristic.

Instincts as "Urges." The notion that human beings are guided by "inner urges" and that such a genotype leads to a variety of phenotypic behaviors was very prevalent in the early part of this century. Psychologists at that time often employed the concept of instinct to account for a broad array of human and nonhuman behavior. Holt (1931, p. 428) satirized the overuse of the word *instinct:* "If he goes with his fellows, it is the 'herd instinct' which activates him; if he walks alone, it is the 'anti-social instinct'; . . . if he twiddles his thumbs, it is the 'thumb-twiddling instinct.' Thus, everything is explained with the facility of magic — word magic." Some even contended that there must be an instinct to believe in instincts!

In the face of such criticisms, the use of instinct as an explanatory construct began to wane (see Beach, 1955). However, in more recent years ethologists, who study animal behavior in natural settings, have presented evidence supporting the notion of internal urges. This concept is perhaps most dramatically illustrated in what has been labeled *vacuum behavior,* or behavior patterns that appear when an appropriate stimulus is *not* present. For example, a starling raised in captivity will sometimes engage in complex sequences of hunting, killing, and even eating prey, even though there is no prey in the cage. The bird thus seems to be acting on an instinctive urge. In a similar manner, caged female birds sometimes take hold of their own feathers and go through the motions of building a nest with them.

Ethologists such as Lorenz (1950) and Tinbergen (1951) account for vacuum behavior by suggesting that such actions have their own energy source. If the action does not occur, the energy accumulates; expressing the action discharges the energy. When energy accumulates, the response is likely to be expressed in inappropriate settings. Hence vacuum behaviors were considered to be goaded by internal agitations or pressures that persist over time. However, this belief is not now accepted by most ethologists.

One might think that the behavior of a captive starling has little to do with complex human actions. Yet Freud contended that humans have an aggressive instinct that increases over time if it is not expressed in action. Indeed, many individuals advocate the creation of socially acceptable channels in which to drain our aggressive energy, such as competition on the football field. This view is examined in detail in subsequent chapters; here we will merely note that the energy models suggested by Lorenz and Tinbergen are not widely accepted (see Hinde, 1960; Lehrman, 1953). Critics argue that the so-called accumulated energy is nowhere to be found. Ethologists, too, have recognized the shortcomings of this mechanical approach, and today few adhere to such energy models. Indeed, there is a growing field of cognitive ethology, and many ethologists now believe that the behavior of nonhumans is as social and intentional as human action.

Instinctive Patterns of Behavior

Recall that instinct, in addition to meaning a genotypic urge, also refers to an unlearned pattern of behavior that is characteristic of all members of a species of the same sex at the same level of development. Birds' responses to mating calls and squirrels' hoarding of food are examples of such unlearned patterns of responses. These behaviors are caused primarily by genetically transmitted physiological states and functions; they are akin to the built-in behaviors exhibited by plants, such as movement toward light. These instinctive behaviors frequently are not single responses, but are action sequences that follow a predetermined, predictable course. Furthermore, the observed behaviors often are crucial for survival and therefore are interpreted in an evolutionary sense. For example, it is known that the stickleback fish will attack any other fish of its color and often any object of this particular color. This behavior results in *species-spacing,* or spreading species members apart so that there is sufficient food available for survival. Distinctive birdsong often also has a species-spacing function.

The *isolation paradigm* is the experimental procedure most often used to demonstrate that behavior is innate. In such studies, nonhuman newborns or infants are reared in isolation so that they cannot observe others or "practice" particular responses. Then they are given the opportunity to engage in a particular behavior. For example, a bird is isolated from other birds of its species, so that it never hears a mating call. Then it is taken from isolation and placed in a situation in which a mating call would be appropriate for other, normally reared birds. If the bird responds, it is exhibiting *innate behavior.* Typically, a response is believed to be innate if it is constant across all members of a species, if it appears even when the animal has been raised in isolation, and if it is elicited the first time that the animal is placed in the appropriate environment. Research has demonstrated many such responses, such as birdsong and nest building, and it has been concluded that these responses have strong genetic determinants.

It often is difficult to prove with certainty that a response is innate or unlearned rather than learned and experience-based (see Lehrman, 1970). In addition, the higher the organism is in the nonhuman-human scale, the more likely that the behavior is influenced by learning. Among human beings one might expect to find few unlearned patterns of behavior, other than reflexive responses such as the eyeblink or knee jerk. However, it is quite possible that there are innate reactions — fears, aversions, preferences for particular stimulus situations — that have significance for human personality. Fear of the grotesque or a child's responsiveness to the mother's breast and the warmth of her body are possible examples of such reaction tendencies.

Infant Features and Maternal Care.   Whether behaviors such as maternal care among humans have genetic determinants cannot be demonstrated with certainty, although it is reasonable to suppose that they do. Such an inborn tendency would have great survival value for the species, in that the young would be protected from danger and starvation. It has been speculated that certain features of the young, particularly facial characteristics, operate as social signals and

Figure 1.1   Contrast in infant and mature faces.

innately elicit complex emotions and behaviors (Berry and McArthur, 1986). A variety of facial features distinguish infants from adults. Infants have large heads in relation to their bodies, their faces are hairless and smooth – skinned, and they have a relatively large forehead and small chin so that the vertical placement of features is low in the infant's face. In addition, infants' eyes are large, they have fine eyebrows, and the nose is small.

Berry and McArthur (1986) have shown that these infant facial features may elicit helping responses and positive emotions that, in turn, promote survival. Consider, for example, your reactions to the faces in the left side of Figure 1.1 (infants), as opposed to their adult counterparts. It is evident that infant features call forth approach reactions and warmth. It has been contended that these features also influence responses toward adults. In one startling finding, it was reported that baby-faced criminal defendants were judged less harshly than mature-faced defendants, even when they had committed the same criminal offense (see Berry and McArthur, 1986).

Sociobiology

In recent years a new scientific discipline, *sociobiology,* has sought to establish that even such social behaviors as conformity, altruism, and cheating have a biological or genetic basis (Wilson, 1975, 1977). Sociobiologists have noted that

Example of grooming, a complex and instinctive pattern of behavior. Sociobiologists might contend that this behavioral pattern also helps to maintain one's gene pool. (M. Krishnan/Animals Animals)

Darwinian principles do account for aggressive behavior. Aggressive individuals are likely to receive food and also can engage in most mating behavior. Hence, it is argued, those most aggressive will survive and pass on this trait to their offspring. However, it is difficult for Darwinian principles to account for altruism. Those with altruistic tendencies decrease their own "fitness" relative to others, and thus altruism would tend to extinguish over time.

Like Darwin, sociobiologists also accept the view that survival-promoting behavior is passed on from one generation to another. But they contend that perpetuation of the genes, rather than the individual organism, is the prime evolutionary tendency. This belief enables them to account for apparently altruistic actions. For example, a bird may risk its own life to warn the rest of the flock of impending danger. In so doing, the individual bird might not survive, but the survival of others with like genes is aided. Why do human beings help others who apparently are not related to them? Sociobiologists argue that an agreement of "reciprocal altruism" has evolved because mutual help-giving augments the genetic pools of all participating parties.

These ideas have been invoked to explain a vast array of puzzling facts. For example, why should female ants devote their lives to helping the queen to breed,

■ Highlight 1.1 ■

The media as well as social scientists are quite aware that facial features elicit positive and negative reactions from others. Mickey Mouse, the most famous of the Disney characters, originally was a rather aggressive character. He was often getting into mischief, fighting and behaving in a less than proper manner. Over his fifty-year career, however, he has become more loving and more lovable. Children want to hug and cuddle him, there is universal demand for Mickey dolls, and so on. It has been noted that Mickey's features also have changed over this period. His face has become rounder, his eyes bigger, and his appearance more youthful as is shown below. That is, his physical characteristics have changed to foster the responses that the Disney people want to elicit.

instead of breeding themselves? Sociobiologists have pointed out that female ants actually share more genes in common with their sisters than they would with their own offspring. Thus, in order to perpetuate genes identical to their own, it is in their self-interest to assist the queen in producing more daughters. Given this view, the queen actually is a reproductive "slave" rather than a "queen."

Sociobiological concepts have also led to reinterpretation of various facets of human sexual behavior. The male, sociobiologists argue, has one prime goal: to transmit as many of his own genes as possible to the next generation. On the other hand, the female must invest a great deal of time in each birth and can have only a very limited number of offspring. Thus, males are in general more promiscuous than females because their promiscuity has a genetic payoff. Furthermore, because females must invest more of themselves in each pregnancy, they are important resources that males must "purchase." As a result, in most cultures older males (who have more necessary resources) marry younger women (who have many years of childbearing left), and women prefer men who are "good providers" (Buss and Barnes, 1986). Sociobiologists point out that males have only one great disadvantage in breeding: they cannot be certain that the offspring are their own. Thus, sexual jealousy is aroused and courtship rituals have emerged to

Highlight 1.2

Sociobiologists have pointed out that different strategies are possible to facilitate the survival of one's genetic pool. These are described under what is called "differential K theory." The symbols "r" and "K" originate in the mathematics of population biology and refer to two ends of a continuum involving a trade-off between egg production and parental care. At one end of this spectrum is the oyster, which produces over 500 millions eggs a year without any parental care. At the other end are the great apes, who produce one infant every five or six years and provide a high degree of parental care. Sociobiologists point out that these strategies are associated with different family, individual, population, and social system characteristics (see table). Clearly humans have evolved with the selection of a K-strategy.

Some life history, social behavior, and physiological differences between *r*- and *K*-strategists (following Pianka, 1970)

r-Strategist	K-Strategist
Family characteristics	
Large litter size	Small litter size
Short spacing between births	Long spacing between births
Many offspring	Few offspring
High rate of infant mortality	Low rate of infant mortality
Low degree of parental care	High degree of parental care
Individual characteristics	
Rapid rate of maturation	Slow rate of maturation
Early sexual reproduction	Delayed sexual reproduction
Short life	Long life
High reproductive effort	Low reproductive effort
High energy utilization	Efficient energy utilization
Low intelligence	High intelligence
Population characteristics	
Opportunistic exploiters of environment	Consistent exploiters of environment
Dispersing colonizers	Stable occupiers of habitat
Variable population size	Stable population size
Competition variable, often lax	Competition keen
Social system characteristics	
Low degree of social organization	High degree of social organization
Low amounts of altruism	High amounts of altruism

Continued.

Highlight 1.2

| 500,000,000 a year | 8,000 a year | 200 a year | 12 a year | 2 a year | 1 every five years |

The r/K continuum of reproductive strategies balancing egg output with parental care.

monopolize the female's time. During this extended courtship the male also can determine if the female is already pregnant. Sociobiologists suggest that the maternal grandparents (the parents of the mother) will be more attached to the offspring than the paternal grandparents (the parents of the father) because of uncertainty regarding the "true" father. It is generally accepted that the mother's mother has prerogatives, such as the first visit to the baby!

Males, in general, have been given the "advantage" by sociobiologists. Even the very act of birth puts females at a disadvantage because the male may leave. This places the female in a "cruel bind": if she leaves, the offspring will die; if she stays, her own "survival fitness" will decrease. However, males may often need to stay to protect the young, particularly if the female is incapable of defense.

Sociobiologists are not reluctant to extend their ideas to explain seemingly unrelated phenomena. For example, they anticipate that child-abuse will be most prevalent toward stepchildren because not only do these offspring not carry the genes of the abuser (most typically the stepfather), they even decrease the "survival fitness" of the stepfather. They contend that rape is a maladaptive form of a more general male mating strategy of frequent copulation, and they predict that male rapists will be those who are generally unfit and unable to attract female company. Further, rape victims will be younger females still able to reproduce (which is true). They even predict who will be most grieved by the loss of a child—the mother (who has few opportunities to reproduce), the maternal grandparents (who can be sure that the deceased child carried their genes), older parents (who can no longer reproduce), and parents following the death of a healthy rather than unhealthy child (since the former was more likely to reproduce itself) (see Crawford, Smith and Krebs, 1987; Littlefield and Rushton, 1986).

Needless to say, these controversial ideas have angered many individuals and groups (Archer, 1988). The controversy involves primarily the extension of sociobiological principles to complex human social behaviors. First, the hypotheses regarding humans are supported by relatively little data. In addition, it is obvious that cultural factors greatly influence human actions (see Washburn, 1978). For example, how can sociobiologists account for the fact that today many males undergo voluntary sterilization and the birthrate in many countries is falling so rapidly that there is zero population growth? In spite of difficulties in explaining such facts, advocating this extreme biological view, which is also present in part in Freudian psychology, has proved exceedingly provocative and has spurred the interpretation and reinterpretation of a variety of phenomena.

Facial Expressions and Emotions

Darwin argued that human facial expressions are inherited and are modified very little by cultural experience. For example, he pointed out that the baring of teeth by humans in situations of anger and contempt is similar to the display of teeth among carnivores prior to a hostile attack or during an aggressive defense.

A number of studies have attempted to verify Darwin's insight. These studies bear on the biological basis of emotional experience as well as on the universality of emotional displays. Two basic paradigms have been followed in this research area: (1) examining the facial expressions of children born deaf and blind; and (2) analyzing the agreement concerning identification of emotions in different cultures.

A baboon in full threat gesture, with teeth bared. Darwin pointed out that a human snarl has a similar facial pattern and suggested that emotional displays are genetically programmed. (Irven Devore/Anthro-Photo)

Figure 1.2

Examples of the photographs used to portray the six primary emotions. These faces express anger (left) and happiness (right). (Ekman and Friesen, *Unmasking the Face,* reprint edition, Consulting Psychologists Press, Palo Alto, California, 1984; right, Dion Ogust/The Image Works.)

Investigations reveal that blind and deaf children do display quite normal facial expressions (Eibl-Eibesfeldt, 1970, Freedman, 1964). Hence, these observations tend to support the universalistic, Darwinian explanation of facial expression. Of course, culture plays some role in the control of facial expression and in determining which situations are appropriate for eliciting and displaying particular emotions and facial expressions.

The cross-cultural research has been guided by identification of the so-called basic human emotions. Ekman and Friesen (1975) isolated six primary emotions — fear, surprise, disgust, anger, happiness, and sadness — and also identified the facial muscles associated with these affective (emotional) states. Photographs showing the facial expressions associated with these emotions (Fig. 1.2 depicts those for anger and happiness) were then shown to people in five different countries — the United States, Brazil, Chile, Argentina, and Japan — and the subjects were asked to identify the emotion portrayed. Table 1.1 shows the percentage of agreement with the labels supplied by Ekman and Friesen. As the table indicates, there is quite high agreement among the five nations. In addition,

Table 1.1   Percentage of identification of depicted emotion across cultures

Emotion	United States (n = 99)	Brazil (n = 40)	Chile (n = 119)	Argentina (n = 168)	Japan (n = 29)
Fear	85	67	68	54	66
Disgust	92	97	92	92	90
Happiness	97	95	95	98	100
Anger	67	90	94	90	90

Source: From the book, *Unmasking the Face* by Paul Ekman and Wallace V. Friesen. © 1975 by Prentice-Hall, Inc. Published by Prentice-Hall, Inc., Englewood Cliffs, N.J.

natives of New Guinea, who did not have reading skills and were not subject to the possible confounding of media exposure, responded similarly to individuals in the other five countries. (However, it must be noted that individuals are more adept at this labeling task when selecting the appropriate emotion from a given list, rather than supplying their own interpretation without the aid of a preselected list.) In sum, it appears that facial expressions of some emotions are to a large extent a genetically based characteristic of the species (also see Ekman 1993), although there is still some controversy about these conclusions (Thompson, 1993).

ALL HUMANS ARE UNIQUE

Despite cross-cultural similarities and the universality of some behaviors, it can equally be said that each human is genetically unique. Given the billions of possible inherited gene patterns, each individual is provided with an idiosyncratic genetic configuration. The resulting variability in genetic structure is manifested in individual differences in characteristics and behavior. Two basic procedures have been followed in studying the genetic determinants of individual differences. One method is experimental, involving the selective breeding of nonhumans. The other is nonexperimental in the sense that there is no intervention in the lives of its human subjects. The nonexperimental procedures include both twin and adoption designs.

The Experimental Study of Heritability

For many years *selective breeding* has been unsystematically performed on domestic animals to enhance certain temperamental or behavioral characteristics, such as ferocity, docility, hunting ability, and so on. In more systematic laboratory settings, animals exhibiting a high or low degree of a certain behavior, such as emotionality, are selectively bred for generations and the emotionality of subsequent generations is then compared. The experimenter thus performs on a compressed time scale what natural selection is presumed to do during the course of evolution. In natural selection, high or low extremes of a characteristic or *directional selection,* may be favored. For example, natural selection in opossums evidently favored inertness in the face of danger; visual aggressive displays or strength and speed are favored in other species. In nature, as in the laboratory, there may also be *balancing selection,* which favors intermediate values of the characteristic in question.

The logic of breeding experiments is straightforward and nicely illustrates what is meant by the concept of *heritability* — the degree to which genetics plays a role in the development of a particular aspect of behavior in a particular population. Assume, for example, that we observe a group of animals learning a maze and that they attain scores of 1–10, based on the number of trials before success. That is, one animal learns the maze in a single trial, another takes two trials, a third requires three trials, and so on. Now, for example, we take the "brightest" animals, which require only one trial to learn, and we inbreed them. Of their offspring, we again inbreed the fastest learners. Assume that this procedure is continued for thirty generations. Now, if the thirtieth generation of animals still gives us scores of 1–10 in maze learning, we know that the ability to learn this maze has no heritability. Rather, the differences among the animals are due entirely to environmental factors. Conversely, assume that for this thirtieth generation, all the animals learn the maze in one trial. In that case, we would assume that maze learning was due entirely to genetic factors; heritability is the determining factor. In actuality in this situation, the variability among the animals, i.e., their differences in how many trials it took them to learn, will most likely decrease over generations, but will not disappear entirely. Thus, there will be both genetic and environmental determinants of learning, with the decrease in variability indicating the degree to which this behavior is influenced by genetic factors.

A representative study of selective breeding for a particular ability is illustrated in an investigation by Thompson (1954). Thompson measured the speed with which rats learned a maze for a food reward. Then he bred the low-error (maze-bright) rats with other maze-bright rats, and the high-error (maze-dull) rats with other maze-dull rats. The offspring of these matings were then tested on the maze. This procedure continued for six generations; by the sixth generation, the error scores of the two breeding populations were dramatically different (see Fig. 1.3). It is interesting to note that rats superior in maze learning do not necessarily master other problems as rapidly. Maze learning appears to be a specific ability.

Figure 1.3   The results of selective breeding for maze learning. (Thompson, 1954, p. 217. Used by permission of the Association for Research in Nervous and Mental Disease, Inc., and the author.)

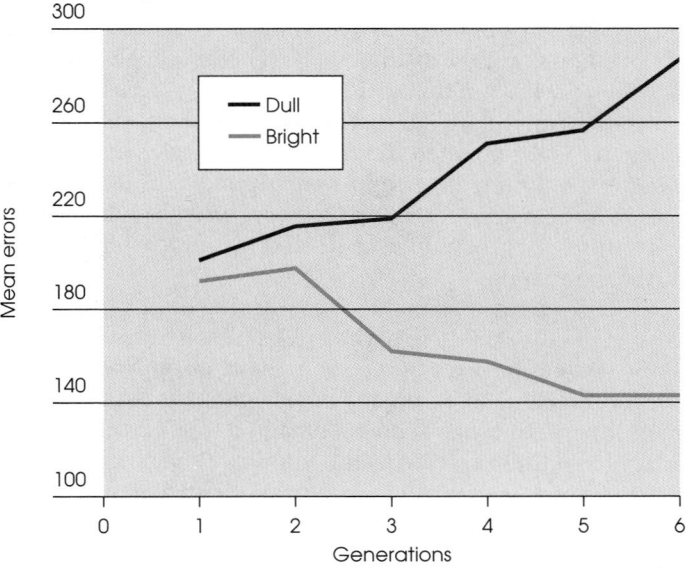

Table 1.2   Mean error scores for maze-bright and maze-dull rats raised in different environments

Rats	Enriched environment	Normal environment	Restricted environment
Bright	111	117	170
Dull	120	164	170

Source: Adapted from Cooper and Zubek, 1958, pp. 160, 161. Used by permission.

The data in Fig. 1.3 indicate that maze learning is influenced by heredity. But this should not be taken to mean that environmental factors have little or no effect on such learning. Cooper and Zubek (1958) took the strains of rats bred by Thompson and reared them in either enriched or impoverished conditions. The enriched environment contained ramps, tunnels, and many movable objects, whereas the restricted environment included only a food box and a water tin. When the maze learning of the rats was assessed (see Table 1.2), the experimenters found that when the groups were reared in either extreme environment, their performance did not differ greatly. The enriched environment primarily raised the performance of the dull rats, while the restricted environment chiefly lowered the performance of the bright rats. Only in the normal environment were there differences due to an innate ability factor. Hence, there is nothing absolute about heritability; an organism's individual sensitivity to disparate environmental conditions may either mask or exacerbate inborn tendencies. What is inherited, then, is the way in which the organism responds to the environment, and heritability is in turn a function of the environment in which the behavior is studied.

Very similar conclusions regarding heritability have been reached in the study of emotionality. Broadhurst (1961) inbred high- and low-emotionality rats, selected on the basis of their defecation in an open field test. In this procedure, rats are placed in an unfamiliar environment, and emotional responses are inferred from the well-documented fact that fear causes defecation and urination. After six generations of inbreeding, there were dramatic differences between the populations, with the data resembling those reported by Thompson (1954) in terms of the magnitude of group differences and the increasing inequality in emotionality over the generations.

While it seems reasonable that learning ability and even emotionality may have a genetic basis, it is perhaps less sensible to believe that preferences or incentive values have a genetic component, as opposed to being entirely learned. However, breeding experiments have demonstrated that alcohol preference also may be inherited. It has been documented that particular strains of mice choose an alcohol solution over a water solution (Rodgers, 1966), while other strains avoid alcohol and prefer water. Furthermore, when strains with high and low alcohol preference are interbred, the offspring display an intermediate desire for alcohol as opposed to water (Rodgers and McClearn, 1962). Later in this chapter we will suggest that alcoholism among humans might also be determined in part by inborn tendencies. Indeed, some have contended that almost any behavior can be selectively bred!

The Study of Heritability Through Human Research

In contrast to studies of nonhumans, research using human populations is nonexperimental in the sense that there is no intervention or manipulation of variables because of obvious ethical constraints. Rather, individuals who vary in their degree of genetic relationship, such as foster parents and their children, natural parents and their children, siblings, fraternal twins, and identical twins, are compared and contrasted. Genetic similarity is a function of degree of kinship, so for genetically influenced characteristics, similarity in behavior and character should increase with biological relatedness.

The basic shortcoming of human genetic research is that the environments are not controlled. As a result, it is often impossible to infer with certainty that observed behavioral similarity is a function of biological relatedness and is due to inborn characteristics. In nonhuman research using inbreeding techniques, the environments are controlled and identical for each group.

Consider, for example, a hypothetical research study demonstrating that emotional mothers have highly emotional children, whereas nonemotional mothers have children with low emotionality. These data might be interpreted as demonstrating that emotionality is heritable. However, it is quite possible that these children had different home environments; perhaps highly emotional mothers create unstable environments which produce highly emotional children, whereas nonemotional mothers establish stable environments which give rise to children low in emotionality. In this investigation, the learning and the genetic contributions to emotionality cannot be separated. To help interpret the ambiguous results of such family studies, twin and adoption studies are often employed to disentangle genetic and environmental contributions.

The central research separating genetic from environmental contributions to human behavior involves a comparison between twins from different eggs (fraternal, or dizygotic twins) with those from the same egg (identical, or monozygotic twins). The latter type share completely identical gene pools; dizygotic twins, on the average, share only about 50 percent of their genes. Hence, monozygotic (MZ) twins should be more alike in behavior than dizygotic (DZ) twins, if the behavior under study has a genetic component. This hypothesis assumes that the environments of DZ twins are as identical as the environments of MZ twins. However, such an assumption, although reasonable, is not always warranted. Identical twins may have more similar social learning histories; it has been found that they are more likely to dress alike, have common friends, and spend more time together than fraternal twins (Smith, 1965). However, this factor may be of limited importance, as shown when parents of twins incorrectly classify their children as MZ or DZ (Scarr and Carter-Saltzman, 1979).

Identical (monozygotic) twins. Evidence indicates that
many aspects of their temperament and behavior also will
be similar. (Erika Stone/Photo Researchers)

In principle, it is possible to study the effects of shared genes by comparing
identical twins reared in similar versus different environments. Although such a
sample is seldom available, some investigations have examined the similarities of
siblings adopted in infancy and reared in foster homes, compared with unrelated
individuals reared in these same homes. Any differences in the similarities within
these two groups, given that all else is equal, are logically attributable to the
genetic similarity of the sibs. Conversely, any differences in the behavior of the
identical twins shows environmental and experiential influences on behavior.

We now turn to some investigations that have compared identical with
fraternal twins. First, some personality characteristics of these groups are examined, and then various psychological problems, such as schizophrenia, criminality and alcoholism, are analyzed for genetic determination.

Temperament. The role of genetics in the development of temperament has long
been noted. In his studies of conditioning experiments, Pavlov examined individual
dogs for long periods of time and observed striking differences in temperament
that he attributed to inborn, neurological inequalities. *Temperament* may be
defined as the "characteristic phenomena of an individual's nature, including his
susceptibility to emotional stimulations, his customary strength and speed of
response, and the quality of his prevailing mood, and all the peculiarities of
fluctuation and intensity of mood" (Allport, 1961, p. 34). Buss, Plomin, and
Willerman (1973) selected four temperaments to study for heritability: emotionality, activity, sociability, and impulsivity. Twenty-item questionnaires were constructed, with five items for each temperament. These questionnaires were given

to mothers of fraternal (DZ) or identical (MZ) twins. The mothers rated items such as "Child cries easily" on a scale of 1 (a little) to 5 (a lot). The items, their corresponding temperaments, and the correlations for the two sets of twins, separated according to sex, are shown in Table 1.3, which reveals that on virtually all the items the correlations were higher for the MZ than for the DZ twins of both sexes.

Table 1.3   Items and correlations on the temperament scales

| | Correlations | | | |
| | Males | | Females | |
A priori scale assignment	MZ*	DZ*	MZ*	DZ*
Emotionality				
Child cries easily.	.56	.10	.47	.23
Child has a quick temper.	.34	.10	.40	.70
Child gets upset quickly.	.64	.10	.66	.00
Child is easily frightened.	.58	.11	.70	.00
Child is easygoing or happy-go-lucky.	.46	.00	.38	.00
Activity				
Child is off and running as soon as he wakes up in the morning.	.88	.41	.86	.00
Child is always on the go.	.48	.02	.72	.01
Child cannot sit still long.	.76	.25	.65	.27
Child prefers quiet games such as coloring or block play to more active games.	.77	.00	.21	.03
Child fidgets at meals and similar occasions.	.67	.38	.68	.31
Sociability				
Child makes friends easily.	.74	.26	.47	.00
Child likes to be with others.	.61	.27	.29	.05
Child tends to be shy.	.57	.10	.51	.00
Child is independent.	.58	.25	.44	.24
Child prefers to play by himself rather than with others.	.55	.10	.73	.46
Impulsivity				
Learning self-control is difficult for the child.	.75	.55	.83	.69
Child tends to be impulsive.	.81	.00	.68	.39
Child gets bored easily.	.83	.13	.49	.59
Child learns to resist temptation easily.	.72	.35	.70	.52
Child goes from toy to toy quickly.	.82	.44	.83	.62

Source: A.H. Buss, R. Plomin, and L. Willerman. "The Inheritance of Temperaments," *Journal of Personality, 41,* 1973, p. 517. Copyright 1973, Duke University Press (Durham, NC).

* MZ = monozygotic
  DZ = dizygotic

At times, the concept of temperament is included within a triad of characteristics labeled emotionality, activity, and sociability. A review of the pertinent genetic data has revealed strong support for the inheritance of these broad characteristics (see Plomin, 1986). However, the magnitude of the genetic effects may be reduced later in life, and research with questionnaires (as shown in Table 1.3) reveals stronger genetic influence than do studies based on actual behavioral observations. Thus, more observational research is surely needed (Plomin, 1989).

Shyness. Kagan (Kagan, 1989; Kagan and Snidman, 1991) and his colleagues have argued for the heritability of a trait which leads to the behavior that we call shyness. They suggest that about 10 percent of healthy white children are born with a predisposition to act in an "inhibited" fashion in the presence of new stimuli such as strange individuals or strange situations. Another 10 percent are born to be more adventuresome and "disinhibited" in such situations.

Kagan and Snidman say that the antecedents of this cautiousness are present at around four months of age and can be seen in both high levels of motor activity and crying to stimuli. These predispositions have a tendency to persist into later life. For instance, while about 50 percent of the children studied at age four months no longer showed extreme fears at age eight years, 80 percent were still not spontaneous. Additionally, about 75 percent of the shy children at age eight had one or more unusual fears—such as fear of speaking in class or fear of attending summer camp—compared to 25 percent of those rated as disinhibited. Generally, shy children also exhibited a variety of physiological correlates such as more motor tension. Kagan (1989) suggests that these are based on brain activity that is easily aroused by unfamiliarity and discrepancy.

Finally, in line with our previous discussion on the difference between phenotype and genotype, Kagan, Arcus, and Snidman (1993) review data indicating that about 35 percent of the variability in the fear score of children at age fourteen months is due to parenting behaviors. Parents who do not comfort their shy and fearful infants too much when they are upset (but who are not harsh) and who set limits have infants who show significantly lower fear scores. Thus both nature and nurture play a role in how fearful an older child is. Many children with an inhibited disposition can learn, for the most part, not to act shyly, although subtle signs of their tendency to act inhibited in strange situations may still be observed.

Introversion-Extraversion and Other Personality Traits. It has been suggested that introversion-extraversion may be the most genetically influenced of the personality traits. Introverts are defined as quiet, retiring, introspective, and not very socially active. Extraverts, on the other hand, are characterized as being outgoing, impulsive, and uninhibited, having many social contacts, and frequently taking part in group activities (Eysenck and Eysenck, 1964).

The best-known theory of introversion-extraversion relates this personality dimension to inherited differences in the functioning of the reticular activating system (RAS). This neurological activating system is located in various areas of the cortex and is responsible for an organism's level of arousal or degree of internal stimulation. Eysenck (1967) has suggested that under normal conditions introverts are more highly aroused than extraverts. Somewhat paradoxically, high arousal results in restraints or inhibited behavior because the cortex is exercising control over the more primitive brain centers (see Wilson, 1978). Extraverts, on the other hand, being less normally aroused, are also subject to less cortical control.

Given this physiological conception, one might anticipate a high degree of heritability in this personality dimension; the twin studies support this belief. Several investigations have compared the similarity of MZ and DZ twins on self-report measures of extraversion (see Shields, 1976; Rose et al., 1988). These measures contain such items as:

- Do you often long for excitement?
- Are you mostly quiet when you are with people?
- Generally, do you prefer reading to meeting people?

Based on a review of over 25,000 pairs of twins, Henderson (1982) has concluded that the typical correlations between tests scores of MZ twins is about $r = .50$, while for DZ, the correlation is about $r = .20$. In one study, Shields (1976) found that identical twins separated from each other actually had slightly more similar scores on the extraversion scale than identical twins reared together, as if parents reacted to the twins or they reacted to each other in a manner that would enhance their differences.

Loehlin and Nichols (1976), making use of personality inventory responses, reported data that support the above conclusion. The subjects, twins who had taken the National Merit Scholarship Qualifying Test, were administered a variety of measures, including the California Psychological Inventory (CPI), which consists of eighteen different scales, some of which relate to the introversion-extraversion dimension. On virtually all of these scales the correlations of the scores for the MZ twins approximated $r = .50$; those for the DZ pairs were $r = .20 - .30$.

Plomin, Chipuer, and Loehlin (1990) have summarized the data from the Swedish Adoption/Twin Study on Aging (SATSA) on nearly 25,000 pairs of twins. Results on eighteen personality scales are summarized in Table 1.4. It is evident from the table that the correlations are generally higher for the MZ than for the DZ twins. The average estimate of heritability (that is, the contribution of genes to personality) from these results in 29 percent. Even empathic concern (human compassion for others) among middle-aged males no longer living together showed correlations near $r = .50$ for MZ twins, and little correlation for DZ twins (Matthews, Batson, Horn, and Rosenman, 1981).

Overall, Plomin et al. conclude that the evidence supports a genetic component to many aspects of personality, with an overall estimate of heritability of about 20 percent. Plomin et al. also note that this means that the majority of the variance in personality is due to the environment. Some interesting examples of the possible impact of genetics on personality are given in Highlight 1.3.

Table 1.4

Summary of SATSA personality correlates for twins reared apart and twins reared together

	MZ twins		DZ twins	
	Apart	Together	Apart	Together
Extraversion	.30	.54	.04	.06
Neuroticism	.25	.41	.28	.24
EAS				
Emotionality — Distress	.30	.52	.26	.16
Emotionality — Fear	.37	.49	.04	.08
Emotionality — Anger	.33	.37	.09	.08
Activity	.27	.38	.00	.18
Sociability	.20	.35	.19	.19
Type A				
Pressure	.20	.42	.29	.23
Hard-Driving	.39	.47	.10	.00
Ambitious	.40	.30	.08	.11
Hostility	.21	.33	.21	.40
Assertiveness	.16	.32	−.08	.20
Locus of control				
Luck	.02	.28	.18	.32
Responsibility	.36	.30	.30	.18
Life Direction	.32	.30	.23	.15
NEO				
Openness	.43	.51	.23	.14
Conscientious	.15	.41	−.03	.23
Agreeableness	.19	.47	.10	.11

Source: Adapted from Plomin, Chipuer, and Loehlin, 1990, p. 231. Reprinted by permission of Guilford Publications.

Highlight 1.3

Similarities Among Monozygotic Twins

A number of striking similarities between monozygotic twins reared apart from infancy have been found in the Minnesota Study of Twins Reared Apart (Bouchard, Lykken, McGue, Segal, and Tellegen, 1990). At their first adult reunion one pair of male twins discovered that they both used Vademecum toothpaste, Canoe shaving lotion, Vitalis hair tonic, and Lucky Strike cigarettes! Later they exchanged birthday gifts in the mail, and discovered each had made the identical choice of gifts. There were two twins who trained and worked with dogs, two gunsmith hobbyists, two women who wore seven rings, and two who were captains of volunteer fire departments. Two male twins discovered that they both had named their sons James Alan (one Allan) and that both chain-smoked Salems while they worked in their basement workshops. While some of these similarities are surely by chance, the dyzygotic twins studied seldom produced such "remarkable coincidences" (Lykken, McGue, Tellegen, and Bouchard, 1992).

Altruism and Aggression. It already has been suggested that aggression and altruism are products of long evolutionary histories. Rushton et al. (1986) examined the heritability of these behaviors in a large study of twins. They mailed questionnaires to adult twin pairs assessing altruism, empathy, nurturance, aggression, and assertiveness. The altruism scale, for example, included items such as: "I have given directions to a stranger" and "I have donated blood." The findings are similar to those already presented in that the correlations for the MZ pairs were near $r = .50$, while for the DZ pairs the correlations approximate $r = .15$.

It appears from the research that many personality traits may have a genetic component. This same research, however, clearly shows that genes do not account for all variations in behavior and that environments also determine personality.

Other Genetic Aspects of Personality and Behavior. Research on the genetics of behavior has become a vigorous and expanding area in recent years. There are now studies which have reported finding genetic aspects of how much television we watch (Plomin, Corley, De Fries, and Fulke, 1990), the likelihood of our getting divorced (McGue and Lykken, 1992), whether we believe in God or not (Tesser, 1993), and even whether we perceive our families as having provided a warm environment (Chipuer, Plomin, Pederson, McClearn, and Nesselroade, 1993).

Mental Illness and Social Problems. The twin-studies of heritability of personality required the assignment of quantitative degrees of the trait under investigation to the individuals being compared. This quantitative trait score was derived from reports of others, self-reports, or actual observations of behavior. Examination of the genetic determination of mental illness and social problems, on the other hand, involves the assignment of individuals to a category, such as schizophrenic, alcoholic, criminal, and so on. Then the rates of *concordance* (both twins classified in the same category) and *discordance* (twins in different categories) are examined. The genetic hypothesis concerning social problems is corroborated when higher concordance rates are displayed as a function of biological relatedness.

The mental illness that has been most extensively investigated from a genetic perspective is schizophrenia. Gottesman (1993) has provided a summary of the nine most recent studies comparing monozygotic and dizygotic twins. The mean concordance rate for monozygotic twins was 39 percent, while for dizygotic twins it was 10 percent. Gottesman suggests that estimates of the heritability of schizophrenia range from .42 to .63, with estimates for the effects of the environment ranging from .29 to .53.

In a discussion of the inborn determinants of schizophrenia, a well-known psychologist (Meehl, 1962, p. 827) wrote:

> Let me begin by putting a question which I find is almost never answered correctly by our clinical students on PhD orals, and the answer to which they seem to dislike when it is offered. Suppose that you were required to write down a procedure for selecting an individual from the population who would be diagnosed as schizophrenic by a psychiatric staff; you have to wager $1,000 on being right; you may not include in your selection procedure any behavioral fact, such as a symptom or trait, manifested by the individual. What would you write down? So far as I have been able to ascertain, there is only one thing you could write down that would give you a better than even chance of winning such a bet—namely, "Find an individual X who has a schizophrenic identical twin." Admittedly, there are many other facts which would raise your odds somewhat above the low base rate of schizophrenia. You might, for example, identify X by first finding mothers who have certain unhealthy child-rearing attitudes; you might enter a subpopulation defined jointly by such demographic variables as age, size of community, religion, ethnic background, or social class. But these would leave you with a pretty unfair wager, as would the rule, "Find an X who has a fraternal twin, of the same sex, diagnosed as schizophrenic."

Even when sibs and twins are reared apart, there are high concordance rates for schizophrenia (see Rosenthal, 1970).

In addition to twin studies, investigations utilizing entire families and adoption studies also support the genetic hypothesis. The logic of the family study approach is straightforward—if schizophrenia is an inherited disorder, relatives of schizophrenics should also exhibit a higher incidence of schizophrenia. Further, the closer the relative in terms of genetic relatedness, the higher should be the concordance rate. It has been estimated that the risk of schizophrenia for first-degree relatives (e.g., parents of a schizophrenic) is about 8 percent and about 2.5 percent for second-degree relatives (e.g., uncles and aunts), as compared to the general population base rate of 1 percent.

In addition, adoption studies reach the same conclusion. The adoption study design removes the possibility of postnatal environmental interaction between the adopted child and biological relatives. One study has shown that when children of a schizophrenic mother are raised by normal mothers, over 10 percent of the adoptees become schizophrenic (see Faraone and Tsuang, 1985; Plomin, 1989).

These findings have resulted in a search for the specific chromosone that may be carrying the schizophrenic gene. However, given that different types of schizophrenia have different concordance rates, the search for a single gene seems unlikely to be successful. In fact, it is now generally believed (Gottesman, 1993) that schizophrenia involves more than one gene.

In a similar manner, manic-depressive psychoses and affective disorders appear to have a genetic component. Recent research has shown the same pattern of data as discussed for schizophrenia, although the strength of the genetic contribution is controversial (see Plomin, 1989). There also is evidence from extensive examination of a closely knit community of Amish that there is a dominant gene resulting in a strong disposition to a manic-depressive disease (see Egeland et al., 1987).

In addition to mental illness, a variety of social problems, including criminality and alcoholism, have some biological bases. Data are quite clear that crime virtually everywhere and throughout history is a young man's pursuit. That is, in greatly diverse cultures, age and sex influence crime rates. There also is evidence that there are general sex differences in aggression that appear to be at least in part traced to biological factors (male sex hormones). In support of the biological approach, twin studies have revealed that identical twins are more similar in delinquency than are fraternal twins, independent of amount of shared activities. In addition, adoption studies have shown that boys with criminal biological parents and noncriminal adopting parents were more likely to have criminal records than those with noncriminal biological parents and criminal adopting parents! (cf. Chapter 18) These studies do not demonstrate that there is a "criminal gene." Rather, other inherited traits such as temperament and intelligence are likely contributors to the tendency to commit criminal acts (Mednick, Brennan, and Kandel, 1989; Mednick, Moffitt, and Stack, 1987; and Wilson and Herrnstein, 1985).

Finally, recall that the preference for alcohol differed greatly among strains of mice. Humans also apparently have inborn preferences or susceptibility to alcoholism, for investigations reveal a marked heritability of this problem. (Of course, preference for alcohol among rats and alcoholism among humans should not be considered identical phenomena.) It has long been recognized that alcoholism is a familial disorder in that rates of alcoholism are far higher among relatives of alcoholics than among the general population. Goodwin et al. (1973) even found that where children have been separated from their biological parents at birth or shortly thereafter, the presence of alcoholism in the biological parents is of far greater predictive significance for the development of this disorder in the children than is the presence of alcoholism among the adoptive parents. An offspring of an alcoholic parent is more likely to become an alcoholic even when raised by nonalcoholic foster parents than is an offspring of nonalcoholic parents when raised by alcoholic foster parents. In general, the data have revealed a threefold to fourfold increased risk for this disorder in sons and daughters of alcoholics, even when raised by nonalcoholic adoptive parents (see Schuckit, 1987).

It is not known how this predisposition might be transmitted and to what degree heritability accounts for the transmission of this illness. Furthermore, it is likely that what is inherited is only a breeding ground where social-cultural factors play a role in the manifestation of alcoholism. The relative roles of genetics and culture are exceedingly complex. For example, it has been suggested that the Chinese drink little because of a genetic propensity to become ill with alcohol intake. Clearly, then, the disentanglement of genetic from cultural factors cannot be readily resolved, and simple instances of a genetic or a cultural influence, on closer inspection, reveal contributions from the other source.

The Nonshared Environment Effect

One of the most startling findings to come out of recent genetic research is the suggestion that the shared environments that siblings grow up in may have very little effect on their personalities (Rowe, 1994). That is, two genetically different siblings growing up in the same family will be no more alike in personality than if they had grown up in different families. This conclusion is based on a variety of researchers' finding of very low correlations between siblings on measures of various personality traits (Loehlin, 1989; Plomin, Chipuer, and Loehlin, 1990; Reiss, 1993).

Low correlations mean that although siblings may share the same family in a general, physical sense, their psychological environments may nonetheless be different. Interest is now shifting to an examination of the impact of nonshared environments on personality. Both Plomin et al. (1990) and Reiss (1993) have suggested that family dynamics play a role. One child is not treated the same as another child, and relationships among siblings vary. In addition, other aspects of the child's environment, such as relationships with peers outside the home or with teachers, probably differ among siblings brought up in the same home.

Criticisms of Genetic Views of Personality

Few would now debate that genetics play a role in personality development. What is debated, however, is the question of how much of a role and how that role is played. Findings that genetics contribute to divorce, belief in God, television watching, and the like would suggest that large proportions of our lives are genetically influenced.

However, this issue is more complex than it seems. First, there is no gene for television watching (how would it have manifested itself one hundred years ago?). Further, two to three centuries ago in western Europe divorce was much more uncommon than it is today. It is likely that if genetic studies had been done on divorce at that time no effects would have been detected because divorce was such a rarity. While genetic causes for behaviors such as television watching and divorce can be found, it is likely that such behaviors are actually mediated by other genetic factors such as personality (McGue and Lykken, 1992).

A number of writers have criticized the concept of *heritability,* the idea that one can give a percent figure to the degree to which a trait is inherited. Bronfrenbenner and Ceci (1993) have pointed out that the degree of heritability of a trait depends on the environment, and others have noted that an estimate of heritability from a given research study holds only for the sample of subjects studied in that investigation. One cannot generalize heritability estimates for the whole population. Others have pointed out that genetically oriented researchers do not adequately measure the environment in their studies and so are not really able to assess the impact of the environment. This has led to the possibility that heritability estimates of various traits are inflated. For instance, in adoption studies twins are separated at birth and adopted by different families. To estimate the heritability of a trait, such as television watching, one then correlates the degree of television watching in each adopted twin. However, twins are typically adopted into families of similar social class that are likely to provide similar environments. While this similarity might not affect the finding that television watching has a genetic component, it might inflate the *magnitude* of the heritability estimate. There is now a call for genetically oriented researchers to more carefully measure environmental factors.

Classification by Type

Biological givens are often relied on to classify individuals. Later in this text one such classification — gender — is examined in detail. Another biological classification scheme is based on body build. Kretschmer (1925) identified four basic constitutional types: pyknic (short and stocky), athletic (strong and well proportioned), leptosomic (tall and slender), and dysplastic (a mixture of the other three). Kretschmer, who believed that body build is related to mental disorders, reported that schizophrenics are often leptosomic and that manic-depressives are typically pyknic.

Guided by Kretschmer, Sheldon and his colleagues (Sheldon and Stevens, 1942); Sheldon, Stevens, and Tucker, 1940) suggested that there are three fundamental physiques and that each physique is associated with a particular temperament.

Physique	*Temperament*
1. Endomorphy (soft and round; digestive viscera overdeveloped)	1. Viscerotonic (relaxed, loves to eat, sociable)
2. Mesomorphy (muscular, rectangular, strong)	2. Somatotonic (energetic, assertive, courageous)
3. Ectomorphy (long and fragile; large brain and sensitive nervous system)	3. Cerebrotonic (restrained, fearful, introverted, artistic)

Relatively sophisticated rating scales have been developed to assess each of these body types.

The idea that physical type influences personality has received relatively little attention from psychologists. This stems in part from the charlatan image created by palmists and phrenologists, as well as from a general reluctance to accept genetic determinism. Nonetheless, there are a number of reasons why body type might influence behavior (see Lindzey, 1967*b*). Some of these reasons implicate social or experiential variables, but others relate directly to genetics.

1. The same experience might influence both physiology and behavior (e.g., maternal overprotection might result in both obesity and overdependence).

2. Factors such as height and weight set limits on behavior as well as influence what behaviors will be rewarded. For example, individuals of a certain biological makeup will be more likely to engage and succeed in sports, which could in turn affect their behavior and self-concept.

3. Society holds certain expectations about the relationship of body characteristics and behavior (e.g., "Fat people are jolly"; "Redheads have hot tempers") that could foster certain biology-behavior linkages.

4. Genetics might influence both physique and behavior. For example, it has been demonstrated that albino mice are especially poor at escape learning (Winston and Lindzey, 1964). In a similar manner, it has been clearly documented that, among humans, mesomorphs are overrepresented among delinquents (see Lindzey, 1967*b*).

Summary

1. A characteristic or a predisposition can be both inherited and modified by environmental factors and experience. For example, early diet manipulation may prevent a genetic mental deficiency known as PKU.

2. *Instinct* has two meanings: (a) an unlearned, fixed pattern of activity such as nest building in birds, and (b) an inner "want" or "urge."

3. The concept of instinct as an inner urge is exemplified by *vacuum behavior,* a behavior pattern undertaken in the absence of the appropriate stimulus. Ethologists have explained these behaviors with the suggestion that energy may accumulate within an organism if a behavior is not expressed.

4. To study whether or not a behavior is innate, the *isolation paradigm* is used. The organism is reared alone and then given the opportunity to engage in the behavior under study.

5. *Sociobiology* seeks to establish that complex social behavior has a biological or genetic basis. Sociobiologists particularly have examined altruism.

6. Some facial expressions appear to be universal. This observation supports the Darwinian belief that expressions are inherited behaviors.

7. *Selective breeding* experiments have demonstrated that specific abilities such as maze learning and traits such as emotionality have genetic components. The offspring in such studies tend to behave similarly to their parents.

8. Research has demonstrated that temperament and personality traits like introversion-extraversion and shyness have genetic components.

9. Studies of social problems using *concordance* and *discordance* rates have demonstrated a genetic basis for mental illnesses like schizophrenia and for social problems like criminality and alcoholism.

10. There is evidence that body type is related to behavior, although it is uncertain whether such a linkage is inherited or is a product of social experience.

11. The nonshared environment effect, that siblings growing up in the same family environment appear to have little in common in terms of their personalities, suggests that siblings may actually experience different environments within the same family.

Thought Questions

1. What are some of the arguments, pro and con, that might be advanced concerning eugenics and the genetic regulation of marriages?

2. Can you think of any apparently instinctive patterns of behavior in pets you have observed?

3. What might a sociobiologist say about falling in love?

4. What evolutionary changes in human personality do you predict will take place in the future?

2 Contextual Aspects of Personality and Behavior

In Chapter 1 we contended that personality structure and behavior are determined in part by a long evolutionary history that predisposes individuals to act in certain ways. People come into the world with genetic givens that influence who and what they are and what they become.

In this chapter we examine the same questions from a totally different perspective: how aspects of the environment into which we are born influence us. These determinants of behavior, which are not genetically transmitted, are part of the impinging physical, social, and cultural milieu. Human beings are versatile in their patterns of adaptation to a variety of physical and social conditions — they dwell in hot or cold climates; they have contrasting social roles; they are brought up in cultures with widely disparate customs and mores. All of these factors produce different modes of behavior. Indeed, it has been said that humans have no nature, only history. It should come as no surprise that environmental conditions influence personality. We know, for example, that even in the plant world such environmental conditions as the composition of soil and amount of rainfall have a significant effect on the characteristics of a plant's root system and leaf structure. In the human world, we may surely expect an even more significant influence from the environment.

In this chapter we first examine interactional and ecological theories of personality. We next consider the impact of the physical world on personality, including the effects of climate, constructed environments, and behavior settings. We then consider the issues of privacy and territoriality. We conclude by considering how aspects of the social world, including social class and culture, affect the study of personality.

ECOLOGICAL AND INTERACTIONAL PERSPECTIVES ON PERSONALITY

Ecological perspectives assume that an individual's behavior is heavily influenced by the surrounding contexts. This context includes both the physical environment and the social environment. It includes the home, the neighborhood, the work environment, the climate, the immediate network of personal relationships, and the culture. Below we consider aspects of the physical and social environments and their impact on individual personality and behavior.

Both Wapner and Hiatt (1993) and Magnusson (1990) have described ecological/interactional views of personality. For Wapner the organism-in-environment is the unit to be studied. This is based on the belief that "every living organism is inextricably embedded in some environment" (p. 2). Magnusson

(1990, p. 196) has suggested the following premises of an interactional perspective:

1. An individual develops and functions as a total, integrated organism; current functioning and development do not take place in single aspects per se, in isolation from the totality.

2. An individual develops and functions in a dynamic, continuous, and reciprocal process of interactions with his or her environment.

3. The characteristic way in which an individual develops and functions, in interaction with the environment, depends on and influences the continuous reciprocal process of interaction among subsystems of mental and biological factors.

These views emphasize that all parts of the person as a system are interrelated in a complex way, and that the whole is greater than the sum of its parts: "[A]n individual functions as a totality at each stage of development and . . . each aspect of the structures and processes that are operating [perceptions, plans, values, goals, motives, biological factors, conduct, etc.] takes on meaning from the role it plays in the total functioning of the individual" (Magnusson, 1990, p. 197).

Illustrating an ecological/interactional perspective, Wapner (1976) makes the following statement about a classroom: "Though the teacher is a very significant part of the classroom situation, the social context of learning goes beyond the teacher and must be treated broadly. The social context encompasses the spirit of a place, its rules and norms which govern the action of its inhabitants, the expectations about how things should be done, the modes of interaction of people, the general atmosphere of the classroom, laboratory, hallways, and the coffee shop" (p. 76). Many of the topics considered in the rest of this chapter also illustrate an ecological/interactive perspective.

THE PHYSICAL WORLD

It is convenient to distinguish between two aspects of the physical world: (1) the natural environment, including the climate, availability of resources, existence of nearby bodies of water, and similar factors; and (2) constructed environments such as offices, homes, and hospitals (Altman, 1976).

The Natural Environment

The natural environment makes demands, sets constraints, and provides resources. In short, it has a great deal to do with how we live our lives and thus tends to affect personality greatly. For example, families in extremely cold climates are more likely to sleep in one bed. This sleeping pattern could influence the closeness of the family, sexual attitudes, and related aspects of personality development.

Individuals typically are not consciously aware of the importance of physical factors as determinants of personality. Thus, both the natural environment and the biological givens discussed in Chapter 1 exert their effect often without the immediate knowledge of those affected.

Climate, Subsistence, and Settlement Patterns. Cross-cultural investigations of the influence of climate on personality nicely illustrate the interlocking of the physical and social worlds. Climate is just one example among many (e.g., physical resources, topography, amount of daylight, ionization of the atmosphere) we could have selected to demonstrate personality's broad environmental context. Climate is particularly appropriate for discussion, however, because its effects on personality and behavior have been clearly documented.

Berry (1976) has shown that one manner in which climate affects personality is through the causal chain of climate → settlement pattern → individuals' personalities. Anthropologists have identified four settlement patterns of societies: fully nomadic (move continuously); seminomadic (move regularly but occupy a fixed settlement for a season); semisedentary (move regularly but less often); and fully sedentary (occupy one settlement for a long period of time). These patterns of adaptation are directly related to the manner in which the society subsists. Societies that live by hunting and gathering are semi- or fully nomadic; agricultural societies are semi- or fully sedentary.

Two climatic variables influence both the means of subsistence and the settlement pattern within a society: the average temperature and the amount of rainfall. The temperature level and amount of rain permit organisms to satisfy their subsistence and shelter needs in diverse ways. In the case of both low rainfall and low temperature, as in polar regions, agriculture is impossible. Hence, the means of satisfying basic nutritional needs are hunting and/or fishing, activities that typically require a nomadic existence. Given low rainfall but high temperature, as in desert regions, neither agriculture nor fishing is possible, but hunger can be satisfied by hunting and gathering; this, too, requires mobility. Given high rainfall, however, agricultural activities are possible for the satisfaction of basic needs.

In sum, the natural environmental factors of temperature and rainfall influence the manner in which food needs are met and, in turn, influence patterns of settlement. Furthermore, these disparate methods of need satisfaction require different personality types in order for the society to survive. In agricultural societies, according to Barry, Child, and Bacon (1959, p. 52):

> Carelessness in performance of routine duties leads to a threat of hunger, not for the day of carelessness itself but for many months to come. Individual initiative attempts to improve techniques may be feared because no one can tell immediately whether the changes will lead to a greater harvest or to a disastrous failure. Under those conditions, there might well be a premium on obedience to the older and wiser, and on responsibility in faithful performance to the routine laid down by custom for one's economic role.

Furthermore, "growing and harvesting crops on a large scale requires teamwork, and rigid organization may be needed to mobilize and direct the people's efforts toward the common goal of an abundant harvest" (Pelto, 1968, p. 40). On the other hand (Barry, Child, and Bacon, 1959, p. 52):

> At an opposite extreme is subsistence through hunting or fishing with no means for extended storing of catch. Here individual initiative and development of high skill seem to be at a premium. Where each day's food comes from that day's catch, variations in the energy and skill exerted in food-getting lead to immediate reward or punishment.

To summarize, societies must cope with disparate environmental demands and may require disparate personality types in order to be successful. Agricultural societies need to bring up children to be reliable and obedient, whereas hunting societies require that their members be self-reliant and autonomous. The research indicates that societies do indeed tend to beget appropriate personalities.

Table 2.1 shows the relationship between degree of food accumulation, which is high in agricultural societies and low in hunting societies, and child-training practices that promote responsibility, obedience, and achievement. Table 2.1 clearly reveals that high food-accumulation societies stress compliance (there is a high positive correlation between amount of food accumulation and responsibility and obedience), whereas low food-accumulation societies emphasize assertion and autonomy (there is a high negative correlation between amount of food accumulation and achievement, self-reliance, and autonomy, meaning that the higher the food accumulation, the lower these other variables).

Table 2.1

Relationship between six child-training practices and degree of food accumulation

Child-training variables	Boys	Girls
Responsibility	+.74	+.62
Obedience	+.50	+.59
Nurturance	−.01	+.10
Achievement	−.60	−.62
Self-reliance	−.21	−.46
Independence	−.41	−.11

Source: H. Barry, I. Child, and M. Bacon, "Relation of Child Training to Subsistence Economy," *American Anthropologist, 61,* 1959, p. 57. Reproduced by permission of the American Anthropological Association from *American Anthropologist 61*:1, February 1959. Not for further reproduction.

The research therefore suggests dramatic relationships among the natural environment, means of need satisfaction, food accumulation, settlement pattern, and socialization practices (see Table 2.2). Although it seems farfetched and requires an understanding of many mediating variables, it is not entirely incorrect to say that personality is determined by the amount of rainfall!

There have also been laboratory attempts to substantiate the linkages shown in Table 2.2. In one investigation (Berry, 1967), individuals from high and low food-accumulating cultures (respectively, the Temne and Eskimo peoples) were tested for conformity in a controlled laboratory setting. The participants were asked to match the length of various lines and in one condition were given false information about others' responses. It was found that only the Temne (high food accumulators) tended to agree with the alleged responses of others, regardless of the information's correctness. Of course, there may be many interpretations of the observed differences in conformity. However, the findings are in accordance with the hypotheses suggested in Table 2.2, thus contributing to a consistent network of theory, support from field observations, and laboratory findings.

Climate, Ions, and Aggression.   We are all familiar with the stereotype that individuals living in a warm climate are much more impulsive and tempestuous than persons living in a cold climate. The phrase *hot-tempered* illustrates this common association between heat and anger. Similarly, tempers are said to "flare" when we fight; we get "hot under the collar" when frustrated; and we might do a "slow burn" when angered. Thus, anger and aggression are often depicted with a heat metaphor.

A great deal of psychological research has explored whether there is a relationship between environmental temperature and aggression. Some studies examine differences in aggressive crime rates as a function of differences in temperatures of geographic regions. Other studies consider crime rates during various time periods, such as season, month, and day. Still other investigations, conducted in laboratories, examine the effects of temperature on the behavior of the participants (see review in Anderson, 1989).

Table 2.2   General overview of relation between ecology and socialization practices

	Low rainfall	High rainfall
Subsistence:	Hunting and gathering	Agriculture
Food accumulation:	Low	High
Settlement pattern:	Nomadic	Sedentary
Socialization emphasis:	Assertion	Compliance

Source: Table adapted from "Human Ecology and Cognitive Style," John W. Berry, p. 60, © 1976, Sage Publications, Beverly Hills, with permission of the author.

◼ **Highlight 2.1** ▬▬▬▬▬▬

Lunacy and the Moon

It has often been suggested that the moon directly influences human behavior. The moon has been thought to increase sexual powers, affect births and deaths, cause the onset of epilepsy, promote mental disturbances and, of course, be responsible for werewolves. These effects have been written about throughout history and in fictional literature. Inasmuch as the moon provides light at night and exerts a powerful gravitational force that influences the tides and weather, these effects could be thought of as having physical mediators.

To examine possible lunar effects on mental disturbances, Campbell and Beets (1978) reviewed the psychological literature related to psychiatric hospital admissions, suicides, and homicides. They found no correlation between a full moon and any of these indicators of psychological disturbance. Perhaps the widespread use of electric lights masks the influence of the presence or absence of a full moon. But for whatever reason, it seems that a full moon has no significant consequences for mental stability. On the other hand, there are data suggesting a relation between the absence of sunlight and depression, and one experimental approach to the alleviation of depression merely bathes the patient in light!

Anderson (1987) examined the effects of both yearly temperature, and temperature between the four seasons of the year, on violent crime. The data clearly revealed that violent crimes were most prevalent in the second and third quarters of the year (the hottest periods). In addition, the differences between violent and nonviolent crimes were highest in these seasons. Figure 2.1 on p. 42 also shows that violent crime was greatest in years that had the hottest number of days, and that the increase in violent crime as a function of yearly temperature exceeded the increase in nonviolent crimes. Anderson (1989) has concluded that hot temperatures increase aggressive tendencies, and this is documented in the fact that hotter regions of the world are associated with more aggression, as are hotter years, quarters of the years, seasons, months, and days. Aggressions, including murders, rapes, assaults, riots, and wife beatings, all occur more frequently given augmented temperature.

Climate is not the only environmental factor that influences aggression-related phenomena. Studies show that negative and positive ions in the air also affect aggression and moods (Baron, 1987; Baron, Russell, and Arms, 1985), as do high ozone levels (Rotton and Frey, 1985). For example, the onset of global winds like the Santa Ana in California and the Chinook in the Pacific Northwest corre-

Figure 2.1 Effects of yearly differences in temperatures on violent and nonviolent crime rates, United States, 1971–1980. (Adapted from Anderson. *Journal of Personality and Social Psychology*, 1987, *52*, p. 1164. Copyright 1987 by the American Psychological Association. Adapted by permission.)

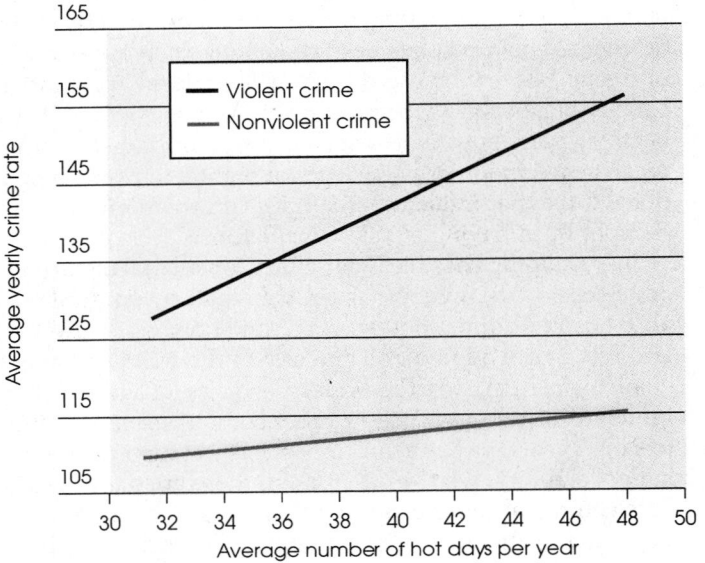

lates with increased crime, suicide, and industrial accidents. It has been suggested that some individuals are particularly sensitive to increased ions and respond with tension and irritability (Charry and Hawkinshire, 1981).

Constructed Environments

The nature of a physical setting promotes a multitude of human actions and feelings. Consider the consequences of working in a windowless office; being confined to a small, dark room; or staying in a cold, impersonal hospital. There are many more research studies about the psychological effects of such constructed physical surroundings than about the natural environment, perhaps because social engineers can change offices and classrooms more readily than the climate or the availability of resources. Again, because of space limitations, we have selected just one example that illustrates the relationships between behavior and a person's physical context.

Psychiatric Wards. What is perhaps most noticeable in a psychiatric ward is the lack of interaction between the patients. They sit alone, wander about by themselves, and remain generally removed from others. Observers attribute this behavior to the patients' states of mind, describing them as "withdrawn," "out of touch," and "incapable of human interaction."

Sommer and Ross (1958) noticed that even in so-called modern wards, with television sets and good lighting, the furniture tended to be arranged with shoulder-to-shoulder seating along the walls of the room or with chairs placed in back-to-back rows, not unlike seating arrangements in public transportation waiting rooms. Given this placement of furniture, interaction is difficult; the geography of the ward promotes psychological withdrawal. Of course, such furniture arrangements might facilitate cleaning and the movement of food carts, but these positive consequences are far removed from the goals of a mental hospital.

To demonstrate the effects of seating arrangements on interpersonal communication, Sommer and Ross changed the position of the furniture in a psychiatric ward. They had the chairs moved from the walls and placed around tables, so that the seated patients would be facing one another. The attractiveness of the tables was also enhanced with flowers and magazines so that the patients would use them as a focal point. Before these changes and two weeks after the alterations were introduced, Sommer and Ross time-sampled verbal communications on the ward. Table 2.3 indicates that the number of both brief and sustained interactions almost doubled given the new physical context. It is thus evident that one's behavior is determined by the immediate geography and that conclusions about a person cannot be divorced from the physical environment. What was thought to be a manifestation of a basic personality pattern (namely, social withdrawal) was found to be significantly influenced by the organization of the physical surroundings. One wonders what the long-term effects on personality might be if one were raised in a home with furniture arranged as in a typical psychiatric ward!

Behavior Settings

Roger Barker (1960, 1965, 1968) has said that the best way to predict human behavior is to know where a person is. In a post office, a person behaves "post office-like"; in church, one's behavior is "churchy"; and in classrooms, one acts

Table 2.3   Total number of verbal interactions during thirty-three five-minute observation periods

	Brief interactions	Sustained interactions
Old arrangement	47	36
New arrangement	73	61

Source: Sommer and Ross, 1958, p. 132.

like a student (or a teacher). Post offices, churches, and schools are all *behavior settings*. A behavior setting has spatial properties and a geographical location, but it also has social properties, such that the setting exists only when people are gathered there to perform certain activities. Hence, a shutdown post office is no longer a behavior setting, even though its physical properties might remain unchanged. Behavior settings vary greatly, from bridge clubs and restaurants to baseball fields and offices. They can be part of the natural environment, such as parks and lakes, or constructed environments, such as schools and offices.

Wicker and Kirmeyer (1977) have described a behavior setting as a place where:

1. One of a number of regularly occurring human activities take place, such as playing bridge at a bridge club or praying in a church.

2. A behavior is coordinated with inanimate objects within the setting, such as card tables at a bridge club or pews in a church.

3. People inhabiting the setting are interchangeable and replaceable. Anyone arriving at a bridge club can enter a game, and Sunday services continue as congregations change. Hence, the behavior exhibited is independent of the particular people within the setting.

Within these settings a variety of personal motivations are satisfied. The motivations of bridge players can vary from aggression and affiliation to achievement and power; the unity of the setting is not derived from the unity of the participants' motivations. But, in spite of motivational differences, the individuals in the setting engage in the same general pattern of behavior.

Overmanning and Undermanning.   The relation between the number of people in a setting and the psychological consequences of being part of that setting has been thoroughly investigated. Settings can be *undermanned, overmanned,* or have an optimal number of members, each determined by the number of people available to perform a setting's essential functions. A bridge club with three members is undermanned, while a baseball team with one hundred members is overmanned.

Consider, for example, some consequences of participating in a baseball game when your team has only four members instead of the usual nine. As a result of this undermanning, each team member's average value is greater and each person has more obligations. For example, the second baseman must also play first base. There is therefore greater variability and more effort required per player than in an optimally manned setting. Because of these demands, more tension is aroused, more responsibility is assumed, and greater insecurities are manifested. And there are more incidents of personal success and failure.

In general, setting size is correlated with degree of manning. Small towns and small schools, for example, tend to be undermanned, whereas urban areas and large schools are overmanned. As Fig. 2.2 demonstrates, there are relatively more

Figure 2.2 Subjective feelings in large and small schools: Relation of degree of undermanning and experiences in behavior settings. (Wicker, 1968, p. 259. Copyright 1968 by the American Psychological Association. Reprinted by permission.)

people performing in responsible positions in small than in large environmental contexts.

Overmanning and undermanning generate forces to bring about an optimal level of manning. For example, if a setting is undermanned, there are pressures to remain in and recruit others to the group. On the other hand, if a setting is overmanned, recruiting tends to be reduced, and eligibility standards may be raised. For example, the drama coach may have to plead with students to participate in a play at a small high school, while at a large school there are tryouts where only the best performers are accepted (see Wicker and Kirmeyer, 1977). These influences on personality and behavior are typically not consciously perceived by the person rejected from, say, the football team. He is less likely to blame the size of the community than to blame himself and to suffer the psychological consequences of this belief.

Total Institutions. A *total institution* is also a behavior setting, but it has certain unique characteristics not found in the types of settings investigated by Barker. A total institution completely encompasses the individual, forming a barrier to the types of social intercourse that occur outside such a setting. Monasteries, jails, homes for the aged, boarding schools, and military academies are a few examples of total institutions.

Total institutions have certain common characteristics (see Goffman, 1961). First, the individuals in such environments must sleep, play, and work within the same setting. These are generally segmented spheres of activity in the lives of most individuals, but within a total institution one sphere of activity overlaps with others. Second, each phase of life takes place in the company of a large group of others. Frequently, sleeping is done in a barracks, food is served in a cafeteria, and so on. In such activities everyone is treated alike and must perform certain essential tasks. Third, activities in an institution are tightly scheduled according to a master plan, with set times to rise, to eat, to exercise, and to sleep. These institutional characteristics result in a bureaucratic society, which requires the hiring of other people for surveillance. What often results is a dichotomous split in

Both prisons and military bases can be total institutions, in which members wear the same clothes and perform identical activities. The institutional world also is divided between those in charge and the "inmates." (left — David Woo/Stock, Boston; right — Owen Franken/Stock, Boston)

the groups within an institution into a large, managed group (*inmates*) and a small supervisory staff. There tends to be great social distance between the groups, who perceive each other according to stereotypes and have severely restricted communications.

The world of the inmate differs greatly from the outside world. When one enters a total institution, all previous roles, such as father or husband, are disrupted. The individual is further depersonalized by the issuance of a uniform, confiscation of belongings, and gathering of personal information, as well as by more subtle touches like doorless toilets, record keeping, and bedchecks. The effects of an institutional setting are so all-encompassing that one can meaningfully speak of an "institutional personality": a persistent manner of behaving compliantly and without emotional involvement.

Of course, there are individual differences in adaptation to the situation. They can be as extreme as psychosis, childlike regression, and depression or as mild as resigned compliance. Most individuals do adjust and build up a system of satisfactions, such as close friendships and cliques. But because of these bonds and the fact that the habits needed to function in the outside world have been lost, inmates face great problems upon leaving an institution. A shift from the top of a small society to the bottom of a larger one may be further demoralizing.

Goffman provides many other fascinating insights into total institutions, but the general message of his work is that, to understand behavior, the environment in which it occurs must be taken into consideration.

Privacy and Territoriality

A number of other key concepts have been identified in the study of the relation between the physical world and behavior; among them are privacy, territoriality, and density (Altman, 1975).

Privacy refers to an individual's freedom to choose what is communicated about the self, to control when this communication will take place, and to limit incoming stimulation. It is evident that when large families live in one or two rooms, or even when houses in good neighborhoods are placed too close to one another, feelings of privacy are sacrificed. In such situations one gives up control over unwanted intrusion (see Ittelson, Proshansky, Rivlin, and Winkel, 1974).

Privacy has a number of functions, including the opportunity for self-evaluation, reflection, and planning. Hence, the absence of sufficient privacy can have serious psychological consequences. It comes as no surprise, then, that cultures provide mechanisms for ensuring privacy, such as locks on doors, curtains, and Do Not Disturb signs. Even primitive cultures have privacy mechanisms, including huts that only one sex or one person is allowed to inhabit. Given some opportunity for privacy, cultures differ markedly in their physical arrangements affecting privacy.

Societies that require economic cooperation and shared decision making tend to have physical arrangements that reduce privacy. The Israeli kibbutz is a modern example of such an arrangement where privacy is hard to come by. Societies that emphasize economic competition and individualism, on the other hand, are more likely to have tall fences to separate different families.

The term *territoriality,* which is derived from the study of nonhumans, assumes that organisms lay claim to a particular territory which they defend from intruders and determine who may or may not enter. A number of nonhuman species, including birds, dogs, and fish, lay claim to territories. Humans also appear to be territorial, although such behavior need not be instinctive. However, common to both humans and nonhumans is the idea that territories encompass a given geographical area, that there is clear ownership of the place, and that the physical location is personalized or marked.

One interesting aspect of territoriality is the reactive behaviors toward intruders or invaders of a territory. Among nonhumans, the defender of a territory is typically the winner of a fight, regardless of the relative physical attributes of the combatants. Among humans, it has been suggested that when in one's own territory one is more dominant, controlling, and powerful.

Edney (1975) experimentally examined whether humans display special behaviors when in a home territory. The study was conducted in college dormitory rooms, where one person was the resident and the other a visitor. Participants who were the residents of a room responded differently to the experimental task than did the visitors, expressing greater feelings of control. In a similar study, Martindale (1971) found that dormitory residents were more successful at a negotiation task when in their own territory. This was found to be true whether the resident was low or high in dominance (Taylor and Lanni, 1981). There is thus some truth to the belief that "people's homes are their castles"; behaviors in a home setting do differ from actions in other physical locations, with individuals more likely to behave like "kings" in terms of increased dominance, power, and hostility. It has even been documented that players in a game arcade exhibit territorial responses like extra touching of their machines to "claim their territory" and ward off intruders (Werner, Brown, and Damron, 1981).

Summary of Environmental Effects

Our initial discussion has examined the relationship between the physical or geographical environment and personality. Natural factors such as average temperature and rainfall influence personality by limiting the available means of subsistence and, in turn, determining what personality types are best suited to survive within these environmental constraints. Constructed environments also influence behavior directly. For example, the placement of furniture or the size of a working area can affect interpersonal communication and friendship patterns.

Another aspect of the environment that shapes behavior is the *behavior setting*. Behavior settings can be characterized by the number of people available to perform important functions. If a setting is undermanned, for instance, more tension and uncertainty are aroused, but there is also a greater sense of responsibility and personal acceptance. A total institution is a particular type of behavior setting where communications with the external world are severely restricted.

Finally, the concepts of privacy, or the freedom to choose and control one's communications, and territoriality, or claim to a particular geographical space, are aspects of the physical environment that have far-reaching psychological consequences on both immediate behavior and long-term adjustment patterns.

THE SOCIAL WORLD

The physical world of climate, terrain, material structures, and space provides the background for diverse cultures, customs, social structures, and roles. We will treat the social world as if it were independent of the physical world, but in fact the two are as intimately connected as nature and nurture. The structure of a society and its cultural traditions exert powerful influences on the personalities of individuals born into it. Social groups and cultures may live in similar physical settings but display quite different behaviors.

The influence of the social world is especially impressive when one considers that the members of quite different social groups can still be quite similar biologically. The infant born into a preliterate New Guinea tribe and the infant born to a sophisticated Parisian family are genetically more alike than different. Indeed, it has been estimated that human races are fifty times more similar than are human and chimpanzee and that even so-called unrelated individuals share more than 99 percent of their genes (Washburn, 1978). After all, all humans have two eyes, one nose, a mouth, and so on. Hence, it remains clear that genetic differences between groups are minor compared with the wide range of behaviors exhibited between social classes and cultures. It is primarily social, not biological, factors that cause members of a social group to behave uniquely.

Because of our flexibility, because humans are adjustable and changeable, the disparate norms and values of a society can be transmitted to and accepted by succeeding generations, ensuring the survival of the culture. Each generation must learn to function within the confines and according to the rules of a given society and social group. Our families, peers, schools, churches, and mass media are among the social agents and institutions that determine who and what we are, or our *socialization*. Some of these influences will be examined in later sections of the text where we analyze personality development and specific behavioral patterns. For the present, we again choose an illustrative topic, social class, and consider the relation between this key social variable and personality to demonstrate the binding of the individual and the social world.

Social Class

All societies are to some extent stratified. *Social stratification* is a relatively stable, hierarchical arrangement of groups of individuals, with the "higher" classes within this hierarchy receiving more social and material rewards than the "lower" classes. Individuals within a class typically perform similar occupations and face the same life conditions and problems. As a result, individuals can be assigned to a social class by using indexes such as education, occupation, income, and prestige. All of these class indicators are intertwined, for education provides access to job opportunities, while jobs, in turn, bring increased income, prestige, and power.

The concepts of social class and social status are so complex that some scholars even differentiate between the two, contending that class has implications for one's *chances* in life, while status has implications for one's *style* of life. Here we will not differentiate between the terms, but assume that assignment to a particular class may reveal place of residence, type of job, level of property ownership, amount of education, friends' social status, and related attributes. Class is also associated with such personal characteristics as values, mode of dress, and even style of speech. Because of the pervasive influence of class membership, knowledge of just this variable can reveal much about an individual's personality. Disparate social classes also expose children to different methods of child rearing, which influence a variety of personality traits.

Although social class membership can be a revealing indicator of a person's life style, speech patterns, and even certain personality attributes, one must keep in mind two cautions when interpreting social-class differences in abilities and behavior:

1. In essentially all instances in which social class differences have been demonstrated, there is a great deal of variation between individuals *within* a particular social class. For example, lower-class children typically obtain, on the average, lower scores on intelligence tests than middle-class children (Scarr and Carter-Saltzman, 1985). However, there are wide differences in intelligence test scores *within* each social class, so that many lower-class children will obtain higher scores than many middle-class children.

2. Style and personality differences that have been observed between lower- and middle-class individuals are not fixed forever. As the challenges that face

different social groups change, and as people change from one social class to another, their life styles, language, and even personality attributes will change also.

Middle Versus Working Class.   There are many contrasts between and implications of middle- and working-class membership in the United States. The middle class often earns income sufficient to permit savings and has both advanced education and marketable skills. Its members have what is called a *conceptual* orientation (Miller and Swanson, 1960), using their mental capacities to solve problems, with their jobs often involving the manipulation of symbols rather than objects. Their working life focus is on occupational advancement and competent performance, and their jobs are often quite specialized and responsible.

Members of the working class, on the other hand, typically have more serious financial concerns and not enough salary to permit savings. They are more likely to have on-the-job training than a formal education. Their orientation toward life is considered to be *motoric,* in that they manipulate objects rather than symbols.

It might be expected that the varied and subtle effects of social class would be evident in the self-concept and self-esteem of the members of the disparate classes — those in the upper classes would be expected to have higher self-esteem than those in the lower classes. However, the relation between social class and sense of self-worth is complex and determined by a multiplicity of factors.

One determinant of a person's sense of self-worth is comparison with others. Children are likely to believe that their external environment is homogeneous and that others are like themselves. On the other hand, adults recognize the differentiations within the larger social environment. Consistent with this fact, among children there is virtually no relation between class and self-esteem, whereas among adults those of the higher classes at times score higher in sense of self-worth than those of the lower classes (Rosenberg and Pearlin, 1978). However, it also has been reported that *within* groups of men with either a high school education or a college education, the self-esteem of successful groups is higher than the self-esteem of unsuccessful groups. However, the overall self-esteem of the college graduates was no higher than that of the high school graduates (Luck and Heiss, 1972). In other words, people compare themselves with others in the same category.

In addition, those of lower class may ascribe their relative failure in life to barriers imposed by others, thus maintaining their own self-worth. Or they may tend to devalue material gains and value other characteristics that they do possess, such as friends.

Finally, changing economic status at various points in life might affect feelings toward oneself, adding still further complexity to any simple relation between class and psychological variables. For example, it has been reported that mother's background status, status at a child's birth, and status before the child is in school all contribute to the child's performance and behavior at age five (Furstenberg, Brooks–Gunn, and Morgan, 1987).

Discipline Patterns. As might be expected, social classes differ in their child-rearing practices. Lower-class mothers impose more restrictions on their children (Waters and Crandall, 1964) and use more negative statements in teaching them (Feshbach, 1973). Evidence of social class differences in parental behavior is provided by a study of adolescents from India (Schludermann and Schludermann, 1983). Lower-class adolescents report significantly greater rule making by their parents and stricter enforcement of these rules, through punishment, than do middle-class adolescents. In addition, contrary to suggestions of earlier studies on Western children (Miller and Swanson, 1960), lower-class Indian parents are perceived as exercising more psychological control, through tactics such as inducing guilt and shame and withdrawing love, than do middle-class Indian parents.

It may be, of course, that lower-class parents are more restrictive because their life circumstances make it difficult for them to behave otherwise. The predicament of the lower-class parent is graphically described by Newson and Newson (1976, p. 338):

> The mother's ability to be "relaxed" over toilet training, for instance, may be more dependent than she likes to think upon an efficient hot water supply, automatic washing machine and plastic pants, or upon disposable napkins or a good nappy service — or, alternatively, upon a warm sun and a culture pattern that allows children to run naked! It is not so easy to remain calm and accepting as the toddler wets nappy after nappy, if washing them involves boiling up water in a kettle and scrubbing away by hand; nor, indeed, can a mother be quite so "friendly and easy-going about the bathroom" (Spock) if the bathroom doesn't exist and the lavatory is the other side of the back yard or down a flight of tenement stairs and shared with three or four other families of careless habits. Again, whether the pre-school child is expected to stand up for himself and hit back when he is among his peers, or whether he is withdrawn from such conflict by his mother, can be seen as partly, though not entirely, a function of the type of housing occupied by the family, according to whether the child can be withdrawn into his own yard or garden and whether neighbouring entrances are separated by fence or hedge.

When considering the relationship between social class and discipline patterns, it should not be thought that the two social class groups are structurally equal. In the lower classes, there is much greater likelihood of there being only one parent in the home, the female. Male absence is a crucial variable in the differential treatment of children, in part because male absence may also change the reactions of the parenting female. In addition, female absence due to wage-earning demands has effects on children, with daughters of employed mothers found to be more independent by some research (Lamb, 1982), while other research has found that maternal absence (but not maternal employment) is related to a deficit in the social connectedness of young adults (Tolman, Diekmann, and McCartney, 1989). In sum, the idea of class differences must be considered within a framework that includes not merely differences in family patterns of behavior, but also differences in what constitutes the family.

Culture

Personality differences between nations and ethnic groups are popularly recognized; there are stereotypes that the people within a particular group or nation are believed to follow. These differences are ascribed to disparities in *culture*: the modes of acting and feeling, or the set of norms and ideals, that are customary for an entire group. Culture therefore involves consistency in the actions of a larger number of people than does social class.

Not all customs that distinguish one culture from another are equally relevant to personality. The fact that it is taboo in some cultures to eat pork while in other cultures it is taboo to eat beef is probably not germane to personality. It is also important to recognize that there is much more variability in personality than in social customs in any society. Consequently, one finds that only *on the average* are people in one culture more aggressive, ambitious, courageous, or conforming than people in another culture. Although phrases like "the fiery Latin American temperament" or "the inscrutable Oriental mind" have varying degrees of correctness when applied to any particular individual, it is still valid to try to determine whether there are sets of personality attributes that most members of a culture have in common. When such common attributes are found, one can speak of a "national character type," recognizing that there are many individuals within that culture who may not conform to that type.

In certain instances the description of the resources or practices of a culture virtually ensures that there will be personality and behavioral differences between cultural groups. For example (Child, 1968, p. 95):

> Suppose we read that a particular society has a very stable economy, with ample food for a longer period always on hand, and efficient and equitable techniques for distributing it. We are strongly tempted to believe that the typical member of that society has little if any anxiety about getting enough to eat. If we read that young children in another society see little of adult men, we will easily believe that some aura of early-instilled femininity will cling to the typical male child as he grows up.

Indeed, our own observations and experience suggest that people in different cultures appear to be dissimilar in certain essential ways. Crossing borders in Europe, one is met with marked and often alarming differences in people. Clearly, an individual's character is determined by time and place of appearance in history. Let us now briefly consider some examples of cultural differences pertinent to personality that have been documented from the study of psychopathology.

Psychopathology. Symptoms of mental disorder vary greatly, depending on the cultural context of the disturbed individual. For example, the hysterical symptoms that were so frequent in Vienna at the time of Freud, and so central in the development of Freudian theory, are now rarely in evidence. Similarly, the incidence of manic-depressive psychoses has greatly decreased in America, but not in England. Although care must be taken in all such comparisons because diagnoses are also subject to change, it is quite clear that there are different rates of mental illness between cultures over time.

Mental disorders may vary between cultures because different cultures give rise to different types of conflict and stress. For example, Weisz and his colleagues (1987) reported that in Thailand, in which children's aggression and other uncontrolled behaviors are severely disapproved, overcontrolled behavioral problems (e.g., fear, worry, nervous movements) are particularly frequent in children. It appears that the traditional emphasis on quietness and inhibition, and the concomitant child-rearing practices, foster the development of problems regarding overcontrol.

In addition, disparate cultural values may result in disparate pathologies. For example, the aged in Ghana have secure positions within the family and are not relegated to a lower status as they grow old. This is not the case in our culture. Thus, in Ghana the tendency toward mental illness is not made worse by aging, while in our culture the aged exhibit a variety of specifically age-related disturbances such as depression.

Pathology takes forms other than mental illness, and again there are marked disparities between cultures. For example, in the United States the homicide rate exceeds that in the Philippines by a factor of almost eight and is ten times that in England (see Chapter 18). In addition, there are wide disparities in rates of alcoholism between cultural groups. For example, it is well documented that Jews and Chinese have very low rates of drinking problems, while the incidence of alcoholism among the Irish is very high (see Opler, 1959).

In sum, cultural differences in psychopathology illustrate the impact of culture on personality.

Culture and the Study of Personality.   It is important to consider how culture influences the study of psychology itself. Smith and Bond (1993) have reviewed attempts to replicate important research findings across cultures. They note that many of the "classic" findings of American psychology do not replicate in other cultures. For instance, in the United States, when individuals work together in groups, a phenomenon called *social loafing* occurs; that is, individuals exert less effort than they do when they work alone. However, this is not found in Taiwan (Gabrenya et al., 1985) or China (Early, 1989). In these cultures individuals work *harder* when they are in groups.

In recent years a rising chorus of voices has been arguing that many of our ideas about personality are based on a view of the individual that is largely a product of Western culture. Furthermore, it is a view that is more reflective of masculine rather than feminine experience. Finally, it has been argued that these cultural biases have also influenced our models of research.

In particular, critics have focused on the Western view of the self and of the individual. Landrine (1992) has noted that in Western culture an unequivocal distinction is drawn between the self on the one hand and the nonself on the other. Our Western view of the self tends to treat it as a ghostly entity inside which has, or should have, absolute power to regulate the individual. The self is thus separate, encapsulated, and godlike, in that it is presumed to be the "originator, creator, and controller of behavior" (p. 402). Such a view of the self puts an enormous emphasis on mastery and control, and healthy individuals are seen as exercising self-control as well as control of any situations they are in.

This self is also seen as having its own stable identity that it maintains independent of the contexts it is in. Therefore it has a structure consisting of traits which are themselves free of contexts. Such a self can be described without reference to other people or to the situations it is in. Such a self can also be reflected on, and Western culture places a high value on abstract self-reflection. Thus there is a premium on ideas such as self-awareness, self-criticism, self-consciousness, self-actualization, self-fulfillment, and self-determination. Finally, this self also puts a premium on rationality (Triandis, 1989).

This view of the self is not only a Western one but is also based more on masculine than on feminine experience (Jordan et al., 1991). It goes hand in hand with a stance that leads to the kind of research model currently valued in psychology, a model that emphasizes distance, objectivity, the study of relatively static objects, and control. In contrast, Gilligan, Brown, and Rogers (1990) argue for a research model that stresses connection, receptivity, understanding, and the flow of interaction over time. In particular they stress the importance of researchers hearing the "voice" of the people they are studying, reflecting the idea that researchers and subjects are more interconnected than our typical models of research assume.

In a recent study of the development of adolescent girls, Brown and Gilligan (1992) repeatedly interviewed girls in a private school over several years. Initially, they tried to follow a formal, rigid interview format, so that they would maintain "objectivity," so that the data-collecting conditions would be the same for all subjects, and so that interviewers could not bias the results by leading subjects in one direction or the other. However, they discovered that they introduced a different kind of bias. By following a formal interview format, they created an inauthentic relationship with the girls, who then did not open up in the ways Brown and Gilligan wanted. Once the interviewers stopped worrying about objectivity and related to the girls in more informal ways, they were better able to hear the voices of the girls, and to obtain data more truly reflective of the girls' experiences.

The Western, masculine view of the self as separate, encapsulated, bounded, existing free of contexts, and controlled from within, is a view of the self not shared by the majority of cultures in the world. In contrast, most cultures hold a *sociocentric* view of the self. This view sees the self as fundamentally interdependent and as existing within a field of forces. Markus and Kitayama (1991) note that the "interdependent view is normative in most cultures . . . seeing oneself as part of an encompassing social relationship and recognizing that one's behavior is determined, contingent on, and, to a large extent organized by what the actor perceives to be the thoughts, feelings, and actions of others in the relationship . . . the view of the self and the relationship between the self and others features the person not as separate from the social context but as more connected and less differentiated from others" (p. 227). This view of the self is more charac-teristic of the African-American (Stevenson, 1993), Hispanic-American (Ramirez, 1991), and Asian-American cultural experiences (Markus and Kitayama, 1991) as well as the experiences of many others, including Native Americans (Markus and Kitayama, 1991).

In Japan, for instance, the word for the self — *jibun* — refers to an individual's share of the shared life space rather than to a substance or attribute with a constant oneness. The self is not a constant, like the ego, but rather a fluid concept which changes as a function of the person's interpersonal relationships (Markus and Kitayama, 1991). To quote Markus and Kitayama, " the Japanese nightmare is exclusion, meaning that one is failing at the normative goal of connecting with others. This is in sharp contrast to the American nightmare, which is to fail at separating from others, as can occur when one is unduly influenced by others, or does not stand up for what one believes, or when one goes unnoticed or undistin-guished" (p. 228).

An implication of the sociocentric view of the self for personality theory is that many of our Western concepts, such as the idea of enduring individual traits, motives, and desires, are revealed to reflect our Western, individualistic view of the self. Landrine (1992) notes that the sociocentric self found in most cultures "has no enduring, trans-situational characteristics, no traits or desires or needs of its own in isolation from its relationships and contexts." Further, self-reflection is not necessarily valued, especially since in some cultures the self is an illusion. In reply to a question such as "Tell me something about yourself," a person from a sociocentric culture would not be likely to give an abstract self-description in terms of personality traits and enduring likes and motivations (for example, "I'm outgoing, I like sports, I'm a high achiever."). Rather, they would be likely to give several long, detailed, concrete descriptions of their interactions with others (for example, "The other day a friend of mine and I were arguing and I lost my temper . . ."). In the process, they might be seen by a Western psychologist as "lacking insight."

Another implication of this discussion for personality theory is that our Western view biases us to see certain kinds of personality traits as more healthy than others. Pederson (1987) has noted that we tend to view independence as more valuable than dependency. Many of our concepts of psychopathology, such as that of co-dependence, revolve around ideas of being excessively dependent, or enmeshed, with others. Yet what a Western therapist sees as excessive depen-dency would be seen as both healthy and absolutely necessary in many cultures. In a similar manner, Ramirez (1983, 1991) has criticized the idea that those whose perceptions are heavily influenced by their context ("field dependence," Witkin and Goodenough, 1981) are "less than" those whose separate their perceptions and judgments out from the context ("field independence"). He has suggested that field dependence is more appropriately thought of as "field sensitivity" and has argued that as a "cognitive style" field sensitivity is more characteristic of non-Western cultures.

Triandis (1989) has studied the differences between cultures that hold individualistic notions about the self and cultures that hold sociocentric or "collectivist" notions. In the West, selves have personal names, while in collectivistic cultures they are often referred to relationally (for example, mother of X). Individualistic cultures see the self in terms of what it *owns* — its possessions, its own experiences, its accomplishments — while in collectivist cultures identity is defined in terms of relationships. In individualistic cultures, to be distinct and different is highly valued. In contrast, in collectivist cultures people try to conform to others in public settings, for instance, ordering the same food at a restaurant.

Two studies point out the differences. In one study, G. V. Marin, Marin, Otero-Sabogal, Sabogal, and Perez-Stable (1987, as referenced in Triandis, 1989) studied individuals' responses to the question of why they should not smoke. Hispanics (from a collectivistic culture) in the United States gave answers emphasizing concern for others, including the negative effects of cigarette smoke and setting a bad example for children. The individualistic sample was more concerned with the effects of smoking on their own physiology.

In a second study of the differences between individualistic and sociocentric cultures, Stipek, Weiner, and Li (1989) asked Chinese and American subjects to describe situations in which they got angry. Americans described situations in which something negative had happened to them personally, while Chinese subjects described situations in which something had happened to others.

Triandis points out that the kind of self valued by a culture depends on its ecology. As cultures become more complex and more affluent, they tend to become more individualistic. However, the more complex the culture, the more confused the individual's identity is likely to be. Other variables that affect whether a culture is individualistic or sociocentric are the degree of population and whether the culture is agricultural or industrialized. Densely populated cultures and agricultural cultures are more likely to be collectivistic in their view of the self.

In sum, the separate, encapsulated, individualistic self of Western culture is not representative of the self of most other cultures, which emphasize a relational, interdependent view. Many of our notions about personality, such as the idea that individuals' behavior primarily reflects individual personality traits that exist independent of situations, or that internal self-control is good, may reflect certain cultural biases. The kind of self a culture values appears to be a function of the ecological nature of that culture.

Individualism and Mental Health.   Not only have critics pointed out that psychology's ideas about self and personality may be culturally biased, but also have a number of critics argued that our culture's emphasis on individualism is the source of some of our mental health problems. Baumeister (1993) argues that in our individualistic culture the self has taken over as the major source of meaning, as other sources of meaning (such as religion and family) have declined. In accord with this, Seligman (1990), has argued that our society has moved toward a value of the "maximal self." The self has come to be the repository of all our hopes. No longer do larger institutions such as family, subgroup, religion, or nation provide a context of meaning for individuals. Now, all meaning must come from the self. Seligman argues that this is too great a burden to place on individual selves, and he blames the recent rise in depression in the United States on this overemphasis on the individual self.

There is not a great deal of research on the healthfulness of an individualistic versus a collectivistic orientation. However some studies have looked at questionnaires that ask whether individuals hold more individualistic or more collectivistic values, and they have found that higher individualism scores correlate with higher (more pathological) scores on the Minnesota Multiphasic Personality Inventory (Johnson and Norem-Hebeisen, 1977; Norem-Hebeisen and Johnson, 1981). On the other hand, Waterman (1981) found that individuals who scored highly on a scale of traditional Western measures of psychological health and development, such as identity achievement, Kohlberg's morality scale, and internal locus of control (all associated with the Western individualistic emphasis on a firm, autonomous, self-chosen identity and set of values), were also rated as more cooperative and altruistic. Anspach (1991), in defending individualism, has noted that while Americans are currently busy criticizing individualism, many other cultures (for example, Eastern Europe and China) are busy striving to achieve the very individualism we are criticizing.

No matter what the outcome of the debate over the nature of the self, and whether one view of the self is healthier than another view, current challenges to our traditional Western perspective should lead to a broader and more comprehensive view of personality.

Summary

1. Ecological/interactional perspectives view the person as embedded in the environment and as in continuous interaction with the environment.

2. Climatic conditions of rainfall and temperature in part determine a society's means of subsistence, which in turn affects settlement patterns and the characteristics of individuals needed for the society to survive. Agricultural societies need obedient and responsible members, whereas hunting societies require self-reliant and autonomous members.

3. Climate also affects behaviors such as aggression.

4. Communication in such constructed environments as psychiatric wards is facilitated by appropriate seating arrangements.

5. *Behavior settings* have spatial properties and a geographical location and exist independent of the specific individuals within the setting. The *overmanning* of behavior settings typical of large towns and large schools leads to exclusion, whereas *undermanning* results in increased participation and responsibility.

6. A *total institution* is a behavior setting, such as a prison or monastery, that completely dominates the individual. Living in a total institution has far-reaching psychological consequences.

7. Privacy, the freedom to choose and control incoming communications; and territoriality, the claim to a particular space, are aspects of the physical environment that also have profound psychological effects.

8. The effects of social stratification into classes are complex but may not influence the self-esteem of children because of the many factors that influence self-esteem and because of the different kinds of social comparison that are or are not possible.

9. The importance of cultural variables in how we conceive of and study personality has become increasingly important. In particular, the Western view of the self as individualistic, autonomous, bounded, and separate has been found to be culture-specific.

Thought Questions

1. Do you think about your self in Western terms as an "egocentric" self or in terms of a "sociocentric" self? Which way of looking at your self do you prefer?

2. List some of the behavior settings in which you act. Are they overmanned, undermanned, or optimally manned? Has this influenced your behavior in the settings?

3. How and when have your reactions been affected by being inside or outside your own territory?

4. Based on your own observations, are people in different cultures really "different"?

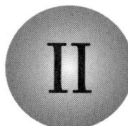

THEORIES OF PERSONALITY

Part 2 presents some of the best-known and most influential theories of personality. Among them are Freudian psychoanalytic theory (Chapter 3); descendants of and dissidents from the psychoanalytic conception, including Jung, Adler, Horney, Fromm, Erikson, Kohut, and Horowitz (Chapter 4); learning theory (Chapter 5); and cognitive approaches to personality as in the work of Carl Rogers, Abraham Maslow, George Kelly, and other phenomenological theorists (Chapter 6). These theories differ in many respects, but at the heart of the differences are contrasting basic assumptions about human nature or the essence of human beings.

Psychoanalytic theorists such as Freud and his followers believed that individuals strive to reduce inner tension, keeping internal agitation to a minimum at all costs. Humans are, in their view, irrational and instinctive biological beings. Psychoanalytic theorists generally believe that:

1. Inasmuch as individuals are unaware of their need states, personality assessment is best conducted by means of indirect or projective techniques.
2. Biological and historical factors play an essential role in behavior, and individuals progress through a fixed sequence of developmental stages.
3. Personality change must deal with the unconscious and the irrational desires of individuals.
4. Conflicts concerning sexual and aggressive instincts and social inhibitions form the heart of the psychoanalytic study of behavioral dynamics. In addition, the frustration experienced because of unsatisfied desires is directly linked with psychopathology.

Learning theory, on the other hand, traditionally asserted in its most extreme form that individuals are mere machines and that the study of personality is part of the more general examination of input-output associations or stimulus-response bonds. Given this basic view of humans, personality assessment, development, change, and dynamics all focus on specific associations:

1. Personality assessment involves the direct recording of behaviors in specific situations.
2. Personality development is based on the formation and strengthening of habits or stimulus-response bonds.
3. Personality change is accomplished by altering stimulus-response connections through the use of rewards to foster acquisition of more functional responses and punishments to extinguish maladaptive responses.

4. Behavioral dynamics involves conflicts between competing habits or response tendencies. Different and incompatible responses may be called forth by the same situation.

In its less extreme, more modern form, which we primarily examine in this book, learning theorists accept the fact that humans are not robots. Many see humans as thinking organisms whose thoughts influence their actions. However, only a few of the higher mental processes are actually incorporated into their theories. The more moderate learning theorists also believe that, although reward and punishment do influence performance, learning can take place through mere observation of others, without the direct influence of reward and punishment. Nevertheless, even these less extreme positions reflect a more mechanistic orientation than do the psychoanalytic and cognitive approaches.

Gestalt, phenomenological, and other cognitive approaches to personality often start with the assumption that individuals are scientists seeking to understand their world and to fulfill their innate potentials. Thus:

1. Personality assessment is concerned with understanding how individuals view the world or ascertaining individuals' subjective experiences.
2. Personality development is synonymous with cognitive growth, accompanied by a movement in the direction of higher goals.
3. Personality change involves altering one's view of the world and oneself. A variety of techniques from group therapy and role playing to more radical forms of sensitivity training that enhance self-awareness can be employed.
4. Personality dynamics considers the influence that beliefs have on actions, focusing on the functional significance of cognitions and subjective meanings.

The theories presented here differ in a number of other respects. Primary among these differences are the phenomena on which they focus and the research methods they have used. Freudian theory led to an examination of defense mechanisms, free associations, dreams, and sexual behavior; social learning theory has examined the effects of different rewards, punishments, and role models on social behaviors; and Gestalt, phenomenological, and other cognitive approaches have been especially concerned with self-concept, self-esteem, self-actualization, and overall human potential. The theories stand side by side, each with unique abilities to account for certain observations. As a result, there is not a clear hierarchical ordering of theories, with one "better" in every respect than the others.

Table 2.1 summarizes some points of comparison in the theories examined in the next four chapters. It will help you to return to this table as you progress through the chapters and the remainder of the text. Some of the terms in the table may be unfamiliar to you now, but they will be introduced and discussed in subsequent chapters.

Table 2.1 Comparison of the major theories of personality

Theory	Chapter	Some major contributors	Focus	Main concepts*	Assessment goal	Assessment instruments	Goals for change
Psychoanalytic	3	Freud	Sexual motivation	Energy, instinct, libido, cathexis, id, ego, superego	Reveal basic unconscious desires	Projective techniques	Insight into desires; new coping techniques
Psychoanalytic Dissidents	4	Jung, Adler, Horney, Sullivan, Fromm, Erikson	Personal growth, social motivations	Archetype, compensation, inferiority, neurotic trend, attachments, authoritarianism	Reveal basic unconscious desires	Projective techniques	Insight into desires; new coping techniques
Learning	5	Miller, Skinner, Bandura, Mischel, Rotter	Learning and the stimulus situation	Reinforcement, expectancy, value, model	Reveal typical ways of responding and their eliciting stimuli	Behavioral observation and objective instruments	Change habits; develop new responses
Cognitive-Phenomenological	6	Rogers, Maslow, Kelly	Humans as scientists; subjective experience	Unconditional regard, positive self-regard, personal constructs	Reveal perceptions of the world	Objective instruments, open-ended questionnaires	Alter cognitions or views of the world

* Not descriptive of all theorists within a category.

3 | Freud's Psychoanalytic Theory of Personality

The greatest figure among personality theorists is Sigmund Freud, the creator of psychoanalysis. Freud's psychoanalytic theory is the most general and best-known conception of personality. His contributions range far beyond psychology; one cannot understand twentieth-century intellectual thought without some knowledge of psychoanalytic theory. Certainly Freud plays a less central role in psychological thinking today than twenty or thirty years ago, but he is by no means relegated to history. Many of his ideas have been absorbed by other personality theorists and incorporated within their theoretical frameworks.

Freud's conception is so vast that it is meaningless to ask whether it is "correct" or "incorrect." Some aspects of the theory have been shown to have reasonable validity, others have no empirical support at all, and still others are beyond empirical test. In this chapter we present an overview of many of Freud's theoretical concepts and examine in detail the area of defense mechanisms in order to illustrate the experimental testing of some of Freud's ideas.

BIOGRAPHY

Sigmund Freud was born in Freiburg, Moravia (now Pribor, Czechoslovakia), on May 6, 1856, and died in London on September 23, 1939. Most of his life was spent in Vienna, which he left only when the Nazis invaded in 1938.

When Freud decided to devote himself to patients suffering from disorders in thought, emotions and behaviors, the prevailing view in medicine was that the cause of illness — whether mental or physical, was fundamentally biological in origin, e.g., a defect in the nervous system. The notion of a psychological basis for psychological symptoms — that traumatic events, internal conflicts, or poor parenting can be the primary cause of many mental and behavioral abnormalities — is a twentieth century concept. This radical change in how mental illness is perceived was introduced primarily by Sigmund Freud, who also introduced radical changes in the conception of the bases of human behavior. These changes are so fundamental that they have been likened to the changes in scientific thought brought about by Darwin's theory of evolution and Einstein's theory of relativity.

Freud began his scientific career as a neurologist and quickly established a reputation in neurological research and medical investigations. In his medical practice he treated patients with various "nervous" disorders by using conventional medical and physical procedures. But he soon became disillusioned with these treatments. In his autobiography (Freud, 1935), he writes:

> "My knowledge of electrotherapy was derived from W. Erb's textbook, which provided detailed instructions for the treatment of all the symptoms of nervous diseases. Unluckily I was soon driven to see that following these instructions was of no help whatever and that what I had taken for an epitome of exact observations was merely the construction of phantasy. The realization that the work of the greatest name in German neuropathology had no more relation to reality than some "Egyptian" dream-book, such as is sold in cheap bookshops, was painful, but it helped to rid me of another shred of the innocent faith in authority from which I was not yet free. So I put my electrical apparatus aside, even before Mobius had solved the problem by explaining that the successes of electric treatment in nervous disorders (in so far as there were any) were the effect of suggestion on the part of the physician" (pp. 27–28).

In an effort to discover new perspectives, he traveled to Paris in 1885 where he attended the lectures of Jean Martin Charcot, a very eminent neurologist. Charcot was a skilled hypnotist whose dramatic demonstrations of the effects of hypnotic treatments so impressed Freud that he made subsequent trips to France to attend the demonstrations of hypnotism by another French physician, Hippolyte Bernheim. But Freud soon became disenchanted with hypnosis as well; many patients were not susceptible to hypnosis, and the effects of treatment frequently did not carry over to the waking state.

Sigmund Freud (1856–1939) with his daughter Anna Freud in 1928. (Mary Evans/Sigmund Freud Copyrights)

■ **Highlight 3.1** ▬▬▬▬▬▬▬▬▬▬▬▬▬▬▬▬▬▬

Anna O.: The Founding Case of Psychoanalysis

In mid-November, 1882, Joseph Breuer told Freud about Anna O., a highly intelligent twenty-one-year-old woman who presented a diverse array of symptoms. Initially, she suffered from headaches, partial paralyses, intervals of excitement, and visual disturbances. Her symptoms then became more exaggerated—mental lapses, hallucinations about black snakes, skulls and skeletons, speech disturbances, and split personalities.

"The turning point in her 'talking cure' came during the spring of 1882, when Anna O. underwent a spell resembling hydrophobia. Though parched with thirst, she was unable to drink until one evening during her hypnotic state she told Breuer she had seen her English lady-companion, whom she disliked, letting her little dog drink out of a glass. Once her suppressed disgust came out into the open, the hydrophobia disappeared" (Gay, 1988, p. 65).

Although Anna's symptoms were not completely relieved through this process, Freud was very impressed by the effectiveness of the "talking" procedure.

Nevertheless, this period was extremely important in Freud's development. First, it was a hypnotic demonstration that provided Freud with key insights into the dynamics of personality. During an experiment conducted by Bernheim, a woman was given the posthypnotic suggestion that, after waking, she should walk to the corner of the room and open an umbrella. Upon awakening, and after the designated time had elapsed, she did exactly that. When questioned about the reason for her behavior, she said that she wanted to see if the umbrella was hers. On the basis of this demonstration, Freud realized that conscious reports do not always indicate the real motivation for an act; that is, an action can be determined by forces that are *unconscious*. A second consequence of Freud's introduction to hypnosis was that he began to use a treatment technique, developed by Joseph Breuer, in which hypnotized patients talked about their symptoms. In the process, patients often recovered disturbing memories that seemed to be the unconscious causes of their illnesses.

From this beginning, Freud gradually discovered the method of *free association,* during which patients are asked, under normal waking conditions, to tell the analyst everything that comes to mind, regardless of how trivial or embarrassing it may seem. Freud found that these free associations could be systematically related to patients' underlying conflicts and overt symptoms. By listening carefully to verbal associations, he was able to detect consistent themes that were manifestations of unconscious wishes and fears. These themes often involved sexual conflicts. The discovery that much of individual behavior is a compromise between wishes and anticipated fears is another of Freud's central contributions.

Freud and Breuer soon parted ways after disagreements over Freud's beliefs about the importance of sexual desires in the development of mental illness. Thereafter, Freud primarily worked alone to formulate startling and original ideas about child development, the incest taboo, the interpretation of dreams, the unconscious, and a wealth of other psychological processes and phenomena. Freud initially surrounded himself with talented individuals, including Carl Jung from Switzerland and Alfred Adler from Austria (see Chapter 4), who were attracted to this new discipline that he was formulating. But his interpersonal relationships were often stormy, and friendships were aborted. His fascinating life history includes his self-analysis, the controversies surrounding his ideas, the founding of the International Psychoanalytic Association, and an invitation to Clark University in Massachusetts (1909) that paved the way for his acceptance after a long period of scientific ostracism. There were a number of reasons why Freud was not initially accepted by the scientific community (see Shakow and Rapaport, 1964). He did not communicate openly with other scientists, having virtually no academic correspondence, and alienated others because of his strong opinions. Furthermore, he did not present carefully accumulated evidence in

Freud (left, front row) with G. Stanley Hall (middle, front row) at Clark University in 1909. At the right in the first row is Carl Gustav Jung. (Mary Evans/Sigmund Freud Copyrights)

support of his ideas, even gathering his data in a mysterious and secretive atmosphere closed to all but his patients. Finally, he came from an unknown Jewish family at a time of religious discrimination that probably contributed to the delay in his being offered a university position.

It is interesting to note that Freud was part of a continuing trend toward relegating humans to lower and lower status levels. First, Copernicus took Earth and its inhabitants from the center of the universe; then Darwin established that humans are not unique; finally, Freud contended that individuals are irrational and unaware of their own motivations. Perhaps the next step, currently in progress, will be to make inanimate objects more intelligent than their makers!

BASIC THEORETICAL CONCEPTS

Homeostasis and Hedonism

It is useful to consider Freud's theories within the context of a biological survival model. For Freud, people are biological creatures driven by fundamental biological needs that produce psychological tensions until the needs are satisfied. Given this viewpoint, which borrows much from Darwin, individuals are viewed as striving to satisfy personal needs within a world of limited resources. To satisfy these needs, behaviors must be undertaken that lead to the desired goals — virtually all of which are located in the external world. Thus, individuals must function within the constraints imposed by the real world in which they find themselves, and acquire a mode of adaptation that will enable them, insofar as possible, to reduce these need-produced tensions.

More specifically, consider a psychological analysis of how behavior is governed by the need for food (although Freud was concerned more with sex and aggression than with tissue deficits). All organisms have a biological need to ingest food, a need made known to the organism because its presence causes discomfort. There is a limited supply of food in the external world, and organisms must compete for these resources. After the organism has engaged in appropriate activities and has eaten, the internal stimulation and pain (e.g., hunger pangs) that accompany food deprivation cease. The organism then feels satisfied and remains in an unmotivated state (at rest) until the next onset of hunger pangs, which follow a cyclical pattern, again generating food-seeking behavior. Freud conceived a similar cyclical model of sexual and aggressive desires and satisfactions.

The model of human behavior proposed by Freud reflects two broad theoretical principles — homeostasis and hedonism. The first is drawn from biology, the second from philosophy. *Homeostasis* is the tendency toward the maintenance of a relatively stable internal environment. That is, there is a propensity for an organism to remain in a state of equilibrium. If, for example, there is a condition of deprivation because food is absent, then a state of disequilibrium exists, and food-related actions are initiated to return the organism to balance, or equilibrium. *Hedonism*, a doctrine associated with the philosopher Jeremy Bentham

(1779), asserts that pleasure and happiness are the chief goals in life. If homeostasis is the governing principle of behavior, then pleasure is the by-product of being in a state of equilibrium, where all one's needs are satisfied. Freud accepted the doctrine of hedonism, which is expressed in his theoretical language as the *pleasure principle.*

In Freud's theory, the principle of homeostasis, which is reflected in efforts to reduce tension, is the basis for human action. For Freud, the satisfied individual typically does not pursue any stimulation, since activity indicates some type of dissatisfaction. On the contrary, the presumed ultimate goal of human striving is the absence of tension or need, which is accompanied by quiescence. One logical extension of this position was Freud's postulating a death instinct or *death wish,* for in death there are no unsatisfied desires. This is similar to the alleged desire to "return to the womb," where all needs are fulfilled.

Psychological Energy

One of the most difficult and debatable features of Freud's theory is his concept of psychological energy. Freud was greatly influenced by Hermann von Helmholtz, the German physicist who argued that physiological events could be explained with the mechanical principles of physics and chemistry. Freud contended that all psychological work, whether attaining a goal or just thinking about it, requires the use of energy. Three energy-related concepts are useful in understanding his explanation of human behavior: conservation of energy, entropy, and a distinction between bound (kinetic) and free (potential) energy.

Freud conceived of humans as closed energy systems. That is, there is a constant amount of energy *(libido)* for any given individual. This idea was derived from the principle of the conservation of energy, which states that energy is neither created nor destroyed. One corollary of this law is that if energy is spent performing one function, then it is unavailable for other functions. It will be seen that this corollary plays an important role in Freud's theory.

Entropy refers to the amount of energy that is not available for doing work. According to Freud, some energy is *bound,* kinetic, or "cathected." A *cathexis* (from the Greek *kathexo,* meaning "to occupy") involves an attachment to some desired but unattained object. The attachment or cathexis does not mean that energy literally leaves the person. Rather, there is a feeling of "longing" for the object, and there are repeated thoughts, images, and fantasies about him or her or some substitute object. A cathexis might be only temporary, for if the desired goal is attained, then there is a freeing of energy. As a result of goal attainment, bound energy is transformed into *free* (potential) *energy* that is then available for use in other functions. If all one's desires are fulfilled, then all energy is free. Thus, energy distribution is related to subjective satisfaction or happiness.

Consider, more specifically, how Freud might analyze the situation in which a loved one must go away for a period of time. Because that person is no longer available as a need satisfier, he or she becomes an object of cathexis. Energy is now bound, and the unsatisfied individual might fantasize about being with the loved one, daydream of their reunion, and so on. The binding of energy is unpleasant, reflecting the fact that needs have not been fulfilled. In addition, the bound energy is not available for other activities. The individual might therefore experience a lack of interest in other friends and hobbies. When the longed-for person returns, then needs are again satisfied, the cathected energy is freed to do other work, and there is a state of subjective pleasure. Note, then, how closely the concepts of homeostasis, hedonism, and the various forms of energy are linked in Freud's theory. If an organism is in equilibrium (homeostasis), then all energy is free, and the maximum pleasure is being experienced (hedonism).

Freud's statements about energy must be considered basic postulates in his conception; they are not amenable to proof or disproof. In other words, it is not possible to test the notion that there is libidinal energy, or that happiness is associated with free energy, or that we are closed energy systems. While these energy concepts have had some utility in enhancing understanding of some aspects of human behavior, modern psychoanalytic theory tends to assign less importance to them.

The Instincts

The hedonistic goals that individuals wish to reach are instinctive, in the sense that instincts are considered internal urges. Freud contended that instincts drive the organism toward action and are represented in the mind as wishes or desires. The *source* of the instincts is bodily metabolism; their *aim* is immediate discharge; and their *objects* typically are external satisfiers.

Freud vacillated in his ideas about instincts, at times postulating one, and at other times two, basic instincts. Initially, he suggested that there are two classes of instincts: those meant to preserve life (hunger) and those directed toward the attainment of pleasure (sex). The sexual instincts also were related to the preservation of the species. In his final analysis he reaffirmed that there are indeed two instincts, but that they are somewhat different from the two he at first postulated. He contended that one instinct represented a life force (*Eros,* or love), while the second represented a death force (*Thanatos,* or death). Freud contended that aggressiveness is one manifestation of the death instinct turned outward. However, the notion of a death instinct, as contrasted with an aggressive instinct, has been accepted by few psychoanalysts. The life instinct, or sexual motivation, was incorporated within Freud's drive-discharge view of behavior. Sexual drives were conceived as biologically rooted, persistent internal stimuli that demand satisfaction. Gratification of sexual desires leads to a state of quiescence, while lack of satisfaction, usually because of an opposing force, could result in maladaptive behaviors and neurotic symptoms.

It is often contended that Freud's concentration on sexual motivation was a result of his living circumstances: repressive Vienna of the late 1800s. But the importance of sexual dilemmas and conflicts appears to be universal, which suggests that powerful drives for sexual expression must be operative in the face of social inhibitions. In addition, Freud pointed to certain clinical findings to defend his concentration on sexual motivation, including his beliefs that neurotic symptoms could be traced to unfulfilled sexual urges and that infants and children also exhibit great interest in sexual matters (Klein, 1969).

Psychological Determinism

Psychological determinism refers to the axiom that thoughts and actions have causes. Freud carried this principle to its extreme, stating not only that *all* psychological events are caused, but also that most of them are caused by unsatisfied desires or drives. Freud maintained that, in order to understand any behavior — be it a neurotic symptom, a free association, or a social act — one must attempt to analyze the motivational function of the behavior. Behavior, moreover, is typically *overdetermined* in that the behavioral act, such as a symptom, serves to satisfy two or more motives, thereby establishing a *compromise* between a wish and fear, or guilt over expressing the wish.

In one of his earliest publications, Freud singled out three apparently different aspects of normal human behavior — humor, slips of the tongue, and dreams — for special attention. According to Freud, all three behaviors serve the same function: vicarious gratification of a forbidden impulse or an unfulfilled wish. They are hidden means of tension reduction. Consider, for example, the following joke: Standing on a green, one golfer is vigorously choking another to death. A third party arrives on the scene and says casually to the aggressor, "Excuse me, but your grip's all wrong." Freud believed that such a joke evokes laughter because unconscious aggressive urges that are usually prevented from expression are being satisfied through the socially acceptable outlet of a joke. In addition (Volosinov, 1976, pp. 58–59), "A good joke needs a listener; its aim is not only to bypass a prohibition, but also to implicate the listener via laughter, to make the laughing listener an accomplice and, as it were, *socialize* the transgression."

Similarly, such mental lapses as slips of the tongue and forgetting also have psychological determinants.

> An error of this sort is said once to have crept into a Social-Democratic newspaper, where, in the account of a festivity, the following words were printed: "Amongst those present was His Highness, the Clown Prince." The next day a correction was attempted. The paper apologized and said: "The sentence should of course have read, the Crow Prince." Again, in a war-correspondent's account of meeting a famous general whose infirmities were pretty well-known, a reference to the general was printed as "this battle-scared veteran." Next day an apology appeared which read "the words of course should have been, the bottle-scarred veteran"! (Freud, 1915, p. 35)

In Freudian theory, dreams are also wish fulfillments, or at least attempts at wish fulfillment, having their origin in sexual and aggressive impulses. Freud argued that the true meaning of a dream, or its *latent* content, is often masked. The *manifest* content of the dream, or what the dreamer reports, is typically a distortion of the "real" dream contents. However, with proper analysis Freud believed that the latent meaning of a dream could be uncovered. He therefore thought that dreams provided the "royal road to the unconscious." Freud also stated that the vicarious satisfaction provided by dreams has the function of preserving sleep. He thought that, in the absence of dreams, unpleasant impulses would disturb and awaken the sleeper (see Chapter 16 for further discussion of the dream state).

Here again one can raise such empirical questions as: Must a "good" joke tap unconscious aggressions and sexual wishes? Are all "Freudian slips" related to unconscious wishes? If I miss an appointment with my girlfriend or with a professor, does it necessarily mean that I did not want to meet with them? Must dreams always fulfill wishes? The answer to these questions appears to be an unqualified "no," but *some* jokes, *some* slips, and *some* dreams do have a motivational basis that are amenable to a Freudian interpretation. Furthermore, Freud's creation of a theory that could interrelate and offer common explanations for such diverse behaviors as jokes, slips of the tongue, and dreams (to which might be added neurotic symptoms, religion, family rivalry, and other behaviors) was a remarkable achievement.

Libido and Developmental Stages

Freud used the term *libido* (Latin for "lust") to stand for the pleasure-seeking instinctive energy that drives human behavior. Freud proposed that sexual impulses undergo four developmental stages: oral, anal, phallic, and genital. During the first year of life, the infant is in the *oral stage,* with libidinal impulses being gratified through the mucous membranes of the mouth (note, then, that Freud might be seen as concerned with sensual pleasure in the broader sense, rather than in the more narrow sexual sense). During the child's second and third years, the *anal-stage* pleasures stemming from the excretion and retention of feces dominate the child's erotic life. Sometime toward the end of the third year and the beginning of the fourth year, the *phallic stage* of development takes place, in which excitation and stimulation of the genital area provides the primary source of erotic pleasure. This stage ends with the resolution of the so-called Oedipal conflict and is followed by a *latency period* during which children appear relatively unconcerned with sexual matters. Finally, after around the age of twelve, the child enters the *genital stage,* which corresponds to adult sexual concerns and pleasures.

The Oedipal Conflict. The psychoanalytic theory about the development of the Oedipal situation is clearest in the case of the male. Around the age of five or six, a boy's sexual impulses are directed toward his mother, and he resents his father, who is perceived as a rival for the mother's affections. Freud labeled this classic rivalry the *Oedipal conflict,* after Sophocles' play in which Oedipus unwittingly

■ **Highlight 3.2** ■

Freud and Fliess

Freud writes in his *The Interpretation of Dreams,* "An intimate friend and a hated enemy have always been necessary requirements of my emotional life." At different times in some of his relationships, the same person came to perform both functions. The critical role which such persons came to play in his professional development is epitomized in the close friendship that he formed with Berlin ear, nose, and throat specialist Wilhelm Fliess, whom he first met in the fall of 1887. Fliess was a very bright, cultivated, and scientifically learned individual who at the same time was given to some unusual medical theories that strike us as peculiar today and were even a bit strange in the latter part of the nineteenth century. He believed that the nose was the dominant human organ affecting health and sickness in other parts of the body. Even less credible were his convictions that males and females are governed by biorhythmic cycles of twenty-three and twenty-eight days and his numerological manipulation of symptom duration and other time indices to conform to these cycles. Yet Fliess also entertained ideas that were consonant with some of Freud's thinking at that time. He proposed that people were fundamentally bisexual, and he also entertained notions of sexual energy. More significant, however, was his role as Freud's confidant, someone to whom Freud could communicate his struggles, insights, and concerns during the period of his great creative efforts in the 1890s. Freud became so uncritically attached to Fliess that he even placed the responsibility for a surgical mistake that Fliess had made on a patient, whom Freud had referred to Fliess, on the patient herself! However, as Freud became intellectually and emotionally independent of Fliess, the relationship cooled and essentially terminated in 1900 in a very emotional quarrel as each man attacked the validity of the other's beliefs (Gay, 1988).

kills his father and marries his mother. According to Freud, the boy also fears that his father will retaliate against these sexual impulses by castrating him. Freud considered this fear, labeled *castration anxiety,* to be the prototype of all subsequent anxieties, in which one is flooded with internal stimulation. To reduce castration anxiety and at the same time gratify his feelings toward his mother, the boy identifies with his father, thereby internalizing his idealized perception of his father's attitudes and values. Clearly, the incest taboo is associated with the resolution of the Oedipal situation.

The same process in a girl—the *Electra complex*—takes an analogous, but more complicated form, with the girl jealous of her mother's relationship with her father and ultimately identifying with her mother. This identification is not as complete as the boy's identification with his father, in part because of an already absent penis; consequently, it is presumed in orthodox psychoanalytic theory that women do not develop as strong a moral sense as men do. Freud also asserted that, because of their lack of a penis, women envy men. Indeed, women emerge as the inferior sex in Freud's theorizing, a facet of the theory that is more a figment of male chauvinism than a result of scientific inquiry and certainly not supported by any empirical evidence. In Freud's defense, however, it must be recalled that at his particular point in history there was great sexual inequality. In addition, Freud clearly was ahead of his time in recognizing and accepting female sexuality at all. And, on a more personal note, Freud used his influence to ensure that women no less than men were eligible to be candidates for psychoanalytic training (Gay, 1988).

Freud's reconstruction of the Oedipal situation from the free associations of his adult clients has provided profound theoretical and clinical insights into the nature of family dynamics. Freud may have been incorrect in assuming that the Oedipal conflict is universal and that sexual jealousy is the primary basis for the child's feelings of rivalry. He certainly failed to take into account the effect of such factors as variations in family structure and the death or absence of a parent on the Oedipal situation. Also, Freud's interpretation of the childhood seductions reported by his patients as being a reflection of early sexual fantasies has been challenged (Masson, 1984). It has been argued that these reports of childhood seduction are not indicative of Oedipal feelings but rather are accounts of actual incestuous episodes. This was Freud's original impression, which he subsequently changed after more extensive experiences with patients.

However, although there may be disagreement regarding Freud's theory of Oedipal conflict, there is little doubt that even in the most loving of households there are rivalrous elements in the family triangle. How the young son resolves the conflict between his envy and fear of his powerful father and his attachment to his mother, and how the young daughter integrates her envy of a mother to whom she is strongly attached with her desire to be the center of her father's attention, play a central role in subsequent personality development.

Fixation.   Many adult emotional problems were traced by Freud to specific disturbances during the oral, anal, and phallic stages. As a result of these disturbances, libidinal energies become tied up, or *fixated,* at a particular stage of development. It is assumed that the greater the fixation at a given psychosexual stage, the less energy the person has available for mature relationships. Freud used the analogy of an advancing army, with the more troops stationed in the rear guard, the fewer troops available to meet new dangers. When defeated, the more likely the army is to retreat to where it has the greatest number of rear-guard troops (i.e., fixated energy). For example, a child with a strong oral fixation who encounters a major source of frustration during the phallic stage — say, the birth of a sibling—may revert to such oral behaviors as thumb sucking, exaggerated dependency, and, in some cases, nursing.

You might well ask, "Do children really have to pass through such a developmental sequence? Is the retention of feces really the primary source of sensual or libidinal satisfaction for two-year-old children?" Such questions related to developmental stages and sequences will be examined in more detail in Chapters 11 and 12, which focus on the growth of personality. However, at this point it can be said that the experiences of feeding, toilet training, and genital exploration are of major significance for the child's development. What is debatable, however, is Freud's hypothesis that these three areas of bodily activity reflect a common sexual motivation. It is also questionable that oral, anal, and phallic transitions are more central to the child's development than are experiences in other areas, such as attachment and independence training.

Personality Structures

According to Freud, human personality has three components: the id, the ego, and the superego. These structures have specific unique functions as well as distinct operating processes. The id, ego, and superego are not to be found in a specific location in the brain or in the body. Rather, they represent interacting, hypothetical structures, proposed by Freud to explain his observation that behaviors result from compromises between libidinal needs and desires, the restrictions of the environment, and the conscience, or internalized moral values.

The Id. Freud conceived of the *id* as the first system to develop within the person. It is most closely related to the biological realm of sexual and aggressive drives. Since the individual is unaware of these inborn drives, the contents of the id are primarily unconscious (see Fig. 3.1 on p. 74).

The id is the reservoir of all psychological energy, or libido. The availability of this energy allows the id to be directly responsive to bodily needs. Internal bodily tension cannot be tolerated by the id, which functions to discharge any internal tension immediately. Thus, the id operates according to the pleasure principle, or the doctrine of hedonism, seeking immediate pleasure through homeostatic processes and tension reduction. For example, a hungry infant will reflexively suck at a bottle or breast, thus reducing its hunger. Although it must be remembered that Freud was concerned primarily with sexual and aggressive instincts, this automatic action, designed to return the organism to equilibrium, reasonably captures Freud's idea of an id-instigated action.

Id functioning is also characterized by *primary process thought,* a mode of thinking perhaps best known to us through our dream experiences. Primary process thought is illogical and timeless, with reality not distinguished from irreality and hallucinations. For example, a dream is not distinguished from actual occurrences. Thus, in the absence of external goal gratification, internal mental

Figure 3.1   Concepts in the same row are all linked to each other. The arrow from Libido,
                    Aggression denotes Freud's proposition that all human motivations are derived from
                    instinctual libidinal and aggressive impulses. The other arrows indicate that ego
                    processes also can be preconscious and unconscious, and superego processes can be
                    preconscious and conscious and both primary and secondary. Thus guilt has
                    unconscious, preconscious, and conscious components.

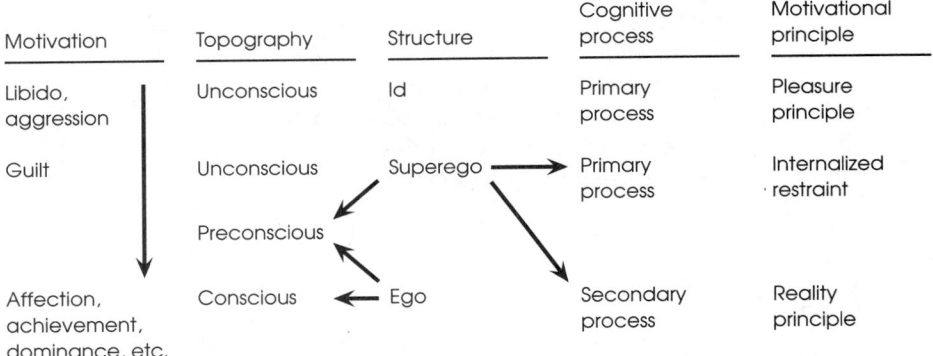

acts can be called on to fulfill wishes. The infant, according to Freud, can imagine
that it is ingesting milk to reduce tension (see Chapters 14 and 16 for a discussion
of imagery). Extensions of this idea suggest that we might dream about great
accomplishments in order to satisfy some of our achievement desires, or daydream of attacking someone in order to gratify aggressive needs.

Freud's view that human beings are driven by biologically rooted id impulses
that seek immediate gratification has profound implications for the relationship
between the individual and society. From the Freudian perspective, society must
inculcate and provide checks to restrain individuals from savagely acting out their
unconscious sexual and aggressive urges.

The Ego. It is evident that organisms must learn to differentiate between milk and
the idea or the image of milk if they are to survive. Fantasy must be distinguished
from reality. In addition, immediate goal gratification sometimes leads to more
pain than pleasure, as when sexual or aggressive actions are later punished by
society. To handle the problems of discrimination and the necessity of delay, the
id develops a new structure that can come to terms with the objective world.
Freud labeled this structure the *ego*.

The ego is governed by the reality principle rather than the pleasure principle.
This does not mean that hedonism is given up. The ego serves the id in its pursuit
of pleasure and tension reduction, but also takes the demands of reality into
account. The ego follows the rules of *secondary process thought*: adult thinking that
is characterized by logic, time orientation, and a distinction between reality and
irreality. The ego also has access to the tools of memory, attention, and the control
of motor activity. Thus, its existence provides a means for delaying gratification
and planning long-term goals.

The contents of the ego are partially conscious (see Fig. 3.1), but the individual is still not aware of all aspects of ego functioning. Most experience is preconscious (not in consciousness), but nevertheless available from memory storage. The ego also includes the defense mechanisms, such as repression, that protect one from psychic pain. These defenses, which are generally not part of the conscious experience, will be examined more fully later in this chapter.

The Superego. According to Freud, the *superego* is the last of the three personality structures to develop. The superego has two main functions, both based on built-in reinforcement processes: (1) to reward individuals for acceptable moral behavior and (2) to punish actions that are not socially sanctioned, by creating guilt. The superego thus represents internalized moral codes, often called the conscience. The superego opposes the expression of unacceptable impulses, rather than merely postponing them, as does the ego.

Freud contended that the development of the superego occurs when the child identifies with the same-sex parent. In doing so, the child internalizes moral ideals, takes on appropriate sex-role behaviors, and resolves the Oedipal conflict with the same-sex parent for the affection of the opposite-sex parent (see also Chapter 12).

Integration of the Structures. Freud was greatly influenced by his training in neurology, where he observed a hierarchical ordering of neural structures. For example, just as the onset of some neural firings can inhibit other neural firings, so can the ego inhibit the strivings of the id. Freud conceived of the ego as the executive agency or "highest" structure in a person, which is responsible for final behavioral decisions. In this capacity it must act as a mediator to satisfy the constant demands of the id, be bound by the constraints of reality, and pacify the ideals of the superego. As Freud (1933, p. 78) noted, "The ego, driven by the id, confined by the superego, repulsed by reality, struggles to master its economic task of bringing about harmony among the forces and influences working in and upon it; we can understand how it is that often we cannot suppress a cry: 'Life is not easy.' "[1]

ANXIETY

The concept of *anxiety* is of central importance in psychoanalytic theory, inasmuch as the dynamics of behavior revolve around the notion of a conflict between expression and inhibition. Inhibition is an ego function that is intimately associated with the experience of anxiety and, in turn, the defense mechanisms.

To understand the relationships among inhibition, anxiety, and the defense mechanisms, it is useful to trace Freud's changing analysis of these concepts.

---

[1] From *New Introductory Lectures in Psychoanalysis* by Sigmund Freud, Translated by James Strachey. Used with the permission of W. W. Norton & Company, Inc. Copyright © 1965, 1964 by James Strachey.

Freud's earliest theorizing argued that anxiety is the result of undischarged libidinal energy. The lack of sexual gratification, which could arise from any number of sources — the absence of wished-for objects, poor relations with others, or, most importantly, inhibitions and repressions — was believed to result in an accumulation of drive energy. The unexpressed libido was then "explosively released in a transformed state, the state of anxiety" (Monte, 1977, p. 120). Anxiety therefore was considered a product of the id, automatically arising from unfulfilled sexual urges. Freud initially considered hypnosis a good therapeutic technique because the patient could relive experiences and discharge libidinal energy when in a hypnotic state, thereby reducing anxiety.

As Freud gave the ego greater importance in his theory, he reversed this sequence of "repression produces anxiety" to "anxiety produces repression" (Freud, 1926). In a later period in his thinking, Freud contended that when drive expression will lead to more pain than pleasure, the ego "inoculates" itself with anxiety. This anxiety serves as a warning that, if the individual engages in the forbidden activity, then the ego will experience a much greater amount of anxiety than it just felt in very modulated form. The anxiety that will be experienced will be similar to that of an earlier danger situation: the "birth trauma," or the overwhelming helplessness that is first experienced when one leaves the protection of the womb. In order to avoid this state, the ego initiates action, activating defense mechanisms that interfere with and delay drive expression. Freud thus made anxiety an ego signal rather than an id discharge.

Stated somewhat differently, whenever an instinct pushes for expression that might lead to significant punishment, pain, or guilt, the organism reacts with alarm in the form of anxiety. A defense will then arise, both to prevent immediate goal gratification and to help resolve the conflict by permitting the urge to be expressed in a socially acceptable form. Thus, anxiety can be directly linked to inhibition and psychological defenses.

DEFENSE MECHANISMS

It has just been suggested that the ego protects the individual from pain that might be experienced as a consequence of direct sexual or aggressive expression. Because the mechanisms used by the ego have a protective function, some of them are called *defense mechanisms,* or simply *psychological defenses.* Psychological understanding of these defenses was one of Freud's major insights and also one of the important contributions of his daughter, Anna Freud.

The psychological defenses that protect an individual from overwhelming anxiety, punishment, and other unpleasant experiences are sometimes quite obvious. For example, fainting is one mechanism that prevents continued exposure to such aversive sensations as the sight of blood or the feelings that accompany the death of a significant other. Any observer can recognize a faint, and the fainter can later readily comprehend what happened, if not the underlying reason for the loss of consciousness. Thus, Freud would not have considered fainting to be a typical psychological defense, although Freud himself fainted on two occasions in uncomfortable interactions with Jung (Gay, 1988), and its function in avoiding unpleasantness was evident to him. Although it is now accepted that not all defenses must be unconscious, Freud contended that defense mechanisms usually operate on an unconscious level, with individuals not consciously aware of the defenses or their functional significance.

Repression and the Unconscious

One of the more provocative, better-known aspects of psychoanalytic theory is the assertion that a significant part of our behavior is governed by forces of which we have no awareness. Our choice of marriage partner, vocation, and even hobbies may reflect the influence of impulses and fears that remain unconscious. Memories associated with unacceptable feelings may also be excluded from awareness. When Freud encouraged his patients to recall painful memories and to confront unacceptable feelings, they appeared to resist his efforts. Freud hypothesized that this resistance was a function of an active force that he called *repression,* which acted to keep thoughts unconscious. The unconscious, of course, is not a place or object situated deep in the recesses of the brain; it is, rather, a property of thought and behavior. People are conscious of some of their thoughts and actions and their underlying reasons, while they may be completely unaware of other thoughts, motivations, attitudes, and actions. (See also Chapter 16.)

Freud believed that repression is the most significant defense mechanism, upon which all the other defenses are based. As he rather poetically described it (1933, pp. 305–306):

> every mental process . . . first exists in an unconscious state or phase, and only develops out of this into a conscious phase, much as a photograph is first a negative and then becomes a picture through the printing of the positive. But not every negative is made into a positive, and it is just as little necessary that every unconscious mental process should convert itself into a conscious one. It may be best expressed as follows: Each single process belongs in the first place to the unconscious psychical system; from this system it can under certain conditions proceed further into the conscious system.
>
> The crudest conception of these systems is the one we shall find most convenient, a spatial one. The unconscious system may therefore be compared to a large ante-room, in which the various mental excitations are crowding upon one another, like individual beings. Adjoining this is a second, smaller apartment, a sort of reception-room, in which consciousness resides. But on the threshold between the two there stands a personage with the office of door-keeper, who examines the various mental excitations, censors them, and denies them admittance to the reception-room when he disapproves of them. You will see at once that it does not make much difference whether the door-keeper turns any one impulse back at the threshold, or drives it out again once it has entered the reception-room; that is merely a matter of the degree of his viligance and

promptness in recognition. Now this metaphor may be employed to widen our terminology. The excitations in the unconscious, in the ante-chamber, are not visible to consciousness, which is of course in the other room, so to begin with they remain unconscious. When they have pressed forward to the threshold and been turned back by the door-keeper, they are "incapable of becoming conscious"; we call them repressed.[2]

Several different kinds of clinical and experimental observations support the belief that unconscious forces may exert significant influences on human behavior. Freud's analyses of his patients' symptoms, dreams, and associations convinced him that they were usually not conscious of the underlying reasons for their actions. They would repeat the same disastrous relationships, the same failures, the same self-destructive life patterns (e.g., alcoholism and drug addiction) without any awareness of the motivational bases for their behavior. Freud further observed that some people were unconsciously attracted to activities or ideas to which they consciously objected. It has been suggested, for example, that those who lead crusades against pornography and spend a good deal of time reading and viewing pornographic material are often unconsciously drawn to such literature. Hypnosis provides still further clinical data suggesting that behavior can be influenced by unconscious motives (see Chapter 16).

There are numerous clinical reports of instances of repression. One dramatic autobiographical example has been provided by the distinguished psychologist Elsa Frenkl-Brunswick. In one session of her psychoanalysis, undertaken in her early twenties, the analyst commented that her conflict and anxiety reflected a kind of "Cordelia" complex, referring to King Lear's youngest daughter. (Shakespeare's King Lear did not appreciate Cordelia's love for him until late in life.) Frenkl-Brunswick, puzzled by the reference to Cordelia, said that she was unfamiliar with the play, and the analyst had to summarize its highlights. Several years later, when sorting through her personal belongings, she came across some old high school notes on *King Lear*. She had not only studied the play, but also copied down the part of Cordelia, word for word!

The Experimental Study of Repression.   In addition to clinical sources of data bearing on unconscious phenomena, there has been a very active study of repression in experimental settings (see Rapaport, 1942; Weiner, 1966). Freud was not very encouraging toward such laboratory investigations, for he felt that his clinical observations provided sufficient evidence and that tests of his ideas could be conducted adequately only during therapeutic sessions. However, others more fully recognized the limitations of drawing inferences where relevant variables are not controlled and where there is opportunity for observer bias.

---

[2] From *New Introductory Lectures in Psychoanalysis* by Sigmund Freud, Translated by James Strachey. Used with the permission of W. W. Norton & Company, Inc. Copyright © 1965, 1964 by James Strachey; Sigmund Freud Copyrights Ltd., The Institute of Psycho-Analysis, and The Hogarth Press, Ltd., from Volume 22 of *The Complete Psychological Works of Sigmund Freud,* edited and translated by James Strachey.

One early technique employed to demonstrate repression was merely asking subjects to recall past events. If they remembered more pleasant than unpleasant experiences, then experimenters inferred that repression was operating to interfere with the memory of unpleasant occurrences. This approach was weak, however, because some of us may indeed have more pleasant than unpleasant experiences. In other words, a subject's recall may be accurate and does not necessarily demonstrate repression.

A second, frequently used procedure in the study of repression is pairing distinctive stimuli, such as digits or words, with pleasant and unpleasant sensations, such as good or bad smells or receiving either money or shock. When subjects are later asked to recall the stimuli, and the stimuli paired with aversive consequences are recalled less often than the stimuli paired with positive consequences, then repression is assumed to have taken place. Note that this procedure is better than merely asking subjects to recall life events, because the positive and negative experiences are controlled and equalized. But these studies are also deficient on several counts. First, consistent data are not reported. At times there is greater recall of stimuli associated with pleasant experiences; at times the reverse is true. In addition, whenever "repression" is demonstrated, it is difficult to argue that the retrieval of the "forgotten" stimuli is opposed by an active restraining force. The experimental stimuli are far removed from the dangerous sexual and aggressive urges discussed by Freud.

A third research procedure for studying repression examines the recall of successful and failed achievement activities. Since it can be reasoned that it is ego-protective to forget failures, repressive forces should impede the retention of poor performances. Subjects in these experiments are given a number of tasks to solve, half of them too long to solve in the allotted time and half more easily solved. Thus, subjects tend to experience success on half the tasks and failure on the other half. Then they are asked to name the tasks on which they worked. Again, however, the findings are inconsistent: at times recall of the incompleted tasks is greater, and at times better recall of the completed tasks is reported.

A fourth experimental procedure involves the recall of "complex-related" words. The notion of a complex-related word was first advanced by Carl Jung (see Chapter 4). Jung read subjects lists of words and asked them to respond with the first associations that came to mind for each word (the *word association* technique). Jung noted that some responses were preceded by unusually long pauses and inferred that, in those instances, the stimulus words were related to a particular personality complex, or area of emotional disturbance and personal difficulty. He believed that the stimulus words were therefore associated with repressed and conflictual material. Because of this association, immediate responses were likely to be censored, resulting in a longer latency period before the appearance of the verbalized response.

Some repression studies examine the recall or retention of complex-related words and their associations, compared with words that are unrelated to particular complexes or conflicts. In one investigation (Clemes, 1964), hypnotized subjects first learned a list of complex- and noncomplex-related words and then were given a posthypnotic suggestion that they would forget about half the words. Subsequent testing in a normal waking state revealed that the subjects were indeed able to recall only about half the words and, of crucial importance, the forgotten words were those specified as complex-related. When the hypnotic suggestion was subsequently lifted, the subjects were able to recall almost all the words. This is a reasonable demonstration of Freud's concept of repression and the unconscious because:

1. The material under study was relevant to each subject's area of emotional disturbance, unlike investigations using smells or shocks.

2. An active inhibiting force was introduced, in this case by means of an experimental instruction during hypnosis. This force interfered with the emergence of threatening thoughts into consciousness.

3. The emotionally related words were retrieved into consciousness when the active inhibiting force subsided, in this case because of the removal of the posthypnotic suggestion.

In sum, although there is a great deal of clinical and anecdotal evidence about the notion of repression, many laboratory studies have failed to support it, except in a few well-designed experimental investigations conducted under controlled conditions. At a later point in this chapter, we will consider individual differences in the tendency to use repression. The individual difference data provide alternative support for the usefulness of the concept of repression.

Childhood Sexual Abuse and Repression

We have previously mentioned that there are those who now believe in Freud's original view that actual childhood sexual abuse was the basis of psychological dysfunction. Recently the controversy over the existence of repression has resurfaced with respect to the issue of childhood sexual abuse. Victims of childhood sexual abuse are often perceived to be unable to recover the memories of such abuse because it has been repressed.

Briere and Conte (1993) found that 59 percent of a sample of 450 women and men who eventually reported forced sexual contact before age sixteen reported amnesia for sexual abuse at some point before age eighteen. This was more likely in those individuals who had been abused at an earlier age, who had been abused over a longer period of time, and whose abuse had been more violent.

Williams (1992) studied one hundred women who had been sexually abused as children and whose abuse had been carefully documented. The children had been brought to city hospital emergency rooms for treatment and collection of forensic evidence. About seventeen years later, the women were located and interviewed. It was found that 38 percent of them did not report memory of the abuse. Williams asserts that qualitative analysis of the interview data suggests that most actually did not remember, and it was not a matter of their simply failing to report on it. In one case, for instance, a woman did not remember that she had been abused by her uncle. What she did remember, however, was that her uncle had sexually assaulted "someone," but not her.

This evidence seems to suggest that many individuals who have been sexually abused as children either partially or completely lose memory of the abuse. Is this evidence of repression? It is not possible to say at this point. Memory is notoriously tricky, and at this point we do not know enough about how memory operates to say what possible mechanisms may be involved in this loss of memory, although repression is certainly one viable explanation.

On the other hand, the fact that many individuals in therapy recover memories of having been abused as children cannot necessarily be taken as evidence of repression. There is now concern that therapists are capable of implanting false memories in their clients. In this regard Loftus (1993) reports a study in which she was able to successfully implant in a fourteen-year-old boy a false memory of an early traumatic experience of being lost in a shopping mall. As part of the research, the boy was told by his older brother that he had been lost in a mall when he was five years old, when in fact this had never happened. The brother offered some general details, including that the boy had been found by an older man wearing a flannel shirt. Within a couple of days the boy began to report more detailed memories of his feelings of being lost, of the man who found him, and of the mall itself. For instance, he described the man who found him as bald with grey hair and glasses, as well as his own feelings of being very scared.

The concept of false memory is highly controversial, and more research is needed to clarify this important phenomenon.

Perceptual Defense

Perceptual defense also refers to a resistance against threatening material. While perceptual defense is not among the ego-protective processes that are usually enumerated when defense mechanisms are presented, it is closely related to denial, which is briefly discussed later in this chapter. Perceptual defense is also similar to repression in that, while repression prevents selected *memories* from becoming conscious, perceptual defense keeps selected *perceptions* from the individual's awareness. This concept has received a vast amount of attention from personality psychologists. Its appeal is due in part to the relationship between perceptual defense and subliminal perception (see also Chapter 16). At one time claims were made that behavior could be controlled by television and movie advertisements processed without the knowledge of the viewer; these ads were flashed quickly across the screen and perceived at a subliminal level, below conscious awareness. These claims, fortunately, are exaggerated.

Nevertheless, there is a great deal of anecdotal and clinical evidence to support the notion of perceptual defense and of perceptual influence below the level of awareness (see also Chapter 4 on psychoanalytic ego psychology). As is true of repression and many other defense mechanisms, the experimental

"Hear no evil, speak no evil, see no evil." Psychological research has concentrated on *visual* perceptual defense. (The Bettmann Archive)

evidence is not always conclusive but, at the same time, there have been some experimental demonstrations that appear convincing, and new ways of thinking about perceptual defense are adding to its validity.

A Controversial Experiment.   An investigation conducted by McGinnies (1949) first aroused interest in the experimental study of perceptual defense and illustrates the goals of research in this area. Subjects were shown words on a tachistoscope, an instrument that allows the exposure of material for durations as short as 0.001 second, so short that the stimuli cannot be identified. Some of the flashed words were neutral, or nonaffective, such as *house* and *flower,* while others were "taboo," such as *whore* and *bitch*. The subjects' task was to identify the words, while the speed of exposure was gradually decreased until the word shown was correctly identified. In addition to word recognition, galvanic skin response (GSR) to the words was recorded. The GSR is a measure of electrical conductance, generally measured from the palm, and is accepted as an index of emotionality. It is one measure taken during a lie detector test, for instance.

     Two interesting findings were reported. First, taboo words were recognized later than neutral words. That is, the duration of the flash needed for the perceiver to be able to identify taboo words was greater than that required for neutral words. A second provocative finding was that heightened GSRs were exhibited on trials in which the subjects did not correctly report the flashed taboo word. In other words, emotion was exhibited without conscious word recognition. These findings posed somewhat of a paradox, for how can a perceiver defend against a stimulus unless that stimulus is first perceived? That is, the material must be sufficiently processed to realize that it produces anxiety, but blocked so that the perceiver is not made anxious!

In part because of this apparent logical inconsistency, investigators attempted to discredit the findings of McGinnies and other reports of perceptual defense. Many opponents argued that perceptual defense is nothing more than a response bias. For example, subjects could have been reluctant to *say* the taboo words. There is also evidence that the frequency of prior exposure to words influences both recognition and what the subject is likely to guess (Howes and Solomon, 1951), and taboo words may be encountered less frequently (recall that the experiment took place in the late 1940s). And finally, it was pointed out that the verbal response was dichotomous; that is, it was scored as either correct or incorrect. On the other hand, the GSR was a continuous measure that allowed for a full range of responses. Thus, for example, an individual could be unsure of whether the exposed word was *bitch* or *bite*. If the subject decided on *bite* while the word was really *bitch,* the answer was scored as incorrect, even though there was likely to be some GSR deflection. It would not be reasonable to label the discrepancy between the incorrect score and the GSR deflection as perceptual defense (see Eriksen, 1958, 1960).

Other investigators have come to the defense of perceptual defense, and it appears that none of the counterarguments attempting to do away with the defense concept has been completely adequate (see Dixon, 1971; Erdelyi, 1974). For example, experimenters controlling for frequency of word exposure also report perceptual defense (Dulany, 1957), and perceptual defense is exhibited when methods are used to eliminate a response suppression explanation (e.g., subjects are required to respond with a taboo word to indicate the perception of a neutral word, and vice versa; see Zigler and Yospe, 1960).

Information Processing and Perceptual Defense.   Perceptual defense becomes logically more acceptable when considered within the framework of more contemporary conceptions of *information processing*. It is now evident that many processes are involved between the perception of a stimulus and a final response, or conscious awareness. These processes include stimulus reception, analysis, and transfer into short-term, then long-term, memory storage.

A process akin to perceptual defense can occur at any stage of this multiprocess system. For example, common observation shows that people frequently avoid traumatic input (as during a horror movie) by fixating away from the stimulus or closing their eyes. In this instance, control over stimulus input is voluntary and conscious, but in other circumstances the avoidance may be neither voluntary nor conscious. For example, it has been documented that pupils expand and contract in different situations as a function of the person's needs and desires (see Hess, 1965), an alteration that influences the perceiver's sensitivity.

In addition, one can scan incoming information and, on the basis of partial analysis, decide whether to encode or to reject the material for additional processing. For example, at a party one might receive different messages in each ear. The contents of one channel can be rejected, even though this rejected information has been "heard." The message content is thus not transferred into memory. In other words, we can perceive without remembering; many more stimuli are apprehended than are put into memory storage (see Chapter 16). This sort of selectivity analysis can readily account for the more esoteric notion of perceptual defense (see Erdelyi, 1974).

Finally, there is increasing evidence from cognitive psychology that information apprehended without awareness is processed differently (parallel processing) from conscious information (sequential processing). This duality is similar in some respects to Freud's distinction between primary and secondary process thought (MacKay, 1987).

Other Defenses

There are many other defenses against painful, anxiety-producing thoughts and feelings in addition to repression and perceptual defense, such as *rationalization, intellectualization* of impulses to strip them of their emotionality, and *isolation* of ideas to separate them from unacceptable related thoughts and attitudes. College students, because of their generally high verbal abilities, are frequently given to intellectualization: discussing threatening topics such as atomic warfare, future careers, and sexual inadequacy in an overly elaborate, rational manner which spares them the anxiety associated with these topics.

Defenses do not have precisely the same meaning or function for each individual. They differ in their consequences, generality, centrality to an individual's personality organization, degree of usage, and many other key dimensions. Suffice it to say that the manner in which one copes with unacceptable impulses is a key area of concern in the fields of personality and abnormal psychology. A few of the more familiar defense mechanisms are discussed in the following paragraphs.

Denial. In *denial,* impulses and associated ideas reach awareness, but their implications are rejected or denied. For example, an unwillingness to check on medical symptoms could indicate the presence of denial, as does "gallows humor," the tendency of soldiers to engage in banter and jest as they near an engagement with the enemy. While denial may be functional for soldiers marching off to combat, it can be damaging for the individual. To deny the possible diagnostic implications of a persistent swelling that may be symptomatic of cancer is to risk the possible consequences of failing to take advantage of early treatment. Denial can also result in profound psychological consequences as, for example, when one refuses to acknowledge negative traits in a potential spouse.

Reaction Formation. *Reaction formation* is the manifestation of behavior that is directly opposite to unconscious feelings and attitudes. A parent who defends against unconscious feelings of resentment toward an unwanted child by reacting with overwhelming affection is exhibiting a reaction formation. Since it is nearly the opposite of genuine expression of feeling, reaction formation is often exaggerated, inflexible, and inappropriate.

Projection. Projection consists of attributing one's own unacceptable, repressed feelings and ideas to others. Experimental studies have shown that perception of others' motives and feelings can be greatly influenced by the perceiver's own feelings and attitudes (Tagiuri, 1969). For example, frightened children are more likely to see other children as frightened (Feshbach and Feshbach, 1963; Murray, 1933). In the strictest definition of projection, the individual is completely unconscious of the impulse that is projected. However, although lack of awareness may facilitate projection, it is not a necessary condition for the attribution of one's own feelings and desires to others.

Displacement. The defense of *displacement* refers to repressed or blocked feelings and actions that are expressed toward an innocent target. In one well-known early study concerned with frustration effects, it was found that children at camp, who were prevented by the camp directors from engaging in a pleasurable activity, attributed fewer favorable traits to minority-group members when judging their characters (Miller and Bugelski, 1948). This defense will be examined in more detail in Chapter 14.

Sublimation. *Sublimation* is a form of displacement in which an unacceptable, unsatisfied impulse is expressed in a socially acceptable form. Freud suggested, for instance, that unsatisfied sexual impulses could be expressed in highly approved artistic ways.

Individual Differences in Defensive Preferences

As might be anticipated, individuals differ in their defensive reactions to threatening stimuli. Defensive preferences can be distinguished in many ways, according to their complexity, generality, effectiveness, and degree of reality distortion. One individual difference that has received much attention from psychologists is *repression-sensitization* (see Byrne, 1961). It is reasoned that some individuals respond to particular kinds of threats with repression and perceptual defense. In so doing, they avoid anxiety-laden information. Hysterical reactions, including symptoms such as blindness and limb paralysis, are generally associated with the use of repressive defenses. Conversely, it appears that one may cope with a particular threat by using sensitizing defenses. The person then becomes more vigilant to threat and remains in close contact with the stressful material. He or she may then be better able to monitor and control the threat. The constant worrier and the obsessive-compulsive neurotic are examples of the use of sensitizing defensive orientations.

Individual differences in repression-sensitization are generally assessed by means of a true/false, self-report inventory called the R-S scale (Byrne, 1961). Some typical items on the scale, with "True" answers indicating repression, are:

- I don't seem to care what happens to me.
- Often I feel as if there were a tight band about my head.

The items on this measure were taken from the Minnesota Multiphasic Personality Inventory (MMPI, see Chapter 8), and many of the items are also included in popular measures of general anxiety, such as the Manifest Anxiety Scale (MAS). Many investigations have examined the behavioral correlates of different responses to the scale items. It has been found, for example, that repressors, as opposed to people labeled as sensitizors, require longer tachistoscopic exposure before recognizing threatening words, remember more successful tasks than failed tasks, and are slower at learning a list of affective arousing words. Thus, the scale has some empirical validity (see Byrne, 1961).

A more recent individual difference approach to the categorization of individuals as repressors has employed two personality scales—a measure of anxiety and a measure of the tendency to respond in a socially desirable fashion (Weinberger, Schwartz, and Davidson, 1979). Individuals who display a pattern of low anxiety coupled with high scores on the social desirability measure are considered to be repressors. There have been a number of studies providing empirical support for this personality index of repressive tendencies; for example, individuals classified as repressors have fewer memories of their feelings and activities (Davis and Schwartz, 1987).

Two other examples follow of individual differences in repressive and defensive tendencies. Morokoff (1985) showed female subjects an erotic videotape and assessed the degree of sexual arousal both by asking them how aroused they were and by measuring their vaginal response with a special vaginal instrument. Women who had previously reported having a lot of guilt over sex reported being less sexually aroused by the videotape than women who reported low sex-guilt, although the women who reported a lot of guilt actually exhibited higher levels of physiological arousal. In a similar fashion, people who report being in excellent mental health, but who are rated by expert clinicians as denying mental distress, respond to stressful experimental procedures with higher levels of blood pressure than individuals who report feeling mentally distressed (Shedler et al., 1993).

Although we really know very little about why or how individuals use one particular defense rather than another, a research investigation by Dulany (1957) has nicely demonstrated the influence of prior learning on defensive preferences. Dulany simultaneously presented four geometric figures on a tachistoscope below the level of recognition, or below what is termed the *threshold level*. The subjects responded by indicating which figure stood out the most. Half the subjects were given an electric shock whenever they designated one particular, "critical," figure as most visible. The other half were shocked when they did *not* select this critical

Figure 3.2

Effects of defense and vigilance training on perceptual recognition. (Adapted from Dulany, 1957, p. 336. From *Introduction to Personality* by Walter Mischel. Copyright © 1971 by Holt, Rinehart and Winston, Inc. Reprinted by permission of the publisher.)

figure. Thus, the subjects in both groups received experiences designed to promote avoidance (repression) or approach (sensitization) behavior. After the training period, the shock apparatus was disconnected; the subjects were quite aware that the shock was no longer contingent on their response. Then the four figures were again presented for recognition. Dulany found that stated recognition of the critical figure was far greater under the sensitization condition than under the repression conditions both during and after training (see Fig. 3.2 above). In sum, it appears that a prior learning experience that has instrumental or functional significance is one antecedent that may produce different defensive preferences and contrasting coping strategies.

GENERAL EVALUATION

What, then, can we conclude about Freud's theory of personality? As was stated at the beginning of the chapter, it is useless to ask whether the theory is "correct" or "incorrect." Some of its concepts, such as that of defense mechanisms, have led to a great deal of research and have gained general acceptance. Other concepts, such as the death wish or the postulation of a closed energy system, have generated no research and have few adherents. In general, the theory's most significant contribution is that it provides a language with which to examine human action. It is therefore a most important step toward the development of a theory of personality, a step that builds a foundation for further work. But it is also just a first step and one with many shortcomings. The theory is often vague and without empirical support, concentrating excessively on particular facets of behavior and neglecting other aspects. As a result, it often leads to false interpretations and overgeneralizations.

There is a tendency to ask too much of this theory. People use it to try to explain why we engage in sports, why we are doing poorly in our interpersonal relationships, and why wars take place. At present, it is impossible for any single theory to account for such diverse phenomena with any degree of accuracy. Thus, rather than criticizing and rejecting Freud's theory out of hand, we should accept it for what it is and was: a monumental attempt to account for a great variety of human behavior by means of a few basic concepts and ideas. Many aspects and modifications of his ideas have been so widely incorporated in psychology and in contemporary thought that they may seem almost commonplace — for example, that we may be often unaware of important motivations that influence our behavior; that we engage in defensive thoughts and behaviors that serve to ward off anxiety and guilt; that experiences in childhood can have a profound effect upon the personality that we display as adults; that family relationships are characterized by anxieties and rivalry as well as by support and love; that disturbances in psychological functioning can have a psychological as well as biological basis; that our dreams, our fantasies, art, literature, and even many of our cultural beliefs and practices, may reflect unconscious impulses and motivations. Whether the overriding importance that Freud placed on libido theory will survive the test of time is questionable. But there is no doubt that Freudian theory has provided abundant insights and will influence psychology and social thought for many years to come.

Summary

1. Freud's ideas were spurred by a hypnotic demonstration that motivations are not always conscious and by the use of *free association,* a method initially derived from having hypnotized subjects talk about their symptoms.

2. *Homeostasis* refers to organisms' tendency to maintain a relatively stable internal environment; the doctrine of *hedonism* asserts that pleasure is the chief goal in life. Freud included both homeostasis and hedonism as basic principles in his conception of human behavior.

3. In Freud's system, if all psychological energy is *free,* then all wishes have been attained and there is a subjective state of pleasure.

4. Instincts are primarily sexual internal urges that strive for expression. They have a source (bodily metabolism), an aim (immediate discharge), and objects (satisfiers residing in the external world).

5. According to Freud, all behavior is determined, including jokes, slips of the tongue, and dreams. This is known as the principle of *psychological determinism.*

6. Humans progress through a fixed developmental sequence of *oral, anal, phallic,* and *genital stages.* The *Oedipal conflict,* which concerns the rivalry between a child and the same-sex parent, is resolved during the phallic stage. *Fixation* can result from specific disturbances during any one of the stages.

7. Freud conceived of personality as composed of three structures: *id, ego,* and *superego.* These structures represent the idea that behavior is in part determined by personal (biological) needs, social reality, and internalized ideals. The ego is the "executive" of these structures, responsible for the individual's overall adaptation.

8. *Repression* is the most important of the psychological defenses. Freud represented repression as a force active in keeping thoughts from consciousness. Many experimental investigations have tested this concept, but only a very few well-conceived studies have provided confirming evidence.

9. *Perceptual defense,* which keeps selective threatening perceptions from conscious awareness, has had a lively experimental history. Contemporary approaches such as *information processing* make this concept less mysterious.

10. There are many *defense mechanisms,* including *denial, reaction formation, projection, displacement,* and *sublimation.*

11. Individual differences on the *repression-sensitization* continuum have been identified by means of personality questionnaires.

Thought Questions

1. Has psychoanalytic theory helped you to understand yourself? In what way?

2. Is repression necessarily "bad" for mental health? When, if at all, can repression facilitate psychological adaptation?

3. Freud maintained that hedonism is the chief goal in life. Can you think of times when you acted in a way that did not maximize pleasure? Could Freud have accounted for your behavior?

4. We have all had the experience of closing our eyes to avoid looking at something terrible or frightening. Can you think of any other methods you have used to avoid anxiety and stress?

4 | Psychoanalytic Dissidents and Descendants

Although psychoanalysis began with Freud, it certainly did not end there. Psychoanalytic theory has undergone significant change since Freud's death, and Freud himself introduced major theoretical revisions during the course of his lifetime. Thus, any response to the question, "What is psychoanalytic theory?" depends on whether one refers to the early writings of Freud, the later writings of Freud, or more contemporary psychoanalytic theory. To complicate matters further, not only has Freud's theory of psychoanalysis undergone substantial revision, but also several similar, but significantly different, rival theories have emerged. Many contemporary modifications of psychoanalytic theory have been introduced in response to criticisms from these rival theories.

RIVALS TO FREUD

Several of Freud's first rivals were early associates, including Carl Jung and Alfred Adler, who were prominent physicians in their own right. Because of their dissent on basic issues, they separated (or were asked to separate) from Freud with the request that they not call their theories "psychoanalytic." It is not always clear why some of Freud's adherents who proposed theoretical changes were able to retain their identification with classic psychoanalysis, while others decided to separate or were excluded from the psychoanalytic movement. In some instances, both personality and theoretical conflicts appear to have been involved. However, one common element in all the dissident movements is the rejection of libido or sexual motivation as the primary source of human conflict, anxiety, and neurosis. The alternatives to libido theory proposed by Jung (1916) and Adler (1927), as well as by such later dissidents as Horney (1937) and Fromm (1941), are diverse. (Highlight 4.1 provides a brief statement of some of these alternative motivations.) In response to their proposals, Freud would not deny that people are motivated by inferiority feelings (Adler) or by a need for relatedness to others (Fromm). But for Freud sexual motivation was primary. The possibility that human beings might have different central motives—with libidinal striving primary for some but ambition, pride, or need for affection dominant for others—was an unacceptable solution for Freud.

◼ **Highlight 4.1** ▮▮▮▮▮▮▮▮▮▮▮▮▮▮▮▮▮▮▮▮▮▮▮▮▮

Basic Human Motivations as Perceived by Psychoanalytically Oriented Theorists

Carl Jung
Striving for self-actualization, as reflected in integrating the "wisdom" of the personal and collective unconscious with the products of conscious experience.

Alfred Adler
Will to power, feelings of inferiority, and striving toward superiority or perfection.

Karen Horney
Basic anxiety, as reflected in exaggerated needs for love (moving toward people), independence (moving away from people), and destruction (moving against people).

Erich Fromm
The expression of one's human, as contrasted to animal, nature; identity and a stable frame of reference for perceiving and comprehending the world, as reflected in the needs for relatedness to and transcendence of other people and physical nature.

There are several possible reasons Freud held so tenaciously to libido theory. First, there is a certain theoretical simplicity and elegance in proposing one basic motive governing all human behavior, from which all desires and goals emerge. Second, transformations in libidinal or sexual impulses and the management and distribution of that energy, as discussed in Chapter 3, were basic premises in Freud's theory; lessening the importance of these impulses would have required substantial modification of the theory. Third, and here we are speculating about Freud's own psychodynamics, Freud had undergone enormous personal sacrifice in bringing the sexual basis of neurotic symptoms to the attention of medical colleagues and in suggesting the radical notion that young children may have sexual fantasies about their parents. Having sacrificed so much for libidinal theory, he must have been strongly motivated to defend that theory in the face of subsequent criticism.

In this chapter we will review some of the major psychoanalytically based alternative theories as well as some of the developments that have taken place in psychoanalytic theory itself subsequent to Freud. We first consider the work of Jung, Adler, Horney, and Fromm. We then move on to consider some of the more recent developments, such as that of ego psychology, the views of Erik Erikson, object relations theory, Kohut's Self Psychology, and Horowitz's concept of states of mind.

A word of precaution, though, before we review these alternatives: most did not arise from systematic empirical research. Most reflect mainly insights, speculations, and assumptions based on each theoretician's own clinical and life experiences. In addition, these theories do not lend themselves to critical empirical comparison, in large part because each stresses a different motivation. Thus, the theories are, in many respects, not *commensurate,* i.e., comparable with one another so that one theory may be judged "correct." Rather, each theory explains some aspects of human behavior better than the other theories do.

The Analytic Psychology of Carl Jung

It would be wrong to presume that the only difference between Freud and his dissenters lay in the motivation believed to be central to human striving. Other revisions, innovations, and concepts were introduced by each theorist. The most comprehensive and formal alternative to Freudian theory is that proposed by Carl Gustav Jung (1875–1961). Jung, like Freud, has had a significant impact on modern thought and was a prolific writer and erudite scholar. Before he pursued a medical and then a psychiatric career, Jung's education and interests lay primarily in humanistic theology, philosophy, anthropology, and archaeology. This orientation became increasingly evident as Jung developed and expounded his own conception of human nature and the limits as well as the possibilities of human potential.

Carl Gustav Jung, (1875–1961), in his study in 1949. (C. G. Jung, *Word and Image,* ed. Aniela Jaffe, Bollingen Series XCVII, Vol. 2. Copyright © 1979 by Princeton University Press, plate 95, p. 114).

Freud and Jung. Jung had already begun a promising career as a leading young psychiatrist in Zurich, Switzerland, when he first became attracted to Freud's writings. It was Freud's interpretation of dreams that particularly intrigued him. Jung had had a long-standing interest in dreams, visions, and other manifestations of human fantasies. In addition, Freud's use of free association to unravel the unconscious meaning of dreams fit with Jung's exploratory investigation of word associations as a means of determining areas of internal conflict. After a lengthy correspondence with Freud, Jung came to visit him in Vienna in 1906. Freud's relationship with Jung had special personal as well as professional meanings for each. For Freud, concerned about the future of the fledgling psychoanalytic discipline, Jung's involvement represented the most important extension of the psychoanalytic movement outside of the Vienna circle. Freud, who was nineteen years Jung's senior, felt paternal toward Jung, an attitude and expectation that facilitated their interaction in the short run but did not bode well for their relationship in the long run.

Freud recognized Jung's brilliance and soon decided that Jung was to be his "crown prince," his successor as head of the psychoanalytic movement. When the International Psychoanalytic Association was founded in 1910, Jung became its first president at Freud's request. But growing theoretical differences began to affect their professional and personal relationship, and Jung withdrew as a member of the association only four years later. Freud thought that Jung's dissent was an expression of Jung's own unresolved Oedipal problem! (See Alexander, 1982.)

There is a sense in which Freud's diagnosis of the basis of his rift with Jung probably has some validity. But it is oversimplified. Jung did have personal difficulties in his relationship with a domineering mother and a troubled father, a pastor who was uncertain about his religious beliefs. He also felt that he was a failure. But Freud's paternalism tended to stimulate any negativism that Jung may have transferred to Freud from his feelings toward his father. In addition, Freud had a history of establishing close relationships with professional peers and then breaking the relationship. This was the case with Breuer and with Fliess (Gay, 1988). Finally, apart from any interpersonal issues, there were genuine and important theoretical differences between Jung and Freud.

Analytic Psychology. Jung saw human beings as guided as much by aims and aspirations as by sexual urges. Jung's formulation of a basic human striving for growth and self-actualization was probably the major factor in his rift with Freud. When Freud asked Jung to become the permanent president of the International Psychoanalytic Association, he also asked for a commitment to the overriding importance of the libido, requesting, "Promise me never to abandon the sexual theory. This is the most essential thing of all. You see, we must make a dogma of it, an unshakable bulwark" (Campbell, 1971, p. xviii). But Jung believed that the unconscious instinctual life embraces more than simply sex and aggression; it includes other urges such as the need to create and to self-actualize. These ideas were subsequently incorporated by humanistic psychologists in America, to the extent that Gordon Allport, one of the original leaders of this movement, spent a year under Jung's tutelage.

To distinguish his approach from classic psychoanalysis, Jung called his theory of personality *analytic psychology.* A basic assumption of this theory is that the personality consists of competing forces and structures that must be balanced. For example, each of us, according to Jung, has both masculine and feminine tendencies; however, an integrated personality balances its more masculine aggressiveness with a more feminine sensitivity. In a similar manner, there must be balance between our conscious and our unconscious. Jung thus emphasized conflicts between opposing forces *within* the individual, rather than between the individual and the demands of society or between the individual and reality. For Jung, a self-actualized individual emerges out of the struggle to balance and integrate the various opposing forces that make up the personality. Moreover, for Jung, the process of development and growth is not resolved in childhood but continues into maturity and later years.

The Collective Unconscious. Jung's interest in archaeology and in ancient cultures and mythology led him to take a much more positive view than Freud of the function of symbols, dreams, and related unconscious processes. One of the most original and controversial concepts in Jung's theory is that of the collective unconscious, which, according to Jung, is the source of much of our vitality, creativity, and neurosis. Jung differentiated the *ego,* or the conscious mind; the *personal unconscious,* which contains repressed memories and desires; and the *collective unconscious,* which includes the psychological residue of the human species' ancestral past. The collective unconscious consists of universal tendencies to respond selectively to particular situations and figures with particular kinds of feelings. Jung contended that "the collective unconscious contains the whole spiritual heritage of mankind's evolution, born anew in the brain structure of each individual" (Campbell, 1971, p. 45).

The collective unconscious is made up of powerful, primordial elements called *archetypes.* Among the many archetypes postulated by Jung are the hero, the wise man, the sun god, the demon, and even each key member of the family. Each archetype is associated with an instinctive tendency to have a particular kind of feeling or thought toward a corresponding object or experience. For example, an infant's image of its mother will consist of aspects of the actual mother infused with the preformed conception of the mother archetype.

Two especially significant archetypes are the animus and anima. The *animus* is the male archetype that is experienced by a woman, while the *anima* is the female archetype experienced by a man. These archetypes imply that, to some extent, women have innate dispositions toward particular ideas and attitudes about men and that men have analogous innate ideas about women. Thus, for example, a woman's response to a man is, according to Jung, a function of her animus archetype as well as a function of the actual man. The same holds true of a male's perceptions of and reactions to a female.

Two additional archetypes that warrant special mention are the shadow and the persona. The *shadow* is the lower, animal side of human nature, or our darker instincts. The passions and impulses associated with the shadow, not unlike those of Freud's id, give rise to socially unacceptable thoughts and behaviors. The *persona,* in contrast, is the socially acceptable mask that each person wears in public. The persona archetype, in conjunction with social conventions, makes individuals tend to adopt masks and conceal their real nature. If this archetype is too powerful, then the individual becomes shallow, playing a role and detached from genuine emotional experience. There must be a balance among the persona, the shadow, and the other archetypes. The archetype of the *self* signifies the innate tendency to balance and integrate the diverse components of the person. The primary symbolic representation of the self archetype, according to Jung, is the magic circle, or *mandala.* This symmetrical circle symbolizes human striving for unity and wholeness. An important component of the path to self-actualization is the development of understanding of and sensitivity to these archetypes that comprise the collective unconscious. It further includes their integration with other facets of one's personality and with the actual attributes of particular men and women with whom one interacts.

It is interesting to consider the specific examples that Jung invoked as evidence for the archetypes. For example, Freud interpreted a da Vinci painting of Saint Anne with the Virgin Mary and the Christ Child as meaning that Leonardo himself had two role mothers. Jung, on the other hand, contended that it was a manifestation of the collectively shared and inherited archetype of the dual mother, or rebirth. There are many myths about dual descent from both human and divine parents. Heracles, according to Greek legend, was born of mortal parents, but unwillingly adopted by the goddess Hera; and Christ, through his baptism in the Jordan, was reborn (Jung, 1936). According to Jung, the practice of giving children godfathers and godmothers is another example of the dual-birth motif. He would no doubt cite the phenomenon of the born-again Christian as still further evidence of the power of the dual-mother, or rebirth, archetype.

Archetypes are reflected in the universal symbols, images, themes, myths, and art of Eastern and Western cultures, as well as in dreams and even in the visions and symptoms of psychotics. Archetypes "create myths, religions, and philosophies that characterize and influence whole nations" (Jung, 1936, p. 68) and influence individual behaviors. These vast sources provided Jung with the needed "proof" for the existence of archetypes. Note again how Jung's training in archaeology and philosophy influenced his ideas, in contrast with the natural sciences that formed Freud's background.

The construct of archetypes is not readily reconcilable with modern psychological science, a factor contributing to the limited input that Jung has had on contemporary psychology. However, the phenomena that the construct of archetypes was invented to explain — the apparent universality of particular attitudes, conflicts, feelings, and images — may well be of fundamental significance and warrant systematic investigation and analysis.

Complexes.   Another of Jung's important, but less controversial, contributions is the concept of the complex. Our common reference today to a "mother complex" or a "guilt complex" are some examples of how Jung has influenced our everyday vocabulary. A *complex* consists of a set of feelings, ideas, memories, and behaviors organized around a common nuclear element that provides the binding power and "pull" of the complex. For example, an adolescent girl seen in a local clinic was unusually attracted to older men. At the same time, she experienced a great deal of conflict and guilt over these relationships. When directly questioned about her late father, she could relate very few memories of him. And when given a word association test, in which she was to respond with the first association that came into her mind, in response to her father's name she blushed and finally uttered a barely audible sound. This cluster of behaviors is a manifestation of what would be called a father complex.

Jung (1904) discovered evidence of these complexes through a clever adaptation of the word association procedure first devised by Galton. Jung presented lists of words to his patients and determined which words produced irregularity in breathing and changes in skin resistance. From an analysis of the content of these words, he was able to infer the existence of specific complexes. There are now a variety of modern word association procedures based on Jung's method. Typically, subjects are asked to give a verbal response to each stimulus in a list of words. Delays in response time and unusual associations are taken to indicate that the stimulus has special meaning for the subject.

Experimenters have found it possible to induce responses similar to complexes through hypnotic techniques, thus lending validation to Jung's idea. For example, Reyker and his associates (Reyker, 1967; Sommershield and Reyker, 1973) induced a sexual complex in hypnotized subjects by administering the posthypnotic suggestion: "After you are awakened, you will not be able to remember anything about the session. However, sexual feelings will well up inside of you whenever words associated with money or metal are mentioned." When subjects were awakened and subsequently presented with words such as *penny,* *dime,* and *lead,* they manifested a variety of symptoms, including headaches, sweating, guilt, and confusion.

Personality Types.   One of Jung's best-known contributions is his personality typology of two basic attitudes, or orientations, toward life: *extroversion* and *introversion.* Both orientations are viewed as existing simultaneously in each person, with one usually dominant. The extrovert's energy is directed toward external objects and events, while the introvert is more concerned with inner experiences. The extrovert is outgoing and makes friends easily; the introvert frequently prefers solitude and cultivates few relationships. Most investigators now view extroversion-introversion as a single personality dimension along which people vary, in contrast to Jung's conception of a pair of opposing attitudes. There is a substantial amount of empirical evidence indicating that extroversion-introversion is indeed a significant personality dimension (e.g., Dicks-Mireaux, 1964; Eysenck, 1947; Wilson, 1978). For example, in anxiety-provoking situations, there is evidence that extroverts are much more likely to choose to be with other people than to be alone (Shapiro and Alexander, 1969).

What happens when introverts and extroverts are paired with partners sharing the same versus opposite personality traits? In a study in which the effects of this variation were explored, extroverts matched with each other had the most upbeat and expansive conversations of all the paired groups (Thorne, 1987). The introverts tended to have more serious discussions that were focused on fewer topics.

Jung extended his typology to include two other pairs of opposing tendencies: *thinking* versus *feeling* and *sensing* versus *intuiting*. These were considered to be psychological functions describing different ways in which extroverts and introverts deal with and perceive their experiences. *Thinking* is intellectual, leading one to ask how things work. Its opposite function, *feeling*, leads one to ask whether an experience feels good or bad (also see Chapter 16 on left-hemisphere versus right-hemisphere functioning). When the feeling function is dominant, one is oriented toward such emotional responses as love, anger, and pleasure. *Sensing* is a reality function; when it is dominant, one deals with the external world in terms of appearance, as if one were a photographer. On the other hand, when the *intuitive* function is prominent, one is responsive to unconscious images, symbols, and the mysteries of experience. Thus, the perceptive functions of sensation and intuition are contrasting ways for the individual to gather data—literal or symbolic—whereas the judgment functions of thinking versus feeling relate to how these data are evaluated.

Two personality measures, the Gray-Wheelwright (1964) questionnaire and the Myers-Briggs Type Indicator (Meyers, 1962), have been constructed to assess these basic functions and have been considered by some to have utility (Maduro and Wheelwright, 1977). As is generally the case in Jungian theory, much more research is needed to establish the validity of this categorization of people according to basic functions. However, the distinctions between thinking, feeling, sensing, and intuiting have been shown to be useful in a number of ways, including the analysis of literary styles (Helson, 1982). There is also evidence that individuals high on *intuiting* recall more dreams categorized as archetypical than individuals high on *sensing* (Cann and Donderi, 1986). This finding is consistent with Jung's proposition regarding the sensitivity of intuitive types to their unconscious experiences.

An Overview of Jung's Theory.   In sum, it is evident that most of Jung's theory remains at the level of conjecture. In contrast to Freudian theory, which stimulated an enormous and varied body of research, Jung's work (with the exception of introversion-extroversion) has given rise to little systematic research. In addition, his concepts of the collective unconscious and archetypes are difficult, if not impossible, to test empirically. Nevertheless, Jung has deepened and expanded our conception of cross-cultural themes, human experience, and human potential. He recognized the positive implications of religious, spiritual, and even mystical experiences for personality growth and can truly be said to be the forerunner of the humanistic movement in psychology (see Chapter 6).

In deviating from Freud's theory, Jung looked further inward, amplifying and reconceptualizing the contents and structure of the psyche. On the other hand, other analysts trained in the psychoanalytic tradition looked outward, maintaining that social motivations, such as the desire for status, approval, and power, can

■ **Highlight 4.2** ■

The Freud and Jung Visit to the United States

In 1909, Clark University sponsored a series of conferences on emerging trends in a number of academic disciplines, including the quite new discipline of psychology. The president of Clark at that time was a psychologist, G. Stanley Hall. In addition to inviting distinguished academic psychologists to these conferences, Hall extended invitations to several eminent practitioners, most notably Sigmund Freud and Carl Jung. Freud was clearly the "star" of the conference, but Jung also had considerable status. Both were awarded honorary degrees; at age thirty-four, Jung became the youngest recipient of an honorary degree from Clark.

Their introductions on receiving their respective degrees provided an interesting comparison. Freud was introduced as "founder of a school of pedagogy, already rich in new methods and achievements, leader today among students of the psychology of sex, and of psychotherapy and analysis," while Jung was introduced as a "specialist in psychiatry, brilliant investigator by the Diagnostische Assoziation-Methode, editor and fruitful contributor to the literature of psychopathology." Freud and, especially, Jung, in their letters to each other, rightfully perceived this conference as an unusual opportunity to spread psychoanalysis across the Atlantic as well as a recognition of their pioneering work (Evans and Koelseh, 1985).

supercede biological urges. Included in this group are such figures as Alfred Adler, Karen Horney, Harry Stack Sullivan, and Erich Fromm. These analysts differ in the particular motivations they believe to be central in human behavior and in how much attention they give to social influence as a determinant of personality. However, these "social theorists" are all sensitive to the role of society in influencing personality and provide valuable, creative insights into personality structure and dynamics.

Alfred Adler's Individual Psychology

Alfred Adler (1870–1937) was a Viennese physician who became associated with Freud shortly after the turn of the century. However, he never fully accepted psychoanalytic theory, and Freud found Adler's criticism difficult to tolerate. Although Adler served as president of the Vienna Psychoanalytic Association in 1910, he severed all relations with psychoanalysis just one year later (Ansbacher

Alfred Adler, (1870–1937), left orthodox Freudian psychoanalysis to found the individual-psychology movement. (The Granger Collection)

and Ansbacher, 1956, 1964). He frequently visited the United States, finally settling in New York in 1933.

A basic tenet of Adler's *individual psychology* is that human beings have an innate social interest (Adler, 1927): it is in the nature of humans to be cooperative and interested in the welfare of other people. This positive, socially oriented image of human nature is in sharp contrast to Freud's depiction of the individual as driven by biological urges that are inevitably in conflict with the requirements of social living. According to Adler, people develop problems because of mistaken goals and patterns of living that block the expression and realization of their social interest — a far cry from Freud's ideas about repression of libidinal impulses.

A Social Interest Personality Scale, based on Adler's ideas, has been shown to have considerable promise in discriminating between groups who clearly differ in social concerns (Crandall, 1980). It can be seen from Table 4.1 that convicted felons have the lowest social-interest scores of all the groups that were sampled. Professional models were anticipated to have low social-interest scores also, an expectation based on the assumption that modeling would tend to attract more self-centered individuals than most occupations. Comparisons with other groups, such as female university employees and female job seekers, were consistent with this expectation. Interestingly, atheists were among the lowest scoring groups. Although atheists can be humanists with strong social interests, concern for people's welfare does not appear to be a strong attribute of the average adult who lacks religious beliefs, according to the results of testing using this particular scale.

Table 4.1   Social-interest scale (means for selected groups)

Group	n	M
Ursuline sisters	6	13.33
Adult church members	147	11.21
Charity volunteers	9	10.78
High school students nominated for high social interest	23	10.22
College students nominated for high social interest	21	9.48
University employees	165	9.24
University students	1784	8.17
Mental hospital patients	25	7.56
College students nominated for low social interest	35	7.40
Female professional models	54	7.06
High school students nominated for low social interest	22	6.86
Adult atheists	30	6.70
Convicted felons	30	6.37

Source: J. E. Crandall, "Adler's Concept of Social Interest: Theory, Measurement, and Implications for Adjustment," *Journal of Personality and Social Psychology, 39,* 1980, p. 484. Copyright 1980 by the American Psychological Association. Reprinted by permission of publisher and author.

Striving for Superiority.   Closely related to the idea of innate positive social motivation is Adler's assumption of a basic human tendency to strive for superiority. Superiority, for Adler, does not necessarily entail power over others or competitive success, but refers to a more general goal of perfection and self-realization. The human being, in his view, constantly strives to move upward. There is a close similarity between this characterization of human motivation and Jung's postulation of a creative energy force motivating the organism toward wholeness and integration. In the neurotic or emotionally disturbed individual, this positive force is misdirected, manifesting itself in the pursuit of power, prestige, and other selfish goals.

Adler's conception of a force moving individuals in the direction of higher goals was the outcome of his own gradual evolution in thinking. Shortly after his association with psychoanalysis, Adler concluded that aggression was a more significant drive than sexuality. However, whereas aggression alone assumed greater importance in Freudian thought, Adler eventually came to view other motivations as more profound and ultimate. Adler replaced aggression with the striving for power, and both power and aggression were subsequently seen as distortions of a more basic urge for superiority or perfection. It was Adler who coined the term *masculine protest* to describe exaggerated, power-oriented behaviors by men or women in response to feelings of inadequacy and inferiority.

Inferiority. The concept of inferiority appeared quite early in Adler's writings. Adler noted that many individuals seem to engage in constant efforts to overcome feelings of inferiority. Initially, he interpreted these as reactions to organ inferiority. As a practicing physician he encountered people who attempted to overcome a physical deficit by intensive exercise of the affected organ or by development of a compensatory skill; e.g., the development of acute hearing as a compensation for poor vision. A famous historical example of compensation for organ inferiority is Demosthenes, who stuttered as a child and is said to have practiced speaking with pebbles in his mouth to overcome his handicap. Thus, in spite, or perhaps because of his handicap, Demosthenes became an outstanding Greek orator.

Adler extended the concept of inferiority to its modern usage, which refers to feelings of psychological and social, as well as physical, inadequacy. Feelings of psychological or social inferiority, like those of physical inferiority, might also have positive consequences, as when a young child's feelings of inadequacy compared with an older sib might lead him or her to learn new skills. Adler, it may be noted, had much more experience working directly with children than Freud did. His focus on ego motivations such as inferiority feelings in contrast to Freud's emphasis on id impulses, coupled with his orientation to the social situation, was reflected in his therapeutic approach, which tended to be more practical and reality oriented than classic psychoanalytic therapy.

Style of Life. The individual's efforts to compensate for real or imagined inferiorities may affect a specific behavior, as in the case of Demosthenes, or the entire organization of personality. Adler referred to the distinctive personality that each of us develops in response to our inferiorities as our *style of life*. Each person is said to have a unique style of life, formed by the age of five, that characterizes the person throughout life and becomes the distinguishing feature of the personality. A related concept is that of the *creative self*, the facet of the individual that provides direction for life by organizing, transforming, and integrating one's experiences. This concept, like some of Jung's notions, is more an affirmation of the human spirit than an explanation of behavior.

An Overview of Adler's Theory. In sum, Adler presents a positive image of human nature and its potential. People are motivated by social interest and by creative efforts to attain perfection and overcome inferiority. These positive urges can turn destructive or neurotic because of deficient child-rearing practices, like rejection

President Theodore Roosevelt overcame early physical weaknesses to become an assertive, physically active adult. (The Bettmann Archive)

or overindulgence, or because of deficiencies in the larger society. Freud, in comparison, presented a more pessimistic, tragic view of development and considered Adler's psychology shallow and superficial. Although Freud recognized social and familial influences, he believed that people are destined to experience conflict between biological urges and the requirements of a civilized society regardless of the mode of child rearing or the organization of society.

Freud's and Adler's contrasting assumptions about human nature do not lend themselves to empirical examination. Which image one considers more valid depends on one's personal experience and worldview rather than on scientific findings. However, Adler's views concerning the importance of such ego or self-based motives as power strivings and inferiority feelings have found acceptance in contemporary views of personality dynamics and psychopathology. Also, Adler's more pragmatic, reality-based approach to psychotherapy is reflected in the work of a number of contemporary psychotherapists (Beck, 1976; Ellis, 1967). In addition, some of Adler's more limited and clinically-based observations have been subject to empirical test and are among his most enduring contributions to psychology (see Highlight 4.3).

Karen Horney

Karen Horney (1885–1952) was a European-trained physician and psychoanalyst who had been psychoanalyzed by a disciple of Freud and emigrated to the United States from Berlin in 1932. Horney's first book, *The Neurotic Personality of*

◼ **Highlight 4.3** ▬▬▬▬▬▬▬▬▬▬▬▬▬▬▬▬▬▬▬

Birth Order and Personality Development

One of Adler's most acute clinical observations was of the importance of birth order in determining personality development. The oldest child, having received the parents' individual attention, has the problem of coping with the birth of the second child. Because one common reaction is concern with maintaining power and the status quo, oldest children are likely to be more conservative, responsible, and socially oriented. The second child, competing to be "number one," is likely to be ambitious; the youngest child is often the family "pet," overindulged and spoiled. Although earlier research failed to provide support for these hypotheses, a classic study by Schachter (1959) reawakened interest in this Adlerian hypothesis and stimulated a large body of research indicating that birth order, in conjunction with such variables as family size and sex, does affect personality. Schachter conducted a number of experimental studies on the effect of anxiety on the need to affiliate with others. Subjects who were led to believe that they would be shocked in a coming experimental session chose to wait for the session with people in a similar situation more often than they chose to wait alone. Of special relevance for Adler's views concerning birth order was the finding that, of first-born subjects, 80 percent chose to wait with others while only 31 percent of later-borns chose to do so. This was believed to demonstrate the greater social orientation of the first-borns.

Our Times, was published in 1937 and provoked enormous controversy among psychoanalysts. Her departures from Freudian theory were no less striking than Adler's, and it was evident, from the perspective of Freud's adherents, that she had left the fold to join the ranks of the heretics.

Horney's and Adler's ideas were fundamentally very similar. Horney was optimistic about the possibilities for human growth, satisfaction, and self-realization. She placed greater emphasis on the role of self-enhancement, personal security, and interpersonal (social) motives than on sexual and biological urges as the principal determinants of adjustment and neurosis. However, the specific interpersonal motives and mechanisms that Horney suggested as central to personality differ from those stressed by Adler. For Horney, *neurosis* was best understood as a pattern of response to basic anxiety, a concept which has some similarity to Adler's notion of inferiority feelings. Horney described basic anxiety as "the feeling a child has of being isolated and helpless in a potentially hostile world" (Horney, 1945, p. 41). The infant's feeling of helplessness is not inevitable but is dependent on the extent of parental warmth, affection, consistency, and other behaviors that contribute to a child's feeling of security.

Karen Horney, (1885–1952), noted early female psychoanalyst who broke away from the Freudian tradition. (The Bettmann Archive)

Just as she felt that basic anxiety is not inescapable, Horney also took exception to the Freudian notion that penis envy in women is preordained by their biological nature. In general, she disagreed with Freud's psychology of women, contending that he failed to appreciate how the socialization of women fosters problems in self-confidence and leads to an exaggerated dependence on the love relationship.

Horney was sensitive to the various neurotic patterns that frequently exist in adult relationships, which she perceived as strategies that the child develops to reduce the distress of feelings of insecurity and helplessness (that is, of basic anxiety). Finding security in trying to please others, manipulating and exploiting others, and even devaluing oneself are examples of such neurotic patterns. What makes these patterns of behavior neurotic or maladaptive is that they are exaggerated and cannot produce satisfaction. In addition, although one of these modes of behavior might be dominant, they tend to conflict with one another, causing additional tension and distress.

Horney categorized neurotic patterns according to three fundamental types:

1. *Moving toward people*—a neurotic need for approval and affection from others; a need to please and defer to others.

2. *Moving against people* — a neurotic need for power; a need to exploit others and constantly feel superior.

3. *Moving away from people* — a neurotic need to be aloof, detached, uninvolved, completely self-sufficient, and independent of others.

All three neurotic patterns result in self-images that are impossible to live up to and trap both the person and those with whom he or she is involved. These patterns may maintain security, but they also serve as ways of expressing the unconscious hostility and rage to which feelings of helplessness give rise. Horney contended that there is a thin line between acting aloof in a social relationship and rejecting someone. Furthermore, one can control and even injure or psychologically destroy another person by excessive demands for affection, help, and support.

Horney neither formulated a comprehensive theory of personality nor attracted a large group of disciples to promote her ideas. However, her descriptions of neurotic patterns and their underlying mechanisms have been incorporated into many contemporary personality theories that address the problems of neurosis and psychopathology. Her views on the importance of the child's early experience of affection and security are reflected in a wealth of research (Bowlby, 1969; Harlow, 1971; Spitz, 1945; see Chapter 12). At the same time, there remains some question of whether Horney's views of personality are superficial and overoptimistic. It is certainly questionable whether *any* child can escape the rivalries within the family triangle of parents and child or avoid conflicts between self-assertion and pleasing others.

Erich Fromm

The last of the social psychological theorists we will consider in this chapter is Erich Fromm (1900–1980). Fromm, like Adler, Horney, and Sullivan, had psychoanalytic training but, unlike the others, came to psychoanalysis with advanced training in sociology rather than with a medical degree (for a succinct description of differences among these theorists, the reader may refer back to Highlight 4.1). Fromm's background in sociology and the related disciplines of philosophy and political science is reflected in his contribution to the understanding of human personality. Fromm's views present an unusual combination of tough-minded Marxian analysis of the impact of economic institutions on personality structure, with warm, almost romantic humanism. While Freud saw social institutions as a mirror or consequence of basic psychological needs, Fromm perceived the individual as essentially victimized by a harmful society. Fromm, a refugee of Nazi Germany, believed that the attraction of so many Germans to extreme political forms was a consequence of the structure of German society, rather than a reflection of uninhibited biological urges.

Personality and Society. Fromm's first book, *Escape from Freedom* (1941), linked changes in basic personality to change in Western society. Fromm suggested that human beings strive for freedom and autonomy but that this very struggle may result in feelings of alienation from nature and society. People need to be free and autonomous, but they also need to feel connected and related to others. The intensity of this conflict and the different ways in which it is resolved, according to Fromm, are dependent on the economic organization of the society.

In preliterate cultures and feudal societies, the individual had few choices. Behavior and opportunity were fully prescribed by one's tribe or one's social and economic position in society. There was little freedom, but also little alienation. With the Renaissance, however, an individual striving for freedom and independence came to the fore. The Protestant Reformation and the rise of capitalism enhanced and emphasized individual opportunity, freedom of choice, and personal responsibility, but the price for this, Fromm argued, was intense feelings of isolation and loneliness.

How do individuals cope with alienation? One way is to surrender individuality and choice. Fromm described a number of personality mechanisms that are unconsciously adopted to "escape freedom." The first of these, *authoritarianism,* is manifested in either masochistic or sadistic tendencies, terms that do not have sexual connotations, as Freud used them, but refer to ways of relating to authority. The masochist behaves in an excessively helpless, submissive, and dependent manner, whereas the sadist strives to control, dominate, and exploit others. Both strivings are typically found in the same person. A highly authoritarian military structure may foster both traits, with the same individual behaving sadistically

Erich Fromm, (1900–1980), at home in Lucerne, Switzerland, in 1968. (Bill Ray/*Life* Magazine © Time Inc.)

toward soldiers of lower rank and masochistically in relation to superior officers. Another escape mechanism that Fromm described is *destructiveness,* in which case a person no longer attempts to relate to others but reduces feelings of powerlessness and alienation by seeking to weaken others. Finally, one can escape through excessive *conformity* to social rules; by being completely conventional and exactly like others, one can reduce feelings of separateness.

Fromm's concept of authoritarianism arose, in large part, from an effort to explain the growth of fascism in pre-World War II Europe and the psychological attraction the Nazi ideology had for many individuals. It provided the stimulus for an extensive body of research on the authoritarian personality that was initiated shortly after that war (Adorno, et al. 1950). Although there was empirical support for such a personality categorization, for various reasons—partly its complex nature, the ambiguity of some of the findings, and changes in the sociopolitical environment—research interest in the authoritarian personality has sharply declined.

The Basic Needs. As Fromm (1955, 1964) developed and elaborated on these ideas in his later work, his humanistic orientation became more evident. The conflict between striving for freedom and striving for security centered on five basic human needs:

1. *A need for relatedness*—to have, care for, share with, and be responsible for others.

2. *A need for transcendence*—to become more creative and rise above one's more animal nature.

3. *A need for rootedness*—to replace our separation from nature with feelings of kinship with others.

4. *A need for identity*—to achieve distinctiveness through one's own efforts or through identification with another person or group.

5. *A need for a frame of reference*—to have a stable structure or framework that will aid in organizing and understanding one's experiences.

Each of these needs can be satisfied in neurotic ways or in a personally and socially productive manner. In Fromm's later work, one finds a consideration of human needs in the context of existential issues such as awareness of death and one's separateness from others (see discussion of humanistic, existential approaches in Chapter 6). Again, the social and economic structure of the surrounding society is critical.

We have already seen, in Chapter 2, that social differences can influence personality. However, there is little evidence indicating that Fromm's character structures are linked with particular social structures. Nevertheless, Fromm's theoretical views are stimulating and appealing. In the tradition of social reformers, he argued that through radical change in the social structure one can create a society in which both the individual's and the society's needs can be met.

Particularly in his later writings, Fromm proposed that humans are essentially good but become corrupted by civilization, a theme reminiscent of Rousseau's "noble savage." For Fromm, true self-love and the love of others are sides of the same coin. In deriving a humanistic code of ethics, Fromm put the matter most succinctly: "Evil constitutes the crippling of man's powers; vice is irresponsibility toward himself" (Fromm, 1947, p. 20). A judgment on whether this positive and optimistic view of human nature is more "correct" than Freud's pessimistic view will have to await the verdict of posterity.

PSYCHOANALYSIS SINCE FREUD

Classic psychoanalysis has never been a static theory. It underwent regular and major changes during the course of Freud's lifetime. For example, the concepts of id, ego, and superego were not introduced until the 1920s, well after Freud had laid the major foundations of his theory. Since Freud's death, psychoanalytic theory has continued to evolve, with new concepts introduced, old ones revised, and new directions taken.

These more recent changes have come from a number of sources. First, psychoanalysis has not been immune to the contributions and criticisms of its dissidents, and efforts have been made to accommodate some of these critiques without altering the basic structure of the theory (Erikson, 1950; Anna Freud, 1946; Kardiner, 1945). Second, psychoanalysis was recognized even by Freud as incomplete. Because it still has areas of inconsistency and ambiguity, a good deal of recent work has been directed toward making the theory more logical and coherent (Hartmann, 1964; Rapaport, 1959; Schafer, 1976). Third, as psychoanalysts experimented with therapeutic techniques and expanded their range of patients, new ideas were introduced to account for their observations (Erikson, 1950; Anna Freud, 1946; Fairbairn, 1952; M. Klein, 1937; Kohut, 1971). Perhaps surprisingly, experimental research has played a very minor role in these changes, even though an enormous number of studies have been directed to the investigation of psychoanalytic propositions (Kline, 1972).

We cannot hope in a few pages or even a few chapters to do justice to the development of psychoanalytic theory during the years since Freud's death. Many of these changes are either technical or involve esoteric controversies of concern only to psychoanalysts. Other changes, however, are of major significance, including a shift in emphasis away from instinctual drive conflicts to the problems posed by social attachments and maintaining one's individuality. There are several directions being taken in contemporary psychoanalytic theory that are of particular interest to students of personality.

1. *The growth of psychoanalytic ego psychology.* Increasing attention is being paid to defense mechanisms; to ego functions such as thinking, perception, and mastery; and to the development of the self and related ego structures. For example, analysts have become as much concerned with coping strate-

gies and modes of adaptation as with basic id-instigated drives; that is, there is as much interest in the ways in which people deal with conflicts and with the effectiveness of their responses or strategies as there is in the motivational source of the conflict. A particularly significant component of this new direction has been object relations theory, which deals with the child's attachment to and thoughts about people, the effect of these attachments and thoughts on the child's individuality and feelings about the self, and how these factors change during the course of development. For example, a question of interest to objects relations theorists would be the developmental effects of a disturbed relationship with the mother when an infant is six months old versus the same disturbed relationship when the infant is eighteen months old. Note that the focus here is on relationships, not solely on impulse frustration or gratification.

2. *Disenchantment with psychic energy and drive therapy.* Modern psychoanalysts do not reject the importance of libidinal impulses and the psychosexual development of the child. However, there has been dissatisfaction with Freud's theory of libidinal energy and its supposed distribution and expenditure. These concepts are far removed from experiences that individuals report and from their perceived sources of conflict. Thus, there have been efforts to bring the theory closer to the perceived world of the patient in therapy.

3. *Greater recognition of the influence of culture and the family.* Although modern psychoanalytic thinking does not attribute the same importance to social variables as do such dissidents as Fromm, Horney, and Sullivan, there is increased acknowledgment of the influence of social institutions on personality. There has been particular interest in the effects of cultural variables on the development of ego functions and self-processes, as evidenced in the writings of Erik Erikson and other psychoanalysts.

The writings of contemporary psychoanalytic theorists reflect these three trends in varying degrees. There is considerable ferment and debate among psychoanalysts over the significance of these theoretical developments. It will become clear in the following pages that contemporary psychoanalysis does not speak with the same unified voice as when Freud was alive and functioning as its principal arbitrator and innovator.

Erik Erikson

Of all the psychoanalytic writers to modify and expand psychoanalytic theory, the best known is German-born Erik H. Erikson (1902–1994). There is some question about whether he should be included among psychoanalytic descendants or psychoanalytic dissidents, with the choice depending on whether one emphasizes the similarities or the differences between his views and those prevailing among post-Freudian analysts. Since Erikson perceived his own views as

Erik H. Erikson, (1902–1994), known for his biographies and his stage conception of personality development. (Historical Pictures Service, Chicago)

expanding rather than radically altering Freudian theory, he has been included in this section of the chapter, rather than in the earlier section on alternatives to psychoanalysis.

Before being trained in psychoanalysis by Anna Freud, Erikson was an art teacher in a progressive private school and a graduate of a training program for teachers in the Montessori method. Erikson's educational background, his direct teaching experiences with children, and the Montessori emphasis on the child's development of intiative through play and work are evident in his later theoretical writings. Following the completion of his psychoanalytic training in Vienna, Erikson emigrated to the United States. At various times he held positions at Yale, at the University of California in Berkeley, at the Austin Riggs Center (a leading psychoanalytically oriented institute), and at Harvard University. His first book, *Childhood and Society* (1950), was a landmark volume, an impressively creative extension of psychoanalytic theory. It contains the essential ideas that provided the framework for his subsequent theoretical writings (1964, 1968, 1976) and his biographies of Luther (1958) and Gandhi (1969). We see in Erikson's writings an emphasis on ego processes and cultural influences, although the significance of libidinal development and biological factors is not denied.

The Stages of Development.   The notion of developmental stages was central to Erikson's thought. He viewed the early stages of development in terms similar to Freud's, but he examined these stages from the perspective of the particular kinds of ego processes involved, rather than in terms of biologically determined libidinal tensions. An emphasis on ego processes leads naturally to consideration of social and cultural forces, for the ego is the mediator between personal needs and the demands of social reality. In addition, Erikson did not view the pattern of personality as essentially completed and unchangeable by the time the child enters school. His analysis of development embraced the full life span, from infancy to maturity.

Erikson proposed eight *psychosocial stages* in personality formation, each stage critical for developing certain fundamental personality characteristics and preparing the individual for later ones. Table 4.2 below shows how basic personality dimensions are related to the psychosocial stages. Each stage involves a crisis or developmental problem; if the crisis is adequately resolved, then the individual acquires a healthy component of personality (e.g., trust or personal initiative); if the crisis is not adequately reconciled, then a negative quality (e.g., mistrust or guilt) is acquired. For example, in the earliest, oral-sensory stage the infant interacts mainly with its mother, and the goal of the interaction is primarily the supplying of food. It is the infant's first interaction with the social world, in which it finds out either that basic needs are fulfilled generously and with affection, or that the world is harsh and unpredictable, giving supplies grudgingly and without love. According to Erikson, the infant develops a sense of trust or mistrust toward the world during this period. That is, the infant is becoming a trusting or a mistrustful person. Although later events can alter the basic disposition that has been established, the first experience of fulfilled or unfulfilled expectations is nevertheless of critical importance.

In later work, Erikson (1976) introduced the concept of *ritualization* to describe a culturally patterned activity or social ritual which each stage fosters. In the oral-sensory stage, the mother recognizes the child through personal but culturally ritualized touching, feeling, and other interactions. This constitutes a significant affirmation of the child and of the mutuality between mother and child.

Table 4.2   Erikson's eight stages and their implications for personality structure

Psychosocial stages	Personality dimensions
1. Oral-sensory (first year)	Basic trust versus mistrust
2. Muscular-anal (ages 2–3)	Autonomy versus shame and doubt
3. Locomotor-genital (ages 3–5)	Initiative versus guilt
4. Latency (ages 5–12)	Industry versus inferiority
5. Puberty and adolescence	Identity versus role confusion
6. Young adulthood	Intimacy versus isolation
7. Adulthood	Generativity versus stagnation
8. Maturity	Ego integrity versus despair

This relationship is believed to form the foundation for subsequent adult ritualizations, such as certain religious ceremonies.

An Overview of Erikson's Work. Erikson's theoretical formulations are especially appealing to contemporary readers because of his emphasis on factors that underscore a sense of identity and relationships with others. If sexual problems can be said to have been the predominant "hangup" in the Victorian era, then problems of confusion over self-identity can be said to be the predominant concern in modern, technologically advanced Western societies.

Erikson, like Freud, thought that conflict was inevitable in the human struggle, but he had a less tragic and pessimistic conception of the outcome of conflict resolution. Self-insight and control, he felt, are important in coping with the dilemmas of living. In addition, the ability to resolve conflict is substantially augmented by the attributes acquired during development, given a positive resolution of each developmental stage. The mature person evolves the attributes, or "virtues," that help him or her to cope with problems: hope, will, purpose, and competence (the rudiments of virtue developed in the four childhood stages); fidelity (the adolescent virtue); and love, care, and wisdom (the central virtues of adulthood) (see Erikson, 1964). These virtues are reminiscent of Old and New Testament preaching, and it is probably not accidental that Erikson's ideal model of the person has counterparts in Western religious thought.

Erikson's work contains a sensitivity to the problems encountered in the course of development that lends credence to his views. Problems of identity and of intimacy are indeed central to many adolescents and young adults as they struggle to determine what they will do with their lives and to establish their independence while, at the same time, they experience a need for close relationships with others. Although there have been a number of investigations regarding issues of identity, intimacy, and other personality dimensions to which Erikson has ascribed importance, his theory has stimulated surprisingly little research that directly address his hypotheses regarding stage-personality linkages. There is some evidence provided by a study of South Africans of an increase in intimacy from adolescence to adulthood. However, this trend did not hold for black males whose intimacy scores were already relatively high in adolescence (Ochse and Plug, 1986). Whether the process of developing intimacy follows a different path for South African black males (and possibly for other cultural groups) than that proposed by Erikson remains to be investigated.

Erikson has been criticized for emphasizing ego attributes and conscious impulses while neglecting sexual and aggressive motivations and unconscious forces. But, in spite of these empirical and theoretical criticisms, Erikson's rich, compassionate, and well-articulated views have had wide-ranging influence, far beyond the sphere of psychoanalysis. In addition, he has compelled psychoanalysis to pay greater attention to cultural factors influencing personality, as well as to the developmental problems that individuals must master at every age in the life span. As we shall see in subsequent chapters, problems of identity are particularly central to the study of development.

Psychoanalytic Ego Psychology

In its early formulation, psychoanalytic theory addressed primarily the issues of libidinal dynamics, psychosexual development, and the expression of unconscious desires in dreams, neurotic symptoms, slips of the tongue, and a variety of other behavioral phenomena. Following World War I, Freud turned his attention to other dimensions of personality and introduced the psychological structures of the id, ego, and superego. The ego, by instigating danger signals, became critical in his concept of defense. Anna Freud then developed and elaborated on the notion of ego defense against threat and considered in detail a variety of mechanisms that children and adults use to reduce threat.

These changes made the ego more central to psychoanalytic theory, but its theoretical status remained unsatisfactory. In classic psychoanalytic theory, all thoughts and actions were derived initially from id desires. Such functions as thinking, perceiving, and mastery, which Freud assigned to the ego system, were secondary processes that arose because of a conflict between reality and the immediate gratification of id impulses. Tying ego functions to the id created theoretical complexities for psychoanalysis, whereas other theories were able to deal with ego functions in a much more straightforward manner. Also, viewing the ego functions as a consequence of conflict and defense tended to make one look at those functions in terms of degree of impairment, rather than as positive, healthy mechanisms for coping with and mastering the environment.

Conflict-Free Ego Functions. Heinz Hartmann (1958) recognized that for psychoanalysis to become a general psychology, it was necessary to conceive of ego functions as independent of the id-reality conflict. He proposed that some ego functions are conflict-free and should be viewed as biological processes that enable human beings to master the various developmental tasks of walking, thinking, concept formation, and motor coordination that are required for effective growth and adaptation. He suggested that ego processes, rather than being derivatives of the id, emerge independent of the id. Because these ego processes were then no longer dependent on drives or conflicts, Hartmann said they had *primary autonomy.* Individuals were believed to derive satisfaction from the pure exercise of their limbs and from acts of perceiving and attending that were analogous to, but independent of, the libidinal pleasure derived from erogenous zones. These ideas provided the theoretical framework for what is currently referred to as *psychoanalytic ego psychology.*

Ego processes become organized into systems or structures that can serve a defensive function, satisfy libidinal impulses, or become instrumental in the satisfaction of other goals. For example, talking can serve a defensive function by obscuring one's true feelings and blocking direct action; satisfy libidinal or oral-sadistic functions, as in the case of sarcasm; and satisfy other goals by serving as an instrument to fame and success, as in the case of a national newscaster. When used instrumentally, these functions are said to acquire *secondary autonomy.* They can become free of the situations and drives that gave rise to them and become significant behaviors in their own right.

Hartmann's work on ego processes and related ideas offered by other psychoanalytic writers (e.g., Rapaport, 1960) contributed significant revisions to psychoanalytic theory. They helped resolve inconsistencies in the theory and provided a more integrated and logical account of normal psychological development. However, in general, psychoanalytic ego psychology has not offered an empirically tested set of hypotheses and predictions. Rather, its theoretical structure permits the study of curiosity, mastery, and perceptual and cognitive processes without relating these activities to id desires. Thus, researchers with a psychoanalytic ego psychology orientation have turned their attention to the ways in which individuals cope with internal feelings and the external world in nondefensive, as well as in threatening contexts.

Cognitive Styles.   As an example of this type of research, George Klein and his associates (see Gardner, et al. 1959) contended that there are systematic individual differences, or *cognitive styles,* in the ways stimuli are perceived. For example, a distinction can be made between *levelers,* who are believed to gloss over perceptual differences, and *sharpeners,* who accentuate these differences. This contrast in cognitive styles is assessed by using a simple perceptual task; levelers, for example, take longer than sharpeners to notice changes introduced by experimenters in the size of simple geometric shapes. There is some debate concerning the generality of this style and its importance for the study of personality; ego psychologists feel that repression is aided by a cognitive style of leveling, although the empirical evidence supporting this belief is weak. Nevertheless, the point to be made is that these studies can stand without reference to classic psychoanalysis.

Subliminal Perceptions.   Another research area explored by psychoanalytic ego psychologists is subliminal perception. Such investigations look at the effects of stimuli presented at levels below the individual's awareness on perceptions, thoughts, and feelings (Luborsky, 1967; Shevrin, 1974; Silverman, 1976; see also Chapter 4).

As we noted in the previous chapter, there is little doubt that verbal and pictorial stimuli can be processed without the person being aware that she or he is responding to these stimuli. There is considerable debate, however, concerning the extent of these unconscious influences and the mechanisms mediating them. The late Lloyd Silverman (1983) carried out a series of studies in which messages of presumed symbolic significance for particular patient groups were utilized (Silverman, 1983). Thus one message, "Mommy and I are one," was hypothesized to symbolize a wish to merge with mother, and was presented to schizophrenic patients inasmuch as the wish to merge is presumed by some psychoanalytic theorists to be particularly intense and a source of conflict for these patients. The data reflected a reduction in several measures of pathological thinking following subliminal exposure of "Mommy and I are one" (Silverman, 1983, 1985). Questions have been raised regarding the implications of these studies due to uncertainty about the reliability of some of the dependent measures of patient thought and behavior and the inconsistency in some of the findings (Balay and Shevrin, 1988; Cordon and Allen, 1980). However, there is nevertheless substantial evidence that communication presented below the level of awareness can influence emotional and thought processes. In a study employing simpler messages, "Loving Daddy is wrong" and "Loving Daddy is okay," with an undergraduate female sample, the subliminal exposure of "Loving Daddy is wrong" was shown to disrupt recall in some of the women (Geisler, 1986). Whether the effects observed in this and related studies are due to the circumvention of ego defenses by subliminal stimuli or to other processes remains to be determined.

Psychoanalytic ego psychology, in contrast with traditional psychoanalytic theory, has also led to interesting and productive research in ego processes in infants and very young children. It has helped psychoanalysts go beyond oral, anal, and genital issues and look at the influence of the type of mothering, the infant's attachment to the mother, and the environment in which the infant is raised on the infant's cognitive and social development. Although the research is not uniquely psychoanalytic in method and implications, the pioneering work in this area has been conducted by psychoanalysts (Escalona, 1968; Mahler, 1958; Ribble, 1943; Spitz, 1945). For example, René Spitz (1945), an early psychoanalytic ego psychologist, drew the attention of psychologists, social workers, and the larger society to the potentially deleterious effects of early institutionalization on the cognitive and emotional development of children. In a classic study, Spitz followed two groups of infants: one raised in an institution where unmarried mothers or adequate substitutes cared for the babies, the other raised in a foundling home with a limited nursing staff (each nurse cared for about ten infants). The foundling home had good hygienic facilities and the infants were not mistreated. Nevertheless, Spitz found dramatic psychological and physical disturbances in this group of children. Thirty-four of the ninety-one babies in the foundling home died within a five-year period, while others displayed various deficits in speech, motor coordination, and other ego functions. While there is some question about the comparability of the babies in the two groups, subsequent work with both humans and nonhumans (Bowlby, 1969; Harlow, 1971) has strongly supported the finding that early attachment plays a critical role in later development.

Object Relations Theory

The theory of object relations is, in part, an aspect of the development in psychoanalytic ego psychology and, in part, reflects other influences in contemporary psychoanalytic theory. Not all features of object relations theory are accepted by all psychoanalysts. There are even subgroups or "schools" that are divided according to which features they accept and the importance placed upon these features relative to other principles in psychoanalytic theory. There are debates about the extent to which object relations are indicative of libidinal investment or are independent of id motivations. However, what is most important is the recognition, by all of the theorists in this area, of the significance of the child's attachment to people and even to inanimate objects in the environment.

This change has profound implications for the way in which psychoanalysts view neuroses and personality development. Instead of focusing on internal conflicts between the id drives and the ego and superego, the question becomes one of the nature of the individual's relationships to other people. Although modern psychoanalysts have not rejected the concept of libido and its oral, anal, and phallic expressions, there is now at least an equal interest in such questions as the degree of psychological separateness from parents; the ability to perceive both positive and negative attributes in the same parent versus perceiving one parent as all "good" and the other parent as all "bad"; and the degree of attachment to and involvement with other people versus self-preoccupation. The question of the nature of one's relationship to others also brings to the fore issues regarding the self—such as the fragility of one's self-concept and the degree of autonomy and independence.

The core of much of object relations theory is the infant's attachment to the mother and other figures. These early attachments provide the basis for the infant's ego development from intense attachment to the mother to a distinct, autonomous self. The characteristics of these attachments are believed to provide the basis for the child's subsequent interpersonal relationships.

Melanie Klein. The potential importance of the infant's early attachments was noted by a number of Freudian analysts who worked with young children. The first systematic theoretical propositions on the role of the infant's social attachments in the development of personality were presented by Melanie Klein (1937). Klein emphasized pre-Oedipal interpersonal experiences, especially mother-child attachment. According to Klein, the infant must pass through two stages of attachment and objects relations during approximately the first year of life. In the first phase, the infant is believed to develop attachments to part objects, such as the mother's breast, and to relate to these objects in terms of gratifications, frustrations, and fears.

Klein agreed with Freud's view on the role of libidinal impulses, but placed even more emphasis than Freud on the importance of aggressive impulses during this period. According to Klein, the child both wishes for the maternal object and is hostile and fearful toward it. The child resolves this conflict by categorizing the world into good and bad objects. This categorization is postulated as a necessary step in the child's ego development. During the next phase, the child begins to integrate objects, no longer splitting them into good and bad components. For instance, the infant now recognizes the mother and relates to the maternal object as a whole rather than as part objects. When the child comes to the realization that good and bad experiences stem from the same object, it must then struggle with feelings of ambivalence. Recognition of the mother as a whole object implies both awareness that she is a separate figure, upon whom one is dependent, as well as awareness of one's separateness. The developmental progress of the infant through these early phases can go awry and become disrupted by hostility and envy if the infant is unloved or if its needs are not gratified.

There is much more to the theoretical views of Klein and her adherents than this brief description of early object relations and ego development. Other aspects of Kleinian theory—the importance of dyadic (mother-child) relationships rather than the triangular (mother-father-child) relationships stressed by Freud, the assumption of pre-Oedipal envy of the parent, the projection of unacceptable impulses onto an object, and subsequent identification with that object—extend beyond the scope of this introduction to object relations theory.

Melanie Klein's theoretical views caused a rift within the Freudian psychoanalytic movement. Her principal rival was Freud's daughter, Anna Freud, who maintained that Klein's elaboration of the internal psychic life of the infant was unwarranted. Both Melanie Klein and Anna Freud, with Freud's encouragement, worked directly with children and derived their theoretical views from observations of children. While Anna Freud focused on the Oedipal and post-Oedipal period and on the ego defenses the child developed and manifested at this stage, Melanie Klein stressed earlier stages. She contended that during the pre-Oedipal period, the child internalized its representation of people and bodily parts and that these internalizations could be loving, envious, or destructive. Some sense of the intensity and complexity of the rivalry between Klein and Anna Freud is conveyed by Melanie Klein's daughter, who was analyzed by her mother and became a psychoanalyst herself, siding with Anna Freud (Grosskurth, 1986).

While Melanie Klein is a significant figure among psychoanalysts, she has had very little impact on the mainstream of developmental psychology because her views on the infant's emotional life are so extreme. She conceived of "an infant from six to twelve months trying to destroy its mother by every method at the disposal of its sadistic endeavor—with its teeth, nails, and excreta and with the whole of its body, transformed by imagination into all kinds of dangerous weapons" (1937, p. 187). This image rightly elicits skepticism and, like many other psychoanalytic conjectures, is not accompanied by empirical support.

Margaret Mahler.   The child not only has feelings toward or libidinal investment in significant objects such as bottle, breast, mother, and father, but also has cognitive images or representations of these objects. These representations may be viewed as the *internalization* of object relations. Feelings and attitudes toward the object become elicited by a representation of the object. However, in the earliest phase, the infant is believed to be unable to differentiate itself from the object (Rapaport, 1950). Mahler (1968) views this primitive level as a period of *symbiosis* in which the infant is attached to and dependent on the mother and cannot differentiate between mother and self. Elements of symbiosis can sometimes be observed in adult relationships; for example, in some marital relationships the partners can no longer determine which feelings and values are their own and which are their spouses'.

Mahler provides a detailed description of the process of separation-individuation through which the infant achieves differentiation and autonomy from its mother, a primary need-satisfying object. Beginning at about four to five months of age, the infant engages in a series of activities characterized by exploration of the environment and seeking security from the mother. By about two years of age, a child who has achieved adequate separation will have established what Mahler refers to as a *rapprochement* between the dependent need for emotional support from the mother and the need to be independent. The attainment of this rapprochement enables the child to consolidate its individuality and develop a permanent sense of self. However, the struggle between dependence-independence is a lifelong one.

Object Representation.   *Object representations* are believed to provide the necessary basis for separation between self and other. They permit the child to tolerate the absence of the mother and of immediate gratification and are the foundation for the development of thinking and symbolic activity. One important element in the process is the development of object constancy. *Perceptual constancy* refers to the recognition and maintenance of a constant perception of a stimulus, even though it is presented at different angles and distances and in varying environments. From a psychoanalytic standpoint, *object constancy* refers to the capacity to evoke a constant representation of an object in its absence, regardless of variations in need for and feelings toward the object. Imagine the child's world if the mother who feeds the child appears different from the mother who disciplines the child, or if each time the mother wears a new dress, she becomes a different person. There is evidence that infants who display greater constancy in their perception of people as compared to their perception of objects have mothers who engage in frequent communication with their offspring and are active in stimulating infant achievements (Chazan, 1981). For psychoanalytic ego psychology, disturbances in object relations are an important antecedent of subsequent neurosis and psychosis.

Empirical Research on Object Representations.   Westen et al. (1990) have studied predictions of object relations theory with respect to object representations. Adolescents who were diagnosed as borderline personality disorder were administered the Thematic Apperception Test (TAT). In this test subjects make up stories in reference to various pictures. A group of nonborderline patients, and a group of normals were also given the test. Object relations theory predicts that borderline personality disorder, a disorder characterized by instability in mood and behavior and unclarity in identity, is derived from developmental problems from early childhood. Therefore, borderlines should have more disturbed representations of relationships with people. Scoring of the TAT stories revealed that borderlines were significantly more likely to represent an object world that was threatening and dangerous; to represent the motives of others in simple, idiosyncratic, and illogical ways; and to portray themselves as investing in others only in terms of getting their own needs met.

Transitional Objects.   Infants develop attachments to their caregivers, but they also have to separate and learn to function without them (see Chapter 7). For many infants and toddlers, attachments to *transitional objects* appear to help them bridge this separation (Winnicott, 1953). Blankets, diapers, and teddy-bears are

Transitional objects provide security in a changing environment. (© Elizabeth Crews)

familiar examples of transitional objects that psychologically seem to have the same function as the mother or another caregiver. These objects are soothing and provide security to the child. As Eagle (1984) notes, "the child knows that the blanket or teddy-bear is not the mother and yet he reacts affectively to these objects and derives comfort from them as if they were the mother. Giving external objects the capacity to soothe and comfort permits a freer and safer exploration of and interest in the external world" (p. 194).

Donald Winnicott (1953), the British pediatrician and psychoanalyst who first gave systematic attention to these phenomena, has argued that interests in transitional objects provide a basis for the later development and internalization of cultural interests and values. Whether Winnicott's speculations concerning the relationship between interest in transitional objects and interest in cultural activities are valid or not, it is likely that transitional objects serve a useful function during the periods of separation throughout the lifespan. A college freshman, living in a completely new setting, may not react to the disappearance of a favored object brought from home with the same intense distress as that of an infant whose blanket has been removed. Nevertheless, that object, though it might be an inexpensive stuffed animal, an old trophy, or even a favorite recording, may have an important transitional function during this period of initial separation and adaptation.

Many children do not develop these early object attachments. How do they differ from those who do? In one study (Passman and Weisberg, 1975), children attached or unattached to a blanket displayed equal stress while playing alone when their mothers were present. The unattached children, however, were much more upset when playing alone, while their mothers were absent. Some data suggest that emotionally disturbed adults had less-than-average transitional object attachments during childhood, but these findings are not consistent (Hong, 1978). Another study relating personality traits of college students to early transitional object attachments indicated that students without such attachments in early childhood tended to be more reserved and aloof as young adults than those with early transitional object attachments. However, the latter group displayed more tension and impatience. It appears that the nature of early transitional object attachments — their intensity, duration, and related characteristics — need to be taken into account in order to determine their adaptive functions.

Narcissism and the Self

Another major deviation from traditional psychoanalytic theory is entailed in the emphasis on the "self" in the work of Heinz Kohut (1971, 1977). For Kohut, the attainment of a cohesive, integrated self takes precedence over psychosexual issues, although the latter remain important. As with other psychoanalytic innovators, Kohut's theoretical views arose out of his work with a particular kind of patient — one who suffers from what Kohut has described as a *narcissistic personality disorder*. These are individuals who feel empty, powerless, and look to others to carry out functions that one normally does for oneself; yet they are given to feelings of primitive grandiosity and boastfulness. Kohut found that traditional psychoanalytic therapy was not effective with these patients, but that he could obtain positive outcomes through manifesting a positive regard for and acceptance of the patient. (It will become evident in Chapter 6 that this approach owes much to the work of Carl Rogers.)

The patient's pathological narcissism stems from parental failure to fully accept the child, so the patient does not develop a truly positive self-regard or *healthy* narcissism. For the self-structure to develop properly, the child requires admiration and acceptance together with an opportunity to idealize a figure with whom it can identify. Effective parents provide these dual functions. Since the parent is not always available to reflect and accept the child's feelings and to soothe and comfort the child, these minor or optimal frustrations, according to Kohut, result in the child internalizing these structures so that it can admire and soothe itself. In this way, self-esteem and internalized values and ideals develop. To this dual or bipolar component structure of the self, Kohut later added a third constituent resulting from the need to be with a similar-age person with shared interests as contrasted with an authority or parental figure (Kohut, 1984).

Kohut's (1984) perspective on the Oedipus complex is different than Freud's. For Freud, the five-year-old child has sexual feelings towards the parent of the opposite sex and aggressive, rivalrous feelings toward the parent of the same sex. For Kohut, this child is interested in exercising his or her capacities for assertion and affection. A male child will practice being assertive with his father and being affectionate with his mother. If the parents respond appropriately to the child, no Oedipus complex develops. However, if the mother has conflicts over the relationship of sex and affection and if the father gets threatened by the son's assertion, the child's assertive tendencies may degenerate into aggressive feelings and the affectionate impulses may become sexualized. For Kohut, Freud's Oedipus complex is not an inevitable aspect of early childhood experience but rather only occurs when parents handle normal developmental processes dysfunctionally.

Kohut's view of the therapeutic process is quite different from that of classical psychoanalysis. For Kohut, the therapist replaces the parent, as it were, and functions as a kind of mirror for the patient. Through the positive mirroring process, the patient's inadequate and wounded self can be restored to a cohesive self with genuine self-esteem. For Kohut, the change from pathological to healthy narcissism makes possible a self-reliant pursuit of one's own talents, ambitions, and values. These, presumably, are the attributes of the genius and the hero. But whether the genius and hero, by virtue of their accomplishments, are the best models for mental health is a matter of some debate.

Ego States and Core Conflict Relationship Themes

Object relations theory and psychoanalytic ego psychology have led to two important shifts in psychodynamic theorizing. First, modern psychoanalysis has become increasingly cognitive. Personality is now seen as resting on the cognitive representations, or *schemas,* of self, other people, and relationships. Second, personality is seen as relational; the most fundamental representations of self involve relationships with others.

Two modern examples of these shifts are the concept of "states of mind" (Horowitz, 1988) and the "core conflict relationship theme" (Luborsky and Crits-Christoph, 1990), both of which are based on empirical research on psychotherapy. Horowitz has suggested that individuals experience their lives in terms of different states of mind. A *state of mind* is a particular organization of experiences and behaviors, and it is typically associated with a particular mood. It may be an organized, harmonious, congruent state of mind or a state of mind in which the individual feels disorganized and where the associated mood may seem ego-alien and intrusive.

A state of mind is associated with a particular self-organization. Horowitz, like many modern theorists, assumes that individuals have many possible self-organizations, or self-schemas (see Chapter 10). In different states of mind different self-schemas are operative. A particular self-organization goes with a particular role-relationship model. A *role-relationship model* is a "mental schematization of the relative characteristics of self and other, and a sort of script of what each may do to the other in a sequence of interactions" (p. 42).

A schematization of the relationship of several different states of mind, self-

Figure 4.1   Different states of mind associated with different role-relationship models for a given individual. (Figure from page 45 from *Introduction to Psychodynamics* by Mardi Horowitz. Copyright © 1988 by Mardi Horowitz. Reprinted by permission of the author.)

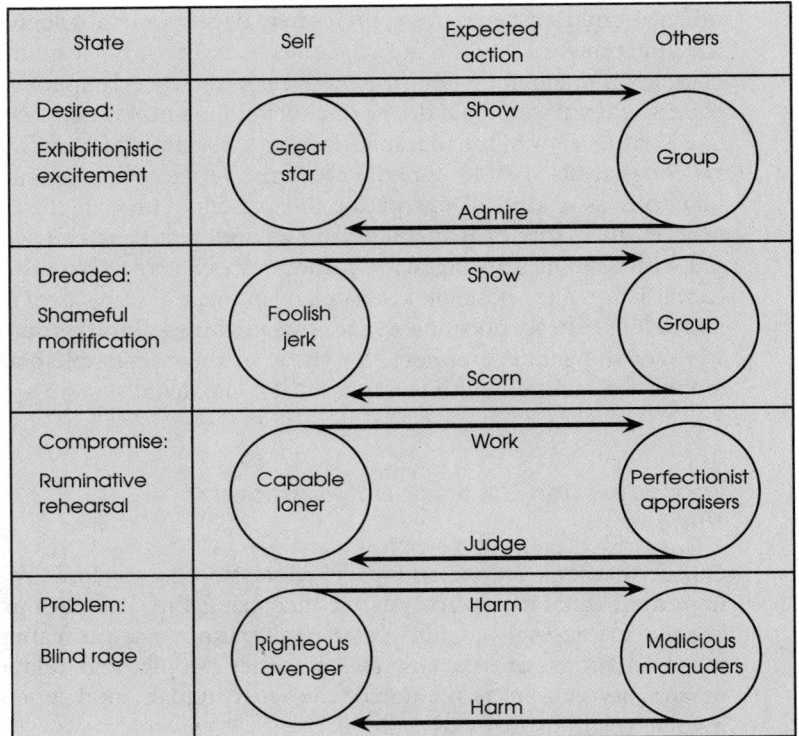

organizations, and role-relationship models for a specific individual is given in Figure 4.1. When this individual is in a desired state of mind — feeling exhibitionistic excitement — his self-representation is one of being a "great star," and his role-relationship model is based on showing himself off to others and receiving admiration. However, states of mind are unstable, and if he does not receive the feedback he expects from others, his state of mind may shift to one of shameful mortification. His self-representation shifts to that of a "foolish jerk," and his role-relationship model now is based on expecting scorn from others. Horowitz and his colleagues have studied tapes of therapy sessions and have documented the shifts in states of mind that individuals undergo.

The idea of a core conflict relationship theme (Luborsky and Crits-Christoph, 1990) refers to the belief that individuals organize their lives primarily around the basis of certain chronic core relationship issues that persist from early childhood. A core conflict relationship theme consists of (1) the individual's main wishes, needs, or intentions toward another person; (2) the (typical) response of the other person; and (3) the response of the individual. These themes are based on unfulfilled wishes from childhood about which the individual experiences conflict. The wishes then become the basis for the individual's interactions with others. For instance, perhaps the individual had unresolved wishes for dependency on his mother and also experienced considerable conflict about the wishes. He will tend to organize his relationships in such a way that this wish for dependency, along with the conflictual elements, dominates how he behaves towards other people. How he behaves will, in turn, "pull" characteristic behavior from others (e.g. perhaps rejection).

By studying transcripts of therapy sessions Luborsky and Crits-Christoph have documented that the same theme shows up in 80 percent of episodes described by a given patient, both in the patient's relationship to the therapist and to other people in the patient's life. Most significantly, the same theme also shows up in patients' discussions of their relationship to their parents.

PSYCHOANALYSIS IN FLUX

The one statement about contemporary psychoanalytic theory that can be made with confidence is that it is in the process of change. One of the most radical departures from traditional psychoanalytic theory has been proposed by Roy Schafer (1976). Schafer stresses the distinction between Freud's clinical insights and his theory (see Klein, 1967). He accepts Freud's theory of infantile sexuality, the importance of the Oedipal situation, the use of defense mechanisms, and similar propositions that are closely related to the reports of people in therapy. However, he rejects Freud's use of psychic energy constructs, of drive, and of terms that imply separate places or entities in the mind. He proposes that "we should not use phrases such as 'a strong ego,' 'the dynamic unconscious,' 'the inner world,' 'libidinal energy,' 'rigid defense,' 'an intense emotion,' 'autonomous ego function,' and 'instinctual drive' " (1976, p. 9). Such phrases make the error of *reification,* that is, making *things* or objects out of psychological processes, experiences, and behaviors that are essentially *actions.* We should use verbs and adverbs, he contends, to designate these as processes. For example, instead of saying, " He cannot control his sex drive," we should say, " He readily engaged in sexual actions even when he knew it would be wise not to do so" (1976, p. 28). This reformulation substitutes sexual behavior for the energy construct of drive and provides a specific meaning — acting despite one's best judgment — for the ambiguous phrase, "cannot control." Phrases such as "internalize an object" and "deeply repressed" attribute to the mind spatial qualities that are properties of physical objects, and such common expressions as "conflict between id and ego" also require translation into action terms.

These changes in language would alter the entire theoretical framework of psychoanalysis. They eliminate a whole array of theoretical structures and mechanisms, many of which are either controversial or simply vague and ill defined. Needless to say, many of the changes proposed by Schafer have not been acceptable to the main body of psychoanalysts. One problem is that Schafer, in his effort to discard surplus theoretical baggage, seems also to have discarded structural concepts such as ego or self that are needed in order to account for the organization and consistency of behavior. Furthermore, by adhering so closely to an action language, one tends to turn a theory into a collection of descriptive statements rather than an organized set of propositions that lead to specific deductions, predictions, and analytic interpretations.

Schafer (1992), along with Donald Spence (1982) and others, has been a contributor to the recent development of narrative approaches to psychoanalysis. Spence and a number of other writers have questioned the idea that the memories recovered in psychoanalysis represent historical truth. Spence has argued that psychoanalysis deals with narrative truth. That is, psychoanalysis is not an archeological enterprise in which one digs into one's past to uncover real, buried memories. Rather it is a storymaking enterprise in which the patient develops new, more functional stories about his or her past and its relationship to the present. We shall have more to say about the narrative approach in Chapter 11.

Although psychoanalysis has profoundly deepened our insight into human experience and behavior, much of the theory is loosely stated and needs to be rooted in clear operations or behavior. In addition, much of the theory has been unresponsive to research. Psychoanalysts do refer to scientific findings, and some are engaged in research inquiries, but psychoanalysts typically do not drop or significantly change a theoretical conjecture simply because of lack of empirical support. They have generally not attempted to separate those aspects of the theory for which there is sound scientific evidence from those portions that remain largely speculative.

Summary

1. According to Jung's *analytic psychology,* each individual has opposing personality tendencies, such as masculine-feminine and introversion-extroversion. The self-actualized individual emerges out of the balance and integration of these opposing forces.

2. The *archetypes* that make up the *collective unconscious* are inherited by all human beings. They are reflected in universal symbols, images, myths, and dreams.

3. Jung conceived of a *complex* as a set of feelings and behaviors organized around a strong, common nuclear element.

4. According to Adler, people are basically motivated by positive social interest and efforts to overcome inferiority. Distortions of positive urges can take place through exaggerated compensation for feelings of inferiority.

5. Horney described three fundamental patterns of response to basic anxiety: moving toward people (exaggerated need for approval); moving against people (hostility, dominance); and moving away from people (aloofness, lack of involvement).

6. In Fromm's view, human beings are basically positive, loving creatures whose positive impulses can be warped by society, particularly by an alienating economic system.

7. Erikson described eight *psychosocial stages* from birth to maturity, each of which poses a particular developmental task. The manner in which developmental problems are resolved provides the basis for specific personality characteristics such as basic trust versus mistrust, initiative versus guilt, and identity versus role confusion.

8. One of the consequences of *psychoanalytic ego psychology* has been an increased emphasis on the infant's early attachment to the mother. This attachment and other *object relations* provide the basis for the child's ego development and subsequent interpersonal relationships.

9. Melanie Klein emphasized the pre-Oedipal period of development, proposing that the young infant resolves its ambivalent feelings toward its caretaker by psychologically splitting that person into good and bad part objects.

10. Heinz Kohut proposed that, for many patients, the primary goal of psychoanalytic therapy should be reparation of the injured self-structure.

11. Two new developments in psychoanalysis are Horowitz's idea of states of mind and Luborsky and Crits-Christoph's core conflict relationship theme. A *state of mind* is a particular organization of experiences and behaviors. A *core conflict relationship theme* is a relationship issue that persists from childhood into adulthood and tends to pervade and organize one's current relationships.

Thought Questions

1. Do you socially present the "real" you and, if not, how do you think your real self differs from your persona?

2. Do you support the Freudian position that society inhibits desires and that people are basically antisocial, or the Adlerian position that society can facilitate personal development and that individuals have social concerns? Why?

3. Assuming that family rivalry is quite common, what other interpretations can you offer of the Oedipal and Electra conflicts besides Freud's hypothesized sexual envy?

4. Do you feel that American society promotes alienation? How might this be changed?

5. Do you think development primarily revolves around sex as Freud thought or around relationships and the development of the self as object relations theory and self-psychology hold?

5

Learning Theory Approaches to Personality

Learning theories of personality have their origins in the laboratory, unlike psychoanalytic theories, which are rooted in the clinical interactions between therapists and patients. However, as we will see, the applicability of these learning theories to personality and clinical problems has become the primary source of their vigor and popularity.

Learning theorists have undertaken the ambitious task of not only accounting for personality development on the basis of principles established in the laboratory, but also applying these principles to changing emotionally disturbed, maladaptive behavior patterns. As we will see, therapeutic procedures based on learning theories have indeed been implemented successfully in clinical situations. In fact, one of the most significant developments in the field of clinical psychology has been the vigorous growth of therapies based on learning principles.

In previous chapters, we have seen how a group of psychodynamic, clinically based theories explained personality development and functioning using complex concepts that were difficult to define and evaluate. In the next chapter, we will cover more cognitive theories that are also clinically based and frequently employ complex terminology not easily translated into concrete concepts. The concepts used by the learning theorists, however, are simpler and more readily tied to observable events. Thus, the learning theorists have in a real sense undertaken a difficult challenge: explaining the phenomena of human personality with a restricted, empirically based vocabulary and a set of well-defined principles. How they have approached this task, the ways in which vocabulary and principles have had to be expanded, and the adequacy of their theoretical accounts of personality are some of the questions to be considered in this chapter.

The learning theories reviewed in this chapter, share a number of characteristics, several of them noted earlier (see the introduction to Part II):

1. The use of concepts and methods that are closely linked to the laboratory, particularly to the experimental analysis of learning.

2. The assumption that the principal behaviors constituting personality are acquired, or learned, during the course of development. More specifically, an individual's behaviors in a given situation are believed to have been acquired through a history of being rewarded or punished in the same or similar situations. For example, the difference in timidity and aggressiveness be-

tween two boys, Robert and John, may be accounted for by differences in their learning histories. Robert may be inhibited and timid because his retreats from threatening social encounters have been rewarded by adults, and his abortive attempts at self-defense have met with punishment from peers. However, John may be a bully at school because his aggressive behavior has been reinforced by his resultant control of others, by his gaining possessions, and by the attention he receives for it. Learning theorists acknowledge that genetic and biological factors may influence individual differences but believe that these are secondary to learning experiences.

3. A theoretical emphasis on observable stimuli and responses. All but the learning theories of personality locate the basic processes of personality inside the individual. Learning theories, however, differ on this point. Some, like Skinner's (1953) operant reinforcement theory, are concerned solely with observables and make no inferences about the mind or what might be occurring inside the organism. Others, like the learning theories of Miller and Dollard (1941) and Bandura (1977), do propose a variety of internal processes that intervene between the onset of the stimulus and the subsequent overt behavior. Nevertheless, even these theories prefer to focus on stimuli and behaviors that are observable to the scientist. They make as few assumptions as possible about mediating elements such as thoughts, feelings, and desires. They particularly try to explain behavior solely in terms of the organism's past learning history and in terms of current circumstances (Hineline, 1980).

4. An emphasis on the importance of the situation as a determinant of action. One of the great controversies in personality research has centered on the role of the situation as a determinant of behavior. How important is the situation compared with the characteristics that an individual brings into it? Whereas personality theorists have by and large paid attention almost exclusively to the attributes of the person, learning theorists have helped to balance this often one-sided emphasis by demonstrating the influence of situational or environmental factors on behavior. Some learning theorists may have pushed this balance between the situation and the person too far to the other extreme by minimizing the role of dispositional (person) variables. The person-situation controversy is a major issue in the study of personality and will be examined at various points in this text (see especially Chapter 9).

Although there are many similarities among learning theories, these are also major differences among them. These differences, which are in some instances as great as those among the various psychoanalytic and psychodynamic theories, will be considered in detail as we review the major learning theory approaches to personality.

In this chapter we begin by considering traditional stimulus-response approaches to learning theory, including the application of Dollard and Miller's work to psychoanalytic theory. We next consider Skinner's radical behaviorist position. We then consider two of the most currently influential perspectives, those of social learning theory and cognitive behavior modification.

ASSOCIATIONIST (STIMULUS-RESPONSE) LEARNING THEORY

The period from the 1930s through the 1960s was one of ferment and controversy surrounding a few major psychological theories, each one offering hope of explaining much of psychology. One of the most influential of these theories was proposed by Clark Hull (1943, 1951, 1952). Hull and other theorists of this period aimed to formulate a theory of behavior that would adequately encompass most species, from the laboratory rat to the human. Indeed, much of the research support for these theories came from studies of the laboratory rat. Hull was not oblivious to the differences between rat and human, but he believed that there are common requirements imposed on every living organism to satisfy biological needs and to adapt to the environment. Clearly, Darwin was an important influence on Hull, who further assumed that for mammals — whether rats or human beings — the mechanisms governing learning are basically identical. Humans as well as lower animals, according to Hull, are creatures of habit.

Habits and Drives

Habits are stable stimulus-response connections. A dog attacking an intruder on sight, a dolphin soaring above the water in response to a verbal command, and a preschooler regularly crying at the sight of another child with a toy he or she wants are all exhibiting habits. Hull proposed that habits are acquired and strengthened whenever a response that occurs together with a stimulus is accompanied or shortly followed by drive reduction. Drive reduction is thus required for a response to be reinforced. *Drive reduction* refers to a decrease in the intensity of a motivation or drive, as when hunger, thirst, or sex is partially or fully satisfied, or when fear is reduced after a threat is overcome. In addition, the effects of drive reduction supposedly work automatically, so that the lowering of drive strengthens any response, adaptive or nonadaptive, that happens to be occurring in that particular stimulus situation.

Hull's own research examined the effects of the reduction of such *primary drives* as thirst and hunger. Since drive reduction in these instances meant that the organism has obtained water when thirsty or food when hungry, the reinforced response was biologically adaptive, aiding the organism in its struggle for survival. But the reinforced response does not have to be instrumental to the attainment of a reward, according to the theory. Irrelevant responses occurring in conjunction with relevant behavior are also expected to be reinforced. For example, a hungry rat that scratches its snout while pressing a bar that releases a food pellet will be more likely to scratch its snout the next time it is hungry and is placed in the same apparatus. B. F. Skinner has suggested that the same mechanism responsible for a hungry rat's pawing at its snout for food, when that response has nothing to do with obtaining a reward, is the basis for superstitious behavior in humans.

The situation is more complex for humans because, in addition to such primary drives as hunger and thirst, there are many *acquired,* or *secondary, drives* such as our desires for love, power, achievement, and money. In addition, people have many learned fears. These secondary drives might even conflict with one another or with primary drives, so that the drive reduction of one motivation may lead to the reinforcement of a behavior that thwarts the satisfaction of other motivations. For example, the response of drinking alcohol may be reinforced by the reduction of painful fears and anxieties. However, habitual drinking may also result in economic loss, family disruptions, and social disgrace; thus, the overall effect of a drinking habit is maladaptive.

Personality Development

Hull provided the basis for a formal theory of learning that could be used to account for both maladaptive and adaptive behavior in humans and nonhumans. Thus, his theory was attractive to psychologists and other behavioral scientists with interests in animal behavior, human personality, and social interaction. For example, sociologists and anthropologists used Hullian principles to analyze how society transmits and maintains particular customs.

Dollard and Miller. Among Hull's associates and students at Yale were John Dollard, a sociologist with an extensive background in cultural anthropology and psychology, and Neal Miller, an experimental psychologist then known for his studies of drive acquisition and reinforcement. These two pioneered in systematically extending and elaborating on Hull's principles to account for personality development, social behavior, and psychopathology (Dollard, et al., 1939; Dollard and Miller, 1950; Miller and Dollard, 1941). In recent years the personality theory formulated by Dollard and Miller has declined in popularity, paralleling the decline of Hullian theory from the central position it once occupied in psychology. However, the Dollard-Miller analysis is still useful and has substantially influenced other learning approaches to personality.

It is helpful to consider how the critical concepts in the Dollard-Miller analysis – cue (stimulus), drive, response, and reinforcement – apply to a concrete situation. Assume that a professor typically responds with sarcasm whenever a student answers a question incorrectly. Even after receiving unfavorable feedback and complaints about his behavior, the professor finds it difficult to change. According to the concepts of Dollard and Miller, the *cue* in this situation is an incorrect answer; the *response,* sarcasm. While the cue and the response are obvious, the operative *drive* in this situation and the *reinforcement* are less apparent. The drive could be a need to impress the class and the reinforcement, class laughter; or the drive could be a need for power and the reinforcement, student fear and docility; or the drive might be aggression and the reinforcement, the expression of pain on the face of the unfortunate student. In examining behavior from the perspective of Dollard and Miller, one seeks to establish the cue that is eliciting a response, the drive that has been gratified in the situation, and the reinforcement that reduces the drive.

Cues. Although the cue that elicited the professor's sarcasm is evident, cues are often so subtle and disguised that neither the respondent nor an outside observer can pinpoint the stimulus that is actually eliciting the behavior. Most of us have experienced feelings of anger or anxiety and have engaged in a compulsive eating binge without being able to identify the stimuli that elicited, or caused, these behaviors. An important task for the clinician dealing with symptoms such as fear, uncontrollable thoughts, and compulsive rituals is to determine the cues that evoke these symptoms. Cues exert a powerful effect on a person's behavior; they "can determine when one will respond and which response one will make" (Dollard and Miller, 1950, p. 32).

Cues can also elicit *mediating responses*: internal, nonobservable responses that are believed to intervene (mediate) between observable stimuli and overt responses. Thoughts, feelings, and the anticipation of events are potential mediating responses which can then serve as cues, eliciting other mediating or overt responses.

Mediating responses can have drive as well as cue functions. For example, for a child who once had been frightened in a dark room by an intruder, any dark area came to elicit the mediating response of fear, through a process of conditioning. Because fear is aversive, the child was driven to reduce the fear, in this case by lighting the room. Thus, the child insisted on sleeping in a well-lit room, never entered a dark area, looked for a flashlight before opening a large closet, and was reluctant to leave the house at night. This process is shown in Fig. 5.1.

Acquired Drives. Fear, as a learned response, is one example of a secondary, or acquired, drive. *Acquired drives* are similar to such primary drives as hunger and thirst in that the organism will strive to reduce them. A response that results in drive reduction will then be reinforced; that is, the probability of that response occurring again in the same situation is increased. This holds true whatever the acquired drive — fear, say, or a need for fame or affiliation.

The cue, or stimulus, value of the fear drive is illustrated by the habits that the darkness-fearing child subsequently developed. He asked his mother to bring along a flashlight whenever he was taken to the dentist, and the dentist found that permitting him to shine a flashlight or placing a bright lamp near the drill helped relax the child. The mediating response of fear was therefore common to both the dental situation and the dark room, and the response of illuminating the area became attached to both the internal cue of fear and the external cue of darkness (see Figure 5.2). That is, when the internal cue (fear) occurred in a context (the dentist's office) other than that in which it was first learned (the dark), the previously learned fear-reducing response (bright light) became generalized to

Figure 5.1   A mediating response with cue functions.

| Observable stimulus cue (dark area) | → | Mediating response (fear) | → | Mediating drive stimulus, or cue, of fear | → | Overt response (lighting room) |

Figure 5.2   The process of mediated generalization.

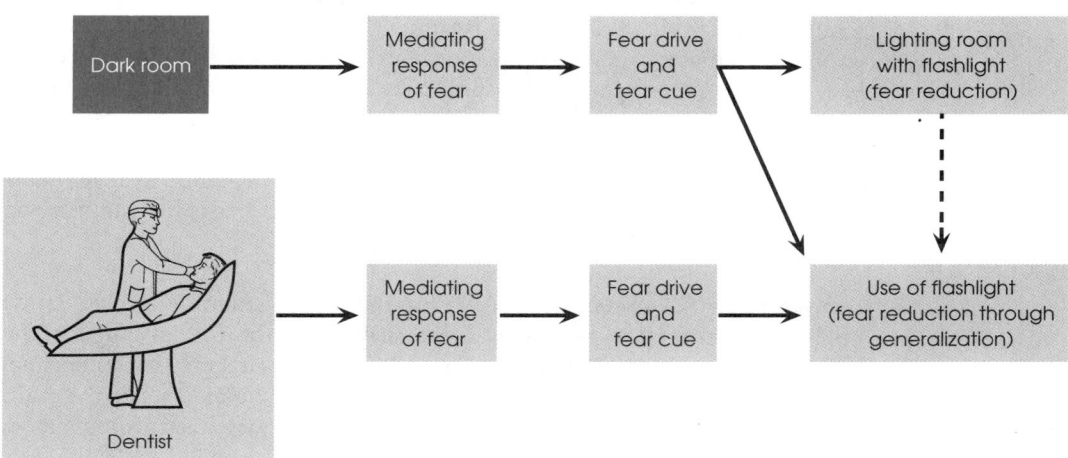

the new context. This process is referred to as *mediated generalization*. Through mediated generalization, very different stimuli — for example, a dark room or a dentist's chair — may come to elicit the same response: use of a flashlight.

From the learning theory perspective of Dollard and Miller, individual differences in personality can be described in terms of differences in the kind and intensity of acquired drives that influence a person's behavior, and in the responses or habits the person has acquired to reduce those drives. One difference between Dollard and Miller and other learning theorists such as Skinner and Bandura is that because of Dollard and Miller's focus on mediating responses, the acquired drives and habits that distinguish individuals may be expressed in a wide range of situations rather than being viewed as highly situation specific. Thus, the concept of personality traits, referring to stable personality attributes that characterize individuals in varied situational contexts, is quite compatible with Dollard and Miller's theoretical orientation.

Comparison with Psychoanalytic Theory.   The examples above illustrating the concepts of cue, drive, response, and reinforcement suggest the applicability of Hull's and Dollard and Miller's learning theory to various aspects of psychoanalytic theory. Although stimulus-response learning theory and psychoanalytic theory come from far different traditions, employ different concepts, and differ sharply in methodology and rigor, they share several assumptions about human nature. Psychoanalytic propositions can therefore be translated into the language and structure of learning theory. Indeed, that translation was one of the goals of Dollard and Miller.

Dollard and Miller's learning theory, like psychoanalytic theory, allows for unconscious determinants of behavior; that is, motivations of which the individual is unaware that affect thought and action. In addition, both learning theory and psychoanalytic theory assert that the ability to label these motivations, or the achievement of insight, will produce more adaptive behavior. Both theories also emphasize the role of drives in governing behavior and the significance of motivational conflict as a cause of psychopathology. Still another point of consistency between the two theoretical approaches is their common assumption of the necessity of drive reduction for reinforcement. Both Hull and psychoanalytic theorists see the organism as striving to reduce tension and as acquiring and maintaining tension-reducing behaviors. Finally, both camps believe that behavior follows laws and is determined, thus providing the basis for scientific analysis and prediction of behavior.

Language and Repression.   It is illuminating to examine the Dollard-Miller analysis of repression because it introduces us to the role of language in their theory and, more generally, to the strategies and concepts that experimentally based learning theories use to explore complex psychoanalytic propositions and observations. We use an example of a male who, through his learning history, has come to feel anxious about sexuality.

Figure 5.3 depicts a number of possible responses that this male might make when confronted with a sexually attractive female. Between the observable cue of an attractive female stimulus and the observable response, different chains of mediating responses might take place. The overt goal response at the end of the chain reduces the experienced anxiety and is therefore reinforced by anxiety reduction. The figure shows that different overt responses are often mediated by disparate covert cognitive statements. For example, a response of indifference might be preceded by the covert statement of "She bores me"; an aggressive remark might be mediated by the covert appraisal, "I don't like her"; and so on. These different anxiety responses can affect behavior at different points in the motivational sequence. Thus, the indifference response might move up in the chain and interfere with the sexual response so that sexual arousal does not even occur. This process might be so automatic that the individual is unaware that he is repressing his sexual feelings.

Figure 5.3   Alternative stimulus-response mediating response chains leading to repression.

This is one type of activity *not* explained by the concept of drive reduction. (Robert Landau/West Light)

Dollard and Miller's incorporation of covert verbal responses in their theoretical analysis anticipated current interest in cognitive behavioral modification, an approach considered later in this chapter. In general, the relative flexibility of their interpretations of Hullian theory has permitted investigators and theorists operating within this framework to address many of the major issues in the study of personality, including frustration, aggression, and conflict (see Chapter 14). The same flexibility, however, made the Dollard and Miller theory vulnerable to criticisms similar to those leveled against psychoanalytic theory, especially since there are too many unobservable concepts that can be made to fit any behavioral outcome. There was also considerable objection to the principle of drive reduction as a prerequisite for learning. A number of apparent exceptions were noted in which people appeared to seek an increase in drive, such as excitement and activity, with these experiences themselves being reinforcing. There was so much dissatisfaction with the drive concept that attention shifted to the analysis of reinforcement. Nevertheless, although the popularity of the Dollard-Miller theory as a whole has waned, many of its concepts have been incorporated into other learning approaches to personality.

REINFORCEMENT THEORY

The learning theory of B. F. Skinner dispenses with the mediating, unobservable processes that Hull, Miller, and Dollard posited as occurring inside the organism.

B. F. Skinner, (1904–1990), the reinforcement theorist most responsible for the application of learning theory to real-life problems of teaching and behavior management. (Monkmeyer Press Photo Service)

The task of psychology, according to Skinner, is to establish lawful relationships between behavior and events in the objective world. Skinner was very precise about what he meant by "lawful" and "objective." Concepts such as tension, feeling, desire, drive, attitude, and intention do not refer to objective, physical events that can be directly observed; they are attributes of a vague entity called the "mind." For Skinner, it was scientifically inappropriate to use nonobjective events as explanations of behavior.

Radical Behaviorism

The *radical behaviorist* position advocated by Skinner had two fundamental components. One asserted that scientific explanation should depend on as few assumptions as possible. Consequently, before assuming the existence of hidden psychological processes, one should first explore the explanatory power of a system based on observables, one that requires no additional assumptions. Skinner noted that when we attribute the "cause" of a behavior to an internal event or tendency, we are doing little more than restating the behavior, instead of explaining it. For example, to say that a child assaults his peers because he is aggressive does not add to our understanding of the assaultive behavior. This statement merely labels or categorizes the behavior.

The second aspect of the radical behaviorist position was more profound in its implications. Skinner's position was that what we commonly refer to as "mind" is either fictional or irrelevant as an explanation of behavior. Skinner contended that human behavior is subject to the same laws as the movement of physical objects and that a sophisticated science, whether of physics or of psychology, should not appeal to mysterious, hidden, inner forces. Skinner (1971, p. 7) wrote:

Although physics soon stopped personifying things in this way, it continued for a long time to speak as if [objects] had wills, impulses, feelings, purposes, and other fragmentary attributes of an indwelling agent. . . . Aristotle argued that a falling body accelerated because it grew more jubilant as it found itself nearer home, and later authorities supposed that a projectile was carried forward by an impetus, sometimes called an "impetuosity." All this was eventually abandoned, and to good effect, but the behavioral sciences still appeal to comparable internal states.

Skinner felt that psychology should primarily be concerned with understanding the functional relationships between events in the environment and behaviors of the organism. Skinnerians do not ignore private events such as thoughts, emotions, choices, or decisions; rather they consider private events to be behaviors under the control of the environment (Hineline, 1980) and not caused by internal factors. What Skinnerians reject is not the existence of internal, private aspects of experience, but rather the idea that these internal aspects are the *causes* of overt behavior. In other words, they reject the idea of mind as a cause. Instead, their focus is on how environmental contingencies cause behavior. Through a functional analysis of the relationship between specific environmental events and specific reactions, one can explain behavior without referring to mechanisms operating within the organism. Hence, if we observe someone eating, instead of asserting that the person is eating because of hunger, we should link the eating to an antecedent environmental event such as hours of food deprivation, the lunch bell's ringing, or the appearance of appetizing food. The objective of functional analysis is to determine which features of the environment are regularly linked to particular behaviors.

Lawfulness and Control

Regularity, the hallmark of a lawful relationship, is the basis for asserting that a particular event is the cause of a particular behavior. Human behavior may often appear chaotic, spontaneous, or free, but according to Skinner, that appearance is only because we have not discovered the events that control the behavior. Skinner deliberately used the word *control* to convey that human behavior is completely determined and predictable, given a knowledge of the stimulus events that are lawfully related to the behavior. A simple example of predictability and control concerns a four-year-old boy who was referred to a clinic because of frequent tantrums. When the child's parents were interviewed, it immediately became evident that the boy threw a tantrum whenever a wish he expressed was denied. His desperate parents ultimately acceded to his demands, permitting him, for example, to stay up late and watch television. The behavior (tantrum) was reinforced (under the control of) his parents' acquiescence. In a similar manner, the parents' acquiescent behavior was reinforced by the child's stopping the tantrum. When the parents learned to ignore the tantrums, they very rapidly disappeared, or *extinguished*.

Operant Conditioning and Reinforcement

The concept of reinforcement is one of Skinner's main theoretical ideas. A *reinforcer* is typically defined as any stimulus that follows some behavior and leads to a change in the behavior's frequency. Reinforcers may be rewards, nonrewards, or punishments. Through the manipulation of reinforcement contingencies, dramatic changes in behavior may be brought about. Removing reinforcements from previously reinforced responses leads to extinction, while the reinforcement of a response will increase the future likelihood of that response.

Learning theorists distinguish between *operant conditioning* and *classical* or *respondent* conditioning. In operant conditioning, a response that operates on the environment so as to change it is controlled or strengthened by the consequences or reinforcers that follow (for example, a rat pressing a bar receives a food reward). In classical conditioning, a conditioned stimulus, such as a bell, is sounded just before an unconditioned stimulus, such as food, is presented. The unconditioned response, or *respondent,* of salivating to the food becomes associated with the bell, which consequently elicits a conditioned response of salivation.

While some learning theorists have emphasized classical conditioning mechanisms in personality development and behavior change, Skinner's principal interest has been in the variables governing operant behavior. The primary factor that he has investigated is scheduling of, or the frequency and patterning of, reinforcement. A reinforcement can be administered after every response, after a specific or variable number of responses, or after a specific or variable time interval. In his first, ground-breaking book, *The Behavior of Organisms,* Skinner (1938) demonstrated lawful, predictable, and quantifiable relationships between different reinforcement schedules and the response rates of the organisms being reinforced. For example, organisms reinforced following every relevant response responded more frequently per unit of time than did organisms given a reward after specified time intervals.

What has all this to do with personality? Skinner and his students have attempted to demonstrate that through appropriate manipulation of reinforcement one can control which responses a human will make and how frequently and vigorously these responses will be made. Personality, then, is viewed simply as the collection of these reinforced operant responses. For Skinner, individual differences in personality are primarily a function of the differences in behaviors that have been reinforced and in the reinforcement schedules governing the emission of those behaviors.

Partial Reinforcement. Although it is frequently argued that the principles of operant reinforcement are less valid because they were derived from studies of rats and pigeons, there is both informal and experimental evidence that humans also respond differentially to different schedules of reinforcement. The effects of *partial reinforcement* (reward schedules in which the relevant response is reinforced less than 100 percent of the time) certainly apply to humans as well as to nonhumans. Extensive research literature indicates that many partially rein-

Behavior thought to be determined by partial reinforcement. (Elizabeth Crews/Stock, Boston)

forced responses are even more difficult to extinguish than responses that have had a history of constant reinforcement. Hence, parents who finally decide to ignore, rather than pick up, a child who cries after being put to bed will find that crying will persist much longer if the child was not picked up every time it cried previously. This consequence of partial reinforcement can also account for the seemingly paradoxical behavior of gamblers who keep betting despite heavy losses; they, too, are intermittently reinforced for their behavior.

Partial reinforcement increases the persistence of positive behaviors as well as such problems as crying and gambling. Given certain tasks, a history of successes interspersed with failures leads to greater persistence in the face of subsequent failures than does a history of 100 percent success. This phenomenon has been observed in the laboratory (Nation, Cooney, and Gartrell, 1979), as well as in everyday life. Compare two politicians, for example: one who has met with both success and defeat in running for political office and one who has always been successful. Suppose that they are both then repeatedly defeated at the polls. According to the partial or intermittent reinforcement effect, the politician with a history of unmixed success will probably give up political life sooner than the politician who experienced failure as well as success. In other words, the "trait" of persistence can be developed by providing the learner with tasks that are neither too easy nor too difficult. Intermediate-level tasks allow learners to experience the pain and challenge of frustration, as well as the pleasure and satisfaction of success.

Discriminative Stimuli. The pattern of reinforcement, or *reinforcement schedule,* which determines the degree of persistent behavior, can vary with different stimulus conditions. Thus, one might have received 100 percent reinforcement when requesting help from one's mother, 50 percent reinforcement from one's father and 0 percent from one's sibling! Mother, father, and sibling then function as *discriminative stimuli* that elicit different patterns of behavior. According to Skinnerian principles, one is then most likely to ask one's mother for help. However, if all three refuse after experiencing these reinforcement contingencies, then one is likely to be most persistent in seeking help from the father.

The fact that some partial reinforcement effects generalize to very dissimilar tasks suggests that there are cognitive factors mediating the effects. For example, the subject may be learning an expectancy or a rule, such as, "If I wait long enough, I will eventually succeed." But from a Skinnerian standpoint, the important question is *whether* particular reinforcement schedules lead to predictable effects, not *how* they produce their effects. This is particularly true if the "how" requires reference to private events.

Shaping.   There are many instances in which a desired behavior is never manifested and therefore is not subject to immediate manipulation through reinforcement. For example, pigeons do not automatically peck at disks, just as rats do not walk into a cage and immediately begin pressing levers. Similarly, a timid person may not make the assertive responses that one wishes to encourage, and a child who fears the water is not even going to try engaging in swimming behaviors that can be conveniently reinforced. To facilitate the emission of these responses, the behavior of an organism can be gradually *shaped* through a process of *successive approximations.*

In a study designed to increase interpersonal behaviors in severely withdrawn schizophrenics (King, Armitage, and Tilton, 1960), patients were first reinforced with social and material rewards for performing a simple motor response. Subsequently, the task was made more complex, and any verbal response, whether directed toward another person or not, was rewarded. The patients' behavior gradually shifted in the direction of more verbal and social responses. Finally, investigators were able to reinforce the patients when they communicated verbally with other patients. This reinforcement technique proved to be more effective than more traditional therapeutic approaches in fostering social behavior in these patients.

The technique of shaping can be very time consuming if one has to wait until the person makes a response before one can reinforce it. The process can be greatly expedited if one prompts the response and uses a combination of prompting and shaping to produce the desired behavior. An example of the effective combining of prompting and shaping is provided by a training program designed to foster social interaction in two youths who were intellectually retarded and also autistic — manifesting serious impairment in language and social attachment (Gaylord-Ross, et al., 1984). First, the youths were trained to use objects that could facilitate social interaction. These objects included the game of Pacman, a Walkman radio, and chewing gum. The discrete steps that were prompted and shaped for each of these objects are detailed in Table 5.1. Following the acquisition of appropriate object skills, the youths were trained to approach, greet, and

Table 5.1   Task analyses for object training

Pacman
1. Turn on machine.
2. Press start.
3. Make Pacman move down.
4. Change direction at wall.
5. Run away from ghost.
6. Read score.
7. Turn game off.

Walkman
1. Turn on radio.
2. Adjust volume control to level 6.
3. Put headphones on.
4. Select rock station.
5. Change station at the beginning or end of a song.
6. Change station at a commercial.
7. Turn off radio and remove headphones.

Gum
1. Take stick of gum out of pocket.
2. Unwrap gum.
3. Put gum in mouth.
4. Chew for 15 s without swallowing. Successively increase time criterion to: 30 s, 1 min, and 3 min.
5. Throw gum away into a receptacle.

Source: From Gaylord-Ross, et al., 1984, p. 238. Reprinted by permission.

interact with a nonhandicapped peer, making use of the three objects. Four months after training, they were observed to determine if the behaviors were maintained without prompting and shaping procedures again being employed.

Applications of Reinforcement Theory

Skinnerian psychology is functional and pragmatic. In an important sense, it is less a theory of personality than a system for behavior change and social engineering. Why, then, should one include Skinner's theory in a text on personality? The answer is that Skinner's approach represents an important theoretical perspective from which to view and analyze the behaviors that are considered to constitute "personality." It views many of the theoretical processes with which the

■ **Highlight 5.1** ▬▬▬▬▬▬▬

Early Intervention with Operant Techniques

Very promising results of a behavioral intervention program have been reported by Lovaas (1987) for a group of very young autistic children. The experimental program was initiated before these children were age four and entailed fully forty hours a week of therapeutic work with the child in the home, school, or community for at least two years. In addition, the parents were extensively trained in all the treatment procedures. The approach consisted of targeting a behavioral deficiency and designing a program to foster development of each targeted behavior. For example, aggressive and self-stimulating behaviors were reduced by ignoring them, by removing the child from the situation for a specified time period, and by the shaping of more acceptable forms of behavior. There was also much instruction in language, communication, and emotional expression. Two control groups of autistic children, one of which had had minor contact with the trainers, were employed for comparison purposes. The principal outcome criteria, summarized in the table below were education level—completion of first grade in regular ("Recovered") or aphasic classes or placement in autistic retarded classes—and I.Q. when post-tested. As the table indicates, almost half the children in

Educational placement and I.Q. at follow-up

Group	Recovered	Aphasic	Autistic/retarded
Experimental			
N	9	8	2
M I.Q.	107	70	30
Range	94–120	56–95	—
Control Group 1			
N	0	8	11
M I.Q.	—	74	36
Range	—	30–102	20–73
Control Group 2			
N	1	10	10
M I.Q.	99	67	44
Range	—	49–81	35–54

Note: Dashes indicate no score or no entry. (Adapted from O. I. Lovaas. *Journal of Consulting and Clinical Psychology,* 1987, *55,* No. 1, p. 7. Copyright 1987 by the American Psychological Association. Reprinted by permission.

Continued

▄ Highlight 5.1 ▄

the experimental treatment group successfully completed first grade in comparison to only one child in the combined control groups. In addition, the I.Q. of the groups classified as ''Recovered'' was well within the normal range. Whether these children are fully recovered and indistinguishable from their normal peers remains to be determined. However, this Skinnerian-based behavioral method has proved its effectiveness in changing the behaviors and competencies of young autistic children who are difficult to treat.

psychoanalytic and other psychodynamic theorists have been concerned to be irrelevant and illusory. However, Skinner sought to explain in Skinnerian terms some of the phenomena observed by Freudians. Skinnerian theory is primarily addressed to the regularities in behaviors and to changes in behavior. It proposes a set of procedures for controlling and shaping behavior and has had a profound impact on a variety of areas, including education, clinical psychology, animal training, and psychopharmacology. Examples of the application of Skinnerian principles to clinical problems have already been cited. Skinnerian methods, sometimes referred to as *behavior modification,* have been used for many different types of behavior difficulties.

Autism. One often finds Skinnerian principles applied to difficult cases that have been unresponsive to other forms of therapy. Work with autistic children, who suffer serious impairment in language and social attachment, is illustrative. Especially distressing to parents is the child's apparent unresponsiveness to and failure to display affection. Other symptoms of autism include stereotyped, ritualized gestures and behaviors (whirling around) and extreme attachment to certain objects. The initial task of determining the environmental stimuli and reinforcements that ''control'' such behavior has proven very difficult in these cases. A great deal of effort is spent simply determining what is reinforcing for the child, say, a favorite food. An experimenter's ''yes'' or smile might be paired with food so that the experimenter's response can also be used as a reinforcer. Through the use of such techniques, detailed shaping procedures, and many learning trials, it has become possible to train autistic children to acquire some speech and some social skills (Gaylord-Ross, et al., 1984; Lovaas, 1968)

Token Economies. Procedures based on Skinnerian principles have also been applied in such social settings and organizations as schools, prisons, and hospitals to foster desired behaviors. The *token economy* is one such innovation in organizational rules and procedures, where tokens are used as interim reinforcers that can eventually be exchanged for a preferred reinforcer. The great advantage of tokens is that they allow for great flexibility in reinforcers—from privileges to material objects—thereby permitting individualization of the reinforcement. The first implementation of a token economy, by Ayllon and Azrin (1965), has become a prototype for numerous programs. Schizophrenic patients in a psychiatric ward were reinforced for a designated set of behaviors including grooming themselves, serving meals, and washing dishes. The tokens the patients received when performing the desired responses could be exchanged for such rewards as passes, television privileges, selection of roommates, candy, and cigarettes. As is characteristic of Skinnerian studies, the responses and reinforcers were carefully specified and objectively recorded and quantified through systematic observation procedures. The results demonstrated substantial improvement in patient behavior with the implementation of a token economy. As soon as the reinforcement procedure was discontinued, however, the patients' behaviors deteriorated, returning almost to their initial levels.

The dependence of new behaviors on the maintenance of reinforcement also illustrates one of the limitations of token economies and other behavior modification techniques. The behavior is frequently dependent on being in the same stimulus situation; that is, positive changes do not generalize to new situations (e.g., the home) where the stimulus conditions are different. For these reasons, investigators working with highly aggressive youngsters have implemented behavioral change programs directly in the home, the setting in which the most difficulty occurred for these children (Patterson, Chamberlain, and Reid, 1982; Patterson, Cobb, and Ray, 1973). The experimenters attempted to modify the family systems of interaction, altering the patterns of provoking stimuli and the ineffective reinforcements employed by both children and parents.

Limitations of Reinforcement Theory

It is evident that many clinical psychologists find Skinnerian techniques to be useful; research using operant theory and methodology is both vigorous and salient. At the same time, however, there are serious limitations in the Skinnerian model as a comprehensive theory of personality and behavior. One fundamental difficulty is the arbitrary relationship it establishes between the particular response to be reinforced and the particular reward used as a reinforcement. Given a particular reinforcer, such as food, the Skinnerian assumption is that this reinforcer will work equally well or poorly for any individual organism, regardless of the response to be learned. However, as was discussed in Chapter 1, this is not the case. Food is an excellent reinforcer to condition the pecking of a pigeon, but a poor reinforcer when one wants to condition wing movements. Organisms are biologically organized so that there are natural reinforcing consequences for particular behaviors (Breland and Breland, 1961). In a similar manner and more germane to present concerns, reinforcing a child for excellent performance with such external rewards as money or candy may not increase subsequent achievement strivings if his or her goals were intrinsic mastery of the task or a desire for parental affection.

A related theoretical difficulty is the failure to consider factors other than external reinforcers that maintain a preferred response. It may be possible, given patience and a sufficient number of reinforcements, to train a child who is temperamentally introverted to be socially outgoing and extroverted (see also Chapter 1). This child might be superficially indistinguishable from a child who responds quickly to reinforcements for extroverted responses. However, there may be costs to the introverted child that would remain hidden unless explicitly assessed. A child whose behavior was difficult to shift might be less happy and spontaneous and have a lower threshold for frustration as an extrovert. Because Skinnerians have ignored the structural or organizational aspects of personality, they have given too little attention to the consequences of behavior modification for aspects of personality other than the specific behaviors that are undergoing modification.

In addition, Skinnerians have failed to ask what some psychologists consider to be a central question in personality, namely: Why are particular events or experiences reinforcing? For example, why is one individual attracted to particular kinds of mates, why is peer approval a powerful reward for child A but not for child B, and so on?

Nevertheless, whatever one's position on the merits of Skinner's ideas as a theory of personality and human behavior, there is no doubt that Skinner's operant reinforcement theory has made important contributions to psychology. In the area of methodology, it has fostered painstaking observations of situations and behaviors so that one can determine and quantify the precise stimulus events that are linked to specific behaviors. It has also encouraged and provided the methods for systematic evaluation of therapeutic and educational programs, just one small aspect of its many applications. In addition, Skinnerian psychology has had the surprising effect of focusing attention on the detailed study of an individual, rather than on the statistical average of a number of individuals. Skinnerian methods enable one to establish precise relationships over time between changes in individual behavior and changes in reinforcement contingencies and other stimulus events. In the traditional controversy between the clinical and scientific approaches, the clinician has typically emphasized individually based case histories, or what is called *idiographic data*. On the other hand, the scientist has emphasized experimental findings that are normative for an entire population, so-called *nomothetic data*. Skinner has combined aspects of both approaches, studying a single individual with scientific procedures. He has therefore helped to make the systematic study of the individual scientifically respectable.

SOCIAL LEARNING THEORY

Although Skinnerians, along with Dollard and Miller, have applied learning principles to complex social behavior, they have been criticized by those learning theorists who are concerned primarily with social behavior. This criticism is based in part on the fact that their analyses are derived from the study of nonhumans. In addition, these critics find fault with Dollard and Miller's emphasis on drives and drive reduction and are especially unsympathetic toward Skinner because of his neglect of cognitive factors in regulating behavior. These shortcomings have been addressed by several related personality approaches which are collectively referred to as *social learning theory.*

Expectancy-Value Theory

Reinforcement Value and Expectancy. The theory proposed by Julian Rotter (1954, 1972) emphasizes the construct of *expectancy,* or an individual's belief in the probability that a specific behavior will lead to satisfactions or valued goals. For example, on the basis of prior experience, a student may have the simultaneous expectancies that diligent study will bring the approval and affection of her parents and the disapproval of her fiancé, who wants to spend more time with her. To predict how hard she will study, one has to know the *reinforcement values* of the goals represented by parental approval and avoidance of her fiancé's disapproval. Each of us has our own hierarchy of values for such common human goals as money, affection, status, entertainment, sex, and power.

The likelihood that a particular behavior will occur, according to Rotter, is a joint function of the person's expectancy that the behavior will lead to one's goals and the values attached to those goals. In other words, people will generally choose actions that, on the basis of previous experience, they expect will lead to valued goals. Hence, children are likely to say "please" in requesting something if previous experience has shown that there is a high probability (expectancy) of getting what they want (highly valued goals) when they do so. Behaviors with low expectancies of satisfaction are not likely to be engaged in unless, under some circumstances, they are associated with high reward. For example, twelve-year-olds are not likely to cry when trying to convince their parents to do something; at this age, they have found that such behavior has low expectancy of bringing satisfaction. But they might cry if crying could result in obtaining some very great satisfaction, such as permission to stay overnight at a friend's house. Characteristics of the specific situation also play a central role in Rotter's theory, inasmuch as expectancy and reinforcement vary according to one's specific environment.

Needs. Reinforcement value and expectancy are terms that Rotter uses to refer to specific goals and behaviors. These specific goals commonly cluster into broader categories that are conceptualized as *needs,* such as the needs for recognition and status, dominance, independence, love and affection, physical comfort, and protection-dependency. For any individual these needs will vary in their *need value,* or the value of their satisfaction for that individual. Personality differences can be described in terms of individual differences in need value. Also contributing to personality differences are differences in the likelihood, or expectancy, of the behavior one has learned to rely upon to achieve satisfaction of a need, referred to as *freedom of movement.* Low freedom of movement coupled with high need value results in a very frustrated individual who feels ineffective in satisfying an important goal. This particular constellation of factors could result in maladaptive and neurotic behavior, such as engaging in excessive amounts of non-productive fantasy.

The concepts of need and need value link Rotter's model to psychoanalytic theories, while the expectancy concept provides links with more cognitive motivational theories. Rotter has been critical of psychoanalytic theorists for not recognizing the role of expectancy as a determinant of behavior. No matter how intense a specific desire or instinct postulated by psychoanalysts might be, if an action has zero subjective likelihood of leading to one's goals, then that action will not be undertaken.

Locus of Control. Rotter's formulation of the concept of freedom of movement was associated with the development of a scale for measuring generalized expectancy concerning the efficacy of one's efforts. This scale has been intensively used to study the properties of a personality dimension labeled internal versus external control of reinforcement. *Internal control* refers to the individual's belief (expectancy) that he or she can significantly determine whether or not a goal will be reached, while *external control* refers to the belief that fate, or external agents, rather than personal factors, are the most important determinants of goal attainment. The research and applications stimulated by the concept of *locus of control* will be examined in more detail in Chapter 17.

Interpersonal Trust. Another generalized expectancy studied by Rotter and his students is that of *interpersonal trust.* Whether or not one believes what someone else says will be strongly influenced by the reputation of that person, as well as by the likely truth of the statements one is asked to believe. However, Rotter suggested that there are stable individual differences in the generalized expectancy that people are trustworthy and developed a questionnaire measure to assess this trait. Research has shown that differences in the degree to which one tends to trust or be suspicious of others is systematically related to a number of attitudes and behaviors. People who are trusting tend to be happier, experience less conflict, are more often sought as friends, are more willing to give people a second chance, and are less likely to lie (Rotter, 1980). High-trust individuals are not necessarily gullible; rather, when there is no reason to be suspicious, they view what others say as trustworthy.

Rotter's model of personality has proved to be very useful. It clearly has limitations. It tends to be restricted in its description of personality structure and personality development. It does not encompass the range of phenomena addressed by psychoanalysis. However, it has stimulated a substantial body of research and, as we shall see, has influenced other social learning models.

Bandura's Social Learning Theory

Another prominent social learning theory was first proposed by Bandura and Walters (1963) and subsequently developed by Bandura and his students, as well as a number of others (e.g., Mischel, 1968; Wolpe, 1958). It now vies with

Skinner's operant reinforcement theory as the principal representative of learning theory approaches to personality. The model places great emphasis on the consequences of a response — that is, the feedback provided by reward or punishment of a behavior. Bandura (1986) has revised and expanded the model so as to incorporate a rich array of cognitive processes such as attention, covert rehearsal of instructions, self-motivation, self-reinforcement, and self-efficacy. For Bandura, people are actively involved in regulating their behavior as well as responding to situational cues which are in turn affected by the consequences of the behavior. This process of mutual interaction between person, situation, and behavior is referred to by Bandura as *reciprocal determination*.

Observational Learning. A number of different learning mechanisms, especially observational learning, are used to account for the social development of the child. *Observational learning* refers to the acquisition of new behaviors through observation of another person performing them. Many social responses and personality characteristics are acquired simply by imitating or copying the behavior of the models one observes. The mechanism of imitation as a significant social learning process was discussed by Miller and Dollard in an early book entitled *Social Learning and Imitation* (1941). However, whereas Miller and Dollard gave only secondary attention to observational learning, Bandura and his students have carried out a systematic series of studies investigating the process of imitation or *modeling;* they assigned this process a central role in social learning theory.

Modeling. When we see a three-year-old boy carrying a briefcase, putting it down, and saying to his mother, "It's been a hard day at the office," we know that the child was not directly taught those behaviors. Rather, he acquired them through observation of a parent's behavior, through modeling. The mechanism of modeling has three properties that give it special significance for the understanding of personality development:

1. Modeling typically involves a social situation (the model and the imitator) and a social relationship. The model can be an actual person or a film or cartoon representation.

2. Modeling is a means by which complex behaviors can be readily acquired. The reinforcement methods proposed by Skinner require careful, time-consuming efforts to shape a complex social behavior. In contrast, imitation can produce very rapid acquisition of social behaviors.

3. Direct reinforcement of imitated behavior is not required for learning to take place.

These properties of modeling have significant consequences for our understanding of behavior change and the process by which children are socialized. According to Bandura (1969, p. 188), "virtually all learning phenomena resulting from direct experiences can occur on a vicarious basis through observation of other persons' behaviors and its consequences to them." Thus, while Skinner would look for reinforcement contingencies in the environment to explain a child's aggressive behavior, Bandura would examine important figures in the child's environment, such as parents, peers, or television heroes, who may serve as aggressive models. In what has become a classic study (Bandura, Ross, and Ross, 1961), nursery school children individually observed an adult engaging in aggressive behavior toward a Bobo doll (a large, inflated plastic clown that uprights itself when knocked down). The adult struck the doll with a mallet and made a number of predetermined aggressive statements such as, "POW! Kick him, sock him down, sock him in the nose!" The child was then mildly frustrated and given an opportunity to play with the Bobo doll while the adults left the room. The degree of modeling displayed by the children was striking, with the children often hitting the doll with exactly the same motions as the model, using precisely the same verbal comments. A comparison of their responses with those of a control group of preschoolers who had merely observed the adult playing with a construction toy revealed much more aggressive behavior in the children who had observed the aggressive model.

A wide variety of behaviors, from self-control and altruistic responses to aggression, can be acquired through modeling. For example, the influence of a model on aiding a "lady in distress" was examined by stationing a woman next to a car with a flat tire. Approximately one-quarter mile closer on the same road, experimenters placed another car with a flat, but this time a young man was helping the female to fix it. The young man thus served as a model. Compared to a control condition without a model, a significantly greater number of drivers stopped to offer assistance to the second woman (Bryan and Test, 1967).

Response Acquisition and Performance. Children do not automatically or consistently imitate. Modeling, like other learning processes, is affected by a number of factors. Among the variables that facilitate modeling are similarity in sex between model and observer (Bandura, Ross, and Ross, 1961); the control of the model (Bandura, Ross, and Ross, 1963); and observation of reinforcement of the model's response (Bandura, 1965; Parke and Walters, 1967). In evaluating the effects of these variables, it is essential to distinguish between *acquisition* and *performance* of the response. Different factors determine whether the response is acquired and, if it is acquired, whether it is performed. Learning, or response acquisition, is influenced by attention to the model and by how well one interprets and rehearses the model's behavior (Bandura and Jeffrey, 1973). Performance, however, depends much more on the nature of the reinforcing consequences to the model and the observer.

In a study bearing directly on this acquisition-performance distinction, preschool children observed a filmed model exhibiting aggressive responses. Under one condition, the model was praised and rewarded with treats, while in a second condition the model was severely punished for the aggressive display. A control condition was included in which there were no response consequences to the model. A test of the degree of imitation following the different modeling conditions revealed significantly less modeling by children in the punished-model condition, compared with children observing the model when reward or nothing followed the behavior. To demonstrate that this effect was not due to differences in learning of the response, the children in all three groups were offered highly attractive incentives to reproduce the responses of the model. When positive incentives were introduced, children in all groups performed the response they had observed. Thus, all three groups learned the model's responses equally, but their performance of the response was dependent on the anticipated consequences of that behavior. (See Bandura, 1965.) It will be noted that although the rewards and punishments were administered only to the model, they nevertheless influenced the observer's behavior. These vicarious consequences — *vicarious reward* and *vicarious punishment* — influence the observer's subsequent behavior through providing information about the effect of an action.

Verbalization and Rules. In contrast to Skinner, social learning theorists emphasize the importance of verbalization, rules, and related symbolic processes that are believed to mediate behavior. Rewards and punishments for behaviors are more effective when they are accompanied by explicitly verbalized rules (Liebert and Allen, 1967; Parke, 1970). To demonstrate the role of verbalization in observational learning, children witnessed a model engaging in a complex sequence of behaviors. They were asked to verbalize the model's novel responses, watch attentively, or count rapidly. The last condition was included to prevent implicit verbal coding of the model's actions (Bandura, Grusec, and Menlove, 1966). Modeling was highest in the verbalization group, next highest in the attentiveness group, and lowest in the rapid-count condition. Verbal statements that are silently rehearsed also have a significant effect on behavior.

Self-Reinforcement. Although Skinner tried to explain self-control in his terms, another point of departure of social learning theory from his theory concerns external versus internal sources of reinforcement. Social learning theorists do not limit reinforcements to external rewards or punishments, but also include self-imposed reinforcing consequences (Bandura, 1977a; Kanfer and Marston, 1963). Human beings have internalized standards of performance which they utilize to evaluate their actions. The self-evaluative statement, "I did well," following a particular test performance is a reinforcement for that performance. One student might make such an evaluation only for a grade of A; another might feel such evaluation was accurate if the grade was C. Conversely, some individuals may be very self-critical, administering self-punishment even though performance might appear excellent to an observer. Depressed adults, for example, tend to evaluate their performances as poorer than the nondepressed do, even for identical accomplishments (Loeb, Beck, Diggory, and Tuthill, 1967).

Self-Efficacy. Feedback from internal and external reinforcements affects one's sense of *self-efficacy,* a concept that has gradually assumed a central role in Bandura's (1977a) thought. Self-efficacy refers to the expectation that one can effectively cope with and master situations, that one can bring about desired outcomes through one's own personal efforts. This clearly relates to Rotter's concept of locus of control, briefly introduced in the previous section.

Bandura maintained that the effects of conditioning and modeling therapies are mediated by the change that occurs in one's sense of self-efficacy, or the belief that "I can." One's perceived degree of self-efficacy, according to Bandura, is influenced by a variety of behaviors in regard to a particular task — e.g., the goals that are set for oneself, the degree of competence or accomplishment in the task, the degree of persistence displayed, and if the task involves something fearful, the degree of fear that is experienced. Thus, through changing self-efficacy, one can hope to bring about significant changes in behavior.

In an illustrative experiment demonstrating the role ascribed to self-efficacy, adults with a snake phobia (severe fear of snakes) were assigned to either a low, medium, or high efficacy-induction experimental condition (Bandura, Reese, and Adams, 1982). The efficacy treatment was conducted by a female experimenter using modeling and prompting procedures with tasks involving a boa constrictor. The tasks on which the subjects rated their ability to perform — that is, indicated their *self-efficacy* — were graded into eighteen progressively more threatening activities that ranged from approaching, to touching, to freely handling the boa. Subjects in the low self-efficacy level group were treated until they made the judgment that they could place their hands in the cage in the vicinity of the snake. In the medium self-efficacy group, the criterion was the judgment that they would be able to touch and lift the snake inside the cage. In the high self-efficacy group, they were treated until they felt that they could let the snake loose and allow it to crawl in their laps. Following the experimental treatments, the subjects responses to a corn snake were recorded. As Figure 5.4 on p. 150 indicates, there was a striking correspondence between the subjects' perceived self-efficacy and their performance in the test situation.

There have been a number of applications of self-efficacy theory to behavior problems besides fear reduction. For example, in a study of participants in a Weight Watchers' program designed to reduce overweight, each week subjects were asked a self-efficacy question regarding their degree of confidence that they would eventually reach their goal weight (Mitchell and Stuart, 1984). Those who dropped out of the program reported significantly lower feelings of self-efficacy than those who remained in the program, despite the fact that their rates of weight loss were generally comparable.

Pain. The importance of self-efficacy is also reflected in studies addressed to the management of pain. In one such study, women enrolled in childbirth classes made self-efficacy judgments of their ability to control pain without medication (Manning and Wright, 1983). The findings indicated that, as anticipated, the use of pain medication was negatively correlated with self-efficacy judgments.

It has also been demonstrated that changes in self-efficacy judgments of pain tolerance, resulting from instruction in different cognitive strategies for alleviating pain, are significantly correlated with changes in measures of actual pain

Figure 5.4

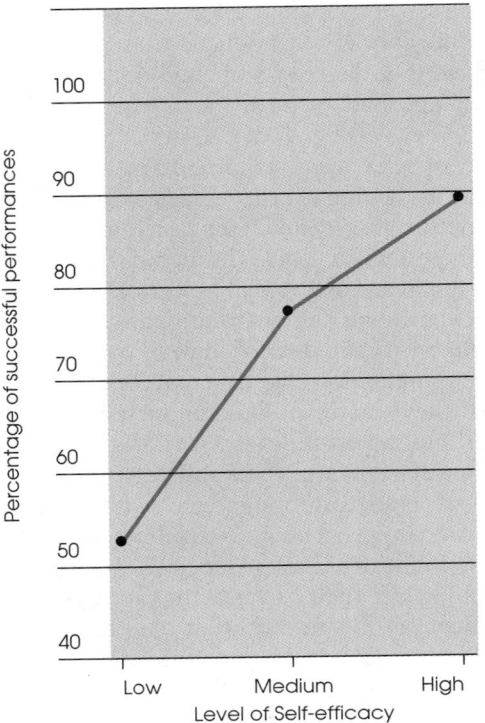

Mean performance attainments as a function of differential levels of perceived self-efficacy. (Adapted from Bandura, Reese, and Adams, 1982, p. 8)

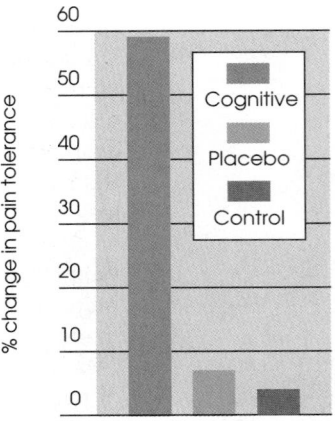

Figure 5.5　　　Effects of Self-Efficacy on Pain Tolerance. (Adapted from Bandura, et al. *Journal of Personality and Social Psychology,* 1987, *53,* p. 567. Copyright 1987 by the American Psychological Association. Adapted by permission.)

tolerance (Fig. 5.5; Bandura, et al., 1987); that is, increases in one's perception of one's ability to endure pain and to reduce pain were accompanied by increases in the amount of time that one tolerated a painful stimulus. One of the interesting features of this study is the evidence indicating that high self-efficacy subjects are able to control pain through cognitive mechanisms that induce secretion of neuro-chemicals called opioids which block pain and through alternative mechanisms such as distraction.

Self-Efficacy Issues.   While there is no doubt that self-efficacy is related to a wide range of mastery behaviors, there remains a question as to its causal role. Perception of self-efficacy is closely related to past performance on a task, and both are related to future performance. What is cause and what is effect? While this question remains to be fully resolved, there are data indicating that while past performance influences both self-efficacy and future performance, self-efficacy has an independent effect on future performance (Bandura and Wood, 1989). A second issue has to do with the difficulty of separating one's expectation of mastery of a behavior (self-efficacy) from one's *outcome expectancies,* that is, the success of the behavior. You may feel in complete mastery of a subject matter, but still feel uncertain as to the *outcome* of an oral examination in that subject if you believe the instructor is biased. It is possible, but difficult, to get independent estimates of *self-efficacy* and outcome *expectations* (Maddux, Norton, and Stoltenberg, 1986; Manning and Wright, 1983). Moreover, features of the environment that affect outcome expectations can also influence perceived self-efficacy. Thus varying information as to the controllability of a situation—in one study, the responsiveness of a group of employees to managerial control—has been shown to have a marked effect on both self-efficacy and performance. Studies show that high controllability elicits greater perceived self-efficacy and better performance than low controllability (Bandura and Wood, 1989). It should be noted that self-efficacy, in Bandura's framework, is significantly related to performance in a specific situation and is not conceived of as a generalized personality trait.

The Situation and Discriminative Cues.   One of the major tenets of social learning theory is that behavior is a function of the situation in which it takes place. Walter Mischel (1968, 1973) has argued cogently and vigorously that the consistency in behavior implied by such concepts as traits or motives is largely illusory. He stated (1968, p. 177) that "response patterns even in highly similar situations often fail to be strongly related. Individuals show far less cross-situational consistency in their behavior than has been assumed." Both Mischel and Bandura reject the "layer" image of personality, the notion that there are basic personality traits underlying the variations observed in overt behavior. If a man is highly aggressive with his peers but docile with his father and other authority figures, social learning theorists would contend that he should not be considered a fundamentally aggressive individual who masks his aggression when dealing with individuals in positions of authority. Rather, they argue, he is more appropriately described as someone who displays different response patterns in situations that present different *discriminative cues.*

For Mischel, behaving the same way in the same situation, or *temporal consistency,* is much more characteristic of behavior than behaving the same way in different situations (Mischel, 1984). We tend to have similar *goals* and *expectancies* when we are in very similar situations; thus we are likely to utilize similar cognitive *strategies* and display similar behaviors. We may believe people display cross-situational consistency because we tend to overgeneralize from some *temporally consistent* behavior. In addition, according to Mischel, we tend to overgeneralize from behavior that we view as representative of or *prototypical* of a particular trait. For example, if a classmate smiles warmly whenever he encounters an acquaintance, we are likely to label him as "friendly." Smiling serves as a *cognitive prototype* of the trait category "friendliness." We might miss or overlook his lack of other friendly behaviors, e.g., welcoming newcomers or expressing interest in other people.

In short, for Mischel, trait generality is not found in actual behaviors, but is a distortion stemming from *temporal consistency* and our tendency to use *cognitive prototypes.* Where Mischel finds the concept of personality to be useful, in the sense of dispositions or attributes that influence behavior cross-situationally, is in regard to certain cognitive attributes such as intelligence and the strategies that individuals use to encode information about people and significant objects in their environment. We discuss the issue of traits versus situations in depth in Chapter 9.

Limitations of Social Learning Theory

Social learning theory, like operant theory, lacks concepts that deal with the organization and structure of personality, concepts that help predict the pattern of interrelationships among the significant components of personality. In general, social learning theory is concerned with the conditions influencing the acquisition and performance of specific responses, rather than with the factors that determine which behaviors or reinforcers are central to the organism. Such questions as the psychological significance of affection, sexuality, the family triangle formed by parents and child, and the development shifts in human striving, remain far outside the scope of social learning theories.

COGNITIVE BEHAVIOR MODIFICATION

The approaches that have been grouped together under the label of *cognitive behavior modification* stress the role of cognitive factors in mediating behavior and attempt to bring about change through alteration of these cognitions (Mahoney, 1974). There is clearly substantial overlap between cognitive behavior modification and social learning theory, and the two approaches are quite compatible. Their difference lies in emphasis and historical background. Cognitive behavior modification was guided by, yet significantly deviates from, Skinner's operant theory. Although Skinner's radical behavioral position either excludes or minimizes the relevance of internal events, the cognitively oriented behaviorists maintained that one can adhere to the objective spirit of Skinner's approach while investigating the role of such internal processes as images, self-monitoring responses, and perceived responsibility.

For example, in one study problem drinkers were taught to be aware of different facets of their drinking behavior by learning to self-monitor their drinking, compute their blood-alcohol level, establish weekly goals for total alcohol consumption, and intersperse drinking of non-alcoholic beverages with alcoholic beverages (Alden, 1988). The experimental treatment resulted in a significant decline in alcohol consumption, which was maintained over a two-year follow-up period. Other strategies may involve systematic efforts to alter the individual's thinking and problem-solving strategies, as in treatments of depressed patients which focus on alteration of patient's illogically negative interpretations of their experiences and their negative views of themselves (Beck, 1976, 1984).

Imagery

During the past two decades, there has been an upsurge of interest in the role of imagery in both experimental (Paivio, 1971) and clinical (Lazarus, 1971; Wolpe, 1969) psychology. *Imagery,* which can include the imagining of pictures, sounds, or even feelings, can be used to facilitate memory and to alter feelings and behavior. Wolpe (1958), in his pursuit of behavioral alternatives to psychoanalytic treatment, pioneered in the utilization of imagery for the *systematic desensitization* of anxiety. Wolpe's objective was to train anxious patients to relax while in the presence of anxiety-provoking stimuli. He theorized that the relaxation response inhibits anxiety and therefore will weaken the bond between the anxiety response and threatening stimuli: a process considered to be an example of the more general principle labeled *reciprocal inhibition.*

Wolpe's treatment requires initial training of the client in deep-muscle relaxation and the construction of an *anxiety hierarchy,* consisting of a series of related situations that are graduated according to the degree of evoked anxiety. The patient first imagines the least anxiety-provoking situation in the hierarchy while maintaining a relaxation response, with the procedure then followed successively for each item in the hierarchy until the patient can relax fully while visualizing the situation that had evoked the most anxiety. Wolpe reported substantial clinical success with this treatment and, in the process, stimulated an extensive clinical and experimental literature applying this technique to a variety of problems. Clinically effective variations of Wolpe's approach include combining his procedures with imagery of pleasurable, relaxing stimuli or with imagery of successful coping with the anxiety-arousing stimuli (Crits-Christoph and Singer, 1983, 1984).

Another variation, used with patients who experienced marked anxiety in social situations, entails relaxation training plus the practice of relaxation skills during role-playing of social situations. The new skills are then used in the natural environment (Jerremalm, Jannson and Ost, 1986).

Cognitive behavioral treatment programs commonly employ combinations of *training* in cognitive strategies, self-monitoring, relaxation, behavioral alternatives, and related skills that help individuals to cope with their pain and fears and to reduce problem behaviors. Examples of the extensive range of problems to which cognitive behavioral approaches have been applied with some success include anti-social behavior (Kazdin, et al., 1989), marital difficulties (Hahlweg and Markman, 1988), back pain (Turner and Clancy, 1988), eating disorders (Agros, et al., 1989, Rodin, et al., 1988), and social anxiety or phobia (Heinberg, 1989).

Other Cognitive Changes

The enormously complex world of images, anticipations, self-perceptions, beliefs, and information offers rich opportunities for changing behavior. We have previously referred to the technique of *self-instruction*. For example, reminding oneself to count to ten before responding in anger is one way in which self-instruction is used to control behavior. Imagery, another cognitive process just discussed in the context of desensitization, can also be used to condition fears and avoidance. For example, one treatment program for obesity required that obese clients visualize appetizing food coupled with a disgust-producing image, a procedure referred to as *aversive imagery* (Cautela, 1977). Aversive imagery has also been used in the treatment of alcoholism (Miller, 1959), smoking (Tongas, 1979), and sexual deviation (Davison, 1968).

The *attribution,* or causal explanation, that individuals make for their success and failure provides another promising area of cognitive intervention. The tendency to attribute failure to one's incompetence, rather than to lack of effort, task difficulty, or luck, is linked to a variety of maladaptive behaviors, ranging from depression (Abramson, Seligman, and Teasdale, 1978; Beck et al., 1979) to poor school achievement (Dweck and Leggett, 1988). In one study, children with poor frustration tolerance and who were having difficulties in school were trained to ascribe their failures to a lack of effort. Effort, as opposed to ability, is under volitional control and can thus be modified and increased. This perception resulted in a substantial improvement in persistence and performance in the face of failure, compared with children not receiving the attributional retraining (Dweck, 1975; see also Chapter 17).

Still another type of cognitive mediator is the logic and strategy used in problem solving. Cognitive strategies are related not only to intellectual performance, but also to the ability to solve social problems (Shure and Spivack, 1972; Spivack and Levine, 1963). Spivack and Shure (1974) developed a program that trained children to think in terms of means-ends relations, that is, in terms of the probable consequences of various behavioral options. They demonstrated a significant improvement in the behavior of disruptive preschoolers who participated in their program.

Some Limitations. Cognitive behavior modification programs vary in their effectiveness, depending upon the behavior to be modified and the length and content of the procedures. Behaviors such as smoking and drug addiction may be so habitual or reinforcing as to be highly resistant to cognitive efforts at modifying them, so that even changes in beliefs and the recognition that the behavior is harmful may not produce a behavioral change. Much more theory and research are required to determine the conditions under which various cognitive behavior modification procedures will be effective and are the preferred mode of therapeutic intervention. There is no doubt that there are significant links among cognitions, desires, feelings, and behavior. But the direction of these links — which elements are causes and which are effects — is a difficult issue. In fact, they may be linked in complex and reciprocally causal ways. Finally, cognitive behavior modification runs the risk of introducing thoughts and responses that are as difficult to define and measure as some of the psychoanalytic concepts that the behavior theorists have so roundly criticized.

Summary

1. Hullian theory asserted that *habits* are acquired when a stimulus-response pairing is followed by *drive reduction,* for both *primary* and *secondary,* or *acquired, drives.*

2. *Drive, cue* (stimulus), *response,* and *reinforcement* are the key concepts in Dollard and Miller's theory.

3. Through a process of *mediated generalization,* dissimilar situations can come to have an equivalent effect because they elicit common *mediating responses.*

4. According to the Dollard-Miller model, the psychoanalytic mechanism of repression can be explained in terms of such overt responses as mislabeling and avoidance, which are elicited by anxiety-evoking stimuli because they reduce the mediating response of anxiety.

5. For Skinner, the concept of "mind" is illusory. Behavior, according to the radical behaviorist position, is a function of reinforcement. Reinforcement of selected responses determines the kinds of behavior elicited in response to a stimulus, and the schedule of reinforcement determines the rate and persistence of responding.

6. Behaviors that cannot be reinforced because they are rarely manifested can be trained through a gradual process called *shaping,* in which *successive approximations* to the behavior are reinforced until the desired response is made.

7. *Behavior modification* procedures based on Skinnerian principles have been applied in cases of severely disturbed children and adults. Autistic children have been taught to respond to social reinforcers, while schizophrenic patients have shown significant improvement in social behaviors through the application of these principles.

8. One limitation of Skinnerian theory is the assumption that any reinforcer should augment any response. In fact, organisms are biologically and developmentally organized so that certain reinforcers are more appropriate for particular behaviors.

9. Among Rotter's significant contributions are the analyses of the constructs of *expectancy, reinforcement value,* and the *internal* versus *external control* of reinforcement.

10. An important property of *observational learning (modeling)* is that it makes possible the very rapid acquisition of complex social behaviors.

11. A distinction must be made between learning and performance. A child may not display a response that has been acquired through modeling if the model was punished for that behavior, but may display that response given situations in which the fear of punishment is reduced.

12. According to Bandura, one's perception of self-efficacy in regard to a particular task or problem is a major determinant of one's mastery of and ability to cope with the task or problem.

13. For Mischel, behavior is primarily a function of specific situational cues and response consequences in that situation, while the view that behavior reflects cross-situational consistency is a misperception stemming from *temporal consistency* and *prototypic* behavior.

14. The recent development of *cognitive behavior modification* procedures offers a less radical Skinnerian approach to behavioral problems. Cognitive processes such as *imagery, self-instruction,* and *attribution* are utilized in clinical procedures applying Skinnerian and related methods.

Thought Questions

1. A student who received a poor grade on an exam began to avoid studying. Analyze this situation using the key concepts of Dollard and Miller.

2. Would you want to live in a society based on Skinner's principles? What might it be like?

3. Can you think of ways in which you control your own behavior through covert self-instructions?

4. What types of behavioral problems seem most amenable to learning theory treatments? Which ones might be better treated with a psychoanalytic approach?

6 | Phenomenological Theories

Many types of personality theories fall within the category of *phenomenology*—the study of subjective experience, or the "meaning" that one gives to events. What these theories have in common is a primary concern with the cognitive, or mental, aspects of behavior and experience. Although most social learning theories have incorporated cognitive variables in their theoretical models, reinforcement mechanisms that influence observable actions remain central to these theories. This is not the case for the phenomenologists. Phenomenological theories are concerned with the "now" of experience. They address the present situation and its meanings rather than the past and how things came to be the way they are (a central quest for both psychoanalytic and learning theories). Humanistic psychology, exemplified in the work of Carl Rogers, Abraham Maslow, and the existentialists, sees the constraints and fears that block full awareness of the "now" of one's experiences as major contributors to neurotic behavior. An important goal of humanistic theories is thus expansion of the individual's consciousness of the present environment and subjective experience.

Theories based on how individuals make sense of the world and themselves are also embraced by phenomenology. The best-known of these theories was formulated by George Kelly, who assumed that individuals go about their everyday activities like scientists, formulating hypotheses about their environments and themselves, gathering information to test these hypotheses, and drawing inferences from the obtained information. Kelly's theory is subsumed within a literature known as *implicit psychology*, which deals with the perceived laws of behavior held by naive observers, or the personality theories of individuals who are untrained psychologists.

One difference between humanistic approaches and the cognitive approach of Kelly stems primarily from their different views on how we "know" the world. While both humanistic theories and Kelly's cognitive theory deal with how people process meaning in their lives, these processes are seen differently. Kelly, in keeping with Western culture's focus on rational, analytic thought, bases his theory on a model of humans as thinking scientists. He assumes that individuals are always thinking at some level, forming concepts or constructs, sorting data, and so on. This thinking may occur quickly and nonconsciously, so quickly that we are not aware that we are perceiving our worlds through our constructs. In contrast, humanists emphasize ways of knowing that are based on direct "felt" experience, emotions, and intuitions. They do not assume these processes are necessarily based upon thinking (Bohart, in press; 1993). In essence, humanistic theories emphasize how people perceive and experience themselves and their worlds; Kelly's cognitive theory emphasizes how people *think about* themselves and their worlds.

Other phenomenological approaches to personality, such as Eastern religious philosophies, are not presented here, primarily because they have not yet made sufficient systematic contributions to our understanding of personality and have not generated supporting research evidence.

HUMANISTIC THEORY

Prior to the 1960s there were two dominant movements in psychology: psychoanalytic and behavioristic. Sociologists of science suggest that the development of both theoretical perspectives was greatly influenced by cultural factors. Psychoanalytic theory originated in the supposedly repressive society of Vienna around the beginning of the twentieth century, a social milieu that may have accounted in part for the psychoanalytic emphasis on repression, conflict, and neurosis. On the other hand, behaviorism was spawned in turn-of-the-century America. It embraced Darwin's concern with adaptation and function, as well as the belief that behavior is completely modifiable, an assumption consistent with the optimistic psychological climate in America at that time.

Around 1960, a so-called third force in psychology came into existence. This third force, *humanistic psychology,* focused not only on what a person is, but also on what a person has the potential to become. Humanism emerged at a time when people were experiencing alienation and dissatisfaction despite (or perhaps because of) economic and technological success. Many individuals began questioning traditional values, including striving for success and achievement. This emphasis on existential problems — basic problems of human values and existence — gave rise to a more humanistic psychology. This psychology focused on problems of the experiencing person living in an uncertain world. Thus, the three major theoretical positions we consider, each having the status of a movement, appear to have arisen directly from the social and cultural themes of their times.

The social precursors to humanistic psychology were in evidence when the Association of Humanistic Psychology was founded in 1962. Four interrelated principles were adopted by the humanists to guide their pursuits:

1. *The experiencing person is of primary interest.* Humanistic psychology begins with the study of individuals in real-life circumstances. Humans are subjects, rather than mere objects, of study. Psychological research, the humanists contend, cannot be modeled after early physics, in which the objects of study were "out there." The person must be examined and described in terms of personal consciousness, which includes subjective experience and how the individual perceives and values himself or herself. The basic question with which each individual must grapple is "Who am I?" Individuals, as travelers in life, must determine where they are and where

they wish to go. As a result, the humanists follow a *holistic* approach in which experiences are not broken down into component parts like single frames within a film, but the entirety of life is considered.

2. *Human choice, creativity, and self-actualization are the preferred topics of investigation.* Humanists argue that the study of psychologically crippled people has led to a crippled psychology, while the study of lower organisms has yielded an incomplete psychology, devoid of consciousness. The humanists believe that psychologists should study wholesome and healthy individuals, people who are creative and fully functioning. People have a real need to push forward in life and to develop their potentials and capabilities. Growth, rather than mere adjustment, is the criterion of health. These self-actualizing tendencies are of particular significance to the humanists.

3. *Meaningfulness must precede objectivity in the selection of research problems.* Psychological research, according to the humanists, has in the past centered on methods rather than on problems. Often research topics have been selected chiefly because objective and convenient methods are available. But research projects should be undertaken because they are significant and pertinent to human issues, even if the methods available are weak. Research cannot be value free; psychologists must study the important issues of people's lives.

4. *Ultimate value is placed on the dignity of the person.* Above all, humans are accepted as unique and as having the potential to be noble. Psychologists must understand people, rather than predict or control their behavior. Individuals are believed by the humanists to have a higher nature with a need for meaningful work, responsibility, and the opportunity for creative expression.

Many prominent psychologists, representing different theoretical viewpoints but sharing a common belief in the importance of the individual's need for meaning and self-actualization, have been attracted to the humanistic movement. They include figures as diverse as Gordon Allport, who, as previously indicated, spent time with Jung; Erich Fromm, whose social psychological deviation from classic psychoanalysis was reviewed in Chapter 4; and Carl Rogers and Abraham Maslow, whose theoretical views lie at the center of the humanistic movement.

THE PERSON-CENTERED THEORY OF CARL ROGERS

Carl Rogers ranks among the most influential contemporary psychologists. Born in 1902, he functioned as an active spokesperson for the "third force" in psychology until his death in 1987. His conception of personality emerged from his work in psychotherapy and reflects the influence of both an early religious background and his early adolescent experience with the study of scientific principles of farming. Rogers, in contrast to the psychoanalysts, communicated a fundamental

Carl R. Rogers, (1902–1987), (at extreme right, facing the camera) conducting a group-therapy session in 1968. (Michael Rougier, *Life* Magazine, © 1968 Time, Inc.)

faith and trust in human nature. While Freud viewed human nature as rooted in the Old Testament, with human beings struggling with the "original sin" of destructive and lustful impulses, Rogers brought the voice of the New Testament to personality. By providing love and fundamental acceptance, Rogers believed, we can help our fellow human beings recognize and ultimately realize the potential for goodness that is in them. He also believed that the fully functioning person acted like a good scientist — continually testing personal ideas and values against experience.

Self-Actualization

For Rogers, as for the other humanists, a core tendency of a person is to actualize his or her own potential. The motive of *self-actualization,* a concept we encountered earlier in the discussions of Jung and Adler, implies that there is an internal, biological driving force to develop one's capacities and talents to the fullest (see Highlight 6.1). The individual's central motivation is to learn from experience and to grow. Growth occurs when individuals confront problems, struggle to master them, and through that struggle develop new aspects of their skills, capacities, and views about life. Life is therefore an endless process of creatively moving forward, even if in only small ways. Fully functioning people are people who are continually learning and developing, much as Rogers, Freud, and Skinner continually learned and developed their own theories. Even if personality were to consist of basic traits, how one expressed and actualized these traits could be continually refined in more and more adaptive directions, and in that sense life is a process of continual growth and change (Bohart, in press).

From the perspective of scientific inquiry, the actualization tendency is a vague, general concept that has not proven to be amenable to measurement or

▬ **Highlight 6.1** ▬▬▬▬▬▬▬▬▬▬▬▬▬▬

The Actualizing Tendency

Rogers once described expression of the actualizing tendency with the following illustration:

During a vacation weekend some months ago I was standing on a headland overlooking one of the rugged coves which dot the coastline of northern California. Several large rock outcroppings were at the mouth of the cove, and these received the full force of the great Pacific combers which, beating upon them, broke into mountains of spray before surging into the cliff-lined shore. As I watched the waves breaking over these large rocks in the distance, I noticed with surprise what appeared to be tiny palm trees on the rocks, no more than two or three feet high, taking the pounding of the breakers. Through my binoculars I saw that these were some type of seaweed, with a slender "trunk" topped off with a head of leaves. As one examined a specimen in the interval between the waves it seemed clear that this fragile, erect, top-heavy plant would be utterly crushed and broken by the next breaker. When the wave crunched down upon it, the trunk bent almost flat, the leaves were whipped into a single line by the torrent of water, yet the moment the wave had passed, here was the plant again, erect, tough, resilient. It seemed incredible that it was able to take this incessant pounding hour after hour, day after night, week after week, perhaps, for all I know, year after year, and all the time nourishing itself, extending its domain, reproducing itself; in short, maintaining and enhancing itself in this position which, in our short-hand, we call growth. Here in this palmlike seaweed was the tenacity of life, the forward thrust of life, the ability to push into an incredibly hostile environment and not only hold its own, but to adapt, develop, and become itself.

Source: Reprinted from 1963 *Nebraska Symposium on Motivation*, edited by Marshall R. Jones.

tests. The reality of an actualization tendency is an axiom of humanistic psychology which is not subject to proof or disproof. Whereas other motivations vary in intensity between individuals and fluctuate within an individual as a function of physiological or situational changes, this is not the case for actualization. Moreover, the form that actualization takes is unique to each individual, making it impossible to establish criteria for the presence or absence of actualization. Despite these methodological limitations, Rogers and other humanists (Maslow, 1971) found the actualizing tendency to be conceptually essential for the understanding of human striving and development.

However, there is evidence for a similar concept, that of a "self-righting tendency," from researchers who have studied the phenomenon of *resilience*. A number of investigators have now found that many children seem to not only survive but also thrive despite the obstacles of adverse circumstances such as poverty or a dysfunctional family life. That is, they seem able to "right themselves" and to continue to grow despite adversity. Masten, Best, and Garmazy (1990) conclude from their research that "studies of psychosocial resilience support the view that human psychological development is highly buffered and self-righting" (p. 438). And Werner and Smith, from their studies of disadvantaged children, conclude that "As we watched these children grow from babyhood to adulthood we could not help but respect the self-righting tendencies within them that produced normal development under all but the most persistently adverse circumstances" (1982, p. 159). While the concepts of self-righting and self-actualization are not identical, they are closely related, as can be seen from the fact that many of Rogers' examples of self-actualization are also examples of self-righting (see Highlight 6.1).

Rather than focusing on the source or strength of the actualizing tendency, Rogers found it more useful to consider what might stand in the way of, or inhibit, this basic human motivation. Rogers (1959) was particularly concerned with blockage of the tendency toward *self*-actualization, which is one component of the more general actualizing tendency. Rogers (1959, p. 200) defined the *self* as the "organized . . . [whole] . . . of the 'I' or 'me.'" It consists of one's self-perceptions (e.g., attractiveness, abilities, achievements, relationships with others) and the range of values attached to these perceptions (e.g., good-bad, worthy-unworthy). Thus, one's self-concept is very dependent on one's learning experiences, especially the kind of feedback and acceptance one receives from others. According to Rogers, human beings have a basic need for others' positive regard in the form of warmth, love, and acceptance. This regard and acceptance, however, is usually offered on a conditional basis. Typically, an individual receives love or recognition as a result of some particular action. Consequently, one's perception of oneself as a valuable human being often depends on these actions and on the resulting evaluations of other people. In contrast, the truly healthy personality perceives his or her whole self in a positive manner. Specific actions can be regarded as good or bad, but the self is always unconditionally valuable.

Positive Regard.   To attain this level of adjustment, the individual needs the experience of *unconditional positive regard,* of being valued for oneself regardless of the degree to which specific behaviors are approved or disapproved. The love of a parent for a child often has such an unconditional quality. A mother may disapprove of her four-year-old's hitting a younger sibling or of the child's sloppy table manners, but she will nevertheless communicate her fundamental love and acceptance of the child. According to Rogers, one should criticize the action, not the person.

Conditional positive regard, that is, acceptance that is dependent on the positive or negative evaluation of a person's actions, leads to the development of

The warmth and affection displayed by this elderly couple convey the feeling of unconditional positive regard advocated by Rogers. (Bruce Davidson/Magnum Photos, Inc.)

conditions of worth. The person experiences "do" or "do not" and "should" or "should not" as necessary in order to feel appreciated and accepted. A condition of worth, in turn, leads to defensive functioning or to the closing off of experiences. The person loses contact with real experiences, reporting what one "should" feel, not what was actually felt. It is quite normal to behave in a way one doesn't feel in order to avoid the disapproval of friends, parents, and other important figures. For instance, you may act as if you enjoy a particular movie or a rock group that you actually dislike because you fear that your friends would think less of you if you expressed your real feelings. The clinical problem arises when one begins to deceive oneself and dissociate the true feelings. This generates discrepancies between the objective and the subjective worlds, producing anxiety and threat, which in turn block self-actualization.

Client-Centered Therapy

Corresponding to Rogers's theory of personality is a psychotherapeutic approach he developed, known as *client-centered therapy*. A key element in this therapy is the therapist's manifestation of unconditional positive regard for the client. The Rogerian therapist is trusting, accepting, and empathic, conveying to the client an understanding and acceptance of the client's perception of and feelings about the problem. Through the therapist's acceptance and empathy, the client becomes better able to accept real feelings that may previously have been distorted or denied because they conflicted with self-perceptions based on the conditional regard of others.

One of Rogers's most important contributions was his initiation of efforts to evaluate client-centered therapy. While studies of the effectiveness of various forms of therapy are now quite common, prior to Rogers's pioneering studies (Rogers and Dymond, 1954), assessment of psychotherapy depended primarily on unsystematic patient and therapist reports. Rogers's investigations both helped stimulate research in psychotherapy and contributed to personality theory.

Self-Concept.   The investigations by Rogers's research group of the efficacy of client-centered therapy focused on the self-concept. Rogers and Dymond (1954) were in part concerned with changes during the course of therapy in the discrepancy between the client's self-concept and *ideal self:* the person the client would like to be, who possesses certain positive attributes and does not have certain negative characteristics. One of the instruments most frequently used to access both self-concept and ideal self is the Q-sort (Stephenson, 1953). In the Q-sort, a large number of statements, such as:

- I am satisfied with myself.
- I have a warm emotional relationship with others.
- I have few values and standards of my own.
- I don't trust my emotions.

are presented to the person. These descriptive statements are written on separate cards, which the test taker then sorts into categories from "least like me" to "most like me," under either "self" (as one is) or "ideal" (as one would like to be) instructions. Typically, there are from nine to eleven categories, each one assigned a number of points — say, from one to eleven. The respondent is required to place a certain number of cards in each category. This procedure permits specific percepts about both the self and the ideal self to be quantified. It is then possible to compare numerically the sorts for the self and the ideal self. The difference between the two sorts is called the *self-ideal discrepancy*. Large discrepancies, a lack of correlation, or a negative correlation reveal feelings of low self-esteem and lack of personal worth, one index of maladjustment. By administering the Q-sort at various times during the course of psychotherapy, the effectiveness of therapy can be examined.

In one frequently cited investigation guided by these ideas, Butler and Haigh (1954), as part of Rogers and Dymond's project, reported that the self-ideal correlation of individuals seeking psychotherapy averaged − .01; that is, their perceptions of the real self were essentially unrelated to the desired, ideal self. This correlation increased to $+.58$ following therapy, while that of a control group not receiving psychotherapy did not change. In the psychotherapy group, the perceived real self changed so that it was closer to the ideal self. This finding provides evidence for the effectiveness of client-centered therapy, gives the Q-sort some validity, and illustrates one of the better research endeavors guided by a concern with the self and acceptance of the notion of a highly general self-concept.

In recent years there has been increasing interest in the structure of the self-concept and in individual differences regarding ideas about the self, as well as the effects of both on behavior. These issues are addressed in greater depth in Chapter 10.

Therapeutic Processes.   Rogers, along with his collaborators and students, addressed the process of psychotherapy in great detail and attempted to link therapeutic processes, or what is done during therapy, with therapeutic outcomes. Scales were developed that could be used to assess the openness of the therapists' communications with the client and the degree of acceptance of the client by the therapist (Rogers, et al., 1967). The question of the therapist's ability to empathize with the client, to experience the world as the client experiences it, has important implications for the selection of therapists as well as for understanding the process and progress of client-centered therapy. As a result, observational scales have also been developed to assess therapists' degree of empathy (Truax, et al., 1966). The importance of empathy extends beyond its role as an attribute of therapists. Thus, several cognitive and behavioral skill-oriented programs have focused on fostering empathy in clients (Feshbach, et al., 1983; Goldstein and Michaels, 1985).

Rogers extended his basic ideas concerning self-actualization and unconditional positive regard to a variety of settings. The principle that self-acceptance and self-actualization are facilitated by full acceptance from others and impeded by conditional regard holds true, according to Rogers, in small-group situations, in educational programs, and in families. In short, it applies to any interpersonal interaction: openness to experience and acceptance of others foster effective interpersonal relations, as well as personal growth (Rogers, 1980, 1983).

In opposition to Freud's belief that some repression is essential for mental health, Rogers argued that defenses help neither adaptation nor successful functioning in life. On the contrary, they interfere with satisfaction. In addition, Rogers was much less pessimistic than Freud regarding the inevitability of conflict between personal growth and society's needs. Society need not be restrictive, but can instead enhance mental health through the development of institutional attitudes of acceptance and trust. In the years before his death, Rogers became actively involved in efforts to foster better Soviet-American relations through the use of empathy, acceptance, and other principles of the person-centered approach.

Abraham Maslow, (1908–1970), in 1968, two years before his untimely death. (Ted Polumbaum, *Life* Magazine, © 1968 Time, Inc.)

MASLOW'S ORGANISMIC HUMANISM

Unlike Rogers, whose theory grew out of his mode of therapy, Abraham Maslow, (1908–1970), another major contributor to humanistic psychology, did not form a specific therapy. When Maslow first embarked on a psychological career, he was drawn to behaviorism and carried out studies on primate sexuality and dominance. He gradually left the confines of the behaviorist method and, after the birth of his first child, remarked that "anyone who [observes] a baby could not be a behaviorist." He was influenced by psychoanalysis, but eventually became critical of the psychoanalytic theory of motivation as well. In developing his own model of motivation and behavior, he incorporated the humanistic notion of self-actualization and eventually embraced humanistic philosophy totally.

The Need Hierarchy

Rather than postulating just one source of motivation, Maslow acknowledged a multiplicity of need systems. More specifically, he delineated a hierarchy of five basic classes or categories of needs, which he defined as physiological, safety, love, esteem, and self-actualization. Arkes and Garske (1977) have pointed out that these needs have common characteristics, such as:

1. Failure to gratify a need results in a related form of dysfunction or disturbance. For example, just as lack of vitamins can produce malnutrition, lack of love can produce depression.

2. Restoration of gratification remedies the dysfunction.

3. In a free-choice situation, gratification of lower needs will normally take precedence over gratification of higher needs. Maslow (1943, p. 372) stated:

If all needs are unsatisfied, and the organism is then dominated by physiological needs, all other needs may become simply non-existent or pushed into the background. It is then fair to characterize the whole organism as saying simply that it is hungry, for consciousness is almost completely preempted by hunger. . . . The urge to write poetry, the desire to acquire an automobile, the interest in American history . . . are . . . forgotten or become of secondary importance.

Table 6.1 shows the hierarchy of needs postulated by Maslow, conditions of deficiency and fulfillment, and a common example of such fulfillment. As already suggested, there is a prepotency of needs, with the lower, physiologically based needs having greater strength and the higher, psychologically based needs relatively weaker. Hence, lower needs must be satisfied before higher ones can be fulfilled. Schultz (1976, pp. 221–222) listed a number of other distinctions between the higher- and lower-order needs:

1. The higher needs appeared later in the evolutionary development of mankind. All living things need food and water, but only humans have a need to self-actualize and to know and understand. Therefore, the higher the need the more distinctly human it is. . . .

2. Higher needs are less necessary for sheer survival, hence their gratification can be postponed longer. Failure to satisfy a higher need does not produce as much of an immediate emergency or a crisis reaction as failure to satisfy a lower need. . . .

3. While they are less necessary for survival, the higher needs nevertheless contribute to survival and growth. Higher-level need satisfaction produces better health, longer life, and a generally enhanced biological efficiency. For this reason, the higher needs are also called growth needs.

4. Higher-need satisfaction is productive or beneficial not only biologically but psychologically as well, because it produces deeper happiness, peace of mind, and fullness in one's inner life.

5. Higher-need gratification involves more preconditions and greater complexity than lower-need satisfaction. The search for self-actualization, for example, has the precondition that all the other needs have first been satisfied and involves more complicated and sophisticated behavior and goals than, say, the search for food.

6. Higher-need gratification requires better external conditions (social, economic, and political) than lower-need gratification. For example, greater freedom of expression and opportunity are required for self-actualization than for safety.

D Values Versus B Values. The list above seems to indicate that lower and higher needs are in some respects qualitatively distinct. Maslow characterized the lower needs as *deficit* (D) *values:* attainment of their desired goal results in tension reduction and returns the organism to a state of equilibrium. Freud was concerned exclusively with D values.

Table 6.1 Need hierarchy and levels of personality functioning

Need hierarchy	Condition of deficiency	Fulfillment	Illustration
Self-Actualization	Alienation Metapathologies Absence of meaning in life Boredom Routine living Limited activities	Healthy curiosity Peak experiences Realization of potentials Work which is pleasurable and embodies values Creative living	Experiencing a profound insight
Esteem	Feeling of incompetence Negativism Feeling of inferiority	Confidence Sense of mastery Positive self-regard	Receiving an award for an outstanding performance on some project
Love	Self-consciousness Feeling of being unwanted Feeling of worthlessness Emptiness Loneliness	Free expression of emotions Sense of wholeness Sense of warmth Renewed sense of life and strength Sense of growing together	Experiencing total acceptance in a love relationship
Safety	Insecurity Yearning Sense of loss Fear Obsession Compulsion	Security Comfort Balance Poise Calm Tranquility	Being secure in a full-time job
Physiological	Hunger, thirst Sexual frustration Tension Illness Lack of proper shelter	Relaxation Release from tension Experiences of pleasure from senses Physical well-being Comfort	Feeling satisfied after a good meal

Source: From *Personality Theories: A Guide to Human Nature* by Nicholoas S. DiCaprio. Copyright © 1983 by Holt, Rinehart, and Winston, Inc. Reprinted by permission of the publisher.

Maslow also postulated that there are *being* (B) *values*. B values are associated with growth motivation, increased tension, and expanded horizons. Among the B values identified by Maslow are wholeness, perfection, justice, beauty, uniqueness, creativity, and truth. One experiences tension from the need to create or to produce beauty, but this tension, Maslow asserted, is associated with positive rather than negative affects.

The Actualized Person

Maslow's wide appeal both within and outside the psychological community has been due largely to his description and elaboration of self-actualization. The B values are associated not only with self-actualization, but also with such qualities as spontaneity and peak experiences, the latter being moments of great ecstasy or awe. Maslow believed that the *peak experience* is elicited by the achievement of real excellence or the movement toward perfect values, not by the "high" attained through the use of drugs.

Maslow attempted to demonstrate the properties of self-actualization by studying individuals who he believed best displayed the qualities of the actualized person. Maslow (1971, p. 7) contended:

> If we want to answer the question of how tall the human species can grow, then obviously it is well to pick out the ones who already are tallest and study them. If we want to know how fast a human being can run, then it is no use to average out the speed of a "good sample" of the population; it is far better to collect Olympic gold medal winners and see how well they can do. If we want to know the possibilities for spiritual growth, or moral development in human beings, then I maintain that we can learn most by studying our most moral, ethical, or saintly people. [Maslow identified anthropologist Ruth Benedict and the Gestalt psychologist Max Wertheimer as two of these "saintly people."]

There are a number of characteristics associated with such self-actualizing or fully functioning individuals. They include such positive qualities as self-awareness, creativity, spontaneity, openness to experience, self-acceptance, and the more specific qualities of democratic character structure and social interest. Adjectives such as *happy* and *satisfied* are less appropriate in describing the lives of these individuals, Maslow contended, than are words like *challenging, exciting,* and *meaningful*.

One may well question whether these characteristics are a consequence of a psychological process called self-actualization or merely are reflections of the particular value systems held by Rogers and Maslow. One might also wonder whether anyone displays these idealized attributes in a consistent manner. Nonetheless, the descriptions of actualizing behavior provided by Rogers and Maslow have called attention to significant aspects of experience and behavior that other personality theorists have neglected.

EXISTENTIAL HUMANISM

We now turn to existential personality theory. This is an outgrowth of the existentialist philosophy developed by Sören Kierkegaard (1813–1855) and subsequently expanded by a number of twentieth-century philosophers and writers, including Paul Tillich, Martin Heidegger, Jean Paul Sartre, Albert Camus, and Martin Buber. We can touch only briefly on the major psychological ideas reflected in these philosophical writings and in the work of personality theorists and clinicians who are identified with the existentialist approach. (For a review of existential psychology, see Kobasa and Maddi, 1977.)

Key words for the existentialists are *freedom, choice, anxiety, meaning, authenticity, responsibility,* and *struggle.* By virtue of our capacity for self-reflection and to perceive our uniqueness and our mortality, we are able to make choices and affect our fate and, thus, must also assume responsibility for the decisions we make. The German term *Dasein* is used to denote this higher, human level of consciousness that captures the whole psychological person. To face the future and contemplate change creates *existential anxiety;* to review the past and one's errors creates *guilt.* While either excessive anxiety or excessive guilt can be crippling, the experiences of anxiety and guilt are conditions of human existence. To change, to grow, and to choose entails *anxiety,* but the willingness or courage to confront anxiety and choose to change is the basis for personal development and the attainment of true maturity, or *authenticity.*

The existential psychologists do not permit us to escape responsibility for our actions, as might the psychoanalysts and the Skinnerians, by attributing the cause for our actions to some past experience or early conditioning. Rather, the cause lies in our present experience. Two Swiss psychiatrists, Ludwig Binswanger (1881–1966) and Medard Boss (b. 1903) pioneered in the development of a form of psychotherapy referred to as existential analysis (Binswanger, 1963), or *Daseinanalysis* (Boss, 1963), which is based on existential ideas. The existential therapists view their primary task as the analysis and clarification of the client's subjective world, of the meanings that the client attributes to events and relationships, and of the alternatives that they believe are available. Existentialists make use of the psychoanalytic method, but they reject psychoanalytic theory, maintaining that theoretical concepts such as the superego and the Oedipus complex, bias the therapist's perceptions and diminish openness to the reality of the client. In addition, the existentialists contend that Freud's views *justify* pathology, rather than giving the person responsibility and choice.

It is the person's existence, his or her "being-in-the-world" (Binswanger, 1963) or consciousness that defines what it is to be human. The person's experiences of the external world of people and objects and of his or her psychological self and body are the essence of being human. From some existential perspectives, there should be a unity or wholeness between the human being and the environment. This notion of oneness with the physical world reflects the influence of Eastern religious thought on existential psychology. Other existentially oriented psychologists point to the feelings of loneliness and separation from others and nature, which may accompany a full existential awareness of one's connectedness and separateness. From either perspective, there are certain conditions that diminish the achievement of authority or existential maturity. These include being treated as a thing or object by social institutions, self-preoccupation interfering with full awareness of people and of nature, and unwillingness to face the anxiety of making difficult choices. These conditions lead to feelings of alienation, loneliness, and despair.

To be authentic, the human being must be willing to recognize his or her unique potentials, desires, and freedom of choice. Authenticity also entails consciousness of the limitations imposed by the environment and one's personal capacities. All things are not possible for all people, but there are individual meanings and choices that can be made even in very limiting circumstances such as in prison or when facing impending death. Viktor Frankl (1963) is a well-known existential theorist and therapist whose views were formulated following his experiences in a concentration camp during World War II. His observations led him to conclude that prisoners who were reflective, fully conscious of their experience, and capable of finding personal meaning in even these extreme circumstances were best able physically and psychologically to survive the concentration camp ordeal.

The existentialist's emphasis on personal struggle, courage, and the unavoidability of anxiety and guilt distinguishes their views from those of self-actualization theorists. Rogers's portrayal of personal growth makes the assumption of a biologically programmed self-actualizing tendency that will result in self-fulfillment if the individual receives unconditional positive regard. The existentialists, however, see the individual as a much more active agent for whom struggle and anxiety are necessary precursors of authenticity. These theoretical differences between the existentialist and self-actualization theorists are a matter more of assumptions and worldviews than of issues that can be put to empirical test. In general, the existentialists see the empirical approach of psychology as irrelevant. However, one can find occasional examples of research efforts guided by existentialist theory.

The personality style of *hardiness,* as formulated and developed by Kobasa and Maddi, is a reflection of existential ideas. *Hardiness* includes three elements — *commitment,* the feeling that some part of what you are doing is interesting and worthwhile, as compared to alienation; a sense of *control* rather than powerlessness; and the experience of life changes as a *challenge* rather than a threat. There have been a number of studies indicating that hardiness helps buffer the impact of stress and moderate its influence on physical illness (Kobasa, et al., 1986), although the significance of the different components of hardiness remains at issue (cf. Chapter 15). While research on hardiness does not address the major principles of existential psychology, the role of personal choice and responsibility has assumed increasing importance in the study of personality (Singer and Kolligian, 1987).

KELLY'S PERSONAL CONSTRUCT THEORY

Humanistic psychologists are particularly concerned with how individuals feel about and perceive themselves in terms of personal value or worth, and with the consequences of disparate self-concepts. *Personal construct theory* addresses how the perceiver organizes his or her world and interprets, or *construes,* events. Thus, personal construct theory is as much a part of the phenomenological approach in psychology as is humanism. However, in contrast to humanistic psychology, thought rather than feeling is stressed, and affect is considered simply one of the consequences of particular thought processes.

The Human as Scientist

George Kelly, (1905–1966), the originator of personal construct theory, contended that the underlying goal of the individual is to predict and control experienced events. Thus, he conceived of individuals as scientists seeking to understand and forecast the events around them.

Kelly noted that it is puzzling that, while psychologists try to explain the behavior of their clients or of people in general, the theories they have formulated cannot account for their own scientific activity. For example, if people are impelled by sexual and aggressive instincts and if all behavior is directed toward the reduction of these primary urges, as the Freudians argue, then what motivated Freud to formulate his theory of personality? Freud did contend that higher intellectual activities, such as scientific pursuits, are derivatives of instinctual drives and are in service of these basic drives. But this analysis is far from convincing. In a similar manner, if humans are mere robots, as behaviorists like Skinner would have us believe, then how did the new ideas formulated by Skinner originate? In sum, the psychoanalytic and strict behaviorist theory that dominated psychology for so many years cannot readily account for the scientific behavior of Freud and Skinner.

As intimated above, Kelly's theory of personal constructs can explain scientific endeavors, for Kelly considered the average person to be an intuitive scientist with the goal of predicting and understanding behavior. To accomplish this aim, naive individuals formulate hypotheses about the world and themselves, collect data that confirm or disconfirm these hypotheses, and then alter their theories to account for the new data. Hence, the average person operates in much the same manner as a professional scientist, although professional scientists may be more accurate and self-conscious in their attempts to achieve cognitive clarity and understanding. Just as scientists sometimes hold bad theories, individuals may entertain bad theories, that is, beliefs that hinder effective behavior and lead to bias in data collection and interpretation. For example, assume that a woman (Nancy) believes that a man (John) has strong negative feelings toward her. When Nancy meets John at a party, she expects that he will ignore her, make an insulting remark, or embarrass her in front of her friends. However, assume that, to Nancy's surprise, John acts friendly and seems happy to see her. Assume, too, that this disconfirmation is repeatedly experienced so that John's displayed friendliness cannot be due to some temporary mood state or to the immediate social pressures of acting "nice." On the basis of these new data, Nancy should reformulate her hypothesis and perceive that John really likes her. The new construction more accurately predicts behavior and allows Nancy to correctly anticipate her interactions with John.

In discussing his conception of the person as a seeker of truth, Kelly (1955, p. 5) asserted:

> It is customary to say that *the scientist's ultimate aim is to predict and to control.* This is a summary statement that psychologists frequently like to quote in characterizing their own aspirations. Yet, curiously enough, psychologists rarely credit the human subjects in their experiments with having similar aspirations. It is as though the psychologist were saying to himself, "I, being a *psychologist,* and therefore a *scientist,* am performing this experiment in order to improve the prediction and control of certain human phenomena; but my subject, being merely a human organism, is obviously propelled by inexorable drives welling up within him, or else he is in gluttonous pursuit of sustenance and shelter."

Many other psychologists besides Kelly implicitly accept the conception of the individual as an intuitive scientist. Of great concern to experimental psychologists is the possibility that the subject will infer what the experimenter is trying to prove and then will consciously or unconsciously comply with this hypothesis (Orne, 1962). The *demand characteristics* of an experiment therefore must be carefully controlled or concealed in many psychological investigations. But the very existence of such controls intimates that subjects search for meaning in their environment, formulate hypotheses, and act on the basis of these belief systems. Of course, if a subject were to perceive the experimenter as a nasty or intrusive person, then he or she might try to "ruin" the experiment by disproving the experimenter's hypothesis. This behavior is also in service of the subject's goal and is based on a particular belief system, as well as on inferences about the purpose of the investigation.

Bannister and Fransella (1971, p. 16), commenting on the human-as-scientist formulation, noted:

> One of the effects of this is to make the model man of personal construct theory look recognizably like you: that is, unless you are the very modest kind of man who can see himself as the stimulus-jerked puppet of learning theory [or] the primitive infant of psychoanalytic theory. . . . If you do not recognize yourself at any point in personal construct theory, you have discovered a major defect in it and are entitled to be suspicious of its claims.

One of the interesting similarities between humanistic theory and personal construct theory is a consequence of the human-as-scientist model. Both the psychologist and the client or an experimental subject are now equal parts of a dyad. That is, the psychologist is no "higher" than the so-called naive person. Hence, psychology is now a metadiscipline, seeking to make sense out of the way that individuals make sense out of the world. The psychologist therefore is engaged in the same interpretive endeavor as non-psychologists.

Note, then, that Kelly proposes a rational image of humans: to understand thoughts is to understand the person. Bruner (1956) speculated that this theory of personality was in part a product of the particular clinical experiences that Kelly encountered. For many years Kelly was a counselor of college students. Rather than facing patients with hysterical paralysis or bizarre dreams, "the young men and women of Professor Kelly's clinical examples are worried about their dates, their studies, and even their conformity" (Bruner, 1956, p. 357). Hence, Kelly spent relatively little time considering the unconscious, deep-seated urges, or even defenses. As with other conceptions presented in this book, he therefore was able to account adequately for some aspects of behavior. However, he could not readily explain a number of other phenomena.

Constructive Alternativism

Kelly labeled his basic philosophical assumption *constructive alternativism*. Meaning, Kelly asserted, is not inherent in an event, but depends on how a person construes or interprets that event. Thus, there is no "reality"; reality truly exists in the eyes of the beholder. Further, people can always revise their constructs — or ideas — about reality, and thus change how they experience it. As a result, some of Kelly's ideas are, perhaps surprisingly, associated with the psychoanalytic notion that needs and values influence our perception of the world.

Because meaning is subject to change, Kelly reasoned that individuals are personally responsible (able to respond) for their own future. Nature does not dictate one's life or, as Kelly contended, "No one needs to be the victim of his biography." This position again links personal construct theory with humanistic and existentialist thinking by placing change processes within the grasp and the capability of the individual. Thus, either credit for a successful life or blame for an unsuccessful one is placed directly on the actor. Each person controls the course of his or her life.

Formal Theory

Kelly outlined a formal theory with one fundamental postulate and eleven corollaries. Here we examine only the postulate and three of the corollaries, selecting those that shed the *most* light on Kelly's conception of personality and behavior.

Fundamental Postulate. Kelly stated that an individual's life or conduct is guided by how the world is construed. Furthermore, the predictive power of that construal is demonstrated or proved by how much sense one has made out of the world, or the accuracy with which one is able to predict future events. Confirmation or disconfirmation of predictions was accorded much greater significance in Kelly's thinking than, for example, drives and drive reduction or reward and punishment.

Individual Corollary. Kelly asserted that people differ from one another in their construction of events. For example, one person might judge others according to their sincerity or wit. Another might use intelligence or kindness as bases for perceiving others. Furthermore, there are individual differences in the complexity of one's construal system, which can be illustrated by considering the perceived properties of light. Humans judge light on the basis of three distinct dimensions: brightness, saturation, and hue. Lower organisms, on the other hand, may have only one dimension or construct available (brightness) to distinguish various light stimuli. Thus, humans have greater cognitive differentiation in their perception of light than some lower organisms. Similarly, some individuals perceive more discriminations, or use more dimensions in their construals, than others.

Inasmuch as individuals perceive the identical objective situation in a different manner, it follows that behavior will also differ between individuals. Furthermore, since no two constructions are exactly alike, each person is unique. This position is in keeping with the humanist position.

Range Corollary. A given construction is not appropriate for all events. For example, the construct "tall-short" may be appropriate for anticipating play on a basketball court but is likely to be quite irrelevant in predicting an individual's honesty. Kelly distinguished between the range of convenience and the focus of convenience of a construct. The *range of convenience* indicates the breadth of different phenomena to which a construct may be applied. The *focus of convenience* refers to the area in which the construct is maximally useful.

Scientists frequently employ the range and focus notions when describing and evaluating psychological theories. Freudians, for example, would argue that the range of convenience of their theory includes war, wit, and slips of the tongue; such generalizability is a positive attribute of any theory. But the Freudian model's focus of convenience concerns sexual and aggressive conflicts. A similar description of the range and focus of convenience of all the theories presented in previous chapters could be made and would prove instructive for comparison and evaluation.

Experience Corollary. A person's construct system is subject to change as a result of successful or unsuccessful construal of events. Given Kelly's perspective, psychotherapy is a process in which one's construct system is altered with the aid of a therapist. The therapist must first discover how the client is perceiving the world and then assist the client in reorganizing the old system and finding new, more functional constructs. The therapist might help the client to design and implement "experiments" to test particular hypotheses. For example, if an individual perceives a parent or a spouse as aggressive or dominating, then special behaviors might be suggested to test whether this perception helps rather than hinders the anticipation of events. Role playing and modeling are frequently used to help alter construct systems. The therapist might suggest, for example, that the client act as if the parent or the spouse were not aggressive or dominant, in order to test an alternative hypothesis. (At an earlier time in his life Kelly was a drama coach, which may account in part for his selection of role playing as a technique for altering construct systems.)

In one social experiment involving the change of constructs, the participants were teachers who believed the children in their classrooms were not learning because they were "lazy" (Kelly, 1958). The experimenters suggested that the teachers give the children nothing to do in the classroom and see what happened. Of course, the pupils would not sit still without any activity. On the basis of this contradictory evidence, the teachers began to consider the school environment and their own inadequacy as causes of poor learning, rather than blaming the problems entirely on the children.

The Role Construct Repertory (REP) Test

Kelly devised an ingenious testing instrument to ascertain an individual's personal construct system. The test reflects Kelly's belief that the tester should not impose his or her constructs on the test taker. Rather, the testee should be allowed to display constructs that are naturally used to give meaning to the world.

In the REP test, the test taker first lists the names of individuals who play or have played certain roles in his or her life, such as mother, father, rejecting person, threatening person, and so on (see Fig. 6.1). On the standard REP grid, shown in

Figure 6.1   Simplified grid form of the REP test.

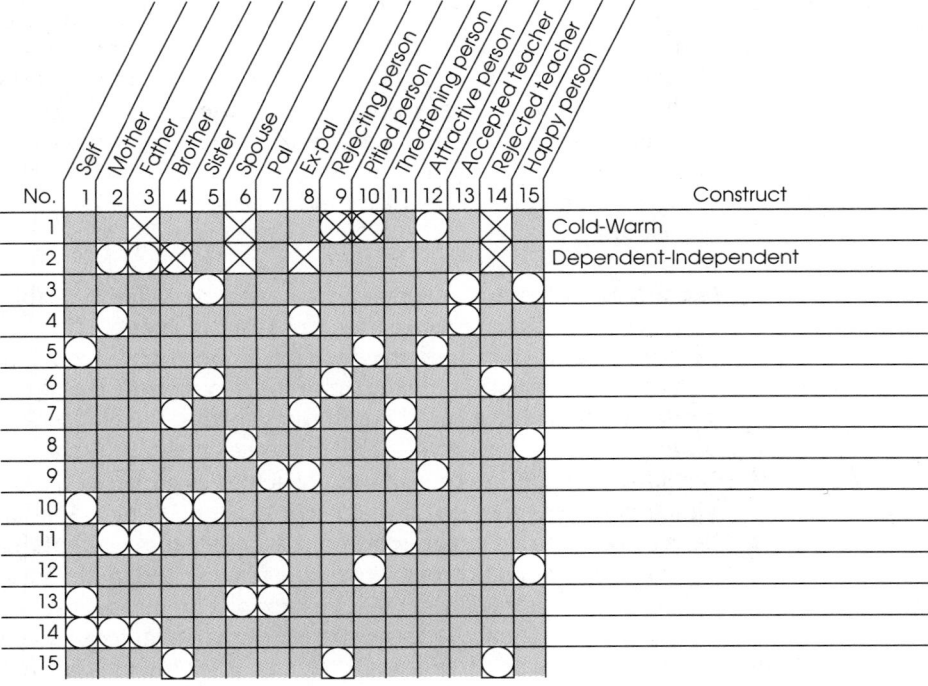

Fig. 6.1, the three circles in each row designate three roles that each subject is to consider as a group. For each triad, the subject determines the construct, such as cold-warm or dominant-submissive, in which two members of that triad are similar yet different from the third. The construct selected by the test taker is assumed to represent a dimension of thought or a construct along which significant people in the respondent's life are ordered or compared. In row 1 of the grid, for example, a respondent might perceive individuals identified as rejecting and pitied to be cold, while attractive people are warm. The respondent then judges the remaining twelve people as having or not having the quality (coldness) of the two linked individuals in the triad, placing an X in the box of that row if that particular characteristic is possessed. Fig. 6.1 shows that father, spouse, and rejected teacher are perceived as cold. The remaining fourteen rows are completed in this manner, with a different construct selected for each triad. Using mathematical techniques, the tester reduces the chosen constructs to a few basic ones representing the respondent's typical way of perceiving and classifying others.

Emotions

Critics have often charged Kelly with ignoring affective states, or "the human passions." This is somewhat incorrect. Kelly focused brief attention on certain specific emotions, namely, anxiety, guilt, threat, fear, and anger, but he defined them all as consequences of construct systems that are in transitional states.

Anxiety, according to Kelly, occurs when one's construct system provides no means for dealing with an experience. Bannister and Fransella (1971, p. 35) elaborated on anxiety as follows:

> We become anxious when we can only partially construe the events which we encounter and too many of their implications are obscure. Sex for the chaste, adulthood for the adolescent, books for the illiterate, power for the humble and death for nearly all of us tend to provoke anxiety. It is the *unknown* aspect of things that go bump in the night that give them their potency.

In a similar manner, interacting with a person whom we cannot understand often gives rise to vague feelings of uneasiness. And even greater anxiety is experienced when starting a new job or confronting a new environment. If anxiety reactions are frequent and severe, then the range of constructs must be broadened so that more phenomena can be incorporated. Disconfirmation of a belief also arouses anxiety because it reveals an inadequacy in the construct system. Anxiety, therefore, is not necessarily bad. It is one precondition for construct change.

Kelly distinguishes between *threat* and anxiety, even though both result from defective, and therefore transitional, construct systems. Threat is experienced when a fundamental change is about to occur in one's construct system, when major beliefs about the nature of one's personal and social world are invalidated. For example, questioning the purpose of life is threatening for it is likely to lead to basic conceptual change. Similarly, a deeply involving extramarital affair may alter one's conception of what it is to be a parent or a spouse, thus engendering a threat. Psychotherapists must be aware of the possibility that they may also be viewed as threatening inasmuch as they are perceived as agents of construct change.

Finally, in Kelly's system *guilt* results from a discrepancy between one's ideal self and one's actions. Thus, one suffers guilt when doing things that are discrepant with the kind of person you thought you were or would like to be.

Overview of Kelly's Theory

Kelly has contended that humans are intuitive scientists, construing the world in idiosyncratic ways to give it meaning. Meaning is the interpretation of events with particular constructs, enabling one to predict, or anticipate, the future. One's construct system is not immutable. Individuals have alternative construction possibilities and are personally responsible for their own well-being. Finally, certain emotions, such as anxiety, threat, and guilt, are products of inadequate and changing construct systems.

Kelly's conception is unique among the theories of personality and provides an alternative language for understanding or construing human action. It has not generated a great deal of research, but it has produced new and valuable insights, as well as a novel method of measurement, and is gaining in popularity.

IMPLICIT PSYCHOLOGY

Compatible with Kelly's theory, some psychologists have recently become interested in the implicit theories that people use to guide their behavior. This interest leads to the distinction between *science* and *ethnoscience*: the reasons people behave the way they do versus *perceived* reasons they behave the way they do, or what is known positively as "folk wisdom" and negatively as "grandma psychology" (see Wegner and Vallacher, 1977). It is evident that individuals have ideas and often elaborate theories about what people are like and what motivates them. Although these theories are "implicit" (Bruner and Tagiuri, 1954), they nevertheless determine social reality.

Implicit theories concerning the interrelationships of traits or attributes have already received much attention from psychological researchers (see Schneider, 1973). Beliefs like "Fat people are jolly," "People who wear glasses are introverts," and "Intelligent people are witty" are examples of such implicit theories of personality. People are often unaware that they hold such theories and thus do not put them systematically to test. Nevertheless, such notions greatly influence expectations and actions. These implicit theories of personality may influence one's responses on a personality scale or one's judgments of another's personality. They can contribute to interrelationships among personality variables that do not exist in reality (Mischel, 1984).

Kelly's REP test represents one attempt to measure implicit theories of person perception by ascertaining the constructs people employ as well as the perceived interrelationships among these constructs. Indeed, Kelly's entire theory rests on the presumption that people are naive scientists, formulating their own idiosyncratic psychological theories. Kelly further contended that at times these theories do *not* work and that the individual must be aided in the construction of better theories.

In addition to implicit theories of person perception, there are implicit theories of child psychology, abnormal psychology, psychodynamics, and virtually any other area within the broad domain of personality psychology. For example, we exhibit our implicit ideas about children in the ways in which we communicate with them. As Wegner and Vallacher (1977, p. 303) state:

> The hostess at a dinner party is not likely to say "Hot, hot!" when she places a steaming dish before a guest, but often makes similar remarks to her five-year-old. She does not say "Look both ways, now" when she sends the guests across the street to their cars, but often will repeat this warning to her child. . . . Many of these wholesome and insipid expressions would be totally inappropriate in adult conversation. [See Gleason, 1973.]

In a similar manner, implicit theories of abnormal psychology abound. Since the layperson has been introduced to Freudian theory, often through "pop psychology" sources, early childhood experiences are typically perceived as an important cause of abnormal adult behavior. For example, schizophrenia or autism is attributed to "bad" child-rearing practices, sibling rivalry, Oedipal wishes, and so forth. The naive psychology of the layperson and the "true" laws of personality, child psychology, and abnormal psychology may or may not be identical. For example, most laypersons are unaware that certain types of schizophrenia have a strong genetic component and that schizophrenia, particularly among this group, may be little related to such early experiences as parent-child interactions (see Chapter 1).

An investigation by Whiteman (1967) illustrates some of the differences between the science of defense mechanisms and defenses as perceived (or not perceived) by younger children. Whiteman presented children with a number of scenarios, such as that for displacement (Whiteman, 1967, pp. 145–146):

> There was once a little girl named Jane. One day her mother promised that Jane's favorite dessert, ice cream, would be served at supper. But Jane's mother forgot to buy the ice cream, and so there wasn't any ice cream for dessert. Jane didn't say anything to her mother about the ice cream. After supper Jane went to play with her dolls and did something she never did before. She spanked her dolls. Why did she spank her dolls?

While the displacement mechanism might be obvious to adults and older children, Whiteman reported that a large percentage of the younger children (ages five to six) did not relate the psychological reaction (spanking the dolls) to the given psychological cause (ice cream deprivation). Rather, in the displacement scenario, the younger children attributed the spanking to, for example, the naughtiness of the doll. In sum, the science of defense mechanisms outlined by Freud and subsequent ego psychologists contrasts with the laws of behavior *perceived* by younger children.

A Concluding Comment

While psychoanalytic theory and its offshoots have focused on unconscious forces and the learning theories on overt behavior, the phenomenological theories have been concerned with the individual's subjective experience. The research that has been stimulated by phenomenological approaches fills an important gap in the description of human personality functioning. The way in which individuals construe their environment, and construe themselves and the reasons for their actions, are major determinants of individual differences in behavior. The phenomenologists' depiction of the individual as an active, striving, developing organism, seeking meaning and growth or mastery, has also served as an important theoretical corrective. The difficulties with the phenomenological approach stem in part from an overemphasis on the "here and now." In general, they have neglected developmental and learning influences. Phenomenology is vulnerable in areas where the other theoretical approaches are strong; that is, insufficient attention is given to unconscious processes and to the relationship between experience and behavior. There is often a discrepancy between people's verbalized intentions and their actions; also, the reasons that people give for their behaviors are sometimes rationalizations for rather than causes of the behavior. Nevertheless, phenomenology provides a needed perspective in our efforts to describe and understand personality.

Phenomenological approaches like behavioristic and psychodynamic approaches, are growing and evolving. Kelly's approach has been an important contributor to the *constructivist* (Mahoney, 1991) movement. Constructivists, in accord with Kelly, hold that we each psychologically "construct" the worlds we live in. By changing how we construct our worlds, we can change both our behavior and our experience. Carl Rogers's client-centered therapy has evolved into a broader approach known as the "person-centered approach" (Levant and Shlien, 1984), which is being applied to education, medicine, and politics. Rogers, in his later years, led groups in which members of warring factions, such as blacks and whites in South Africa, were brought together to foster dialogue. New approaches to therapy, which integrate ideas from other approaches but are based on Rogers's ideas, are being developed (e.g., Greenberg, Rice, and Elliott, 1993).

Summary

1. *Humanistic psychology* is governed by the tenets that the experiencing person is of primary interest, that creativity and self-actualization are the preferred topics of investigation, that meaningful research topics should be selected, and that the dignity of the person is an essential aspect of research inquiry.

2. *Self-actualization* denotes the internal driving force to develop one's capacities and talents to the fullest. It is central in the theory of Carl Rogers.

3. *Unconditional positive regard,* or being valued for oneself, facilitates self-actualization. On the other hand, *conditions of worth* where acceptance is dependent on particular actions decrease the possibility of self-actualization.

4. The *self-ideal discrepancy* refers to the differences between how one perceives oneself and how one would like to be. There is some evidence that this discrepancy decreases following *client-centered therapy.*

5. Maslow postulated a need hierarchy with physiological needs at the bottom and self-actualization needs at the highest level. Lower needs must be gratified prior to the full pursuit of higher-order needs. Higher needs, although aiding adjustment and satisfaction, are not necessary for survival.

6. There is a distinction between *deficit* (D) and *being* (B) *values,* the former associated with tension reduction and the latter with increased tension and expanded horizons.

7. Existentialists contend that we must assume responsibility for our actions and that we cannot escape anxiety and guilt.

8. *Personal construct theory* as formulated by George Kelly addresses the issue of how a person construes (perceives, organizes) his or her world. It is based on the assumption that individuals act as scientists, formulating hypotheses and gathering data relevant to those hypotheses.

9. Individuals differ in their construction of events and these constructions are not fixed. The REP test was devised to assess construct systems.

10. The emotions of *anxiety* and *threat* have been interpreted by Kelly with the aid of personal construct theory. Anxiety indicates that one's construct system does not allow one to deal with an experience, while threat is experienced when the construct system is about to undergo fundamental change.

11. *Implicit psychology* refers to the theories of behavior held by untrained psychologists or laypersons.

Thought Questions

1. Who among your acquaintances is the most self-actualized? On what evidence do you base this judgment?

2. What do you think of the humanistic belief that people are fundamentally good? How do the humanists account for evil?

3. Many psychologists believe that the humanistic approach to personality can never attain the status of a science. Do you agree with this belief and, if so, is it a "fatal" flaw?

4. Do you believe that our significant behaviors are primarily (1) conscious and rational, (2) conditioned and mechanistic, or (3) unconscious and irrational?

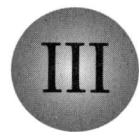

THE STRUCTURE OF PERSONALITY

The word *personality* connotes what one is "like": the characteristics, traits, or general manner of thinking and behaving that define who one is. Psychologists sometimes refer to this as the structure of personality. Webster defines *structure* as an arrangement of parts organized in some meaningful way. The next three chapters, then, are concerned with this construction of the parts of the person. This rather analytic aspect of the study of personality contrasts with the explanation of how personality traits develop, which has just been discussed, and with the manner in which personality structures influence behavior, which falls under the dynamics of personality, analyzed in the next part of the text.

The study of the structure of personality is intimately linked with the measurement of personality. To determine the degree to which one is introverted, aggressive, or high in need for achievement, there must be appropriate instruments to assess these concepts. In Chapter 7 the basic principles of measurement are introduced. Reliability, which refers to how well a concept is being measured, and validity, which is concerned with whether a test is measuring what it is supposed to measure, are examined in detail. This is followed, in Chapter 8, by a discussion of the types of instruments used to assess personality. Objective tests are distinguished from projective tests; other ways to measure personality are suggested; and the reliability and validity of these different approaches are considered. Then, in Chapter 9, traits are examined in detail. There has been a movement in psychology to deny the existence of traits, based on apparent evidence that behavior is neither general across situations nor enduring. The accuracy of this position is debated and some newer conceptions of traits and their assessment are presented in Chapter 9.

In some texts, trait approaches, such as the ones covered in Chapter 9, are considered among the theories of personality. While trait approaches are indeed theories of personality, we consider them in this part because they are so intimately linked to issues of measurement and assessment and because they tend to be empirically based.

In sum, the chapters in this part of the text progress from the basics of measurement, to an examination of specific measures being employed, to a discussion of traits, or what is being measured. The field of personality structure is exceedingly complex. Because so many issues remain to be resolved, it is one of the most active areas in the field of personality.

7 | Foundations of Personality Measurement

In earlier chapters we frequently referred to specific studies of personality, describing the measures used in these studies and the results obtained. To interpret these results properly, however, it is necessary to be able to evaluate the measures and how well they assess whatever it is they are supposed to assess. One must also have an understanding of the meaning of the numerical relations that are reported. In the next three chapters, we will discuss some of the methods that psychologists use to measure aspects of personality, with measurements typically expressed in terms of scores, ratings, and other quantitative values. Quantitative methods allow us to evaluate theories and hypotheses more systematically. As a result, they also allow us to learn more about characteristics of individuals as well as how these characteristics are the same as or different from those of other individuals.

In this chapter we present some of the foundations for research in the measurement of personality. First, we discuss some of the history of personality assessment. Next, we discuss the reliability and validity of psychological assessment procedures.

Before considering these issues, remember that one of the most important purposes of personality assessment is to help investigators make decisions about people. Thus, a college student may be asked to take a test to help a counselor decide what career to recommend; a clinician may administer a test to help decide whether or not a person should be hospitalized or simply placed under psychiatric care. But such decisions involving selection or classification must also take risks and benefits into account. For example, a test score may classify an individual as suicidal. The therapist must then determine whether the person should be placed in a hospital, which is quite costly and has serious implications for both the individual and the community. While making this decision, the therapist takes into account the fact that suicide is quite rare (it has a low "base rate"). Because even good tests are imperfect and the chances of suicide are in general so low, usually the best prediction concerning this individual, regardless of his or her test score, is that suicide will not be attempted. Given only probability or likelihood as the basis for a decision, it would be best not to recommend hospitalization; but in view of the severity of loss in the event of suicide, the therapist may suggest hospitalization in spite of the low probability of that behavior. That is, the clinician would much rather err in the direction of hospitalizing a patient who would not have attempted suicide than in not hospitalizing a client who later does attempt suicide. In sum, testing must be considered within the broader context of decision making and cannot be divorced from the overall values of society.

THE PRESCIENTIFIC ERA

The prescientific era in the examination of personality structure, which extended to the middle of the nineteenth century, produced a number of interesting ideas that provided the foundation for modern personality testing. The origins of testing for mental abilities actually go back more than 2,000 years, to the practices of the Chinese emperors of the Qin or early Han dynasties, roughly around 150 B.C. It is said that the emperor himself gave written examinations to all nominees for government offices, and it is thought that the tests were more for literacy than for knowledge. These examinations then fell into disuse for several hundred years, but reappeared around 900 A.D. Modern scholars believe that the system ensured a supply of talented men from the provinces to serve in the national government and also formed a power group the emperor controlled as a counterbalance to the hereditary aristocracy. The tests were quite elaborate and required the use of abstract arguments and word games (Bowman, 1989).

Better known to us are the developments that first took place in Europe. Consider, for example, the interesting and creative conception of Theophrastus (372–287 B.C.), Aristotle's successor as head of the Lyceum in Athens, who is best known for his collection of personality sketches called "characters." Theophrastus was struck by the observation that, while all of Greece had the same climate and Greeks had the same general upbringing, they did not all have the same personality. He proposed a set of thirty personality types, each one presented in the form of a character vignette with one outstanding personality attribute. Each sketch opened with a brief definition of the dominant characteristic and continued with examples of this style in action (see Highlight 7.1). Among the characters sketched were the Liar, the Surly Man, the Tasteless Man, and the Flatterer. These exaggerated, unidimensional depictions of character also became common literary devices, as in the romantic heroism of Cervantes's Don Quixote and the blind loyalty of his vassal, Sancho Panza.

Despite our sense that we know people who fit some of these character types, there are many difficulties with Theophrastus' approach. Some of these same difficulties apply to modern character typology. One obvious problem with these unidimensional sketches is that they are caricatures, appropriate perhaps for dramatic purposes but grossly inadequate for objective scientific description. The concept of type has an either-or quality; one is or is not a particular personality type. In contrast, the concept of trait implies a continuum of the quality in question, with some people displaying very little of the trait, others more, and so on. Individuals are more appropriately and accurately described by their position on a continuum of trait dimensions rather than as belonging to one particular type.

■ **Highlight 7.1** ■

The Penurious Man
Theophrastus

Penuriousness is economy carried beyond all measure. A Penurious Man is one who goes to a debtor to ask for his half-obol interest before the end of the month. At a dinner where expenses are shared, he counts the number of cups each person drinks, and he makes a smaller libation to Artemis than anyone. If someone has made a good bargain on his account and presents him with the bill he says it is too much.

When his servant breaks a pot or a plate, he deducts the value from his food. If his wife drops a copper, he moves furniture, beds, chests and hunts in the curtains. If he has something to sell he puts such a price on it that the buyer has no profit. He forbids anyone to pick a fig in his garden, to walk on his land, to pick up an olive or a date. Every day he goes to see that the boundary marks of his property have not been moved. He will destrain on a debtor and exact compound interest. When he entertains the members of his deme, he is careful to serve very small pieces of meat to them. If he goes marketing, he returns without having bought anything. He forbids his wife to lend anything — neither salt nor lamp-wick nor cinnamon nor marjoram nor meal nor garlands nor cakes for sacrifices. "All these trifles," he says, "mount up in a year." To sum up, the coffers of the penurious men are moldy and the keys rust; they wear cloaks which hardly reach the thigh; a very little oil-bottle supplies them for anointing; they have hair cut short and do not put on their shoes until midday; and when they take their cloak to the fuller they urge him to use plenty of earth so that it will not be spotted so soon.

Aside from the unidimensionality of Theophrastus' character types, one has no way of knowing whether the number of types should be ten or one hundred or one thousand. Five centuries later, in fact, the physician Galen (A.D. 130–200) proposed only a fourfold classificatory system based on Hippocrates' doctrine of the four basic "humors" of the body: black bile, an imaginary fluid; yellow bile, a fluid secreted by the liver; phlegm, secreted by mucous membranes; and blood. Galen's theory of *temperament* asserted that an excess of black bile makes a person melancholic; an excess of yellow bile produces a choleric temperament, quick to anger and action; the predominance of phlegm results in a phlegmatic (calm and stolid) individual; and the predominance of the fourth humor, blood, makes one sanguine (warm-hearted and confident). Galen's effort to relate biological characteristics to personality traits anticipates modern theories of the relationship between physique and temperament and the role of biochemical factors in personality. But Galen, like Theophrastus, failed to provide any evidence in support of his particular physical and psychological typology. There was no way to determine or measure the dominant humor or temperament, much less demonstrate that particular humors were associated with particular temperaments (also see Chapter 9).

Unfortunately, measurement in itself does not guarantee a scientific basis for a theory; that basis depends on how the measurements are obtained and the ability of other investigators to produce the same findings. When the measurement of personality is based on the judgments of a human observer, then the measurements are subject to serious distortion by possible observer bias. An observer, when viewing an event or another person, does so selectively, attending to some stimuli in the situation and not to others. There is always a danger that the observer may attend primarily to those events and stimuli that support any hypotheses or biases that may be brought to the situation.

Phrenology

There are several episodes in the history of psychology that exemplify the fallibility of measurements obtained without controlling for observer bias and other sources of error. None is more telling than the pseudoscientific movement of *phrenology* that achieved wide acceptance during the first half of the nineteenth century. Even Edgar Allan Poe attempted to "explain" some of the behavior of his book characters by including a description of their head shapes.

The early phrenologists drew numerous conclusions about an individual's personality from bumps in the shape of the head. They assumed that the mind could be broken down into numerous essential elements, or faculties, of human nature (Franz Joseph Gall, 1758–1828). Each of these faculties corresponded to enlargements of particular areas on the surface of the brain and skull (see Fig. 7.1). While some phrenologists were charlatans, many were genuinely convinced that their discipline was a science that employed the same methods as any other natural science. The following excerpt from O. L. Fowler's "Practical Phrenology" is illustrative:

> Like all other exact sciences, large portions of it was discovered and brought to its present state of perfection, entirely by induction . . . by an observation and a classification of facts . . . the following is the method adopted by Dr. Gall in the discovering of competitiveness . . . after collecting a promiscuous company of ordinary persons from the streets, he assertained from them which were cowardly and which courageous. He then placed the former by themselves, and proceeded to examine and compare the respective developments of the different portions of

Figure 7.1   A typical phrenological chart, showing the correspondence between parts of the skull and personality and behavioral characteristics. (Courtesy, The Francis A. Countway Library of Medicine, Harvard University)

NUMBERING AND DEFINITION
OF THE ORGANS.

1. AMATIVENESS, Sexual and connubial love.
2. PHILOPROGENITIVENESS, Parental love.
3. ADHESIVENESS, Friendship—sociability.
4. UNION FOR LIFE, Love of one only.
5. INHABITIVENESS, Love of home.
5. CONTINUITY, One thing at a time.
6. COMBATIVENESS, Resistance—defence.
7. DESTRUCTIVENESS, Executiveness-force.
8. ALIMENTIVENESS, Appetite, hunger.
9. ACQUISITIVENESS, Accumulation.
10. SECRETIVENESS, Policy—management.
11. CAUTIOUSNESS, Prudence, provision.
12. APPROBATIVENESS, Ambition—display.
13. SELF-ESTEEM, Self-respect—dignity.
14. FIRMNESS, Decision—perseverance.
15. CONSCIENTIOUSNESS, Justice—equity
16. HOPE, Expectation—enterprise.
17. SPIRITUALITY, Intuition--spiritual revery.
18. VENERATION, Devotion—respect.
19. BENEVOLENCE, Kindness—goodness.
20. CONSTRUCTIVENESS Mechanical ingenuity
21. IDEALITY, Refinement—taste—purity
B. SUBLIMITY, Love of grandeur.
22. IMITATION, Copying—patterning.
23. MIRTHFULNESS, Jocoseness—wit—fun.
24. INDIVIDUALITY, Observation.
25. FORM, Recollection of shape.
26. SIZE, Measuring by the eye.
27. WEIGHT, Balancing—climbing.
28. COLOR, Judgment of colors.
29. ORDER, Method—system—arrangement
30. CALCULATION, Mental arithmetic.
31. LOCALITY, Recollection of places.
32. EVENTUALITY, Memory of facts.
33. TIME, Cognizance of duration.
34. TUNE, MUSIC—melody by ear.
35. LANGUAGE, Expression of ideas.
36. CAUSALITY, Applying causes to effects
37. COMPARISON, inductive reasoning.
C. HUMAN NATURE, perception of motives.
D. AGREEABLENESS, Pleasantness— suavity

their heads, until he assertained that not withstanding the great diversity of shape in other parts, yet the heads of the courageous ones all displayed a fullness and thickness just behind the top of the ear, and that the heads of the cowardly were all thin and depressed in that particular region. This discovery . . . was then applied to innumerable other subjects, until its correctness was fully established.

The errors that led Gall to these completely fallacious conclusions are numerous. He used a questionable self-report procedure to determine who was cowardly and who was courageous and neither recorded his measurements nor determined the variability in his groups. Fowler also cites a number of case histories that are testimonials to the remarkable "success" of the phrenologists' approach. We know, of course, that there are great dangers in using anecdotal individual case material as a principal source of evidence. Judging from the popularity of such modern pseudo-sciences as scientology and astrology, the lesson to be learned from phrenology is a difficult one.

THE SCIENTIFIC ERA

The scientific era in the testing of individual differences may have begun with the work of Sir Francis Galton (1822–1911), a cousin of Charles Darwin. In 1869 he published the first edition of *Hereditary Genius,* in which he marshaled evidence that eminence ran in families. He then assumed that this familial pattern was due to the inheritance of ability. Galton investigated many aspects of individual differences, such as the richness and range of verbal associations, and developed mental tests to measure these differences. He also proposed the use of physiological measures of blood pressure and heart rate to assess individual differences in emotionality and temperament.

Galton was able to accomplish his work through the establishment of a laboratory in the South Kensington Museum in London. Each visitor to the museum paid three pence for his or her assessment on a variety of attributes, including strength, breathing capacity, eyesight, and so on. This provided data for over 17,000 individuals, and increased Galton's preoccupation with measuring almost everything. To describe these data quantitatively, Galton invented the concepts of the median and percentiles (see Johnson, et al., 1985).

Later, the work of the French with the mentally retarded led in 1905 to Alfred Binet's (1857–1911) development of a test of intelligence to establish a more accurate diagnosis of this disorder. Intelligence testing had a profound effect on the field of personality in that it highlighted the possibility and the importance of assessing individual differences.

Sir Francis Galton, pioneer in the study of individual differences. (The Granger Collection)

Military needs were a significant stimulus in the development of testing. These World War II recruits are taking an aptitude test. (The Bettmann Archive)

World War I served as an impetus to the development of personality tests. To screen and classify soldiers, army psychologists constructed the first group-administered intelligence test: the Army Alpha. And since it was not feasible for each recruit to receive an individual psychiatric interview to screen mental disorders, a test including more than one hundred items was developed based on questions that would have been asked in such an interview. This first personality questionnaire was the Woodworth Personal Data Sheet. The test included the following items (Hollingworth, 1920):

- Do you usually feel well and strong?
- Do you ever walk in your sleep?
- Do you have nightmares?

A "no" answer to the first item and a "yes" answer to the second and third items were believed to be indications of psychopathology. If there were many responses in this direction, the soldier was seen by a psychiatrist.

The 1920s and 1930s witnessed the development of a great variety of personality tests, some designed to assess psychological disturbance and others to measure individual differences in intelligence, personal values, and personality traits. These tests used increasingly sophisticated techniques, including complex methodologies that supposedly permitted the investigator to uncover the basic structure of personality.

Among the obstacles faced by test developers is that the "data" are typically provided by verbal reports of the respondents. Freud found that many of the reports of his patients were inaccurate because they were not consciously aware of the truth. In a similar manner, many of the results of psychological tests are invalid because the truth either is consciously withheld or is not consciously known. Thus, test developers had to construct tests that would overcome these difficulties. The methodology in the area of psychological testing has become more sophisticated over time because of our increasing scientific knowledge; such advancement is less characteristic of the area of general personality theory. Psychological testing is now one of the major subdivisions within the field of personality.

One of the hallmarks of science is measurement. Psychologists, no less than physicists, chemists, and biologists, need to quantify the variables they wish to investigate. That quantification can consist of crude statements of mere "presence" or "absence" or quite precise terms such as "twice as much." When one deals with traits such as dependency and introversion, the task of measurement becomes especially difficult and challenging. Indeed, some would argue that the task is impossible. According to one eminent scholar (Barzun, 1954, p. 143), "the love of a parent for a child, or any other kind of attachment, repulsion, fear, joy, faith . . . these are realities that are visible, non-material and non-measurable." Yet these are precisely the "realities" that are at the very heart of the study of personality.

Psychologists recognize that personality measures cannot do full justice to the richness and individuality of human beings. However, relatively meaningful measurements can be made. Quantification is essential because it both permits comparison between people on given dimensions and also allows one to determine which factors are associated with these personality dimensions and how strong the associations are.

The measurement of personality traits is a major scientific challenge. There are no X rays available that will penetrate our psyche and reveal our innermost hopes, secrets, and passions. Useful measures have been developed for some facets of personality but not for others. No measure of personality is perfect; psychologists are engaged in an ongoing effort to improve and refine their measuring procedures and tests.

RELIABILITY AND VALIDITY

There are two critical features of a measure that determine its quality: reliability and validity. *Reliability* refers to the consistency or measurement error of the measuring instrument. A test of introversion that yielded very different scores for a sample of individuals every time they were tested would have low reliability and would not be very useful. *Validity* refers to the degree to which a measure actually assesses what it is intended to assess. The measure of introversion could be highly reliable but would lack validity if it were precisely assessing anxiety or fatigue or nonconformity — attributes other than introversion. A major concern of personality investigators is the reliability and validity of the measures they use.

Reliability

Measurement error occurs in almost all forms of observation. It is assumed that for each quality we attempt to measure, there is a *true* score; the researcher's task is to make an observation that is used as the measure of this true quality. The *observed score* is usually not exactly the same as the true score. The deviation of the observed score from the true score is regarded as *measurement error*. In some fields of inquiry the measurement error may be quite small, whereas in other fields it tends to be great. An example of a situation in which measurement error might be minimal would be the measurement of height. In this case there is a standard measurement device such as a ruler or yardstick. The true height of an object or a person might be the number of inches it stands above the floor. Using a yardstick, it is possible to obtain a measure of height which is close to, if not exactly the same as, the true score. Even in this example, however, there might still be some sources of error. For instance, the person using the yardstick might have made

Height can be measured accurately because a valid and reliable measuring instrument exists. Unfortunately, in the study of personality traits, such unambiguous yardsticks are not yet available. (© Peter Vandermark)

some small error in applying the stick to the second three feet after the first three feet had been marked. In addition, he or she might have recorded, say, 69 inches even though the true measurement was 69½ inches, or have made some clerical error in recording the measurement. All things considered, however, there is little error in the recording of height, because height is clearly defined and can be measured quite simply.

Contrast this with some of the qualities that the social sciences attempt to measure. Usually, the concept under consideration is not defined in terms of any single measure. There is no unambiguous yardstick to tell us how depressed or aggressive someone is, but we can attempt to build yardsticks to measure these characteristics. Developing a measure that correctly assesses what it is supposed to is a problem of *validity*. Assessing the error in application of the yardstick is a problem in *reliability*.

The scores yielded by a measure are of interest only if they vary between people. If they did not vary, then all persons would be scored exactly the same. However, not all of the variability in a score is really what we want it to be. We are interested only in true variability, or real differences between people. Usually, some observed variability is unwanted, random variability, or *error variance*. The study of reliability can help determine how much of what is being measured is such unwanted error.

Sources of Error.   There are many potential sources of error. Concepts like depression and aggressiveness include many kinds of behaviors and ways of thinking; it is unlikely that any small set of items will accurately represent all that is implied by these concepts. The first major component of measurement error occurs when items do not fully represent a concept.

A second source of error results from inconsistent use of the measure by different test takers. For example, a questionnaire may contain ambiguous items that permit varying interpretations by different individuals. On the item "I like to fight," respondents are permitted two alternatives: "Yes" or "No." Some test takers might interpret this item as referring to fist fights; others, to verbal arguments. Some might read standing up for one's rights into the item, and some who like to box in amateur prizefights, but dislike fighting in other contexts, might be uncertain how to answer the question. And, if a third alternative to the item, such as "?" or "Unsure," were permitted, as is sometimes the case, there might be significant individual differences in the tendency to use this alternative. In fact, some people tend to mark items "Yes" when they are confused, while others mark them "No."

A third source of error is introduced when a measure is used in different settings. For instance, a person might score as more depressed if a test were given in a hospital than if it were administered in a private clinic or at home. All of these problems cause a measure to become less accurate than is desirable. In effect, measuring aggressiveness with an unreliable measure would be like trying to measure height with a rubber yardstick: sometimes the yardstick would be stretched too long, sometimes it would be squeezed too short (Nunnally, 1978).

Since the turn of the century, psychologists have attempted to formalize theories of measurement error and to express how error affects other aspects of investigations.

Variability. Reliability is one of the most fundamental concepts in science. If personality measures are unreliable, it becomes impossible to find correlations between the variables that are assessed by these measures. Suppose, for example, we hypothesize that people with high anxiety have a poorer memory of immediate events than people with low anxiety. Suppose further that every time we administer the measure, with repeated administrations only a few minutes apart, the scores vary so widely that the same person sometimes obtains the highest anxiety score, a middle-range anxiety score, or the lowest anxiety score. Since individual scores on the anxiety measure are so unstable, it would be impossible to establish a correlation between memory and anxiety, even if the hypothesis relating memory and anxiety were true.

Another way of describing our anxiety measure is in terms of the meaning of the different individual scores obtained on the measure. Let us suppose that some individuals obtain very high scores on the measure, others score in the middle range, and others fall into the lower range. These score differences can reflect the exact or true differences among individuals, if the measure is completely accurate, or they can reflect measurement error. The variability, which is based on individual differences, can therefore be divided into two components: *true variability* (representing real differences) and *error variability*. The reliability of a measure can be stated in terms of the relationship between these two components of variability; the greater the proportion of true variability relative to error variability, the more reliable the measure. This relationship can be expressed in simple quantitative form as follows:

$$\text{Reliability} = \frac{\text{True variability}}{\text{True variability} + \text{Error variability}} \quad \text{or}$$

$$= \frac{\text{True variability}}{\text{Observed variability}}$$

As can be seen in this formula, reliability expresses the proportion of the total variation that is true variability. The greater the error, the smaller the reliability ratio will be.

It is, of course, desirable to improve measures so that the proportion of total variability that is true variability increases, while the proportion that is error decreases. Unfortunately, it is no simple matter to find out which aspects of variability are true and which aspects are error.

Evaluating Reliability. There are many methods for evaluating reliability, with the choice of method depending on the potential source of measurement error. One source of error is time sampling. Errors arise from time sampling when a test is given at only one point in time and when a different score might be obtained if the test were given at some other time. Differences in an individual's responses might arise because of differences in mood, in interpersonal relationships, in physical condition, and in myriad other factors that can influence responses on a set of personality items. For example, consider the following items:

1. I like to spend a good deal of time by myself.
2. I feel uncomfortable in large social gatherings.
3. I have many friends.

Let us assume that, at time A, life is running fairly smoothly for a given extrovert. At time B, however, he or she has just experienced a very distressful break in a close relationship. At time A, the extrovert responds "No" to items 1 and 2 and "Yes" to item 3. But at time B, because of preoccupation with the disrupted relationship, he or she responds "Yes" to items 1 and 2 and, although hesitant, still responds "Yes" to item 3. Another extrovert, who might have responded in the direction of extroversion at time A, could have just moved to a new community at time B. He or she might have no friends in the community and might have just attended a social gathering that was cliquish and unresponsive to strangers. While still answering "No" to item 1, this person would answer "Yes" to item 2 and "No" to item 3. There are many other factors that can influence the consistency of responses from time A to time B: inattentiveness on one of the testing occasions; different interpretations of an ambiguous item (Does "friends" mean "close friends"? How many is "many friends"?); the sex of the tester; the degree of rapport with the tester; ad infinitum. One of the reasons for having many items on a test is to reduce the influence of changes on a few items on the overall test score.

For a measure to be reliable, there must be some individual stability in the responses given. If people changed their responses every time a test was administered, the measure would be highly unreliable. A quantitative determination of a test's degree of reliability can be made by giving the measure on two occasions to the same group of individuals. The correlation between scores obtained at two times is an estimate of *test-retest reliability*. However, there are certain inherently unstable personality attributes for which the test-retest method of assessing reliability may be inappropriate. Emotions and moods such as joy, sadness, anger, fear, boredom, and fatigue are expected to fluctuate even though there may be individual differences in the basic tendency to be happy, angry, bored, or tired.

A second method of determining reliability, which is applicable to measures of mood and emotional change, is evaluating the *internal consistency* of a test, using a variety of methods. One method is *split-half* reliability in which test items are divided into two groups (such as odd- and even-numbered items), and the correlation between scores for these halves is obtained. The higher the split-half correlation, the greater the reliability.

Reliability of Observations.   In addition to the reliability of tests, psychologists are also interested in the reliability of behavioral observations, which are used in many kinds of situations. Behavioral observations have the advantage of being closer to the actual behaviors of individuals than self-report questionnaires. However, if they are to be useful, they must meet the same criteria of reliability. Here the sources of error are associated with different observers' recording the same behavior and with time-sampling issues.

The Skinnerian psychologist who is studying the effects of a particular reinforcement program on attentive behaviors in a primary-grade classroom needs to define attention in terms of behaviors that can be reliably scored by classroom observers. The investigator who wishes to determine whether a questionnaire measure of aggression in hospitalized patients is related to the actual frequency of aggressive behaviors observed on the ward is confronted with a similar problem. If a single observer is used, it is important that the observer score the same behavior in the same way whenever it occurs. Inconsistency in observer scoring can become especially problematic when different observers are used. To ensure the reliability of observations, observers typically are required to take a training program in which they practice the observational scoring system and correct inconsistent scoring of the same behavior before the observational procedure is used in an actual experiment.

In addition to minimizing potential observer error, it is also important to observe representative samples of behavior. If some preschool children are aggressive primarily before mealtime and others when they arrive each morning after being left by the parent who has brought them, it is important that both of these time periods are sampled in addition to other times.

Validity

It is not acceptable for scientific psychology to merely offer opinions about human behavior; psychologists must substantiate their claims, just as lawyers must provide evidence for the particular positions they advocate. There are many personality tests and it is important that psychologists become good consumers of these materials, which requires careful evaluation of the evidence used to support the claims of any given test.

Validity defines the meaning of a test or measure. What does it mean to have a test that measures anxiety, moral values, leadership potential, manic-depressive psychosis, or the likelihood that one will fail a flight training program? The meaning, or validity, of a test of anxiety is determined by the behaviors considered to be indicative of anxiety that the test uncovers. Thus, high scorers on a test of anxiety might be more likely than low scorers to forget painful events, to manifest increased heart rate and trembling of the hands while taking an examination, and to be heavy smokers. If high scorers were no different from low scorers on these and other measures, our anxiety test would have no validity. Alternatively, if the anxiety test was found to be correlated with aggressive behaviors and not with anxiety indicators, we would then have to change its name and its claim.

Evidence for validity is derived from demonstrating clear associations between a test and other measures of behavior. These associations or correlations define the meaning of the test. The same principle applies to our test of flight-training success even though the criterion is more evident than in the case of anxiety. Does our test predict success and failure in any kind of flight training context, or only in one particular military flight school? The more behaviors and measures that are associated with a test, the more confident we can be and the more things we are willing to say about its connotations. There are several types of validity that give different types of evidence about the significance of tests: content, criterion, and construct validity.

Content Validity. A test has *content validity* if it adequately covers the content area it is supposed to measure. For example, if you are being tested on what you learned in a personality course, the test is content valid to the extent that it represents all the material covered in the course. Traditionally, content validity has been of greatest concern in the area of educational testing. However, there are many instances in personality testing in which content validity is important. For example, if it is concluded that someone is compulsive solely on the basis of responses to a set of test questions, then, at the very least, there must be some assurance that the items on the test of compulsiveness adequately represent the behaviors encompassed by the diagnostic label "compulsive."

Content validity is the only type of validity for which the evidence is logical rather than statistical; inferences are often more about test construction than about test scores (Tenopyr, 1977). Establishing whether a test has content validity with regard to the inferences a test constructor wants to make requires good logic and intuitive skills. Establishing content validity for tests of knowledge, such as spelling competency, is more straightforward than for a test of a personality dimension like anxiety, where there is less agreement about the range of content that the test should sample. However, there can also be disagreement over the content validity of a test of knowledge. For instance, students often disagree with an instructor about whether the items on a particular examination adequately represented the material covered in lectures and readings. As will be shown in the following sections, other types of validity depend more on statistical methods, such as correlation, and less on intuition. Content validity is insufficient in itself to establish the validity of a test; other types of validity must also be used as the basis of making inferences about validity.

Criterion Validity. Some psychological tests have a very specific purpose; many are used exclusively to make predictions. A good example of a test used for a predictive purpose is the Scholastic Aptitude Test (SAT). Most of you took SATs to allow colleges and universities to evaluate your potential. To justify using SATs, the Educational Testing Service and the College Board, which are responsible for this instrument, had to provide some evidence that the test really was successful in forecasting future success in college. To do this they chose some index of success, such as grade-point average (GPA) during the first year of college, as the criterion against which the test was to be validated; thus the term *criterion validity*. The variables used to forecast the criterion are called predictor variables.

The correlation between the predictor variables and the criterion defines the criterion validity of a test.

Tests should not be labeled as simply valid or invalid. Validity is not absolute; rather, it defines what can be inferred on the basis of a test or measure. Usually, tests have some validity for making certain specific statements. The SAT example will help illustrate this point. At one large California university, it was shown that high school SAT scores correlated .40 with success in the first year of college. This means that the SAT can be expected to forecast about 16 percent of the variability in the first-year college GPA and that 84 percent of the variability cannot be explained by SAT scores.

Is the SAT valid for predicting who will do well in the first year of college? Yes, the test predicts performance better than just guessing. However, most of the variation in college performance is left unexplained. If the validity or the correlation between SAT score and first-year college GPA had been 1.0, then the SAT would be considered the perfect predictor of college success. Thus, a wise college might want to continue using the SAT because it gives them one significant predictor of college success, allowing admissions officers to make better predictions about who will do well in college than they would have been able to make without the test information. However, the Educational Testing Service also advises colleges that the evidence for validity suggests they consider other information about potential students in addition to SAT scores.

When a test is used to predict some criterion that will occur in the future, the problem is one of *predictive validity*. The SAT example is a problem in predictive validity because the test is given to high school students to predict how well they will do in college. Studies of predictive validity are also common in industry, where tests are given to potential employees to predict which people will have the most success on the job.

A related type of criterion validity does not attempt to forecast what will happen in the future. Instead, the criterion measurement and the assessment of the predictor may occur at the same point in time. This is called *concurrent validity*. The Minnesota Multiphasic Personality Inventory (MMPI), a measure discussed more extensively in the next chapter, is an example of a test based *primarily* on concurrent validity. The MMPI is used to diagnose specific forms of psychopathology and covers both the less severe forms of mental disturbance (neuroses) and more severe forms in which there is disruption in thought processes and contact with reality (psychoses). For example, the test might be used to screen a large sample of military recruits. On the basis of scores on particular subscales of the test, some recruits might be diagnosed as schizophrenic (a psychosis characterized by disordered thinking and a split, or dissociation, between one's thoughts and feelings). This diagnosis might be validated through concurrent psychiatric interviews. The MMPI might also be used for predictive purposes, e.g., to predict which students, independent of college grades and measures of ability, will succeed in a clinical psychology graduate training program. We often find both concurrent and predictive procedures used to validate a test.

Construct Validity. About twenty years ago, psychologist Zick Rubin (1970) wanted to develop a measure of romantic love (See Chapter 18). To do this, he had to define exactly what it was that he was attempting to measure. The problem Rubin faced was quite perplexing. After reviewing what many popular authors, playwrights, and famous people had to say about love, Rubin discovered that nearly everyone had his or her own definition. The index of *Bartlett's Familiar Quotations* lists more citations for *love* (769) than for any other word except *man* (843) (Rubin, 1973). Among all these quotations about love, there were some common themes, but no standard definition.

The problem Rubin faced is quite common among psychologists. Frequently, we want to measure something but are not clear about exactly what it is we want to measure. Measuring the width of a table or the length of a car is straightforward because we can directly observe cars and tables and there is little disagreement about what their length and width are. There are also standardized instruments for such measurement, like the familiar yardstick. The problems of psychological measurement are much more difficult because psychologists try to measure unobservable and ambiguous constructs like assertiveness or intelligence. In *construct validity,* there is a simultaneous attempt to define these constructs and to develop assessment devices to measure them.

There is a constant interplay between the validation of the measure of a psychological construct and the specification of the properties of the construct. Consider a questionnaire such as the Repression-Sensitization (R-S) scale, designed to differentiate individuals who tend to be repressors and those who tend to be sensitizers (Byrne, 1961) in their defenses against anxiety (see Chapter 3). Repressors are hypothesized as using a cluster of defense strategies characterized by avoidance of a threatening stimulus. Thus, they can be expected to deny threats; to forget painful, anxiety-evoking events; and to have difficulty verbalizing feelings of anxiety. Sensitizers, in contrast, are hypothesized as being especially wary of and attuned to possible threatening stimuli. They are likely to be overly preoccupied with threat, to be worriers, and to be obsessed with ideas and possibilities that evoke anxiety. They try to cope with threat, not by avoidance, but by preoccupation with the potential consequences of danger. They err on the side of alertness.

The measurement of this construct of repression-sensitization simultaneously poses two sets of issues. One set of issues has to do with the specification and demonstration of the properties of the construct. Does the concept apply to all threatening events or only to particular kinds of threats, such as threats to self-esteem? What are the specific ways in which avoidance and sensitization are manifested behaviorally? Do individuals consistently avoid or consistently behave in an oversensitized manner? Are some people repressors when faced with certain threatening stimuli and sensitizers when confronted with another type of threat? A second, related set of issues has to do with the validity of the Repression-Sensitization scale in differentiating between individuals who display the characteristics of repressors and those who manifest the characteristics of sensitizers. The two sets of issues are interconnected because, in order to study the construct of repression-sensitization, we must first have some way of determining the degree to which an individual is a repressor or a sensitizer. So we begin with one test that we have reason to believe might be a useful measure of this personality dimension. As we find out more about the correlates of the measure with other behaviors, we learn more about the properties of the construct. On the basis of a number of research studies (e.g., Bell and Byrne, 1978; Haley, 1974), it has been possible to gain a better understanding of the validity of both the R-S scale and the repression-sensitization construct.

It is evident that the construct validation of a test is a complex process with several steps. First, the concept of interest is carefully considered and items are generated that represent various aspects of the concept. At this point, the real work of construct validation begins. In a series of studies, scores on the test or measure are correlated with scores on other tests, measures, and behaviors. Each time a correlation is demonstrated, the meaning of the test is further defined and amplified. For example, if a measure of test anxiety is found to correlate $-.40$ with grade-point average and $+.30$ with number of illnesses experienced per year, then two new implications for the anxiety scale are found. The observed correlations define what the test measures; each time a new correlation is observed, the test takes on some new meaning. In this way, the test itself and the underlying theory or significance of the test develop together (Kaplan and Saccuzzo, 1981).

Construct validation is a never-ending process, in many ways similar to amassing evidence in support of a scientific theory. The researcher continually advances hypotheses, such as "If I am really measuring anxiety, then I would expect those scoring high on the anxiety scale to have more psychosomatic problems than those scoring low on the scale." This hypothesis is then evaluated in a systematic study, with each new study adding some meaning to the test.

In construct validation, two types of correlation are important to observe: convergent and discriminant. *Convergent validity* comes from demonstrating that a test measures the same thing as other tests. However, if the test correlates too well with other measures, then it might be unnecessary. If, for example, our anxiety scale correlated perfectly with one used for psychosomatic illness, then it might not be needed; the psychosomatic measure could be used in its place.

Discriminant validity, on the other hand, establishes that a test is measuring a different construct than that assessed by other measures. For example, if the anxiety scale correlated highly with a well-established test of achievement, it could be measuring achievement motivation instead of test anxiety. But a moderate or low correlation would tell us that the tests are distinctive and thus that the anxiety scale is measuring something other than achievement motivation.

How Low Reliability Affects Validity

As previously indicated, a scientific investigator is working under a handicap when reliability is less than perfect. In most studies, one attempts to find relationships between variables. Finding these relationships is greatly hampered if one or more of the variables is measured unreliably. Over the years, psychologists have systematically defined the ways in which measurement error serves to hamper other aspects of research. To have validity, there must be a reasonably high correlation between two measures of a construct. An earlier example of the relation between a test of anxiety and a measure of immediate memory indicated that, when one of the measures is not reliable, the observed correlation will be lowered. This means that the correlation is less than would be expected if the quantities were measured without error.

Measurement theory allows one to estimate the maximum correlation between variables if one or both variables is assumed to have been measured with some error. For example, if television violence and viewer aggression were correlated perfectly in nature but the reliability of each measure were .60, then the observed correlation would be only .60. Thus, 64 percent of the variance or predictability of one measure from the other would have been lost due to measurement error. A measure with a reliability of .50 on one variable would reveal only a moderate relationship with any other measure, even if the true association between them were perfect (+1.0). This tells us that, without reliability, it is impossible to obtain convincing evidence for validity. In other words, reliability is required in order to demonstrate that a measure has meaning.

Summary

1. The field of testing has a long history, dating back to early China. An especially important contributor was Sir Francis Galton.

2. The first questionnaire measure of personality arose out of a need during World War I to develop a test that could be used to screen soldiers for emotional disturbances.

3. *Reliability* refers to the degree of *measurement error,* or the degree to which the observed score deviates from the true score. Sources of error include inconsistent interpretation of items by test takers and the effects of the testing environment on test answers.

4. Types of reliability include *test-retest reliability,* in which the source of unreliability is differences in testing times, and *internal consistency,* which refers to the degree of consistency within a test at any given time period.

5. *Validity* defines the meaning of a test or measure; it indicates whether a test is in fact measuring what it is supposed to measure.

6. *Content validity* refers to whether a test adequately represents the content it is supposed to assess. The evidence for content validity is logical rather than statistical.

7. *Criterion validity* refers to the degree to which a test predicts (correlates with) a subsequent factor (*predictive validity*), as well as the degree to which a test is associated with other indexes that exist at the same point in time (*concurrent validity*).

8. A more complex type of validity is known as *construct validity*. In *construct validation* the meaning of a construct and the test measuring the construct are developed simultaneously. Test validation provides better understanding of the construct, while elaboration of the construct results in changes in the test.

9. Reliability places constraints on validity; for an instrument to have validity, measurement error must be minimized.

Thought Questions

1. What advice would you give teachers who want to make their examinations more reliable and valid?

2. Describe a test that would have appropriate content validity as an instrument for selecting a good teacher or a good executive.

3. SAT scores predict subsequent grade-point averages, but leave much of the variation in grades unaccounted for. What factors might be responsible for this less-than-perfect validity? Could a test be constructed to assess these other factors?

8 | Personality Assessment

Psychologists frequently use tests to obtain information about clients. There are now thousands of personality tests that attempt to measure every imaginable human characteristic. It would not be feasible to describe each of them, but we will focus on some of the best-known general approaches to testing and the most widely recognized tests.

With few exceptions, traditional approaches to assessment assume that human characteristics can be measured independently of the situation or environment. If, for example, someone scores high on a personality assessment instrument of outgoingness, it is assumed that this individual is outgoing in many different situations and that the tested characteristic is one that the person brings to any situation. Such environment-independent characteristics are typically referred to as *traits,* or enduring tendencies to respond in a particular manner.

Personality measures designed to assess traits also view these characteristics of personality as *stable over time.* The developers of many measures assume, as did Freud and other psychoanalytic theorists, that personality is formed early in life. Once characteristics are established, they are not expected to change significantly. If, for example, a personality test reveals that Fred is aggressive, then it is expected that Fred will also be aggressive in the future. Fred will supposedly not display aggression for one month, followed by two months of passivity, followed by one week of aggression, and so on. The aggression should occur with some stability, or it will be concluded that Fred is unpredictable.

Most personality assessment techniques also assume that all humans possess the *same* characteristics. People differ from one another only in the degree to which they possess these common traits, such as anxiety, aggression, or the need for achievement. On the other hand, there are some personality assessment techniques that allow for the possibility that, while certain characteristics exist to some degree in all humans, there are some specific characteristics that may occur in only a few. For example, perhaps only a few people display true altruism, the sacrifice of personal pleasure for the betterment of others. This assumption is consistent with the position that humans are at the same time like all other humans, like some other humans, and like no other humans. In addition to these assumptions, the predominant view is that an individual's personality represents the sum total of the variety and degrees of the relatively stable, consistent traits that he or she possesses.

Most personality assessment instruments are referred to more simply as personality tests. Traditionally, two major types of personality tests have evolved: objective and projective. In recent years, however, a number of newer approaches to human personality assessment have appeared. The two major types of personality tests, as well as the newer approaches (which are not really "tests" in the traditional sense) are discussed in this chapter.

OBJECTIVE PERSONALITY TESTS

You no doubt already have a good idea of what an *objective* test is; most college instructors give objective exams, with questions of the multiple-choice or true-false variety. This type of question requires that students recognize or remember items, rather than produce anything original, as in a term paper or essay test. In an objective test, one usually chooses from two or more designated alternatives. The response can be made on a standard answer sheet and can be machine- or computer-scored. The scoring is objective rather than subjective, with no judgments or evaluations required.

Like objective college exams, objective personality tests provide a written stimulus. The test taker is then asked to choose among two or more alternative responses, or to compare one written stimulus with one or more alternatives, selecting one or more of these choices according to a set of criteria. In some personality tests, people are asked to indicate which of two statements is more characteristic of them. For example, the following pair of alternatives appears in a test (the internal-external (I-E) locus of control scale) designed to assess individual differences in whether people believe that one can influence and control rewards and punishments or that they are externally controlled (see Chapter 17):

1. Many people can be described as victims of circumstances.
2. What happens to other people is pretty much of their own making.

The test taker is asked to select the alternative in which he or she more strongly believes. Another test provides three statements and asks the individual to indicate which is most and which is least characteristic. In all objective personality tests, the stimulus is a word, phrase, or statement, and the response requires selection among provided alternatives. Unlike objective college exams, however, there are no right or wrong answers. Subjects simply recall or determine the responses they believe are the best according to the instructions given. The test usually contains a number of items related to each of several personality characteristics. All items related to a single personality characteristic are known collectively as a *scale*. Some objective personality tests contain only one scale; however, most consist of several. If a person marks a greater than average number of items in the appropriate or scored direction on a scale, then that person is assumed to possess a greater than average degree of the trait measured by that scale.

Although they are widely used, there are many problems with objective personality tests. Early objective personality tests were particularly crude and inadequate by today's standards. But even the best of modern objective personality tests are not without recognized flaws. Psychologists continually strive to improve them, either through revision of existing scales or through development of new ones. Efforts to develop accurate objective personality tests have produced four major models or approaches to objective personality testing, each with its own unique assumptions.

Tests Based on Face Validity

Personality testing was used on a large scale in the United States during World War I. These early tests assumed that a person's response to an objective test item could be taken at face value. This assumption of *face validity* viewed the content of a test item as a straightforward indicator of a person's personality. If a person endorsed the item "I am outgoing," then it was assumed that this person was indeed outgoing. Linked to the assumption of face validity are the additional assumptions that people are honest, aware of their own characteristics, objective in evaluating these characteristics, and interpret the word *outgoing* in the same way as others taking the test and evaluating the test responses.

The first objective personality test to assume face validity of test responses (see Chapter 7) was the Woodworth Personal Data Sheet (Woodworth, 1920). By the 1930s, however, many of the problems with the face validity approach had become apparent. Some of the problems were that people differ in their interpretations of an item's meaning and are limited in their ability to accurately observe and objectively report their own behavior. Other problems concern honesty. Tests based on face validity assume that a person is so open, flexible, and nondefensive that he or she responds as honestly as possible to each item. However, when tests are used to select people for jobs or, more dramatically, in criminal cases, honesty is not always in the test taker's best interests!

Closely related to the honesty of a test response is the notion of *social desirability*. A person might be honest but, without even being totally aware of it, might endorse the response believed to be the one the examiner wants to hear or the response that reflects most favorably on the subject. Edwards (1957, 1962, 1964) has most clearly articulated the importance of this factor in a person's response to an objective personality test. He argued that the meaning of any response on an objective personality test is influenced by the number of acceptable, expected, flattering, and complimentary responses that are selected. When endorsing the socially desirable rather than the true or realistic alternative response, the test score simply reflects the individual's need to present desired and culturally valued qualities. If correct, Edwards's notion of social desirability suggests that objective personality tests measure the need to be accepted and approved, which tends to be confounded with the other behavioral tendencies that the tester wants to assess. Although not without criticism (see Block, 1965; Norman, 1967), the concept of social desirability has been a problem with which practically every major objective personality test has had to cope.

Related to the concept of social desirability is the problem of response tendencies or biases. A *response bias* is the tendency to respond in a particular way, regardless of item content. Some individuals, for example, tend to agree or to say "Yes" regardless of the content of an item (see Jackson and Messick, 1962; Messick and Jackson, 1961). This tendency to agree with or mark "True" on an item regardless of the item's content is called *acquiescence*. There are many other biased response dispositions as well. For example, the corresponding negativistic response bias is the tendency to say "No," while the tendency to endorse the opposite of what a person believes to be true is known as *oppositional bias*. These response tendencies may in themselves reflect an individual's personality characteristics; e.g., acquiescence may reflect a tendency toward conformity and compliance, while a negativistic response bias may indicate hostile, oppositional tendencies. However, the main implication of response bias is that objective personality tests may measure factors other than those the test constructor intended to measure; that is, the possibility always exists that these response patterns have influenced a person's test score to such an extent that the meaning of a test score is subject to some doubt.

Empirical Approaches

The psychologists who developed early personality tests were unaware of problems like social desirability and response bias. However, years of research gradually eroded faith in face validity approaches to personality testing. Twenty years of experience with these early tests gave way to the introduction of various *empirical* approaches, which began around 1940 (see Dahlstrom, 1969). Objective personality tests based on face validity were replaced by tests such as the Minnesota Multiphasic Personality Inventory (MMPI), Cattell's Sixteen Personality-Factor Questionnaire (16 P-F), and other personality measures whose validity was based on research procedures and findings.

Objective personality tests vary in the extent to which they are based on theoretical considerations as well as empirical findings. Some tests are almost completely empirically based, with the theoretical rationale for the content and structure of the test items irrelevant. The critical question is the relationship of test responses to some criterion; e.g., a test of depression should differentiate depressed and nondepressed populations, and a test of the successful salesperson's personality should differentiate known groups of good and poor salespeople.

The empirical approach to objective personality testing attempts to find the behavioral correlates of certain test responses. For example, a test constructor interested in developing a measure of aggressiveness might identify a group of people assumed to be aggressive because they have been in three or more fights during the past year. Then a second group of nonaggressive people might be selected from individuals who have never been in a fight. A set of items is given to both groups and the items or scales marked more often by the aggressive than by the nonaggressive individuals could be used as an indicator or "test" of aggressive tendencies. It need not matter what the actual content of the items is; perhaps aggressive individuals tend to endorse the item "I like carrots" more often than the nonaggressive. This nevertheless becomes a valid test indicator of aggressiveness under the empirical approach. In most instances, however, one can perceive the connection between items on empirically based tests and the criterion behavior.

The MMPI. The *Minnesota Multiphasic Personality Inventory (MMPI)* is perhaps the best-known and most widely used empirically based personality test. This test was introduced at a time when the problems facing objective personality tests seemed all but insurmountable. The MMPI not only came to the rescue, but actually kindled new interest in objective personality testing by providing solutions to the problems intrinsic to the earlier, face validity approach.

The MMPI is a true-false questionnaire consisting of more than five hundred self-reference items. The subject is instructed to respond true or false to each item as it applies to him or her. The items vary widely in content, such as:

- I like to read news magazines.
- I never had trouble falling asleep.
- People are out to get me.

The test contains four validity scales and ten clinical scales. The validity scales of the MMPI were designed to meet the problems inherent in its predecessors. The first validity scale, the "cannot say" scale, records the number of items in which no response is made. This scale is related to the person's level of defensiveness, that is, his or her tendency to avoid revealing personal information. As more items are omitted, the validity of the MMPI results becomes increasingly questionable. If too many items are omitted, then no effort is made to interpret the test, since what has been measured cannot be a true reflection of the person's personality. In more recent uses of the MMPI, respondents are encouraged not to omit any of the items.

A second validity scale, perhaps the most important MMPI scale, is the F scale. The F scale consists of sixty-four items that are rarely endorsed by the general population, such as:

- Everything tastes the same.
- I see things, animals, or people around me that others do not see.

The items cover many content areas, ranging from paranoid thinking to hostility and poor health habits. On the average, the general population endorses about four F-scale items per test (Dahlstrom, Welsh, and Dahlstrom, 1972), while psychiatrically disturbed individuals might endorse eight to sixteen of them, reflecting the nature and severity of their psychological impairment. Furthermore, persons who see themselves as in need of assistance may indicate this by responding to as many as twenty-five of the sixty-four F-scale items in the scored direction (Graham, 1977). However, even the most severely emotionally disturbed individual rarely, if ever, would have enough symptoms to justify marking more than sixteen to eighteen items, and even this many endorsements on the F scale is questionable.

By determining the number of F-scale items endorsed in the scored direction, it becomes possible to evaluate possible response tendencies, as well as a person's approach to the test. If the subject fails to comply with the instructions or cannot read and understand the items, then about half the F-scale items would be endorsed, since these problems result in a random response to the items. In a similar manner, if a person deliberately fakes, in order to appear more disturbed than is warranted, then again there would be far more items endorsed in the scored direction than would realistically be justified.

The F scale is used in combination with the two remaining MMPI validity scales, the K and the "Lie" (L) scales. The K scale is related to social desirability and includes items like:

- At times I feel like swearing.
- At times I feel like smashing things.

Extremely high scores ("No" responses) suggest a defensive approach in which the person is trying to fake a "good" profile. The L scale is similar to the K scale, but much less subtle. An example of an L-scale item is "I always tell the truth." It is assumed that everyone has lied at some time. Thus, responding "Yes," in which case the person claims that he or she never lies, would in fact indicate that the person is lying in order to look good. With the use of these validity scales, errors in measuring a person's personality can be markedly reduced so that the test user can feel more confident that the test scores actually reflect designated behavioral tendencies or personality characteristics.

The ten clinical scales of the MMPI (see Table 8.1) are used to measure specific personality disorders and related personality characteristics. It should be noted, however, that the MMPI was originally designed to measure abnormal or disturbed personality. Eight of the clinical scales of the MMPI were formed by the criterion-keying method, in which, as we mentioned, groups of people known to manifest a certain abnormal behavior, such as depression or schizophrenia, were given the items of the MMPI. Items that were more frequently endorsed in a certain direction by these groups than by a control group were then selected to form a scale that purportedly measured the characteristics (e.g., depression or schizophrenia) of the criterion groups. In other words, each scale consisted of those items discriminating the criterion groups from the normal group.

In spite of its apparent strengths and widespread use in clinical settings (Lubin, Wallis, and Paine, 1971), the MMPI also has a number of important limitations and problems. A detailed analysis of its limitations in terms of the various types of reliability reveals that test-retest reliability over short periods of time is acceptable, but often marginally so. And for longer time intervals, there is substantial unreliability. For most of the scales, individual scores are not stable

Table 8.1   The meaning of the clinical scales of the MMPI

Scale number	Scale name	Important meanings
1	Hypochondriasis	Preoccupation with body and fears of illness
2	Depression	Symptomatic depression; dissatisfaction; low morale
3	Hysteria	Immaturity; denial of problem
4	Psychopathic deviate	Delinquency; antisocial tendencies; family problems
5	Masculinity-femininity	Male and female interests
6	Paranoia	Suspiciousness; hostility; paranoid symptoms such as delusions (false beliefs)
7	Psychasthenia	Anxiety; psychological discomfort
8	Schizophrenia	Alienation; bizarre behavior or thoughts
9	Hypomania	Elevated mood; hyperactivity
10	Social introversion	Tendency to withdraw or become uninvolved in social relationships

Source: Adapted from *The MMPI-2: Assessing Personality and Psychopathology,* Second Edition, by John R. Graham. Copyright © 1993 by Oxford University Press, Inc. Used by permission of the publisher.

(Dahlstrom and Welsh, 1960). The reasons for the poor long-term reliability of the MMPI have not been clearly established. One important factor that must be taken into consideration in interpreting the long-term unreliability of the MMPI is its dual use as a measure of psychopathology and as a measure of personality attributes. One would expect fluctuations over time in the degree of psychological disturbance as individuals seek treatment, as they mature and develop better skills in coping with their problems, as crises disappear, and as new stresses arise. There clearly are lower stabilities for measures of pathologies when compared with those measures of normal personality traits (Schuerger, Zarrella, and Hotz, 1989). These fluctuations in the individual's psychological state may obscure relative stabilities of the psychological traits that are also assessed by the MMPI.

In addition to poor long-term reliability, there are other significant problems with the MMPI. First, many items can be found on more than one scale, in some cases on as many as six. Paralleling this problem, the ten clinical scales are highly intercorrelated, so that some analyses of the interrelationships among the scales indicate that as few as two underlying dispositions are being measured (Dahl-strom, Welsh, and Dahlstrom, 1975): a general psychological adjustment variable and the degree to which the individual exercises control over feelings and actions. Furthermore, the meaning of MMPI scores varies as a function of demographic characteristics such as age and sex (Webb, 1970). For example, standardized interpretations of specific MMPI profiles seem to fit males better than females (Kelley and King, 1979). In addition, as personality measures, most of the sub-scales can have several different meanings. For example, the overall masculinity-femininity score obscures the important distinction between a person's *identity* as a male or female and his or her *interests,* which may be socially defined as masculine or feminine. A well-adjusted female may be interested in math and sports, and a male with no sexual identity problems may have interests in cooking and art. In fact, one study has shown that well-adjusted college students of both sexes have strong interests in both traditionally feminine and traditionally mascu-line activities (Bem, 1975). Nevertheless, despite these limitations, the MMPI has proved to be a useful instrument. Thousands of studies have been conducted using the MMPI (Dahlstrom et al., 1975), providing ample documentation of its validity. Most of the studies demonstrate that the MMPI does sort people into appropriate diagnostic categories.

Usage of the MMPI has extended far beyond its initial purpose. It is now being used for the screening of persons for sensitive occupations such as pilots or policemen, for the classification of prison inmates, and in cross-cultural studies of personality. Cross-cultural research with this instrument is possible because the MMPI has been translated into so many languages, including Chinese and Turkish (see Butcher, 1979). Newer investigations also attempt to find relationships be-tween MMPI categories and personality types that were not included in the original scales. A study of *anhedonia* (a term used to describe the inability to experience pleasure) exemplifies this type of research. Although it is common to think of anhedonia as a form of depression, it has been suggested that groups experiencing this condition share many of the same characteristics as schizo-phrenics. Thus, it was hypothesized that anhedonia would be associated with an MMPI profile pattern that included a high score on the schizophrenia scale. Data have tended to confirm this pattern (Penk, Carpenter, and Rylee, 1979), thus defining a new meaning for a particular MMPI pattern. In addition, because the MMPI has a large number of items, it has become possible to derive new personal-ity scales using subsets of these items. These new measures include several important research instruments such as the previously cited Repression-Sensiti-zation scale (Byrne, 1961) and the Taylor Manifest Anxiety scale (Taylor, 1953).

In 1989 a new version of the MMPI, the MMPI-2, was introduced. While the basic structure of the test remains the same, some offensive items have been deleted, sexist wording has been eliminated, and some new items have been added. Most importantly, the norms for the new version are based on a much broader and more representative sample of the population of the United States, one that takes ethnic diversity more into account. In addition, a version of the test appropriate for adolescents, the MMPI-A, has recently been developed.

Factor Analysis

Some approaches to the study of personality depend on sophisticated methods such as *factor analysis,* a statistical procedure taking large amounts of data from tests, rating scales, or behavioral observations and reducing them down into smaller, more manageable, chunks.

Factor analysis reduces the redundancy or overlap in a set of scores or data. If two variables are correlated, this means that the two overlap in measuring some common characteristic. For example, there is a correlation between how fast a person runs and how far he or she can jump. If we took a group of people and recorded their speeds in the hundred-yard dash and their distances in the broad jump, we would no doubt find a positive correlation. This correlation would mean that those who run faster also jump farther. The association or correlation between performance on these two track events suggests that some common process or ability, such as leg strength, underlies both running and jumping. Each event requires its own unique abilities, or the two would be perfectly correlated; however, a common factor, such as leg strength, is related to both. The correlation tells us the extent to which some common factor or factors underlie performance in both events; the higher the correlation, the more the two have in common.

It may be helpful to think of factor analysis as analogous to finding basic elements in chemistry. A chemist might use technical methods to find what elements or combinations of elements are parts of a given compound. In factor analysis, the "compounds" are large samples of behaviors or responses to tests and scales. Submitting such sets of data to factor analysis is like reducing a large array of information to its basic elements. Objective personality tests based on factor analysis assume that all the descriptive characteristics found in personality test scales can be reduced to just a few common factors that describe the underlying and fundamental aspects of human personality. Factor-analytic procedures are used to ascertain these fundamental aspects of human personality. The dimensions of personality obtained by a particular factor analyst can be viewed as a theory of personality; thus factor analysts often are considered to be personality theorists as well as investigators who use a particular technique to determine the structure of personality.

Guilford's Work. The pioneer in the factor analytic model of objective personality assessment was J. P. Guilford. Guilford's approach was to intercorrelate the results of a wide variety of existing personality tests to develop a single test that measured the essentials of all the other existing tests. Guilford's initial efforts were published in the early 1940s (Guilford, 1940; Guilford and Martin, 1943) and culminated in the Guilford-Zimmerman Temperament Survey (Guilford and Zimmerman, 1956). Presumably, the Guilford-Zimmerman scale reduced human personality to ten basic characteristics or dimensions: general activity, restraint, ascendance (leadership), sociability, emotional stability, objectivity, friendliness, thoughtfulness, personal relations, and masculinity. But despite the careful work and laborious effort that went into the Guilford-Zimmerman scale, the test failed to find widespread acceptance from either researchers or test users. Part of the problem may have been the measure's limited utility for clinical populations. The test market was far greater for tests like the MMPI, which measured abnormal personality and was appropriate for clinical settings. Another problem with the Guilford-Zimmerman scale was that very limited data were produced in support of the test's stability over time. In other words, if Guilford's ten factors did indeed represent the basics of human personality, there was little evidence that what was being measured remained stable features of the individual whose personality had been assessed.

The 16 P-F. Following Guilford's early work, R. B. Cattell also used the factor-analytic method to ascertain and measure the fundamental characteristics of human personality. Cattell's starting point consisted of an analysis by Allport and Odbert (1936) of over 4,500 adjectives applicable to human beings listed in an unabridged dictionary. Cattell first added to this list other descriptive adjectives taken from psychiatric and psychological literature and then reduced the list to approximately 170 items which he believed were relatively independent and captured the meaning of all the words on the original list. He then asked college students to describe their friends according to the terms on the reduced list and factor analyzed the results. Cattell reported that the items could be reduced to 36 dimensions that were labeled *surface traits* (see Cattell, 1957). Subsequent attempts to further reduce this list ultimately uncovered 16 dimensions, or factors, labeled *source traits.*

Presumably, Cattel's 16 source traits, including intelligence and ego strength, provided the same information that Guilford's ten dimensions of personality supposedly measured. In 1949, the items most strongly related to each of the 16 factors were identified and selected for inclusion in the 16 Personality-Factor Questionnaire, better known as the 16 P-F (see Cattell, 1949). However, even the factors of the 16 P-F intercorrelated, so that these 16 factors were themselves factor analyzed. The results of these additional factor analyses of the 16 P-F scale have yielded from 4 to 8 so-called second-order factors. Among the factors that were identified are introversion-extroversion, anxiety, affectivity, and free will versus resignation (Cattell, Eber, and Tatsuoka, 1970). Of these, the first two factors are best replicated, that is, most often found in other factor-analytic studies.

In considering the reliability of the 16 P-F, the question of stability over time is again at issue. For the short term, the test-retest scores are relatively higher than for the MMPI. Indeed, the 16 P-F is perhaps the soundest and most carefully constructed personality trait test. Nevertheless, as in the case of the MMPI, long-term stability is lacking. This issue will be explored in greater detail in the next chapter.

The Theoretical Model

Another model of objective personality assessment uses theories of human personality in selecting test items. If, for example, a given theory divides human

▰ Highlight 8.1 ▰▰▰▰▰▰▰▰▰▰▰▰▰▰

Fun With Personality Tests

Objective personality tests include questions about a wide array of beliefs, feelings, and experiences. At times certain questions may be perceived by the test taker as trivial or inconsequential. The apparent pointlessness of some test items has generated a parlor game of devising personality inventories composed of only facetious queries. One publicized true-false list contains the following questions:

1. When I was younger, I used to tease vegetables.
2. Sometimes I am unable to prevent clean thoughts from entering my mind.
3. I am not unwilling to work for a jackass.
4. I would enjoy the work of a chicken flicker.
5. I think beavers work too hard.
6. It is important to wash your hands before washing your hands.
7. It is hard for me to say the right thing when I find myself in a room full of mice.
8. I use shoe polish to excess.
9. The sight of blood no longer excites me.
10. It makes me furious to see an innocent man escape the chair.
11. As a child, I used to wet the ceiling.
12. I am aroused by persons of the opposite sexes.
13. I believe I smell as good as most people.
14. When I was a child, I was an imaginary playmate.

Source: *American Psychologist* 20, 1965, p. 990.

personality into three components — mood, thought, and behavior — then items would be selected to measure each of these components. A test that illustrates this approach, although not used as often as it once was, is the Edwards Personal Preference Schedule (EPPS; Edwards, 1954, 1959).

Murray (1938) theorized that a number of basic needs underlie human personality, including such motivations as the need to achieve, conform, affiliate, gain power, and be nurtured. Selecting from Murray's list of human needs, Edwards chose fifteen and constructed items to assess the extent to which each of these was present in any person. Like the MMPI and the 16 P-F, the resulting EPPS contained a number of validity items designed to detect response biases. Furthermore, to eliminate social desirability, the EPPS was constructed so that each person had to choose between two items in a pair, selecting the more characteristic one. Each item in the pair reflected a different need, and an effort was made to equate the items on social desirability in order to reduce the influence of this bias on the test results. An example of an item pair is:

1. I feel depressed when I fail at something.
2. I feel nervous when giving a talk before a group.

One difference between the EPPS and other objective tests is that the scores assessing each need are interdependent, reflecting each individual's own preference hierarchy. If some needs receive high scores, then others must receive low scores for a given person because of the forced-choice methodology that is used. For example, in pairing an achievement and an affiliation item, selection of the achievement item augments the achievement scale score while not adding to the affiliation scale score. In contrast, on other tests it is possible to obtain high scores on all the subscales. Although the EPPS is a well-designed instrument from a technical standpoint, it also does not have a good record for long-term stability. Thus, like the MMPI and the 16 P-F, it is subject so some of the same factors that limit the usefulness of these tests as measures of enduring personality traits.

PROJECTIVE PERSONALITY TESTS AND METHODS

Long before objective personality tests based on face validity were replaced by better objective instruments, an entirely new and different idea about personality assessment had emerged. This second major traditional approach is known as the *projective* method. In projective methods, the person's task is to produce something spontaneously, through such procedures as associating to test stimuli. Rather than selecting among written alternatives, the test taker has few guidelines for the type of response required; therefore, almost any response can be obtained. Given such a wide range of possible responses, it is difficult to formulate a set of rules for scoring purposes; subjective evaluation is often the most workable solution. As a result, agreement in scoring between testers and between responses is often far from perfect, even though some objective scoring techniques have been developed.

Projective tests begin by presenting a person with an ambiguous stimulus like an inkblot or a picture with some indeterminate elements. The examiner might ask a question as simple as "Tell me what this might be," or the subject might be asked to make up a story about an ambiguous picture. In either case, the person must use his or her creative and analytical capacities in providing an answer; alternatives are not provided. In exchange for the loss of objectivity in scoring and evaluating a person's response, projective tests provide much more opportunity for the expression of individuality. They therefore are thought to be potentially capable of detecting more subtle and varied aspects of personality than is possible with objective tests.

All projective tests are based on the hypothesis that the person's response to an ambiguous or vague stimulus is a reflection (i.e., projection) of his or her own needs and feelings. That is, the person, in giving meaning to an ambiguous stimulus, "projects" onto that stimulus his or her needs, feelings, strivings, and thought processes. Moreover, the projection can take place without the individual's being aware that significant aspects of the personality are being revealed. Thus, it is assumed that projective tests provide more access to the kinds of unconscious impulses and attitudes with which psychoanalysis is concerned.

The Rorschach Inkblot Test

The *Rorschach Inkblot Test,* in which subjects are asked to respond to ambiguous inkblots, may be the first formal projective method. One of the earliest references to the possibility of using inkblots to assess individual differences dates back to the Civil War (Keiner, 1857). Keiner noted that, when asked to interpret the meaning of an inkblot, each individual tended to produce unique and idiosyncratic responses. Inasmuch as responses to inkblots were different for each individual, it seemed reasonable to conclude that different interpretations reflected differences between individual interpreters. If most subjects had provided the same or even similar responses to the same inkblot stimulus, then the obvious conclusion would have been that the interpretations were simply a reflection of the characteristics of the inkblot. For example, asking subjects to describe a table or a chair would not reveal much about the subjects because all responses would be relatively similar.

Objective personality tests attempt to measure individual differences in specific attributes. The Rorschach Inkblot Test, on the other hand, makes no assumptions concerning the characteristics that should or will be measured. Instead, the Rorschach is so flexible that it leaves open the possibility of assessing the most unique aspects of an individual. There are, however, certain broad dimensions of personality, including impulse control, sensitivity to internal thoughts and feelings, sensitivity to external inputs, and the tendency to distort reality, that the test attempts to assess in all individuals.

The Rorschach consists of ten cards, each displaying a meaningless, bilaterally symmetrical inkblot. To get an idea of what the cards look like, you can simply repeat the same method Hermann Rorschach used to construct the original test (Rorschach, 1921). Place a few drops of ink on a white card or piece of paper, carefully fold the card in half, open it, and then let it dry. What emerges is an apparently meaningless blob that is symmetrical on both sides of the crease, so that each half looks like the mirror image of the other half. A little inspection soon seems to reveal meaning, and all or parts of the inkblot will begin to resemble familiar shapes and objects (see Fig. 8.1 on p. 216).

The Rorschach test contains five black-and-gray inkblots; two that are black,

Figure 8.1   An inkblot similar to those used in the Rorschach test. (Mussen and Rosenzweig, 1977, p. 152. Used by permission.)

gray, and red; and three cards consisting of a variety of pastel colors. The Rorschach is administered with minimal instructions since it is designed to be ambiguous and unstructured. Unlike objective personality tests, the Rorschach is typically administered individually, testing one person at a time. Throughout the sometimes-lengthy testing period, the examiner writes down each response, at the same time offering no clues to the type of response required. In the typical situation, the card is presented and the examiner asks, "What might this be?" The subject is then free to give one or several responses to each of the ten cards, responding to the entire inkblot, to some portion of it, or to both.

After the subject has responded to each of the ten cards, without information or comments from the examiner, the examiner goes through the cards a second time and asks a set of carefully worded questions, often getting the subject to elaborate on responses. The purpose of this second phase is to provide the examiner with sufficient information to score the test. Responses are evaluated in terms of location (area of the blot used); whether or not color or shading is used in formulating the response; kind of object described (animal, human, inanimate); presence of activity or movement; correspondence of the percept to real objects; and how typical or atypical the response is. Each of these dimensions of scoring is believed to be associated with personality characteristics.

The person's scores, which can be summarized in terms of the frequency of each of the various dimensions, are referred to as the quantitative aspects of the test. Of equal significance, however, is an analysis of the actual content of the person's responses, which is referred to as the qualitative aspect of the test. Rorschach interpretation is based on an evaluation of each scoring category as well as the quality and specific content of each response and how this varies from card to card. Considering the scoring categories, the human movement response (for example, "A man dancing") is thought by some to reveal introversion, in that the perception of movement is believed to indicate inner-directedness. A response like "That is a bat, but not a good one" might lead to inferences about obsessiveness. According to a proponent of the Rorschach, an experienced examiner can make some rather detailed and specific descriptions of the person's personality and emotional functioning. Although it is suitable for assessing normal personality, the Rorschach, like the MMPI, finds its most extensive use in clinical settings in which there is a need to assess maladaptive thought processes, motivational conflicts, and problems in emotional and behavioral control.

The Rorschach is an extremely complex and subjective method of personality assessment. From the very start, it has been a highly controversial personality

This child is responding to a Rorschach inkblot, one of the principal methods of projective measurement. (Sybil Shelton/Monkmeyer Press Photo Service)

instrument. It has been extremely difficult to evaluate its reliability and validity, in part because there are no universally accepted methods of administration, scoring, and interpretation. In addition, because the number of responses can vary widely, it is difficult to be certain about the meaning of the frequency of particular response characteristics. For example, the number of human movement responses in a Rorschach record will vary with the total number of responses given as well as with the tendency to perceive human movement in the blots. Also, test-retest studies reflect considerable instability in Rorschach responses over time. As a result of these and other problems, there is little consensus among psychologists concerning the soundness of the Rorschach and its validity as a measure of human personality. In the case of an instrument as flexible and complex as the Rorschach, one must ask: validity for what? For each dimension of personality? For the assessment of psychopathology? For the prediction of reactions to the stress of pilot training? The evidence bearing on the utility of the Rorschach in various personnel selection programs has been largely negative, while evidence for its utility as a personality measure has been variable. For example, its validity is questionable as an indicator of self-concept and sensitivity to others, but the Rorschach has proved to be somewhat effective in assessing self-control and ego strength (Klopfer, 1954; Zubin, Eron, and Schumer, 1965). In addition, there are also data indicating that specified combinations of Rorschach scores can reliably distinguish schizophrenics from neurotics (Fisher, 1967), even though there are many negative findings concerning the assessment of psychopathology. The Rorschach Prognostic Rating Scale, an index based on the assignment of weights to such features of the response scale as human movement and the match between the response and the ink-blot stimulus, has proved to be a promising predictor of response to therapy (Fisher, 1967; Klopfer and Taulbee, 1976). In general, however, the Rorschach is a better instrument for assessing the person as he or she is currently functioning, not as he or she will function at some future time (Exner, 1974).

It is interesting to note that a projective test like the Rorschach is subject to some of the same difficulties as objective measures: both reflect substantial instability over time. An individual's response to an inkblot (projective test) or to an MMPI item (objective test) can be seen as a function of one's personality disposition, a more temporary personality state, the specific stimulus (inkblot or test item), and the situational context in which the test takes place. When the stimulus remains constant, as in test-retest studies, variability in the subject's response can reflect changes in any of the remaining three determinants of test performance.

The Thematic Apperception Test (TAT)

The *Thematic Apperception Test* (*TAT*) was first published in 1935 by Christiana Morgan and Henry Murray of Harvard University. Like the objective EPPS, the TAT is based on Murray's (1938) theory of needs. Murray proposed that human beings have to deal with the expression, satisfaction, and frustration of a number of psychological needs such as aggression, nurturance, affiliation, achievement, dependency, power, and sex. The TAT was specifically developed as a vehicle that would permit individuals to express these needs. The TAT purports to be a measure of human personality functioning that can be used in the assessment of normal as well as abnormal personality. Unlike the Rorschach, the TAT is not widely used in determining the extent of emotional disturbances, although it is used to ascertain the content of an individual's conflict and the defenses employed in coping with psychological conflicts.

The TAT contains thirty cards, each showing a picture or scene. In addition, one blank card is included. Although vague, each picture contains a specific type of content in which the dominant feature is usually one or more humans; e.g., a picture of a seated boy and a violin resting on a table. Some pictures contain only a child and others, only adults. The ages and sexes of the characters are sometimes mixed, such as a middle-aged woman and an older girl, or a young man and an older woman. Although some of the cards can be used for any age group or either sex, others are specifically designed for men, women, boys, or girls. Inasmuch as the pictures of the TAT are more meaningful or structured than the Rorschach inkblots, each picture tends to elicit a certain type of response. Thus, for example, a picture of an older and a younger man together typically elicits stories about father-son relationships. However, there is sufficient variability between individuals' interpretations of the cards to yield information about personalities

Figure 8.2   A card similar to TAT stimulus cards. (Mussen and Rosenzweig, 1977, p. 153. Used by permission. Photo by Ted Polumbaum.)

and problems. A card similar to some of the TAT stimulus cards is shown in Fig. 8.2.

When administering the TAT, the examiner presents the cards one at a time. The subject is requested to make up a story about each picture, stating what led up to the story, what is happening, what the characters are thinking and feeling, and what the outcome will be. Responses are recorded word for word.

The TAT is similar to the Rorschach in several respects. Neither test has a universally accepted, standardized scoring or interpretation. However, both have a number of commonly accepted scoring techniques. Scoring of the TAT can be more difficult and complex than scoring of the Rorschach. Most scoring systems tend to require that the hero, needs, environmental forces or press, themes, and outcomes be identified. The hero is the central character in each picture; it is assumed that the storyteller will identify with the hero. Therefore, the needs and motives of the hero, particularly those that recur from story to story, are assumed to reflect the needs and motives of the storyteller. *Press* refers to the environmental forces or obstacles facing the hero. Again, as the same types of such obstacles recur in several stories, the likelihood increases that the storyteller perceives similar difficulties in his or her own life. Recurrent conflicts and outcomes also are believed to reflect characteristics of the storyteller. In sum, what the examiner looks for in the TAT are themes concerning needs, motivations, obstacles, conflicts, or outcomes that recur in the individual's stories for different pictures. These repeated themes are interpreted as reflecting the basic underlying motivations and conflicts of the storyteller.

As an example of how the TAT is used, consider the following story told by a person we will call Robert. The stimulus card to which his story was given depicts a young man with bowed head and an older woman looking into the distance.

> The fellow has just told the woman some bad news. He is a friend of her son who was living in another town. I'm not sure why. Perhaps he was in the service or maybe he had taken a job in that town. The son has been in an accident. He was a passenger in the car that his friend was driving. His friend had been drinking, not heavily, but had taken a couple for the road, as it were. Anyway, he was driving pretty fast and didn't see the sign for an approaching S curve. When he tried to slow down, he skidded into a tree. He luckily had only a few scratches, but the woman's son was badly injured and is in a coma. The friend naturally feels guilty and it was very hard for him to tell the mother about the accident. (Q: What happens?) The mother is extremely upset but she manages to maintain her self-control. She rushes to the hospital where she keeps watch at his bedside. After 24 hours, he comes out of the coma and eventually recovers.

There are a number of themes and needs that can be inferred from this story. One might be the untrustworthiness of friends and frustration of the need for affiliation. Another theme bears on the relationship of a young man to a mother figure. The core sequence of events consists of a son separated from his mother; a very negative, painful experience; reunion with the mother; and then a positive outcome. One might infer from this sequence that separation from his mother is very painful for Robert. He cannot acknowledge the frustration of his dependency needs and can express it only indirectly, through physical injury and through the visit of his friend in the story. The guilt expressed by the friend, a central character in the TAT picture, may be a displaced expression of his own guilt about his anger over frustration of dependency needs. There are other features of the story that might also be revealing: drinking, self-destruction, displacement of responsibility (the accident was the friend's fault). In all cases, however, one looks for repeated expressions of a theme in a number of stories before drawing inferences about an individual's basic needs and conflicts.

In reviews of the TAT, Exner (1974) and Murstein (1963) noted that test-retest reliability can be quite high under the specific condition that only a particular variable is studied. But even under such a specific condition, data are still insufficient for drawing firm conclusions about the test's value. There is nevertheless extensive research bearing on the validity of the TAT. For example, several experimental studies have manipulated such needs as hunger, aggression, and sex in order to examine the effects of need arousal on stories elicited in response to a subset of TAT stimuli. In general, the results of these studies indicate that aroused subjects make more responses relating to the aroused need than do nonaroused subjects (McClelland and Atkinson, 1948). These findings contribute to the construct validity of the TAT. At the same time, though, they indicate that the TAT is subject to situational or temporary influences, a fact inconsistent with the traditional assessment goal of measuring enduring personality traits. An enormous amount of data also bear on the relation between TAT measures of need and behaviors reflecting that same need (see Chapter 17).

In general, as in the case of the Rorschach, validity studies have yielded variable findings. It is clear that there are circumstances under which the TAT and the Rorschach are predictive of significant aspects of personality. The problem lies in specifying those circumstances in order to tell in advance when the TAT and the Rorschach will provide valid pictures of a subject's personality.

OTHER APPROACHES TO PERSONALITY ASSESSMENT

The Interview

The *interview* is without doubt the oldest technique for assessing personality. The original objective personality test, the Woodworth Personality Data Sheet (1920), was actually an attempt to develop a standard psychiatric interview. Before the Woodworth, the only substantial tool available for assessing personality was the interview, which was most commonly employed by psychiatrists in determining an individual's emotional stability. The Woodworth attempted to specify a number of questions common to the psychiatric interview and to put these questions in paper-and-pencil form.

Interview techniques are commonly used in conjunction with objective and projective tests in the assessment of personality. Like the tests themselves, inter-

Clinical Versus Statistical Prediction

In the clinical method of predicting behavior, the assessor uses various sources of information, such as the TAT and interview data as well as structured tests. There are no set rules for combining this information, and so judgments are guided by intuition, hypotheses about personality dynamics, and common sense. In the statistical procedure, relationships are established between particular tests and a behavior. Then a formula is uniformly applied to predict individual behavior.

Adherents to the clinical approach describe it as dynamic, global, meaningful, configural, and sensitive, as opposed to mechanical, artificial, academic, static, and oversimplified. On the other hand, advocates of the statistical procedure describe it as verifiable, objective, scientific, precise, and empirical, as opposed to vague, subjective, unscientific, unreliable, and private.

Which procedure in fact has proved more effective in predicting behavior? Carefully conducted research studies using a variety of predictor variables and sources of information have repeatedly found evidence supporting the superiority of the statistical method. In general, the greater the involvement of humans in the assessment process, the less the validity of the prediction.

Critical research studies typically involve predictions of one of three kinds of behavior: grade point average, recidivism (committing criminal acts after release from prison), and recovery from psychoses. In one representative investigation involving predictions of college grade point average (Sarbin, 1942), adherents to the statistical method applied a formula derived from prior studies relating high school rank, aptitude test score, and grade point average. Supporters of the clinical approach interviewed the students and used other kinds of information, such as projective test scores — as well as the high school rank and aptitude scores used in the statistical method. The results of this investigation favored the statistical procedure; predictions were more accurate when based upon the previously derived formula.

Sometimes, however, clinical judgments allow one to take account of data never before used. The following case, reported by the noted psychoanalyst Theodore Reik, illustrates one prediction that could not have been made with a statistical procedure.

> One session at this time took the following course. After a few sentences about the uneventful day, the patient fell into a long silence. She assured
>
> *Continued*

■ **Highlight 8.2** ■

me that nothing was in her thoughts. Silence from me. After many minutes she continued about a toothache. She told me that she had been to the dentist yesterday. He had given her an injection and then had pulled a wisdom tooth. The spot was hurting again. New and longer silence. She pointed to my bookcase in the corner and said, "There is a book standing on its head." Without the slightest hesitation and in a reproachful voice I said, "But why did you not tell me you had an abortion?" (Meehl, 1954).

Source: Adapted from Meehl, 1962. Reprinted by permission.

view techniques have improved, and considerable data have accumulated in recent years concerning the nature of the interview (e.g., Marsden, 1971; Wiens, 1976). The evidence suggests that effective interviews are those in which the interviewer is able to display such attitudes as warmth, involvement, interest, and commitment (Orlinsky and Howard, 1967; Saccuzzo, 1975; Tyler, 1969). It is also important for the interviewer to communicate a feeling of empathy or understanding to the person being interviewed (e.g., Truax and Mitchell, 1971). The success of the interview has been shown to be related to the feelings, mood, nonverbal behavior, and even activity level of the interviewer (Bandura, 1971; Heller, Davis, and Myers, 1966). Good interviewers tend to remain calm, relaxed, and confident throughout the interview, while communicating interest, concern, and a sense of mutual sharing.

Although much is known about effective interviewing, there is no standard or universally accepted method for conducting an interview. As a result, interviewers have practically unlimited opportunity to explore any area they believe will aid in the assessment of personality. Interviews vary from the highly structured to the totally unstructured. In the most structured type of interview, the interviewer asks the same set of questions in a particular order. This type of interview is much like a test such as the Woodworth except that the examiner reads the questions and then records the responses. A totally unstructured interview, on the other hand, might begin anywhere, proceed in any direction, change topic at any time, and focus on whatever content the interviewer wishes.

There are little available data concerning the long-term reliability and validity of conclusions based solely on interview data. The variety of interview procedures, the wide differences among interviewers, and the unlimited focus of interviews have limited researchers' ability to produce convincing results concerning the interview's value. There is general consensus, however, that the less structured the interview, the less reliable the information it yields (Wiens, 1976). The less structured the interview, the greater the inconsistency between the information obtained by different interviewers. If different questions are asked with different goals in mind, then the results cannot help but be different. On the other hand, it is difficult to conceive how even the most structured interview can be any more reliable than the best-constructed personality test. At best, an interview might approach the reliability of personality tests, but no real evidence exists that this is the case.

Among the problems of assessing personality via interview is that the interviewer can and does affect the verbal (Greenspoon, 1962) as well as the nonverbal (Matarazzo, Wiens, Matarazzo, and Saslow, 1968) behavior of the person being interviewed (see also Matarazzo and Wiens, 1972). The interviewer can influence the interviewee through subtle expression of interest, approval, or disapproval conveyed by movements of the head and the body, and by voice intonation — without either interviewer or interviewee being aware of the interaction or its effects. Also, a specific explanation or theory held by the interviewer may create a set in which those beliefs are artificially confirmed. As a result, the validity of interview data is often suspect.

The interview is a valuable tool that will no doubt continue to play a role in efforts to assess human personality. However, in providing the most flexible method for assessing individuals, the interview is grossly limited in terms of the true meaning of its results. In its major strength also lies its most serious weakness. Consequently, even though our knowledge of it has grown rapidly in the last two decades, the interview, like traditional personality tests, leaves much to be desired in the area of personality assessment.

Behavioral Techniques

In an effort to solve the difficult problems inherent in the assessment of personality, there has been new and increasing interest in more nontraditional techniques. Perhaps the most important and best developed of these are the *behavioral techniques,* which tend to make few assumptions about the nature of human personality (see Chapter 5). Indeed, contrary to traditional tests, these newer approaches do not necessarily assume that the characteristics being measured are even stable. Nor do they assume that human personality can be assessed independently of the environment. On the contrary, most behavioral procedures are based on the assumption that situations play an integral role in behavior, so that human behavior and thus human personality can be measured only within the context in which they occur. The behaviorist approach to assessment, therefore, is that behavior should be studied directly, rather than determined indirectly through test or talk procedures.

Common to most procedures that employ behavioral observations is the recording of behavioral samples that can be readily quantified. Typically, an observer notes and records the actual behavior of a subject, making no inferences like those usually involved in a rating scale. In assessing a child's aggression, for example, an observer might count the number of fist fights, arguments, destructions of objects, and similar behaviors over a particular time period (Feshbach, 1970; Lovaas et al., 1965). The experimental modification of behavior stemming from the application of learning theories has facilitated the development of sys-

Behavioral Assessment in Action

The following is a report of a behavioral assessment procedure in a natural environment:

Issue. Investigation of the feasibility of treatment in the natural setting (the home) where the child's behavior problem appeared, with the mother serving as the therapeutic agent. The child (C), a four-year-old boy, was brought by his mother (M) to the university clinic because she felt helpless to deal with his frequent tantrums and general disobedience.

Observations. Experimenters (Es) observed M and C in the home and noted that many of C's undesirable behaviors appeared to be maintained by attention from the mother. If C behaved objectionably, M would try to explain to him why he shouldn't do something or would try to distract him by offering him toys or food. Observation in the home indicated that the following responses made up a large portion of C's repertoire of undesirable behavior: (1) biting his shirt or arm, (2) sticking out his tongue, (3) kicking or biting himself, others, or objects, (4) calling someone or something a derogatory name, (5) removing or threatening to remove his clothing, (6) saying no loudly and vigorously, (7) threatening to damage objects or persons, (8) throwing objects, (9) pushing his sister. These nine responses collectively are called objectionable behavior (OB). The frequency of occurrence is measured by recording, for each ten-second interval, whether or not an OB occurred. Observations are made during one-hour sessions conducted two to three times a week. Two Es are employed as observers on eight occasions and three on one occasion to check the reliability of the response scoring. Reliability is found to range from .70 to 1.00 with an average of .88, indicative of high observer reliability.

Treatment. After an initial *baseline period* of sixteen sessions during which C and M interact in their usual way, the *first experimental period* is begun. Every time C emits an OB, M is signalled by E to tell him to stop or to put him in his room by himself and without toys. (This isolation is viewed as a period of "time out" from stimuli associated with positive reinforcement.) When E notices that C is playing in a particularly desirable way, M is signalled to give C attention and approval. During the *second baseline period* M is told to interact with C as she did prior to the experimental period. This is followed by the *second experimental period,* which is the same as in the first except that special attention for desirable play is excluded, save for one accidental instance. Finally, there is a *follow-up period* after twenty-four days without contact between E and M.

Continued

▪ Highlight 8.3 ▬▬▬▬▬▬

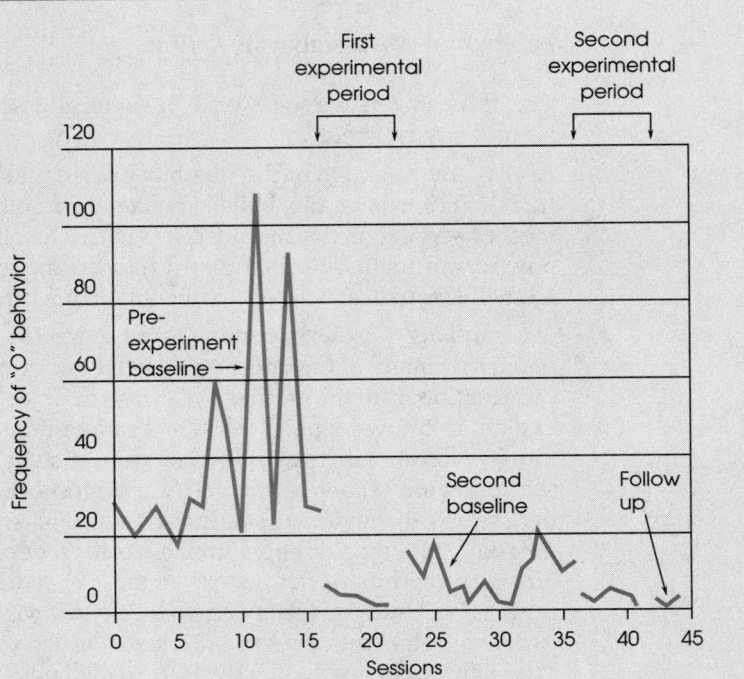

Number of ten-second intervals, per one-hour session, in which objectionable behavior occurred.

Results.   During the baseline period, OB varied between 18 and 113 per session (one hour). During the first experimental period, the rate of OB ranged from 1 to 8 per session. Special attention was given ten times. During the second baseline period, the rate of OB varied between 2 and 24 per session. M reported that she had trouble responding in her previous way because she now felt more sure of herself. She now gives C firm commands and does not give in after denying a request. She also gives more affection, mostly in response to an increase in affectionate overtures from C. During the second experimental period, the rate of OB varied between 2 and 8 per session. The rate of OB remained low after the twenty-four-day interval (follow-up period) and M reports C is well-behaved and less demanding.

Summary. The results of this study show that it is possible to observe and treat behavioral problems in the home, with the parent as the therapeutic

Continued

◼ **Highlight 8.3** ▬▬▬▬▬▬▬▬▬▬▬▬▬▬▬▬▬▬▬

agent. Since it is widely held that many of the child's problems originate in the home environment, direct modification of this environment (including the behavior of other family members) may arrest the difficulty at its source.

Source: Hawkins, Peterson, Schweid, and Bijou, 1966, p. 105. Reprinted by permission.

tematic and sophisticated behavioral observation techniques. Before an experimental procedure is introduced to modify some designated behavior — e.g., rewarding a withdrawn child whenever an approach response to another child is made — the frequency of the behavior is recorded over a particular time interval to provide a *baseline*. Stimulus events that precede, coexist with, or follow the designated behavior can also be recorded. Following the experimental intervention, changes in these stimulus events (e.g., friendly actions by other children) and any corresponding changes in the frequency of the designated behavior can be determined through analysis of the behavioral observations. By recording those factors that maintain or reduce particular behaviors, behavioral observation techniques provide a different perspective than traditional tests. This process is specifically illustrated in Highlight 8.3.

Behavioral assessment procedures are relatively new and many of their problems have yet to be solved. First, like the interview, there is no standard or universally accepted technique for observing behavior. Guidelines do not exist to indicate which behaviors should be recorded and which are irrelevant. Furthermore, just as an interview can influence the person being interviewed, so too can an observer influence the behavior of the person being observed. As early as 1949, a study by Polansky and his colleagues provided strong evidence that the presence of an observer does alter the behavior of the individual being watched. This has been confirmed in a number of other studies (Goldfried, 1976; Wiggins, 1973).

Kanfer and Saslow (1969) have presented a model and guidelines for observing behavior. These authors contend that behavior can be viewed as adaptive (facilitating the accomplishment of goals) or maladaptive. In addition, behavior can be defined in terms of excesses or deficits. Behavioral excesses occur with such frequency, duration, or intensity that they impede the individual in some way. Behavioral deficits, on the other hand, would enhance goal attainment if they occurred more frequently. In attempting to define the components of behavioral observations and to identify the important elements, Kanfer and Saslow have taken positive steps in the development of behavioral observation as a technique in personality assessment. Other steps are following, inasmuch as this remains an area of rapid growth and change.

The polygraph is used to assess emotional reactions and to detect lying. (Paul Conklin/Monkmeyer Press Photo Service)

Physiological Assessment

Another relatively new behaviorally oriented approach to personality assessment involves the evaluation of such physiological changes as heart rate, blood pressure, skin temperature, and perspiration (Lang, 1971). The rationale for *physiological assessment* is that changes in bodily processes reflect changes in psychological, particularly emotional, states (Kallman and Feuerstein, 1977). The major tool for such assessment is the polygraph, an instrument used to monitor various physiological indicators. The lie detector, for example, is a polygraph. It uses a number of physiological recordings and its application is based on the assumption that a lie will produce a marked emotional reaction. Perhaps the most commonly used physiological measure in personality assessment is the galvanic skin response (GSR). The GSR reflects relatively minute changes in the electrical characteristics of the skin related to sweating and therefore is frequently used as an indicator of emotional arousal or anxiety. While self-descriptions of emotional states and even actions can be altered to disguise true feelings, it is extremely difficult to control one's GSR or other physiological responses.

Although the GSR, pulse rate, and other physiological indications assessed by the polygraph may reflect emotional reactions when a subject is lying, they may also reflect emotional reactions when the subject is upset, angered, anxious, or even amused. Consequently, polygraph methods have only limited validity as lie-detection procedures (Kleinmuntz and Szucko, 1984b). The fallibility of lie detectors is nicely illustrated by a naturalistic study (Kleinmutz and Szucko,

■ **Highlight 8.4** ■■■■■■■■■■■■■■■■■

Primitive Methods of Lie Detection

Throughout history there have been efforts to distinguish the guilty from the innocent and to tell the liars from the truthful. Many of these methods relied (unknowingly) on the basic physiological principles that also guided the creation of the polygraph. For example, a method of lie detection practiced in Asia involved giving those suspected of a crime a handful of raw rice to chew. After chewing for some time, the persons were instructed to spit out the rice. The innocent person was anticipated to do this easily, whereas the guilty party was expected to have grains of rice sticking to the roof of the mouth and tongue. This technique relied on the increased sympathetic nervous system activity in the presumably fearful and guilty person. This activity would result in the drying up of saliva that, in turn, would cause grains of rice to stick in the mouth. A similar but more frightening technique involved placing a heated knife blade briefly against the tongue, another method used for criminal detection. An innocent person would not be burned while the guilty party would immediately feel pain, again because of the relative dryness of the mouth.

A more primitive but functional technique for detecting liars was supposedly used by a Persian king. He was presumed to have a donkey with the ability to tell an innocent person from the guilty. When a crime was committed, the suspects would be gathered in a hall next to the room that held the donkey. Each suspect would enter the room alone, find the donkey in the dark, and was told to pull its tail. If an innocent person pulled the tail, the donkey was said to remain silent, whereas when the guilty person pulled the tail, the donkey would bray loudly. In fact, the donkey's tail was dusted with graphite. When the guilty person emerged with clean hands, because he wanted to avoid detection, the criminal was caught.

1984*a*). The polygraph charts of fifty innocent and fifty guilty subjects with regard to some theft-related action were submitted for interpretation to six polygraph trainees at the completion of their training. Confession to the full amount of the theft was considered verification of guilt, and confession by another to an offense of which the subject had been accused was used as the criterion for the latter's innocence. On the average, the polygraph interpreters misclassified 37 percent of the innocent subjects as guilty! The lie detector, then, has the same limitations as any psychological test and must be used with great caution when applied to a particular case.

A variety of new techniques for measuring bodily changes have recently been developed (Epstein, 1976). For example, following Masters and Johnson's (1966) finding establishing a link between human sexual arousal and the flow of blood into the genitalia, a number of tools have been developed to measure this flow of blood in order to assess sexual arousal (Kallman and Feuerstein, 1977). These physiological measures made studies of the antecedents and consequences of sexual arousal possible that could not otherwise have been carried out.

Physiological methods, no less than other personality assessment techniques, are subject to the requirements of reliability and validity. However, in terms of development and supporting evidence, many physiological techniques are only in their infancy. Much more research is needed before even the first steps can be taken in evaluating their role and value as personality assessment devices.

Summary

1. Psychologists measuring personality typically assume that personality *traits* are stable and general (exhibited regardless of situation).

2. *Objective* personality tests provide a set of responses to a particular item, to which the test taker responds by selecting the most appropriate alternative. The construction of the test may be guided by *face validity,* empirical evidence, or the search for underlying structure (*factor analytic* instruments).

3. Tests having face validity suffer from a number of problems because items may be interpreted differently or not honestly answered by the respondents. There may be a tendency to answer in a way that reflects most favorably on the self (*social desirability*). In addition, *response biases* have been identified, such as *acquiescence* (agreeing with an item regardless of its content) and *oppositional bias* (disagreeing with an item regardless of its content).

4. Tests based on *empirical* approaches first identify groups that differ on a particular behavior or set of behaviors. Items given to both groups that are differentially endorsed are then included in the measuring instrument, regardless of the specific content or meaning of that item.

5. The *MMPI* is the most widely used of the empirically based questionnaires. In addition to ten clinical scales, the MMPI includes four validity scales: (a) the "cannot say" scale (the inability to endorse either alternative); (b) the F scale (items rarely endorsed by the general population); (c) the K scale (socially desirable items); and (d) the "Lie" (L) scale (less subtle, socially desirable items). A new form, the *MMPI-2,* is now available.

6. *Factor analysis* is a statistical method that enables the investigator to identify the fundamental aspects of personality. Instruments constructed by Guilford and Cattell are among the best-known factor-analytic batteries.

7. In *projective* tests, the test taker spontaneously produces a response, such as a story, for which scoring is often subjective. Projective tests are based on the

assumption that a person's response to an ambiguous stimulus reflects his or her own needs and conflicts.

8. The *Rorschach Inkblot Test* was the first formal projective instrument. Responses to symmetrical inkblots are evaluated in terms of location, inclusion of color, the kind of object described, movement, the "accuracy" of the percept, and how typical the response is. The validity of this test is questionable, although it appears to have validity for the assessment of personality characteristics like self-control and ego strength.

9. In the *Thematic Apperception Test (TAT)*, one of the most widely used projective instruments, the subject tells stories about a set of somewhat ambiguous pictures. As with the Rorschach, the validity of the TAT is unclear.

10. All the traditional tests of personality suffer in that long-term, test-retest reliabilities are low, a fact in conflict with the traditional belief in enduring personality traits.

11. Included among additional approaches to personality assessment are the *interview,* which is generally believed to be a poor assessment technique, *behavior techniques,* and *physiological assessment.* The lie detector, a frequently used instrument, has serious limitations.

Thought Questions

1. Why do you think personality measures have low long-term reliability? Is personality unstable, or does the fault lie in the measures? If the latter, what might these faults be?

2. Can you think of a time when you were less than completely honest on a personality test, or when you answered in a socially desirable manner? Under what conditions are these types of responses most likely?

3. Different factor-analytic batteries tend to find different underlying personality structures. Do you think that there are certain basic aspects of personality that describe all individuals? What do you think they are?

4. Tell a story about the TAT picture shown in this chapter. Do you think that your response is meaningful and reveals your current needs and conflicts?

9 Traits, Situations, and Their Interaction

Suppose that someone is about to introduce you to one of her best friends. A common inquiry in such circumstances is "What is she like?" In other words, what *traits* characterize her? Is she kind, aggressive, honest? Traits provide us with convenient methods of organizing information about others, of describing how they have behaved in the past, and of making predictions about how they will behave in the future (Jones and Nisbett, 1971; Kelley, 1967). Throughout the history of the study of personality, considerable effort has been devoted to building taxonomies of traits, developing methods for measuring traits, and finding the ways in which groups of traits cluster together. Indeed, the very concept of personality assumes that there are characteristics or traits that remain stable over time.

Even though the search for traits has a long and rich history, their utility has been questioned since at least the turn of the century. Edward Thorndike, one of the pioneers of measurement, wrote in 1906 (p. 248):

> Training the mind means the development of thousands of particular, independent capacities, the formation of countless particular habits. . . . The amount of identical elements in different mental functions and the amount of general influence from special training are much less than common opinion supposes.

In this short passage, Thorndike challenged the predominant trait orientation as well as the notion of general intelligence, suggesting instead that behavior is influenced more by situations or training for specific situations than was acknowledged in his time.

By 1934, trait approaches to personality were under serious question. For example, the use of personality tests was attacked at that time because they were unreliable and undependable in classifying individuals (Lehman and Witty, 1934). It was suggested that it was not necessarily the tests that were at fault, but rather the concept of traits. The question arose as to whether people really were consistent over time and between situations. Nevertheless, the trait approach remained dominant in personality theory for several decades. World War I saw the development of huge testing batteries for the classification of servicemen. World War II was also an impetus for expansion of psychological assessment, and the development of trait classification systems flourished in the period immediately after the war.

A variety of other events helped to establish the stature of trait psychology. First, Harvard personologist Gordon Allport (1937) was an extremely influential psychologist who was also a firm believer in traits. In addition, prominent factor-analytic methodologists like Raymond Cattell, whose work was introduced in the preceding chapter, were concerned with trait classification. During the period after the second world war, there was also a growth spurt in clinical psychology. Following the medical model, clinical psychologists began to find traits useful for classifying people, in much the same way physicians classified patients into disease categories.

However, a major critique of trait psychology appeared with the publication of Mischel's (1968) book, *Personality and Assessment.* Mischel's review of the personality literature indicated that personality measures were very poor at predicting behavior in specific situations. Following the publication of Mischel's book and his severe criticisms of the trait notion, the field of personality had to rethink many of its most basic assumptions. As the issues were argued and debated, some clarification began to emerge, but the debate about the existence of traits continues to be one of the most active areas of research in personality psychology. We will present some of the basic issues in the trait-situation debate (also see Endler and Magnusson, 1976; Magnusson and Endler, 1977).

In this chapter we first consider attempts to classify different kinds of human personalities in terms of *types.* This is related to the current concept of *personality disorders* in the field of abnormal psychology. Then we consider some of the most influential attempts to classify personality in terms of *traits,* those of Cattell, Eysenck, and the Big Five model. From there we move on to consider the debate over the usefulness of trait notions.

PERSONALITY TYPES

The origins of theories of personality go back to Hippocrates and later Galen. Galen suggested there were four personality types associated with the four bodily fluids (humors) as well as with the four physical elements (see Table 9.1, below,

Table 9.1 Relationship between bodily humors, personality types, and elements, as suggested by Galen

Bodily humor	Personality type	Characteristics	Elements
Yellow bile	Choleric	Irritable	Fire
Black bile	Melancholic	Depressed	Earth
Blood	Sanguine	Optimistic	Air
Phlegm	Phlegmatic	Calm; listless	Water

■ **Highlight 9.1** ▬▬▬▬▬▬▬▬▬▬

Elements and Temperament

The four physical elements identified by the Greeks — earth, air, fire, and water — were arranged according to the doctine of opposites. Fire was perceived as the opposite of water, and earth as the opposite of air. As indicated in Table 9.1, each element was associated with a particular fluid and temperament. These associations were the basis of the prime theory of individual differences throughout the Middle Ages, and the distinctions are still persistent today. For example, literary critics have analyzed the elements predominant in the works of famous writers. It has been suggested that Nietzsche focused on air imagery, Flaubert on earth, and Poe on water.

Perhaps surprisingly, the associations postulated by Galen between elements and temperament have given rise to some recent research (Martindale and Martindale, 1988). These investigators asked subjects to combine adjective descriptions of the four temperaments (see Table 9.1) with words representing typical forms of the four elements. The college-aged subjects did combine the words (sort them into piles) in a manner consistent with the model proposed by Galen and the Greeks. For example, the pile containing words related to water (e.g., bath, ocean, rain) also included adjectives such as calm, controlled, and unemotional.

and Highlight 9.1 above). The belief in a relationship between body type and personality has persisted into the present (see also Chapter 1). Toward the end of the last century, a German psychiatrist (Kretschmer, 1925) argued that people who were thin had a tendency to become schizophrenic, while those who were fat were more likely to tend toward manic depression. A more recent and better-known effort regarding body types was that of William Sheldon (1954; Sheldon and Stevens, 1942). Sheldon had people rated according to three physical structure types and then attempted to relate these body types to temperaments. Sheldon reported that people who had *mesomorphic* physiques (strong, athletic, and muscular) tended to have somatotonic temperaments (energetic, assertive, and courageous). *Endomorphic* body builds (soft, round, and with large stomachs) were associated with viscerotonic personalities (relaxed, gregarious, and food-loving). And *ectomorphic* physiques (tall, thin, and fragile) were common among cerebrotonic personality types (fearful, introverted, and restrained).

In Sheldon's investigations, individuals were photographed and rated on the extent to which they possessed each of the three body types. Then untrained observers rated the personality characteristics of these same people. Sheldon then found correlations between the physique and personality ratings. However, these

A medieval woodcut portraying the four temperaments and the elements traditionally associated with them: left — phlegmatic (water) and melancholic (earth); right — sanguine (air) and choleric (fire). (Zentralbibliothek Zurich, Ms. C 101)

findings have come into question because the raters may have been biased by predominant contemporary stereotypes, such as that round body types are jolly and athletic body types are aggressive. In fact, studies in which individuals are rated on specific behaviors rather than on global traits tend not to show strong associations between body types and personality (Mischel, 1968). This statement does not mean, however, that everyone has given up on somatotypes. For example, Sheldon's system has been extended (Carter and Heath, 1971) to provide more accurate measurements of body type, and there are theories of sport motivation based on the Sheldon data.

Not all type theorists base their classification system on physique. Although Jung (see Chapter 4) believed that introversion and extroversion are both present in each individual, he speculated that one of these dispositions would be dominant. Thus, he felt it appropriate to categorize individuals as primarily introverts or extroverts. Nevertheless, typologies like those proposed by Sheldon and Jung are used less frequently in current psychology. The complexity of human behavior makes it difficult to fit individuals neatly into a few simple categories. The description of someone as introverted or extroverted gives us too little information about the person. For most personality characteristics, people fit at some point on a continuous distribution of that characteristic rather than into the either-or categories provided by type concepts. A more scientific extension of the typology approach is represented in the work of trait-oriented psychologists.

Personality Disorders

While earlier typologies of personality no longer are influential in psychology, a typological approach is still used in the field of psychological disorders, where the concept of personality disorder has become popular over the last fifteen years. A *personality disorder* is "an enduring pattern of inner experience and behavior that deviates markedly from the expectations of the individual's culture, is pervasive and inflexible — is stable over time, and leads to distress or impairment" (American Psychiatric Association, 1994, p. 629). The Diagnostic and Statistical Manual of the American Psychiatric Association (1994) lists up to fourteen different personality disorders.

A personality disorder is a personality type in that it constitutes the extreme of a pervasive, organized pattern of traits. In addition, individuals manifesting a particular personality disorder are considered to have a fundamentally different constellation of character traits than do people with other personality disorders. A borderline personality, for instance, manifests the characteristics of impulsivity, emotional instability, identity confusion, inappropriate or intense anger, chronic feelings of emptiness or boredom, intense fears of being abandoned, engagement in self-mutilation or suicidal behaviors, and intense and unstable interpersonal relationships. In contrast, a paranoid personality is described as having the tendency to interpret the actions of others as deliberately demeaning or threatening and the tendency to be suspicious, mistrustful, hypervigilant, and argumentative (American Psychiatric Association, 1994).

However, like earlier typologies, the personality disorder concept has problems, including the fact that the categories overlap considerably in many cases. People, generally, cannot be neatly typed by a single personality disorder. Most individuals are given multiple diagnoses (the average number has been found in different studies to be between 2.8–4.6, Widiger and Frances, 1994). Recently, some have argued that it is better to think of personality disorders not as distinct character types but rather as representing different patterns of high and low scores on various trait dimensions (Widiger and Frances, 1994). For instance, instead of seeing borderline personality as a character type, the person who is labeled borderline could be described as showing an elevated profile on the traits of hostility, vulnerability, depression, anxiety, and impulsivity. The person diagnosed as a paranoid personality would be expected to score low on agreeableness, openness, and extraversion and high on hostility. The argument is that clinicians who describe individuals by their scores on various trait dimensions rather than by classifying them by character types, such as borderline or paranoid, will avoid many of the problems associated with a categorical model.

TRAIT THEORIES

There have been many psychologists who have believed that personality is best understood by studying the organization of traits within an individual. Perhaps the most influential of the trait psychologists was Gordon Allport. Trait psychologists believe that there are characteristics of individuals that remain consistent over time and across situations. If you are an aggressive person, for example, trait theories imply that you will be aggressive in many different settings. In their study of behavior, trait psychologists use a trait as the unit of analysis or the basic focus of examination. Their task is to determine which traits occur together and how patterns of traits are organized within an individual. This taxonomic approach shares with the periodic table in chemistry the goal of identifying basic elements and expressing all compounds (traits) as elements or amalgams of the basic factors.

Cattell and Factor Analysis

To study the organization of traits, many psychologists have turned to complex statistical methods such as factor analysis, discussed in the previous chapter. The work of Raymond Cattell (1965) is among the best-known work of this type. In his search for the basic elements of personality, Cattell performed extensive factor analyses of three types of data: life records (ratings of behavior in everyday situations), self-ratings on personality scales, and scores on objective tests. As indicated earlier, to determine the nature and the organization of traits, Cattell first examined a list of 4,500 trait names and then reduced this list to less than 200 by grouping synonyms or near-synonyms. Then scores were obtained on the degree to which individuals possessed these traits, and the results were factor analyzed. This procedure yielded 36 *surface traits* (clusters of responses or overt behaviors that fit together) and a smaller number of *source traits* (more basic organizing structures that underlie and determine surface traits).

    Various investigations by Cattell using life record and self-report data have produced a similar list of basic traits, shown in Table 9.2. It is clear from Table 9.2 that Cattell had a fondness for coining words, to the extent that his technical titles needed to be translated into more popular labels. For example, the trait label *premsia* is short for "protected emotional sensitivity."

    Most of Cattell's research has been directed toward the identification of source traits, some of which he has called *environment mold traits,* or traits formed by the environment. Others, determined by factors within the individual, are called *constitutional source traits.* Another distinction Cattell has made is between *specific* source traits, which describe how a person operates in a particular situation, and *general* source traits, which affect behavior in many different situations. Thus, in interpreting his factor analytic findings, the idea of trait consistency remains fundamental to Cattell's work and is reflected in the concept of a general source trait.

Eysenck's Hierarchy

Hans J. Eysenck is one of the more controversial figures in contemporary psychology. In his many active years as a psychologist he took strong positions against traditional psychotherapy (Eysneck, 1952), was one of the earliest advocates of

Table 9.2   Cattell's major personality factors found

A	Affectothymia-Sizothymia	Outgoing-reserved
B	Intelligence	More intelligent-less intelligent
C	Ego strength	Stable-emotional
E	Dominance-Submissiveness	Assertive-humble
F	Surgency-Desurgency	Happy-go-lucky-sober
G	Super-ego strength	Conscientious-expedient
H	Parmia-Threctia	Venturesome-shy
I	Premsia-Harria	Tender-minded – tough-minded
L	Protension-Alaxia	Suspicious-trusting
M	Autia-Praxernia	Imaginative-practical
N	Shrewdness-Artlessness	Shrewd-forthright
O	Guilt proneness-Assurance	Apprehensive-placid

Source: Hall and Lindzey, 1970, p. 390. Reprinted by permission.

behavior therapy, and strongly supported the notion of intelligence as an inherited trait.

Eysenck's view of personality is in many ways similar to Cattell's, with behavior viewed hierarchically. At the bottom of the hierarchy are the *specific responses* that are actually observed. Just above these are *habitual responses*. At the next level in the pyramid are *traits* that are analogous to Cattell's source traits, and at the top level are types. *Types* for Eysenck are basic behavior dimensions which are continuous rather than typological categories. Eysenck identified three types or dimensions that he regarded as the basic units of personality: neuroticism, extroversion-introversion, and psychoticism.

Using a variety of data sources, such as ratings, questionnaires, and physiological measures, Eysenck repeatedly identified the same dimensions in factor analytic studies. Most of his attention was devoted to classifying people along the dimensions of neuroticism and extroversion-introversion. Since neuroticism can be viewed as corresponding to emotional stability, individuals were classified along a continuum from stable to unstable. An unstable personality is seen as moody, touchy, anxious, and restless, while a stable person is characterized as calm, even-tempered, and carefree. With regard to extroversion and introversion, extroverts are seen as sociable, active, outgoing, and optimistic, while introverts are characterized as passive, quiet, careful, and unsociable. In many respects, the basic personality dimensions identified by Eysenck are similar to those described by Cattell. Eysenck acknowledged this but also contended that his approach was more dependable and more theoretically meaningful and parsimonious.

The Big Five

More recently, a number of researchers have converged on the idea that there are five basic trait dimensions to personality. This concept is increasingly referred to as the *Big Five* model of personality.

Development of the Big Five model had its roots in the analysis of natural, everyday language (John, 1990). A number of investigators over the years have collected words from the dictionary that represent personality traits (e.g., *strong-willed, assertive, introspective*) and then, using a technique called factor analysis, have sorted them into categories. Five factors have frequently appeared.

Others have arrived at a five-factor solution by factor analyses of personality tests. In a personality test, the subject rates the degree to which a *statement* about someone, rather than simply a single word, describes the person. One of the most well known examples of this type of research is the work of McCrae and Costa (1990), who have developed their "NEO-PI-R" personality inventory to measure their version of the Big Five. McCrae and Costa's five factors are: Neuroticism, Extraversion, Openness to Experience, Aggreeableness, and Conscientiousness. The following list describes the basics of each of these five factors (from Costa and Widiger, 1994).

1. Neuroticism versus emotional stability. People high on this scale may manifest anxiety, angry hostility, depression, self-consciousness, impulsivity, or vulnerability.

2. Extraversion. People high on this scale might be sociable, talkative, active, person-oriented, optimistic, or fun-loving. People low on this scale might be reserved, sober, independent, quiet, or aloof.

3. Openness to experience. People high on this scale are imaginative, curious, and willing to entertain novel ideas. They experience a whole spectrum of emotions. People low on this scale tend to be conventional, conservative, set in their ways, and emotionally unresponsive.

4. Agreeableness. People high on this scale tend to be good natured, altruistic, helpful, forgiving, and trusting. People low on this scale tend to be suspicious, uncooperative, irritable, cynical, or rude.

5. Conscientiousness. People high on this scale tend to be reliable, self-directed, punctual, scrupulous, ambitious, and hard-working. People low on this scale tend to be aimless, lazy, lax, negligent, and unreliable.

The identification of these five basic traits, then, has come from two sources: analysis of the *words* and analysis of the *descriptions* that individuals make of themselves and of others. An immediate question that occurs is the degree to which the Big Five represent how the average English-speaking person views personality compared to how people in other cultures view personality. In other words, how universal are these Big Five traits? There are currently several research projects underway to answer this question. Past studies have found overall congruence for the Dutch and German languages, as well as for Japan and China (John, 1990). Neuroticism and extraversion have been replicated for languages of the Solomon Islands and of India; and there have been mixed results for Filipinos (John, 1990). John (1990) notes that so far the weakest evidence for universality is found for openness to experience. Overall, though, the results are encouraging for some degree of universality.

Big Five advocates view these traits as the basic structure of personality. However, if you look at the descriptions of the five factors, you will note that each broad factor includes a number of more specific traits. For instance, neuroticism includes such disparate emotional states as anxiety, hostility, and depression. Conscientiousness includes being reliable and punctual but also being ambitious and self-directed. This is because the five factors are conceived of as being *broad band* personality traits. That is, they are seen as forming the *general* underlying structure of personality, even though they encompass many, more *specific* traits. For most Big Five advocates, nested within each factor are more specific factors. John (1990) notes that the Big Five is similar to taxonomies in the natural world. The five factors are equivalent to terms such as *plant* and *animal*. Under *animal,* for instance, we have lions, tigers, dogs, and so on. In a similar manner, under *conscientiousness* we have *ambitious* and *reliable*. Advocates of the Big Five do not mean to imply that personality can be described *only* in terms of these five traits any more than the world of living beings can be described only in terms of plants and animals. In fact, many Big Five advocates have said that in order to actually predict an individual's behavior, the Big Five is too broad and general. One needs measures of the more specific traits within each factor.

While writers such as McCrae and John (1992) have argued that the field should now assume that the five-factor model is the correct representation of personality trait structure and move on to using it to explore other topics, there are those (e.g., Block, unpublished) who believe that this conclusion is premature. Others, such as Eysenck and Cattell, whose personality tests are respectively based on three, and sixteen factors, would agree. We shall briefly note some of the criticisms Block has raised concerning the Big Five.

First, advocates of the Big Five have argued that one of the strongest sources of evidence for the existence of the Big Five is that it has been found *empirically*. That is, it was not based on someone's theoretical preconceptions, but simply found by factor analyzing words and sentences people use to describe other people. However, Block has noted that before these factor analyses were done, investigators had made numerous assumptions that may well have biased the outcome in favor of finding five factors.

Second, while many investigators have found five factors, they are not the *same* five factors. Block notes some important discrepancies among the various five-factor models. For instance, McCrae and Costa place *warmth* under *extraversion,* but Goldberg (another five-factor theorist) places it under *agreeableness*. They place *impulsivity* in *neuroticism,* but Goldberg places it in *extraversion*.

Third, while advocates of the Big Five claim that five factors consistently emerge, others have disagreed. We have already mentioned that Cattell bases his personality test on sixteen factors and that Eysenck claims there are three main factors. Block's analysis of the personality assessment device he uses, the California Q Sort, finds eight factors. And Hogan and Hogan (1992) have found that they must use six factors to describe their data adequately. Block argues that this suggests that there are important aspects of personality that are not being encompassed by the Big Five.

Despite criticisms, there is much enthusiasm for the Big Five model of personality. Only further research will clarify whether that enthusiasm is well founded.

Although trait and type classifications are commonly recognized by psychologist and layperson alike, their value has been a matter of serious debate. The next section of this chapter examines the attack on traditional trait psychology and introduces some new approaches to personality assessment that have arisen out of this debate.

THE ATTACK ON TRAITS: SITUATIONAL THEORIES

Mischel's Argument

Mischel's (1968) book on the assessment of personality has often been interpreted as an all-out attack on the concept of traits. Mischel, however, repeatedly denied this extreme position. Rather, he maintained that the evidence for the existence of traits is weak and that the methods for their assessment need reevaluation. Furthermore, he acknowledged the value of cognitive traits, such as intelligence and speed of processing and encoding information.

The essence of Mischel's argument is that trait measures are not valid predictors of behavior in specific situations. Although personality tests do well at predicting how people will score on similar personality tests, they do poorly at predicting how someone will actually behave in a given situation. One finds that questionnaire and projective measures of aggression are not very effective predictors of an individual's aggressive behavior on the athletic field, in confrontations with authority, in response to a friend's arriving late for an appointment, and in a myriad of other concrete situations in which variations in aggressive behavior can be observed. Moreover, observational measures of aggression are not very effective in predicting aggressive behaviors in situations other than the one in which aggression was initially assessed. Similar low predictability of behaviors in specific situations can be found for measures of impulsivity, achievement motivation, anxiety, and other personality characteristics. It can be maintained that if such tests are really meaningful, they should be able to forecast how people will behave in the specific tasks that psychologists create for laboratory studies.

Mischel reported that many investigations demonstrate that the correlation between test scores and behavior in specific situations is rarely greater than .30, or that around 91 percent of the variance in behavior is unexplained by the test score. Mischel called these low correlations *personality coefficients* and suggested that knowledge of personal characteristics tells us little about how a person will actually behave. Mischel was more impressed with the amount of variation that would be explained by knowing about the situation in which the behavior is observed, rather than knowing about the person in that situation. Thus, he championed what is known as the *situational* critique of the concept of traits.

Mischel's original position led to many responses, some in support, others in contradiction. Below we consider other positions in response to his attack on traits.

Attribution Theory

Another perspective suggesting the need to modify traditional trait theories derives from *attribution theory*. Originally, attribution theory was concerned primarily with the judgments people make about others, in particular their inferences about others' intentions. However, research in this area now covers all aspects of how people attempt to understand the causes of events in their lives.

The basic ideas of attribution theory were first formulated in the mid-1940s and 1950s (Heider, 1944, 1958) but became popular only in the late 1960s (Jones and Davis, 1965; Kelley, 1967). Kelley offered a model to capture how the layperson determines causation. He suggested that events are perceived as caused by three potential sources: persons, entities (aspects of the environment), or circumstances. To determine which of these, or which combination of sources, has caused an event, the person uses three criteria called distinctiveness, consensus, and consistency. If, for example, we wanted to explain why John enjoys the food at a particular restaurant so much, it would be helpful to ask if he always feels this way in restaurants (distinctiveness), whether others in the same restaurant also enjoy the food (consensus), and whether John enjoyed the food when he ate in this restaurant before (consistency). If all people enjoy the food in this eating establishment, then John's enjoyment would be attributed to the entity (it is a good restaurant); if John always enjoys food at restaurants, then the enjoyment would be attributed to him (he is a glutton); and if John usually dislikes this restaurant, then his present enjoyment would be ascribed to special circumstances, such as unusual hunger, the presence of friends, or some special dish (Kelley, 1967; Orvis, Cunningham, and Kelley, 1975).

Actor-Observer Differences. Jones and Nisbett (1971) have suggested that the selection of a trait or a situational explanation for behavior also depends on the role played by the person making the judgment. When people are observers and are making judgments about others, they tend to use dispositional or trait explanations. However, they use fewer trait concepts and more situational concepts to explain their own behavior. Thus, one might say, "You hit him because you are aggressive" (a trait explanation), but, "I hit him because he did something wrong" (a situation explanation).

Why should there be a difference between the attributions of actors and observers? Jones and Nisbett suggest that this is so because people know more about their own behavior than they know about the behavior of others. Searching in memory, a person can recall behaving differently in many different situations in the past. Information regarding the distinctiveness and inconsistency of behavior fosters situation attributions. Note, however, that this analysis assumes that individuals find little consistency in their behaviors across situations! Observers, on the other hand, are less likely to have the information available about others to rule out situational causes of behavior, and therefore make trait attributions for other people.

Another explanation of actor-observer differences in attributions is that the sensory apparatus (eyes and ears) of the actor are focused on the environment rather than on the self. Thus, the actor observes the environment, while the observer views the actor. Videotapes have been used to demonstrate that when actors are shown a situation from the vantage point of the observer, they describe their own behavior in terms of traits (Storms, 1973). In a similar manner, when the observer is shown one situation from the vantage point of the actor, situational attributions are more likely. In sum, attributions are in part dependent on the focus of attention and the information available to the observer.

Attribution Theory and Trait Psychology.   Attribution theorists have not been concerned with the inadequacy of traditional trait tests for predicting behavior. Rather, traits are important because people use them to describe the behavior of others; they are part of the implicit or "naive" psychology that the layperson uses (see Chapter 6). Extensive research has demonstrated that both laypeople and experienced clinical psychologists favor explaining behavior in terms of enduring dispositions instead of in terms of the situation. The tendency to overestimate the importance of traits and underestimate the importance of the situation in causing behavior has been labeled the *fundamental attributional error* (Ross, 1977).

Indeed, it appears that our first, relatively automatic reaction is to attribute what a person does to his or her traits. Only with conscious effort and thought do we take the situation into account (Gilbert, 1989). Gilbert has argued that when we are under stress, we are more likely to ignore situational contributions to behavior and to overattribute the behavior to an individual's personality traits.

For instance, in a study by Gilbert, Pelham, and Krull (1988) subjects watched a silent videotape of a woman engaged in conversation with a stranger. The woman exhibited various visual signs of distress and anxiety: tapping her fingers, twirling her hair, biting her nails. In one condition, where subjects were told that the woman had been asked to talk about her sexual fantasies, it was assumed that the subjects would attribute her distress to the *situation,* that is, to having to talk about one's sexual fantasies to a stranger. In another condition, where subjects were told that the woman had been asked to talk about bland topics, it was assumed that the woman's distress would be attributed to her *personality,* that is, the woman acts anxious because she is an anxious person. These differences in behavior attribution were found as long as the subjects were not under stress themselves. However, when subjects had to engage in a memory task as they watched the video, all subjects tended to attribute the woman's anxiety to her personality, as if they had not bothered to take into account whether or not she was in an anxiety-producing situation (e.g., talking about sexual fantasies to a stranger).

Other research even suggests that the manner in which we make judgments about others is not strongly associated with either past experiences or our observations of these others. For example, one study examined peer ratings given by different groups of men (Norman, 1963). One group had lived together in the same fraternity for three years, while another group was less closely associated. Although the two groups had differing amounts of contact, they used very similar dimensions for making judgments about one another. Indeed, these same dimensions of judgment emerge when subjects rate complete strangers (Passini and Norman, 1966). These studies demonstrate that the same dimensions or traits are used to rate others whether or not the subjects are familiar with the people they are evaluating. These findings do not necessarily mean that the trait dimensions are being misapplied; rather, they suggest that trait ratings might tell us more about the raters than about the people being rated. But whether or not traits are valuable for understanding behavior, observers *believe* that they are and tend to perceive information in a manner that supports trait interpretations.

If traits are not useful concepts, then why is there such a persistent need for people to refer to them? The following possible explanations for this behavior have been suggested (Epstein, 1979, pp. 1099-1100):

1. It is emotionally satisfying to believe that behavior is predictable, particularly when it is someone else's.

2. It is simpler to classify behavior by people than by situations.

3. People have implicit personality theories that assume stability in personality, and their theories bias their perceptions.

4. A primacy effect operates to make new impressions conform to old ones.

5. The observer is always present in the situations that he or she observes in real life, thereby presenting the observer with a biased sample of behavior.

6. There is a tendency for observers to equate behavior that elicits the same emotional reactions in them.

7. There is a tendency for judges to generalize from a few attributes that are stable, such as intelligence, to others that are not.

8. There are more terms for classifying people than for classifying situations, which leads to a bias toward attributing behavior more often to characteristics of people than to characteristics of situations.

NEWER ASSESSMENT STRATEGIES

Despite arguments against the notion of traits, few psychologists have actually shelved their faith in personality dispositions. Mischel (1979) and others contend that psychologists have tended to predict too much from traits alone. While the concept of traits may still have utility, it does appear that trait categorization is an oversimplification that can lead to incorrect predictions of behavior in a variety of situations. Although there is consistency and constancy in our lives, better measurement techniques are needed to forecast future behavior. This requires methodologies that consider and include the evaluations of situations, the interaction of traits and situations, and new approaches to trait assessment.

Situational Assessment

There is little doubt that behavior is influenced by the situation in which it occurs. Some investigators have attempted to create taxonomies of situations, similar to trait taxonomies. Just as trait psychologists attempted to determine which traits predicted behavior, *situational* psychologists attempted to build classification systems to relate environments and situations to behavior. For example, one taxonomy (see Table 9.3) has been developed in which environments are classified according to six characteristics (Moos, 1973). Each aspect of the environment has been shown to have pronounced impact on individual or group behavior.

The situational orientation emphasizes the impact of situations over the impact of personality characteristics in determining behavior. For example, consider the question "Is Fred motivated at work?" Trait-oriented psychologists would want to know something about Fred's characteristics. How high does he

Table 9.3 Six characteristics of environments

Characteristics	Examples
1. Ecological dimensions	Architectural design, geographic location, weather conditions.
2. Behavior settings	The office, the home, the store.
3. Organizational structure	Percentage of women in the student body, number of people per household, average age of group.
4. Characteristics of milieu inhabitants	Proportion of students in your university who date, drink, or vote.
5. Psychosocial and organization climate	Work pressure, encouragement of participation, orientation toward helping with personal problems.
6. Functional or reinforcing properties of the environment	Is aggression reinforced on the football field? Is it reinforced at home?

Source: Derived from Moos, 1973, pp. 652–665. Copyright 1973 by the American Psychological Association. Reprinted by permission.

score on scales that measure need for achievement, need for power, and other work-related traits? In contrast, situation-oriented psychologists would want to measure characteristics of Fred's work environment. What is the psychosocial climate? Are Fred's work efforts appropriately reinforced?

An emphasis on environments or situations brings with it a whole new set of measurement problems. Just as trait psychologists had to struggle with methods for the evaluation of people, those with a situational orientation need to find quantitative expressions for environmental characteristics. Unfortunately, research has not revealed that studying the characteristics of the environment lead to much better predictions of behavior than studying the characteristics of the people inhabiting those environments (Endler and Magnusson, 1976). However, the study of situations has made it clear that both situational and personal characteristics influence behavior. The obvious next step is to consider both traits and situations as determinants of action.

The Interactionist Position

To a growing number of psychologists, whether traits or situations are more important in determining behavior is a moot question (Endler, 1973). It is meaningless to ask which is more important when it is evident that behavior is always a joint function of characteristics of the person and of the situation. This *interactionist* position is a rapprochement between trait and situational approaches to personality assessment which acknowledges the importance of personality dispositions as well as the role of situations.

The interactionist position takes several different forms, each with different implications. The most complete and sophisticated form is the *transactional* approach (Magnusson, 1990, cf. Chapter 2). Whenever interaction is described in these terms, it refers to the reciprocal sequence of actions that take place between person and situation. Each situation poses its own demands and cues and tends to call for a particular set of behaviors. The relaxed setting of an informal gathering will elicit very different behaviors than a formal dinner party; the athletic field elicits different responses than the classroom; and comparable differences are obtained between home and office. Each individual brings his or her own set of unique personality traits to each of these situations. These traits influence how the situation is perceived; different people will see different aspects of the situation as most important. Thus, at the dinner party, person A, who is characterized by anxiety over status and acceptance by others, will be oriented to the seating arrangement and to the amount of attention given by the host and hostess; person B, a "hail-fellow-well-met" extrovert, will find the stiffness and formality particularly frustrating.

The transactional process does not end with individual differences in perceptions of situations. Individuals behave on the basis of these perceptions and their behaviors elicit reactions from others; the feedback from these behaviors and reactions will then influence subsequent behaviors. The behavioral outcome that is finally observed is a result of a sequence of reciprocal transactions between the individual, with his or her uniqueness, and the situation, with its uniqueness. This formulation of the trait-situation interaction is consonant with the views of situation-oriented theorists like Mischel, as well as with those of many trait-oriented theorists (Endler and Magnusson, 1976; Magnusson and Endler, 1977).

There is a common but more limited meaning of the term *interaction* that is also applicable to the trait-situation issue. In the statistical sense, interaction refers to a *differential* effect that the same situation may have on different people or the differential effect of the same disposition in response to different situations. For example, a highly insulting, frustrating situation will elicit more aggressive behavior than a nonfrustrating situation. However, the effects of the frustration are likely to be much more pronounced in individuals who have a strong disposition to respond with anger and aggression than in individuals who are low on this trait dimension. The difference in aggressive behavior between the high-aggressive and low-aggressive individuals under nonfrustrating conditions may be negligible; it is under conditions of frustration that the difference in personality traits becomes evident.

In comparison to the transactional model, the more limited interactional model is easier to investigate. Using this model, evidence for the interactionist position is obtained by comparing the proportion of variance in behavior that is explained by person, by situation, and by interaction between person and situation. One might think of this by drawing a pie and dividing it to represent all of the different influences on human behavior. Figure 9.1 shows such a pie. One slice represents the proportion of variance attributable to personality traits; another slice represents the proportion of variance caused by situational influences; and a

Figure 9.1   Factors influencing behavior.

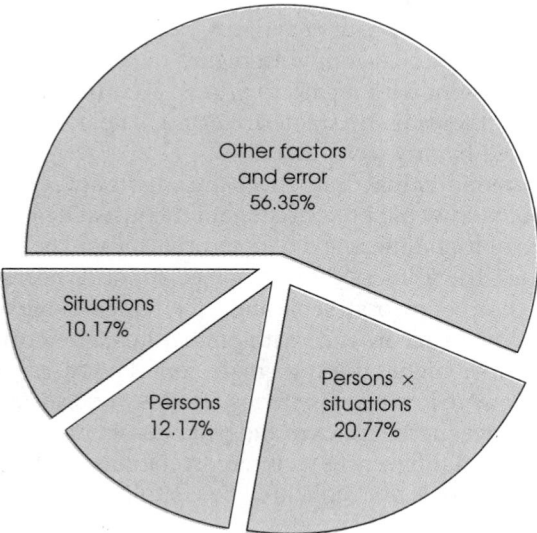

third slice is for the interaction between situational and dispositional influences. The interaction is due to unique combinations of traits and situations. Careful studies designed for application of the statistical method known as *analysis of variance* have separated the proportion of variance attributable to each of these factors. As shown in Fig. 9.1, interaction accounts for a larger proportion of the variance in behavior than either person or situation (Magnusson and Endler, 1977).

Although it is revealing that unique combinations of persons and situations explain more of the variation than either influence by itself, the interaction position still explains only some of the behavior of some of the people some of the time (Bem and Allen, 1974). As Fig. 9.1 reveals, the largest slice of the pie is reserved for error variance: the proportion of the total that is not explained in terms of the three specified sources of influence. After reviewing many studies of the influence of the person versus the influence of the situation versus the person × situation interaction, Sarason, Smith, and Diener (1975) concluded that none of the three sources accounts for an impressive share in the variation of accounted-for behavior, as compared to the amount of variation that is left unexplained. Although the interaction is a better predictor than either the trait or the situation, it is only slightly better. Thus, there is still a need for measurement methods that can be used to predict more of the people more of the time.

The Moderator Variable Approach

One solution to the dilemma of accounting for such little variance in predicting behavior from traits is to propose *moderator variables* (i.e., identify factors that are responsible for the lack of predictability of trait indexes) and then take them into account when attempting to predict behavior (see Cheek, 1982). One such moderator proposed by Bem and Allen (1974) is the reported consistency of each person's behavior in each domain of activity. Bem and Allen proposed that some individuals may be very consistent with regard to some personality characteristics, yet very inconsistent with regard to others. That is, some traits characterize some people while other traits characterize other people. And some people might not be characterized by any traits at all!

To demonstrate individual differences in consistency, college students rated whether their behavior would be consistent or inconsistent across different situations for the traits of friendliness and conscientiousness. They then examined the correlations among friendliness measures (self-reports, peers' and parents' reports, and objective behaviors) separately for subjects high and low in self-reported consistency. In accordance with predictions, intercorrelations of friendliness measures were higher for the high consistency group than for those declaring that they were low in consistency. That is, reported consistency moderated the relation between trait indexes and behavior. However, this procedure did not yield the predicted differences in intercorrelations for conscientiousness. In addition, the findings were not replicated by Chaplin and Goldberg (1985) or by Paunonen and Jackson (1985).

Individuals vary in the consistency of their behavior. (© Elizabeth Crews)

Guided by this approach, Zuckerman et al. (1988) demonstrated that self-reported consistency as well as subjective trait importance moderates cross-situational consistency. If the individual reports that he or she is highly consistent and the trait has high relevance, then there is cross-situational consistency in behavior and a relation between trait measures and actions. These investigators recommend that psychologists search for an array of moderator variables; predictions of behavior from traits will then be enhanced.

The Template Matching Technique. Subsequently, Bem and Funder (1978) introduced a descriptive system of measurement that could be used to take advantage of the ability to predict our own behavior in particular situations. Their approach, called the *template-matching technique,* attempts to match personality to a specific template of behavior. To employ the technique, one must specify how a person would behave in a particular situation without any information about the particular person. For example, consider the question "Should Cathy see the movie *War Correspondent*?" Perhaps the best way to guide Cathy would be to describe the movie in terms of how several hypothetical people might react to it. People who are squeamish might enjoy the movie but have bad dreams about it for a few nights. Or people with certain political beliefs might not like it because it presents a specific perspective about our involvement in wars. Now Cathy can predict her own reaction to the movie by matching her characteristics with this set of "templates" that have been provided for her.

Bem and Funder (p. 486) proposed that situations can be characterized as sets of template-behavior pairs, each template being a personality description of how an idealized type of person is specifically expected to behave in that setting. The probability that a particular person will behave in a particular way in a situation will be a function of the match between his or her characteristics and the template. For example, if Cathy's personality characteristics matched the template for those who would hate *War Correspondent,* then she might be best advised to avoid it.

The experiments by Bem and Funder indicated that by asking the appropriate question it is possible to predict the behavior of more of the people more of the time. This research acknowledged that there are personality characteristics that aid in the prediction of behavior in particular situations and is consistent with the findings of Bem and Allen. The difficulty with this approach is that there are so many potential combinations of persons and situations. Bem and Funder were able to demonstrate that they could predict behavior very well in three particular situations, yet the number of potential person-situation combinations staggers the mind (Cronbach, 1975).

Aggregation Techniques

The fact that behavior varies with situations suggests a strategy for reducing the variability contributed by the situation and maximizing the variability contributed by the person — namely, by averaging, or aggregating, behavior across different situations. This is essentially the strategy used in the development of objective personality tests, which typically have large numbers of items. In general, the larger the number of items, the more reliable the test. For example, each item of the MMPI scale of depression can be assumed to tap a generalized dimension of depression and also a reaction specific to that item. By using a large number of items, the influence of any single item relative to the general dimension of depression is reduced, and the reliability thereby enhanced. Epstein (1979, 1980) has cogently argued that situations are analogous to questionnaire items, and that one can enhance the reliability of trait measures and their intercorrelations by averaging across situations.

There has been some controversy regarding the implications of this increased reliability for trait correlations when aggregated over many, very different situations, for aggregation seems to acknowledge that behavior in a specific situation cannot be predicted from a trait measure. However, a number of investigations have shown that aggregation procedures improve predictions and contribute to stronger trait relationships (Cheek, 1982; Rushton, Brainerd, and Pressley, 1983). For example, the correlation between self-ratings and ratings by fraternity peers on a number of personality dimensions increases as a function of the number of items being rated and the number of raters (see Table 9.4 on p. 251, from Cheek, 1982).

Measurement Error.   Aggregation has been shown to make a difference in the implications of the classic series of studies conducted in the 1920s (Hartshorne and May, 1928, 1929; Hartshorne, May, and Shuttleworth, 1930). This large longitudinal study of honesty remains one of the most thorough and widely cited pieces of research in the field (see Chapter 12). Over the course of six years, a national sample of eight thousand children was repeatedly evaluated on a series of

Table 9.4   The effects of aggregation over items and raters on correlations between self-ratings and peer ratings

	Rating dimensions				
No. of items and raters	Extro-version	Agree-ableness	Conscien-tiousness	Emotional stability	Average
Single item, single rater	.43	.22	.27	.22	.29
Two items, two raters	.53	.33	.40	.25	.38
Three items, three raters	.59	.39	.47	.27	.44

Source: From Cheek, 1982, p. 1261. Copyright 1982 by the American Psychological Association. Reprinted by permission.

measures of honesty which included cheating during a game, cheating at school, cheating on a take-home exam, taking money, lying, and falsifying records. Epstein (1979) noted that this study is widely cited as evidence that personality is not general because honesty in any specific situation was not found to be a good predictor of honesty in any other specific situation. What is seldom mentioned, however, is that when several measures of honesty are combined into a single score, honesty at one point in time and across situations becomes a very good predictor of honesty at another time and across situations. In sum, the problems of inconsistency across situations and of instability over time may both result from measurement error. More reliable indicators can be created by averaging together behaviors in several situations.

TRAIT PSYCHOLOGY REVISITED

It would be worthwhile now to review the various approaches that have already been examined in this chapter. First, we presented the work of traditional trait psychologists who felt that personality measures accurately assess personality traits. Next, Mischel's challenge to personality tests was presented. Although it appeared to many psychologists that personality was neither stable over time nor consistent across situations, it was also suggested that most people do perceive stable and general personality patterns. Bem and Allen, Bem and Funder, and Epstein have now forced us to reconsider whether the notion of traits was ever completely wrong in the first place.

Again there is a paradox. On the one hand, few people seriously deny the importance of personality characteristics. On the other hand, there is still little evidence that personality tests can predict behavior in particular situations. Nevertheless, many psychologists remain unconvinced by Mischel's critique of trait psychology and believe that personality dimensions can be demonstrated to be meaningful predictors of behavior. In a strong defense of traits and the personality tests used to measure them, it has been acknowledged that poor research does not support the existence of traits but that many well-conducted studies are supportive (Hogan, DeSoto, and Solano, 1977). For example, Gough (1965) demonstrated that the sociability scale of his inventory correlated .73 with delinquency in a study of over ten thousand youths. And other investigators have reported that the creativity of architects as assessed by other architects' ratings can be predicted very well on the basis of a few personality variables (Hall and MacKinnon, 1969).

There is also evidence that behavior patterns are stable. Some studies, in which people's self-reports are monitored over the years, have found that people's views of themselves remain constant. However, consistency in self-perception may not mean consistency in behavior. Without resorting to self-report studies, there are well-conducted longitudinal studies that demonstrate the stability of behavioral patterns (see also Chapter 13). Perhaps the most important of these used a set of data maintained at the University of California, Berkeley. As discussed earlier, subjects in this study were first evaluated in junior high school, then again in senior high school, and once again when they were in their midthirties. In all, persons in the sample were rated on 114 personality variables by different observers at three different points in time. The results clearly demonstrated that many personality characteristics are stable. Indeed, between junior and senior high school nearly 60 percent of the personality characteristics measured remained consistent.

A European study on aggressive behavior in boys produced even more convincing results with regard to personality stability. Over two hundred boys were rated on their tendency to start fights and other characteristics of aggressive behavior. The ratings were obtained when the boys were in the sixth grade and then again three years later. In each case, at least three raters were used. The results showed that aggressive tendencies were quite stable over the three-year period, with a correlation of .66 across the two time periods. When error of measurement was corrected, the correlation became even stronger, reaching a level of .80 (Olweus, 1973, 1974, 1977a, 1977b).

Finally, Funder (1989, 1991; Funder and Colvin, 1991) has forcefully defended the concept of traits. He has shown that if different people who know an individual well rate that individual's personality traits, there is considerable agreement among them. This is true even when the people doing the rating know the individual from different situations in his or her life. For instance, agreement on the item "enjoys aesthetic impressions" had a correlation of .64. In addition, Funder points out there are numerous correlations between trait ratings and specific behaviors. For instance, those individuals who took longest to complete the tests in his studies had been described by acquaintances as "tending to interpret basically simple situations in complex ways." Similarly, those who took the least time had been described by acquaintances as irritable, over-reactive, and prone to give up in the face of adversity.

State versus Trait

One factor that has been responsible in part for the low correlations between some trait measures and actual behavior is the failure to distinguish between states and traits. *States* refer to transitory conditions of the organism, to emotions and moods that vary in intensity and fluctuate over time, such as anger, panic, depression, and boredom. *Traits* refer to more enduring individual differences in behavior disposition, in the individual's *tendency* to be angry, afraid, depressed, or bored. A clearer understanding of the manifestations of a trait and of the relationship of the trait to behavior is obtained when a state measure is distinguished from a trait measure. This is best exemplified by the extensive amount of research that has been carried out on the distinction between state anxiety and trait anxiety (Spielberger, 1971*a*, 1971*b*; Spielberger, Gorsuch, and Lushene, 1970).

The difference between state and trait anxiety is made evident in the different ways in which they are assessed. Items on the state anxiety scale are answered in terms of the *intensity* of the individual's feelings and how the person feels at the moment. For instance, for the item "I am tense," the individual is given a choice among four alternatives ranging from "Not at all" to "Very much so." In contrast, items on the trait anxiety scale are answered in terms of the frequency of the feeling and how the individual generally feels. For example, for the item "I take disappointments so keenly that I can't put them out of my mind," the individual's four choices range from "Almost never" to "Almost always."

Spielberger and his associates (1970, p. 3) defined trait anxiety in terms of "differences between people in a tendency to respond to situations perceived as threatening with elevations in state anxiety intensity." Whether anxiety will be elicited at any particular time and its manifestation in behavior depends on the strength of trait anxiety and the presence of situational stimuli that will evoke state anxiety. Furthermore, the influence of trait anxiety and of external stimulus stressors are mediated by the process of *cognitive appraisal*. If a stimulus is perceived as nonthreatening (e.g., "He wants to get back at me but he's powerless"), then no anxiety is elicited. If the stimulus is appraised as threatening, then the individual may respond with feelings of anxiety or automatically react with defensive behaviors that minimize the experience of anxiety. Extensive research has been carried out on the process of cognitive appraisal, and it has been shown that it is possible to reduce physiological and other anxiety indicators by manipulating the cognitive appraisal of an ordinarily highly threatening stimulus. For example, people exposed to a stressful film depicting the subincision rites of a preliterate culture were asked to perceive the film within an anthropological context. This introduces a method of coping with anxiety similar to that of intellectualization, which lets the viewers detach themselves from a threat that is otherwise reacted to in personal terms (Lazarus and Alfert, 1964; Lazarus and

Averill, 1972). In Spielberger's terms, the cognitive appraisal that mediates state anxiety can be modified by situational, experimentally induced, defensive approaches or by variations in trait anxiety and accompanying defensive tendencies.

In accordance with the theoretical attributes of state and trait anxiety, there is a substantial amount of research indicating that trait anxiety is a stable measure while state anxiety varies markedly with changes in situational stresses (Lamb, 1978). There is also evidence that individuals who differ in trait anxiety also differ, as expected, in the intensity of their state anxiety reactions to stressors, particularly to psychological rather than physical threats. These and other relationships indicating the value of the state-trait distinction for the study of anxiety suggest that a similar distinction can be fruitfully applied in helping clarify the trait-situation interaction for other personality attributes. Eliminating state components from the trait measure and taking state changes into account results in more stable trait indicators and stronger relationships between traits and behaviors. Assessing both trait and state also helps reduce measurement error.

Attribution theory, introduced earlier in this chapter, also has implications for the trait-state distinction. Chaplin, John, and Goldberg (1988) asked subjects to rate a series of acknowledged traits and states on a variety of characteristics. They found that stability over time, consistency of behavior, and perceptions of internal or personal causality were linked with traits, whereas instability, inconsistency, and external causality were associated with states. Hence, an anxious person is perceived as always anxious in a variety of situations and that reaction is caused by the self. However, when a person reacts with anxiety in a specific situation, then that reaction is perceived to be temporary, different than in other situations, and is caused by something external to the person. Chaplin et al. (1988) suggest that trait perceptions enable people to predict behavior over time and situations and thus lead to social actions based on the person (e.g., seek out or avoid people with that characteristic). On the other hand, state reactions, being unstable over time, cannot be predicted from past experience with the person, but may be controlled by manipulating the situation.

Figure 9.2   Conceptualizing traits.

Conceptualizing Traits

We have considered the consistency of traits and the relative influences of traits and situations on behavior. The interaction between traits and situations can provide a basis for conceptualizing the theoretical properties and functions of traits. Figure 9.2 depicts a chain of processes that can mediate between an observable stimulus and an overt response made to that stimulus. The stimulus first must be perceived and categorized (information processing); the organism's appraisal of the stimulus then has motivational consequences; alternative means for satisfying the motivation elicited may then be considered; and the final link in the chain is the overt response. Individual differences in the overt response may arise from trait differences that can influence any of the processes in the sequence.

Consider the following stimulus situation. A male college student approaches several female students after class and asks each for the class assignment and reading list. Student A sharply tells him to go elsewhere. Student B also refuses, excusing herself to rush to an appointment. Student C agrees to his request. The differences in behaviors among these three students can reflect various trait influences. The students may have reacted differently because they perceived the situation differently. Student C might have a cognitive style characterized by scanning of stimuli rather than focusing on details and might not have perceived subtle cues of intonation and body movement indicative of a social overture. Among other traits that can influence the organism at the information-processing stage, the most extensively studied is the dimension of field dependence-independence (Witkin et al., 1962) The perceptions of the field-dependent person are strongly influenced by the context in which stimuli are presented, while the field-independent person is better able to separate figures from their context.

Returning to our example, the students may have interpreted the information similarly but the information may have elicited different feelings and motivations. Student A might be high in aggressive motivation and might have resented the indirect social approach that was taken. Student B might have anxiety over sexual impulses and reacts with avoidance to most social overtures by members of the opposite sex. The dotted arrow in Fig. 9.2 indicates that motivational traits can also influence information processing. For example, Student B might be a repressive on the repression-sensitization dimension, block out awareness of the heterosexual aspects of the interaction, and fail to recognize her avoidant behavior. Student C might be more comfortable in the sexual area or experience anxiety over asserting her feelings and refusing moderate impositions.

The differences in behavior among the three women could also have arisen from traits operating at the behavior regulation level. Student A might be high on impulsivity and have difficulty in controlling the expression of her feelings, while B might be at the opposite end of this continuum. C might be impulsive or playful or, conversely, overcontrolled. Finally, part of the difference in behavior may be a reflection of behavioral style at the overt response level. Student C might simply have learned to be more polite than A and B. These trait attributes at the overt response level do not influence or cause the behavior; they are intrinsic to it. Traits at this level are *descriptive* of behavior rather than explanatory. However, traits influencing information processing, motivation, or the regulation of behavior can be considered as determinants of or contributing causes to the observed behavioral differences.

This classification of traits in terms of the nature of their influence is schematic and, in many instances, an oversimplified representation. Trait dimensions such as aggression, anxiety, achievement, introversion, or rigidity are complex constructs with elements and feedback loops that may influence the individual at several points along the sequence between stimulus and response. Thus, individuals with a strong tendency toward anger and aggression might be highly selective in their perception, being quick to perceive slights and humiliations. They also might have difficulty in controlling their behavior and have learned aggressive styles of responding. Nevertheless, the schema in Fig. 9.2 is useful in that it provides a context for the analysis of the functions and modes of influence of different traits.

Furthermore, the schema implies that behavior in a given situation results from a complex interaction of that particular situation with the whole set of one's personality traits. Therefore one would never expect a simple relationship between any one trait and a particular behavior. In fact, Ahadi and Diener (1989) showed that if a given behavior is totally caused by only four traits, the maximum correlation one could expect between any one trait and the behavior is .45. Considering that most psychologists believe that personality consists of at least five global traits, and many more specific traits, we begin to see that a .30 correlation between a given trait and behavior in a specific situation is meaningful. A person's behavior in a given situation can be thought of as a "final common pathway" resulting from the interaction of many factors, just as many other events in the world are the final product of many interacting causal contributors. (Consider, for example, that many diseases, such as cancer, arise from complex interactions of genetic predispositions, environmental pollutants, and aspects of a person's life style — such as whether or not they smoke.) In sum, while personality traits may be imperfect for predicting behavior in a given situation, they are not meaningless psychological constructs.

Summary

1. Sheldon contended that three body types—labeled *mesomorphic, endomorphic,* and *ectomorphic*—are related, respectively, to energetic, relaxed, and introverted personality types. Typologies no longer play a central role in psychology because they fail to capture the complexity of personality.

2. Trait psychologists believe that characteristics of individuals are general over situations and endure over time. Cattell distinguished a number of different traits and sources of traits, while Eysenck suggested three higher-order types of traits: neuroticism, introversion-extroversion, and psychoticism.

3. The Big Five model of personality traits has come to be widely accepted as the basic structure of personality. These five traits include neuroticism versus emotional stability, extraversion, openness to experience, agreeableness, and conscientiousness. However, not all personality theorists believe there are only five basic personality traits.

4. Mischel caused psychologists to rethink the trait issue by documenting that generalized trait measures are poor predictors of behavior in specific situations. The magnitude of the correlation between a trait and behavior tended not to exceed .30.

5. *Attribution theorists* believe that observers tend to see the behavior of others as caused by trait characteristics and their own behavior as due to environmental conditions. This disparity may be due to the greater information held by actors about themselves or to the differential perceptual focuses of actors and observers.

6. Among the newer assessment strategies is *situational* assessment, in which taxonomies of situations, similar to taxonomies of traits, are created. However, situational assessment alone is not sufficient to accurately predict behavior.

7. *Interactionists* contend that behavior is governed by both the properties of the person and the situation in which that person is acting. The *transactional* approach emphasizes the reciprocal influence of the person and the environment on each other. Interactionism, however, typically refers to the fact that variation in behavior is best accounted for by considering both the person and the environment simultaneously.

8. Individuals differ in the consistency of their behavior across situations. In addition, within any individual there may be consistency in some characteristics and inconsistencies in others across different settings.

9. The *template-matching technique* identifies ideal types who would be most likely to behave in a given manner in a given setting. Individuals can then be matched with this ideal type to predict their behavior in that setting.

10. *Traits* are distinguished from *states* in that states are unstable, temporary conditions of the organism. Anxiety is considered to be both a trait and a state. As a state, anxiety is assessed with queries about current intensity of feeling; as a trait, it is measured with questions about frequency and generality across situations.

11. Behavior appears to be more consistent over time and across situations when many instances are sampled. Small samples of behavior, like tests with an insufficient number of items, result in error of measurement, which reduces correlations between the behaviors under study.

Thought Questions ◼▬▬▬▬▬▬▬▬

1. Do you believe that body type might "cause" personality characteristics? Why might this be the case?

2. Is your behavior consistent across different settings? Can you think of some behaviors that are consistent and others that are inconsistent?

3. Answer the above question about any friend. Why might the question be difficult to answer about another person, and what implications might this have for how you perceive that individual?

4. Create a personality template for a good teacher or businessperson. Now predict who among your friends best fits this description.

PERSONALITY DEVELOPMENT

Part 4 is concerned with the genesis or antecedents of personality and with changes in personality that occur during the course of life. The development of the self is presented as a key process for the development of personality because it contributes in different ways to almost all of the personality theories that have been reviewed. To understand personality, one should have some understanding of its developmental roots. There is a vast gap in behavior and personality between the newborn and the adult. Children must be socialized through the process of child-rearing and other influences so that they function effectively in a particular social and cultural setting. As children grow older, they are confronted with new requirements and new problems that must somehow be mastered. And personality development does not end in childhood or adolescence. The adult years also present unique demands and opportunities for personality growth and change.

The chapters in Part 4 examine the major changes in personality that take place over the developmental life span and the various processes involved in bringing out these changes. Developmental changes are examined from the perspectives of (1) behavior changes that characterize most individuals in an age group and (2) individual differences in personality development.

Part 4 begins with Chapter 10 on the development of the self and its significance for personality. Chapter 11 addresses the development of identity in general and various aspects of identity, such as gender and ethnic identity, in particular. Chapter 12 begins with a discussion of attachment and its role in the beginning socialization of the child. It then continues with a discussion of topics such as moral development, the antecedents of other prosocial behaviors such as empathy and caring, and the influence of child-rearing practices on socialization. Chapter 13 considers development across the life span, beginning with a discussion of change and continuity in personality over time and then considering the developmental periods of adolescence, adulthood, and old age. Overall, these chapters are based on the ideas that personality undergoes constant change and development and that particular experiences are associated with particular ages. A principal objective of all four chapters is to convey the relevance of a developmental perspective for the understanding of personality. We will have frequent occasion to refer back to developmental issues in subsequent chapters.

10 | The Development and Functions of the Self

The self has increasingly become a central topic of both theory and research in psychology in recent years. Before 1960 there were relatively few references to the self, although there were some theorists, such as Carl Jung and Carl Rogers, who did emphasize the concept. Freud's theory did not specifically have a concept of self. Instead, it partitioned the mind into id, ego, and superego. Behaviorist theories (see Chapter 5) until very recently also did not utilize a concept of self.

In recent years the concept of *self* has become a central focus of attention in many areas of psychology, including personality, social, developmental, and clinical psychology. An indication of this increased attention is that the number of topics that include the prefix *self* in the Psychological Abstracts has increased from eight in 1969 to thirty-three in 1989 (Hoare, 1990).

However the concept of self is anything but easy to define and study. In the first part of this chapter we address the various meanings of the term *self*. We then proceed to discuss how the self develops. We look at the development of an experiential sense of self, self-boundaries, the self-concept, and self-esteem. We also consider various aspects of the self-concept. Next we study various self-processes, including self-monitoring, self-control, self-awareness, self-consciousness, self-enhancement, and self-consistency. We conclude by considering the role of the self in various theories of personality.

THE SELF

We all have an intuitive sense of the importance of the self for the understanding of human experience and behavior. To help make this intuitive sense more concrete, it is instructive to perform the following "thought" experiment. Imagine that you had no sense of self or self-concept. What difference would that make in your plans? You could not think meaningfully about getting a degree, or going to graduate school, or getting married, or becoming rich or famous because planning for each of these objectives requires that you project *yourself* into the future. You would be different in a great many other ways as well. If you are religious, your worship would become rote and devoid of significance. Whatever is personal in the religious experience — grace, redemption, sin, guilt — would be lost. A basic element in the human tragic experience, the knowledge of one's mortality, would be gone.

Culture and the Self

In spite of the intuitive reasonableness of the idea of a "self" to those raised in Western culture, this concept is held with lesser degrees of strength and certainty in other cultures, and it has evolved and changed over time. We have already seen in Chapter 2 how different cultures have vastly different views of what the self is. Western culture sees the self as an inner entity, occupying an inner space, capable of controlling the body and of actualizing itself. It is bounded, separated from others, and should be autonomous, firmly defined, and stable. In contrast, many other cultures see the self as more inclusively defined in terms of one's connections with others. In some cultures there is no individual self; the self is largely a repository for spirits and ancestors.

In addition, the American emphasis on the importance of self-esteem may be culture-specific. Both Campbell (1993) and Markus and Kitayama (1993) have suggested that self-esteem may be a Western concept. Markus and Kitayama, for instance, have found that Japanese students did not exhibit the "false uniqueness" bias commonly found among Americans (Taylor and Brown, 1988). That is, when asked to compare themselves to others, most Americans tended to see themselves as "above average," whereas Japanese students did not. Self-effacement, rather than self-enhancement, seems to be more prevalent in Japanese society than in American society. Psychologists' emphasis on the importance of high self-esteem and on the tendency of individuals to strive to enhance and protect their self esteem may be culture-specific (see the section later in this chapter on protection and enhancement of the self).

There have been efforts to trace the historical development in Western society of the concept of self and of self-related issues (Baumeister, 1987). The development of the individual, autonomous self is seen as beginning in the sixteenth century, with the emergence of the Renaissance. Changes that appear to have taken place between the medieval and modern eras in one's conception of the self and view of self-knowledge, and in the conception of self-fulfillment and means of attaining fulfillment are outlined in Table 10.1. One notes that the notion of an "inner" self that is hidden and inaccessible to the conscious self is a relatively recent one, and that issues of self-deception do not emerge until the Puritan era. One also notes dramatic changes in how one seeks fulfillment — from being guided by religious and societal goals and standards to more personal, individualistic objectives. The sense that society can deter self-fulfillment, with consequent feelings of alienation and separation of work from self-fulfillment emerges after the Industrial Revolution. Although scholars may not necessarily agree with the self attributes and issues that are ascribed to particular time periods, there seems little doubt that self issues and attributes vary as a function of historical context and culture.

Definitions of Self

Two different meanings of the self have been used by psychologists. Sometimes the term *self* is used as an *object,* in which case an individual is depicted as having

Table 10.1   Issues of selfhood and historical stages

Historical era	Self-knowledge, self-conception	Fulfillment
Late medieval	Unproblematic Increased sense of unity of single life	Christian salvation (in heaven) (Possible) public acclaim
Early modern (16th to 18th century)	Unproblematic for own self; for others, question of inner *true* self vs. outer *apparent* self Increased interest in individuality, uniqueness of self	Christian salvation Incipient secular fulfillment, as in creativity
Puritan	Self-consciousness Concern with self-deception (henceforth, self-knowledge uncertain)	Christian salvation: but individual is helpless Inner struggle to overcome sin and weakness
Romantic (late 18th, early 19th centuries)	Need to discover own destiny and fulfill it (duty)	Creativity Passion ("romantic" love) Thus, grope for secularized concept of fulfillment
Victorian (mid & late 19th century)	Repression, hypocrisy Involuntary self-disclosure	Seek fulfillment alone (transcendentalism) Private, family life is paramount
Early 20th century	Devaluation of self Impossibility of complete self-knowledge (Freud)	Society prevents fulfillment (alienation) Emotional fulfillment in family Work as unfulfilling
Recent 20th century	Belief in personal uniqueness Values of self-exploration	Quest for celebrity Quest for means of self-actualization

(Adapted from Baumeister, 1987.)

knowledge of and evaluating the self-as-object in much the same way one has knowledge of and evaluates another person. One can like or dislike another person; one can like and dislike oneself. We entertain beliefs about and concepts of other people, such as "She's bright," "He's ambitious," "The instructor is fair." Similarly, one has such beliefs about oneself. In this sense, the self becomes the object of one's attitudes, beliefs, and feelings. This set of attitudes, beliefs, and feelings about the self is referred to as the *self-concept.*

Is the self-concept always conscious, part of our phenomenal experience? The answer is no. We, of course, do have a conscious self-concept, but there may well be feelings about ourselves of which we are unaware. For example, we may have an unconscious perception of ourselves as physically unattractive, based on childhood experiences, even though we have physically changed and consciously judge ourselves, in accordance with the feedback from others, as attractive.

Self as Agent

Another usage of the self is as an *agent* or *process;* that is, as a mechanism that does something. Thus, the self is said to influence perception and judgment and to screen out threatening or inconsistent information. Related to this usage is the notion of the self as an organized structure or personality component, much like the psychoanalytic concept of the ego. And, as we indicated in the chapters on personality theories, there are even broader usages of self—for example, in the motive for self-actualization and in the search for self-identity.

Sometimes the question is asked: "Why do we need a concept of self as agent? Isn't the whole person the agent?" In fact, however, sometimes we experience some of our behaviors as self-initiated, while we experience others as outside the self. For example, one may be beset by an impulse or an idea that is experienced as "foreign" and that one cannot control. One may feel a loss of agency or responsibility for one's behavior, and even a loss of individuality. Hence, the organism does not always conceive of itself as an agent, and a concept of self is needed.

The terms "self" and "self-concept" are often used interchangeably (cf. Markus and Wurf, 1987). We believe it helpful to restrict the term *self* to its properties as an agent and organized structure of personality and the term *self-concept* to the attitudes, beliefs, and feelings about the self as object. From this perspective, the self-concept becomes one component, a very important one, of the self-system. It then becomes meaningful to refer to the self-concept of the self.

One major objective of personality theory and research is to provide a clearer, more precise definition of the self and the self-concept. Better definitions would help improve measuring procedures that are now only barely satisfactory (Wylie, 1974) and also lead to more agreement about the psychological properties of the self. In the meantime, we can review the process of development of the self and examine some of the principal ways in which the self is significant for an understanding of personality. We need to recognize, however, that there are ambiguities in how the self is defined and serious difficulties in our methods of assessment. In some overviews of the field of personality, very little attention is given to the self because of definitional ambiguities and measurement problems. It is our view that the concept of the self is critical to any comprehensive theory of personality development and function. The self provides a key to much of human motivation,

The Proprium: The "Self" Model of Gordon Allport

Gordon Allport was among the pioneers in the study of personality. He attempted to integrate humanistic interests and empirical approaches in his work. His research on individual differences in expressive behaviors — in handwriting styles, in one's stride and gait — was influential in early efforts to develop an objective approach to the study of personality. In his writings, Allport emphasized the individuality of traits and the uniqueness of personality. The critical element in human uniqueness, according to Allport, is the individual's self, for which he used the term "proprium." Allport (1955; 1961) enumerates eight aspects of the Proprium:

1. Bodily sense (the bodily "me")
2. Self-identity
3. Ego-enhancement (self-enhancement)
4. Ego-extension (identification with family, groups, nation)
5. Rational agent
6. Self-image (self-concept)
7. Propriate striving (motivations that are central to the self)
8. The knower (awareness of self as conscious being)

Propriate strivings are of particular importance in Allport's theory. He cogently argues that a propriate striving can function as a guide to one's life and dominate other motives. As an illustration, he cites the example of the explorer Raold Amundsen, who surmounted many obstacles to reach the South Pole. After achieving this goal, he went on, against extreme discouragement, to accomplish the objective of flying over the North Pole. Amundsen died in an attempt to rescue another explorer from death in the Arctic. His life was characterized by a particular propriate striving, what Alfred Adler might describe as "style of life."

social understanding, and personality disturbances. Basic to the personality development of both the child and the adult are changes in the self. Hence, this chapter examines the process of the development of the self and its significance in the understanding of personality. In Highlight 10.1, we present one famous theorist's model of the self, that of Gordon Allport.

BEGINNINGS OF THE SELF: A BASIC EXPERIENTIAL SENSE OF SELF

Many psychologists long believed that the newborn infant is unable to tell itself apart from its surroundings, particularly from its mother. Object relations theorists (see Chapter 4) for instance, have held that infants experience themselves and their mothers as "one." Development is presumably a matter of gradually coming to learn that one is separate and distinct from one's mother and, by extension, from other people and the environment. According to Mahler's object relations theory (also discussed in Chapter 4) this achievement is not fully established until about eighteen months of age.

However, several recent writers on self-development argue that this is not true. Both Stern (1985) and Neisser (1988), basing their views on research studies of infant development and perception, have proposed that there are several different aspects of the self, which develop at different times. Both Stern and Neisser believe that infants never experience a period of total self/other undifferentiation. What Stern calls the "emergent" self and Neisser calls the "ecological self" is present from birth. Neisser claims, "The old hypothesis that a young infant cannot tell the difference between itself and the environment, or between itself and its mother, can be decisively rejected. The ecological self is present from the first" (p. 7).

This sense of self is based on the infant's ability to directly perceive its environment and to act in relation to it. We now know that infants' awareness of their environments is present from birth and that they already have many basic perceptual skills. Within a few weeks the infant can watch objects move towards and away from it; it can hear sounds and orient toward them. These experiences lead to its "knowing" that it is an object physically separate from other objects.

Within the first few months the infant is also developing a sense of itself as an organized bodily *agent*. The infant learns that it can track objects with its eyes. When it moves its hands and arms, it receives internal muscular feedback that gradually helps it learn that it can control its own movements. These experiences help develop a basic sense of itself as an agent — as a being capable of initiating actions.

Along with a sense of agency, the infant also gradually develops an integrated organized sense of itself as a bodily entity. This sense of self involves perceptions of the body's shape and size, of its boundaries, and of the interconnectedness of its parts. The young child also learns that the body is a stable structure that has continuity over time, despite developmental changes in physique. In its early months, the infant acts as if objects do not exist when they are hidden from sight. By around eight months of age, the infant has developed the ability to preserve the memory of objects that are no longer present, a capacity Piaget calls *object permanence*. It is likely that this same capacity applies to the self-as-object (Lewis and Brooks, 1975).

Although the child may have acquired a sense of *self-permanence* by the end of its first year, the body image is far from complete. For example, the child does not yet have a clear, stable conception of its own gender. More learning about the self must take place before the child has a full understanding of its sex identity, and realizes that boys cannot be transformed into girls and vice versa simply by changing activity or clothing (Gerardo and Bohan, 1971; Kohlberg, 1966). Further, it is not until the infant is about eighteen months old that it gives evidence of recognizing a mirror image or a picture of itself (Amsterdam, 1972; Lewis and Brooks, 1975).

Both Stern and Neisser hold that a basic *interpersonal sense of self,* what Trevarthen (1983) calls "primary intersubjectivity," also develops very early. This occurs through the infant's direct experience of its relationship with another living being like itself, most typically the mother (or primary caretaker). Infants are asserted to be "hard-wired," that is, genetically predisposed, to respond to nonverbal communications from the mother. Infants orient to the mother's voice very early in development. Eye contact is sought by infants within about six weeks of birth, and after this they respond to a complex array of expressive signals from the mother (Trevarthen, 1983). Trevarthen notes that mothers reciprocate by aligning their faces with their babies' faces and by exaggerating their expressions, thus eliciting obvious signs of response from the infant. If a mother makes her face immobile, the baby will stop smiling and maybe even begin to show signs of distress. This indicates that the infant is aware of being "in dialogue" with the mother and is distressed when that dialogue is disrupted.

Mothers mirror back to their child their experience of what the child is experiencing in such a manner as to make it a shared experience. (© Dion Ogust/The Image Works)

■ **Highlight 10.2** ■

Affect Attunement

A 9-month-old girl becomes very excited about a toy and reaches for it. As she grabs it, she lets out an exubertant "aaaah!" and looks at her mother. Her mother looks back, scrunches up her shoulders, and performs a terrific shimmy with her upper body, like a go-go dancer. The shimmy lasts only about as long as her daughter's "aaaah!" but is equally excited, joyful, and intense . . .

An 8½-month-old boy reaches for a toy just beyond reach. Silently he stretches toward it, leaning and extending arms and fingers out fully. Still short of the toy, he tenses his body to squeeze out the extra inch he needs to reach it. At the moment, his mother says "uuuuuh . . . uuuuuh!" with a crescendo of vocal effort, the expiration of air pushing against her tensed torso. The mother's accelerating vocal-respiratory effort matches the infant's accelerating physical effort.

Source: Stern, 1985, p. 140.

What Trevarthen has called "primary intersubjectivity" consists of the fact that "the participants respond to each other immediately and coherently, in both action and feeling. Their reciprocal activities are closely coordinated in time. The result is a shared structure of action—a structure that both participants enjoy, and that neither could have produced alone. Indeed, "the contributions of the individual partners would be useless and foolish if they occurred by themselves" (Neisser, 1988, p. 45). It is through this interaction that infants begin to gain a basic interpersonal sense of self at a very early age.

In a similar manner, Stern (1985) talks about "affect attunement" between mother and infant. Mothers "mirror" back to the child their experience of what the child is experiencing, in such a manner as to make it a shared experience. Two examples of affect attunement are given in Highlight 10.2.

For both Stern and Neisser, the two early senses of self—the ecological and the interpersonal—are perceptual and experiential. The infant knows about these aspects of the self in the same basic perceptual way that it knows where one object begins and another leaves off and knows the direction an object is moving when it follows the object with its eyes. Infants do not yet have a concept of self. It is not until around eighteen months of age that infants develop the capacity to form representations of themselves and therefore begin to develop a self-concept, based on their developing ability to be aware of themselves.

DEVELOPMENT OF THE SELF-CONCEPT

Self-Awareness

The development of the capacity for self-awareness appears to be crucial for the development of the self-concept (Lewis, 1990). This capacity, as we have said, seems to develop around eighteen months of age; and it appears to be unique to humans and to higher primates. This conclusion is based on a series of clever research studies by Gallup (1970, 1975, 1979) in which animals and human infants observe themselves in mirrors.

Most of us have seen a dog staring at, sometimes snarling at, and approaching a reflection of itself. For most animals, seeing their own image in a mirror acts as a social stimulus. But does the dog recognize itself, or does the reflection simply signal a potential companion or threat? The evidence indicates that dogs and almost all other nonhumans do not recognize themselves. In his series of experiments, however, Gallup has shown that the chimpanzee does have this capacity. Gallup exposed chimpanzees in a small cage to a full-length mirror for ten consecutive days. It was observed that over this period of time the number of self-directed responses increased. These behaviors included grooming parts of the body while watching the results, guiding fingers in the mirror, and picking at teeth with the aid of the mirror. Describing one chimp, Gallup (1975, p. 324) said, "Marge used the mirror to play with and inspect the bottom of her feet; she also looked at herself upside down in the mirror while suspended by her feet from the top of the cage; . . . she was also observed to stuff celery leaves up her nose using the mirror for purposes of visually guiding the stems into each nostril."

Then the researchers devised a further test of self-recognition. The chimps were anesthetized and marks were placed over their eyebrows and behind their ears, areas the chimps could not directly observe. The mirror was temporarily removed from the cage, and baseline data regarding their attempts to touch these areas were recorded. Figure 10.1 shows the number of touch attempts both before and after reintroduction of the mirror. The data clearly suggest that chimps do recognize themselves, or are self-aware, for their attempts to touch the marks increased when they viewed themselves. Citing further evidence for this argument, Gallup noted that chimpanzees with no prior mirror experience did not direct behavior to the marks when they were first exposed to the mirror (Figure 10.1); that is, the other chimpanzees appeared to have remembered what they looked like and to have responded to the marks because they noticed changes in their appearance.

An analogous procedure incorporated in a study of human infants clearly reveals the role of developmental influences on this form of self-recognition (Lewis and Brooks-Gunn, 1979). Heavy rouge was applied to the noses of ninety-six infants, ranging in age from nine months to twenty-four months. The infants' actions when exposed to a mirror were observed prior to and after the application of rouge. Figure 10.2 indicates the difference between the percentage of infants in each age group who engaged in directed behavior in the rouge condition and the

Figure 10.1

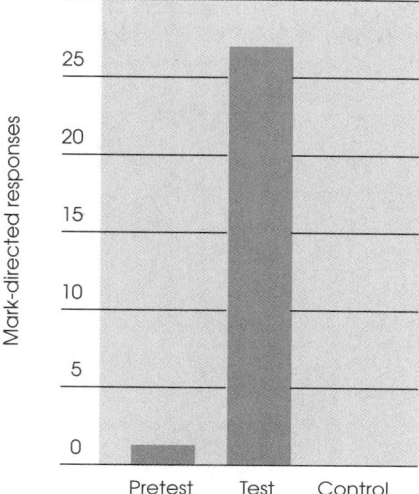

Number of mark-directed responses made by experimental animals before being exposed to a mirror and by experimental and control animals during the test of self-recognition; controls made no responses. (Gallup, 1975, p. 326. Used by permission.)

Two-year-old babies recognize their images in a mirror; among nonhumans, only chimpanzees appear to exhibit similar recognition. (left — © Elizabeth Crews; right — Ylla/Rapho-Photo Researchers, Inc.)

Figure 10.2   Nose-directed behavior: Percentage difference between the no-rouge and rouge conditions by age. (Lewis & Brooks-Gunn, 1979, p. 41. Used by permission.)

percentage who attempted to touch their noses in the no-rouge condition. While the nine- and twelve-month-old infants were unresponsive to the rouge condition, a dramatic change in responses indicative of self-recognition occurred during the latter half of the infants' second year.

Boundaries

For some psychoanalytic thinkers, the most fundamental part of the self-concept is one's sense of boundaries. The concept of *boundaries* is based on a definition of what is "self" and what is "not self" — where one draws the line between "self" and "others." Psychological boundaries of the self can be conceived of as having properties similar to physical boundaries. That is, good self-boundaries are firm and distinctive, drawing a clear line between self and others, yet not so rigid or impermeable that they block connection with others.

Boundaries are difficult to test empirically (see Fisher and Cleveland, 1968). Despite the empirical difficulties in assessing boundaries, the concept remains clinically useful in describing certain personality patterns and interpersonal relations. In some close relationships between child and parent, and even between adults, the self-other-boundary may be so weakened that the person may be unable to discriminate between his or her own feelings and ideas and those of the partner. The person, in an almost automatic fashion, assumes the opinions and attitudes expressed by the partner. This process of loss of boundaries is amusingly and perceptively depicted, albeit in exaggerated form, in the film *Zelig* by the writer-director-actor, Woody Allen. Zelig, the main character, is unable to maintain any stable personality pattern of his own, taking on the personality and physical expressions of significant individuals in his environment. It is as if the boundaries defining his self were completely porous.

Loss of self-boundaries need not necessarily be maladaptive; it may entail a widening of self to include others. According to Maslow (cf. Chapter 6), for example, the highest level of self-actualization is achieved in those moments when one is able to transcend the self and merge, as it were, with humankind. Maslow's conception is similar to that of Eastern religions that also place the loss of self or ego at the pinnacle of human consciousness. These religions have developed systematic and lengthy training procedures that facilitate the attainment of this level of consciousness. However, the loss of boundaries is not maladaptive in these instances because it is controlled and disciplined rather than automatic. The process is more of a merger rather than a total identification; and one is merging with a higher order structure (humanity or, depending on the religion, universal energy). On another level is the example of a particular kind of positive feeling that is often elicited when we identify with some larger group or function, such as when we lose ourselves as part of an inspiring chorus or as a group participant.

However, as we have previously indicated, the emphasis on firm self-boundaries appears to be a distinctly Western phenomenon. In contrast, many other cultures as well as women in this culture emphasize fluid self-boundaries. These self-boundaries are inclusive rather than exclusive and typically include one's relationships. A number of feminist theorists have argued that the emphasis on firm, exclusive self-boundaries is a reflection of masculine values that do not fit women well. Instead of emphasizing separation as a goal in therapy, these writers believe that psychotherapy should work to increase a sense of connection between people. Problems are seen as fundamentally relational in nature, both for men and women (Jordan, et al., 1991).

Further Developments of the Self-Concept

The self-concept can be considered one's description of who one is. It includes feelings, attitudes, desires, judgments, and behaviors that the individual considers to be characteristic of himself or herself.

Developing a concept of who one is as a person is important. Consider what happens when one behaves in a way that is very different from one's typical patterns—for example, a sudden outburst of rage and profanity in a man who sees himself as calm, rational, and well-spoken. He might say, "This isn't like me," "Something must have come over me," or "I wasn't myself." If his behaviors persist, he may change his self-concept, integrating these new feelings and behaviors into his conception of his personality. However, this integration is not always easily accomplished, and the individual could feel that he is beset by strange, incomprehensible feelings, even that he is going crazy. What is important in terms of the development and dynamics of personality is that a developing image of who we are as persons is a useful tool for helping us understand and predict our reactions to situations and experiences in our life. We learn to recognize and to count on our images of who we are, much in the same way we learn to recognize and count on our physical selves. And we work to maintain stability in these self-images.

The self-concept develops over time as the child has experiences that interact with its increasing cognitive understanding and development of language. Harter (1990) reports that there are changes in the content of the self-concept from childhood through adolescence. In childhood, the self-concept is primarily focused on the social exterior — what is observable from outside. Young children describe themselves primarily in terms of their behaviors, their achievements, their preferences, their possessions, and their physical attributes. Older children tend to emphasize traits such as "shy" and "outgoing."

In adolescence, when the ability to think abstractly increases, a number of changes in the self-concept occur. First, the psychological interior is emphasized. The self-concept includes an increasing emphasis on emotions, attitudes, beliefs, wishes, and motives.

Second, the self-concept becomes more complex and multidimensional. In early and middle childhood there are four general domains of the self-concept. By adolescence this has become differentiated into at least nine: scholastic competence, job competence, athletic competence, physical appearance, peer social acceptance, close friendship, romantic appeal, relationship to parents, and behavioral conduct (Harter, 1990).

Third, aspects of the self-concept become more abstract. Montemayor and Eisen (1977) asked students between fourth grade and high school to give twenty answers to the question "Who am I?" Adolescents' descriptions included more abstract elements than those of the younger groups. Highlight 10.3 shows several examples of responses from this study.

Fourth, adolescents struggle to integrate their self-concept. Harter (1990) notes that children around the age of eleven do not detect conflicts in their personality. By ages fourteen through sixteen, however, adolescents are vividly aware of contradictions among various aspects of their self-concept and they are troubled by these contradictions. In fact, it is at this age that individuals experience the most conflict over contradictions. It is hard for them to reconcile, for instance, the fact that they are "cheerful" with their friends but "depressed" with their parents. In late adolescence they are able to begin to create abstract systems of self-descriptions that integrate the contradictions experienced at an earlier age. For instance, "cheerful" and "depressed" may be synthesized as "flexible" or "moody."

◼ **Highlight 10.3** ◼

Development in the Self-Concept

9-year-old: My name is Bruce C. I have brown eyes. I have brown hair. I love! sports. I have seven people in my family. I have great! eye site. I have lots! of friends. I live at. . . . I have an uncle who is almost 7 feet tall. My teacher is Mrs. V. I play hockey! I'm almost the smartest boy in the class. I live! food. . . . I love! school.

11½-year old: My name is A. I'm a human being . . . a girl . . . a truthful person. I'm not pretty. I do so-so in my studies. I'm a very good cellist. I'm a little tall for my age. I like several boys. . . . I'm old fashioned. I am a very good swimmer. . . . I try to be helpful. . . . Mostly I'm good, but I lose my temper. I'm not well liked by some girls and boys. I don't know if boys like me. . . .

17-year-old: I am a human being . . . a girl . . . an individual. . . . I am a Pisces. I am a moody person . . . an indecisive person . . . an ambitious person. I am a big curious person. . . . I am lonely. I am an American (God help me). I am a Democrat. I am a liberal person. I am a radical. I am conservative. I am a pseudoliberal. I am an Atheist. I am not a classifiable person (i.e., I don't want to be).

Source: Montemayor and Eisen, 1977, pp. 317–318.

Finally, one other aspect of the development of the self-concept at adolescence is the increased importance of the distinction between the "true" and "false" self. Harter (1990) reports that sixth-graders have little insight into the true-false self distinction. However, by eighth grade virtually all adolescents find the distinction compelling. Harter found that most of her adolescents defined the true self as one who acts naturally, or is what one is inside, while a false self is one who acts primarily to please others.

Self-Schemata. Currently, the self-concept is thought of in cognitive terms in psychology. It is conceived of as a "knowledge structure" and consists of cognitive generalizations about the self. These are often referred to as *self-schemata* (see Markus, 1977). These schemata are believed to filter incoming information, organize new experiences, and guide subsequent action. For example, a person with a self-schema of independence is likely to interpret personal behaviors as indicative of being independent and is not likely to accept evidence from others that he or she is dependent. In addition, information will be readily available from memory to support the self-perception of independence. It has been demonstrated that people who regard themselves as masculine, or as feminine, can recall many instances in their lives when they acted in accordance with this self-perception. On the other hand, androgynous individuals (persons not sex-typed) or those without a schema with regards to gender (that is, gender is not a salient aspect of their self-concept) have few memories of instances in which they acted in a masculine or feminine manner (Markus, Crane, Bernstein, and Siladi, 1982).

Dramatic effects of self-schema have been studied in depressive populations (see Kuiper, MacDonald, and Derry, 1983). Depressives have self-schema that include personal deficiencies, such as low ability, poor personality, unattractiveness, and the like. Information not congruent with these schema tends to be rejected, so that positive (but not negative) performance feedback is underestimated. In addition, unpleasant past experiences and failures are readily accessible from memory, which results in the anticipation of such experiences. These consequences of a negative self-view are believed to aid in maintaining the depressed state.

There is a substantial body of research documenting the selective effects of the self-structure on the processing of information (Markus and Wurf, 1987). For example, in one study subjects were presented with a series of pairs of letters, each pair containing a letter from either their first or last name (Nuttin, Jr., 1985). The subjects' task was to choose as quickly as they could which letter of the pair they preferred. While the subjects displayed no awareness of the relationship between their name and the letter pairs, they nevertheless selected more often letters from their own name. Other cognitive processes that have been shown to be selectively influenced by self-relevant stimuli include discrimination, memory, and judgment (Marcus and Wurf, 1987). One also tends to process more efficiently information that is congruent with one's own personality. Thus individuals scoring higher on a personality scale measuring manipulative tendencies and given stories to read were significantly faster in reading a story depicting high manipulative tendencies than in reading one depicting low manipulative tendencies. The opposite difference was obtained for low manipulative individuals (cited in Markus and Wurf, 1987).

Through the agency of the self, the self-concept acts as an important filter, selectively screening the information that we receive from the external and internal environment. The self selectively influences information processing not only through a self defense function but also, as we have seen, through its sensitivity to self-relevant stimuli. At a later point in this chapter, some important self-processes will be discussed in greater detail.

Multiple Self-Concepts.   In referring to a person's self image, it is common practice to use the singular term, self-concept. However, current psychological perspectives suggest that the self-concept is multiple. There is the body image and the psychological self-concept. Further distinctions can be made between the unconscious and conscious aspects of the self-concept, between our perception of our past self and our perception of our current self, and between the different elements that constitute the psychological self. And there are all the different roles that constitute vital parts of our self — our role as a student, as an offspring, as a male or female, as a citizen. One can also speak of our social self, our work self, our play self, our athletic self. While these different aspects of the self may be interrelated and organized into a more or less unitary self-structure, different features of the self become more salient and operative depending upon the particular context and circumstances.

A number of studies provide evidence that the self-concept is multiple. Research by Harter (1990) and Rosenberg (1985) shows that the self-concept appears to have multiple dimensions. Rosenberg (1985), based on his study of 5,000 adolescents, identifies the following components of the self-concept: self-esteem, a sense of "mattering" to others, a sense of certitude about who one is, feelings of control, "plane coordination" (the degree to which different aspects of the self are coordinated), how vulnerable one feels as a self, and the degree of anxiety or self-consciousness one feels.

A study by Smollar and Youness (1985) shows that we experience ourselves somewhat differently in different relationships in our lives. The authors asked adolescents to complete the statement "When I am with my (mother/father/close friend) I am. . . . " The adolescents showed much variability in who they experienced themselves to be in reference to different contexts. With fathers, for instance, adolescents typically reported being "capable, serious, and anxious." These aspects did not show up in reference to best friends, where they viewed themselves as "intimate and spontaneous," qualities that they did not typically experience with their parents.

Markus and Kunda (1986) have suggested that we have a whole set of self-concepts, but that at any one time, in any given context, one self-concept is active and "working." They use a computer metaphor: A computer may have many programs on its hard disk, but usually at a given moment only one is "working." An example from the Smollar and Youness study would be that with one's close friend, one's concept of self as intimate and spontaneous is working, that is, it becomes active and guides one's behavior. With one's father, one's concept of self as serious is active and working.

To say that we have multiple self-concepts is not to say that there is no overlap among them. Physically, one will see oneself as a man or as a woman with both one's father and one's close friend, while psychologically, one may see oneself as reliable in both relationships. Therefore, while we may have multiple self-concepts, in most cases they are not completely distinct from one another or exclusive.

The richness and complexity of the self-concept, or self-concepts, are further conveyed by the distinction that has been made between one's representation of: (a) one's actual self, (b) one's ideal self, the self one wants to be, and (c) one's ought self, the attributes and behaviors that we believe are our obligations or duty to possess (Higgins, 1987). Discrepancies between these self-concepts and the actual, ideal, and ought concepts that significant others (parents, close friends) may have of you can be a source of discomfort and distress. In one study, college students were administered these different self-concept measures. Six to eight

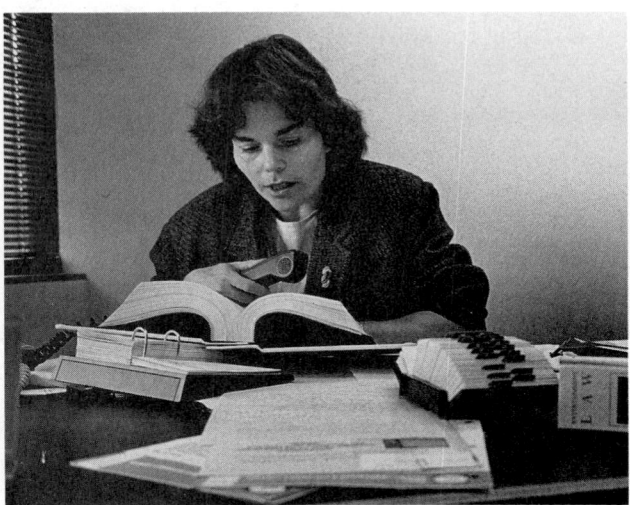

Example of multiple roles and multiple selves: a family self and a work self. (© Elizabeth Crews)

weeks later, they completed a questionnaire in which they indicated the frequency with which they experienced various emotional-motivational states (Van Hook and Higgins, 1988). The students were divided into two groups depending upon whether there was a marked discrepancy between any pair of self-concept measures. It can be seen from Table 10.2 that the Discrepancy-present group experienced more negative kinds of feelings than the Discrepancy-absent group. This difference was especially marked for confusion-related items (i.e., unsure of self, uncertain about goals, confused about identity).

Table 10.2   Mean frequency of experiencing different emotional-motivational states

Motivational state	Discrepancy-present group	Discrepancy-absent group
Confusion	1.87	0.77
Dejection	1.15	0.80
Agitation	1.60	1.20
Anger	1.22	0.62

Note: Scale range: 0 (almost never) to 4 (almost always).

Possible Selves. Still another way to conceive of self-concepts that may function as important guides to behavior and sources of motivation and conflict is the notion of *possible selves* (Markus and Nurius, 1986). There are possible selves that we hope for and possible selves that we fear. Thus we may hope for a particular career, lifestyle, income level, and close interpersonal relations while we may fear loneliness, failure, or other life possibilities that we perceive as negative. Although there may be some overlap between these possible selves and the ideal self, there are sufficient differences to warrant a different label and, most important, a different measure. Table 10.3 lists the percentages of students endorsing some examples of actual ("Does this describe you now?") and possible ("Have you ever considered this a possible self?") self items used in a study exploring the utility of questions about possible selves (Markus and Nurius, 1986). The investigators found that one's perceptions of one's "now" self and of one's "possible" future selves correlated with one's current emotional and motivational state. However, images of possible future selves may sometimes predict a person's current behavior better than does the person's current self-concept. For instance, Oyserman and Markus (as referenced in Markus and Nurius, 1986) found that juvenile delinquents had positive current self-images (positive self-esteem) but were deficient in their images of positive possible future self-images. This is reminiscent of members of gangs, who may have positive self-concepts but act in an antisocial and dangerous manner because they believe that they will probably be dead by age twenty.

Complexity and Clarity of the Self-Concept. We have seen that the self-concept includes a variety of aspects and dimensions. How a self-concept is organized in terms of its complexity, integration, and clarity is important in terms of how well it functions. Linville (1985) has found that those who have more complex self-concepts show greater emotional stability in the face of both emotionally positive and negative experiences. Linville measured self-complexity by having individuals sort cards, each of which had the name of a personality trait on it, into piles describing the self. The same trait could be placed in multiple piles. More piles indicated greater self-complexity. Subjects then were exposed to either a success or a failure experience and then rated their emotional responses. Subjects whose self-complexity scores were low showed greater fluctuations in mood following success or failure than subjects who scored higher in self-complexity.

Other studies have found that individuals high in cognitive complexity in general are less likely to become depressed (Marsh and Weary, 1989) and that those with more integrated (Showers, 1992) and more clearly articulated (Campbell, 1993) self-concepts have higher self-esteem, which is an important aspect of the self-concept.

Self-Esteem

While self-concept refers to a complex, multifaceted organization of percepts regarding oneself, *self-esteem* usually connotes a generalized, overall attitude toward oneself. *Self-esteem* connotes the value that one places on oneself. Just as

Table 10.3   Percentages of respondents endorsing selected self items

	Question	
Item	Does this describe you now?	Have you ever considered this a possible self?
Personality		
Happy	88.0	100.0
Confident	83.8	100.0
Depressed	40.2	49.6
Lazy	36.2	48.3
Life style		
Travel widely	43.6	94.0
Have lots of friends	74.6	91.2
Be destitute	4.5	19.6
Have nervous breakdown	11.1	42.7
Physical		
Sexy	51.7	73.5
In good shape	66.7	96.5
Wrinkled	12.0	41.0
Paralyzed	2.6	44.8
General abilities		
Speak well publicly	59.0	80.3
Make own decisions	93.2	99.1
Manipulate people	53.5	56.6
Cheat on taxes	9.4	17.9
Others' feelings toward you		
Powerful	33.3	75.2
Trusted	95.7	99.1
Unimportant	12.8	24.8
Offensive	24.8	32.5
Occupation		
Media personality	2.2	56.1
Owner of a business	1.4	80.3
Janitor	2.6	6.8
Prison guard	0.0	4.3

there are variations in the degree to which one values another person, whether we hold them in high or low regard and feel that they are worthy or unworthy, so there is variation in the degree to which one values oneself.

Neither children nor adults feel neutral about all their self-characteristics. Positive and negative values are placed on particular attributes that we see in others and in ourselves. It is good to be tall (but not too tall), attractive, strong, intelligent, and socially skillful, and it is bad to be unathletic, shy, or poor. The evaluations we place on these self-attributes contribute to our feelings of self-esteem. It thus becomes evident that self-esteem is closely related to and depends on the self-concept, but self-esteem is not the same as self-concept. We can have beliefs about ourselves that are important elements in our self-concept but that do not affect the value we place on ourselves (self-esteem). For example, one may perceive oneself as introverted or emotionally expressive without feeling particularly good or bad about that self-perception. Whether success or failure at an activity will affect self-esteem is very much dependent on how important one perceives that activity to be (Harter and Engstrom, cited in Harter, 1983).

In a study of sixth-grade children, McGuire and Padawer-Singer (1976) found that only a minimal part of the self-concept involved self-evaluative responses such as "I am smart" or "I am a nice person." The types of self-descriptions given by children in response to the question "Tell us about yourself" are enumerated in Table 10.4. The self-descriptions were consistent with the authors' hypothesis that an especially important determinant of self-concept is distinctiveness. Thus, children born in cities other than the one in which their school was located, and especially in foreign countries, were much more likely to mention their birthplace in describing themselves than were children who were native to the community. McGuire and Padawer-Singer also hypothesized that momentary and situational factors, as well as more stable characteristics and enduring values, will affect the self-concept.

In contrast to the characteristics that do not influence self-esteem, others have isolated the personal and situational factors that do influence how one feels about oneself. About a century ago, William James defined self-esteem by the following formula (cited in Harter, 1983, p. 320):

$$\text{Self-Esteem} = \frac{\text{Success}}{\text{Pretensions}}$$

James is asserting that one's feelings of worth are determined by the ratio of one's achievements to one's aspirations. James's analysis still has merit although one also needs to take into account the extent to which one is valued by significant others.

The analysis of self-esteem must also reflect the complexity of the self. Epstein (1973) has proposed a hierarchical structure for self-esteem. At the summit of the hierarchy are feelings about the worthiness of the overall self-concept. Below this generalized attitude are more specific evaluations pertaining to four major areas of the self: general competence, moral self-approval, power, and love worthiness. Within each of these four areas, even more specific differentiations can be made. Thus, within the competence area, one can distinguish between the self-esteem associated with intellectual, artistic, and athletic competence, and make even further distinctions within these specifications—for example, between verbal and mathematical competence.

The relationship between overall self-esteem (the degree of high or low regard in which one holds oneself) and the positive and negative values placed on specific components of the self-concept remains an interesting and unresolved issue. Some individuals' view of their academic skills might be the most important contributor to self-esteem, while for others it might be perceived popularity. However, there is a connection between one's appraisal of specific self-attributes and one's overall self-esteem. Studies have shown that the sum of an individual's evaluations of specific attributes—school performance, athletic skills, social interactions, physical attractiveness, and so on—is predictive of the person's overall sense of self-esteem (Coopersmith, 1967). Yet, though predictive of general self-esteem, it is important to recognize that the different areas of self-esteem are not the same as *general* self-esteem. A measure of a child's general feelings of self-worth has been shown to be only moderately related to feelings of competence in the cognitive, physical, and social skills areas (Harter, 1982).

As previously suggested, the experience of being accepted by significant others is also related to overall self-esteem; it may well be the most important factor in self-esteem, as Carl Rogers has proposed. In an extensive study of the

Table 10.4   Categorization of sixth graders' response to "Tell us about yourself"

Category	Percentage of children	Category	Percentage of children
Own activities		*Miscellaneous*	5
Hobbies, amusements	48		
Sports	43	*Demographic*	
Daily schedule	43	Age, birthdate	25
Places lived	5	Name	19
Skills	8	Residence	16
TV	10	Birthplace	11
Books	6	Health	11
Jobs	3	Sex	10
Miscellaneous experiences	6	Race, ethnic	5
		Religion	3
Significant others		*Self-evaluation*	
Family	38	Moral	20
Friends	43	Physical	15
Pets	22	Intellectual	10
Teachers	16	Emotional	2
Public figures	0		
		Physical characteristics	
Attitudes			
Likes and dislikes	52	Hair color	13
Vocational	18	Weight	11
Hopes and desires	12	Height	10
		Eye color	11
School (excluding teachers)	71		

Source: McGuire and Padawer-Singer, 1976, p. 748. Adapted by permission.

Self-worth and self-esteem in a growing child. (© Jean-Claude Lejeune/Stock, Boston)

antecedents of self-esteem in a group of boys, aged ten to twelve, Coopersmith (1967) found that parents of boys with high self-esteem conveyed total or nearly total acceptance of their children. Other child-rearing factors linked to the boys' self-esteem were "clearly defined and enforced limits, and the respect and latitude for individual acts that exist within the defined limits" (p. 236). Although there are a number of methodological problems with this study (Wylie, 1979, p. 348), the data make intuitive sense. In addition, the findings of other investigators (Ritu and Sukhdeep, 1986) are consistent with those reported by Coopersmith.

Parents are not the only "significant others" who contribute to variations in self-esteem. The culture provides an important source of influence that is only beginning to be understood. One might expect that members of subgroups in a culture who are the objects of discrimination would experience decreased self-esteem. But the effects of culture are complex, and such propositions, even if made by prominent authorities, require empirical verification. Thus it has been postulated that Blacks living in the United States will suffer from self-derogation and even self-hatred because of the social prejudice and hostility to which they are subjected. Rainwater (1966) writes, "Black comes to stand for a sense of identity as no better than these destructive others. The individual feels he must embrace an unattractive self in order to function at all." (p. 205) Erik Erikson (1966) similarly states, "There is ample evidence of 'inferiority' feelings and of morbid self-hate in all minority groups" (p. 155). In a subsequent article on Blacks, other commentators point to "the heavy psychological costs of low self-esteem, feelings of helplessness and basic identity conflict" (Proshansky and Newton, 1973, p. 176).

These assertions regarding the self-esteem of African-Americans, however, are not supported by a review of the empirical data (Wylie, 1979). The data are mixed and, if anything, tend to indicate that black children and youth, the ethnic group most extensively studied, have higher self-esteem than whites. It is unclear why this might be the case. However one reason may be that negative messages from others are often attributed to the prejudices of those individuals, rather than to characteristics of the self.

Self-Esteem and Negative Affects.   There are a substantial number of studies reflecting a relationship between low self-esteem and feelings of anxiety and depression (Wylie, 1979). High self-esteem appears to facilitate coping with stressful situations. Thus high self-esteem in a sample of pregnant women was associated with lesser feelings of depression at time of delivery, whether normal or with complications, and three months after delivery (Hobfoll and Leiberman, 1987). At the same time, an individual with high self-esteem is likely to have higher expectations for achievement and rewards than an individual with low self-esteem. One would then expect the high self-esteem person to be less accepting of an unfair environment and to display greater resentment, anger, and disappointment when subjected to prejudice and injustice than a low self-esteem person.

SELF-PROCESSES

The development of self-awareness leads not only to the development of a self-concept but also to the development of several other important personality processes. In Western culture in particular, the development of the ability to reflect upon oneself is seen as a useful skill (Landrine, 1992). It can be used to monitor one's internal states and behavior and to enhance one's ability to control oneself. This ability can function in both positive and negative ways, though. Negatively, it can lead to painful self-awareness and self-consciousness. But, positively, it can lead to strivings to protect one's self-esteem and to maintain self-consistency. In this section, we consider each of these self-processes.

Self-Monitoring

One of the unique properties of humans to which we have already alluded is the capacity to observe and regulate our own behavior. When faced with temptation, young children can say to themselves, "Don't take a cookie; opening the cookie jar is naughty." For the older child and adult, these various prohibitions have been internalized in the form of a "conscience" which functions as a built-in self-monitor, as it were. Monitoring can also be a guide as well as a defense. Long distance runners observe when they need to slow down and pace themselves for the end of the race; dieters record their caloric intake and modify their eating behavior accordingly. Self-monitoring in varying degrees is an important part of our every-day activities and, as we have seen in the review of social learning theories, can be an important component of a cognitive behavior modification therapeutic approach.

Snyder and his associates (Snyder, 1974; Snyder and Gangestad, 1986) have focused on a specific aspect of the general activity of self-monitoring. They have developed a scale assessing individual differences in self-monitoring tendencies. This scale has focused on the monitoring of the social presentation aspects of the self. It was designed to assess the degree to which individuals regulate their social behavior in order to make a particular social impression.

The items address the ability to control or manage expressive behavior, e.g., "I would probably make a good actor;" the tendency to perform in social situations and attract attention, e.g., "In a group of people I am rarely the center of attention" (scored in the reverse direction); and the tendency to behave as others expect and contrary to the way one might feel, e.g., "I may deceive people by being friendly when I really dislike them."

High self-monitors would be expected to alter their behavior in response to specific situational demands and therefore to display less consistency in their actions. While there are some exceptions, the data are generally consistent with this prediction (Snyder, 1987). There are numerous studies, ranging from responsiveness to advertising, to dating behavior (cf. Chapter 18), to the degree of consistency between beliefs and actions that verify the utility of this measure. However, there is considerable controversy as to the personality dimension or dimensions that are being assessed by the self-monitoring instrument (Briggs and Cheek, 1988). There is debate as to whether the scale measures one personality dimension or is a combination of several different dimensions. For example, the self-monitoring scale is significantly correlated with such personality factors as extroversion and exhibitionism (Briggs and Cheek, 1988). These personality indicators would appear to relate more to temperament than to self-monitoring. The fact that there is a significantly greater correlation between identical twins on the self-monitoring measure than between fraternal twins suggests a genetic basis for this trait (Gangestad and Snyder, 1985); biological causation would be consistent with a personality temperament interpretation of what the self-monitoring instrument assesses.

Temperament and self-monitoring factors are probably both assessed by the scale. An important question for future research to resolve is whether temperamental traits such as extroversion are primary, and the self-monitoring behavior subsequently develops in the course of managing the extroversive and related temperamental dispositions.

Self-Control

There is a close relationship between self-monitoring and *self-control*. We have already alluded to the internal monitor or conscience. Self-monitoring refers primarily to the attention paid to one's behavior and feelings, while self-control refers to the ability to inhibit immediate gratification and alter one's behaviors appropriately. Self-control is also frequently used synonymously with self-regulation to connote future planning and the guiding of one's behavior in accordance with one's standards and situational demands. A number of theoretical explanations of self-control or self-regulation consider the monitoring of behavior as the first step in a three stage cycle (Bandura, 1978; Kanfer, 1970). For the second step, the observed behavior is then judged against a criterion based on one's own standards or the standards of significant others. The last step consists of the person reinforcing or criticizing the self for the behavior. Self-criticism then leads to efforts to modify the behavior so that it meets the standard.

Some theories consider the role of the third stage to be in its information rather than reward value (Carver and Sheier, 1982). A significant discrepancy between the observed behavior and the standard then elicits a motivation to reduce the discrepancy, resulting in efforts to modify the behavior.

Development of Self-Control.   As the infant matures, it acquires increasing mastery of its behavior. It also, as discussed earlier, develops an awareness of self and self-concept. The self system in turn greatly enhances the human organism's ability to regulate its behaviors. These changes in the pattern of control have been documented in a detailed, intensive study of the emergence of self-control (Kopp, 1987). Eighteen 24- and 36-month-olds were given a series of laboratory tasks requiring some inhibition or delay in the child's response; for example, the child is instructed not to touch an attractive telephone or not to search for raisins hidden under a cup until given a cue. By age 36 months, these children have developed strategies that they employ to help them conform to the delay requirement. They employ such tactics as sitting on their hands, distracting themselves by singing, and talking to themselves.

Mischel has carried out a series of studies of delay of gratification (cf. Chapter 14) in which children have been observed to employ the tactic of self-instruction or talking to themselves in coping with temptation (Mischel, 1974). He and his co-workers have shown that pre-school children can effectively use self-instructional plans given to them to pay attention to a repetitive task and to avoid looking at an attractive toy (Patterson and Mischel, 1976). One of the reasons that young children find it so difficult to exercise self-control in naturalistic situations is that they have not yet learned why particular strategies are effective and which to employ (Patterson, 1982). By age eight they display an understanding of plans which they can use to regulate their behavior (Mischel and Mischel, 1977).

Positive and Negative Effects of Self-Awareness

Does self-awareness always facilitate an individual's behaving effectively? The answer is no. There are conditions under which individuals appear to function more effectively if they are not self-aware. For instance, athletes usually attempt to blot out awareness of the self. Baseball hitters cannot be conscious of every aspect of their batting techniques while swinging the bat and still be successful. There is a movement among athletic coaches to emphasize the Zen aspect of the sport; that is, to have players transcend any awareness of the self and to lose their identity by completely merging with the game. A best-selling tennis book stressed that the player should be aware of the seams on the tennis ball and nothing else. Self-statements after missing a shot, such as "I am a lousy player" or "I can't seem to hit a backhand today," are believed to impede performance.

There is a large body of research addressing the effects of self-awareness on personal functioning. One clear finding is that focusing awareness on the self produces more acceptance of oneself as the cause of events. For example, Duval and Wicklund (1973, p. 26) had subjects read several scenarios, such as:

1. Imagine that you have selected and purchased a race horse. You enter the horse in a major race and hire a good jockey to ride him. The horse wins first place. To what degree did your actions cause the victory and to what degree did the actions of the jockey cause the victory?

2. Imagine that a friend of yours wants to get you a date. You tell her what characteristics you like in a date and she selects one of her friends. You go out with him and have a very good time. To what degree did your actions cause the successful date and to what degree did the actions of your friend cause the successful date?

Half of the subjects read these stories under normal conditions; the remainder read the passages in front of a conspicuous mirror. The presence of a mirror was expected to shift the focus of attention to oneself. In accordance with their predictions, Duval and Wicklund found that individuals in the mirror condition made relatively more self-attributions than did subjects in the normal condition.

Duval and Wicklund (1972) also proposed that heightened self-awareness is an aversive state, inasmuch as it makes us consciously aware of our shortcomings. In a related theoretical development, Wine (1971) and Sarason (1978) contended that when a stressful event arouses self-preoccupying thoughts, there will be performance decrements because task-relevant thoughts are diminished. Further, they stated that highly anxious persons focus on the self during test performance, which may account for their relatively poor scores in test situations.

In this regard, Hamilton et al. (1993), Barlow (1988), and Baumeister (1990), among others, have argued that excessive self-awareness plays a role in depression, anxiety, suicide, substance abuse, and other psychological disorders. Among other things, self-awareness intensifies emotions. If one is feeling anxious or depressed, then excessive self-awareness will magnify those feelings. In addition, because self-awareness increases the tendency to see oneself as the cause of some event, if something goes wrong one is more likely to blame it on oneself. At the extreme, this can lead to excessive self-criticism and self-blame. Excessive self-focused attention can be so aversive under certain circumstances that one will strive to escape it, for instance by committing suicide (Baumeister, 1990) or by abusing substances.

However, the effects of self-awareness on behavior are far from settled. Carver, Scheier, and their colleagues (e.g., Carver, Blaney, and Scheier, 1979*a*, 1979*b*) have argued that if self-confidence and performance expectancy are high, then self-focus of attention will increase performance, whereas low confidence combined with self-focus will give rise to performance decrements. To test these ideas in an experimental investigation, people with snake phobias were asked to approach and pick up a snake. Some of these individuals were confident about their ability to overcome the phobia, while others were quite apprehensive and doubting. In one of the experimental conditions a mirror was present to heighten self-awareness. The data were as predicted: the mirror enhanced the likelihood of picking up the snake among the confident subjects but impeded snake handling among the nonconfident subjects, relative to the behavior of persons without feedback from a mirror.

In sum, common situations such as placement in front of a mirror, camera, or audience can heighten self-awareness. Changes in awareness or self-consciousness can have profound positive or negative behavioral effects. We next consider some of the negative aspects, of the related concept of self-consciousness.

Self-Consciousness.   Self-awareness, in addition to its reflection in self-evaluation, is also manifested in *self-consciousness* — the extent to which awareness of self enters into one's thoughts and behaviors. For example, one is less likely to feel self-conscious joining a group of good friends who are having a party than in joining a group of strangers. In the latter case, thoughts of the impression one is making are more likely to arise as one interacts with the group. Of course, one can be self-conscious with one's friends — e.g., wondering about their reaction to some new clothes you're wearing, or expecting congratulations from them regarding a recent award.

In addition to situational factors affecting self-consciousness, there are also personality differences in the tendency to be self-conscious. Some individuals are more insecure about the impression they make, constantly worrying what others think about them. A personality scale has been developed to assess these individual differences, distinguishing between differences in public self-consciousness and private self-consciousness (Fenigstein, 1987). Individuals who are highly conscious of the public aspects of one's self as contrasted to being conscious of private aspects, such as one's feelings and desires, display much more sensitivity to the behavior of others. For example, such individuals may react in a very personal and negative manner when ignored. At the extreme of public self-consciousness are the *paranoid* individuals, who believe that others are always talking about or plotting against them, or that they are actually an extraordinarily powerful and important figure — for example, the President or Jesus Christ. The former reaction, being talked about, is called *delusions of persecution* and the latter, *delusions of grandeur*. In both instances, the self is the center of the person's experiential world.

Protection and Enhancement of the Self.   One aspect of awareness of the self is that it can lead to a tendency to want to protect and enhance the self. We want to engage in behaviors and seek situations that will maximize feelings of self-esteem and minimize threats to our self-esteem. There are many ways in which self-esteem can be enhanced or threatened, depending on the particular culture and on one's personal values and competencies. One can achieve self-esteem through financial success, through fame, through popularity, through mastery of a difficult task, through social dedication, and so on. How we maintain and enhance self-esteem is highly influenced by learning, but the need for self-esteem is a consequence of the emergent development of the self-concept.

Both psychoanalytic and humanistic theories have long held that individuals act in ways to protect their self-images. The theories suggest that individuals will selectively distort information positively in their favor and reject information that is threatening to their self-images. A good deal of research has been done and there is now a large body of evidence supporting these assertions. People generally prefer and seek out positive feedback and attempt to reduce the impact of negative feedback (Snyder, et al, 1983). Studies of success and failure indicate that we tend to attribute success to our personal efforts and ability, while we are likely to attribute failure to the difficulty of the task or to bad luck (Weary, 1978). Research on what is called the "social comparison process" indicates that people make downward comparisons when they compare themselves to others in order to assess how well they are doing. That is, they compare themselves with others perceived as less able than, inferior to, or less fortunate than themselves, to enhance their own self-esteem (Gibbon, 1986).

Taylor and Brown (1988), summarizing research evidence, have argued that humans show a tendency to have unrealistically positive views of the self. When negative aspects of the self are acknowledged, these aspects tend to be dismissed as inconsequential. A study by Lewinsohn, Mischel, Chaplin, and Barton (1980) is illustrative of people's tendency to have unrealistically positive self-views. In this study, observers watched subjects complete a group-interaction task. Each subject was then rated on a number of personality dimensions by the observers, as well as by the subjects themselves. Subjects' self ratings were significantly more positive than the observers' ratings.

There is much controversy over what actually causes us to "self-servingly" interpret information in this fashion. While some have argued that we do it because of our self-serving desire to enhance or protect the self-image, others suggest that it has to do with how people process information. For instance, those who are used to success might logically attribute success at a particular task to their own efforts and failure to external factors. Numerous studies have tried to unravel which of these two explanations is correct. The conclusion drawn by most psychologists is that both factors are involved. People interpret evidence in a manner favorable to their self-concepts, both because they are acting logically based on the way they interpret experience and because they are trying to enhance their self-images. Once again we caution, however, that the phenomenon of a self-serving bias may be culture-specific.

Even in our culture, however, not all individuals interpret evidence in a manner favorable to a positive self-image. Taylor and Brown (1988) point out that depressed individuals are actually often more "realistic" in their self-assessments than nondepressed individuals, who distort information positively. Swann, et al. (1987), based on their self-consistency view (see next section) have suggested that individuals with low self esteem will actually reject positive information about themselves in order to preserve their negative self-image and, conversely, will accept negative information about themselves. Several decades ago, Lecky (1945) proposed that an important factor governing socially maladaptive behavioral symptoms in children was their tendency to act consistently with a negative self-image. Thus, children who see themselves as poor spellers or stutterers may spell poorly or stutter to maintain consistency with their self-images. Similarly, children who believe themselves to be "bad" may behave delinquently in accordance with their self-concepts, perhaps without being conscious at all of the process. Therapies based on Lecky's approach attempt to help the child become aware of these maladaptive efforts to maintain consistency and, in addition, to help the child modify a negative self-concept. The fact that some individuals appear to strive to maintain a *negative* self-image is compatible with the self-consistency motive, to which we now turn.

SELF-CONSISTENCY

How we perceive ourselves shapes our judgments and behaviors through still another psychological mechanism: the motivation for *self-consistency*. Psychologists have found that inconsistencies in one's beliefs or between one's beliefs and behavior are a source of tension and discomfort (Heider, 1958). People are motivated to resolve such inconsistencies and to maintain consistency. For example, a miserly individual who sees himself as very generous can maintain consistency between his behavior and his self-image by perceiving himself as very poor, by exaggerating the significance of any pittance given to charity, by believing that people will be corrupted by gifts, by viewing others as exceptionally greedy and demanding of his resources, and so on. The motivation for cognitive consistency appears to be quite pervasive and is central to a number of personality and social psychological theories (Festinger, 1957; Heider, 1958). Although the development of this motivation has not been systematically studied, the motivations for consistency probably become stronger with developmental changes in the level of cognitive functioning. Inconsistencies need to be understood before one can be concerned about them. In addition, the motivation for consistency is probably influenced by social learning inasmuch as children are encouraged to be logical and consistent.

In recent years, an extensive body of theory and research has arisen bearing on the motivation for self-consistency. While much of this research is considered within the domain of social psychology, it also is germane to central issues in personality regarding the functions of the self and individual differences in self-concept. The striving for consistency has been documented in a series of experiments by Swann and his colleagues (Swann, et al., 1987; Swann and Hill, 1982; Swann and Read, 1981). For example, in one study (Swann and Hill, 1982) college students participating in an experiment were given feedback from an experimental confederate that they seemed either dominant or submissive. When the feedback confirmed the self-concept, the appraisal was accepted. However, if it was discrepant, the students resisted the feedback by exaggerating the behaviors indicative of the personality that they felt truly characterized them. Thus subjects who saw themselves as dominant and were told they were submissive responded in an especially dominant manner while those with a submissive self-concept, who were labeled dominant, became especially submissive.

This research suggests that there are at least two motives relevant to the self-concept: the motive to enhance one's self-esteem and the motive to preserve the consistency of one's view of the self. The challenge is to determine, particularly for negative self-concept, low self-esteem individuals, the conditions under which each of these tendencies will be paramount. There has been some effort to address this problem. There is evidence that cognitive responses tend to be mediated by self-consistency and affective responses by self-enhancement (Swann, et al., 1987). Subjects, after their self-esteem was assessed, were asked to make a brief speech and then given positive or negative feedback regarding their self-confidence. Both the high and low self-esteem subjects felt happier and less hostile and anxious after positive rather than after negative feedback, manifesting a preference for self-enhancing information. However, as one would predict from a consistency model, the cognitive reactions of the high and low self-esteem subjects differed. The high self-esteem subjects rated the favorable feedback as more accurate than the unfavorable feedback and their evaluation of the feedback procedure was commensurate with this difference. The low self-esteem subjects, in contrast, considered the unfavorable feedback to be more accurate than the favorable feedback. They also viewed the evaluator providing the unfavorable feedback as more competent than the favorable evaluator.

PERSONALITY THEORIES AND THE SELF

The *self* has become an increasingly important concept in the study of personality and social behavior. One will find the properties of the self structure relevant to issues concerning personality development and personality dynamics that will be considered in the ensuing chapters. The self is also pertinent to personality measurement in that many measurement procedures require individuals to appraise themselves, and most of the personality traits that are measured are self attributes.

We have also seen that properties of the self are important in almost all of the personality theories that have been reviewed in the preceding chapters. The only theorist who does not employ any self-related concepts is Skinner. However, the other learning theorists all refer implicitly or explicitly to some aspect of the self in their theoretical models. For Dollard and Miller, self-references are largely implicit. However, the notion of self-based motivations and affects such as pride, achievement, dependency, insecurity, in addition to defenses that reduce threats to the self are quite compatible with their theoretical approach to personality. In the case of Rotter, we find more explicit references to self-based motivation such as needs for recognition, dominance, and dependency. In addition, Rotter introduces an important self-agency concept in his distinction between belief in internal versus external control of reinforcement. For Bandura, the self enters into his theory primarily through its agency functions. Self-efficacy beliefs and self-monitoring and self-regulation of one's behavior in terms of one's standards and goals have assumed an increasingly important place in his social learning theory (Bandura, 1989).

For the phenomenological theorists, the self is a central concept. However, the phenomenologists differ as well as share similarities in their treatment of the self. Whereas Rogers and Maslow both emphasize self-actualization and Kelly does not, both Rogers and Kelly place importance on one's self-concept and its function as a frame of reference.

A comparison of the role of the self in the different personality theories that have been reviewed in the previous chapters is instructive. The various theorists and the role of the self in their theories are outlined in Table 10.5 (pp. 291 – 292) in the order in which the theorists were discussed. Table 10.5 indicates properties of the self that are important in the theories. Freud was well aware of self-based motives, but these were completely subordinated to instinctual, id motives, and hence self-based motives are not specified in the table. Adler was certainly aware of self-love, and both Freud and Adler recognized that personal attributes functioned as a frame of reference, but these were not central processes in their theories. In one instance, Freud's concept of narcissim was cited, although not previously introduced in the text, since Freud coined the term and since it has an important although not a central role in his theory. Finally, Table 10.5 is limited in that not all of a theorist's concepts relevant to a particular aspect or function of the self were listed.

Table 10.5 does not list those concepts of a theorist that are not germane to the "self" (e.g., Freud's libido, Jung's "anima"), or processes that affect both self and non-self behaviors (e.g., partial reinforcement). Nevertheless, it is apparent that almost every personality theorist addresses some aspect of the self. It is of interest that most of the differences between personality theorists lie in the particular function of the self that is emphasized rather than in different interpretations of the same function.

It is primarily in the category of specific self-based motives that we see differences between theorists in the motives that are deemed most important. Most of the theorists address only one or two functions of the self while none, including Freud, whose theory is the most comprehensive, addresses all of the self's properties.

Table 10.5 Personality theorists and the self

	Cognitive Aspects and properties of Self			Emotional and motivational properties of Self					
	Differentiation of Self from Other; Structure of Self	Cognitive Agency Function of Self	Description of Self-Concept; Frame of Reference	Self-Actualization; Mastery; Pride	Self-Enhancement Bias; Self-Love	Specific Self-based Motives	Self-Defense	Self-Other; Self-ideal Discrepancy	Self-Consistency
Freud	Ego; Superego	Ego functions			Self-Love ("Narcissism")		Ego-Defenses	Guilt ("internalized other")	
Jung			Archetype of Persona Extrovert, Introvert	Self-Actualization, Mandala			Concept of Balance		
Adler				Striving for superiority		Inferiority	Compensation		
Horney					Self-Enhancement	Basic Anxiety (Personal Insecurity)	Moving towards, against, or away from people		
Fromm			Need for frame of reference	Need for Transcendence	Self-love basis for love of others	Relatedness; Rootedness; Identity; Alienation	Authoritarian personality type		
Erikson		Initiative; Generativity	Identity	Autonomy; Ego Integrity		Industry-Inferiority; Intimacy-Isolation	Defenses against guilt, inferiority, isolation	Guilt	
Mahler	Separation; Differentiation	Individuation					Varied		

Continued

Table 10.5 Personality theorists and the self (cont.)

	Cognitive Aspects and properties of Self			Emotional and motivational properties of Self					
	Differentiation of Self from Other; Structure of Self	Cognitive Agency Function of Self	Description of Self-Concept; Frame of Reference	Self-Actualization; Mastery; Pride	Self-Enhancement Bias; Self-Love	Specific Self-based Motives	Self-Defense	Self-Other; Self-ideal Discrepancy	Self-Consistency
Klein	Separation from mother; Internalization of concepts of mother				Self-love		Projective Identification		
Kohut	Fragile self-boundaries				Narcissism; need for Mirroring		Varied		
Dollard-Miller						Implicit	Defense-mechanisms		
Skinner									
Rotter		Internal vs. External Control of Reinforcement				Needs for recognition; dominance; dependency, etc.	Varied		
Bandura		Self-Efficacy; Self-Monitoring							
Rogers			Self-Concept descriptions; frame of reference	Self-Actualization		Positive and Negative Self-regard		Self-ideal	
Maslow				B values; Self-Actualization		Safety; Love; Esteem	Defenses against deficits in safety, love, esteem		
Kelly			Constructs of self; frame of reference						Consistency with self-constructs

Summary

1. An experiential sense of self as distinct from other objects, as an agent, and as an interpersonal organism, develops very early.

2. The self-concept, one's description or image of oneself, begins to develop at around eighteen months of age. It appears to begin to develop when human infants become self-aware, and it continues to develop into adulthood, becoming more complex and differentiated.

3. One of the most basic characteristics of the self-concept is the sharpness and permeability of its *boundaries*. If the boundaries are too permeable, the individual becomes excessively influenced by other people and other situations, with an accompanying loss of individuality. However, how boundaries are drawn around the self varies from culture to culture, and is even different for men and women.

4. *Self schemata* are cognitive generalizations about the self that serve to filter incoming information, organize experience, and guide subsequent action.

5. Of the many components and features that make up the self-concept, only a small segment is germane to a particular situation and becomes accessible at any given moment. The self-concept that is operative is referred to as the *working self-concept.*

6. Discrepancies between the *actual self,* the *ideal self* and the *ought self,* and between *actual* and *possible* selves are an important source of motivation and of one's affective state.

7. *Self-esteem* is based on one's generalized positive and negative evaluation of the various features of the self-concept. Not all elements of the self-concept contribute to self-esteem inasmuch as many elements of the self are only descriptive.

8. Low self-esteem is not necessarily correlated with experiences of discrimination and minority status.

9. *Self-awareness* is a prerequisite for the development of self-monitoring and self-control. Self-awareness can function in positive and negative ways.

10. The *self-monitoring scale* is predictive of a wide range of behaviors bearing on the social presentation aspects of the self. High self-monitors are more responsive to situational demands and tend to display less consistency in their behavior. Because the self-monitoring scale is substantially correlated with extroversion and exhibitionism, there is some question as to whether it primarily measures temperament traits, both temperament and self-monitoring, or primarily self-monitoring.

11. The motivation for *self-consistency* can conflict with the motivation for *self-enhancement* in individuals with low self-esteem. There is some evidence that cognitive responses in situations in which these tendencies are operative are mediated by self-consistency while affective responses are mediated by self-enhancement.

12. The *self* is a key concept for almost all personality theories. However, the particular property of the self that has been addressed varies markedly with the personality theory.

Thought Questions

1. Do you think chimpanzees may eventually be shown to have a psychological self? If not, why not?

2. Can you think of any character in fiction or drama, or television or movies, where there is a significant discrepancy between that individual's self-concept and others' concept of that person? What are the consequences of that discrepancy?

3. Which leads to more effective behavior and better psychological adjustment in individuals with actual minimal competencies — a self-concept that matches one's actual skills and behaviors or a self-concept that is more positive and over-estimates one's competencies? Justify your response.

4. What kind of society do you think is preferable — one that maximizes individuality and individual accomplishments or one that subordinates individual uniqueness, privacy, etc. to the practices and goals of the groups? Why?

11 | Identity

In the previous chapter we considered the development and functions of the self. In this chapter we consider aspects of the development of identity.

Identity deals with that which we consider to be most basic to our sense of self—the things that identify who we are, both to ourselves and to others. It includes our most basic values and goals and our ethnic and gender identifications. As fans of science-fiction movies or amnesia victims know, there is nothing more terrifying than the sense of losing one's identity. Identity involves the fundamental sense of *continuity* in one's life: I am who I was yesterday, and I am who I will be tomorrow. It provides a framework for taking action in the future.

Self-concept and identity are closely related ideas. Both can provide answers to the question "Who am I?" Yet they differ. *Self-concept* is one's *description* of who one is. *Identity* is one's *definition* of who one is (Baumeister, 1986); it consists of those things that most basically define who we are. Something can be part of one's self-concept ("I am sloppy") but not part of one's identity ("I don't consider sloppiness an integral part of who I am"). Identity is defined by our connection to various aspects of our life, and it helps us locate ourselves in terms of who we are and where we belong (Lewis, 1990).

Many psychologists believe that adolescence is the key developmental time period for the formation of identity. While individuals begin to develop an identity in early childhood and may continue to modify their identities throughout their lives, adolescence is thought to be the most crucial organizational period for forming an identity. This view characterizes the perspectives of Erik Erikson, James Marcia, Dan McAdams, and those who have developed models of ethnic identity formation. However, gender identity, as we shall see, appears to develop considerably earlier.

In this chapter we first consider Erik Erikson's view of identity as a global, internalized psychological structure, and Marcia's extension of Erickson's ideas. Then we consider narrative perspectives on personality in general and identity in particular. We next turn to a consideration of the development of ethnic identity and follow that with an overview of the development of gender identity. We conclude by considering current research on how identity concerns affect everyday life.

STAGES OF IDENTITY FORMATION: ERIKSON AND MARCIA

Erik Erikson has been the most influential theorist of identity (see Chapter 4). Erikson emphasized the ability to experience oneself as having continuity and sameness as an important aspect of identity. Identity includes one's bodily identity, the ability to sustain loyalties, and a sense of having a future. It also includes having a stable sense of self versus feeling self-conscious, being able to pursue a career versus feeling paralyzed in terms of work, being able to experiment with various roles versus rigidly locking oneself into a fixed role, feeling clear about one's sexual identity versus being confused about one's sexual identity, and having ideological commitments versus being confused about one's values.

Erikson believed that late adolescence was the time of identity achievement, although earlier developmental periods played a role. Identity achievement precedes the development of the capacity for intimacy, which occurs in early adulthood. However, Erikson held that this sequence is more characteristic of males than of females. For females, interpersonal aspects are at the core of their identity. Men therefore achieve identity first and intimacy second, while women achieve identity and intimacy concurrently, or intimacy first. Erikson also assumed that women do not complete an identity in adolescence because marriage and having children complete their identities.

James Marcia (1980), using an interview format, studied Erikson's ideas on the development of identity in adolescence. Others have subsequently developed objective measures based on Marcia's interview format (Grotevant and Adams, 1984). An example of items from one of these measures is given in Table 11.1.

Marcia's original research involved interviewing adolescents about their vocational plans and goals, and their values and beliefs. They were asked about the degree to which they had explored each of these areas and the degree to which they had made a commitment in each area. Initially, consistent with a masculine bias, the identity interview focused on vocational achievement. Later, to correct for this bias, interpersonal elements were added to the interview. Currently the interview includes questions about vocational plans, avocations, religious beliefs, political ideologies, sex-role orientation, sexuality, values, friendships, dating, marriage, parenting, family and career, setting priorities, and ethnicity.

Marcia identifies four identity *statuses* during adolescence: diffusion, foreclosure, moratorium, and identity achievement. These four statuses vary along two dimensions: commitment and exploration. *Identity diffusion* is characterized by low levels of both commitment and exploration. The person neither has a set of commitments to goals or values nor is actively struggling with the process of forming such commitments. *Foreclosure* is characterized by a high level of commitment and a low level of exploration. Individuals in this stage are most likely those who have adopted an identity from their parents or culture without actively exploring and choosing. *Moratorium* is what we typically think of as an identity crisis and is characterized by high levels of exploration but a low level of commitment. The person is in the process of exploring who he or she is and what he or she wants to be but has not come to any stable set of commitments yet. *Identity achievement* is arrived at through exploration which results in a personally chosen commitment to a set of values and goals for one's life.

In Marcia's scheme, identity achievement is the "highest" level, with moratorium the next, foreclosure third, and diffusion the lowest. However a number of writers have noted that this order may be culturally biased. Only in Western

Table 11.1   Sample items from the objective measure of ego-identity status

Status	Item
Diffusion	I haven't chosen the occupation I really want to get into, but I'm working toward becoming a ＿＿＿ until something better comes along.
	When it comes to religion, I just haven't found any that I'm really into myself.
Foreclosure	I guess I'm pretty much like my folks when it comes to politics. I follow what they do in terms of voting and such.
	I've never really questioned my religion. If it's right for my parents, it must be right for me.
Moratorium	I just can't decide how capable I am as a person and what jobs I'll be right for.
	There are so many different political parties and ideals, I can't decide which to follow until I figure it all out.
Identity-achievement	A person's faith is unique to each individual. I've considered and reconsidered it myself and know what I can believe.
	It took me a while to figure it out, but now I really know what I want for a career.

Source: Adams, Gullota, and Markstrom-Adams, 1994, p. 274.

society must one achieve an identity. In many other cultures, one attains one's identity from the culture and the role one plays in it (foreclosure). Therefore, for many cultures a foreclosed identity may be the healthiest. In fact, it has been found that for minorities in the United States a foreclosed identity is more common than an achieved one. It has been argued that foreclosure may be a more functional identity for minorities in a hostile society (Hauser and Kasendorf, 1983; Markstrom-Adams, Berman, and Brusch, 1993). Taking on an identity provided by one's group may be more adaptive than trying to individually achieve an identity in a society that blocks opportunities and conveys negative messages about one's minority status. This topic is discussed further in the section on ethnic identity.

Each of the four identity statuses can be thought of either as the state that a person is in or as a developmental stage. For some individuals, identity status remains relatively constant with time. In one study (Adams and Montemayor,

Figure 11.1

Figure 11.1

Trajectories in identity
development beginning
with the freshman year
in college. (Adapted
from G. R. Adams &
Montemayor, 1988.)

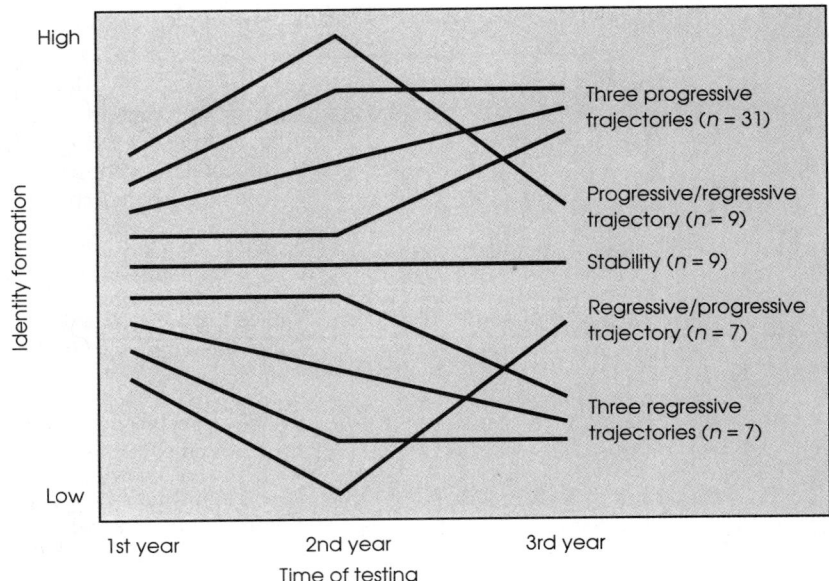

High

Identity formation

Three progressive
trajectories (*n* = 31)

Progressive/regressive
trajectory (*n* = 9)

Stability (*n* = 9)

Regressive/progressive
trajectory (*n* = 7)

Three regressive
trajectories (*n* = 7)

Low

1st year   2nd year   3rd year

Time of testing

1988, see Fig. 11.1), constancy of identity status was found to occur for about 15 percent of the adolescents studied. For other individuals, the identity statuses form a kind of stage model, in which the individuals progress upwards through the four stages over time. About 50 percent of individuals were found to show steady progression over time. Still others showed an up and down pattern of progression and regression through the four statuses.

Researchers have found a variety of correlates of the four identity statuses. Identity diffused individuals tend to show signs of poor psychological adjustment, such as feelings of inferiority and poorly articulated self-concepts. They are more likely to have parents who are rejecting or not affectionate and are more likely to have problems with substance abuse (Adams, Gullota, and Markstrom-Adams, 1994; Markstrom-Adams, 1992; Jones, 1992). Foreclosed individuals are more likely to be hardworking, quiet, obedient, respectful of authority, and industrious. They tend to come from families that are warm and supportive but that appear to stifle autonomous growth (Adams, et al., 1994). Individuals in the moratorium status tend to be the most anxious, which is not surprising because they are in the midst of questioning their identity status. They appear to be high in self-directiveness while open to exploring alternative perspectives. They also tend to be introspective and emotionally responsive (Adams, et al., 1994). Their families are likely to be democratically organized, but there is liable to be strain between the adolescent and the parents (Fuhrmann, 1986).

Identity achieved students have been found in many studies to have high levels of self-esteem, moral reasoning, self-confidence, psychological integration, emotional maturity, and social adeptness. They are also most likely to have established strong intimate relationships (Adams, et al., 1994; Waterman, 1992). As with adolescents in the moratorium status, they are likely to have come from democratic homes (Fuhrmann, 1986). However, while the vast majority of the evidence indicates that identity achievement is associated with positive qualities, the findings are not entirely uniform. Kroger (1992) reports that some studies have found a high percentage of identity achieved subjects to be excessively self-sufficient or detached.

Differences between men and women have been a major focus of investigation. As we have noted, Erikson assumed that interpersonal issues were at the core of women's identity, suggesting that their identities might not be completely formed until the intimacy stage in early adulthood. Research indeed supports the idea that identity and intimacy tend to merge for many women, while for men they are separated, that is, identity first and intimacy second (Patterson, Sochting, and Marcia, 1992). However, these researchers also conclude that the task of identity *begins* in adolescence both for women and for men. Further, for nontraditional women, late adolescence is the optimal time for resolution of the identity, as it is for men. For traditional women, whom Erikson expected would complete their identities when they married and had children, the evidence suggests that marriage and children do not complete their identities. Rather, these women put their identities "on hold" until their children have grown up, when they resume the task of identity completion. Josselson (1988) has studied identity formation in women by interviewing them in college and again when they were in their mid-thirties. She found that identity development for women does involve issues of interpersonal connection.

In early research on identity status it was found that for men, identity achievement and moratorium were the most "healthy" patterns (e.g., high self-esteem, etc.), while for women identity achievement and foreclosure were the most healthy (Patterson, et al., 1992). At the time, Marcia (1980) suggested that the foreclosure status might be adaptive for women because society did not provide support for women, as it did for men, to explore and choose their identities. He predicted that if society changed, so would the pattern of these early research findings. Making Marcia look like a prophet, recent findings show that for women, as well as for men, identity achievement and moratorium are the more adaptive patterns. Patterson et al. (1992) note that this might be due to the fact that the identity status interview was changed over the years to take interpersonal issues more into account. However they think this shift is more likely due to societal changes that now provide more support for women to choose careers.

There are several problems with the research done on identity statuses from Marcia's perspective. One problem is that most of the research has been done on college students, typically between the ages of eighteen and twenty-two. There is less research on adolescents not in college. In one study, Morash (1980) examined working-class youths and college students. It was found that working-class youths were more likely to be either identity achieved or diffused, while college students were more likely to be in moratorium or foreclosure. Working-class youths were also more likely to have experienced shorter, more concrete moratoriums. It may be that being in college allows one the luxury of a more leisurely moratorium period in which one can explore one's identity before making commitments. However much more research is needed on adolescents not in college.

From a feminist perspective, Archer (1992) has criticized the research on identity statuses. She argues that focusing on differences between the sexes is not fruitful. Individual men and women vary among themselves enormously, and the differences that have been found between men and women as groups are minimal. She believes it is more interesting to look at the question of how *individuals* pattern their identity achievement rather than at group comparison of genders. For instance, some of her research has found that reasoning about identity is "domain specific." This means that an individual's reasoning about identity in one area, such as vocation, is not necessarily the same as his or her reasoning in another area, such as relationships.

One criticism of identity status theory and research has previously been mentioned. That is that the whole concept of achieving an identity has a distinctly Western flavor. Myers, Speight, Highlen, Cox, Reynolds, Adams, and Hanley (1990), working from an Afro-centric paradigm, have noted that in Western culture one must establish one's worth through one's activities, while in other cultures one is valued just because one is. They believe that the Western idea is a product of our cultural assumptions, which separate self from others and separate the material from the spiritual. As previously noted, the foreclosure stage, therefore, may not necessarily be a less developed stage than the identity achieved stage in many cultures.

In conclusion, Marcia's theory of identity statuses has led to research that has helped clarify the process of identity development in adolescence. At the same time many issues remain to be clarified. We next turn to an alternative view of identity in adolescence, and of human functioning in general, that of a narrative perspective.

NARRATIVE AND IDENTITY

Dan McAdams (1989) has focused on the "narrative" aspects of identity. He has suggested that one's identity is grounded in a personal "life story." This reflects a recent more general trend towards viewing individual experience in terms of narrative constructions (Smith, 1988; Howard, 1991). This in turn is part of a larger set of views variously called "postmodernist," "constructivist," and "constructionist" (Mahoney, 1991). What these views all have in common is the idea that people's personal realities are "constructed." How we construct our experiences of self, others, and the world determines the world we inhabit. Our constructions are significantly influenced by the cultures or subcultures in which we live. As we have seen, the self is constructed differently by different cultures. Even our experience of gender is now being seen as a social construction (Ashmore, 1990).

Mair, and others who adopt a narrative perspective, assumes that our constructions of reality take the form of stories.

> Stories are habitations. We live in and through stories. They conjure worlds. We do not know the world other than as story world. Stories inform life. They hold us together and keep us apart. We inhabit the great stories of our culture. We live through stories. We are *lived* by the stories of our race and place. It is this enveloping and constituting function of stories that is especially important to sense more fully. We are, each of us, locations where the stories of our place and time become partially tellable. (1988, p. 127)

Therefore, life experience is constructed along the lines of stories. Lives have plots and subplots, and main characters and minor characters. Paul Ricoeur, a French psychoanalyst, has argued that it is how we "emplot" our lives that provides meaning for the events in it. An event without being embedded in a "plot" has no meaning. He says:

> . . . a story is made out of events to the extent that plot makes events into a story. An event, consequently, must be more than a singular occurrence, a unique happening. It receives its definition from its contribution to the development of a plot. A story, on the other hand, must be more than an enumeration of events in a serial order; it must make an intelligible whole of incidents. (1983, p. 152)

One's life can have a well-organized plot, a poorly organized plot, a plot that has few leads towards a productive future, or a plot poorly connected to the past.

The narrative perspective on personality is having an important influence on psychotherapy. Therapists representing psychodynamic, humanistic, and cognitive points of view have begun to view therapy as the "restorying" of an individual's life. Ricoeur (Smith, 1988) sees therapy as a process of reorganizing one's plot through sharing it with another. An important part of the healing process is the sharing of one's "untold" stories. What might be called "repressed experience" is really experience that has not previously been articulated and shared with another.

An example of how people can utilize narrative accounts to deal with a life problem is provided by Harvey, Orbuch, and Weber (1993). They studied hundreds of individuals dealing with traumatic experiences such as incest, armed combat, an airline crash, or the loss of a loved one. They argue that it is in developing an account of the incident that the victim learns how to cope with the event and to restore a sense of meaning to life. An *account* is a "story-like construction containing attributions, trait inferences, descriptions, emotional expressions, and related material regarding self and outside world" (pp. 1–2). Confiding in others as one develops the account appears also to be an essential part of the healing process. One study by Harvey et al. (1991) found that there was greater recovery if the individual engaged in account-making through diary work, confiding in responsive, empathic others, or participating in support groups. Feelings of completion appear to be associated with accepting loss and appear to be crucial to recovery.

Psychotherapy can be seen as the process of restorying one's life. (© Michael New-man/Photo Edit)

As we have noted, the narrative perspective has been applied to the study of identity by Dan McAdams (1989), who argues that identity is a narrative construction based on one's "life story." Our sense of ourselves, how we interpret events and experiences in our lives, comes from the sense of the "stories" we see ourselves as living. Further, our goals and motives only take on meaning in terms of our life story.

McAdams (1988) has researched this theory by collecting life stories from individuals. He had students enrolled in his developmental psychology courses complete "identity journals" in which they had to write about issues relevant to the class material. For instance, when the issue of consistency in personality was being discussed, students were asked to think about it in terms of themselves by trying to remember an incident in which they had done something completely out of character. McAdams has also interviewed midlife adults (see the interview format in Table 11.2). McAdams' research is a good example of the *personological* tradition of research in personality. That is, his interest has been in studying the life paths of whole individuals rather than in studying one aspect of behavior (say, achievement motivation) across large groups of individuals.

McAdams, like Erikson, argues that adolescence is the major period of identity and life-story construction, although one continues this process for the rest of one's life. Infancy contributes the "feeling tone" of the story — such as funda-

Table 11.2   McAdams' life story interview format

I.	Life Chapters
II.	Specific Scenes

A. Peak Experience (High Point)
B. Nadir Experience (Low Point)
C. Turning Point
D. Earliest Memory
E. Significant Childhood Memory
F. Significant Adolescent Memory
G. Significant Adult Memory
H. Significant Other Memory

III.	Important Persons
IV.	Future Script
V.	Stresses and Problems
VI.	Personal Ideology
VII.	Life Motif or Message
VIII.	Other

Source: McAdams, 1993.

mentally hopeful or frightening—based on early experiences with caretakers. Early childhood contributes a variety of images (see Highlight 11.1). In late childhood children are able to work with themes, and they begin to construct more truly storylike narratives about themselves and the events in their lives.

During adolescence individuals rearrange their past to develop a story of self which will help them face the future. As individuals progress into adulthood they have a number of different *imagoes,* or self-images, of themselves inside. This set of self-images acts like a Greek chorus—commenting on and guiding behavior. McAdams (1988) found in his study of midlife adults that, although they were relatively normal individuals, their life story accounts were described as if they were "multiple personalities." In particular they often had two conflicting primary self-images.

Some of the polarities in self-images found were: adventurer/housewife, humanist/barbarian, good citizen/bum, and worker/escapist. One subject, for instance, struggled with his two conflicting images, one of himself as an artist (with all its bohemian connotations) and the other of himself as a "successful, worldly money maker." Ultimately individuals integrate the various imagoes into one.

■ **Highlight 11.1** ■■■■■■

Early Childhood Roots of the Life Story

A turning point in my daughter's life was the day she saw *Snow White*. It was almost a year ago; she was 3 years old. The original Walt Disney version of the fairy tale was playing at a local theater, so I took the opportunity to escort Ruth Megan to her first full-length movie. . . .

Since that day, my family has lived with Snow White and the Seven Dwarfs. All seven of the dwarfs ride with us in the car to nursery school —Grumpy, Happy, Doc, Bashful, Sleepy, Sneezy, and Dopey. The Wicked Queen, the Peddler Woman (who is the Queen in disguise), the Queen's Huntsman, and the Handsome Prince frequently show up for dinner. When she first met a classmate named William, Ruth told him that she lived in a little cottage (like the Dwarfs') tucked far away in the woods. (Incredulous, William told her she was crazy, and then reported that he would be traveling to nursery school next week in his flying car.) When William comes over for lunch these days, Ruth pretends that she is the Wicked Queen and he is the Queen's Huntsman, and the two of them terrorize her little sister, Amanda, who is 1½ and cast in the pitiful role of Snow White. They steal her stuffed animals and threaten to lock her up, even kill her, (William's idea, I am sure); they hide poisoned apples under her pillow. On other days, Ruth herself is Snow White, organizing regular birthday parties for Grumpy, her favorite dwarf, taping pink crepe paper all over the dining room, making birthday cakes out of sugar, pepper, oregano, and water.

My daughter is obsessed with the story of Snow White! Yet it is not so much the integrated story—from beginning to end—that so fascinates her. Rather, it is various pieces of the story, easily divorced from their coherent narrative context, that she appropriates into her daily life of fantasy, play, and fun. One day she is the Wicked Queen. The next day she is Bashful. Her identification with each of these characters is ephemeral and idiosyncratic. Recently she was Grumpy, rescuing three of the "Little Ponies" who were stranded on a cliff. Yet in *Snow White*, Grumpy never rescues anybody. And there are no ponies in the movie—they originate from a popular television show.

Although Ruth seems to recognize that stories have a certain canonical form, she does not insist that her own renditions conform to the canon. Her make-believe world is inconsistent, illogical, and very fluid. It is populated by a rich and ever-expanding repertoire of *images*. It is the images in stories—not the stories themselves—that Ruth zeroes in on. This is not to say that she cannot follow a story's plot or that she fails to appreciate the dramatic building of tension in narrative, the climax, and

Continued

the denouement. Ruth has a pretty good sense of the whole story, from beginning to end, of Snow White and the Seven Dwarfs. But it is not the whole story that captures her imagination, for it is too big and complex, too systematic and progressive, to find its way *in toto* into her daily world of imagination and play. Instead, Ruth dwells on the images, reworking them daily into her own fantastical plots.

Source: McAdams, 1990.

ETHNIC IDENTITY

We now turn to an important specific component of identity: ethnic identity. Ethnic identity has to do with those aspects of one's identity that relate to one's identification with one's ethnic group. Not everyone has specifically worked out an ethnic identity. However, it is a particularly important issue for minority group members in our culture.

Individuals who are members of minority groups in our society face a particularly complicated task in forming an identity. First, they are often confronted with conflicting messages concerning important life values. For instance, the minority culture may hold the value that an individual's choice of careers should be influenced by the family, while the dominant culture in the United States emphasizes individual choice. Second, we have already seen that different cultural groups hold different views of what a self is: is it a ''we'' interconnected with others, or is it an ''I,'' a separate, autonomous entity? Third, such individuals are often confronted with the social devaluation of their minority group status. In various implicit and explicit ways they are told that they are ''less than'' because

Young children begin to develop their life stories by playing the role of fantasy characters. (© Toni Michaels/The Image Works)

they are members of a particular minority group. This message might be conveyed, for instance, through stereotypic television portrayals or perhaps even through the invisibility of their group in television shows. Fourth, they face some objective limitations to their hopes and aspirations because of their minority group status and various concomitants, such as economic inequality. Malcolm X, for instance, although clearly more intelligent than many of his fellow white students, was told by one of his teachers (who had previously been supportive of him) that he could not hope to be a lawyer but should pursue some kind of manual labor occupation (Jenkins, 1982).

There are two interrelated aspects to the formation of an identity for ethnic minority members. First is the issue of forming a positive, proactive identification with one's ethnic group. This is the issue that most models of ethnic identity formation have focused on. A second issue is that of acculturation — the degree to which the individual attempts to integrate with the dominant culture or chooses to remain separate and identify exclusively with the minority culture.

Ethnic identity, according to Phinney (1991), includes one's sense of self-identification as a group member, attitudes and values in relation to one's group, attitudes about oneself as a group member, the adoption of ethnic behaviors and practices, and the extent of one's ethnic knowledge and degree of commitment to one's group.

There is a commonality to many models of ethnic identity development. This commonality is shared by models of identity development for nonethnic minority groups as well, such as for gays and lesbians. Individuals are seen as first experiencing a stage in which they either deny, devalue, or are unaware of their oppressed identity. Then they move into a stage of questioning their oppressed identity followed by a stage of strongly identifying with their oppressed identity. Often in this stage there is a great deal of anger and rejection of the larger oppressive culture. Finally, in the last stage, the previously devalued part of themselves is integrated into their larger identity (Myers, Speight, Highlen, Cox, Reynolds, Adams, and Hanley, 1990).

Phinney (Phinney, 1991; Phinney and Rosenthal, 1992) has proposed a model of ethnic identity development that is synthesized from other models but is also based on the work of Erikson and Marcia. A schematization of it is given in Table 11.3. The first stage is that of an unexamined ethnic identity, which could be likened to Marcia's either foreclosed or diffused status. The adolescent either adopts an unexamined commitment to his or her ethnicity from the parents and is therefore foreclosed, or has no clear sense of commitment to ethnic identity but is not exploring it either and is therefore in a diffused state. In the second stage, some event (perhaps some act of discrimination) triggers the adolescent's awareness of his or her ethnic identity, and he or she begins to think about it. This stage is equivalent to the moratorium stage in Marcia's model. In the third stage of ethnic identity development, some kind of commitment to an ethnic identity occurs. This follows a process of resolving conflicts and contradictions involved in being a minority in a majority culture where minorities have often experienced discrimination. A recent study (Phinney and Chavira, in press, reported in Phinney and

Table 11.3 Ethnic identity as a continuum

High, strong, secure, or achieved ethnic identity:
Involvement in ethnic behaviors and practices
Positive evaluation of the group
Preference for own group; happy with one's membership
Interest in and knowledge about the group
Commitment, sense of belonging to the group

Low, weak, or diffuse ethnic identity:
Little involvement in ethnic behaviors
Negative evaluation of group
Preference for majority group; unhappy with one's membership
Little interest in or knowledge about group
Little commitment or sense of belonging to group

Source: Phinney, 1991.

Rosenthal, 1992) studied the development of ethnic identity in minority youths between the ages of sixteen and nineteen and found movement from lower to higher stages, as predicted.

Phinney (1991) has reviewed the literature on the relationship between self-esteem and ethnic identity status. She notes that a fundamental question is whether ethnic identity status has a positive or negative impact on psychological adjustment. Phinney asks, "Is a strong sense of identification with one's ethnic culture likely to act as a positive influence on well-being, by providing a sense of belonging and serving as a buffer against the negative impact of prejudice and discrimination? Or, conversely, might this sense of belonging promote internalization of negative stereotypes and serve to emphasize one's difference from the dominant culture, thus increasing the stress of minority status?" (p. 193). In her review it was found that not all components of a positive ethnic identity correlated with high self-esteem, but the trend was that individuals with a strong ethnic identity were more likely to have high self-esteem. However the strength of the relationship varied from ethnic group to ethnic group and from component to component. Therefore there were no clear universal patterns.

With respect to acculturation, Berry and his colleagues (Berry, et al., 1989) have defined four modes of acculturation. Those who strongly identify only with their ethnic group are in a state of separation. Those who strongly identify only

Having a sense of identification with one's own culture can have a positive influence on one's own identity. (© Robert Clay/Monkmeyer)

with the dominant culture are in a state of assimilation. Those who identify with both their own group and the dominant culture are considered to be bicultural. Finally, those who identify with neither are considered to be in a state of marginalization. In general, most theorists now hold that biculturation is the most adaptive mode. For instance, LaFromboise, Coleman, and Gerton (1993) have argued that biculturated individuals are those who have developed the competencies to function both in their culture of origin and in the larger majority culture. They are able to utilize the best of both cultures. In this sense they will have also developed a more complex, differentiated, and integrated identity. Several empirical studies, reviewed by Phinney (1991) have supported the contention that biculturated individuals generally show better psychological adjustment.

In sum, a strong, achieved ethnic identity along with a bicultural state of acculturation appears to be psychologically healthy. But does a strong ethnic identity develop primarily through encounters with racism, as several of the models have suggested? Stevenson (1993) has argued that many models of racial identity have focused on individuals' reactions to racism and discrimination. In so doing, they have neglected the socialization aspects of the family.

Stevenson argues that the major factor of African-American life is the importance of the family. Individuals have an extended self, a sense of "WE"; thus, their identity is closely connected to their family and culture. This connection is based on what Nobles (1989) has said are the two key principles of African-American life: survival of the tribe and "oneness of being." A mature sense of identity includes a sense of "WE."

Thus, to measure identity one must measure not only what an individual thinks of him or herself but also how he or she sees him or herself in an interpersonal context. For African Americans the family is the most important institution, especially for adolescents who are struggling to resolve the issue of their identity. Stevenson says, "A self that is extended is more prepared to meet the demands of a racist, sexist, or age-ist society" (p. 8). Racial socialization by the family is important in developing a strong ethnic identity. That is, a strong ethnic identity is not merely a result of the individual confronting his or her ethnic identity upon experiencing discrimination. Stevenson cites research suggesting that individuals who received positive racial socialization experiences from their families appear to have more positive ethnic identities. Compatible with this, Markstrom-Adams and her colleagues (Markstrom-Adams and Berman, 1993; Markstrom-Adams, Berman, and Brusch, 1993) found that adolescents who grow up in neighborhoods made up of members of their ethnic group have stronger ethnic identities than adolescents who grow up in neighborhoods dominated by members of other cultural groups.

In sum, there is some evidence that minority youths progress in development of an ethnic identity during adolescence. However, it appears that the establishment of an ethnic identity involves not only confronting one's ethnic identity as a result of discrimination experiences but also positive socialization experiences by the family and growing up among members of one's cultural group. Having a strong ethnic identity and being bicultural appear to be psychologically advantageous.

GENDER IDENTITY, SEX TYPING, AND SEX DIFFERENCES

Some of the most active current research in developmental psychology concerns the development of gender identity and the related issues of sex differences and sex typing. While gender identity has to do with individuals' self-perceptions of who they are as males or as females, sex differences have to do with the question of whether there are objective differences in psychological functioning between the two sexes. The issue of sex-typing has to do with how males and females develop their masculine or feminine identities, attributes, or behaviors. The issue of whether there are sex differences and how sex typing occurs are intimately related to the development of gender identity. We first examine gender identity, then consider the issue of sex differences, and finally reflect upon how sex differences and gender identity develop, i.e., the issue of sextyping.

Gender Identity

One of the most important components of identity is gender identity. In introducing his model of gender identity, Ashmore (1990), says that "it is assumed that sex and gender pervade most aspects of daily life and can shape many aspects of psychological structure and function" (p. 512).

One's *gender identity* is defined by how one's perception of gender influences or plays a role in other aspects of identity. It could be said to be the answer to the issue of what it means to me to be a man or woman. It is how one's view of oneself as male or female is interwoven with all the various other aspects of one's identity. According to Ashmore (1990), gender identity consists of five general content areas. The first is the biological and physical attributes associated with gender, including aspects of appearance and dress. The second area is "symbolic and stylistic behaviors," including how one walks, one's body bearing, and how one communicates nonverbally. The third area consists of the interests and abilities that one sees as relevant to and characteristic of one's gender. The fourth area is "social relationships," which includes images of how one will differentially relate to men and women as well as how one's sense of masculinity or femininity are organized and expressed in relationship with others. The fifth area is perception of one's personal and social attributes — for instance, one's personality traits and how these relate to masculinity and femininity.

Sex Differences

Many differences can be observed between boys and girls and men and women in terms of "typical" behavior. More boys play with blocks and fire trucks than do girls, who tend to play with dolls and paper cutouts more than do boys; boys prefer football, while girls prefer dramatic play. Sex differences in toy and activity preference can be observed early in development, well before the age of three (Lewis, 1987). Later in life, more men than women study to be architects and engineers, while more women become nurses and school teachers than do men. There are many exceptions and, although changes are occurring in traditional gender roles, there are still gender differences in preferred activities and in such diverse domains as child-care responsibilities, work roles, and occupations. These differences are most likely a reflection of the contrasting social roles ascribed to men and women. Comparable kinds of gender differences in social roles are observed in other societies, both modern and preliterate.

We know that these sex differences exist at the social level. The intriguing question is what they are related to at the psychological level. To what extent do boys and girls differ in intellectual abilities, motivation, social skills, and other personality attributes? There are many popular stereotypes concerning gender differences in personality. For example, males have been regarded as aggressive, rational, and ambitious, while females have been described as passive, emotional, and nurturant. These stereotypes are opinions and are in part responsible for the differential occupational roles, income levels, and statuses of the sexes. But to what extent do these gender stereotypes have a basis in fact?

Sex-typing begins early in life. (© 1976 Suzanne Szasz/Photo Researchers)

One task undertaken by psychologists has been to determine possible personality and cognitive attributes that distinguish the two sexes and, in addition, to discern the age levels at which gender differences appear. This empirical task has proved to be far more complex than it initially seemed. First, one must assume that the samples of the sexes studied are comparable on such variables as socioeconomic status and educational opportunity. It is also important to sample different ethnic and economic groups to establish that the findings are representative of boys and girls in general, rather than restricted to some particular segment of society. To add a further complication, as the culture undergoes economic and social change, there may be corresponding alterations in personality traits. For example, differences in dependency between the sexes seem to have been greater in previous decades, indicating that gender differences reported at one time may not hold for another. Conversely, where there once were similarities, differences may suddenly appear. Finally, some of the psychological attributes distinguishing the sexes are subtle and difficult to measure.

A second and even more challenging task for psychologists is determining how differences between the sexes have come about, or how sex typing occurs. The role of biological versus social factors in determining behavioral differences between the sexes is an especially critical social issue. The phrase "anatomy is destiny" crystallizes the view that women's personality and role in society are fundamentally caused by their biological structure. This explanation has often been used to justify women's subordination and sex discrimination. It is evident from the extensive amount of research that has been conducted on gender differences that there is a great deal of overlap between the sexes with regard to virtually any behavior. Because of individual variability within a sex and the overlap between sexes, gender discrimination is psychologically, as well as legally, unjustified.

In the sections that follow, we consider research studies on sex differences and on the development of sex differences and gender identity.

Studies of Sex Differences.   We are all aware that men and women are socialized to be different in a number of ways, such as in how they dress. However, are there basic *psychological* differences? A good deal of research has been done to determine whether there are such differences. In a comprehensive review of the literature on human gender differences, Maccoby and Jacklin (1974) concluded that the following differences are well established by research data.

1. Girls excel in verbal ability.
2. Boys excel in visual-spatial ability.
3. Boys are superior in mathematical ability.
4. Males are more aggressive than females.

However, more recent findings have led to questions about some of these conclusions. Recent research has indicated that men and women are now closer to equal in the areas of both verbal and mathematical ability (Feingold, 1988; Jacklin, 1989). In addition, even the finding that males are more aggressive does not appear to be as strong a difference as was once supposed. Based on a summary of "meta-analytic" findings on gender differences, Ashmore (1990) notes that the difference in degree between male and female aggression is in the "small to moderate" range. Nonetheless, the data still indicate that men are more likely to be aggressive than women, although such a difference may depend on how aggression is measured (see the following discussion of how sex differences develop).

Ashmore's (1990) summary of research indicates that, overall, few psychological sex differences have been found that are of more than "small to moderate" size. There are differences between men and women in "social stylistic" behaviors, such as smiling and facial expressiveness. Women report themselves to be more empathic than men, although when empathy is objectively measured only small differences are found. The largest differences found between men and women are in physical variables, such as in the distance to which they are able to throw a ball.

Other researchers have concluded that girls are more timid than boys in certain situations (Christophersen, 1989; Ginsburg and Miller, 1982) and are not as physically active as boys (Eaton and Enns, 1986; Eaton and Yu, 1989). There is also evidence that girls appear to be more compliant than boys to the demands of teachers, parents, and other authority figures during childhood (Cowan and Avants, 1988; Maccoby, 1988). Yet Maccoby (1988) says that girls are not more compliant to the demands of agemates.

In general, most researchers believe that there are far fewer differences in basic psychological attributes between the sexes than there are similarities. For instance, Hyde (1984) notes that gender accounts for about 5 percent of the variation in aggressive behavior in children, which means that about 95 percent of the variation in aggressive behavior is due to factors other than gender.

While there may be relatively few basic psychological differences between the sexes, some differences in behaviors begin to develop very early. Boys between the ages of fourteen and twenty-two months already prefer trucks and cars to play with, while girls prefer dolls and soft toys (Smith and Daglish, 1977). Two-year-old girls prefer to play with other girls, and by age three boys prefer to play with boys (La Freniere, Strayer, and Gauthier, 1984).

Sex Typing: Development of Sex Differences and Gender Identity

There have been a number of different theories that try to account for differences that are observed between the sexes. Biological theories hold that differences in the sexes are based in biology and are observable as soon as children begin to interact and play with peers (around the age of two). Yet the role of biological factors is controversial and complex.

Evidence from primate studies indicates that male monkeys engage in more rough-and-tumble play than females do and that even male infants display more aggressive behavior when attacked than females do (Aldis, 1975; Devore, 1965). But whether these observations of monkey behavior are applicable to humans is uncertain. In humans in this culture, the process of treating males and females differently begins at birth, with pink and blue blankets. Girls and boys are not only differently identified through the use of different colors and clothing, but also reacted to with different expectations and behaviors. Thus, even these early sex differences in aggression may be attributed to social rather than biological factors.

In Chapter 18, the question of gender differences in aggression and the role of biological and social factors are examined in more detail. At this point, it is useful to keep in mind that the greater aggressiveness noted in males is based on observations of direct physical and verbal aggression. Although the gender differences in direct aggression before the age of six have been questioned (Tieger, 1980), extensive evidence can be presented indicating that this difference is reliable (Maccoby and Jacklin, 1980) and can be observed in children as young as age three (Fagot, Leinbach, and Hagan, 1986). However, when one examines more indirect, subtle forms of aggressiveness, such as snubbing or ignoring peers or gossiping, there is some evidence that aggression is greater in females than in males (N. Feshbach, 1969; Lagerspetz, Björkqvist, and Peltorer, 1988).

According to Freud, the process by which boys and girls develop sex differences and their gender identities is rooted in biology. For him, identification was the principal mechanism leading to sex typing. As a result of the process of identification, children acquire the attributes and orientations of their sex. The biological difference between boys and girls leads not only to their making a different choice of which parent to identify with, but also to a less satisfactory identification for females (see Chapter 3). Therefore, the process of identification has biological roots. Freud did recognize some influence of learning processes in the development of gender differences, however, and contemporary psychoanalysts acknowledge the importance of social variables to an even greater extent.

The social learning theorists stress the importance of the differential reinforcement boys and girls receive for "appropriately" imitating male and female models and for behaving in accordance with the norms and expectations of society. The behaviors that define the female and male roles are very much influenced by the culture in which a child is socialized. Sex role norms vary from society to society, but in each case children are rewarded for those behaviors that will help them fit the particular roles prescribed by society. This differential reinforcement begins very early. It is manifest in the disparate ways that males and females are handled by their parents, in the unequal rough-and-tumble play of fathers with boys versus girls, and in the reinforcements given for engaging in appropriate sex-typed activities. One of the earliest gender differences that is consistently observed is that a greater amount of physical stimulation and gross motor play is directed toward male infants than toward female infants (see Block, 1979; Parke and Suomi, 1980). Studies of child-rearing practices in this and other cultures (Antill, 1987; Block, 1973; Whiting, 1963) clearly indicate that parents have different expectations for boys and girls and respond differentially according to the sex of their child. It is inevitable that these socialization practices define and shape male and female behavior.

At the same time, it should be noted that in many instances of gender differences it is very difficult to disentangle the influence of biological and social variables. Parental practices may reinforce and enhance subtle biologically based sex differences or may obscure them. Application of the twin method (cf. Chapter 1) to the analysis of individual differences in masculine and feminine personality attributes enables one to at least partially separate the independent roles of biological and environmental influence. In one study, monozygotic and dizygotic twins ranging in age from eight to fifteen years were administered several questionnaire measures of masculinity and femininity (Mitchell, Baker, and Jacklin, 1989). These self-report measures, adaptations of instruments used for older populations, are based on attributes which men and women believe to be more typical of and appropriate to males and to females. An example of a masculine item is "I am often the leader among my friends," and a feminine item, "I am a kind and gentle person." The relationships between monozygotic twins proved to be much stronger than that for dizygotic twins for both femininity and, especially, masculinity scores, thus providing evidence of a genetic influence. Analysis of the data also reflected significant environmental influences.

It may be noted that masculinity and femininity are separate dimensions or traits rather than opposite ends of a single continuum. Thus, while boys tend to be higher in masculinity and girls higher in femininity, it is quite possible for a boy or a girl to obtain both high masculinity and high femininity scores. While masculinity and femininity as personality traits appear to have genetic components, this finding does not automatically establish a genetic linkage between gender and masculinity or femininity. It seems likely that boys have more of whatever the genes are that make for "masculine" behavior and girls more of the genes that influence "feminine" behavior. However, research has yet to demonstrate a clear relationship between the hormonal and other biochemical differences between males and females and masculine or feminine behavior. In any case, even if biological influences were to be reliably established, there is considerable variability within each sex for degree of masculinity and femininity, and substantial overlap between sexes.

The development of gender typing and gender-linked behaviors is a complex process in which maturational and cognitive factors are involved as well as gender and social influences. A study by Fagot and Leinbach (1989) illustrates the interaction of several of these factors. A sample of boys and girls and their parents were seen when the children were approximately eighteen months, twenty-seven months, and forty-eight months of age. At age twenty-seven months, half the children, designated as "early labelers," were able to successfully identify the gender of children and adults in photographs presented to them. The other half, who made several errors in identifying males and females, were designated as "late labelers." Differences between boys and girls, and between early and late labelers, in gender-linked behaviors at eighteen and at twenty-seven months are presented in Table 11.4. At eighteen months, there were no significant differences between the groups. However, at twenty-seven months, gender differences in male- and female-typed toy play and in aggressive behavior can be seen. In addition, these differences are strongly influenced by whether the child can successfully identify gender. The largest sex differences in gender-typed behaviors are between the boys and girls who can successfully identify gender (early labelers). Clearly, learning factors are entailed in the development of gender typing.

The powerful influence of learning and cultural variables in gender typing is particularly reflected in studies of *hermaphrodites,* infants born with two sets of genitalia. Some of these infants with external female organs and internal male organs are genetically males according to chromosome tests. Conversely, others are genetically female and have internal female organs and external male organs. Studies of these children consistently indicate that children reared according to their external sexual characteristics develop a gender role and orientation corresponding to the manner in which they are raised, even though this gender role is contrary to their biological constitution (Hampson, 1965; Money, 1965).

But there are at least two major problems with the social learning explanation of sex typing. First, it implies that the many behaviors associated with being male or female have to be differentially reinforced or systematically modeled. It seems

Table 11.4   Mean percent of time children spent in sex-stereotyped behaviors

	Boy		Girl	
Child activity and child age	Early Labeler	Late Labeler	Early Labeler	Late Labeler
Male-typed toy play:				
18 months	4.1	6.8	.8	3.0
27 months	23.8	11.2	4.6	7.6
Female-typed toy play:				
18 months	2.7	4.7	4.5	4.1
27 months	1.9	5.1	20.8	10.2
Aggessive behavior:				
18 months	.8	2.5	1.1	.9
27 months	2.1	2.2	.4	1.9

unlikely that these vast differences have all been due to reinforcement mechanisms. Second, and perhaps more important, sexual identity is acquired quite early in the child's development and is remarkably stable and difficult to change. The child establishes its *gender* identity and subsequently acquires the set of behaviors that constitute gender role identity. Guided by this observation, Kohlberg (1966) proposed that the child first learns to identify itself as a boy or a girl and then models itself after males or females.

Kohlberg proposed that children pass through three stages as they acquire an understanding of what it means to be a male or female. The first stage is that of "basic gender identity," which consists of acquiring the basic label of oneself as a boy or girl, usually achieved by about age three. The second stage is that of "gender stability." A number of researchers have found that very young children, even when they understand that they are boys or girls, do not understand that gender is a stable attribute that does not change over time. This developmental achievement occurs somewhat later, around five or six. The third stage is "gender consistency," which is the understanding that one's sex is stable across situations. That is, one's sex is not changed by dressing in clothes of the opposite sex or by engaging in play activities preferred by the opposite sex. This is typically achieved by age six to seven. Some research has found that the gender concept does indeed develop sequentially, passing through the stages, and that this sequence has been observed across cultures (Munroe, Shimmin, and Munroe, 1984).

However there are problems with Kohlberg's model of the development of gender identity. First, it cannot account for the great variation in masculine or feminine qualities within each sex. Second, we have already seen evidence that children are beginning to develop sex-typed behaviors (such as choosing particular toys to play with) before they acquire a mature gender identity. As an alternative to Kohlberg's view, Martin and Halverson (1981, 1987) have developed *gender schema theory*. They suggest that children develop a set of gender schemas, which are organized sets of concepts about males and females. Children begin very early to develop a basic gender identity based on a simple classification of toys and behaviors as "for males" or "for females." Using this basic categorization, they then begin to explore and gradually add more and more information to their gender schemas until they have developed a stable and consistent gender identity by about the age of seven. Of course, this does not signal the end of learning about gender, which continues throughout childhood and adolescence.

A study by Stangor and Ruble (1989) tested the gender schema model. One of the properties of a schema is that it selectively influences the kind of information one pays attention to and remembers. In this study, it was found that the proportion of pictures remembered by children that were consistent with their gender-role in contrast to pictures that were inconsistent with it, increased with age.

As we have mentioned, although gender schema theory suggests that a stable and consistent basic gender identity is established by about age seven, new aspects of gender identity continue to develop as one grows older. Brown and Gilligan (1992) have showed that adolescence is an important time for socialization of certain aspects of the gender identity of girls. They studied how girls lose their "voice" during the transition from late childhood to adolescence. Nearly one hundred girls between the ages of seven and eighteen at a private girls' school were interviewed over a five-year period. It was found that as girls entered adolescence, they increasingly received pressure from their teachers and other adults to "be nice." They learned that in order to keep relationships, they had to lose an important part of relationships — authenticity. One of the girls says, "I do not want the image of a 'perfect girl' to hinder myself from being a truly effective human being, . . . yet, I still want to be nice, and I never want to cause any problems" (p. 41). In sum, girls' gender identity during adolescence comes to include "being nice" at the expense of being authentic.

Androgyny. Is there such a thing as a "healthy" gender identity? We have already seen how young girls making the transition from childhood to adolescence are socialized to lose a part of themselves that has traditionally been considered to be masculine — their assertiveness. At the same time it is likely that boys are being trained to lose a "feminine" part of themselves. Would it be better if children were able to retain both their masculine and feminine sides? Precisely this issue has been raised in the study of *androgyny*.

In early research, it was assumed that masculinity and femininity were two opposite ends of the same pole. If one was high in masculinity (that is, possessed traits characteristic of the male stereotype), one could not be high in femininity. Bem (1974), however, asserted that masculinity and femininity were two separate dimensions, and, therefore, a person could be high in both masculinity and femininity. As part of their gender identities, individuals could have traits characteristic of both the stereotypical male and the stereotypical female. Bem assumed that individuals who were high in both masculinity and femininity would be more flexible and adaptive. Using an inventory designed to measure both masculinity and femininity, it was found that such "androgynous" individuals did exist. Several research studies also found that individuals who were androgynous did appear to be more well-adjusted. However, there are a number of methodological problems that have made it difficult to conclude at this point that androgyny is indeed uniquely associated with better psychological adjustment (Ashmore, 1990).

Conclusions on the Development of Gender Identity and Sex Typing.   Ashmore (1990) has pointed out that the development of gender identity is a product of a number of different factors, including general cultural factors, specific interactions with specific individuals (e.g., parents, teachers, etc.), and one's own self-guided activities. The result is that individuals' gender identities will vary from person to person, and it may be meaningless to talk about "masculinity" and "femininity" as if they were global traits that individuals simply have more or less of. Ashmore suggests that culture has often been treated as if it were homogeneous, when in fact different subcultures in the United States may have different beliefs and expectations about the behavior of males and females. Individuals socialized in these subcultures may therefore have different concepts of male and female gender identities than do individuals socialized in the dominant or mainstream culture.

It is quite likely that gender typing and gender identity are functions of all the mechanisms that have been discussed: identification, selective reinforcement, cognitive labeling, and gender schemas. In addition, one cannot ignore the contribution of biological factors, even if they may be overridden by social reinforcement. In sum, sex typing and gender identity are the result of the interaction between social and biological processes, leading to personality differences between the sexes and variations within each sex.

IDENTITY, LIFE TASKS, AND GOALS

Up to this point we have been considering the more global aspects of identity, such as ethnic or gender identity. We turn now to the study of some specific aspects of identity. Among the most important components of identity are the goals that structure an individual's behavior. In recent years many psychologists have become concerned with the study of goals in personality (Pervin, 1989), and a number of researchers have begun to study goals and goal behavior at an individual level. This research is focused on units that are much more specific and idiosyncratic than the global issues considered in assessing an individual's identity status. For instance, Klinger (1987) has studied the *current concerns* that influence a person's moment to moment behavior by sampling what the person is thinking about from moment to moment. Emmons (1989) has studied individuals' *personal strivings,* the chronic enduring goals or concerns that underlie individuals' everyday behavior. Emmons and King (1988) found that the more conflict and ambivalence people had associated with their personal strivings, the more likely they were to score high on measures of neuroticism, depression, negative affect, and psychosomatic complaints. Little (1989) examined the *personal projects* of individuals by asking them to list their current personal projects. These might include projects such as: watch baseball games, make new friends, or develop a philosophy of life. Little's research has found that personal well-being is enhanced to the degree that individuals are engaged in personal projects that are meaningful, well-structured, supported by others, not excessively stressful, and that lead to a sense of personal efficacy. Below we consider one other concept, that of life tasks, in greater detail.

The concept of life tasks has been influenced by Erikson's model of identity development (Cantor, 1994). *Life tasks* are "self-articulated problems that individuals are motivated to try to solve, to which they devote energy and time, and that they see as organizing their current daily life activity" (Cantor and Zirkel, 1990, p. 150). For instance, for college students, life tasks include "being on my own away from my family" and "setting career goals." Cantor (1990) sees life tasks as issues that become particularly important at specific life transitions. They are embedded in the agendas of cultures and social groups at particular developmental times. For instance, "becoming independent" means something different and is worked on in different ways during different life transitions, such as leaving home to go to college or getting a first full-time job.

Being on one's own away from one's family is an important task for many college students. (© Dean Abramson/Stock Boston)

Cantor (1994) reports research done by herself and her colleagues in which the "life task" of achieving intimacy was studied in college students. Cantor suggests that how individuals frame the goals involved in the life task will determine how they go about achieving it. For achieving intimacy, some may adopt a more "communal" view, in which the goal is to learn how to share thoughts and feelings. Others may adopt a more "agentic" view, in which the goal is to learn how to maintain one's independence while in relationships. Depending on how one defines the task, one's behavior differs. Those who define the task more communally are more likely to engage in more serious relationships of longer duration. Those who identify the task more agentically are more likely to have a greater number of casual partners. These differences in orientation are also associated with safe sex practices. Those who adopt a communal orientation are less likely to engage in safe sex activity than those who adopt an agentic orientation. Cantor and her graduate students used this information to design an HIV/AIDS intervention program. For more communally oriented individuals, the program focused on skills of negotiation and communication about condom use, while for agentically oriented individuals, the program focused on technical skills designed to make a person feel more efficacious about the use of condoms. It was found that when the intervention corresponded to the student's definition of the life task, the student was more likely to report greater favorable attitudes towards condom use at a three-month followup (Cantor, 1994).

In contrast to a focus on global themes of life goals and tasks, researchers such as Cantor and her colleagues have been more interested in the day-to-day business of how individuals weave goals into their everyday life. Their studies provide a more complete picture of how individuals function than do the studies that focus on more global, general issues and values.

At the same time, the Cantor work is consistent with the work on gender identity, ethnic identity, and identity statuses in demonstrating the psychological importance of different aspects of identity. The work on identity further demonstrates how different methodological approaches can be fruitfully applied to investigate and give meaning to subtle and elusive psychological constructs such as that of identity.

Summary

1. *Identity,* in contrast to self-concept, consists of all the things one identifies with—the things one considers to define who one is. An important component of identity is the sense of continuity in one's life.

2. Erikson felt that continuity and experiencing oneself are important aspects of identity. He believed that late adolescence is the time of much identity achievement. Marcia, extending the work of Erik Erickson, postulates that there are four different *identity statuses* during adolescence: diffusion, foreclosure, moratorium, and identity achievement.

3. Research has shown different patterns on how individuals move through the four identity statuses.

4. Erickson predicted that identity development would be more closely tied to the development of intimacy for women than for men. While some research has supported this, the results are complex and there are no clear patterns that characterize all or most of one sex in contrast to the other.

5. Narrative approaches to personality assume that people's lives are bound together by the stories they tell about themselves. McAdams's narrative approach to identity assumes that identity is a *life story.*

6. Ethnic identity development appears to pass through stages, going from a diffused or unquestioned state to a clearly defined and worked-out state. Strong ethnic identity appears to be associated with higher levels of self-esteem.

7. Biculturated individuals, who are able to flexibly utilize the best from both the majority culture and from their own minority culture, appear to be the most healthy psychologically.

8. There appear to be relatively few basic psychological differences between the sexes, although members of the two sexes are socialized to behave in different ways.

9. Biological theories of sex differences assume that these differences have a genetic basis. Psychodynamic theories focus on identification with the parent. Social learning theories focus on the reinforcement of sex-typed behaviors. Cognitive labeling and gender schema theories assume that children develop concepts about what behaviors characterize being a member of a given sex. Children then assimilate information to these concepts.

10. A recent focus of personality research has been on variables that are components of one's identity, such as current concerns, personal strivings, personal projects, and life tasks. These specific components are more easily researchable than is the more global concept of identity itself.

Thought Questions

1. Do you think your identity can be easily classified into one of the four major identity statuses: diffusion, foreclosure, moratorium, or achievement? Or do you think your identity may include components from more than one stage?

2. How have you struggled with the issue of your ethnic identity?

3. In what way do you think you have constructed a "life story" that helps you make sense out of who you are?

4. What do you think accounts for differences between the sexes?

Social Development and Patterns of Childrearing

The study of adult personality inevitably leads back to the study of personality development. One reason for this is the assumption, made by most personality theorists, that the roots of adult personality are laid in childhood. A second, related reason is that a number of issues and processes that are central to the understanding of adult personality are also encountered in the study of personality development. One such issue, the nature/nurture question reviewed in Chapter 1, becomes immediately salient as one explores behavior among infants, young children, and adults. Another recurring issue throughout the life span is whether there are critical periods of development and developmental stages, characterized by relatively marked transitions from one level of development to another, as contrasted with a process of gradual, continuous change.

These issues will be considered in this chapter along with the processes basic to the development of social behavior. Particular attention is paid to the process of attachment, a key construct in personality development with implications for phenomena that will be discussed later in the text. Moral development and the development of prosocial behavior, is also considered. The development of a healthy, functional, moral, and prosocial adult has been a central concern of most personality theories. The chapter concludes with a consideration of the role of the family in socialization.

ISSUES IN PERSONALITY DEVELOPMENT

Nature or Nurture?

Examining personality from a developmental perspective highlights certain issues in the emergence and development of personality. One familiar and significant issue is the question of nature versus nurture. Is personality primarily a process of biological maturation; or is it influenced by environmental factors? Forces of nature are involved in the child's progression from a state of helpless infancy to that of an autonomous individual with language, logic, familial attachments, and social involvements. But, as many of the points raised in Chapter 2 suggest, nature does not operate in a vacuum. Children in different cultures learn to speak very different languages and, if deprived of social contact, will develop only the most primitive of communication skills. Children raised outside a social milieu are not likely to develop ambition, conscience, and social concern. The tracing of interactions between biology and environment, between the given and the experiential, and the determination of each influence's role, are the primary scientific tasks of developmental psychologists.

The nature/nurture question is illustrated by the often striking individual differences among children. Some babies are highly active, others are calm and placid, and still others are sensitive and easily distressed (Chess, Thomas, and Birch, 1965; Matheny, Jr., Wilson, and Thaben, 1987). What parents with a "different" child have not wondered what mistakes they made in bringing up the child? Other parents, whose children are quite unlike, wonder if they played any role at all in influencing the personality of each child. Developmental studies bear directly on the question of the causes or antecedents of individual differences and on the analogous question of group differences, such as those between males and females, which we considered in the previous chapter.

The observation of marked differences in temperament among children at infancy strongly suggests the influence of biological factors on personality. The calmness of some infants is reminiscent of the phlegmatic temperament described by the Roman physician Galen, while the irritability of other infants is suggestive of a choleric temperament. However, there are many features of infants' differences in temperament that do not correspond neatly to the ancient classification of temperaments. There are some babies — about one out of every ten (Thomas, Chess, and Birch, 1968) — who, for want of a better term, have been categorized as "difficult." These infants are characterized by extensive crying, unpredictable fluctuations in emotional state, intense reactions when aroused, and resistance to consolation and soothing. They are more likely than other infants to develop a subsequent behavior disturbance.

Although infants with difficult temperaments have a higher probability of manifesting later behavior problems, it would be misleading to conclude that these children display behavioral problems solely because "they were born that way." The data show only a weak relationship between early infant disturbances and subsequent psychopathology (Chess and Thomas, 1984; Sameroff and Chandler, 1975). Whether such infants will later develop behavior problems very much depends on the parents' response to an infant's behavior, on cultural resources and values, and on the particular experiences of the child with peers, in school, and in other contexts. This is not to say merely that a good environment will modify the effects of poor endowment or a birth injury; rather, there is a constant interaction over time between the child and its environment. The characteristics of a child may influence its environment; a difficult infant will evoke a range of responses from its caretakers different from those evoked by an infant with a more placid temperament. The responses from others will in turn modify the child. One mother's patient, warm, and consistent pattern of responding may, after time, foster positive changes in the child's emotional response, which in turn may modify the mother's behavior. Another mother's ambivalent response of oscillating between oversolicitousness and avoidance may exacerbate the infant's difficult behaviors, which in turn may intensify the mother's ambivalence.

Figure 12.1   Transactional model. (Adapted from Sameroff, 1975, p. 282.)

There are many other factors that influence the transactions between a child and its environment. A child with a biological handicap may develop a compensatory skill (cf. Adler, Chapter 4). Among a group of infants with difficult temperaments, one difficult child who initially had a very negative interaction with her father subsequently developed a strong interest in the piano. Her excellent skills as a pianist helped change her father's attitude from anger and rejection to pride and acceptance (cited in Sameroff, 1979).

This formulation of the nature/nurture issue in terms of a continuous series of reciprocal interactions between the child and its environment is referred to as the *transactional model* (Sameroff, 1975). The essential elements of the transactional model are shown in Fig. 12.1, which illustrates the continuing interaction between constitution and environment over time.

Continuity or Stages?

A related developmental issue of importance to personality is whether the changes in behavior observed during childhood reflect a gradual, continuous process or are marked by discrete stages that introduce new patterns of behavior. For example, most children at the age of seven display a strong sense of conscience, internalized standards of conduct, and guilt feelings. In contrast, three-year-olds display only the barest rudiments of conscience, with few signs of guilt. Psychologists who perceive development as continuous, that is, as developing gradually, account for this change in terms of the specific learning experiences to which a child has been exposed. Conversely, those who consider development as discontinuous, discrete developmental stages favor an interpretation based on changes in the child's psychological structure. The role of learning is not ignored, but the emphasis is on interactions of learning and biological maturation that produce new capacities and relationships that are *qualitatively* different from those that existed before. These emergent stages make possible very different types of behavior than those the child could exhibit before entering the new stage of development.

The personality theories reviewed in Chapters 3 through 6 hold disparate positions on the continuity/discontinuity controversy. Perhaps the two most opposing views are represented by the psychoanalytic and the learning theory schools. Psychoanalytic theory, which views the libido as progressing through a series of transformations in the oral, anal, phallic, and genital stages, reflects the discontinuity position. Learning theories, on the other hand, portray development as a continuous process of change, determined by the particular behaviors that are reinforced or learned by the child. From a learning theory standpoint, personality development is not inherently "progressive"; rather, the direction that development takes is a function of the child's socialization experiences.

Critical Periods. The concept of *critical periods* suggests another way of looking at the continuity-discontinuity issue or the question of stages. Experiences occurring during critical periods are believed to have greater impact than those occurring at other times during development. Psychoanalysts, for example, believe that the first five years of a child's life are critical for personality development. The basic features of one's personality are believed to be formed during this early period, with later experiences having only a secondary impact. A less extreme view held by most psychologists asserts that, while early childhood experiences are especially influential, significant changes in personality can occur throughout life.

A second implication of conceptualizing critical periods as a significant factor in development is the view that certain skills and competencies can be acquired during these periods. If they are not, then the child may suffer a permanent deficit or one that is extremely difficult to remedy. These deficits may be emotional and social as well as cognitive. For example, according to Erikson (cf. Chapter 4), a child who does not experience affection and nurturance during the oral-sensory stage will develop a basic mistrust of others and will have difficulty in responding to love and affection in later years.

For some behaviors and competencies, the critical period may cover a wide age range. Thus, it has been proposed that language must be acquired by early adolescence. If not, which may be the case if a child is raised in isolation, then language, according to this view, can never be taught to that child (Lennenberg, 1967). Exploration of this issue is one reason why feral children (children raised by packs of animals like wolves) are of such great psychological interest. Unfortunately, these children are typically brain damaged as well, limiting the clear testing of the critical period-language acquisition hypothesis. Nevertheless, there have been a number of documented instances of individuals acquiring language after the supposed critical period (Snow, 1987).

Does this mean that there is no critical period in language development? The answer to that depends upon how we define critical. It is certainly easier to acquire language before adolescence than after it. Similarly, some personality patterns, such as aggressiveness and a basic feeling of security and self-confidence, appear to be particularly influenced by experiences in childhood, although later experiences also influence these behaviors. These early experiences are critical in that they exert a profound effect upon personality development which may be, but are not necessarily, irreversible. A more recent and descriptive phrase referring to time periods during which particular experiences have an especially important influence on the organism's structure and future behavior is *"Sensitive Periods"* (Bornstein, 1989). While the term "critical" has an all or none implication, the term "sensitive" allows for more variation in the significance of a time period for the organism's development. Although the conception of sensitive or critical periods is in keeping with a good deal of animal and human data, many questions remain regarding the specification of sensitive periods and the kinds of behaviors and skills to which the sensitive period notion is relevant. These issues will become salient in the following discussion of attachment.

The question of whether personality develops in a continuous or stage-like fashion is currently unresolved, and, as with many psychological issues, the answer will probably involve both processes.

PROCESSES OF PERSONAL AND SOCIAL DEVELOPMENT

Attachment

We turn now from an examination of the continuity of personality to a key process in the infant's early socialization and personality development: the formation of attachments to others. We will find evidence of continuity here as well; the kinds of attachments established in infancy are reflected at subsequent developmental periods.

Among the special characteristics of infancy are the infant's helplessness and prolonged dependency on its parents and other caretakers for food, protection, satisfaction of needs, and relief of discomforts. Prolonged dependency is one of the hallmarks of human as opposed to nonhuman development. There is evidence that the greater the cognitive ability of a species, the longer the period of dependency. A human infant could not survive for very long without the support and care provided by others. To facilitate survival in the first few months of life, an infant is equipped with a set of reflexive biological responses, such as crying, sucking in response to lip stimulation, head movements, thrashing about, babbling, and smiling. These behaviors directly modify the environment and function as signals to caretakers, informing them of distress and satisfaction. A caretaker must, of course, be able to interpret the signals correctly and to be appropriately motivated. Indeed, what sound is more compelling to parents than their baby's crying?

There are two broad implications of the infant's situation and behavior that warrant special notice. First, the human infant is thrust into a social situation from the moment of birth; social interaction is the normal state of affairs. Second, although dependent, the infant is not a passive creature totally subject to the

Infants' reactions of smiling and crying communicate states and needs to those who care for them, and elicit attention and care. (© Ken Robert Buck, 1981)

whims of the environment. Through its cries and smiles the baby can significantly influence the behavior of its caretakers. While the mother's control of reinforcement contingencies is much greater than that of the infant, the baby's responses can also be said to shape the mother's behavior (Gewirtz and Boyd, 1977; Isabella, Belsky, and von Eye, 1989). While the mother has control over such reinforcements as food, attention, and relief of irritation, the infant can reinforce the mother and other caretakers through its responsiveness, the skills it acquires, and a pleasant versus an unhappy disposition. The amount of attention or even affection that parents give their infant will be influenced by the infant's reinforcing and aversive reactions. There is much evidence that the child-rearing practices of parents are to a great extent *determined by* the behavior of the child (Bell, 1968), as well as the more often discussed opposite sequence of child-rearing practices *determining* the behavior of the child.

During the first few months of development, the infant attends to the presence of people, observing them and perhaps smiling or becoming excited in their presence. But the infant does not yet discriminate between its mother or father or other people. There is no innate *attachment* by the infant to the mother, although this early period of social responding may be considered the first phase in the development of attachment to significant people in the infant's world (Bowlby, 1958, 1969). The formation of selective attachments to caregivers, or *bonding,* is usually manifested after three months of age. This bonding is considered to be of paramount importance for the infant's social development and, in the views of many personality theorists, is a prime determinant of the child's basic personality structure.

Characteristics of Attachment.   How do we know when a child is attached to someone, and exactly what does it mean to say that a child has an attachment? These questions have been the subject of considerable theoretical debate and investigation, and there are no simple answers. The most comprehensive and influential analysis of attachment has been provided by British psychiatrist John Bowlby. The essence of attachment, according to Bowlby, is the maintenance of proximity to the caregiver, usually the mother. This proximity can be in terms of physical contact (e.g., touching the mother) or psychological contact (e.g., seeing the mother and knowing that she is close by). In addition to maintain proximity, the baby performs a set of attachment behaviors, including babbling, smiling, looking at the caretaker, and following or clinging to him or her.

One main characteristic of attachment to a person, then, is an effort to approach or maintain proximity to that person. A second characteristic is distress and protest when the infant is separated from the individual to whom it is attached. The same person is able to soothe the child when it is upset. Finally, when the caretaker is present, the infant is able to explore novel surroundings without displaying anxiety. It is as if the special caretaker provides the infant with a base of security that enables it to leave the safe and familiar and to explore new, potentially threatening environments.

The child's early attachments, although formed in infancy, are predicted to be evident in later periods of development as well. Theorists believe that early attachments provide the basis upon which children develop their basic "working models" of relationships. How early attachments are later manifested will depend on the age, the particular culture, and the idiosyncratic avenues of expression of the child. Consider, for example, the following expression of a young boy's attachment to his father (Lewis, 1961, p. 65):

> Although I haven't been able to show it, I not only love my father, I idolize him. . . . My father was always very dry with us; he didn't talk much. . . . Only twice in my life did my father speak intimately to me. He asked me, "Son, what troubles you? What is the matter? Tell me your trouble." I felt the most important and happy person in the world to hear him call me "son" so affectionately.

The Universality of Attachment.   Attachment behaviors are characteristic not only of infants in every culture, but also of many nonhuman species, especially mammalians. The comparability between the attachment behaviors of primates and those of human infants has stimulated extensive primate investigations of the variables involved in the formation of attachments and the consequences of separation (Simonds, 1977; Suomi, 1977). The following description (Jensen and Tolman, 1962, pp. 132–33) of separation in rhesus monkeys conveys the flavor of attachment in a nonhuman primate species:

Separation of mother and infant monkeys is an extremely stressful event for both mother and infant as well as for the attendants and for all other monkeys within sight or earshot of the experience. The mother becomes ferocious towards attendants and extremely protective of her infant. The infant's screams can be heard over almost the entire building. The mother struggles and attacks the separators. The baby clings tightly to the mother and to any object which it can grasp to avoid being held or removed by the attendant. With the baby gone, the mother paces the cage almost constantly, charges the cage occasionally, bites at it, and makes continual attempts to escape. She also lets out occasional mooing-like sounds. The infant emits high pitched screams intermittently and almost continuously for the period of separation.

Similar behaviors have been observed in lambs and puppies (Cairns, 1977). The evidence of attachment behavior in nonhumans suggests that there are important biological factors influencing the human infant's attachment response. From an ethological standpoint, the mother might be considered the stimulus that releases the innate smiling response from the infant while the smile, in turn, releases biologically programmed approach and loving responses. Thus, there is a complex chaining of events. In a similar manner, the baby's cry releases approach and comforting responses from the mother. The attachment responses thus increase the likelihood of the newborn's receiving protection and sustenance, thereby increasing its chances of survival.

The foregoing discussion is not meant to imply, however, that learning does not affect attachment. Bowlby (1969) noted that the child has to *learn* to discriminate mother from other adults and stressed the importance of the quality and pattern of the child's interaction with the mother in determining the nature of the attachment bond between them. If the mother, for example, is depressed or for some other reason unresponsive to the infant's smile, then the attachment relationship will take an atypical course. Some theorists believe that the biological explanation and the notion of an affective bond is superfluous and have attempted to account for attachment behavior on the basis of Skinner's principles of mutual reinforcement and operant conditioning (Gewirtz and Boyd, 1977). However, as we examine variations in attachment, it will become clear that although operant conditioning principles are pertinent, they cannot readily account for many attachment phenomena.

Feeding and Attachment. From a theoretical perspective, the question of why and how the child becomes attached to the mother, and the mother to the child, has not been fully resolved. Early explanations by learning theorists (Miller and Dollard, 1941) emphasized the primary reinforcement provided by nursing and bottle feeding. This reinforcement then generalizes to the caretaker, so that the mere presence or voice of the caretaker could serve to reduce the child's tensions and elicit positive reactions. However, there is much more taking place in the interaction between child and caregiver than feeding. The infant is typically held and soothed and its attention and motor responses are directed toward the caregiver, usually the mother. Thus, the child receives a great deal of stimulation from the mother, in addition to being fed.

The well-known cloth-versus-wire-mother experiments carried out by Harry Harlow of the University of Wisconsin provide compelling evidence that feeding is not central to the development of attachment. Harlow (1958, 1971) separated infant monkeys from their mothers immediately after birth. The infants were then fed through a bottle connected to a dummy that functioned as a substitute, or surrogate, mother. These "mother" dummies were constructed of either wire mesh or wire mesh covered with terrycloth (see Fig. 12.2). If reduction of the infant's hunger drive is the primary basis for attachment, then the infant monkeys should have become attached to the mother surrogates associated with the giving of milk. But this was not the case. The animals fed by the wire mothers went to them only when they were hungry. But both wire-fed and terrycloth-fed infants preferred the terrycloth mothers and spent most of the day with them. When upset, both groups also were more readily comforted by the terrycloth mothers. Other research has indicated that the critical variable influencing monkey attachment is an opportunity to cling. Monkeys and chimpanzees have a strong tendency to cling, especially when upset, and the terrycloth surrogates were much better than the wire mother substitutes for this response. But, as will be documented later, even the monkeys fed by the cloth mothers manifested severe social problems, demonstrating that a real monkey mother is best.

Physiological studies also indicate that the lack of tactile stimulation, rather than food deprivation, is the critical factor mediating the adverse effects of separation from the mother (Shanberg and Kuhn, 1980). These studies demon-

Figure 12.2   The clinging response of Harlow's monkeys to a cloth "mother" and of a human infant to an adult. (left — Harry F. Harlow, University of Wisconsin Primate Laboratory; right — © George Goodwin/Monkmeyer)

 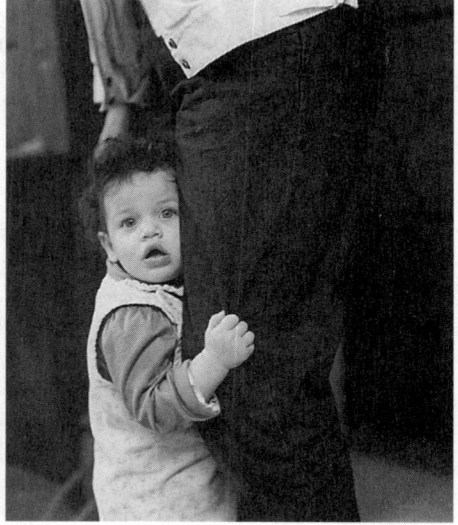

strate that tactile stimulation of rat pups can counteract the negative biochemical effects of maternal deprivation. Similarly, other studies have shown that tactile stimulation of premature human infants significantly increases their weight gain (White and LaBarba, 1976).

Variations in Attachment. An important challenge in the study of attachment is the development of procedures that will capture the attachment relationship of the child to its caretaker. Mary Ainsworth, who has had extensive experience in naturalistic observations of mother-child interactions among a group of East African Ganda living in the bush, noted differences in the attachment manifested by these Ganda infants as compared to American infants. She then developed a simple but ingenious set of procedures for assessing attachment that could be implemented in a laboratory context. Ainsworth and her colleagues (Ainsworth, Bell, and Stayton, 1971) employed the following standard series of laboratory episodes in their studies. A mother and an infant enter an unfamiliar room; the infant plays with the mother present; a stranger enters and the stranger and mother are both present for a while; the mother leaves and the infant is left with the stranger; the mother returns and the stranger leaves; the infant is left alone; the stranger returns; and finally, the mother also returns.

Observation of one-year-old infants' behavior during this sequence of events led Ainsworth to classify the babies into three groups: *securely attached, insecurely attached,* and *avoidant* (Ainsworth, et al., 1971). Infant crying on separation from the mother is *not* a critical factor in distinguishing the three groups. Rather, the significant factors are: (1) the ease with which the infant recovers from the distress of separation upon reunion with the mother; (2) how comforting contact with the mother is; and (3) the degree to which the mother serves as a secure base for the infant's explorations. The infants in these three groups seemed not only quantitatively, but also *qualitatively,* different in their attachment to their mothers (Sroufe and Waters, 1977*a*). Avoidant infants differ from others in that they are the only babies to avoid proximity with the mother in the reunion situation. But this does not mean that avoidant infants are indifferent to their mothers. Recordings of infants' heart rates in laboratory situations indicate relatively long-lasting heart rate acceleration in avoidant infants when the mother returns, suggesting emotional arousal rather than indifference (Sroufe and Waters, 1977*b*). In comparison, the heart rates of most attached infants recover to a normal level more rapidly.

Several studies have shown that the classification of infants into securely attached, insecurely attached, and avoidant categories is predictive of their subsequent behavior. In one study of the stability of attachment behavior, fifty infants were classified at both twelve and eighteen months on the basis of their responses in the laboratory (Waters, 1978). Forty-eight of the fifty infants were assigned to the same groups during both of these time periods. A followup on these infants at age two revealed that the securely attached group was more enthusiastic, persistent, cooperative, and effective than the insecurely attached children (Matas, Arend, and Sroufe, 1978). Findings from other longitudinal studies indicate substantial consistency between attachment patterns assessed at age six and the attachment behaviors developed in The Strange Situation at infancy (Main, Kaplan, and Cassidy, 1985). Indeed, studies of attachment patterns in adult love relationships indicate that these adult patterns are significantly related to reports of early attachment relationships (Hazan and Shrader, 1987, cf. Chapter 18). Inferences from such studies are of course limited because of the retrospective nature of the adult subjects' reports about their early attachment relationships.

Clinical evidence also suggests that the security of early attachment has a fundamental influence on subsequent manifestations of security and insecurity. There are data indicating that children who display insecure attachments at twelve and eighteen months of age behave in an overdependent manner when assessed three years later. In Table 12.1, the mean ratings by the childrens' pre-school teachers on a series of dependency scales are presented for the children who earlier had been classified as anxious or avoidant (Groups A and C) and the children classified as securely attached (Group B). The secure children are significantly higher only on the positive attention-getting scale, which reflects such behaviors as active greeting of teachers on arrival, positive exchanges with the teachers, and seeking contact when injured or ill. Whether these particular early patterns of attachment are linked to social interaction in later periods of life, reflecting what Erikson called the development of basic trust and mistrust (Chapter 4), remains to be established in future research.

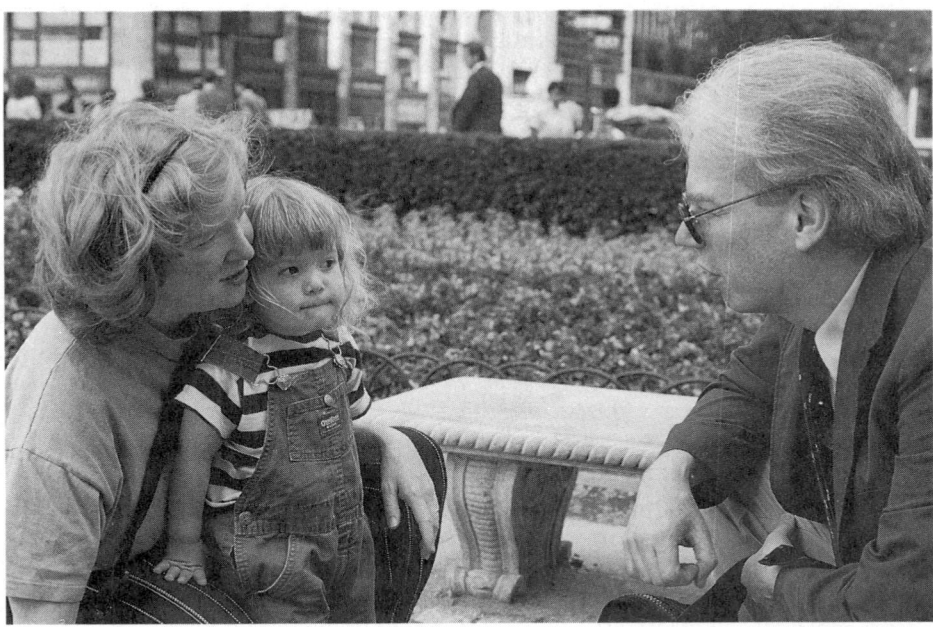

Children display attachment in the presence of strangers. (© Robert Brenner/PhotoEdit)

Table 12.1   Means for dependency items (7-point scales)

	A (Anxious)	B (Secure attachment)	C (Avoidant)
Help seeking in self-management	4.70	3.02	3.93
Help seeking (interpersonal)	4.41	3.30	4.00
Recognition seeking	4.30	4.23	4.10
Contact seeking	4.59	3.53	4.08
Seeking to be near	4.50	3.77	4.40
Positive attention seeking	3.48	5.02	3.98

Source: Adapted from Sroufe, Fox, and Pancake, 1983, p. 1621. Reprinted by permission.

The quality of attachment also appears to affect the child's cognitive development. The securely attached child, for instance, tends to be more developmentally advanced (Belsky, Garduque, and Hrncir, 1984). For example, children at around age two who had been classified as secure infants engage in more advanced symbolic play activity than children who had been classified as insecure or avoidant (Slade, 1987). Children who are rated as securely attached at age seven performed better as adolescents on a variety of cognitive tasks, such as deductive reasoning, compared to those rated as insecurely attached at age seven (Jacobsen, Edelstein, and Hofmann, 1994).

Researchers have found, too, that the quality of attachment is related to the behavior of the caregiver. Mothers of securely attached children were observed to respond more readily to their infants' crying than mothers of insecure and avoidant children (Ainsworth et al., 1978). Furthermore, securely attached infants do not cry as much as the others. This finding is difficult for learning theorists to explain, inasmuch as greater responsiveness to crying should reinforce and increase the frequency and duration of crying.

Studies of maternal responsiveness to their infant indicates that mothers of secure infants are sensitive to a variety of cues provided by their infant besides crying (Smith and Pederson, 1988). In addition, relationships have been demonstrated between behaviors of the mother toward a three-month-old infant, prior to the manifestation of the attachment relationship, and the infant's attachment behaviors when one year old (Lewis and Feisking, 1989). However, at the same time, behaviors of the child manifested at three months were more highly correlated than were maternal behaviors with the child's attachment behaviors at year one.

This latter finding relates to one of the theoretical controversies that has developed in attachment research—are the attachment behaviors manifested by the child a consequence of the caretaker's sensitivity, involvement in the child, and child-rearing behaviors or are they a reflection of temperament and related biologically-based attributes that the child brings to the attachment situation? While a number of investigators report little evidence of infant temperament correlates of the attachment behavior patterns displayed by the infant, there are also findings of significant relationships between infant temperament and infant attachment behaviors (Thompson, Connell, and Bridger, 1988). Several investigators have attempted to reconcile these conflicting findings regarding the role of temperament by separating the assessment of the infant's attachment classification from assessment of the infant's emotional and social behaviors in The Strange Situation. Their findings indicate that temperament affects the manner in which security and insecurity is expressed. For example, how much the infant cries when separated from the mother, rather than whether or not the infant develops a secure or insecure attachment is of interest. (Belsky and Rovine, 1987; Vaughn, et al., 1989).

In view of the transactional model of the interaction between the child and its environment that has been described earlier, it is very likely that the attachment relationship is a function of the interaction of both infant and caretaker characteristics. Some infants may present such difficult temperaments that the most sensitive and skilled caretakers are necessary in order to form a secure attachment. The temperament of most infants is probably such that reasonable parenting is sufficient for a secure attachment to develop. In the case of severely deficient parenting, exceptional infant stability may be required for a secure attachment to be formed. While one should take into account the child's temperament and other features of the personality in explaining the development of attachments, caretaker attributes and behaviors remain important.

Cultural Variations. Attachment is believed to be a universal phenomenon. While most attachment research has been carried out in the United States, there have been a substantial number of studies carried out in other countries. Table 12.2 presents a summary of the distribution of attachment patterns of infants, based on summing the results of different studies carried out in each of six countries. It may be noted that the number of infants studied in the United States is greater than the sum of all of the infants studied in other countries combined. The data indicate that the majority of infants in each of the countries listed are classified as "Secure." The predominant cultural difference that emerges is in the proportions of "Insecure" versus "Avoidant" infants. For the West European nations, a much higher proportion of infants display Insecure as compared to Avoidant patterns, while the reverse holds for Japan and Israel. The proportions for United States' infants fall in between, with more infants classified as Insecure than Avoidant, and with the proportional difference being much smaller than that for the West European nations.

Table 12.2   Distribution of Attachment Patterns

Country	Insecure	Secure	Avoidant
Federal Rep. of Germany	48	77	11
Great Britain	16	54	2
Netherlands	66	169	16
United States	260	797	173
Japan	5	65	26
Israel	8	76	34

(Adapted from Ijzendoorn and Kroonenberg, 1988, pp. 150–151.)

The implications of this difference for the development of children in these different cultural contexts have yet to be determined. In addition, it remains for future research to determine the specific features of the culture, and possibly the specific temperamental attributes of infants in that culture, that bring about these differences in attachment patterns.

Attachment as a Theoretical Construct. It is also the task of future research to clarify the theoretical properties of attachment and help resolve theoretical controversies over its usefulness. Some investigators maintain that there is little value in postulating an underlying bond called "attachment" that mediates behavior. Rather, what is significant, they suggest, is the behavioral interaction that takes place between infant and caretaker in a concrete situation and the principles that govern this interaction (Cairns, 1972; Weinraub, Brooks, and Lewis, 1977). They point to the weak correlations among different indicators of attachment as evidence that discrete behaviors, rather than a single, underlying dimension, are involved in attachment behavior. Furthermore, attachments are established to the father as well as to the mother and, along with other aspects of the infant's development, vary with the nature of the marital relationship or family system (Belsky, 1981).

Others, amplifying and extending Bowlby's theory, emphasize the affective nature of the attachment bond (Ainsworth et al., 1978; Sroufe and Waters, 1977a). They point to the evidence for stability of attachment-related behaviors and to the indications of goal-directed activity; that is, striving to be near the object of attachment when the organism's security is threatened. It is further proposed that it is useful to think of attachment as a flexible organization of behaviors, mediated by the affective attachment bond (Sroufe and Waters, 1977). How children display and maintain attachments will vary with the individual characteristics of the child, with situational factors, and with developmental level. Consequently, one must distinguish between the underlying attachment bond and the overt attachment behaviors and expect variations in the indicators of attachment.

From the perspective of those who see attachment as a key organizing dimension of behavior, attachment bonds not only protect the child and maintain its security, but also form an integral part of subsequent love relationships. "When people are attached to another, they want to be with their loved one. They may be content for a while to be apart in the pursuit of other interests and activities, but the attachment is not worthy of the name if they do not want to spend a substantial amount of time with their attachment figures — that is to say, in proximity and interaction with them" (Ainsworth et al., 1978, p. 14). Indeed, attachment is hypothesized to be a key element in the formation of stable, affectionate bonds with siblings and friends, as well as in marital relationships (Ainsworth, 1989).

MORAL DEVELOPMENT

In the previous section, we saw how the infant develops significant attachments to adult figures, usually its parents. Attachment theorists believe that a secure attachment to a parent provides a secure base for the child to develop in a prosocial manner. Further, the model of a good relationship with a parent provides a basis for having a fundamentally positive and trusting attitude towards others. We now consider in more detail how infants are socialized into being moral and prosocial adults.

How does the infant develop from a creature dominated by biological urges, seeking immediate satisfaction, to an individual with a sense of right and wrong? How does a child become a moral being? The major theoretical approaches to personality — psychoanalytic, cognitive, and social learning theory — offer very different explanations of the process of moral development. In part, these different theoretical explanations arise from their emphases on different aspects of morality. The psychoanalysts have been concerned with the emotional and motivational aspects of morality, particularly the acquisition of guilt and conscience. Cognitive theorists have focused on the development of understanding of moral conduct or rules, or changes in the child's perception of right and wrong. Social learning approaches have been more concerned with the child's moral behaviors and good or bad actions, as well as with mechanisms for the acquisition of these behaviors.

The Superego and Moral Development

The key element in the psychoanalytic theory of moral development is the superego. As noted earlier (see Chapter 3), the superego refers to an internalized set of prohibitions and standards acquired by the child in the resolution of the

Oedipal conflict through identification with the same-sex parent. There are a number of interesting implications of Freud's formulation that have led to considerable debate. These implications have to do with the role of identification in superego formation, sex differences, and the age at which superego formation takes place. Specifically, Freud's theory implies that:

1. Identification with a parent plays a major role in the development of the internalized moral standards that comprise the superego.

2. Defensive identification (identification out of fear) is more central in superego formation than is anaclitic identification (identification out of affection).

3. Boys develop a stronger, more integrated superego than girls do because the Oedipal conflict is more intense in boys than in girls and because boys fear their fathers more than girls fear their mothers.

4. Superego formation, or the internalization of moral standards, is characterized by rapid development around the age of four or five, during the phallic period.

Only the first of these implications is supported by empirical evidence, and even in that instance the support is slight. The other three derivations from psychoanalytic theory are contradicted by the available evidence.

Concerning defensive versus anaclitic identification, neither has been shown to be linked directly to moral behavior. However, in contrast to the psychoanalytic expectation, defensive identification, which is associated with a more punitive household in which fear of physical punishment prevails, tends to be related to weak moral development in the child. Children raised in affectionate, nurturant households, in comparison, tend to have greater internalization of moral standards (Hoffman, 1970). The latter children are influenced primarily by fear of loss of parental love rather than by fear of parental aggressive coercion.

With regard to the implication that boys display a more integrated set of moral standards and behaviors than girls do, the evidence suggests the contrary: girls tend to be more consistent in their moral attitudes and behavior than are boys (Maccoby and Jacklin, 1974). Finally, concerning the psychoanalytic belief that superego formation does not occur until the age of four or five, it is evident that children show indications of conscience well before those ages. Younger children use self-monitoring to resist forbidden acts and often "confess" when the resistance was insufficient to inhibit the act (Sears, Rau, and Alpert, 1965).

Given the available evidence, one can conclude that the classic Freudian explanation of the acquisition of conscience or superego is seriously inadequate and, in important respects, incorrect. Moreover, the concept of the superego as an unconscious, unrelenting internal censor that blocks and punishes the expression of id and egoistic impulses requires modification. Even Freud tempered this fire-and-brimstone image of the nature of conscience by introducing the concept of *ego ideal* to convey the positive aspects of conscience. The ego ideal refers to standards that guide behavior because they are believed to be worthy. Other analysts have suggested that the positive ideals and moral values reflected in the ego ideal arise out of the child's identification with the loving aspects of the parents (Schafer, 1960) and that the ego ideal is a part of the superego that is in harmony with healthy personality development. More generally, however, psychoanalysis offers an inconsistent and ambiguous picture of the neurotic versus healthy implications of guilt, conscience, and responsibility. There is the suggestion in psychoanalytic writings, as well as in the writings of some self-actualization and cognitive theorists, that rigidly held "ought" and "should" rules of behavior have no place in a truly healthy personality.

Stages of Moral Development: The Cognitive Approach

In addition to feeling guilty, confessing wrongdoings, telling the truth, and not cheating, conscience involves an understanding of moral issues, including what it means to be good or bad.

Kohlberg's Contribution.   One of the most influential cognitive models of how people think and reason about moral issues is that of Lawrence Kohlberg (1969b), who based his work on an earlier cognitive model of moral development developed by the Swiss developmental psychologist Jean Piaget (Cowan, 1978). Kohlberg postulated six stages of moral development, each characterized by qualitatively distinctive modes of thinking. In the course of development, which extends into adolescence, more advanced stages supercede earlier, more immature stages. The six developmental stages, described in the following paragraphs, are grouped into three moral levels: the preconventional, or premoral; the conventional; and the postconventional, or principled.

At level 1, rules and expectations are perceived as external to the self. The child does make a distinction between right and wrong, but defines right first on the basis of what authorities such as parents and the law demand (stage 1) and subsequently on the basis of *concrete reciprocal hedonism,* characterized by the phrase, "If I do something for you, then it's right that you do something for me" (stage 2). Level 2 begins at approximately age nine and, according to Kohlberg, is the level of most adolescents and adults. Morality here is based on good intentions and obtaining social approval (stage 3) and on a recognition of the importance of laws and rules as means of maintaining the social order (stage 4). The minority of individuals achieving level 3 do so in late adolescence, supposedly around the age of twenty. At this highest level, morality is perceived in terms of contractual obligations and laws based on democratic participation (stage 5). Ultimately, morality is a matter of individual conscience and universal ethics (stage 6). Stage 6 morality is characterized by reasoning from a set of principles that both are universally acceptable and stem from the individual's formulation of moral standards. These stages of moral development are summarized in Table 12.3.

Kohlberg derived these stages from an analysis of responses to a series of

Table 12.3   Kohlberg's Stages of Moral Development

Level I (Preconventional Morality)
Stage 1. Moral judgments based on conformity to authority figures.
Stage 2. Moral judgments based on concrete reciprocal hedonism.

Level II (Conventional Morality)
Stage 3. Moral judgments based on desire for social approval.
Stage 4. Moral judgments based on law and order orientation.

Level III (Postconventional Morality)
Stage 5. Moral judgments based on achieving the good of all.
Stage 6. Moral judgments based on the development of one's own set of ethical
    principles.

stories that posed moral dilemmas. Children of different ages and cultures had to
arrive at moral judgments based on the content of these stories. For example, in
one story a man's wife is desperately in need of a drug recently discovered by a
local druggist. The druggist, however, has priced the drug very high in order to
make a substantial profit. The husband cannot pay the price and breaks into the
man's store to steal the drug for his wife. The question posed is whether the
husband should have stolen the drug. Some children argue that the man is
justified in stealing the drugs. Others say he is not. However, what is important is
the *reasoning* the child uses to arrive at a conclusion.

Kohlberg and his associates have found that the stages observed in samples of
American children also characterize the developmental pattern of moral understanding in children from other cultures, including those of Mexico, Taiwan, and
Turkey. There is also some empirical support for the assumption that the sequence of stages is invariant, maintaining the same sequential order, and that
most of a child's moral judgments consistently reflect a particular stage (Kohlberg, 1976; Turiel, 1966). For example, in a longitudinal follow-up of a sample of
Turkish children and adolescents, developmental changes in stage sequence took
place in accordance with Kohlberg's hierarchy (Nisan and Kohlberg, 1982). This
sequence was manifested by both village and city subjects, although the rate of
development in the village sample was slower.

However, much more evidence is required to substantiate the notion of a
moral stage and the implication that stages follow a fixed developmental sequence. There is some question as to whether the superiority of the highest stage
is a function of social and cognitive development or is largely a matter of an
arbitrarily imposed cultural value. In addition, there is evidence that people use
different rules for different situations and that the stages are not sequential
(Kurtines and Greif, 1974). Finally, the stage approach is limited in that it focuses
on moral *thought* and does not consider the motivational and affective aspects of
moral *actions*.

Gender Differences. A major critique of Kohlberg's stage theory has been voiced by Gilligan (1982) in her book *In a Different Voice.* She contends that the stages of moral development postulated by Kohlberg are based more on how men reason than on how women reason about moral issues. Gilligan asserts that males and females differ fundamentally in their orientation to moral issues; that males approach issues of morality in terms of justice and rights, while females see moral issues more in interpersonal terms of degree of helping and caring for others. As a consequence, females are more likely to be found at stage 3 in Kohlberg's scheme in which concern for others is preeminent, and fewer females than males will be at the "higher" stages. While Gilligan's arguments seem cogent and she reports on research findings that appear supportive of her views, considerable controversy has arisen regarding the evidence for gender differences and its interpretation (Baumrind, 1986; Walker, 1984, 1989). Relatively few gender differences in cognitive moral stage attainment have been reported, and these become minimal when education is controlled (Walker, 1984). If instead of using the standardized Kohlberg hypothetical dilemma, participants are asked to recall and discuss a recent real-life moral dilemma from their own experience, then differences in moral orientation are found between adult females and males that are consistent with Gilligan's view (Walker, 1989). However, these differences reflect differences in the kinds of moral dilemmas that females and males are concerned with rather than gender differences in moral reasoning or level of cognitive moral stage attainment.

Kohlberg's cognitive stage theory of moral thought does not appear to be sex biased, although general questions regarding the validity of the stage approach, the role of cultural influences, and the relation between moral thought and moral action remain.

The Social Learning Approach

For social learning theorists, moral behavior is not fundamentally different from any other class of social behavior. It is acquired through punishment for deviation from social rules and through reinforcement for conforming to these standards. Through a process of conditioning, in which rule breaking is first followed by punishment, the child learns to experience discomfort and fear even when thinking about or anticipating breaking a rule. This discomfort inhibits the deviant action even in the absence of likely discovery and punishment. Furthermore, the child comes to feel guilty following a transgression and learns to reduce that guilt through self-punitive remarks and confession (Aronfreed, 1964). Finally, the child also learns to covertly verbalize statements that help control and inhibit socially disapproved actions. These statements, such as "Don't hit the baby" or "Don't take the candy" are often initially voiced aloud. But they eventually become silent and provide the basis for the voice of conscience.

There are a number of studies indicating that moral behaviors and judgments in children can be influenced through the observation and imitation of models

(Bandura and McDonald, 1963). From a social learning standpoint, each society's norms and models form the primary source of moral behavior, but social influence is insufficient to account for all aspects of morality. Social learning theorists point out that the child must develop the cognitive competence required to understand moral rules, as well as the behavioral competence, such as self-control, required to comply with those rules (Mischel and Mischel, 1976). It has been suggested by social learning theorists that variations in mental age and IQ might account for the developmental stage sequence postulated by Kohlberg. However, while IQ is undoubtedly one determinant of moral level, it has also been demonstrated that there are meaningful differences between children at different moral stages even with the influence of IQ eliminated (Kohlberg, 1958).

Social learning theorists also favor a specificity model of moral behavior, maintaining that behaviors such as stealing, cheating, and lying are differentially reinforced and depend on the situation. A classic pioneering study addressed to the question of the generality versus specificity of moral behavior was conducted many years ago by Hartshorne and May (1928). Their study bears on the broader issue of the trait/situation controversy (see Chapter 9), as well as on the more pointed question of the generality of moral behavior. Hartshorne and May obtained a variety of different measures, on a very large sample of children, of lying, cheating, and stealing in several different settings, such as home, school, and so on. The correlations between the different measures were unimpressive, and it was concluded that honesty is essentially situationally determined; that is, it is not meaningful to describe one child as honest and another as dishonest.

Reanalyses of these data (Burton, 1963; Epstein, 1979), using the more reliable of their measures or multiple measures, yielded greater evidence of consistency than was initially reported (see also Chapter 9). Yet some psychologists remain unimpressed by the results of the reanalyses and argue that the data from Hartshorne and May's study are still consistent with a social learning, specificity position. Whether one is more impressed by the fact that disparate moral behaviors are significantly related or by the relative weakness of the relationship is very much dependent on one's theoretical orientation and beliefs, a case of a cup that is half empty also being perceived as half full. Efforts to relate Kohlberg's all-encompassing stages of moral development to specific moral behaviors have yielded similarly small but significant and consistent correlations (Blasi, 1980).

In any case, many people are able to articulate the higher levels of Kohlberg's stages, but behave in a less moral fashion than do individuals at lower levels. Thus, "ripping off" was a not uncommon practice among sophisticated college students during the late 1960s and early 1970s. The gap between cognitive stages and moral behavior poses a problem for stage theory. On the other hand, it is difficult for learning theorists to account for individuals who maintain moral beliefs and actions that are contrary to the prevailing norm and that may even subject them to ridicule and physical retaliation. What is required in this important area of personality development is a better understanding of the social and individual factors that make possible the attainment of the highest stages of

"Here, have some of mine!" This photograph shows an example of prosocial behavior. (Frank Siteman/Stock, Boston)

moral judgment and the courage to behave in accordance with those moral beliefs.

PROSOCIAL BEHAVIORS

The discussion of moral behavior focused on prohibitions, conformity to social rules, and developmental changes in children's concepts of what constitutes good and evil. We now turn to positive social behaviors, such as generosity, caring, and helping, which frequently are socially prescribed and viewed as moral kinds of actions. The four-year-old preschooler sharing her lunch with a peer is engaging in prosocial behavior, as are the young opponents of an injured football player who pat him on the back as he is helped from the field. There are, of course, many other behaviors that are included in the prosocial category, such as dedication to improving the lot of the poor, efforts to overcome social injustice, and struggles to eliminate brutality. More generally, "pro-social behaviors refer to actions that are intended to aid or benefit another person or group of people without the actor's anticipation of external rewards" (Mussen and Eisenberg-Berg, 1977). One can never completely eliminate the possibility of "anticipation of external rewards"; even in the biblical parable of charity, the bread cast upon the waters ultimately benefits the giver. Nevertheless, the definition is a useful one. It helps orient research toward investigating the internal reward systems — the pride, the sense of obligation, the intrinsic satisfaction, and perhaps even the reduction of guilt — that may motivate or accompany prosocial behavior.

Evolution of Positive Social Behaviors

Whenever the question of what human beings have inherited from their animal ancestors arises, characteristics such as aggression, sex drive, and territorial competition are typically cited. Rarely does one think of such positive social behaviors as cooperation, generosity, and altruism as part of our animal heritage. Yet there is no doubt that many animal species display cooperative social patterns; even instances of self-sacrifice are not uncommon. However, whether the same biological factors that govern nonhuman prosocial behaviors are relevant to human prosocial behaviors is debatable.

The complex cooperative societies of social insects like the ant and the bee have been described in countless popular articles, and the interaction of genetic programming with environmental influences in these insects has been extensively studied. But cooperation and sharing are by no means restricted to social insects. Chimpanzees, for example, display unusual cooperation and coordination when in pursuit of prey (Teleki, 1973). Also, when the food supply is limited, chimpanzees will beg from one another and share food (Wilson, 1975). Positive social behaviors are common even among African elephants. "Young calves of both sexes are treated equally and each is permitted to suckle from any nursing mother in the group. Adolescent cows serve as 'aunts', restraining the calves from running about and nudging others awake from their naps" (Wilson, 1975, p. 494). When a young bull elephant was felled with an anesthetic dart, "the adult cows rushed to his aid and tried to raise him to his feet" (p. 494). The African wild dog provides a striking contrast between savage behavior displayed when attacking prey and gentle, nurturant behavior extended to others in its pack. When the pack have eaten their prey, they return to the den and regurgitate, making it possible for the young and other adults who remained behind to share in the bounty. The sick and the crippled, unable to participate in the hunt, are thus maintained by the pack. As the incident described in Highlight 12.1 on p. 344 illustrates, a similar kind of cooperative behavior can be observed in dolphins.

Many of these behaviors can be considered instances of altruism, since, in an effort to save members of their own species, these animals risk their own well-being. But perhaps the most striking examples of altruism are provided by the social insects. Honeybee workers that embed their barbed stings in an intruder threatening the hive will die as a result but, in the process, perhaps save the rest of the hive. Similarly, termite soldiers spray predators with a glandular secretion fatal to both themselves and their enemies. The colony's king and queen are thereby protected and remain able to preserve and expand the colony through breeding. The insects sacrificing themselves are relatives of and share common genes with the surviving insects. The altruistic organism is therefore contributing

■ **Highlight 12.1** ■■■■■■■■■■■■■■■■■■■■■■

Prosocial Behavior in Dolphins

A school of approximately 50 *Delphinus delphis* was sighted. As soon as the Zodiac (our boat) approached, they increased speed, dived and changed direction under water. The school reassembled behind the Zodiac. The yacht took over the chase and an animal was wounded by the harpoon. We saw quite clearly how other dolphins came immediately to the help of the wounded animal on the starboard side of the yacht. They supported the wounded dolphin with their flippers and bodies and carried it to the surface. It blew 2–3 times and then dived. The whole incident lasted about 30 seconds and was repeated twice when the animal appeared unable to surface alone. All the animals including the wounded dolphin then dived and swam quickly out of sight.

Source: Pilleri and Knuckey, 1969, from Wilson, 1975, p. 475.

to the survival of its own gene pool (see also Chapter 1). Sociobiologists argue that such acts of altruism are built into organisms because they perpetuate the gene pool.

Sociobiologists like Wilson have extended this argument to suggest that there is a genetic basis for altruism and other prosocial behaviors among humans. However, while one can draw a crude analogy between self-sacrifice in nonhumans and humans, it is pure speculation to propose that the same mechanisms are operative in both species. Human altruism takes many different forms and is affected by a great range of social influences. Rather, the importance of animal studies lies in their demonstration that prosocial behaviors are as natural to many animal species as are the more often cited examples of destructive, antisocial behaviors. Human tenderness, caring, attachment, and self-sacrifice are, then, just as "animalistic" as are human competitiveness, selfishness, and brutality.

Self-report questionnaire measures of altruism have been used to determine whether there are genetic influences on altruism as a personality trait. A study of degree of similarity between identical twins versus fraternal twins in altruism personality test scores indicated a much higher correlation between the identical than the fraternal twins (Rushton et al., 1986). These findings, based on twins reared in the same household, provide evidence of a genetic factor in altruism. However, demonstration of a genetic factor does not mean that there is an "altruism" gene. There may be genetic differences in temperament and in cognitive abilities that contribute to the development of altruistic attitudes and behavior. Much more research needs to be done about the nature of the genetic influence before one can conclude that altruistic tendencies are directly inherited (also see Chapter 1).

Cooperation

Describing behavior as "natural" does not necessarily mean that it is inborn; rather, it implies that the organism has the potential for developing this pattern of behavior and will do so under normal environmental circumstances. Infants are not cooperative, but preschool children display sharing, reciprocity, and other forms of cooperation in their play behavior. In an observational study of a twenty-minute interaction between children and parents on a cooperative game, one of eight one-year-olds and seven of eight two-year-olds participated in at least one cooperative interchange (Hay, 1979). By two years of age, children verbalize sympathy to individuals in distress and make efforts to assist them (Zahn-Waxler and Radke-Yarrow, 1982). A poignant description of young children's shared concerns and cooperativeness is provided by Anna Freud, who helped bring orphaned German-Jewish preschool-age children to hostels in England during World War II (Freud and Daun, 1951).

> "On walks they were concerned for each other's safety in traffic, looked after children who lagged behind, helped each other over ditches. . . . In the nursery they picked up each other's toys. . . . Behavior of this kind was the rule, not the exception." (p. 134)

These positive social behaviors are related to the child's general mental development (Emmerich, Cocking, and Sigel, 1979) and personal adjustment (Block and Block, 1980). An extensive longitudinal study of nursery school children indicated that children rated by their teachers as high in such characteristics as helpfulness and cooperativeness obtained low scores on measures of impulsiveness and high scores on an index of their capacity to recover to a state of normalcy after a stressful experience (Block and Block, 1980). Moreover, four-year-old children described as dependable, calm, and cooperative tended to behave generously at age five on a measure of sharing and distributing rewards. However, four-year-old children described as overreactive and not competent in handling stress tended to be low in generosity at age five.

Cross-Cultural Cooperative Behaviors. Cooperative behaviors are strongly influenced by the larger culture as well as by individual traits of the child. Whiting and Whiting (1975) gathered detailed, naturalistic, observational data of children between the ages of three and eleven in six different cultures: Kenya, Mexico, the Philippines, Okinawa, India, and a New England community. The majority of the children observed in Kenya, Mexico, and the Philippines were above average on such behaviors as "offers help" and "offers support." The children in the other three cultures scored low on this constellation of prosocial responses. Children from Okinawa, India, and the New England community were more self-seeking and dominance oriented in their social interactions.

Laboratory studies of cooperation and competition by Madsen and his colleagues (Kagan and Madsen, 1971; Madsen and Shapira, 1970) have helped sharpen our understanding of the nature of some of these cultural differences. In several experimental studies of Mexican and American children, in which a child

Examples of children cooperating on a task can be found in many different cultures around the world. (© Tony Arruza/The Image Works)

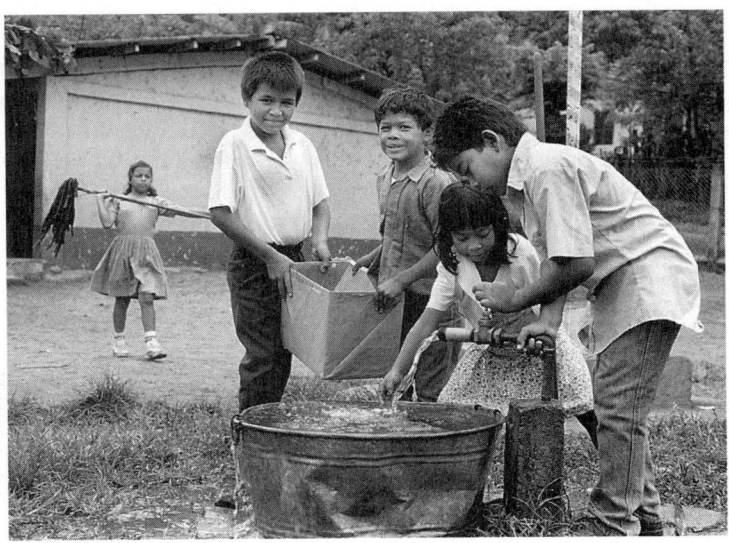

must choose either to cooperate or to compete with a peer, Mexican children were found to be much more cooperative than Americans. In general, the closer the culture of the Mexican child to the prevailing culture of United States children, the less cooperation was manifested by the Mexican child (Knight and Kagan, 1977). These laboratory findings therefore are consistent with the cultural differences reported by the Whitings, using naturalistic observations, and illustrate how both laboratory and field research methodologies can mutually contribute to understanding. However, it is still unclear whether the greater cooperativeness of the Mexican children was due to the fact that they were less competitive or was an indication of a stronger tendency to be cooperative. In one study bearing on this issue, children were given a task in which they could prevent their partner from receiving a toy. This was done twice as often by American as by Mexican children. In another investigation it was revealed that, in an effort to avoid conflict, Mexican children would give their toys up to their partner when only one could receive a toy, while this was not the case with the American children. Hence, the Mexican and the American children apparently differed in competitiveness. But why these Mexican and American children differed in their behavior — whether the critical factors were cultural norms, family structure, or rural-urban background — remains an unresolved question.

Antecedents of Cooperation.   As already suggested, cooperation and other prosocial behaviors are related to the child's cognitive and social-emotional competence. In addition, cooperative behavior is affected by situational factors, particularly the presence of competitive goals. A dramatic demonstration of the role of situational context in determining cooperative versus competitive behavior is provided by a classic social psychological field experiment conducted at a camp (Sherif et al., 1961). After the male campers arrived, they were assigned to one of two groups, either the Bull Dogs or the Red Devils. A series of cooperative activities was introduced *within* each group to promote intragroup solidarity. In addition, competitive games and contests were initiated *between* the two groups. Strong hostility between the Bull Dogs and the Red Devils began to accompany competition.

Several methods for reducing hostility and competition and fostering cooperativeness were then introduced. One of the most effective involved taking both groups on an overnight camping trip and having an old food truck break down. Both groups then worked together to pull the truck, using a heavy rope that had previously been used for tug-of-war contests between the groups. When this truck later appeared with the food, the two groups spontaneously engaged in cooperative behavior by preparing meals together.

Members of a culture may also perceive themselves as either Bull Dogs or Red Devils in competition with each other, or they may perceive themselves as part of a larger cultural group cooperating to achieve mutual goals. How different cultures instill a self-centered, competitive orientation versus a socially oriented, cooperative orientation has not been precisely determined. However, some characteristics of society have been described (Mussen and Eisenberg-Berg, 1977) that could enhance cooperation, social responsibility, and other prosocial behaviors:

1. Stress by parents, peers, and other agents of socialization on consideration for others, sharing, and group orientation.

2. A simple social organization like that found in traditional, rural settings.

3. Members of extended family living together.

4. Early assignment of tasks and responsibilities to children.

Generosity and Caring

People who are cooperative also tend to be more generous in their willingness to come to the aid of others in distress. In addition, many of the variables that influence cooperation, such as personal adjustment, cognitive level, imitation, and cultural background, also influence generosity and caring behavior. However, generosity toward others and responsiveness to distress are sufficiently different from cooperation to warrant separate discussion.

A common experimental procedure in the study of generosity is to have children win a prize or earn some reward, such as crayons, pennies, or candy. Then the children are asked to make a donation from their earnings to help needy children. The amount that each child donates serves as a measure of generosity. This procedure has the advantage of providing an objective, quantitative measure that can be readily used in experimental settings, but it also has the disadvantage of a lack of naturalism, for children are not usually called on to make donations to charity. Their generosity is more typically expressed in interactions with playmates and siblings. Nonetheless, this methodology has yielded some interesting findings. For example, relatively brief exposure to an adult model who donates generously has been shown to have a surprisingly strong positive effect on children's generosity. This increased generosity has been reported even months after the observation of the model (Midlarsky and Bryan, 1972; Rushton, 1976). It therefore seems reasonable that children with a generous parent or parents, who identify with that parent, will be high in generosity. In support of this, it has been found that when parents place a high value on prosocial behaviors, their children are more generous and caring (Feshbach, 1975; Hoffman, 1975). A very different and dramatic source of data reflecting parental influence on prosocial behavior is provided by a study of Christians who rescued Jews from the Nazis (London, 1970; Oliner and Oliner, 1988). In their interviews, the rescuers conveyed a strong identification with moral, principled parents.

A common method used by teachers, ministers, and others to encourage generosity is exhortation and preaching. How effective is this approach with children? Mild exhortations, simply stating what the child ought to do, are generally ineffective. On the other hand, strong, forceful preaching, especially when reasons for the request and the positive consequences of a donation are made explicit, can have some positive effects on children's generosity. In one pertinent investigation (Eisenberg-Berg and Geisheker, 1979), third- and fourth-grade children observed a model donating some money to a UNICEF collection bank. The collection bank was placed next to a poster showing poor children. The model made either an *empathic* appeal including reasons ("They would be so happy and excited if they could buy food and toys.") or a *normative* appeal ("Sharing is the right thing to do."). The data revealed that children hearing the empathic appeal donated more money. In addition, fourth graders donated more than third graders did, which is consistent with the general finding that generosity increases with age. But the effects of preaching are weak when compared to the behavior of a model. In one investigation (Bryan and Walbek, 1970), third- and fourth-grade girls were exposed to either a model who preached charity but acted in a stingy manner or a model who preached stinginess but behaved generously. The children followed the model's behavior rather than the preaching!

Empathy

One can be generous, supportive, and cooperative because these responses are encouraged and reinforced by the culture. But one can also engage in these same prosocial behaviors because of an understanding of other people's needs and feelings and because one shares in those feelings. The term *empathy* has been used to describe the process of social understanding and common emotional responses. In some theoretical treatments of empathy, the cognitive or social-comprehension aspect of empathy is stressed, while in other treatments the emotional aspect receives greater emphasis. But it appears that empathic responses involve the ability (1) to discriminate and label feelings in others; (2) to assume the perspective and role of another person; and (3) to experience and respond with feeling (N. Feshbach, 1978).

Altruistic Persons

The recent movie, *Schindler's List,* presented a portrait of a man who becomes altruistic and bankrupts his business to save Jews from extermination in Nazi Germany.

A unique study of prosocial, altruistic individuals entailed a comparison of other individuals in Nazi-controlled countries during World War II who rescued Jews with individuals from these same countries who remained bystanders (Oliner and Oliner, 1988). These acts of rescue took various forms — hiding Jewish children and adults, transporting them to a safer place, falsification of records, deceiving friends as well as authorities, but all constituted truly altruistic acts in that they entailed risk of imprisonment and a very real risk of being condemned to death. Following the destruction of the entire Jewish community in his town, the senior author, then a 12-year-old boy, was able to escape and obtain refuge in the home of a Polish peasant woman.

The difficult task of identifying rescuers had already been made by an Israeli commission using the following criteria: (1) the rescuer had to be motivated by humanitarian considerations only; (2) risked his or her own life; (3) received no remuneration of any kind. Some 6,000 such rescuers have been formally identified, although the actual number is considerably larger. A sample of several hundred rescuers from eight different countries and a smaller group of bystanders were interviewed.

The focus of the study was to determine whether one could identify an "altruistic personality," although recognizing that opportunity and other situational factors were also relevant. On the one standard personality scale that was administered, the Internal/External locus of control scale (see Chapters 5 and 17), the rescuers obtained significantly higher "internal" scores than the bystanders, reflecting a stronger sense in the rescuers that one's own efforts affect the rewards one receives. Also, in their self-descriptions, rescuers perceived themselves as being more honest and helpful than did bystanders. Questions regarding family influences were particularly revealing. Rescuers were three times as likely as bystanders to report that their parents taught them to care for other people while a significantly higher proportion of bystanders indicated that their parents placed importance on self-oriented values such as economic achievement. Differences in degree of attachment to the family and others were particularly striking. Seventy-eight percent of the rescuers in comparison to 52 percent of the bystanders report being very close to their family, while 76 percent of rescuers in contrast to only 44 percent of the bystanders indicate a close relationship with an influential person other than their parents.

Continued

■ **Highlight 12.2** ■

> These findings reflect a much stronger association between emotional relationships and altruistic behavior than between stages of cognitive moral development and altruistic behavior. Being able to conceptualize moral issues at Kohlberg's higher stages may contribute to moral behavior but is insufficient. More important appears to be the degree to which one is concerned about other people, the kind of moral orientation that Gilligan has emphasized.

Evidence of the emotional component of empathy, particularly the response to distress, can be discerned rather early in the child's development (Hoffman, 1981; Sagi and Hoffman, 1976). Although before twelve months general agitation is the principal response to another infant's cries, by twenty-four months one can observe more differential and more frequent empathic-like responses, such as patting and bringing objects to the distressed child (Zahn-Waxler and Radke-Yarrow, 1982). To study empathy in older children, a test has been developed that involves presenting the children with a series of slides depicting happiness, sadness, fear, or anger (N. Feshbach, 1978). After each sequence, the child was asked how he or she felt. The number of times the child's reported affect matched the depicted emotion was the measure of empathy. Children scoring high on this measure of empathy were rated by their teachers as high in cooperation, and children scoring low in this measure were rated as high in competitiveness (Barnett, Matthews, and Howard, 1979; Marcus, Telleen, and Poke, 1979). Empathic children tend to be low in aggressiveness (N. Feshbach, 1978; Feshbach and Feshbach, 1969). However, the relationship between empathy and prosocial behaviors is variable and appears to depend on a number of factors (Radke-Yarrow, Zahn-Waxler, and Chapman, 1983). With older children and using other measures of empathy, fairly consistent positive relationships have been found between empathy and prosocial behaviors and inverse relationships with aggressiveness (Eisenberg and Miller, 1987; Miller and Eisenberg, 1988). Empathy, in addition, has been shown to be associated with higher levels of moral reasoning (Eisenberg et al., 1987), consistent with the view that empathy in older children and adults has an important cognitive component as well as an emotional component (N. Feshbach, 1978).

Situational factors also influence empathic responses. For example, higher empathy scores appear to be a function of the degree of similarity between the person depicted in the slide sequence and the child; boys respond with more empathy to slide sequences of boys, girls to girls. Even black children respond more to pictures of blacks, and white children to pictures of whites (Feshbach and Roe, 1968; Klein, 1970). Thus, it might be expected that children will be less cooperative and caring when interacting with other children of a different sex or race.

There have been a number of attempts at empathy training which demonstrate that this approach holds considerable promise for the development of prosocial behavior (Feshbach, Feshbach, Fauvre, and Ballard-Campbell, 1983; Pitkänen-Pulkkinen, 1979; Staub, 1971). For example, Staub (1971) had children participate in training sessions in which they played the role of helper to an individual in need of aid. Girls with role-taking experience subsequently responded more frequently to cries of distress on a recording in an adjacent room than did girls without such experience, while boys with experimental training displayed more subsequent sharing than did boys with no role-playing experience.

SOCIALIZATION AND THE FAMILY

It has been indicated that children do not automatically behave in a moral, cooperative, and generous manner. These characteristics have to be acquired and reinforced through a process of socialization. There are a number of socializing agents in society, such as school, church, peers, and the mass media. We turn now to an examination of probably the most powerful socializing agent: the family. Families in which children are reared are very complex social systems, varying in size, stability, economic status, stress, misfortune, the personalities of and relationships between parents, openness of communication, and the practices used to train children. Since we cannot do justice to this complexity here, we will focus on one major source of family influence: child-rearing procedures.

It is useful to distinguish two related categories of child-rearing or socialization practices. The first encompasses broad characteristics or overall patterns of child-rearing activities, such as degree of warmth, control, or punitiveness. The second refers to the specific practices used to train certain behaviors; for example, the methods used to wean or toilet train the child, control aggression, inhibit sexuality, and so on. The broader patterns are obviously reflected in the more specific training practices, but to varying degrees and with varying relevance to the behavior being trained.

Child-Rearing Patterns

Society assigns parents the critical role of child care and child training. It is a parent's responsibility to ensure that the child is adequately fed, clothed, and sheltered. A parent is also responsible for the child's health and safety and may not neglect the child by leaving it unattended, isolated in a locked room, or subjected to comparably severe experiences. If a parent fails to meet these responsibilities, then society may remove a child from the parent's care. In addition, the culture expects much more from a parent than mere adherence to these basic responsibilities. A parent is expected to provide emotional security, guidance, and instruction, as well as to train the child to control bodily functions, act independently, and abide by the standards and values of the culture. While these responsibilities are enormous and although many parents are quite unprepared for them, they are assumed by parents when they decide to have a child.

There are many differences between parents' approaches to the task of child rearing. Some are warm and affectionate, others are cold and aloof; some are strict, others are permissive; some believe that the child should participate in decisions, others favor a more authoritarian style; some are anxious, others are assured; many are gentle, a few are cruel. Parents bring to their child-rearing role completely different personalities, values, and expectations. A basic theoretical and empirical question for the psychologist concerns the influence of all these factors on the personality development of the child.

Our review of attachment has indicated that if a child does not experience the warmth and security of attachment, there can be negative effects on development and adjustment. But there are significant variations within the less extreme, more normal range of child-rearing practices that also warrant attention. In assessing these child-rearing practices by interviewing parents or directly observing parent-child interactions, it has been found that many aspects of child rearing are interrelated and tend to cluster together. Thus, it is possible to describe the differences in child-rearing practices between families with reference to just a few basic characteristics. One such characteristic is degree of permissiveness versus strictness; another is degree of warmth and nurturance versus coldness and hostility (Becker, 1964). With just these two dimensions, a given child-rearing pattern could be described as permissive and warm, strict and warm, permissive and cold, or strict and cold.

Is it better for the child's development if parents are strict in their demands and discipline, or will the child have better psychological adjustment if parents are more permissive and less authoritarian in their behavior? Research has not provided a consistent or simple answer to such questions. It is known that the effects of both permissiveness and strictness are negative if the family environment tends to be cold and hostile. A hostile and permissive environment is likely to produce an aggressive and delinquent child, while a hostile-suppressive or restrictive family environment fosters children who are anxious and inhibited. In warm and nurturant family environments, the effects of permissiveness versus strictness are less clear. Several early studies (e.g., Baldwin, 1949; Watson, 1957) revealed that children raised in warm and reasonably permissive, democratic families that allowed the child freedom of choice tended to be friendly, assertive, and creative, whereas children raised in warm but strict and controlling homes tended to be conforming, low in curiosity, and well behaved.

Authoritative Parenting. However, the results of more recent work by Baumrind (1971, 1972, 1978) and by other investigators (Dornbusch, et al., 1987; Steinberg, Elmen and Mounts, 1989) suggest that the exercise of strong parental controls may have more positive developmental consequences than a permissive approach. Baumrind divided a sample of nursery school children into three personality groups on the basis of observations of their behavior. Children in one group were described as competent, self-reliant, content, inquiring, and assertive. A second group of children was described as moderately competent and mature, but also somewhat fearful, disoriented, and withdrawn. Finally, the least mature children formed a third group. They were highly dependent, fearful of novel situations, and displayed little self-control. Baumrind then assessed the child-rearing practices of the parents through interviews, home visits, and controlled laboratory observations. She found striking differences in the child-rearing procedures used by the parents in the three groups of children. Child-rearing practices among the mature, competent children were characterized by high levels of control and maturity demands (parental pressures to behave at intellectual and social levels congruent with the children's capacities). But control and demands were accompanied by a high degree of communication clarity; explanations and reasons were used to influence the children's behavior and feelings. The communication dimension most differentiated the parents of this mature group of children from the parents of children in the two other groups. The parents of the highly mature children were also the most nurturant, displaying warmth and involvement with their children. Baumrind's description of the parents of well-adjusted children is partially inconsistent with earlier data on the effects of permissiveness. Consistent with prior evidence, the "better" parents used reason and communicated openly with their children, but were higher in control than the permissive parents described in earlier studies. These data suggest that control is not necessarily associated with arbitrary or highly punitive discipline; one can be *authoritative* without being authoritarian.

It has become clear that the two-dimensional analysis of child-rearing attitudes and practice (degree of permissiveness-strictness and degree of warmth-hostility) is a useful initial tool for the analysis of parental behavior, but more refined analyses are now required. For example, the degree to which parents are intrusive and controlling, thereby encouraging dependency, is an important child-rearing variable (Parker, Tupling, and Brown, 1979). The responsiveness of the parent to the child, particularly in providing reinforcements that are linked to the child's behavior (contingent reinforcement), is another important factor that is believed to contribute to the child's development of controls over the environment and over himself or herself (Cairns, 1979; Patterson, 1982). A related dimension is the degree of parental involvement in the child, the extent to which the parents are child-centered versus parent-centered. The following items that contribute to a child-centered guidance score may help amplify the meaning of this concept:

- Parent is interested in events at child's school.
- Parent knows child's whereabouts, activities, and associates when child is away from home.
- Parent considers child's opinion.

At fourteen, children of child-oriented parents were, on the average, responsible, achievement-oriented, and socially competent, whereas children of parent-centered parents tended to lack concentration and to be impulsive, truant from school, and given to aggressive outbursts (Pitkänen-Pulkkinen, 1982). Six years later, similar differences in adjustment between children of child-centered versus parent-centered parents were observed.

These and related findings suggest an alternative classification of parenting patterns. Table 12.4 describes the patterns resulting from the different combinations of the two dimensions of accepting-rejecting and demanding-undemanding. In this context, the child-rearing pattern that is the most conducive to the child's development is the combination of demanding and accepting. Additional evidence for the adaptive effects of a parental *authoritative* approach to child rearing is provided in studies of adolescent school performance. An extensive survey of a large and socioeconomically and ethnically diverse group of adolescents reflected a consistent positive relationship between authoritative parenting and school success in adolescents whereas authoritarian and permissive parenting were negatively related to the offspring's school success (Dornbusch, et al., 1987). A longitudinal approach to adolescent school performance confirmed this finding and, in addition, strongly suggested that the mediating factor between authoritative parenting and school success was psychosocial maturity; that is, authoritative parenting fostered greater psychosocial maturity (as assessed by a Psychosocial Maturity Inventory) and the latter, in turn, contributed to the adolescent's success in school.

Despite these findings, one must be cautious in directly extending them to other cultures. The same parental behavior may be interpreted differently, and as a consequence, have different effects in a different culture. Thus, cross-cultural studies have indicated that in cultures where strict parental discipline is the norm, the discipline is perceived by children as an expression of parental concern rather than arbitrariness or rejection. The same behavior in more child autonomy and communication-oriented cultures is perceived as unfair and rejecting (Kagitcibasi and Berry, 1989, Rohner, 1986).

Table 12.4   A two-dimensional classification of parenting patterns.

	Accepting, responsive, child-centered	Rejecting, unresponsive, parent-centered
Demanding, controlling	Authoritative, reciprocal, high in bidirectional communication	Authoritarian, power-assertive
Undemanding, low in control attempts	Indulgent	Neglecting, ignoring, indifferent, uninvolved

Source: From Maccoby & Martin, 1983, p. 39. Reprinted by permission.

Summary

1. The *transactional model* of development views the interaction between nature and nurture, or the organism and its environment, as a reciprocal and continuous process.

2. Psychoanalytic theory offers a stage or discontinuity conception of development, while learning theories new development as a continuous process of change.

3. While many developmental psychologists believe that early childhood experiences are critical for the child's subsequent cognitive, emotional, and social development, there is still considerable debate over the usefulness of the concept of *critical periods.*

4. The evidence of *attachment* behavior in nonhumans suggests that there are important biological factors influencing attachment in human infants. From a biological standpoint, the infant's attachment to a caregiver increases the likelihood of receiving nourishment and protection and therefore increases the infant's chances of survival.

5. Harlow's studies indicate that the reduction of an infant's hunger through the caretaker's provision of food is not a critical factor in the development of attachment in monkeys. Comforting physical contact, particularly the opportunity to cling, appears to be the major contributing element.

6. Research indicates that there are significant differences among infants in the quality of their attachment behavior and that the classification of infants into *securely attached, insecurely attached,* and *avoidant* categories is predictive of subsequent attachment behavior and adjustment.

7. Cross-cultural studies based on Kohlberg's moral-dilemmas test reflect a developmental pattern that is consistent with Kohlberg's postulated six stages of moral development.

8. Reward and punishment, exposure to models, and verbalization of moral rules and prohibitions are processes that social learning theorists suggest are relevant to moral behavior.

9. The Hartshorne and May studies of the degree of consistency among different measures of honesty are frequently cited as evidence that honesty is situationally determined rather than a general trait reflected in many kinds of situations. However, reanalyses of these data have provided more evidence of consistency or generality than was initially reported.

10. Sociobiologists, citing evidence of altruistic behavior among nonhuman species, have suggested that there is a genetic basis for human altruism. They argue that acts of altruism have evolved because, despite the individual sacrifices involved, the survival of one genetic pool is facilitated.

11. Cooperative behavior in children varies significantly with cultural background and situational factors.

12. Children's generosity is markedly enhanced by exposure to models displaying generosity. Advocacy of generosity by the model is less effective than an actual display of generous behavior.

13. Empathy is facilitated by situational factors such as similarity between people. Empathy also has some of the characteristics of a personality trait, in that children high in empathy tend to be more cooperative and less competitive than children low in empathy.

14. The effects of parental control depend on the degree of parental acceptance and the clarity of parental communication to the child.

15. Authoritative parenting, consisting of a combination of parental acceptance and understanding of the child and of guidance, communication, and appropriate controls, fosters psychosocial maturity and effective school performance in the child, while authoritarian and permissive parenting tend to have negative developmental effects.

Thought Questions

1. There are some philosophies, mostly Eastern, that argue that we must unlearn attachments and that attachments limit our freedom of choice. How do you feel about this position?

2. Why aren't moral beliefs and moral understanding more closely related to actual moral behaviors?

3. Is teaching children to be cooperative and generous likely to handicap them if the culture at large is highly competitive and self-oriented?

4. Is there a "best way" to raise children, a set of socialization practices that all parents should use? What variations from these child-rearing practices would you allow?

13 | Development Through the Life Span

This chapter begins with a consideration of the issue of the degree to which personality stays the same or changes over time. It then extends the discussion of developmental changes germane to personality into the adolescent period, adulthood, and old age. Adolescence is a period marked by substantial changes in the self (cf. Chapter 10). Issues of self-definition and self-integration also emerge in adulthood and old age. Attention is directed to the particular problems and issues that confront most people during maturity and old age and to how resolving these problems and issues can contribute to personality change and growth. The chapter concludes with a discussion of psychobiography, which is an effort to analyze the development of particular individuals over time.

PERSONALITY CONTINUITY AND CHANGE

In the previous chapter we considered the issue of whether personality developed in a continuous or in a stage-like fashion. The term *continuity* has another meaning besides that of gradual change. It also refers to the constancy, or stability, of behavior over time. Are traits displayed by children during the early years predictive of similar behaviors during later periods of development? Is a fearful and timid child likely to develop into an anxious adult? Similarly, are aggressive children likely to remain aggressive adolescents and adults? Are other traits such as intelligence and dependency relatively enduring over the life span?

The answers to these questions, like those for most psychological questions, depend on a number of factors. First, answers depend on *what* aspects of personality are measured and how. For instance, McCrae and Costa (1990) define personality as the individual's underlying set of personality traits. Using measures of traits, they argue that personality stabilizes in early adulthood and then does not change very much thereafter. On the other hand, Helson (1993) defines personality as "the relatively enduring organization of motivations and resources" (p. 97) and uses different measures than do McCrae and Costa. She finds evidence of change in certain aspects of personality during the adult years. For instance, women show drops in "succorance" (the degree to which they are motivated to help others) from the time they are new parents to the time when their children have grown up.

Second, answers depend on *when* measures of personality are made. Block (1993), for instance, found significant correlations between childhood and adulthood for his measures of ego-resiliency and ego-control in males, but not in females. *Ego-resiliency* refers to the degree of flexibility in coping. *Ego-control* refers to the degree of impulse control exhibited by individuals. For females, there was consistency through the childhood years, but that consistency did not extend into adolescence. From adolescence on, there was again consistency, but there was no relation between consistency in the two time periods of childhood and adolescence/adulthood. These findings also suggest that gender can make a difference in whether or not there is continuity.

Third, answers depend on what is meant by stability and change. For instance, while Block (1993) found significant correlations between measures of male ego-resiliency in early childhood and in adulthood, suggesting continuity, there was nonetheless change. Individuals tended to maintain their relative rankings with respect to one another in the degree of ego-resiliency. However, all individuals showed increases in this capacity from childhood to adulthood.

Furthermore, psychologists distinguish between *absolute stability* and *coherence* (Caspi and Bem, 1990). If a person throws temper tantrums both as a child and as an adult, that is an illustration of *absolute stability*—the behavior in childhood is closely related to or similar to the behavior in adulthood. *Coherence* refers to the idea that the adult will exhibit behaviors that are *conceptually* similar to those in childhood but different in form, thus suggesting that there is some degree of change in the manifestation of an underlying trait. For instance, a child who throws temper tantrums may grow up to be an irritable, uncooperative adult, but the adult does not throw temper tantrums. As an example of coherence, Caspi, Bem, and Elder (1989) found that men who were rated as acting dependent in childhood tended to be more nurturant and more stable marital partners as adults. How is nurturance and marital stability linked to dependency? Once could argue that dependent individuals are invested in maintaining relationships and develop more mature ways of doing this with age. In general, psychologists believe it is more likely that coherence, and not absolute stability, between childhood and adulthood characterizes the development of personality. Coherence is a concept that encompasses both continuity and change.

Finally, whether personality changes or is stable from childhood to adulthood may vary among individuals (Ozer and Gjerde, 1989). For instance, Sampson and Laub (1990) studied 500 delinquent children and compared them to 500 controls. As adults, the former delinquents were more likely to have had unstable employment histories, to have been arrested, and to drink excessively. However, there was considerable heterogenity among the subjects studied. That is, while many exhibited consistency, many were found to have undergone considerable positive change, becoming reliable adults. Similarly, women who worked were found to exhibit increases in independence between the ages of twenty-one and forty-three, while women who were homemakers did not (Helson and Stewart, 1994).

Other factors that influence continuity include the time intervals at which change is measured and what statistical procedures are used (Weinberger, 1994).

The sheer numbers of factors that can influence the stability of a behavior pattern over time make it difficult to interpret the relationship between the childhood manifestation of a trait and later displays of that trait. It is known that certain traits, such as intelligence and aggression, are stable over time; that is, a child who is aggressive at age five also tends to be aggressive at age ten and age sixteen (see also Chapters 9 and 18). This finding of continuity in aggression is particularly true for boys. Similarly, children having high IQs at the age of five tend to score high on IQ tests during the rest of their lives, as well. This continuity can be accounted for by genetic factors. Psychoanalytic theory also argues that the early formation of personality accounts for similar manifestations of personality in later life. According to Freud, basic personality is formed in the first five or six years of life. Subsequent experiences are of secondary importance compared to the overwhelming influence of those early experiences. One might also assume a less extreme position, acknowledging the importance of experiences later in life, while maintaining that early influences are much more powerful than later ones.

A contrasting position, and one held by many social learning theorists, asserts that behavior is continuously shaped by the reinforcements in our environment, by the models to whom we are exposed, and by the cognitive feedback they provide. From this perspective, personality is largely environmentally determined (see Chapter 5) and therefore subject to major changes throughout life. Hence, whereas psychoanalytically or genetically oriented theorists expect stability in personality over time, social learning theorists anticipate situational influences. But even if personality stability in social behavior is uncovered, social learning theorists still may contend that, in these instances, there has been constancy in environmental reinforcers and external stimuli. There are some family environmental factors that influence aggression, for example, and it may be that the continuity of these family influences is responsible for the continuity observed in this personality disposition. Thus, the stability observed in aggressive behavior over long periods could be due to consistency of the deprivation and frustration experienced by the child or to the family's consistent reinforcement of aggressive responses.

Humanistic theory (see Chapter 6) also holds that personality should change over time. For Carl Rogers, the person is an "open system," continually learning and integrating new experience into the personality. Personality will therefore evolve, although this does not mean that earlier forms of coping will be abandoned. Rather, as documented in the Caspi et al. study of men who were dependent as children, earlier forms of coping will develop into more mature forms.

Genetic theory seems to hold that if personality is genetically based, it will be fixed and unchanging from early childhood on. This implication, however, is incorrect. In fact, behavior geneticists argue that the tendency to change is itself heritable, and changes in personality over the childhood years are genetically based (Brody, 1994).

The research strategy most often used to address the question of stability is the *longitudinal study*. Measures of personality are taken in the child's early years and again at subsequent periods of development. A number of longitudinal studies have extended through adolescence and well into adulthood (Kagan and Moss, 1962; Macfarlane, Allen, and Honzik, 1954). Initial data yielded by these investigations have not proved conclusive, partly because some personality traits are more stable over time than others, partly because stability decreases as the time period between testings is extended, and partly because of the limitations of the measures used to assess personality. It is difficult to find measures of introversion or achievement that are comparable for young children and adults. Nevertheless, later investigations using sophisticated analyses have yielded significant correlations between personality measures obtained at different times (Baumrind, 1972; Block, Block and Keyes, 1988; Olweus, 1979). For example, in the investigation by Baumrind, children's social behaviors were assessed both at nursery school age and again in the third or fourth grade. The degree of measured competence, social responsibility, and prosocial behaviors manifested by the children at both times were similar. Similarly, Block, Block, and Keyes (1988) found striking relationships between the inability to delay gratification and related characteristics at ages 4–5, and drug use at age 14.

A major longitudinal project at the Institute of Human Development of the University of California, Berkeley, has been able to provide data for a number of investigators interested in the continuity issue. One of these studies (Block, 1971) compared personality ratings obtained at three different times: when the subjects were in junior high school, in senior high school, and thirty to forty years old. The data provided evidence of consistency. About 60 percent of the personality items on which the subjects were assessed in junior high school were substantially correlated with the senior high school ratings, and about 30 percent of the senior high school ratings were comparable to the ratings obtained during adulthood. For males, substantial consistencies emerged on ratings of such items as, "Is a genuinely dependable and responsible person," "Tends toward undercontrol of needs and impulses, unable to delay gratification," and "Enjoys aesthetic impressions, is aesthetically reactive." Examples of items on which stable ratings were obtained for females include "Basically submissive," "Emphasizes being with others, gregarious," and "Rebellious and nonconforming."

While Block's (1971) findings are often taken as evidence of consistency, the finding that only 30 percent of the traits showed substantial correlations from adolescence to adulthood suggests the presence of change as well. Other studies have found evidence of changes in personality from childhood into adulthood (Chess and Thomas, 1984), and most researchers now agree that personality does not stabilize until sometime between the ages of twenty and thirty. Even after age thirty, as we shall consider in a later section of this chapter, there is evidence of further personality change. With regard to other data on stability, Caspi and Bem (1990) conclude, "In general, differences in aggression, dominance, dependency, sociability, and shyness are preserved from middle and late childhood through adolescence and adulthood" (p. 558).

When there is change, what is the nature of that change? Generally it is most likely to be gradual and subtle (Heatherton and Nichols, 1994). However there are cases where change is sudden and dramatic (Miller and C'deBaca, 1994; see Highlight 13.1).

The study of the consistency of personality over time indicates both stability and change. But what are the mechanisms that underlie stability over time? One possibility is that early childhood experiences form personality traits that persist. Many current psychologists, however, favor more complex explanations involving the series of transactions between the person and his or her environment over time (Caspi, 1993; Sroufe, Carlson, and Shulman, 1993). For instance, children

Sudden Personality Change

Can personality change occur suddenly? Literature is replete with examples of people, such as Ebenezer Scrooge, whose personality changes. Miller and C'deBaca (1994) located fifty-five individuals through responses to a newspaper article who reported having experienced a sudden and major change. The researchers found that these changes were usually preceded by a period of emotional distress and that some "focal incident" had precipitated the change. (Scrooge's focal incident, of course, would have been the appearance of the three spirits.) Barlow, Abel, and Blanchard (1977) reported a study of a male transsexual undergoing hormonal therapy in order to change. After a single two-to-three-hour prayer and healing session with a physician, the man experienced an immediate shift from a female to a male identity. He started dressing as a man and discontinued hormonal therapy. At a four-year followup he not only was dating women but also, using a scale designed to measure motor behaviors, was walking like a man instead of a woman. Such sudden changes are also reported by recovering alcoholics, who often "hit bottom" (the focal incident) before changing.

who show early antisocial, aggressive behaviors tend to interpret others as treating them negatively. They may then react aggressively to these other people, thus provoking negative reactions that sustain and reinforce the child's antisocial, aggressive tendencies. As the child gets older he or she may gravitate to a peer group of like others, who further reinforce and support the antisocial behavior. It is now believed that while there are chains of continuity between childhood and adulthood, these chains are complexly forged out of a whole series of interacting experiences.

In sum, the question — Is there continuity and stability in personality from childhood to adulthood? — needs to be rephrased. A more productive question is: What are the factors that make for stability or discontinuity? Some attitudes and behaviors are likely to be more stable than others. For example, child behaviors that are closely related to physiology, such as activity level and emotionality or what is commonly called temperament, are personality characteristics that are likely to remain relatively stable over time (Chess, Thomas, and Birch, 1965). The scientist's task is to be able to predict which kinds of behaviors for which kinds of individuals under which kinds of circumstances will show stability.

ADOLESCENCE

We now turn to a consideration of developmental aspects of personality in adolescence. There are those who now believe that adolescence, as much as or perhaps even more than early childhood, is a key developmental period for personality. Measures of personality in early adolescence predict adult personality more accurately than do measures in early childhood (Livson and Peskin, 1980). Caspi (1993) says, "It may be no coincidence that studies grappling with the puzzle of life-course change have pointed to experiences in late adolescence and young adulthood that appear to deflect life trajectories" (p. 364).

Adolescence is a period of transition; the adolescent is in the process of moving from the status of child to the status of adult. It is a period of development marked by profound physical, psychological, and social changes. Physical changes in sexuality and body size are often rapid and dramatic; though welcome, they can nevertheless be disquieting until they are fully incorporated in the adolescent's altered body image. At the same time, adolescence brings with it a new social role, with increased independence, choice, and responsibilities. This new role is in fact a reflection of society's recognition of: (1) the psychological development that has taken place when the individual enters adolescence; (2) the adolescent's increased physical and cognitive powers; and (3) the fact that the adolescent has entered a higher level of cognitive and moral development, and can see situations in their full complexity (Elkind, 1970; Kohlberg, 1969b).

These changes in the physical, social, and psychological spheres affect and upset the self-concept and tend to produce a state of uncertainty in the adolescent as to his or her true self. "Who am I?" "What can I do?" "What do I really want?" are questions with which the adolescent is suddenly confronted. Much of adolescent behavior can be understood as efforts to resolve these questions. However, it must be emphasized that the degree of disruption entailed by the changing self-concept, the amount of emotional turmoil experienced by the adolescent, and the extremeness of behaviors are strongly influenced by cultural and familial factors. While adolescence is frequently described as a period of *Sturm and Drang* (the German equivalent of "storm and stress"), this does not have to be the case. Social and biological variables interact in determining the pattern of behavior displayed in adolescence (Petersen, 1988). And, as we will see, even the biological changes that occur in adolescence are influenced by cultural variables.

Biological Changes

Adolescence begins with the onset of puberty, the period of maturation of the sex organs and other sexual characteristics. Actually, two closely related changes in physical development are occurring, both stimulated by an increase in a particular hormonal secretion. The *gonadotropic* hormones, secreted by the pituitary gland, stimulate and enlarge the gonads—the ovary in females and the testes in males—which then release larger amounts of sex hormones. These hormones, in turn, regulate the changes taking place in masculine and feminine bodily characteristics: the enlargement of breasts, the rounded contours and, most dramatically, the menstrual flow in females and the growth of body hair, the deepening of voice, and ejaculation in males. Testosterone (the masculinizing hormone) and

Sexual maturation and sexual interest characterize adolescence. (Mimi Forsyth/ Monkmeyer Press Photo Service)

estrogen (the feminizing hormone) are necessary for normal sexual development in both males and females. The proportions differ, however, with more testosterone secreted in boys and more estrogen in girls.

At the same time, working in conjunction with the sex hormones, growth hormones secreted by the pituitary initiate a growth spurt. The increase in muscle tissue is greater in boys than in girls so that males, on the average, become biologically stronger than females. Augmenting these biological differences in strength are greater heart and lung size in males than females and corresponding differences in other vital capacities. These changes culminate in the maximum physical size the individual will achieve (excluding weight gains) during the course of his or her development. While it may be an exaggeration to say that one's decline begins as one enters the twenties and adulthood, we certainly cannot look forward to an increase in physical size and capacity at that point. However, in contrast to the pattern for physical development, one can grow psychologically throughout one's lifetime.

Hormonal Changes and Behavior. There is little doubt that the hormonal changes that occur in connection with puberty exert a significant influence on sexual interest and activities. However, the relation between these hormonal changes and other aspects of the adolescent's behavior, such as aggressiveness and psychological adjustment, remains very much at issue. While there is some evidence of a correlation between testosterone level and aggressive attributes (Olweus, et al., 1980), other studies have reported only a complex, indirect relationship for males and a negligible relationship for females (Susman, et al., 1987). There is suggestive evidence of a depressive effect in some adolescent boys following puberty that may be due to hormone secretion (Rutter, 1980; Susman, et al., 1987). Nevertheless, most boys do not become depressed and, more generally, puberty does not appear to be a significant cause of psychological distress. One writer puts it, "Developing adolescents like most pubertal changes" (Petersen, 1988, p. 595). There are, of course, individual differences, and important exceptions to this generalization.

Individual Variations

Pubertal change entails the most extensive and rapid change in postnatal life. The responses of the self and others to these physical changes may be more important than the physical changes themselves (Petersen, 1988).

Having experienced the changes of puberty and observed them in our peers, most of us are quite aware of the marked individual variations in the onset and termination of sexual growth. Early-maturing girls may begin to menstruate at age ten while, for some late-maturing girls, menstruation may not begin until age seventeen. Similar variations occur in the initiation and completion of other physical changes. Boys show corresponding variations in their sexual maturation and growth spurts, although as a group they reach puberty about two years later than girls. These differences in rate of physical maturation have consequences for the adolescent's changing self-concept. Early pubertal onset in boys has been found to be related to enhanced body image, higher self-esteem, and improved moods (Blyth, et al., 1981; Petersen, 1988). There are, of course, many individual exceptions to these generalizations. The early maturer who is physically awkward or suffers excessively from blackheads and acne will not see himself as highly attractive. For girls, early pubertal development is associated with decreased feeling of attractiveness, while later maturation is associated with positive psychological outcomes such as higher self-esteem (Simmons and Blyth, 1987). Also, girls who are very early or unprepared for their menarche report more negative reactions and symptoms than average maturers (Ruble and Brooks-Gunn, 1982).

Autonomy and Conformity

Over a relatively short period of time, the adolescent acquires new physical powers, matching those of the adults who are the controlling forces in society. The adolescent is beset with intense sexual feelings that motivate sexual interests and behaviors that remain largely prohibited by adult society. The drive toward assertion of one's powers and self-definition as an independent decision maker, and toward autonomy from parents and from social rules that are seen as controlling and repressive, is therefore strong. The adolescent may express this drive in a number of different ways: through career choice, political action, sexual experimentation, defiance of speed limits, cigarette smoking, or experimenting with alcohol or drugs. How an adolescent manages his or her independence striving, whether in a socially acceptable or a socially deviant manner, whether with rebelliousness and parental conflict or in the context of maintenance of strong family ties, depends on (1) the stresses and transition structures that exist in the culture, (2) the family atmosphere and response to the adolescent's efforts at independence, and (3) the personality of the individual adolescent.

But the adolescent's search for independence is only half the struggle; the adolescent also needs a support system and a place in society. The adolescent needs feedback on the new self that is in the process of definition (Hamachek, 1976), including answers to questions of self-uncertainty, such as "Am I attractive?" "Am I as powerful as I think I am?" "Can I make intelligent decisions on my own?" "Am I capable of assuming the responsibility of an adult?" In addition, the process of separation from family controls and protection can be painful and isolating. To reduce pain and loneliness, the adolescent is often motivated to seek out some group with which to affiliate. This group can be one's immediate peers, a political organization, a new religious movement, or the military. Paradoxically, in some cases it can even be one's immediate family. There is evidence that adolescents with a cohesive family to whom they have a secure attachment (cf. Chapter 12) have a more favorable self-concept than adolescents who are insecurely attached or emotionally detached, and are better prepared for independence and autonomy (Ryan and Lynch, 1989). The emotionally detached adolescent appears to be less self-reliant and more dependent on peers for self-expression (Steinberg and Silverberg, 1986).

Thus, the adolescent who is on the one hand striving for independence, on the other hand needs a group that can provide feedback, validation of the self, and emotional support. Under these circumstances, strong attachments to the group can develop, with the group exercising powerful conformity pressures on its individual members. The adolescent asserting his or her independence from adult norms and prohibitions may also adopt every new fad in style of dress, in rock music, in hair length, even in jargon (Remmers and Radler, 1957). In a real sense, the adolescent is dependent on a social group in order to achieve independence. Some psychologists (Riegel, 1975) have used the term *dialectic,* borrowed from philosophers Hegel and Marx, to describe this developmental interplay between two opposing forces. Out of this dialectic between the need for independence and the pressures toward conformity will emerge a more mature individual, able to conform or act independently in a more adaptive, realistic fashion. The struggles and changes of adolescence, then, provide the groundwork necessary for psychological growth in adulthood.

Idealism

One of the striking characteristics of adolescents is a strong measure of idealism (Horrocks, 1969). Of course, not all adolescents are idealists. Some follow conventional values and activities; others are predominantly oriented to self-gratification and may display very little in the way of social conscience. Surveys of adolescent attitudes and opinions, in fact, indicate that in the two decades between 1967 and 1987, a decline has taken place in adolescent idealism coupled with a corresponding rise in material interest (Astin, Green and Korn, 1987; Conger, 1988). This trend may be reaching a plateau and may reverse itself in the 1990s. In any event, the idealism that many adolescents manifest — their dissatisfaction with the state of the world and their desire to improve on society and to adopt life styles that are more genuine and fulfilling — is a special feature of this period of development. How idealism is expressed is as dependent on social conditions and social structure as it is on the degree of individual extremism versus individual willingness to work "within the system."

In the 1940s, the United States was engaged in a war supported by a majority of its population. Adolescents with strong idealistic feelings could express them through participation in the war effort: early enlistment, identification with a noble cause, and often through acts of sacrifice and heroism. Pacifists whose values permitted joined the medical corps or served in a nonmilitary capacity. In the 1960s, on the other hand, the United States was engaged in an unpopular war in Vietnam. Adolescent idealism could find an outlet more readily through opposition than through support of the war. There were other important social and economic differences between the 1940s and the 1960s that influenced the expression of adolescent idealism. A major step in race relations had taken place in the United States during World War II, with the integration of the armed forces. But progress in this area moved slowly during the postwar years until the civil rights movement emerged, providing adolescents with still another opportunity to work toward a more ideal society. A further difference between these two periods was the long economic depression that preceded World War II, in contrast to the almost two decades of economic prosperity preceding the sixties. The latter situation permitted young people to concern themselves with inner experience and growth, with the development of authentic life styles, rather than with the workaday constraints of striving for economic security and advancement. In brief, the contrast between adolescent behavior during the 1940s and the 1960s illustrates the powerful role that historical and socioeconomic conditions play. As we will see again and again, adolescence is not merely a matter of hormones.

But how do we explain this intensified drive toward a better world, a more just society, a more honest life style that so many adolescents experience? Where does this idealism come from? There are studies linking adolescent involvement in civil rights activities and the student protest movement of the sixties to family background. But, by and large, these studies do not tell us what it is about the adolescent period of development that fosters intense idealistic impulses. There are a number of different factors that one can suggest, but further research is needed to determine which are the critical variables promoting idealism. Probably, it is a combination of several of the following factors:

1. *Greater cognitive skills.* According to Kohlberg, some adolescents during this period attain a higher stage of cognitive and moral development. Adolescents

are capable of dealing with statements that have double meanings and enjoy manipulating verbal symbols (Elkind, 1970). One might expect the adolescent to be better able than pre-adolescents to recognize inconsistencies, which he or she is then motivated to resolve.

2. *Increased independence.* One characteristic of independence is the ability to think for oneself. Adolescents, in establishing their autonomy and independence from parents and authority, can now begin to evaluate critically ideas and values expressed by their parents and by society, which had previously been accepted without question. Seeing imperfections, like recognizing inconsistencies, is the first step toward eliminating these imperfections.

3. *Rivalry with parents and between generations.* Whereas, in the preteen years, the child sees the adult as a source of both support and control, a new ingredient is added in the adolescent years: the adult becomes a rival. Physically, the adolescent is the peer of the parent and is perhaps even stronger and more attractive. Psychoanalytic theory sees adolescence as a period in which the Oedipal impulse and conflicts are reawakened. One difference from the earlier Oedipal situation is that the parents may now feel threatened by the same-sex child: the mother by her sexually mature daughter and the father by his physically adult son. Going beyond the immediate family, rivalry between adult society and adolescents is fostered by the fact that the adolescent is about to enter the labor force and can be an economic threat. In addition, adolescents identify with their peer groups and display tastes and values that may challenge those of the adult society. Thus, part of the fervor of adolescent idealism may be a kind of competitive assertiveness with adult rivals: an "I-can-do-better-than-you-can" response. Contributing to this rivalry with adults and to the adolescent sense of moral superiority is the adolescent's recognition of parental and adult fallibility. This recognition in turn gives rise to *cognitive conceit,* a defensive belief in one's own greater intelligence and insight (Elkind, 1979).

4. *Reaction formation.* Adolescence is a period when impulses — especially sexual ones, whose expression has been prohibited — are intensified and brought to the fore. Aggression, too, may become exacerbated with the stimulation of rivalry and competitiveness, with efforts to establish autonomy, and with an increase in physical strength. Further, the adolescent's attention quite naturally turns inward to cope with these new feelings, powers, and insecurities. The adolescent has to struggle against being self-centered, seeing oneself as the center of the universe. The intensified idealism of some adolescents may then be one way of coping with sexual, aggressive, and egocentric impulses that the adolescent cannot fully accept. To the extent that the defense of reaction formation is operating, the adolescent may display in exaggerated form a concern with the welfare of others rather than oneself, an opposition to any form of aggression, and a search for "pure" relationships in which sexual passion is minimized or absent. Anna Freud (1958) has described the *ascetic adolescent* as in a transitory period in which

there is a lack of differentiation between the pleasurable, id aspects of life and the vital biological drives such as the need to eat and to sleep. In defending against id impulses, the adolescent overreacts, rejecting the satisfaction of significant bodily needs. It should be emphasized that we are not saying that asceticism, pacifism, and social concern are necessarily reaction formations, only that these idealistic tendencies can be exaggerated in adolescence through the process of reaction formation.

Continuity Between Adolescents and Parents

We have focused on the adolescent's efforts to separate from the parents and to establish his or her own identity. However, adolescents also have attachments to their parents and, in most societies, the parents have been the most influential adults in the adolescent's life. Consequently, one might expect some similarities between adolescent and parent in attitudes, values, and preferences. In a major study of adolescents, in which fourteen-year-olds were followed through school and, in most cases, through age twenty-two, Offer (1969; Offer and Offer, 1975) found that the values and social orientation expressed by most teenagers were fundamentally similar to their parents'. There were value conflicts, of course, and occasionally severe disagreements and discord, but, on the whole, the teenagers shared their parents' value structures. "The goals they were striving toward were very appropriate in the sense that they fitted very nicely into the cultural milieu in which they were living, and were almost always in accordance with the parents' expectations" (Offer, 1969, pp. 60–61).

We must remember that adolescents share their parents' socioeconomic status, religious affiliation, and residential area — all sociological, demographic factors that exert a powerful influence on social values. In this regard, teenage children of a southern farmer who is a member of a Fundamentalist church are likely to have more in common with their parents than with upper-middle-class, urban adolescents on the East and West coasts. But even when adolescents are matched on demographic factors, one still finds evidence of similarity between parental values and those of their offspring (Troll, Neugarten, and Kraines, 1969). Studies of political activists during the 1960s and early 1970s also revealed a continuity in values between parent and child. The difference between activist students and their parents was most often in the greater willingness of youth to take militant action on beliefs their parents shared (Keniston, 1967). Thus, the difference between generations appears to be more on issues of style than on questions of basic values. But style — how we go about realizing our values, the sacrifices we are prepared to make, the risks we are willing to take — is by no means a trivial matter.

Discontinuities in Adolescent Development

Although most adolescents conform in general to the value structure of their parents and to that of the larger society, many deviate and engage in behaviors that are socially disapproved or illegal. Generation differences became especially marked during the 1960s with regard to sex and drugs. We must be especially careful here to distinguish between behaviors that are characteristic of the long period of development we call adolescence and behaviors that are confined to a particular period of history. To understand the "drug revolution" and the "sexual revolution," one would have to go beyond the adolescent, to examine the social, political, and economic forces that were prevalent during the 1960s: economic affluence, an unpopular war, threat of nuclear destruction, and depletion of natural resources, to cite some of the more evident factors. At the same time, it was the youth of the Western nations who sparked the changes in sex practices and use of drugs. For the psychological reasons that have been reviewed—the search for self-identity, increased physical and cognitive competence, the need for autonomy and independence, idealism, and its corollary, disillusionment— young people are likely to be in the forefront of both social and political revolutions.

ADULT DEVELOPMENT

Concern with personality development throughout the life span is relatively recent in psychology. Adolescence was recognized as a period of self-uncertainty and self-change that finally culminated in the crystallization of the self upon entrance into young adulthood. There were some studies of personality and attitude change during the college years (Newcomb, 1943), but it was implicitly assumed that by the time one graduated from college, if not before then, personality was more or less "set" until one reached old age. Research on even this latter period remained quite limited until the increase in elderly people in the population gave special social and economic significance to the physical and psychological changes that occur with aging.

Because of the newness of the life-span approach to personality development, there is uncertainty and debate as to what the important issues and questions are (Baltes and Schaie, 1973). Just what does a developmental approach to personality in the adult years contribute to our understanding, beyond simply studying the changes and continuities in personality over time? Certainly we can expect that the personalities of adults will be affected by repeated experiences of success versus failure, by prolonged unemployment, by tragedies and serious illness, by positions of prestige and responsibility, and so on. What, then, does it mean to talk about personality *development* in the adult years?

There are three kinds, or levels, of answers that have been given to this question, depending on how closely the personality change is linked to a particular age period and how regular or inevitable the change is seen as being:

1. One can examine the effects on adult personality of unusual life events such as a prisoner-of-war experience (Hunter, 1976), an untimely death in the family (Weisman, 1973), or exposure to severe persecution (Ostwald and Bittner, 1968). Developmental considerations become relevant to the extent

that one takes into account age-related variations in the social, emotional, and cognitive status of individuals; for example, the fact that these severely stressful events may have occurred to recently married couples, or to men and women with well-established positions and growing families, or to elderly residents of a nursing home.

2. One can focus on the implications for personality change of experiences that occur only or primarily to all those of adult status or to particular age groups within the adult category. Marriage, divorce, becoming a parent, job dissatisfaction, career achievement, and retirement are examples of such experiences. Of course, there is no simple, one-to-one relationship between these experiences and their effects on personality. The personality consequences of marriage, divorce, or a new job depend in part on other personality attributes of the individual. Nevertheless, these events have powerful meanings for adults; they satisfy or frustrate significant needs and may enlarge or narrow one's self-understanding and sensitivity to others.

3. From the most explicitly developmental viewpoint, one can conceive of adult personality as a series of age periods in which specific aspects of personality are acquired, enhanced, or modified. Some investigators maintain that there is a regular sequence in the patterning and fluctuations of personality over time (Bühler, 1962; Erikson, 1950; Gould, 1972; Levinson, 1978). Just as adolescence and the preceding developmental periods have special significance for the formation of personality, so are the periods of early adulthood, middle adulthood, and old age characterized by their own growth-related issues of marriage, parenthood, career, and retirement. In this section, we will focus to a large extent on research that approaches the adult personality from this perspective.

Adult Developmental Stages

In *As You Like It,* Shakespeare described seven ages of man (see Highlight 13.2). You will recall, too, that Erikson (Chapter 4) proposed a sequence of three psychosocial tasks and corresponding age periods with which the developing adult must deal: intimacy-early adulthood (20–40); generativity-middle adulthood (40–65); and integrity-later adulthood (65–). According to Erikson, the principal problem faced by young adults, in their twenties and thirties, is the achievement and maintenance of a close personal relationship or, alternatively, the living of one's life as an independent but emotionally isolated individual. On entering the forties, the individual's problems shift. Will one cling to established routines, to old patterns and old habits, or will one look forward to and pursue different satisfactions and future opportunities? Old age presents both the most difficult challenge and possibly the highest level of self-realization: recognizing one's limitations and the ultimate finality of life. At the same time experiencing life as meaningful and integrating the mosaic of tragedies and joys that life presents is equally fulfilling.

■ **Highlight 13.2** ■

The Seven Ages of Man
William Shakespeare

All the world's a stage,
And all the men and women merely players.
They have their exits and their entrances,
And one man in his time plays many parts,
His acts being seven ages. At first the infant,
Mewling and puking in the nurse's arms.
Then the whining schoolboy, with his satchel
And shining morning face, creeping like snail
Unwillingly to school. And then the lover,
Sighing like furnace, with a woeful ballad
Made to his mistress' eyebrow. Then a soldier,
Full of strange oaths and bearded like the pard,
Jealous in honor, sudden and quick in quarrel,
Seeking the bubble reputation
Even in the cannon's mouth. And then the justice,
In fair round belly with good capon lined,
With eyes severe and beard of formal cut,
Full of wise saws and modern instances,
And so he plays his part. The sixth age shifts
Into the lean and slippered Pantaloon,
With spectacles on nose and pouch on side,
His youthful hose, well saved, a world too wide
For his shrunk shank, and his big manly voice,
Turning again toward childish treble, pipes
And whistles in his sound. Last scene of all,
That ends this strange eventful history,
Is second childishness and mere oblivion,
Sans teeth, sans eyes, sans taste, sans everything.

Source: *As You Like It,* act 2, sc. 7, lines 139–166.

Erikson, then, saw adulthood as a series of age-related stages, each presenting its own developmental task. The successful resolution of these tasks results in the individual's progressive attainment of higher levels of self-realization. Despite the value that Erikson placed on the greater maturity that aging offers, however, adults over thirty in this culture generally prefer to be somewhat younger (Kastenbaum, Derbin, Sabatini, and Artt, 1972). Young adults, the middle aged, and the aged have nevertheless been shown to report the same degree of life satisfaction (Cameron, 1972). Furthermore, in that same study, the middle aged were considered by the other groups to be the happiest.

The degree of life satisfaction that one attributes to different stages in life is one component of the way in which different age periods are perceived. Another component is the changes that are believed to occur at different life stages. A study of the perception of age changes in a sample of young (20–36), middle-aged (40–55), and older adults (60–85) indicated that these adults do not see personality as fixed (Heckhauser, Dixon and Baltes, 1989). Rather, they believe that substantial personality changes take place during the course of adult development, and that most of these changes are positive. While the percentage of "gains" in comparison to "losses" is seen to decline with increasing age, developmental gains were perceived to outnumber losses throughout adulthood, with the exception of very advanced age (beyond 80). In addition, the middle aged and older adults perceived more and varied changes occurring during adulthood than did the young adults.

These studies of satisfaction, age perception, and preferences tell us that people do find meaning in such a division of adult life into different age periods. However, we have to look to other kinds of data to determine whether there are stages of personality development associated with these different age periods. One source of data has been the study of individual biographies. Charlotte Bühler (1962) initiated the collection of life histories from elderly people in Vienna in the early 1930s and continued working on life-span development after emigrating to the United States. Her approach in inferring personality patterns from these life histories was essentially clinical and impressionistic, and her theoretical orientation was in the humanistic tradition. She postulated five basic life tendencies: need satisfaction, adaptive self-limitation or adjustment, creative expansion, establishment of inner order, and self-fulfillment. These life tendencies were assumed to emerge and become dominant at different age periods, and the way in which they were reflected in behavior also varied with age period. For instance, need satisfaction is assumed to be dominant in the first year and a half of life, again during the adolescent years, and once again in very old age. Adaptation and adjustment are assumed to be dominant in early childhood (ages 1.5–4) and again in the early adult years. Creative expansion is assumed to be dominant in late childhood, and between the ages of twenty-five and fifty. Research findings that are consistent with Bühler's analysis (Ryff, 1982) reflect changes in values and in the needs for achievement, dominance, and social recognition as one moves from middle age to old age.

Midlife Crisis

The work of Daniel Levinson and his collaborators (Levinson, 1978) is a more contemporary, sophisticated use of biography. In this study, adult males between the ages of thirty-five and forty-five were interviewed. (Due to limited resources, the investigators reluctantly limited their sample to men). The sample of forty individuals was equally divided among four occupational groups: executives, biologists, novelists, and factory workers. Occupation was chosen as a major variable because of the central importance of work to a man's status and income. In the investigators' view, the life cycle as reflected in personality development during this midlife period, as well as in the conflicts and struggles along the way, is affected by the social structure and social context, particularly the work setting and occupational role. As was the case in Bühler's theory, the self played a critical role in Levinson's theoretical formulation, and it is through the self-concept that occupation exerts its influence on adult personality development (Levinson, 1978, p. 45):

> Occupation has important sources within the self and important consequences for the self. It is often the primary medium in which a young man's dreams for the future are defined, and the vehicle he uses to pursue those dreams. At best, his occupation permits the fulfillment of basic values and life goals. At worst, a man's work life over the years is oppressive and corrupting, and contributes to a growing alienation from self, work and society. In studying a man's life, we need to understand the meaning of work and the multiple ways in which it may serve to fulfill, to barely sustain or to destroy the self.

To analyze the individual biographies, Levinson found it useful to employ the concept of *life structure,* or the basic pattern at a given developmental period in a person's life: how the person deals with issues concerning work, close relationships, changing perceptions of the self and of the future, and other critical matters that regularly arise as one progresses from youth to old age. The different developmental tasks posed by early, middle, and late adulthood require the individual to build a life structure through certain key choices and decisions, to keep options open or to make commitments, to settle down or to strive to attain greater heights. The most significant conclusion of this study is the finding of an orderly sequence of development, of an evolution of life structure during the adult years, and further that "the essential character of the sequence is the same for all the men in our study and for the other men whose biographies we examined" (Levinson, 1978, p. 49). Whether or not these investigators' findings are as universal as they claimed, they offered many rich observations and stimulating hypotheses regarding the nature of personality development during the adult years. They saw development as marked by stable periods in which the individual copes with particular developmental tasks and by transition periods, or stressful times when one must change from one level of adult development to the next. Although these observations were based on interviews with males, they would seem to have considerable relevance for females as well.

On the basis of the biographies they obtained and others' studies of the later segments of adult life, the Levinson group divided the adult life span into five transition and five developmental periods (see Fig. 13.1 on p. 374). After making the transition from adolescence to early adulthood, one's initial task on entering the adult world is to resolve the struggle between exploring a variety of alternatives — in personal relationships, jobs, life style — and making a commit-

Figure 13.1   Developmental periods in early and middle adulthood. (Levinson, 1978, p. 57.)

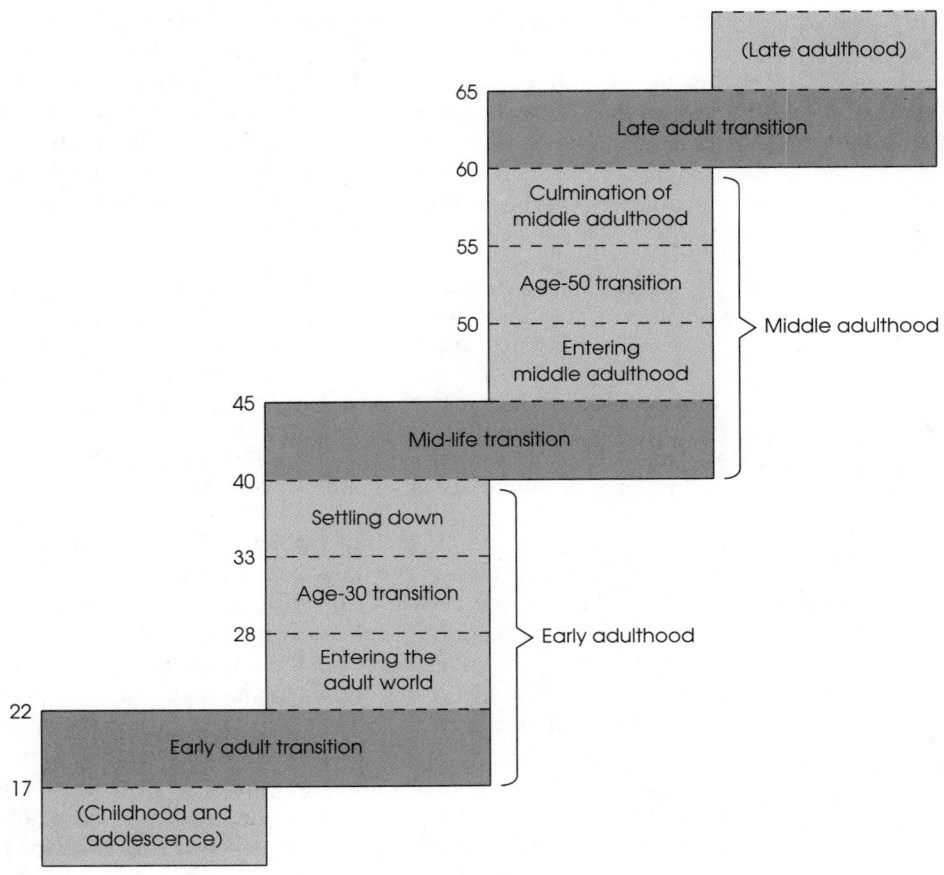

ment to a stable structure—getting married, choosing a career. The next transition period (ages twenty-eight to thirty-three), the so-called age-thirty transition, can be particularly stressful as one begins to move toward "really" settling down. The flaws and mistakes that one may have made—an unsatisfactory marriage, a frustrating occupation, or no commitment at all—take on a more serious quality as one advances from a provisional, "try-out" status to more stable, permanent commitments.

In the next adult stage, which lasts until approximately age forty, a man is most concerned with settling down. This is the period in which he attempts to realize his goals and aspirations, whether in terms of income, status, fame, creative work, or social contributions, and to "build" on his home and family. Then, roughly from age forty to forty-five, he enters the midlife transition period, characterized in a majority of men by a review and questioning of basic life structure. "What have I accomplished?" "Does my work matter?" "What do I really get from and give to my wife and children?" "Am I getting what I want out of life?" "What happened to my dreams?" This is the period of the so-called *midlife crisis,* a theme popularized in films and books in the 1970s (Sheehy, 1976). The turmoil and despair that many men (and women, as well) may experience during this period is not to be confused with mental illness. The crisis is normal and, if successfully resolved, healthy. Some men emerge from this crisis defeated and resigned to a life of decline; others emerge with an acceptance of mortality, loss of youth, and realistic limits to aspirations, but with renewed energy and purpose. This period of middle adulthood flows into the age-fifty transition, which can be a period of difficulty for men who have failed to come to grips with the issues of the midlife crisis. However, the decade of the fifties can be a period of rejuvenation and fulfillment as one approaches the later years of one's life span.

The picture of adult development painted by Levinson and his colleagues, although based on intensive biographical studies, must be considered hypothetical until supported by more exact, quantitative data. In one major study of four specific stages of life, from high school seniors to people nearing retirement, it was found that sex was a much more important determinant of issues than age or stage (Lowenthal, Thurnher, and Chiriboga, 1975). In the particular cultural context in which this study was carried out, marriage, parenting, and career achievement were some of the issues that differed in significance for men and women. However, some of the data yielded by this study were consistent with the Levinson observations, particularly the notion of midlife crisis. Experience of a midlife crisis was especially evident in the case of bright, talented women who felt trapped in their parental and housekeeping roles.

Roger Gould (1975, 1978), a psychiatrist who has carried out both clinical and questionnaire studies of adults in midlife, reports that men and women in this period no longer feel that "there's still plenty of time to do most of the things I want to do." Gould's clinical observations are consistent with Levinson's research findings. But there is also evidence in the case of women that the period of midlife change may be one of generativity and opportunity, women having new energies for extrafamilial involvement such as engaging in political activities and devoting additional time to careers (Harris, Ellicott, and Holmes, 1986; Stewart and Gold-Steinberg, in press). Indirect support for one component of the midlife transition period is provided by studies of personality change, which consistently indicate that people become more reflective and self-appraising in the second half of life (Costa and McCrae, 1977; Guttman, 1977).

There is much in literature and history, too, to support the notion of a midlife crisis. Certainly, an ebb in physical powers and other biological changes become clearly noticeable as one enters one's forties. Stamina, reaction time, and strength have all declined. There are also changes in physical contours and in the surface of the skin. If you haven't already won the Davis Cup or a figure skating medal, you will have to adapt to the probability that you never will. There are also biologically linked changes in sexual virility: in males' ability to obtain and maintain an erection, in the force of ejaculation, and so on. It seems reasonable that these biological changes can become linked with the recognition that one's life is at least half over and that this begets a midlife crisis. However, it is also quite likely that crisis is as strongly influenced by cultural features as by individual differences in personality. In cultures with clearly established, age-related social rules and expectations, in which the individual has few alternatives or choices, we might not expect to find a midlife crisis. Individuals living in economically marginal contexts, who are constantly concerned with physical survival, would probably not experience the pattern of adult development that has been described by the adult stage theorists. Concepts such as the midlife crisis are insightful, but our theoretical and research task is to discover the conditions that determine this phenomenon rather than to assume its inevitability as a stage of life.

Continuity and Change in Adulthood

The theoretical debate as to whether development in childhood is best character- ized by discrete stages has its counterpart in competing views of adult develop- ment. Erikson's and Charlotte Bühler's stage models assert that adult develop- ment is marked by age periods that pose particular developmental issues, and that the resolution of these issues are steps in a sequential path of increasing self-ful- fillment. Levinson (1986) agrees with the view that certain age periods are critical in that personality changes are most likely to occur during these periods.

Others, on the basis of data indicating continuity in personality and the failure to find evidence of systematic transformations in adult personality, have argued against the notion of age-linked developmental stages (McCrae and Costa, 1984). McCrae and Costa (1990) have argued that there is little change in personality at all during the adult years. In one study, these investigators administered the Guilford-Zimmerman Temperament Survey to adult subjects three times over a twelve-year period. The correlations they found between the first administration and the third administration twelve years later were quite high, ranging from .68 to .85 on the traits measured. Data from other investigators cited by McCrae and Costa show lower relationships, ranging from median correlations of .34 to .71, but generally provide evidence for relative consistency in personality over the adult years.

However, we have already mentioned data from Helson (1993) suggesting change in some characteristics over time. Helson and Stewart (1994) cite a variety of studies showing changes in impulsiveness and flexibility (Dudek and Hall, 1991), ambition and autonomy (Howard and Bray, 1988), and the need to achieve (Franz, 1994) during the adult years. Franz (1994) found a change towards being more relationship oriented between the ages of thirty-one and forty-one, and McAdams, de St. Aubin, and Logan (1993) found that individuals became more concerned with "generativity"—the desire to take care of others, as they aged (see Highlight 13.3 for other evidence of adult personality change).

In addition, the fact that personality *traits* may not generally change over the adult years does not mean *personality* does not change. It depends on what we define personality to be (Heatherton and Nichols, 1994; McAdams, 1994). We could conceive of personality as the overall organization of one's traits, values, and motivations. Changes can occur in goals, values, and motivations, as well as

◼ Highlight 13.3 ◼

Psychological Resilience

In recent years there has been a great deal of research interest in the topic of psychological resilience. Is a child permanently scarred and inevitably doomed by having a dysfunctional early childhood? Apparently not. A number of researchers have found that many children appear to thrive despite highly unfavorable early childhood experiences. George Vaillant (1993) has studied a sample of 456 individuals who were followed from age fifteen into their sixties. Eleven men were identified as having the poorest risk histories, including low self-esteem, low socioeconomic status as children, and a dysfunctional family life. At age twenty-five all appeared to be "broken beyond repair" (Vaillant, 1993, p. 287). However, by their sixties, eight of the eleven had "self-righted" themselves, and all but one were in the top 25 percent in terms of mental health. In general, researchers who have studied resilience have identified a number of factors that seem to "buffer" children against unfavorable circumstances. These include the temperament and disposition of the child, the presence of an adult (not necessarily a parent) who provides support and encouragement, the attributional style of the child (see Chapter 17), and good physical health.

in the overall organization of personality, while trait structures remain relatively constant. The kinds of changes Bühler and Levinson describe have more to do with the overall goals and organization of the person's personality at different times in the life sequence than they do with changes in particular traits.

As an example of how personality can change, Elder (1986) has shown that the opportunity for military service provided by the Korean War tended to have a positive effect on the personality development of men who joined military service before the age of twenty-one. These were young men whose parents had been particularly hard hit by the Great Depression of the 1930s. Most of them as high school adolescents had below average grades and were less assertive and less self-confident than either late joiners or non-veterans. But military service helped reshape the life course for many of these veterans. Full-time employment, marriage, and children all started later in life: the early veteran also changed his educational aspirations. Although almost a third had entered the service before completing high school, all of the early joiner sample earned their high school diploma. In addition, a fourth went on to enroll in a university, while almost one-half continued through junior college or vocational school. This change in educational goals is accompanied by evidence of marital stability and also by dramatic gains in psychological competence when assessed around age forty. The early joiners had increased significantly on measures of self-confidence and goal-orientation, while showing a decrease in submissiveness and feelings of inadequacy. If one excludes the role of combat, these data indicate that military service fostered the personal growth of men who had little to look forward to as adolescents.

More broadly, the findings of Elder and other investigators are supportive of the view that personality change in adulthood does occur and that these changes are related to the interaction of significant social events with the personality and age-related stage of the individual.

OLD AGE

The miracles of modern medicine and public health programs have made possible the extension of the life cycle into old age for increasing numbers of people, a change that in the United States is sometimes referred to as the "graying of America" (Datan, Rodeheaver, and Hughes, 1987). Sheer numbers have posed enormous medical, economic, and social problems for Western society, which places such a premium on productivity and youth. In addition, the urbanization and mobility of the American family make it difficult for the family to accommodate an elderly parent in the household. To further complicate the role and status of the elderly, the larger society's vision of older people is distorted by myths, half-truths, and stereotypes. The elderly themselves may accept these commonly held half-truths about their own intellectual functioning and emotional life.

Thus, in examining the question of personality change in old age, we do so within a particular social context in which attributes such as the wisdom of the elderly are not highly valued, in which old age is a time of economic hardship for many, and in which large numbers of the elderly live in nursing homes and retirement communities, segregated from younger age groups in society. We have the very difficult task of determining the extent to which behavioral changes in the elderly are due to the process of aging and the extent to which they are attributable to the particular social conditions experienced by the elderly in this society.

Many changes take place simultaneously during old age. There is a noticeable slowdown in reactivity and movement (Hicks and Birren, 1970); the skin is wrinkled and spotted; there is typically a decline in visual acuity and hearing. The aged are very vulnerable to illness and to such chronic diseases as diabetes, arthritis, and heart impairments. Mental illness also increases after the age of sixty-five. Much of this increase is due to biological disorders such as *cerebral arteriosclerosis,* in which the blood vessels thicken and blood flow to the brain is reduced. In disorders such as Alzheimer's, there is a decrement in brain cell function. But there are also mental disorders among the aged that are reversible: anxiety, depressive reactions to the loss of loved ones, and disturbances brought on by alcohol or drugs.

Aging Versus Illness

The biological and behavioral changes that occur in the aged are closely related (Fillenbaum, 1977), supporting a holistic approach to the problems of aging. The field of *gerontology,* which addresses the phenomena associated with old age, draws its experts from various biological and behavioral disciplines. A pioneering study carried out by James E. Birren and his colleagues (1963) illustrates the value of a multidisciplinary, gerontological approach to aging. A major objective of the study was to separate the effects of aging from the effects of the illnesses from which old people frequently suffer. Volunteer males, at least sixty-five years old, were screened for evidence of medical disorders, and only the healthier men were retained for inclusion in the study. The mean age of the final group of forty-seven "healthy" individuals was 71.5 and all were living independently in the community, in most instances in households with their wives. Detailed physiological and psychological evaluations of the men were carried out. The results were quite striking. These old men constituted a vigorous, alert, even optimistic group of individuals who were very much involved in their daily lives. The image of rigid, confused oldsters certainly did not apply to this sample. There was evidence of depression and distress in some of the men, but these reactions seemed appropriately linked to personal losses. More intensive analyses and comparisons with a sample of young men reflected differences on some physiological measures but

Active senior citizens in marathon competition. Illness, rather than aging per se, accounts for many of the differences observed between younger and older people. (Martine Franck/Magnum Photos, Inc.)

similarities on many others. For example, elevations in blood pressure did not discriminate between healthy old men and healthy young men and therefore can be taken as a sign of pathology rather than a result of a process of aging. The Birren findings, while based on a small sample and therefore to be taken as preliminary and suggestive, nevertheless point to the importance of separating the effects of illness from the effects of aging. What does seem to be true about the process of aging is that the organism becomes increasingly *vulnerable* to disease, accident, and life's hazards.

Competence and Survival

An interesting followup of survivors in the Birren sample was carried out eleven years after the initial study (Granick and Patterson, 1971). Although the sample of elderly men had been selected on the basis of healthiness, there were still variations in the degree of the men's physical health and in their psychological status. These factors were then examined to determine which factors differentiated survivors and nonsurvivors. As one might expect, physical symptoms such as elevated blood pressure and arteriosclerosis were more common among the nonsurvivors. However, psychological factors also predicted survival. Those among the elderly who had obtained higher scores on an intelligence scale, who were evaluated as more resourceful, and who had more social supports were more likely to be among the survivors. Perhaps this should not be too surprising, since as we have previously noted, physical and psychological functioning are closely interrelated among the aged.

An intriguing experimental study by Judith Rodin and Ellen J. Langer (1977) also bears on psychological factors in the aged that may be associated with survival. A group of elderly nursing home residents were given a talk by the hospital administrator which emphasized the responsibility the residents had for themselves. A contrasting talk was given to a control group of residents in the same institution which stressed the staff's responsibility to the residents as patients of a nursing home. In addition, the experimental group that received the communication emphasizing self-responsibility was offered plants to care for, while the comparison group was given plants that were watered by the staff. There were a number of significant immediate effects of the experimental manipulation of responsibility on the attitudes and behavior of the elderly patients. The elderly residents in the responsibility-induced group became more active, displayed greater alertness, and reported feeling happier than the control group. Patients in the responsibility-induced group also showed an increase in involvement in different kinds of social activities such as movie attendance, social interaction with friends and with staff, and participation in contests (Langer and Rodin, 1976).

Eighteen months later, a followup evaluation indicated that the experimental effects still persisted. The survivors who had been in the responsibility-induced group were judged to be more self-initiating, sociable, involved, and vigorous than those survivors who had been in the control group. The most striking result was the finding that a significantly smaller proportion of patients in the responsibility-induced group (seven out of forty-seven) had died in the eighteen-month period than in the comparison group (thirteen out of forty-four). It would be premature to conclude on the basis of this one study that a single talk, or that responsibility for a plant, will increase longevity. There were all kinds of factors in the nursing home that were not under experimental control that could have influenced the outcome of the study. Nevertheless, the findings indicate that it is possible to improve the psychological status and physical well-being of the elderly; programs designed to encourage the assumption of greater self-responsibility are a promising avenue for accomplishing these goals (see also Chapter 17).

Changes in attitudes toward the elderly, particularly the labels used to describe them, constitute another important avenue for enhancing the way older age groups in our society function. In other experiments that have been carried out, Langer and Rodin (1980) have shown that labels such as "senile" foster negative stereotypes and expectations of the elderly, and may, in turn, influence their self-concept and behavior. In contrast, positive expectations of the elderly motivate them to increase their cognitive activity and can lead to significant improvements in memory functioning and in feelings of wellbeing.

To Disengage or Not to Disengage

For many years, the prevailing view of how to grow old most effectively was a *disengagement* model (Cumming and Henry, 1961). The disengagement theory held that, since slowing down was a natural aspect of aging, the psychologically healthy response for the aging individual was to gradually reduce his or her activities and social involvements. The theory stimulated a good deal of research which nevertheless failed to support the disengagement model. Old people, for example, regret the reduction in their level of activity (Havighurst, Neugarten, and Tobin, 1968) and, in fact, the degree of activity and social engagement is positively related to reports of satisfaction with life.

Subsequent research has revealed that there is no simple prescription — "Keep busy" or "Cut back" — that can be applied generally to the elderly. Although keeping up one's activity tends to go together with positive feelings about life, there are many exceptions to this relationship. Some people need to and should cut back; their heightened activity is often a defense against the idea of growing old. Personality factors, such as the way one relates to one's activity, are more important than activity level. We have already noted that assuming responsibility for oneself can be a major factor in determining adjustment during old age. The elderly who *choose* to become less active or *choose* particular activities in which to become involved are more contented, better-adjusted individuals than the aged who feel dependent on other people to help and make decisions for them (Neugarten, Havighurst, and Tobin, 1968).

Recently Brandstädter and Greve (1994) have pointed out that while many believe that aging will bring with it reduced well-being, self-esteem problems, and a sense of loss of control, research has generally failed to support these beliefs.

These authors suggest that aging individuals utilize three processes to maintain a positive attitude towards life and thus cope with developmental losses and changes. First, they utilize instrumental and compensatory actions to prevent or alleviate losses in functioning. These actions might include, for instance, changes in diet and exercise. Second, they modify their goals and aspirations to more realistically reflect what they can hope to accomplish. Third, they utilize psychological self-protective mechanisms, such as interpreting evidence in self-protective ways, to minimize experiences of loss.

From the perspective of Bühler's and Erikson's conceptions of adult stages of development, old age offers an opportunity to attain a higher level of self-development than is usually possible at younger ages. It entails a level of maturity and wisdom that Erikson refers to as *ego integrity*. Individuals who have achieved this stage have accepted their fate in life, see the inevitability and meaning of their life's course, and realize the inescapability of their triumphs and defeats. They do not engage in fantasies of "If only I had done ——— rather than ——— ." They experience order in their lives. They find satisfaction in life but are also prepared to accept the inevitable finality of life. Young and middle-aged adults may try to approximate some of these attitudes toward life through the adoption of non-Western philosophies such as Zen Buddhism and training in disciplines such as yoga. However, according to Erikson, there is no substitute for the experiences of the life cycle and the review and acceptance of that span of experience if one is to realize this highest stage of self-development.

Demography and Ethnicity

The process and problems of aging have been described as if they were uniform for the elderly, with the exception only of personality differences in how individuals cope with the psychological and social role changes. However, the problems and consequences of aging undoubtedly vary with cultural factors that influence the social role, status, and economic welfare of the elderly. Thus the problems of aging that confront women, while sharing similarities with those confronting men, may also differ in important respects.

Women aged sixty-five and above experience significantly greater distress than men in this age group (Levy, 1981). Women, in fact, tend to report greater distress than males throughout the adult lifespan. However, the factors responsible for greater female distress may differ at different stages of adult life. For middle-aged women, anxieties concerning separation and divorce, feelings of loss over the departure of children from the home (the "empty nest" syndrome), and concerns over the lack of economic skills are among the major sources of distress. For the elderly female, problems of poverty, loneliness, and isolation emerge as significant issues. The elderly female is three times as likely as her male peer to live in a nursing home. Because the lifespan of women is longer than that for men, the elderly female is more likely than the elderly male to have to cope with the loss of her partner. Also, while there are relatively few studies of the effects of retirement on women compared to the more extensive literature on male retirement, available data indicate that women are less likely to look forward to retirement than men. Women are more likely to express dissatisfaction with their lives as a whole, and to express wishes that they had done something differently, such as completing their education or marrying later (Levy, 1981). At the same time, elderly women also tend to display greater coping strength than elderly males, appearing to have a greater capacity than males to overcome the limitations of body illness.

Culture and life events also influence the adaptation of the elderly female, as they do that of the elderly male. A study of elderly Vietnamese and Japanese women living in America indicated that they felt less control over their lives and more helpless than a sample of elderly women of British background (Yee, 1987). This effect was particularly pronounced for the Vietnamese elderly — the older the Vietnamese woman, the less control she felt she had (the importance of feelings of control as a personality dimension is elaborated in Chapter 17). To understand the bases of this difference in control between the women of Asian and British background, one has to look at the patterns of socialization within their respective cultures, the experiences they have had in the United States, and the timing of those experiences in their lives. The sex roles of women as defined by Asiatic cultures are more traditional than those defined by the prevailing American culture. Older Asian women are likely to be more traditional than younger generations, even within their own families. Other factors that one would have to consider in the case of the Japanese women is whether they had experienced internment during World War II and whether they came to the United States as part of an arranged marriage — as so-called "picture brides" who exchanged pictures and then on arrival in the United States often found that they had been deceived by the intended bridegroom. These experiences, as well as socialization patterns, might well influence one's sense of one's ability to control one's destiny.

If we consider the multiplicity of factors that can influence coping patterns and adjustment in the elderly, the study of aging can become the study of individual life history (Neugarten, cited in Datan, et al., 1987).

PSYCHOBIOGRAPHY: THE INTEGRATION OF LIVES

There is a growing interest among psychologists in the study of lives — the history of a particular individual from birth to death (see White, 1966). In addition to providing insights about one individual's life, these case studies also are used to reach generalizations about personality and development. In a parallel advancement, historians are increasingly using psychological principles in their studies of people. This cross-fertilization between psychology and history has led to a hybrid field called *psychobiography,* or more broadly, *psychohistory.* A psychobiographer uses psychological theory to explain individual lives, whereas a psychohistorian makes formal use of psychology in attempting to explain aspects of historical behavior.

Life histories often show the continuity and organization of personality that are not evident when only one action or one period of a person's life is analyzed. Life histories also help to elucidate developmental processes—for example, the subtle influence of experience and maturation on subsequent thinking, feeling, and acting. At the same time, in-depth studies of single individuals also can highlight discontinuities in behavior and the importance of unique experiences on later personality.

Psychobiographical writings have primarily been guided by psychoanalytic principles and hypotheses. This is in part the case because Freud launched this field with his studies of da Vinci, Michelangelo, and Moses. Later, Erikson applied psychoanalytic techniques and ideas in his influential analyses of Luther and Gandhi. The breadth of psychoanalytic theory, its speculative nature, and its assumption of permanent effects of child-rearing practices readily make this approach useful in the study of lives. But more recently, the full gamut of psychological principles, especially concepts related to the self and its development, are being used to understand people throughout history. It should be evident from the names cited earlier that people throughout history who have been examined by psychobiographers typically are well-known figures, whether famous, such as Jesus, Jefferson, or Roosevelt, or more infamous, such as Hitler and Stalin. One advantage of studying the famous is the wealth of material available to biographers. However, ordinary people and groups also have been the target of study, such as the people of Germany during the rule of Hitler.

One popular approach to history from the psychoanalytic perspective is to search for repeated themes, or characteristic modes of action and reaction, during the course of a life. This tendency is then traced to child-rearing episodes or relationships with parents or siblings. For example, psychobiographers have pointed out that Woodrow Wilson experienced a repeated pattern of important accomplishments when first in a new position, followed by a series of devastating setbacks. This pattern describes his tenure when he was President of Princeton University, Governor of New Jersey, and President of the United States. His most serious defeat as president was his failure to obtain Senate ratification of the League of Nations Charter; this prevented the United States from becoming a member of the League, which Wilson himself had been the driving force in creating!

To explain this recurrent theme, George and George (1964) suggested that Wilson's power desires were based on a need to compensate for his low self-esteem. This need was traced to his father, a severe minister, who often ridiculed him during his formative years. Because of this low self-esteem, it has been speculated that when others opposed him, Wilson felt threatened. Rather than facing and solving the task, he focused on himself. He then reacted with an uncompromising rigidity, holding himself in a morally elevated position. This alienated him from others and ultimately led to his self-defeat. Note that in this analysis a "lifescript" is repeatedly played out, based upon an inferred sense of low personal worth that was established early in childhood from interactions with his father. This interpersonal childhood experience was presumed to be the antecedent for a lifelong consistency in his manner of dealing with stress and personal threat.

The life of Richard Nixon also has been subject to close psychological scrutiny (Brodie, 1981). Brodie speculates that there may have been a repeated tendency for Nixon to lie. For example, during his last, wrenching speech at the White House on August 10, 1974, just prior to stepping down from office, Nixon talked at some length about his mother and father. One of the stories he told was of the lemon ranch his father owned for a short time — "the poorest lemon ranch in California, I can assure you." Nixon said that, typical of his father's bad luck in business, the ranch was sold before oil was discovered on the land. The story, according to Mrs. Brodie, is simply not true; she says no oil was ever found on the land. Even the opening lines of his memoirs have been subject to some doubt. The book begins: "I was born in a house my father built"; but many residents of his home town of Yorba Linda question that recollection. Brodie was unsure of what experiences in his past produced this behavior, but also cites evidence of a feared father and a restrained relationship with his mother.

As the reader might imagine, some have felt that the speculations of Brodie and other psychobiographers are strained and lack empirical support. Often, childhood interactions are inferred from adult behavior (direct evidence is typically sparse), and then later, the same inferred interactions are used to explain adult behavior. Also, the psychoanalytic hypotheses relating early childhood experience to adult personality have not received empirical support. Finally, what evidence is available often is contradictory, so that there are as many warm interactions between Nixon and his mother that are documented as there are cold or rejecting interactions.

It should be noted that psychobiographical research can make use of diverse methods, some of which may offer more substantial empirical support for the personality attributions made. In another study of President Nixon, inferences were made regarding his underlying motivations on the basis of qualitative and quantitative analysis of the imagery in some of his key speeches (cf. Chapter 8 for a discussion of motivation imagery in verbal material such as Thematic Apperception Test stories). Nixon's First and Second Inaugural Addresses were analyzed for the frequency of achievement, affiliation/intimacy, and power motivation related images (Winter & Carlson, 1988). The data indicated that Nixon is high in achievement motivation and in need for affiliation/intimacy but is only average in power motivation. The investigators then went on to analyze behaviors described as characteristic of Nixon in memoirs of Nixon by people who had worked directly with him. Analysis of these behaviors revealed a close correspondence with the motivation profile based on the analysis of his speeches.

Another common flaw in psychobiographies, especially those written from a psychoanalytic perspective, is that often religious, economic, political, and social influences on behavior are minimized. For example, it has been suggested that Hitler's hatred of the Jews stemmed from his mother's death while being treated by a Jewish doctor. Clearly, this would be insufficient to account for his part in the Holocaust. On the other hand, more careful psychohistorians call upon multiple sources of evidence and carefully examine the available evidence to support more guarded claims. They also typically recognize that behavior has many determinants, and therefore seek multiple or alternative explanations.

This search for evidence and multiple determinants of an action often is best illustrated when psychohistorians attempt to explain some circumscribed event. One ingenious account has examined a shocking act performed by Vincent van Gogh—he cut off part of his ear and presented it to a prostitute at a brothel. Runyan (1982) uncovered a variety of explanations for this incident, some very speculative and guided by psychoanalytic theory, and others more mundane and based on common sense or simple psychological principles such as modeling. Some of the explanations are:

1. He was frustrated by his inadequate relationship with the artist Gauguin and took his aggressive impulses out on himself.

2. He had a conflict over homosexual impulses and cutting off part of his ear was a symbolic self-castration.

3. He both hated and identified with his father. Cutting off his ear and presenting it at a brothel also symbolically fulfilled his wish to sleep with his mother.

4. Influenced by his observations of bullfights, he cut off his ear and presented it to the lady of his choice (as does the victorious bullfighter).

5. This was an emulation of the recent activities of Jack the Ripper, performed on himself.

6. This was a strategy for getting the attention of others, particularly his brother, and dramatically highlighting his need for money.

7. He was experiencing auditory hallucinations and during a psychotic episode cut off his ear to silence the disturbing sounds.

These are just a few of the alternative hypotheses uncovered in the literature by Runyan (1982). How can these alternative explanations of an incident in history be evaluated, and which is (are) correct? According to Runyan, explanations can be evaluated in terms of their logical soundness, comprehensiveness in accounting for all aspects of the event, and consistency with the available evidence. For example, Runyan doubts the "Jack the Ripper" explanation because only two newspaper reports mentioned ear mutilation, and then merely in passing; thus, they were unlikely to have been seen by van Gogh. On the other hand, it is known that he attended many bullfights and admired the conquering bullfighter. Other explanations that Runyan questions revolve around the idea of an ear as a symbol of his penis, which seems logically unlikely. Runyan most accepts the hypothesis that the ear-cutting mutilation relates to the perceived loss of his brother's care. In van Gogh's life, the ear incident and two later breakdowns corresponded, respectively, with his brother's engagement, marriage, and birth of a child. These events threatened his main source of both financial and emotional support. Recently, support for the hypothesis of a severely pained ear also has been documented.

Vincent van Gogh, *Self-Portrait.*
(The Granger Collection)

In sum, it appears that some of the hypotheses do receive support from what is known about the life of van Gogh, whereas other explanations can be more assuredly rejected on the basis of their lack of logic, comprehensiveness, and consistency with historical evidence. Other investigators, carrying out psycho-biographical studies, have suggested the additional utility of a systematic clinical mode of analysis (Alexander, 1988). Like the clinician analyzing the associations of a client or the client's dreams or fantasies, particular significance is given to such features of a statement as its primacy (e.g., initial statements, opening sentences), frequency of occurrence, its unusualness or uniqueness, and the degree of emphasis it is given. Psychohistory, therefore, applies not only the theories of psychology, but also the clinical methods of psychology and, in addition, some of the rules of social science in its reconstruction of historical events.

Summary

1. The issue of whether personality remains stable or changes from early childhood to adulthood is complex. The answer depends on what is meant by change and stability and on when one measures personality. However, evidence indicates that personality both changes and remains stable.

2. The physical changes of puberty are brought about by an increase in the pituitary gland's secretion of growth hormones and gonadotropic hormones. The latter, in turn, stimulate the gonads to secrete masculinizing and feminizing hormones in differing proportions for males and females.

3. The psychological changes in puberty are only weakly linked to direct effects of hormonal changes and are more closely linked to the responses of self and

others to the hormonal and accompanying physical changes. The timing of puberty affects the response to puberty, early pubertal onset having favorable effects for boys and tending to have negative effects for girls.

4. The adolescent is confronted with a conflict between the need to express sexual feelings and establish and assert autonomy on the one hand and the need for support and conformity to social rules on the other. The intensity and mode of resolution of the conflict will vary with cultural, familial, and personality factors.

5. The *idealism* that many adolescents display may be a reflection of their independence, their recognition of adult inconsistencies, and their *cognitive conceit* that they "can do it better." It may also be in part a reaction formation against unacceptable sexual and aggressive impulses.

6. Despite the conflict and discord that may occur in adolescence, there is considerable continuity or similarity between the values of parents and those of their adolescent offspring.

7. There is some empirical evidence for the hypothesis proposed by several theorists that adulthood can be divided into a sequence of periods or stages, each posing a particular set of problems and issues. Coping with these issues can stimulate personality change and growth in adults.

8. The *midlife crisis* that many adults are reported to experience during their early forties should not be confused with mental illness, but should rather be considered as a normal experience for that age group that can result in positive personality development.

9. There are suggestive findings indicating that many of the so-called "effects of aging" are actually a manifestation of the effects of illness to which old people happen to be vulnerable. Relatively healthy elderly individuals do not display the rigidity and mental confusion that often accompanies aging.

10. There is no single prescription for how old people should live their lives. For some, it is best to maintain a certain activity level; for others, it is best to disengage.

11. To understand personality development and change in the elderly and in other stages of adult life, one has to take into account cultural factors and significant historical events as well as personality differences.

12. Psychobiography is the study of peoples' lives that explicitly uses psychological (and often psychoanalytical) principles.

Thought Questions

1. Do you think personality is stable or changeable from childhood to adulthood?

2. Is it better for an adolescent's personality development if the adolescent period is marked by "storm and stress" rather than by relative calm?

3. How might cultural factors influence the stages of adult development observed among samples of adults studied in the United States?

4. Do you think it is wise for society to organize separate residential communities for the elderly? Why or why not?

5. Do you think psychobiography is a "scientific" method of psychobiological study? Why yes or why no?

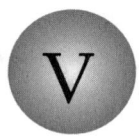

PERSONALITY
DYNAMICS

So far, we have examined the determinants of behavior that individuals encounter as soon as they enter the world: their genetic predispositions and the physical and social context in which they are placed. Then, after reviewing some of the major theories of personality, we turned to the structure and development of behavior and its measurement. Now we ask: how are these structures expressed in thought and action? What is the dynamic interaction between an individual, attempting to adapt, satisfy needs, and survive, and the environment, which provides the need satisfiers? Here we encounter themes of conflict, impulse control, substitute gratification, emotion, and stress.

In addition, in this section of the book we deal with questions of consciousness and awareness. Although we must adapt to the environment, often we are not consciously aware of the information that it provides or, for that matter, of the informational signals that our own body sends us. There are multiple levels of awareness. Furthermore, it is often apparent that we are operating within different realms of consciousness, as during dream, and hypnotic states. In these latter instances, environmental information is almost totally blocked or, on the other hand, there may be a heightened focus of attention.

Dynamics is defined in the dictionary as forces that produce motion. In this Part, we are concerned with the forces acting on the individual that produce psychological "motion": the expression and inhibition of needs and feelings, the entering or leaving of a particular state of consciousness, and the goals and functions of behavior.

14 | The Dynamics of Behavior

PERSONALITY DYNAMICS: A HISTORICAL INTRODUCTION

There is an intimate relationship between the structure and the dynamics of personality, although the terms refer to different aspects of the study of personality. The *structure* or "anatomy" of personality concerns basic dispositions and interrelationships of the different elements of personality. Personality *dynamics,* on the other hand, is concerned with the meaning and function of behavior. In considering personality dynamics, one looks for the purpose or the objective of an act — *why* the individual behaves the way he or she does. Questions of dynamics are also typically addressed to the immediate situation in which the action occurs, whereas questions about the structure of personality generally deal with relatively enduring and stable aspects of behavior. Three research traditions are linked with the study of psychodynamics: behaviorism, Gestalt psychology, and psychoanalytic psychology.

Behaviorism

The fields of clinical psychology and personality assessment were born in Europe, particularly France, Austria, and England. But in the early 1900s America began to develop its own special brand of psychology, known as *behaviorism.* Whereas psychoanalysis envisioned the mind as filled with unconscious fantasies and early childhood residues, the behaviorists emptied the mind of its contents, even rejecting the very concept of mind. (It is sometimes said that psychology first lost its soul and then its mind!) In a famous article that appeared in 1913, John B. Watson criticized prevailing psychology as subjective and unreliable; he argued for a *science* of psychology based on objective measures of observable behaviors and of the external, stimulus situation. The task of psychology, he contended, was to (1) predict the response, given the stimulus; (2) identify the stimulus, given the response; and (3) predict the change in the response, given a change in the stimulus. Watson's views on psychoanalysis were especially severe. He predicted that "twenty years from now an analyst using Freudian concepts and Freudian terminology will be placed upon the same plane as a phrenologist" (1930, p. 27).

Watson, like Freud, was willing to pursue the implications of his theory and observations wherever they might lead. And, also like Freud, he had a profound influence on the psychology of personality.

Behaviorism was also strongly influenced by the ideas of Darwin. Prior to the Darwinian period, humans were perceived as intelligent and "good," while non-humans were considered "evil" and merely governed by instinctive urges. The behaviorists believed in Darwin's proposal of a human-nonhuman continuum. Thus lower organisms, just as humans, were thought to have some degree of intelligence. Behaviorists therefore paid much attention to learning and the ability of nonhumans to adapt to their environment. When studying lower organisms, such as rats and pigeons, it was assumed that something was being learned about human behavior and its causes.

The behaviorists also differed from the early personality theorists and assessment psychologists in their methodological approach. Rats or pigeons cannot report on their wishes, desires, or values; these must be evidenced in, or inferred from, their behavior. Thus the method of gathering data shifted, with increased ingenuity demanded of the experimenter to obtain the kind of evidence that was desired.

The behaviorist school gave rise to several related but competing theories. Efforts to translate psychoanalytic concepts into a form that could be empirically tested were undertaken by a group of Yale University psychologists, including John Dollard and Neal Miller (see Chapter 5), influenced by Watson but advocating a more elaborate theoretical perspective. In contrast to Freud, this group stressed the importance of a laboratory-based learning theory. Learning theory places great emphasis on the significance of situational factors, postulates few mental processes, and attempts to deal with personality processes within a rigorous and objective experimental framework. The Yale psychologists conducted a number of experiments linking aggression to the occurrence of frustration. The hypothesis of a relation between frustration and aggression was a significant advance over the Freudian position, which postulated an instinctive aggressive drive. Conflict, fixation, and other complex behaviors and processes also were studied by the behaviorists.

Gestalt Psychology

Gestalt psychology primarily developed in Berlin after the start of the 1900s and reached its heights in the 1920s and 1930s. In opposition to the behaviorists, the Gestaltists did not want to empty the mind; rather, they asserted behavior is influenced by how a person interprets the world. A horseback rider might ride over a snow-covered, frozen lake without worry, they contended, if he or she thought they were merely crossing a field. Thus, they embraced the idea that a person acts on the basis of his or her perception of reality. This position challenged the contention of the behaviorists that behavior could be predicted from knowing the objective, external situation.

Another essential aspect of Gestalt psychology was its assumption that the determinants of behavior are interrelated. For example, the near simultaneous flashing of two lights in close proximity, as on a movie marquee, gives the illusion of movement. Analysis of each light independently would not explain the phenomenon of perceived movement. The whole, Gestaltists argued, cannot be neglected and is different than the sum of the parts. Personality theorists with a Gestalt orientation thus consider the "whole person," and consider specific problems in relation to an integrated personality.

Kurt Lewin (1890–1947) brought the principles of Gestalt psychology to bear upon the study of psychodynamics. He was the first psychologist to experimentally test some of Freud's ideas. Lewin initially examined the Freudian notion that a wish, once aroused, persists until it is either directly satisfied or is indirectly fulfilled by the attainment of substitute gratifications. In his exploration of this area, as well as in the study of such topics as frustration and conflict, Lewin always considered the total "field of forces" acting on an individual and how a change in one force affects other aspects of the situation.

Gestalt psychology, as elaborated by Lewin, subsequently influenced the study of personal aspirations, achievement strivings, and other topics considered in some detail later in this text. Unlike behaviorism, Gestalt psychology did not create a dramatic following and then largely fade from the center of psychology. Rather, it has remained in the background as a subtle yet persistent influence.

Psychodynamics from a Psychoanalytic Perspective

The influence of the French upon Freud already has been discussed. The French interest in hypnosis and hysteria continued with more detailed studies of *dissociation,* or the split between behavior and awareness that occurs under these conditions. American interest in dissociation was spurred by Morton Prince, who reported a number of intriguing cases of multiple or split personalities. Patients exhibiting amnesias, automatic writing, sleepwalking, and related dissociation symptoms were also studied by Prince. Particularly significant for the emerging field of personality was Prince's founding of the Harvard Psychological Clinic in 1927. Here Henry Murray, Prince's successor, demonstrated how the ideas and observations of Charcot, Prince, and, most importantly, Sigmund Freud could be studied experimentally.

Henry Murray developed a theory of personality that emphasized the full range of human motivation. He also pioneered in the measurement of human motivation and developed the well-known Thematic Apperception Test (TAT). In Murray one can see again that the various areas in personality do overlap, because Murray was a personality theorist who developed an instrument to assess individual differences to further the experimental study of conflict and related areas.

Researchers following the psychoanalytic tradition in the study of psychodynamics have been particularly guided by the idea of unconscious motivation.

Thus, they have examined subliminal perception, repression, and other phenomena that often demonstrate an individual's lack of awareness of the determinants of his or her behavior. Many of these phenomena are examined in this text.

TOPICS IN THE STUDY OF PERSONALITY DYNAMICS

Why are people motivated to think and behave as they do? One widely accepted and broad answer to this question is that thoughts and actions serve to maximize pleasure and minimize pain, a position most explicitly assumed by Freud (1920, p. 1), who stated: "The impressions that underly the hypothesis of the pleasure principle are so obvious that they cannot be overlooked."

There are two components of the pleasure principle that dictate the directions of our behavior. One indicates that we want to approach and get more of desirable objects and feelings; the second is that we want to avoid or withdraw from undesirable objects and negative emotions. But, to complicate matters, it is often not in our best interests to attain pleasurable goals or to avoid unwanted events *immediately*. That is, it may be functional and adaptive to forgo immediate pleasure in the pursuit of more sustained happiness. Thus, we study to attain a distant career rather than putting down our books and going to a good movie; we do not hit someone when we are angry, because it may lead to retaliation; and so on. In other words, we develop controls over our pleasure-seeking impulses; our defenses inhibit immediate goal attainment but enhance the likelihood of reaching long-term satisfactions. And to further aid in the pursuit of pleasure, if a desired goal is not attained, alternative goals may be established that partially or perhaps entirely satisfy unfulfilled needs. Unfortunately, however, it is also often the case that neither desired goals nor satisfactory substitutes are reached, and frustration is experienced.

Each step in this chain of events — from the arousal of feelings and desires to their frustration and gratification — raises a host of interrelated theoretical and empirical questions. Consider a student who must choose between studying for an exam and going out on a date. Each behavior satisfies a different set of goals related to achievement and academic success versus affiliation and social satisfaction. The student is in conflict between which behavior to choose and which motivation to pursue. What are the properties of such psychological conflict? What kinds of conflict are there? What determines how conflict is resolved? How is the student able to delay the impulse toward being with his girlfriend? The choice the student makes also has important consequences. When a decision is made, some goals are temporarily, or perhaps more permanently, frustrated. Does the desire for the unselected alternative persist? What are the possible responses to frustration? How do these responses influence our student's effectiveness? And how is the unsatisfied desire finally gratified? Through substitute behavior, or even just fantasizing about the postponed desire?

Although a great many questions about the dynamics of behavior have been raised here, the analysis of the situation is still not complete. Given a particular choice, how will the student feel after taking action? Happy? Sad? Angry? Guilty? What determines his or her emotional response? And, beyond the specific context of choice and the feelings involved, there are further questions about the effects of the tension and stress generated by the experience of conflict. Such stress can accompany the decision and become even more intense following the choice. Of course, in this example the stress might have been minimal, but consider the stress associated with a decision between maintaining a close relationship versus accepting a distant job opportunity.

This chapter is concerned with the topics of conflict, impulse control, substitution, and frustration. In the following chapter we examine emotion and stress. All of these topics are subsumed under the general heading of the dynamics of personality, or *psychodynamics*.

CONFLICT

We live in a world of conflict. Should we marry or remain single? Whom should we marry? What career should we pursue? Should we lie about a wrongdoing or honestly take our punishment? At any given moment in time there are many possible alternatives from which to choose, even in everyday activities. For example, you might be deciding now whether to stay in and study or to go join some friends. If your decision is to study, should you continue with psychology or move on to some other subject? These are conscious conflicts that do not involve any violation of social standards or norms. Other conflicts, however, involve unconscious desires and inhibitions and are of fundamental importance to personality.

Conflicts vary in strength. Some are serious and difficult to resolve, while others are relatively meaningless and easy to settle. The magnitude of a conflict is determined by a number of factors. Assume, for example, that you want to go to a movie, that there is only one movie playing that you have not seen, and that it is precisely the movie you have been waiting for. It is intuitively clear that little conflict exists in this situation. But if two movies are showing that you haven't seen, then more conflict is generated. In general, we can state that *the greater the number of alternatives available, the greater the degree of conflict* (see Berlyne, 1960).

There are other determinants of conflict magnitude in addition to number of alternatives. For example, contrast the situation in which none of the movies except one is considered good with the situation in which many of the movies have been favorably reviewed. Again, there is intuitively more conflict in the latter instance. A second law determining the magnitude of conflict therefore is: *the greater the equality in the attractiveness of the alternatives, the greater the degree of conflict.*

Now suppose you are deciding which college to attend, which job to accept, or which person to marry, as opposed to which movie to attend. Much greater conflict will be aroused in the former instances. Thus, *the greater the importance of a decision, the greater the degree of conflict.*

Temporal, Spatial, and Discriminative Conflict

There are many types of conflicts and different schemes have been proposed that group them into categories. This is an essential scientific step, for it points out the underlying similarities and differences between the various conflict types. One interesting classification scheme distinguishes temporal, spatial, and discriminative conflict (Brown, 1957).

Temporal conflict exists when the attractiveness of alternative choices changes over time. For example, an engaged couple might become more and more uncertain about their decision to marry as the date of the wedding draws near. Job shifts and moving also tend to be perceived with increasing or decreasing favorableness as the time of change approaches.

Spatial conflict varies as a function of physical distance. A teen-ager might decide to fight the neighborhood bully, for example, but as he approaches him begins to doubt the wisdom of his decision.

Discriminative conflict is best illustrated by an experiment conducted by Ivan Pavlov. Pavlov presented dogs with food following a 600-cycle-frequency tone. A second, 800-cycle-frequency tone was also presented to the animals, but was not followed by any reward. Then, on the conflict trials, a tone of 700 cycles was presented. The dogs had to decide if this was a "food" or a "no-food" tone. Pavlov reported that this conflict gave rise to emotionality and disturbance in his laboratory dogs. He compared these behaviors to the neurotic actions of humans and suggested that certain forms of mental illness might be a result of insoluble discriminative conflicts. Other investigators subsequently contended that schizophrenia can be promoted by a mother who sends both acceptance and rejection signals to a child (a *schizophrenogenic* mother), so that the child does not know if rewards or punishments will be forthcoming (Bateson, Jackson, Haley, and Weakland, 1956).

Lewin's Classification System

A more complete taxonomy of conflict has been proposed by Kurt Lewin, who is considered to be one of the founders of experimental psychodynamics. Lewin (1935) differentiated three types of conflict: approach-approach, avoidance-avoidance, and approach-avoidance. *Approach-approach conflicts* occur when there are two or more positive alternatives from which to choose: for example, the proverbial donkey choosing between two bundles of hay or someone deciding which of two award-winning movies to see. *Avoidance-avoidance conflicts* are created when a choice is confined to two or more unattractive alternatives, such as a command to either wash the dishes or vacuum the rug.

Lewin contended that approach-approach conflicts are easy to resolve and labeled them *unstable conflicts,* whereas avoidance-avoidance conflicts are difficult-to-resolve, *stable conflicts.* Lewin reasoned that, in approach-approach conflicts, as one comes closer to one of the goals, the attractiveness of that goal increases. For example, as one drives to a restaurant, enters the door, reads the menu, and finally sees the food, that food is more and more desired. Thus, in an approach-approach conflict, when an alternative is selected, its attractiveness increases, while the attractiveness of the unselected alternative decreases because one is psychologically further from it. The conflict therefore is readily resolved, as illustrated in Fig. 14.1, which shows that the difference in the relative attractiveness of alternatives increases as one comes closer to either of the goals.

On the other hand, given an avoidance-avoidance conflict (see Fig. 14.1), as one of the aversive alternatives is approached, it becomes increasingly negative. For example, anxiety increases dramatically as one gets closer and closer to the edge of a cliff; less dramatically, washing the dishes will appear increasingly unattractive as the soap and hot water are experienced. In addition, the aversiveness of the unselected alternative decreases, for one is getting psychologically further from it. This change in the perceived aversiveness of the alternatives will cause one to oscillate and repeatedly shift choices. This analysis assumes that escape from both negative alternatives is impossible. Lewin argued that one of the great disadvantages of using negative alternatives and punishments is that energy must be expended to ensure that the individual does not attempt to leave the situation, thereby avoiding both alternatives.

To test the idea that approach-approach conflicts are easier to resolve than avoidance-avoidance conflicts, Arkoff (1957) presented subjects with a number of hypothetical choices representing both types of conflict, such as "Would you rather be more attractive *or* more intelligent?" and "Would you rather be less

Figure 14.1   The attractiveness of alternatives, according to Lewin.

Should I or shouldn't I? A stable approach-avoid-ance conflict, thus making one wonder how long this young diver will remain on the board. (Peter Vandermark)

attractive *or* less intelligent?'' The time taken to make a choice or resolve the hypothetical conflicts was much less in approach-approach than in avoidance-avoidance situations.

The third type of conflict identified by Lewin, *approach-avoidance conflict,* was the basis for a well-known theory presented by Neal Miller (1944, 1959). Miller, previously discussed in Chapter 5 on learning theory approaches to personality, used learning theory terminology to explain complex conflicts.

Miller's Conflict Model

The most prevalent type of conflict is *approach-avoidance conflict,* which occurs when both positive and negative consequences are associated with the same action. For example, we like to buy new clothes, but they are expensive; we want to eat a candy bar, but it is fattening; we would like to hit people we are angry at, but this is likely to be punished. Observation of approach-avoidance conflicts often reveals ambivalent behavior; the organism approaches the desired object, only to turn away, reapproach, and so on. The behavior oscillates from approach to withdrawal and hence is labeled *ambivalent*. Miller's model is able to account for this behavior.

In accordance with Fig. 14.1, Miller assumed that the tendency to approach a positive goal, as well as the tendency to avoid a negative goal, is stronger the nearer the organism is to those goals. However, he asserted that the strength of avoidance increases more rapidly with nearness to the goal than does the strength of approach. This process is depicted in Fig. 14.2. The differential steepness of the slopes in Fig. 14.2 is based on the fact that avoidance behavior is determined, in part, by one's level of fear. Fear is a learned drive which varies as a function of one's nearness to the feared situation. For example, fear is great when one is at the edge of a cliff, or perhaps in a dark room, but decreases rapidly when one steps a few feet from the edge of the cliff or turns on a light. On the other hand, approach behavior is typically based on internal drives, such as hunger, which remain relatively constant even though the external environment may change. For these reasons, Miller posited that the avoidance tendency would be steeper than that of approach. Further inspection of the approach-avoidance conflict gradients shown in Fig. 14.2 reveals that the organism should approach the goal until reaching point X, the place where the strengths of both tendencies are equal. Beyond that point, the strength of avoidance exceeds that of approach and the organism should begin to withdraw, thus producing oscillation and the appearance of ambivalence.

Miller, Brown, and others have conducted a number of experiments to test this model. Often rats have been used as the experimental subjects, so that rather severe hours of deprivation as well as the strength of a shock could be varied. In one of the original investigations, Brown (1948) developed a technique for measuring the strength of the approach and avoidance tendencies in rats. The rats were fitted with a harness that allowed the experimenter to test how hard they

Figure 14.2   Goal strengths in approach-avoidance conflicts.

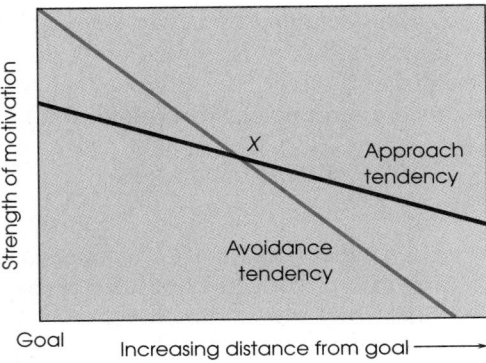

Figure 14.3   Differences in approach gradients.

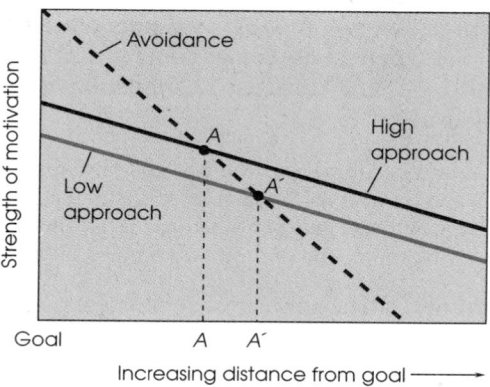

pulled. Animals had been trained in separate goal boxes either to approach food or to avoid shock and were then placed at various distances from the food or shock. As hypothesized, the strength of pull varied as a function of distance from the goal, and the distance from the shocked compartment influenced the intensity of pull more than distance from the rewarded compartment.

Other tests and derivations of the model have concerned the effects of the degree of hunger or strength of shock on conflict resolution. Figure 14.3 repeats Fig. 14.2, except that a second approach gradient has been added. The two approach gradients differ in magnitude, showing the difference in intensity of motivation caused by, for example, unequal levels of hunger. The distance between points A and A' represents the differential distance of approach to the goal. As the figure shows, the intersection of the approach and avoidance gradients occurs at a point closer to the goal when the approach desire is heightened.

The situation depicted in Fig. 14.3 has some interesting behavioral implications. Suppose, for example, that the figure represents strength differences in the aggressive approach tendencies of two individuals. Because the avoidance gradient at the goal is greater than either of the approach gradients, neither individual will engage in overt hostile actions. However, because the individual with the stronger drive comes closer to the goal, he or she experiences more fear and more conflict. Thus, the amount of fear and conflict displayed by an individual can be an index of his or her attraction to that situation. The Miller conflict model therefore can account for Freud's paradoxical observation that the intensity of avoidance behavior is often a direct reflection of the intensity of temptation.

Conflict and Displacement.   The term *displacement* refers to the observation that one's goals may change, even though the desire to reach the original goal has not subsided (see Chapter 3). Freud contended that there are "vicissitudes of the instincts''; in other words, there are a variety of objects that may satisfy an underlying wish. The most frequently cited example of such displacement activity is in the study of aggression, where it is often pointed out that someone who cannot express anger at his or her boss comes home to take it out on an unsuspecting spouse. Freud (1915, pp. 174–175) used a similar but more humorous example to illustrate displacement:

> There was a blacksmith in the village who had committed a capital offense. The Court decided that the crime must be punished; but as the blacksmith was the only one in the village and was indispensable, and as on the other hand there were three tailors living there, one of *them* was hanged instead.

Displacement activity, or the shifting of goal objects, has been incorporated into Miller's conflict model. Consider the employee angry at the boss but not directly expressing this hostility. Miller would reason that the aggressive tendency directed toward the boss is inhibited by a stronger avoidance tendency. Thus, the person responds aggressively to someone other than the boss, as depicted in Fig. 14.4. In Fig. 14.4, the horizontal or *X* axis, which represented physical (spatial) distance in previous figures, now depicts "psychological" distance or "similarity" to the figure eliciting hostility. Of course, Fig. 14.4 is a simplified analysis of what can be a very complex process, inasmuch as displacement is affected by a number of psychological factors such as previous experience with the displaced object, the availability of alternative goal satisfiers, and the like.

In situations of conflict, one often must forego a desired goal, as was the case when our hypothetical student decided to study rather than to join his girlfriend. In the next section of this chapter, we examine impulse control and factors that enhance or decrease our ability to delay gratification.

Figure 14.4   Displacement.

IMPULSE CONTROL AND DELAY OF GRATIFICATION

If all our wishes could be acted on immediately, and if appropriate goal objects existed in the external world, then there would be little conflict of any psychological import. Of course, there are different ways of satisfying desires, and there are competing wishes and goal objects, but approach-approach conflicts typically are easily resolved. Conversely, when avoidance tendencies are elicited and barriers preventing goal attainment are imposed, as is the case when there are social norms prohibiting desired actions, then the potential for severe psychological consequences exists. On the one hand, wishes may be left unfulfilled, while on the other hand, goal satisfaction might entail such great personal cost as retribution, punishment, and loss.

From the perspective of psychoanalytic theory, ego mechanisms recognize the demands of the social world and impose restraints on behavior. Ego constraints postpone goal-directed actions until external conditions are more suitable for the expression of one's drives. Repression, which was discussed in detail in Chapter 3, is the main mechanism responsible for preventing the immediate gratification of wishes. Recall that the defenses often intervene so that a wish does not enter consciousness and thus is not directly acted upon.

Ego controls are necessary if the organism is to function in society and avoid the punishment that might accompany immediate sexual or aggressive gratification. With the individual's increasing cognitive development and maturity, such controls become a virtue as well as a necessity, for the ability to delay enables one to attain highly desirable long-term goals that require the abandonment of immediate gratification. For example, studying to do well on an exam might require foregoing a pleasant social encounter, and enrollment in graduate or medical school necessitates giving up immediate monetary gain for a better position in the future. Thus, ego functions include not only the recognition of appropriate external conditions for drive expression, but also more general self-imposed constraints, or everyday "will power" (Loevinger, 1976).

Hallucinatory Images

Freud (1911) argued that in the absence of satisfying external objects, images of these objects are called forth and pleasure is attained through hallucinations or fantasy activity. Hallucinations, therefore, are one way to cope temporarily with lack of gratification; they bridge the delay between one's desires and their expression — a function frequently referred to as *time binding*.

The effects of mental representations of rewards on the ability to delay gratification have been examined experimentally by Mischel and his colleagues (Mischel, 1974a, 1974b; Mischel and Ebbesen, 1970). In these studies, children were placed in a choice dilemma in which they might have received either a smaller, immediate reward (a candy bar) or a larger reward (two candy bars) at a later time, in exchange for their cooperation at a task. A variety of factors then were manipulated to assess their effects on the choices the children made (see Chapter 5).

To examine the influence of the visual presence of the reward on delay of gratification, Mischel and Ebbesen (1970) created situations in which the delayed reward, the immediate reward, both rewards, or neither reward was in the subject's visual field during the delay period. In this study, the child could wait for the experimenter to return with the larger reward or signal for him to return and immediately receive the smaller reward. The results of this investigation are shown in Fig. 14.5. The graph clearly reveals that waiting time was maximal when neither of the rewards was visible, and minimal when both rewards could be seen. In a subsequent investigation of the effects of mental representation of a reward, the researchers devised two experimental conditions in which the rewards were not visible and the subjects were instructed to either think about the rewards or think "fun" (Mischel, Ebbesen, and Zeiss, 1972). Figure 14.6 shows that thinking about a reward retards the ability to delay gratification.

On the basis of these and other data, Mischel contended that one consequence of the mental representation of a reward object during the delay interval is frustration. The additional frustration then decreases the ability to delay gratification. Any activity that distracts the person from thinking about the reward should therefore lessen frustration and increase delay behavior. Perhaps we intuitively realize this; when we want something that is unobtainable, we may go to the movies to forget about it. Furthermore, even given the visual appearance of the desired reward, the individual may engage in coping activities that help delay gratification. For example, when children had a potential reward of pretzels and thought about them as logs or other objects, delay ability was enhanced. However, it can be contended that a choice between candy bars does not reflect any

Figure 14.5   Mean minutes of voluntary waiting time for the delayed reward in each attention condition. (From Mischel and Ebbesen, 1970, p. 333. Copyright 1970 by the American Psychological Association.)

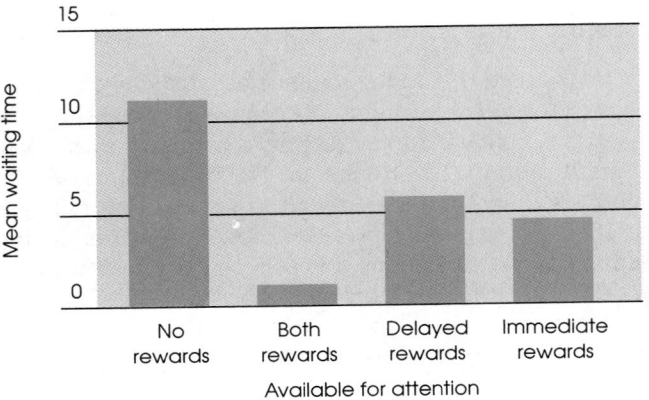

Figure 14.6   Mean minutes of voluntary waiting time for treatment conditions and controls. (From Mischel, Ebbesen, and Zeiss, 1972, p. 213. Copyright 1972 by the American Psychological Association.)

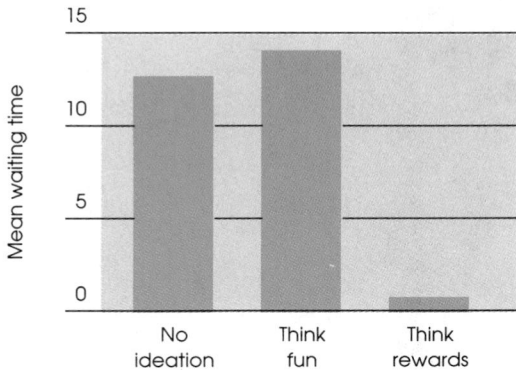

strong internalized desires and does not quite capture the problems that Freud addressed. Thus, one must be careful in the generalization of these data to more intense need situations.

In more recent research, Mischel, Shoda, and Peake (1988) contacted some of the children first used in the delay experiments ten years earlier. The children were now in their early adolescence. It was found that the subjects who were able to wait longer at the age of four or five were rated by their parents as more academically competent, verbally fluent, rational, attentive, and planful when in their teens. Mischel et al. (1988) suggest that the ingredients necessary for effective delay — ability to divert and control attention and to purposefully distract oneself from frustration — influence long-term development.

Learning Theory Approaches

It is evident from the previous discussion that, according to psychoanalytic theory, delay is an ego function determined by intrapsychic factors. Mischel (1968, p. 153) contrasted this position with that of the social learning theorists:

> According to the psychoanalytic theory of delay behavior, aroused impulses press for immediate discharge of tension through overt motoric activity. . . . The psychoanalytic approach . . . leads one to seek determinants of delay behavior in such hypothetical internal events as ego organizations and energy-binding ideations [hallucinations]. In contrast, social behavior theory . . . views manipulable social-stimulus events as the critical determinants of self-controlling behavior.

In the tradition of social learning (see Chapter 5), Bandura and Mischel (1965) examined the role of a model in altering delay behavior. These investigators first identified children who were willing to delay reward and others who sought

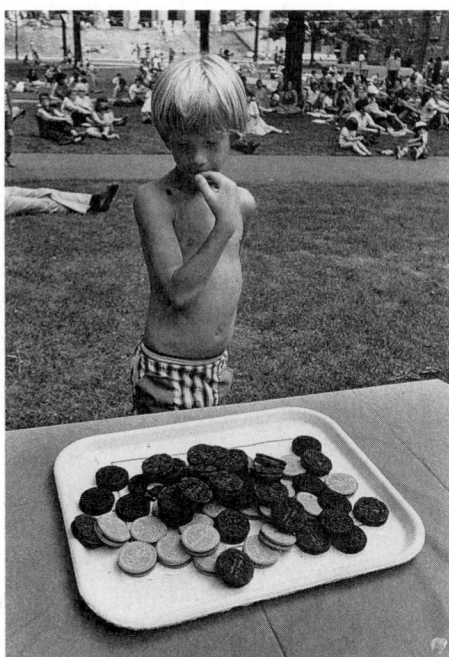

What strategies can this child use to delay gratification? (Christopher S. Johnson/Stock, Boston)

immediate gratification. The children then observed a model displaying behavior inconsistent with their own delay preferences. For example, the high-delay children observed a model choosing cheaper, plastic chess figures without delay rather than waiting one week for a more attractive chess set. In one condition the model was "live," while in a second condition the model's responses were read rather than actually observed. Both before and immediately after the model's performance, and one month later, delay of gratification was assessed. Figure 14.7, which depicts only the responses of the high-delay children, indicates that their preference for immediate, less valuable rewards increased dramatically in the model conditions. Furthermore, the influence of the live model remained effective at the one-month retest period, or postexposure, and at a related choice task (a "generalization" condition).

In addition to observational learning, there are other procedures and contingencies that can establish self-control. For example, guided by Skinnerian principles, one woman who had problems controlling her "cussing" fined herself a dollar every time she swore. This money was immediately put aside for charity. Other control techniques that manipulate the environment, like putting a lock on the refrigerator, have been used to prevent impulsive expression. And cognitive behavior modification techniques such as covert self-statements (see Chapter 5) have been used effectively to control motoric discharge ("If I miss this shot, I will not throw my racquet").

Figure 14.7

Effects of modeling on delay of gratification. (From Bandura and Mischel, 1965, p. 702. Copyright 1965 by the American Psychological Association.)

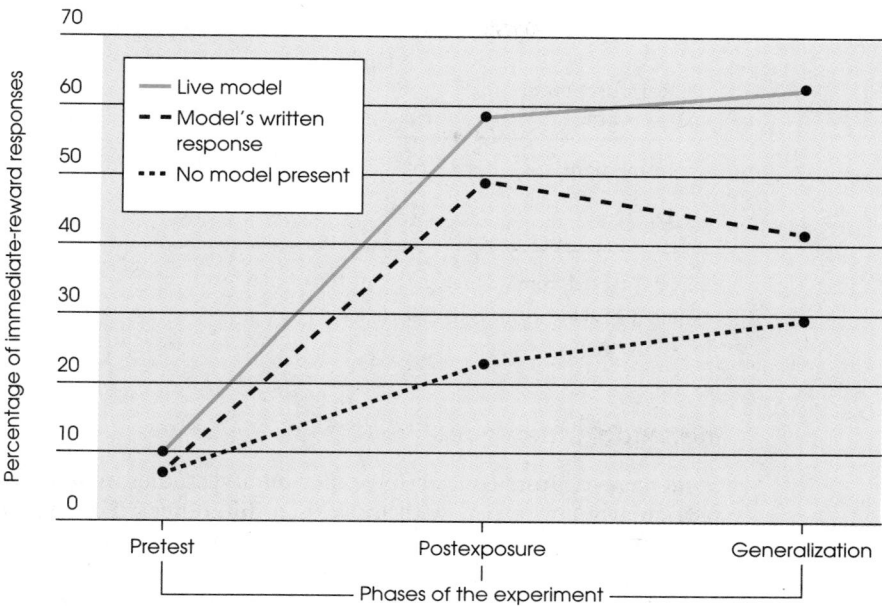

Expectancy and Delay of Gratification

Rotter's social learning theory (see Chapter 5) also has been applied to the study of delay behavior. Mahrer (1956) demonstrated that delay behavior is in part determined by the expectation of reinforcement. Children seven to nine years old were offered a choice between a smaller immediate reward and a more attractive delayed reward. Before the choice dilemma, three levels of expectancy for the receipt of a promised reward were induced. On each of five consecutive days the experimenter told the children that for performing an activity they would receive a small balloon on the following day. To develop groups of high, moderate, and low expectancy for delayed reward, this promise was kept variously 100 percent, 50 percent, or none of the time. Three days later, the same subjects were offered a choice between the immediate and the delayed reward. Furthermore, the experimenter offering the choices was either the same one (experimenter A) who conducted the training session or a person differing from A in sex and age (experimenter B). The results of this study are shown in Table 14.1 on p. 408. The table shows that the groups of subjects tested by the different experimenter (E_B) all exhibited the same delay behavior, regardless of prior training. On the other hand, responses to experimenter A (E_A) were consistent with the expectancies based on prior experiences, with higher expectancies leading to greater delay behavior.

Table 14.1   Choices of immediate and delayed reinforcement

	Expectancy					
	High		Moderate		Low	
Reinforcement choice	E_A	E_B	E_A	E_B	E_A	E_B
Immediate	6*	6	15	5	18	7
Delayed	19	14	11	15	6	15

Source: Adapted from Mahrer, 1956, p. 104.

* Number of subjects making that choice.

Individual Differences

Some investigators conducting experimental studies in delay behavior have been particularly concerned with individual differences. For example, Kagan (1966) identified reflective as opposed to impulsive children on the basis of their delay in answering difficult visual discrimination problems. Reflective children were reported as less distractible in school and displayed better attention and concentration on tasks. Subsequent work with this personality dimension suggested that not only response time, but also rate of errors, is important in distinguishing reflective from impulsive children (Kagan and Kogan, 1970). It has been speculated that impulsive children are anxious over their ability and therefore work with excess speed to remove themselves from the task situation. This results in a high rate of errors. However, children working quickly who make many errors must be distinguished from those who work with equal speed but with few errors (see Block, Block, and Harrington, 1974). Indeed, one of the contentions of the Block study was that accuracy, rather than speed, of response has important personality correlates and determinants.

SUBSTITUTION

If one's wishes are not attained, either because of conflict and impulse control or because the goal object is not available, then psychological processes are elicited to help one cope with the situation. One such process, considered in the previous section, is hallucination. Freud contended that hallucinations about goal objects serve to gratify one's wishes (although the experiments by Mischel and his associates might be considered as evidence contradicting this notion). Other fantasy activity such as dreaming (which is examined in detail in a later chapter) has also been considered to have wish-fulfillment functions. And, as discussed in the chapter on psychoanalytic theory, even such diverse behaviors as slips of the tongue and jokes were thought to reduce aggressive and sexual urges.

But perhaps the most prevalent, most adaptive way of coping with goal frustration is to establish alternative goals. Freudian theory, as has been pointed out, posits that the object of a desire may change. A forbidden, unfulfilled wish can, for example, become directed toward objects that have some similarity to the desired object yet permit expression of the original wish. Freud stated that ultimately a libidinal tendency might even be expressed in cultural activities such as painting or composing. In his analyses of Michelangelo and da Vinci, Freud contended that these great artists had strong unfulfilled sexual urges toward their mothers that were deflected into socially acceptable channels. Freud labeled this defense, included among the defense mechanisms in Chapter 3, *sublimation*.

Displacement activity, examined in the section on conflict, and also one of the defense mechanisms, concerns desires that are deflected from a primary goal because of conflict. Displacement refers to the direction of behavior, or the goals that one selects. The study of alternative goal gratification, or *substitution,* concerns a related, yet different problem; namely, does the attainment of substitute goals satisfy one's desires? That is, is the original wish partially or completely satisfied? More specifically, assume that you want to aggress against an authority figure like your father, but are prevented from doing so by conflict. Aggression is now displaced toward your brother. Is this displacement activity of motivational value; that is, are your aggressive tendencies satisfied through the substitute goal gratification? The latter question is the focus of the study of substitution.

Kurt Lewin and his students conducted a series of experiments that examined the properties and functions of substitute goals. Although these investigations were conducted nearly fifty-five years ago, they remain classics in the field. Lewin (1935, pp. 180–181) believed that substitution is manifested in many different ways.

> There is, for instance, the man who dreams of a palace and brings a few pieces of marble into his kitchen. There is the man who cannot buy a piano, but who collects piano catalogs. Again, we find the delinquent boy who knows that he will not be allowed to leave his reform school but who asks for a traveling bag as a birthday present. . . . These and a hundred other examples make us realize how important and far-reaching the problem of substitution is in regard to psychological needs as well as with reference to bodily needs such as hunger and sex.

To examine the value of substitution in a laboratory experiment, Lewin and his students first allowed their subjects, typically children, to engage in an attractive, gamelike task, such as a building activity, and then interrupted the children before the task was completed. Earlier research had established that there is a strong motivational force to return and complete such interrupted tasks. Then, before allowing the children to finish their task, the experimenters permitted them to engage in some other activity. After this, the children had the opportunity to resume the interrupted activity. If the children resumed the previously unfinished task, then the intervening activity did not serve as a substitute. But if the originally unfinished activity was not undertaken, then the intervening activity had substitute value. Thus, resumption became the behavioral indicator identifying substitute goals and their effects.

One of the first experimental studies of substitution was conducted by Lissner (1933). In her experiment, children were interrupted while making a figure from clay. Then, after they had made a different figure, they were tested for resumption. Lissner identified two factors that influence the substitute value of an activity: its similarity to the first activity and its level of difficulty. The more similar and difficult the intervening task, the greater its substitute value and the less likely the resumption of the unfinished task. Mahler (1933) gave subjects an intervening activity that could be completed in ways that differed in how closely they resembled the original, overt behavior. Subjects could think about doing the task, talk through its completion, or actually do it. In general, substitute value varied directly with the degree of reality of the substitute action, with the least substitution value provided by the imaginative task. This implies that daydreams and other fantasy activity may have little (yet *some*) value for the reduction of persisting desires.

In sum, these studies demonstrate that goals can substitute for one another. Further, some of the relevant dimensions and determinants of substitute value have been identified. There clearly are interrelationships between psychological needs, as Freud and Lewin argued. Unfortunately, while there has been some followup of the work of Lewin and his students, there has been very little recent research on the problem of substitution. One exception has been investigations of the catharsis or discharge of aggression through fantasy, particularly studies that examine the effects of violence on television. This will be discussed in detail in Chapter 18.

One should not conclude from the dearth of research on substitution that it is a minor element in the dynamics of personality. The research techniques developed by Lewin's research team were appropriate to rather minor, experimentally induced motivations and goals, such as cutting out paper dolls, making clay figures, and so on. However, making substitute choices is intrinsic to human experience; questions of the factors determining the value of substitutions are fundamental for human motivation. If we fail to make the football team but play on the baseball team, is our desire to play on the football team thereby less intense? If we aspire to be a novelist but, after a series of rejection slips, shift to a successful career in business, will the desire to write abate? Clearly there are many fundamental unanswered questions concerning the value of substitute choices, and this should be a fertile area of study for future personality psychologists.

FRUSTRATION

So far we have examined the dynamics of conflict and how coping with conflict is aided by means of impulse control and the establishment of substitute goals.

However, goals must frequently be forsaken. In those cases, there is likely to be frustration as well as a number of more well-defined emotions, including anger, disappointment, and guilt.

Frustration has diverse meanings for psychologists. It may refer to an independent variable, or experimental manipulation. Often this involves blocking the attainment of a goal, inducing failure, or delivering a personal insult. Hence, the definition refers to the situation. Performance of a "frustrated" group is then compared to the performance of a "nonfrustrated" control group. Frustration may also refer to a dependent variable, in which case the researcher measures the amount of frustrated behavior. For example, one might examine whether individuals high in anxiety display more frustrated behavior than persons low in anxiety. This definition therefore refers to the condition of the organism. Finally, frustration frequently pertains to an intervening variable, or a complex process inferred from certain observable responses. For example, on the basis of observed aggressive behavior, one might conclude that an individual is frustrated.

In the 1940s, 1950s, and 1960s a good deal of research was done on frustration. In laboratory situations the association of frustration to other variables such as aggression, fixation, enhanced goal strivings, and regression was studied. The relationship of frustration to aggression was found to be a complex one, and it is documented more thoroughly in Chapter 18.

In recent years, the relationship of frustration to the other variables has been studied in the context of other issues. The relationship of frustration to both fixation and enhanced goal strivings is being examined within the framework of feelings of helplessness, competence, and mastery (see Chapter 17). The relationship of frustration to regression is now being studied within the framework of stress (see Chapter 15).

Fixation is the tendency of an organism to persist in responding the same way even when those responses are ineffectual in achieving a goal. Fixated behavior is maladaptive, in that it does not flexibly respond to the demands of the situation or task and it can often be seen in people experiencing psychological problems. In Maier's (1949) early research with animals, frustration was induced by giving rewards and punishments to animals in a completely random fashion, no matter what they did. Maier found that frustration increased the probability of animals responding in a persistently maladaptive manner.

Enhanced goal strivings refers to the tendency of some individuals to respond to frustrating obstacles by enhancing their efforts and by being more creative. Both fixation and enhanced goal strivings now appear to be a function of whether an individual feels helpless or competent when he or she encounters frustration (see Chapter 17). They do not appear to be a function of frustration per se.

Regression is the tendency to repeat earlier, more primitive modes of behavior when under stress. An example might be running home to mother when one experiences difficult circumstances. Studies by Lewin and his colleagues (e.g., Barker, Dembo, and Lewin, 1943) found that children's play became more primitive when they were under stress. More up-to-date research (see Chapter 15) has found that stress can lead to lower levels of thinking — thinking in more concrete rather than abstract terms.

Summary

1. Three historical movements in psychology: behaviorism, Gestalt psychology, and psychoanalysis have influenced the study of psychodynamics.

2. The strength of a *conflict* is in part determined by the number of available alternatives, the relative attractiveness of those alternatives, and the importance of the decision involved.

3. *Approach-approach conflicts* involve a choice between two or more attractive alternatives; *avoidance-avoidance conflicts* involve a choice between two or more aversive alternatives. The latter are especially difficult to resolve.

4. *Approach-avoidance conflicts* occur in situations where an alternative has both positive and negative characteristics; they tend to produce ambivalent behavior. According to Miller, the observed ambivalence can be accounted for by postulating that the gradient of avoidance, or the change in motivational strength as a function of distance from the goal, is steeper than the gradient of approach.

5. Evidence suggests that the visual presence of desired goals increases frustration and reduces the ability to delay gratification. Hallucinatory images, the behavior of models, social engineering techniques, and expectancy of future goal attainment all influence delay of gratification.

6. *Substitution* refers to the gratification provided by goals attained in place of the original one. Substitution is greatest when the substitute goal is similar to the original goal and is actually attained, rather than imagined.

7. *Frustration* can refer to an independent (manipulated), an intervening (inferred), or a dependent (measured) variable. It produces behaviors as disparate as aggression, fixation, regression, and enhanced goal striving.

Thought Questions

1. Think of some conflicts you have had recently. Can you classify them according to any of the types of conflict discussed in this chapter? If so, does your classification help you to understand the dynamics of your conflict better?

2. Individuals trapped in an approach-avoidance conflict sometimes resolve the conflict after a few drinks. How does the ingestion of alcohol make conflict resolution possible?

3. In what ways are the concepts of conflict, frustration, displacement, and substitution interrelated?

Emotion and Stress

The topics examined in the prior chapter, particularly conflict, delay of gratification, and frustration, are all intimately related to the study of emotion and stress. Certainly these are negative states — they are experiences we generally would prefer not to undergo, and they create stress. In addition, as will be seen, actions are guided by either current emotional states, such as guilt and shame, or by the anticipation of positive and negative emotional outcomes. Hence, emotions are a central topic in the study of personality and psychodynamics, as are the stresses that we all face in everyday life.

In this chapter we first consider the definition of emotion. We then consider different theoretical perspectives on emotion, including arousal theories, cognitive theories, and recent developments in theories of emotion. We next consider the structure of emotion, including individual differences in emotional reactivity, and move on to consider mood. We conclude with an examination of stress and methods of coping with stress.

EMOTION

Emotion has increasingly become an important topic of study for psychologists (Thompson, 1993). For many years emotion was seen primarily in terms of its capacity to be problematic and disruptive of conscious, rational self-control. Or, emotion was seen as a relatively peripheral or secondary aspect of behavior. Current views of emotion, however, stress its often central role in the organization and activation of behavior. For *Star Trek* aficionados, the shift in psychologists' perceptions of emotion can be likened to the shift from the character Spock in the original *Star Trek* series, for whom emotion was a distracting, irrational annoyance, to Data in the recent *Star Trek: The Next Generation* series, who was fascinated by emotion and saw much value in the capacity to feel (Todd and Bohart, 1994).

Definition

The word *emotion* is derived from the Latin *emovere* ("to move out"). Young (1943), as noted in Cofer and Appley (1964, p. 25), described how the word *emotion* found its way into the field of psychology:

> Originally the word meant a moving out of one place into another, in the sense of a migration. Thus: "The divers emotions of that people (the Turks)" (1603). . . . The word [then] came to mean a moving, stirring, agitation, perturbation, and was used in a strictly physical sense. Thus: "Thunder . . . caused so great an

413

Emotion in the air" (1708). . . . This physical meaning was transferred to political and social agitation, the word coming to mean *tumult,* popular disturbance. Thus: "There were . . . great stirres and emocions in Lombardye". . . . Finally, the word came to be used to designate any agitated, vehement, or excited mental state of the individual. Thus: "The joy of gratification is properly called an emotion" (1762).

An array of emotion-related terms have been distinguished by psychologists, including affect, feeling, evaluation, mood, and, of course, emotion. In this chapter we will use these synonymously, with the exception of mood. Mood is considered of longer duration than an affect and it is not centered around a particular object or event. Thus, moods may be thought of as diffuse background experiences. But what about affects, or emotions, or feelings?

Averill (1982) points out that emotions are interpreted as passions, rather than actions. An action is something a person does deliberately. A passion, however, is something the person suffers. Thus, a disease is a "passion," and it is of interest to note that the words passion, patient, and passivity all stem from the same root. Hence, a person is "gripped" by fear, "falls" in love, is "torn" by jealousy, is "dragged down" by grief, and so on. In these examples, something happens to the person that does not appear to be subject to volitional control.

A number of distinguishing characteristics are also associated with emotions. Not all emotions are described by all the characteristics, but if all the characteristics are evident, then an emotional state can be inferred with some certainty.

1. Emotions have a positive or negative experiential quality. That is, they are something the person likes and wants to get more of (joy, love, pride) or something the person dislikes and wants to be rid of (sadness, hatred, guilt).

2. The positive and negative characteristics vary in magnitude. Thus, one can feel a little or a great deal of happiness, somewhat sad or very sad, and so on.

3. The feelings might be accompanied by certain facial expressions and body postures. Smiling often accompanies positive emotions; curled lips and tightened facial muscles are linked with anger; and pride may be displayed with an upright posture.

4. The emotions signal certain types of behavior. Thus, for example, one strikes out in order to "eliminate" the object of anger; gratitude gives rise to a reciprocal favor; and so on. Tomkins (1970) has proposed that emotions, not drives or desires, are the chief movers of behavior. He made his point powerfully with the following anecdote (1970, pp. 101–102):

Consider anoxic deprivation. Almost any interference with normal breathing will immediately arouse the most desperate gasping for breath. Is there any motivational claim more urgent than the demand of one who is drowning or choking to death for want of air? Yet it is not simply the imperious demand for oxygen that we observe under such circumstances. We also are observing the rapidly mounting panic ordinarily recruited whenever the air supply is suddenly jeopardized. . . . We have only to change the rate of anoxic deprivation to change the nature of the recruited affect. . . . Thus, in the Second World War, those pilots who refused to wear their oxygen masks at 30,000 feet suffered a more gradual anoxic deprivation. They did not panic for want of oxygen. They became euphoric. It was the affect of enjoyment which the more slowly developing anoxic signal recruited. Some of these men, therefore, met their death with smiles on their lips.

5. Emotions often follow particular thoughts. For example, if you fail an exam because you believe that others hindered you, anger is a likely reaction; success ascribed to help from others elicits gratitude; both success and failure believed to be due to luck bring about surprise; and so on. Thus, one's feelings are determined in part by one's thoughts. The subjective interpretation, not the objective facts, determines emotions. For example, one may fail because of insufficient studying, yet anger (rather than, say, guilt and self-blame) is experienced if the failure is believed to be due to the teacher's bias.

This complexity in the definition and determination of an emotion reminds one of a story about a new student first visiting a university. The student is given a tour and told "This is the administration building; this is the student union; this is the gymnasium; . . . " After the tour is over, the student asks: "But where is the university?" In a similar manner, the antecedent thoughts, the facial expression, the behavioral consequence, and so on of an emotion can be pointed out. But the emotion itself is an amalgam; it represents the entire system and the way in which the components are organized.

One final definitional issue should be addressed, namely, the distinction between a "cold" thought ("This is a table") and a "hot" emotion ("I feel angry"). Intuitively, the condition of the person in these two contexts differs. But what if one is described as relaxed, or curious, or tired, or interested, or abandoned? When these terms are applied, is the individual in a "cold" cognitive state or in a "hot" emotional state?

Emotion theorists differ on the answer to this question. For example, some have considered "interest" to be a very basic emotion, while others do not even classify "interest" as an emotion. In one investigation attempting to resolve this issue, Clore, Ortony, and Foss (1987) searched for a criterion that distinguishes emotional labels from other words. They proposed that "genuine" emotions are equally judged as emotions when presented in the context of feeling or being. For example, one can be described as feeling angry or being angry, as feeling proud or being proud, and in both instances the label of emotion is judged as equally applicable. But other words, such as interested, are not equally judged as emotions when accompanied by the states of feeling and being. Feeling interested, for example, is considered more of an emotional state than being interested, which is thought of as a cognitive state. Of course, there remain grey areas, but this is an important step in distinguishing between emotional and nonemotional labels.

Areas of Study

The study of emotion, like the study of the entire field of personality, is quite diverse and mirrors the subdivisions of the field of personality. Some researchers have been interested in the evolutionary and biological determinants of emotional states and expression, as previously reviewed in Chapter 1. There it was indicated that some emotional expressions appear to be universal, hence implicating genetic or inborn influences. Others have examined the cultural determinants of emotions and emotional expression. It is known, for example, that overt expressions of joy are often masked in Thailand, consistent with their tendency to be very controlled, as discussed in Chapter 2. Different cultures have different "display rules," including, for example, what amount of grief is appropriate at funerals depending on the genetic closeness with the person who has died. Hochschild (1983) has even shown that different occupational subcultures within the United States, such as flight attendants, are in part paid to feel, or at least pretend to feel, certain emotions such as cheerfulness.

Still other schools of emotional thought examine the structure of emotions. How should emotions be classified or taxonomized? How many dimensions of emotions are there? This is quite similar to the search for the basic dimensions of personality structure and the fundamental trait dimensions. Yet others study the function of emotions and their role as instigators of behavior. And finally, there are general emotion theorists who consider what emotions "are" and attempt to describe all emotional states with a few general principles.

In the following pages, we will first consider two theoretical approaches in the field, arousal theories and cognitive theories, and then briefly consider some recent theoretical developments and controversies over the nature of emotion.

AROUSAL THEORIES

The concept of arousal has been one of the most dominant themes in the study of emotion and is the basis for various theories of emotion. Arousal refers to the intensity, state of activation, or general drive level characterizing an individual.

An early theory of emotion specified that too high an activation level would result in overexcitement, while too low a level would produce depression. Furthermore, emotions were believed to lead to either behavioral organization or disorganization, depending on the intensity of the emotion or the person's level of arousal. Schlosberg (1954, pp. 82–83) illustrated this position with the following vignette:

> [A sleeping man] . . . is near the zero level of action. . . . As a result of this general condition, he doesn't respond to ordinary stimuli; he is unconscious.
>
> Now let the alarm clock ring. . . . The individual is awake and responsive to stimulation. . . . Let us assume that our hero has reached an optimum level of activation by 10:00 A.M. He is alert, and responds efficiently to his environment. But now he finds that a book he needs is missing from his shelf. This frustration

produces an increment in level of activation, perhaps not high enough at first to be dignified by the name of anger. But as he continues to search for the book the level of activation builds up until he is "blind with rage."

This conception of emotions, however, proved to be inadequate. First of all, emotions do not necessarily disrupt behavior. As indicated in Tomkins's quote about pilots, even emotions of great intensity may be quite adaptive and survival relevant. Equally important, given the same level of arousal, there are different emotional reactions. For example, high arousal might be accompanied by intense hate, intense love, or excitement. Arousal is therefore not a sufficient explanation of experienced emotions; it does not provide the conceptual tools to distinguish between emotions.

Schachter (1964) and Schachter and Singer (1962) supplemented arousal theory so that it could differentiate between emotions. They proposed that emotions are a function of two factors: level of arousal and cognitions about the arousing situation. In real-life situations the situational cues that arouse an organism also provide the information necessary for understanding the event. For example, the appearance of a birthday cake may heighten arousal and act as a stimulus for positive affect (joy); the sight of a gun is likely to cause heightened arousal and act as a cue for fear. However, in laboratory settings, Schachter and his colleagues were able to manipulate arousal and cognitive factors independently and thereby study their joint effect on emotional expression.

In the best-known of their studies, Schachter and Singer (1962) injected subjects with epinephrine (an activating agent that often produces autonomic arousal and a general "high" feeling), under the guise of studying "how vitamin supplements affect the visual skills" (p. 382). Some subjects were told of the effects of the drug and could thus appropriately label the source of their feelings. But other subjects were either uninformed or misinformed about the drug's effects, and control subjects were injected with a placebo. The subjects then awaited their "visual test" in the presence of a stooge subject. The stooge either acted in a very euphoric manner or feigned anger at some personal inquiries that were part of a questionnaire administered during the waiting period. During this interval, the subjects' behaviors were observed and rated for euphoria or anger. The main reported findings were that uninformed, epinephrine-injected subjects (aroused, but "unlabeled") were relatively angrier in the anger-inducing situation and relatively more euphoric when the stooge acted in a euphoric manner than control subjects. Thus, emotion is a function of arousal level, and individuals in an aroused state may experience disparate emotions as a function of the social (cognitive) situation in which they find themselves.

Schachter's theory suggests that emotional experience results from the following sequence:

1. There is a bodily reaction (arousal).
2. The individual becomes aware of this reaction.
3. There is a need to seek a reason or explanation of the reaction.

4. An external cue is identified and the internal reaction is labeled. This labeling provides the quality or the naming of the emotional feeling and is thus a key determinant of experienced emotions.

A number of other so-called "misattribution" paradigms have evolved to study emotional experience. In an experiment by Nisbett and Schachter (1966), subjects were given a placebo after being told that they were about to receive a series of electric shocks. All of the subjects were informed that the placebo had side-effects. In one condition, the side-effects were described as tremors, shaky hands, pounding heart, and other effects identical with symptoms of fear arousal. In a second condition, the side-effects were described as itching, headache, and other reactions unrelated to fear. Subjects were then given a series of shocks that progressively increased in intensity. The dependent variables included the point at which pain was first experienced and the intensity at which the shock was reported to be unendurable. The data revealed that, within the range of shock at which the subjects reasonably could attribute their arousal symptoms to the two possible causal sources (pill or shock), the individuals in the pill-attribution condition reported that they first experienced pain at a higher level of intensity and had a higher tolerance level than subjects who could attribute their arousal reactions only to the fear of shock. That is, the misattribution of the fear symptoms (which were objectively due only to the shock) to the pill resulted in a reduction of fear itself.

Studies in the aggression area have shown the influence of misattribution on hostile responding and feelings of anger (see Rule and Neasdale, 1976). In these studies, a subject is treated badly by another (typically, a confederate). In addition, there is heightened arousal from an extraneous source, such as loud noise, erotic stimuli, or physical exercise. Under the heightened arousal conditions, angered subjects acted more aggressively than subjects who lacked additional arousal. However, the additional arousal did not have this effect if it was attributed to its true source (see Zillman, 1978).

The arousal-plus-cognition theory of emotions proposed by Schachter has been severely challenged (see Marshall and Zimbardo, 1979; Maslach, 1979, and Reisenzein, 1983). These investigators pointed out some of the weaknesses in the data analysis carried out by Schachter and Singer and were unable to replicate their reported results. In addition, Maslach and Marshall and Zimbardo offered the following strong objections to the Schachter position:

1. Unexplained arousal is akin to free-floating anxiety and has a negative quality, rather than being a neutral state to which any emotional label can be applied.

2. When individuals seek to explain a state of arousal, they do not use merely the behavior of others in their environment. Rather, many other sources of information are called on, particularly their own personal histories. That is, they search for prior occasions on which they felt this negative arousal state to explain its occurrence now. The behavior of others may dictate or suggest

how one should behave in the situation, but it does not provide information for why one feels as one does. For example, if a confederate were behaving in a completely inappropriate manner, the subject would not use this action to infer something about his or her own emotional state. In this instance, the attribution for the confederate's behavior may not be at all applicable to the subject.

A number of other investigations contradict Schachter's position and suggest that cognitions are sufficient to produce emotional behavior. To demonstrate that the energizing, physiological effects of arousal do not influence emotional expression, Valins (1966) presented fraudulent information to his subjects. At times the subjects overheard bogus heart-rate information indicating that they were in a heightened state of arousal while viewing slides of seminude females. After viewing the stimuli, the subjects rated the attractiveness of the nudes. It was found that the nudes associated with a perceived change in heart rate were rated more attractive than the pictures of nudes not linked with this bogus information. Valins therefore concluded that internal events such as arousal act only as a source of information to the actor; actual arousal is not necessary for emotional experience.

Further evidence that arousal is not necessary for the experience of emotion comes from recent studies of spinal cord injured patients (Chwalisz, Diener, and Gallagher, 1988). This injury prevents autonomic feedback to the brain, depending on the degree of the injury. According to Schachter's theory of emotion, these individuals should not experience emotion, or should experience it in greatly reduced intensity. However, Chwalisz et al. (1988) report intense emotional feelings, thus contradicting the Schachter theory and some earlier studies that were not well-controlled.

The data from Valins (1966), Chwalisz et al. (1988), and others suggest that cognitions are sufficient to produce emotional behavior. Thus, we turn to the cognitive (at times called "structural") approach to emotional experience.

COGNITIVE THEORIES

The cognitive position concerning emotions is relatively straightforward — emotions depend on the interpretation or meaning of an event. Thus, "cold" knowledge, or "hot" appraisal (which includes an interpretation of the personal significance of an event) determine feelings (Lazarus and Smith, 1988).

Consider, for example, a simple classification of emotions proposed by Mowrer (1960). Mowrer distinguished between situations connoting increases or decreases in the likelihood of undergoing positive or negative experiences. Increases in the perceived likelihood of experiencing positive events gives rise to hope, while decreases in this estimate produce disappointment. Considering negative events, increased likelihood promotes fear, while decreases in their anticipated appearance produces relief (see Fig. 15.1). Note, then, that the only

Figure 15.1

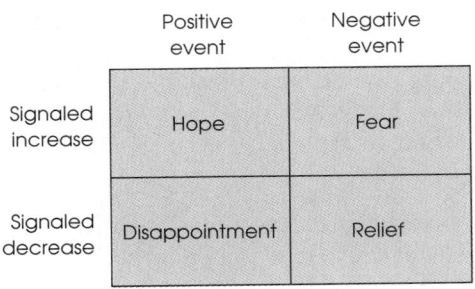

Mowrer's (1960) analysis of four emotions.

determinants of emotion are cognitions about the change in probability of an event and the perception of the positivity of that event. Arousal is not discussed as a determinant of these emotions.

The scheme proposed by Mowrer (1960) is obviously limited in that it addresses only four among the many, many emotions. In a similar manner, Higgins, Strauman, and Klein (1986) have developed a classification scheme that examines four emotions, but the emotions are quite different from those addressed by Mowrer.

Like Mowrer, Higgins et al. first differentiate two cognitive determinants of emotion. They state that the self is differentiated according to an "ideal" self (how one would ideally like to be) and an "ought" self (a representation of the attributes that someone should possess; see Chapter 10). They also distinguish between the frames of reference according to which one is judged—from the perspective of the self or from the perspective of others. This again results in a 2 × 2 classification scheme, as shown in Figure 15.2. Figure 15.2 reveals that if there is a discrepancy between an ideal and a perceived actual self when judged from one's personal point of view, then dissatisfaction is experienced. Thus, for example, if one would like to be smarter than he or she is, then the affect is to feel dissatisfied. However, when this shortcoming is considered from the viewpoint of others, then one experiences shame. Turning next to the ought self, if one thinks he or she is less honest than should be, then guilt is felt. However, if judged from the perspective of others, then the emotional experience is insecurity. Note then, that just as Mowrer proposed, a simple division of thinking is brought creatively to bear on a small subset of feelings.

Figure 15.2

	Ideal self	Ought self
Judged by Self	Dissatisfaction	Guilt
Judged by Others	Shame	Insecurity

Four emotions as interpreted by Higgins et al. (1986).

When comparing the disparate emotions addressed by Mowrer (1960) and Higgins et al. (1986), one becomes aware of the difficulties of a cognitive approach to emotion: one must be able to specify which cognitions are linked to which emotions. Inasmuch as there are myriads of pertinent thoughts, there also must be classification systems that reduce the number of thoughts to underlying dimensions, yet this classification system must remain rich and diverse enough to account for a wide range of emotions. Mowrer and Higgins et al. had rather sparse classification systems, based respectively on dimensions of changes in probability of an event as well as perceived valence of the event, and types of self and perspective of evaluation. Other theorists have developed more complex cognitive schemes, and thus have been able to account for more emotions. However, these systems also have only met with partial success.

An Attributional Approach to Emotions

Attribution theory was previously introduced in this text when traits and the trait-state distinction were discussed. And it will be elaborated in the following chapters on perceived responsibility and achievement motivation. Here, we want to consider how attribution theorists relate their ideas to emotion (see Weiner, 1985, 1986).

Attribution theory is concerned with perceptions of causality. This approach embraces two basic questions: First, how are causal beliefs reached? For example, how does one "know" that failure was due to lack of ability, as opposed to insufficient effort? The second question relates to the function of attributions. For example, what difference does it make, or what are the consequences, of an attribution to low ability as opposed to lack of effort?

Attribution theorists have argued that causes such as ability and effort can be compared and contrasted on three dimensions of thought: locus (is the cause inside or outside of the person?); stability (is the cause temporary or stable?); and controllability (is the cause something the person can volitionally change?). Ability (or aptitude) typically is construed as inside the person, stable, and uncontrollable, while effort also is thought of as internal to the person, but unstable and controllable. Each of the causal dimensions has been related to particular emotions and actions.

1. *Locus of causality.* It has been argued that internal attributions for success are necessary for the experience of pride. Thus, for example, one feels proud if high performance on an exam is attributed to ability or effort. However, if that high performance was because the exam was very easy (all the other students also did well), then pride will not be felt. Pride, in turn, is a reinforcer that increases the likelihood that similar actions will be undertaken again. Hence, attribution of success in achievement domains to ability and/or effort will raise the likelihood that the individual will engage in future achievement actions.

The relation between internal attributions and self-esteem is part of common knowledge and is used in everyday interactions. Thus, when rejecting a person for a date, the rejector does not say: "You are too (tall, short, fat, thin, dumb, etc.)." It is known that these internal attributions will hurt the feelings of the rejected other. Instead, an external attribution (and perhaps a lie) is communicated that does not result in a loss of self-esteem for the other (e.g., "My parents are in town; The teacher is giving an exam tomorrow") (see Folkes, 1982).

2. *Causal stability.* The stability of a cause connotes whether the cause might change in the future. Failure at math attributed to low math aptitude, for example, intimates that the cause will not change so that there will be future failures. On the other hand, failure perceived as due to lack of effort gives rise to the belief that the future might produce a better outcome, inasmuch as effort can be augmented. It therefore follows that hope (failure ascribed to something unstable) and hopelessness (failure ascribed to something unchanging) are related to perceived causal stability.

3. *Causal controllability.* Some causes, such as effort and strategy, can be volitionally changed. On the other hand, causes such as aptitude, the weather conditions, luck, etc. cannot be willfully altered. Perceived controllability relates to a variety of affects including:

   a. *Anger.* If negative self-related outcomes are controllably caused by others, then anger is experienced. One is angry at a roommate who has not cleaned the house, at others for lying, and so on. Anger gives rise to the desire to "eliminate" the other. This association also is part of common knowledge. Hence, if one has broken a social contract by, for example, arriving late for an appointment, an uncontrollable reason is communicated (e.g., "The traffic was heavy"). One would not reveal "I took my time because it was a nice day," for this would arouse anger.

   b. *Pity.* Pity is experienced when a victim has no control over his or her fate. Thus, we pity the elderly, the sick, those struck by natural disasters, etc. Pity (sympathy) gives rise to desires to help others, to put the situation back into a state of balance.

   c. *Guilt.* Guilt is linked to self-blame regarding the violation of moral codes and values. Thus, one is guilty for lying, or cheating, or other situations in which there was personal controllability. Guilt gives rise to the desire to make amends; under usual conditions, therefore, it is a positive motivator.

   d. *Shame.* Unlike guilt, shame is associated with uncontrollable causes. Thus, failure because of lack of aptitude produces shame and humiliation. Shame tends to produce withdrawal; one wants to "curl up in a ball." At times it is difficult to distinguish guilt from shame, inasmuch as both are negative self-evaluations. However, in addition to the disparities in perceived controllability, there are other differentiating characteristics of these two emotions (see Table 15.1 on p. 423).

Table 15.1   Comparison of Guilt and Shame

	Guilt	Shame
Antecedents		
Audience	Not necessary	Necessary
Sanctions	Internal	External
Source	Action of self	Action or characteristic of self
Cause	Controllable	Uncontrollable
Experience and consequence	Seek control, make amends	Submission, feel inferior, helpless, withdrawal
Achievement attribution	Lack of effort	Lack of ability
Affect from other	Anger	Pity

There are linkages between anger and guilt, as well as between pity and shame. If one conveys anger to another, and that anger is accepted, then the receiver of this emotional communication should feel guilty. Similarly, communicated pity tends to give rise to shame and embarrassment. Helen Keller is said to have stated: "I do not want your pity," for she realized that this brought about humiliation and task withdrawal. These associations are shown in Figure 15.3 at the bottom of this page.

In sum, attribution theorists have provided a classification system of thoughts that is able to account for a variety of affects. Of course, many emotions are not interpretable from an attributional point of view. Nevertheless, this conception is able to incorporate some of the most prevalent of the human emotions.

Appraisal Approach to Emotions

Attributions are one type of *appraisal*—they refer to the meaning a person imposes on the environment (see Lazarus, 1982). But attributions are only one

Figure 15.3

Attribution

	Lack of effort	Lack of ability
Self-generated emotion	Guilt	Shame
Other-generated emotion	Anger	Pity

Self- and other-affected consequences of failure due to lack of effort versus lack of ability.

among many possible types of appraisal, each with emotional significance. Smith and Ellsworth (1985, 1987) have proposed eight dimensions of appraisal in differentiating emotional responses. The dimensions are:

1. pleasantness: the extent to which a situation is perceived positively
2. anticipated effort: the extent to which the person feels effort is needed
3. attentional activity: the extent to which the person wants to attend
4. certainty: the extent to which the person understands what will happen
5. responsibility: who brought about the situation
6. control: who the person perceives is controlling the situation
7. legitimacy: the extent to which the situation is perceived as fair or unfair
8. perceived obstacles: the extent to which the person perceives problems that hamper goal attainment

These dimensions have been found to be associated with (produce) a wide variety of emotional experience. For example, it has been reported that hope is correlated with appraisals of personal control, certainty, and anticipated effort. Surprise, on the other hand, is associated with uncertainty and external control. It is evident that the appraisal approach, by including many dimensions of thinking, is the most complex of the cognitive approaches presented thus far. However, as might be anticipated, it is in an early stage of development.

RECENT DEVELOPMENTS IN THEORIES OF EMOTION

Currently there is a great deal of ferment in the field of emotion studies. Some hold that while cognitions can and do influence emotional experience, the cognition and emotion systems are fundamentally separate (Posner and Rothbart, 1989; Zajonc, 1980), at least at the neurological level. On the other hand, a number of theorists argue that emotional experience and expression are heavily influenced by learning and sociocultural factors (Thompson, 1993).

Most of the recent views on emotion adopt an integrative stance, seeing emotional experience as a complex *system* in which biologically-based body states such as physiological arousal, expressive motor behaviors such as facial expressions, and patterns of activation in the body and in the nervous system interact with cognitions, perceptions, and memories to create a particular emotional reaction (Greenberg and Safran, 1987; Leventhal, 1984). Therefore, the body, learning, culture, and cognition can all play a role in a given emotional experience.

Emotions are also seen by many as being a product of evolution and therefore as having a biological basis (Izard, 1992). This implies that emotions are not merely distracting annoyances to effective functioning but biologically adaptive; and several theorists hold that emotions organize and activate the organism to take adaptive action. Frijda and Swagerman (1987) feel that "emotions are parts of a provision for ensuring the safeguarding and satisfaction of the [organism's] goals" (p. 237).

While there have been many recent developments in the study of emotion, consensus on its exact nature has yet to be reached.

THE STRUCTURE OF EMOTION

Basic Emotions

Rather than asking about the dimensions of emotions, some have suggested that there are "basic" or fundamental emotions, with the other emotions derived from these. Based on his study of facial expressions and observations of children, Izard (1977) suggested ten fundamental emotions: interest, enjoyment, surprise, distress, anger, disgust, contempt, fear, shame/shyness, and guilt. Quite similarly, as discussed briefly in Chapter 1, Ekman and Friesen (1975) isolated six primary emotions — fear, surprise, disgust, anger, happiness, and sadness (see Highlight 15.1 on the emotion of disgust).

In more recent research based on emotional classifications by subjects, Shaver and his colleagues (e.g., Shaver, Schwartz, Kirson, and O'Connor, 1987) have identified six basic clusters of emotion: love, joy, surprise, anger, sadness, and fear. Included, for example, within the fear category are labels such as alarm, fright, horror, panic, dread, etc., while sadness incorporates emotions such as depression, despair, grief, sorrow, misery, etc. According to Shaver et al., emotions are represented mentally and are grouped into categories of different inclusiveness, just as lounge chair, chair, and furniture represent different levels of abstractness. The basic emotions they identified are the most abstract categories of grouping.

However, there are those who question whether there are any emotions that could be considered basic (Ortony and Turner, 1990). For instance, Ortony and Turner note that different theorists produce different lists of basic emotions. Even the evidence that various facial expressions are associated with discrete emotional states (see Chapter 1) is being challenged by recent research that does not find such clear relationships in young children (Thompson, 1993). Instead of experiencing discrete, separable emotions, some suggest that we experience subtly nuanced blends of emotional states (Thompson, 1993).

Therefore, while it is probably safe to say that most theorists still believe that there are basic emotions, the issue may be more complex than previously thought. If there are basic emotions, there does appear to be some convergence that fear, anger, surprise, and a positive general emotion such as happiness are among them.

◢ **Highlight 15.1** ▰▰▰▰▰▰▰▰▰▰▰▰▰▰▰▰▰▰▰

Experiences of Disgust

Rozin and Fallon (1987) have recently reported research on the emotion
of disgust. In a series of studies they and their colleagues have found that
individuals: prefer not to drink a glass of juice in which a sterilized
cockroach has been placed and then removed; prefer not to consume
chocolate fudge shaped as dog feces; prefer not to wear a clean, laundered
shirt of someone whom they dislike, such as Hitler; prefer not to drink
from a bowl of soup that they have spit in with their own saliva; prefer not
to lick their own blood from a bandage (though they will lick fresh blood
from a pricked finger); prefer to hold a rubber drain mat in their lips
rather than a piece of rubber imitation vomit from a novelty store; and
prefer not to eat soup out of a brand-new bed pan nor to eat soup stirred
by a brand-new fly swatter.
  Rozin and Fallon believe that the emotion of disgust is ultimately
based on the eating of food and includes as an important part the avoidance of contamination. They claim that virtually all the above reactions
are based on a kind of superstitious avoidance of contamination, and they
note that individuals tend to base such reactions more on the laws of
magical thinking than on strict rationality.

Individual Differences in
Emotional Reactivity

People differ consistently in the intensity of their emotional responses (see Larson
and Diener, 1985, 1987). We all know of individuals who seem to be highly
emotional and react to each situation as though it were a matter of life and death,
while others are quite "cool" in the face of either great adversity or great gain.
Research has shown that the same individuals who react so strongly to positive
events also react strongly to negative events. Furthermore, individual differences
in affective intensity are stable over time and across situations.
  What might account for this emotional difference? Larson, Diener, and Cropanzano (1987) suggested that particular cognitions augment the intensity of
emotionality. They contend that tendencies to personalize events (overestimate
the degree that events are related to themselves and be excessively absorbed in
personal meanings), to selectively attend to the most emotional aspects of events,
and to see the event as quite general (or "blowing the situation out of proportion")
increase the level of emotional responding. Research has supported these hypoth-

eses, thus documenting that not only do cognitions determine the direction or kind of feeling that is experienced, but also the intensity of that experience.

A quite different approach to the issue of individual differences in affective intensity has been taken by Linville (1982). The following situation will help to illustrate her viewpoint. Assume that there are a number of important goals in your life that you are now undertaking—be a good student; have a well-developed social life; become accomplished at some sport, hobby, musical endeavor; etc. If there is success or failure at one of these, your emotional reaction will be modulated when compared to the situation in which there was attainment or nonattainment of your only life goal.

Linville focuses on informational rather than goal complexity, but her analysis is similar. She states that the more complex you perceive others, then the more modulated will be your emotional and evaluative reaction to them when you receive some pertinent information. For example, if you think that a "good" person must be sincere, outgoing, even-tempered, etc., the less extreme will be your evaluative reaction when finding out about one of these attributes as compared to the condition where you think "goodness" is determined only by that one characteristic. In the latter case, that evidence will entirely decide your evaluation, which will be highly positive or highly negative. Hence, individual differences in cognitive complexity are a general affective moderator. Linville focuses upon complexity with respect to specific situations or others. However, individual differences in general complexity are possible that would then mediate affective reactivity across situations.

MOOD

As indicated earlier in this chapter, mood differs from emotion in that it is of greater duration and not tied to any specific object. Hence, surprise and pity are not considered mood states, since they have a short time span and a specific elicitor. However, happy, sad, and even angry are terms that can refer to mood states.

To study the effects of mood on cognition and behavior, psychologists have devised a number of ways to induce positive and negative moods in the laboratory. One method is to have subjects read a series of positive or negative statements to themselves, such as "things will get better and better today" or "everything seems empty and futile." They might also be told to then think about the most positive or negative of these statements. A second methodology is to play music that elicits positive or negative states. Still a third procedure is to induce mood via hypnotic induction, instructing participants that they will feel happy or sad when awakened. And still a fourth procedure used in field investigations is to have subjects find money in a phone booth, be handed a gift by a "survey taker," or have some other small but positive event take place. In all these situations, the experimenter then examines the effect of the positive or negative mood induction on other variables of psychological interest.

It has been well-documented that background mood states exert profound influences over a wide variety of thoughts and behaviors. For example, individuals in depressed mood states exhibit less interest in social, leisure, intimate, and strenuous activities than those exposed to a positive mood induction (Cunningham, 1988). In addition, and perhaps unexpectedly, persons in positive mood states take less risk than those in negative states (Isen, Nygren, and Ashby, 1988). It appears that people feeling happy are cautious optimists: they report higher probabilities of gains and lower probabilities of losses, yet they avoid risk. They are especially sensitive to loss, so that taking a chance seems not to be worth the risk.

But perhaps the best-documented effects of mood are on memory and judgments of others. When in a happy mood, people make more positive judgments about others and recall more positive facts about them than when they are in a sad mood (Forgas and Bower, 1987). This also is the case with one's self — individuals in depressed moods tend to retrieve negative past events and negative characteristics about themselves to a greater extent than those in a positive mood. Thus, mood tends to be self-perpetuating, which obviously has implications for mental health, coping, and emotional well-being.

We now turn from the topic of emotion to that of stress, which obviously also has emotional significance. Just as in the study of emotion, the way one appraises a stressful situation has important implication for the consequences of that stress, and individual differences also influence this process.

STRESS

In physics, *stress* is a force that acts on a body, producing some kind of strain. In the social world, it also is the case that stressors such as war, fire, and impoverished conditions put a "strain" on the organism. In addition, there is accumulating evidence that any circumstances requiring a change in life pattern, such as marriage, a new job, or the birth of a child, are stressors.

Stress connotes an organism's response to stressful conditions. Stress reactions are determined by many factors, including the characteristics of the stressor, such as its intensity and duration; the availability of social support systems, such as the family and the church; and characteristics of the person, such as prior experience and the ability to use coping defenses.

Life-Event Stress

The role of stressful life events in the etiology of various illnesses has been a prominent field of investigation in the last decade, although the possibility of a connection between stress and illness has long been suspected (see Kobasa, 1979). This research has focused on the relationship between recent life events that require personal change and the onset of an illness. It has been contended that the more such events have occurred in the recent past, the greater the likelihood that one will become seriously ill.

Many of these investigations have used some version of a scale constructed by Holmes and Rahe (1967); see Table 15.2 on p. 430. The items on the scale represent typical incidents of stressful change; the respondent reports which of these events happened within the last six to twenty-four months, depending on the study. Each stressor is given a value, usually determined by judges' ratings, indicating the necessary readjustment that the event requires. Note from Table 15.2 that death of spouse and divorce were judged to require great readjustment, whereas a vacation or a minor law violation were believed to involve little change in one's normal routine.

A great deal of research has demonstrated that scores on the scale shown in Table 15.2 on p. 430 relate significantly to the onset of illness. For example, Rahe (1974) found that sailors who began a cruise with a high score on the scale suffered more illnesses at sea than sailors who started the voyage with low stress scores. This general finding has been replicated many times, using procedures that are both retrospective (data concerning subjects' remembrance of stressful events and illness in the past are collected at the same time) and prospective (stressful events are assessed before illness) (see reviews in Maddi, Bartone, and Puccetti, 1987; Rabkin and Streuning, 1976). It also has been found that at times a severe stressor, such as the unexpected loss of a spouse or child, can result in long-term distress. In one study interviewing people who had lost their spouse in an automobile accident, depression and lack of resolution of the event were evident among some respondents four-to-seven years after the loss (Lehman, Wortman, and Williams, 1987).

Although the reported research findings have been quite consistent, the investigations are not without their critics. The Holmes and Rahe scale includes both positive and negative, and controllable and noncontrollable, events. Many investigators have argued that these should be separated, and that uncontrollable negative events are the important precursors to illness. In addition, respondents often do not answer the questions in the same way at a second testing session (low test-retest reliability), and it has been found that the correlation between a wife's responses about her husband and a husband's responses about himself are lower than desired (low interrater reliability). That is, there is likely to be inaccuracy of reporting. Another problem is that both a life event and an illness could be due to a third cause. For example, both being fired from work and subsequent illness might be brought about by fatigue, in which case job change does not *cause* illness, even though the two factors vary together. Finally, some of the question items, such as mortgage payment and pregnancy, may be irrelevant to particular classes or groups. Most people in the lower class are renters rather than owners and, of course, pregnancy is not applicable to males. These are all reasonable criticisms that require careful consideration before the meaning of the reported findings can be fully understood.

Table 15.2   The Holmes-Rahe schedule of recent life events

Life event	Scale value	Life event	Scale value
Death of spouse	100	Son or daughter leaving home	29
Divorce	73	Trouble with in-laws	29
Marital separation	65	Outstanding personal achievement	28
Jail term	63	Spouse begins or stops work	26
Death of close family member	63	Starting or finishing school	26
Personal injury or illness	53	Change in living conditions	25
Marriage	50	Revision of personal habits	24
Fired from work	47	Trouble with boss	23
Marital reconciliation	45	Change in work hours or conditions	20
Retirement	45	Change in residence	20
Change in family member's health	44	Change in schools	20
Pregnancy	40	Change in recreation habits	19
Sex difficulties	39	Change in church activities	19
Gain of new family member	39	Change in social activities	18
Business readjustment	39	Mortgage or loan less than $10,000	17
Change in financial state	38	Change in sleeping habits	16
Death of close friend	37	Change in number of family gatherings	15
Career change	36	Change in eating habits	15
Change in number of arguments with spouse	35	Vacation	13
Mortgage over $10,000	31	Christmas season	12
Foreclosure of mortgage or loan	30	Minor violations of the law	11
Change in responsibilities at work	29		

The model relating life stress to health thus far has been relatively simple:

Stressful life events $\longrightarrow$ Adverse health change

To increase the predictability of adverse health change, two additional contributors have been studied by psychologists: daily social situations (or life hassles) and personal dispositions, particularly the Type A personality. Some investigators (e.g., Lazarus, 1985) have in fact shifted focus from major stressful events to the ongoing stresses and strains of daily living. Daily hassles with family, work, physical abilities, money, and even weather are considered proximal or immediate determinants of stress, whereas major life events are more distal influences and almost have the status of moods in the sense of being background determinants of lasting duration.

Investigations of daily hassles typically ask participants to complete a daily hassle scale each night before going to bed. In addition, a daily health record also is kept which asks about a number of health-related symptoms such as headaches, digestive system complaints, etc. It has often been reported that there are significant relations between daily stress and the occurrence of both concurrent and subsequent health problems (e.g., DeLongis, Folkman, and Lazarus, 1988).

Rather than focusing on external psychosocial factors that might increase health problems, others have been concerned with factors within the person that augment health risk. Foremost among these has been the so-called Type A personality and its relation to coronary heart disease. About thirty years ago, clinical observations of cardiac patients led two cardiologists to suggest a coronary-prone behavioral pattern that might explain the association between high-pressure job environments and coronary heart disease. The early observations indicated that a type of person who engages in a continuous struggle to do more and more in less and less time is prone to a coronary heart attack. This behavioral pattern includes time urgency, competitiveness, and aggression and hostility that are aroused when obstacles are encountered (Matthews, 1988).

Since its original postulation, there has been a huge literature regarding the Type A personality and its relation to heart disease. At the present time, however, clear answers about the existence of this hypothesized association are not available. There is evidence both for and against the hypothesis that Type A behavior is a reliable predictor of coronary heart disease (see Booth-Kewley and Friedman, 1987; Matthews, 1988). There was a time period when it was thought that the key component of Type A behavior that resulted in heart disease was hostility, however that also is now under question (see Friedman and Booth-Kewley, 1988). It also is not known if this disposition should be thought of as an independent contributor to heart disease (see Model A on p. 432), or whether Type A behavior should be considered a "vulnerability" factor (see Model B on p. 432); that is, these individuals are more vulnerable to harm caused by stressful life events and daily hassles than are others by reacting with exaggerated physiological responses (see Houston, 1988). Model A and Model B are contrasted as follows:

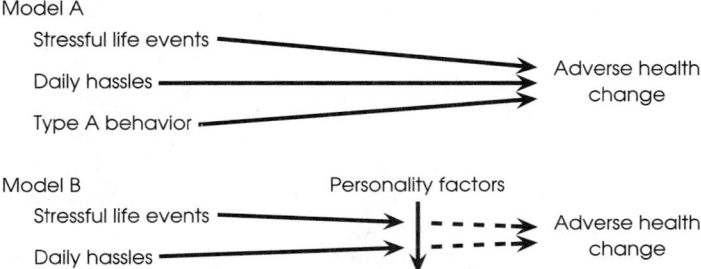

Effects of Stress on Thinking

Stress can have negative impacts on other aspects of functioning such as thinking and problem solving. Under stress, individuals often make mistakes, become obsessed with detail, and are easily distracted from the task at hand. Recently, Pennebaker (1989) argued that there are different levels of thought ranging from more abstract and complex levels to more concrete and specific levels, and he has suggested that stress affects the *level* of one's thinking. He assesses level of thinking by having subjects write their thoughts out in a "stream of consciousness" manner. In one research study, subjects heard a loud noise as they wrote out their thoughts. Half of the subjects were told that they had control over the noise — they could turn it off if it became unbearable — and the other half believed they had no control over the noise. While no subjects turned the noise off, those who believed they had control wrote thoughts at a higher level of thinking than subjects who believed they had no control.

Coping with Stress

Thus far the factors that contribute to stress and, in turn, illness have been examined. But we have failed to consider how individuals deal with stress and how that process influences the onset of illness. As Folkman and Lazarus (1988) state:

> There is a long-standing and widely held conviction among researchers and practitioners in the fields of mental health and behavioral medicine that the ways people cope with the demands of stressful events make a difference in how they feel emotionally (p. 466).

The addition of such coping processes complicates both Models A and B, for additional mediating processes are proposed that act as buffers to stress, as shown in Model C on p. 433, which builds on Model A.

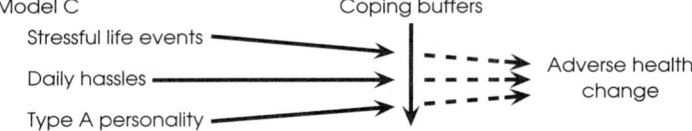

A number of coping strategies to deal with stress have been identified, including confrontation (standing one's ground), distancing (acting as if nothing happened), self-control (keeping feelings to oneself), seeking social support from others, accepting responsibility, escaping and avoiding (eating, taking drugs, etc.), planful problem solving, and reappraisal (growing as a person as a result of the action) (see Folkman, Lazarus, Dunkel-Shetter, DeLongis, and Gruen, 1986).

Consider, for example, the following program of experimental research conducted by Lazarus (1966). In these studies, denial and intellectualization, two of the defense mechanisms considered in Chapter 3, were experimentally manipulated to demonstrate their mediating effects on stress reactions. Here we will only present research on denial, which occurs when the implications of a thought are rejected so that, for example, the existence of a threat is not accepted, as when one refuses to believe that he can be killed during battle.

The general experimental procedure used by Lazarus was to have subjects view a film that gives rise to stress reactions. Lazarus used two films that yield similar results: an anthropological movie showing a stone-age subincision ritual (similar to circumcision) and a safety movie depicting workshop accidents. While subjects view either movie, various measures of autonomic arousal, such as heart rate and galvanic skin response, are continuously recorded. A sound track preceding or accompanying each film presentation evokes the psychological defenses of denial or intellectualization. The denial theme indicates that the subincision operation is not harmful or that the participants in the safety film are only actors. Lazarus then examined whether emotional reactivity to each film was lowered when the defense was introduced.

Figure 15.4 on p. 434 shows the results of one study that induced the defensive orientation of denial (Lazarus and Alfert, 1964). The subincision film was used, and the denial theme was introduced either as a denial orientation before the film or as a denial commentary during the film. Skin conductance (change in the electrical resistance of the skin) was used to measure emotional reactivity. The figure shows that (1) the denial defense reduced reactivity to the stressor among subjects in the experimental groups, compared to subjects in the control group, who did not receive the defensive sound track; and (2) the reduction of emotional reactivity was greatest when the defense was introduced in its entirety before the subjects viewed the film. These data indicate that the amount of emotion we experience in fear-inducing situations will be influenced by how we cope in that situation. The activation of defenses results in disparate ways of thinking about the situation, which will often determine the way we end up feeling.

Figure 15.4

Skin conductance curves. "Denial orientation" indicates that the sound track was presented in its entirety before the film began. "Denial commentary" indicates that the denial sound track accompanied, rather than preceded, the film. The control condition is designated as "silent"; that is, there was no accompanying sound track. (Adapted from Lazarus and Alfert, 1964.)

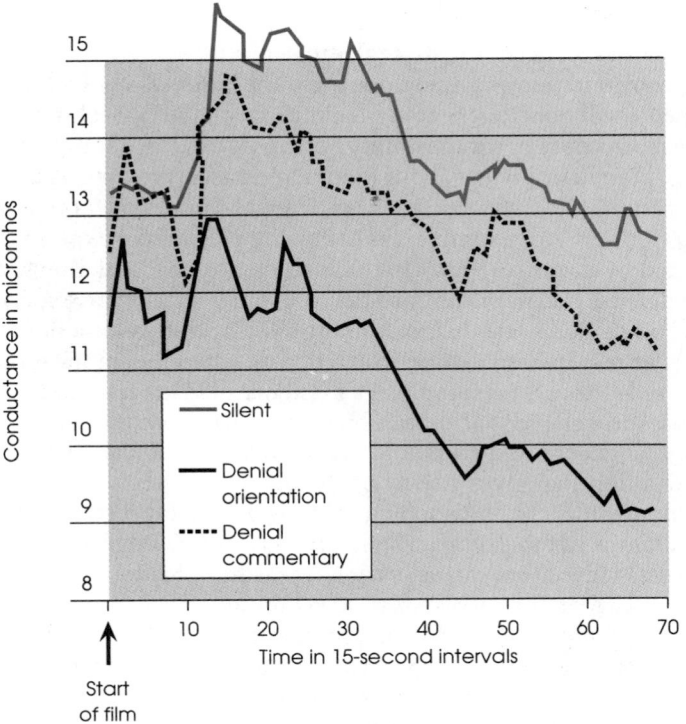

In field research, it has also been documented that coping strategies mediate the relation between stress and outcomes. That is, strategies generated during or after an encounter change the relationship between the stressor and its effects. For example, Folkman and Lazarus (1988) assessed how various types of coping affect emotions of worried/fearful, disgusted/angry, confident, and pleased/happy. Both coping and affect were assessed with retrospective reports. It was found, for example, that planful problem-solving was positively associated with confidence and their pleased/happy scale, while confrontive coping and distancing were positively associated with a disgust/anger scale and negatively related to confidence and happiness among younger married couples.

But the coping research has primarily concentrated on two potential buffers of stress reaction, one internal to the individual undergoing stress and the other external. The personal factor concerns individual differences in what has been

■ **Highlight 15.2** ■

The Myths of Coping with Loss

There are a number of assumptions that people maintain about how others respond to serious loss, such as death of a loved one. It is expected that there will be a period of intense distress and that failure to experience such distress indicates a psychological problem. Further, it is assumed that successful adjustment to loss requires that persons "work through" their feelings of grief and not deny them. However, it also is anticipated that within a reasonable period of time people recover from their loss and return to their typical level of functioning (see Wortman and Silver, 1989). In contrast to these naive beliefs, it has been found that: (a) there is not invariably intense distress after a major loss or after a severe disabling injury; (b) those who fail to experience distress do not necessarily have difficulties later; to the contrary, those most depressed following a loss also are most depressed one or two years later; (c) a substantial minority of individuals continue to exhibit distress for a much longer time period than is normally assumed; and (d) individuals are not always able to achieve some resolution to the loss. In sum, contrary to universal stage theories of distress, some persons do not show distress initially or even following a period of time, while others continue to remain in a state of high distress. There are some individuals who follow the predicted course from high to low stress, but other patterns are quite prevalent.

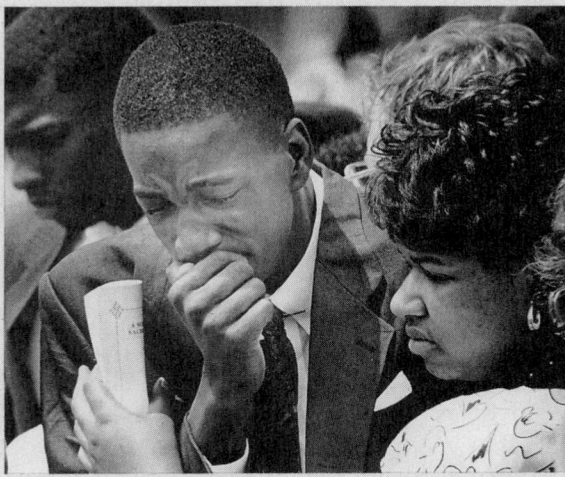

Grief is a common initial reaction to the stress of loss. (Michael Grecco/Stock, Boston)

■ **Highlight 15.3** ■■■■■■■■■■■■

Why Do People Cry?

Although the eyes of all mammals are moistened and soothed by tears, only human beings shed tears in response to emotional stress; yet we know nothing about this uniquely human behavior. A recent theory suggests that tears help to relieve stress by ridding the body of potentially harmful stress-induced chemicals. Thus far, it has been demonstrated that emotionally induced tears have a higher protein content than tears produced in response to eye irritation, such as that caused by a cut onion. However, stress-related chemical differences have yet to be identified.

Other provocative evidence supports this idea. For example, one report found that people with stress-related illnesses cry less than their healthy counterparts. In addition, it is well known that people feel better "after a good cry." In our society, it has been documented that men cry much less frequently than women, and they appear more susceptible to ulcers and some other stress-related problems. In America, the most frequent triggers of crying episodes involve interpersonal relations, such as arguments, and movie or television scenes. Thus, the peak crying time is between seven and ten in the evening, when people are likely to be with others and/or watching television.

called "hardiness," while the external factor relates to the amount, type, etc. of social support that is available to the person.

Individual Differences In Stress Reactions and Hardiness

Inasmuch as there are individual differences in the preference and use of defenses, it might be expected that some persons are better able to cope with stress than others. There is accumulating evidence that the *manner* in which one copes with stress is as important as the *amount* of objective stress encountered. Kobasa (1979) examined the impact of stressful life events on the onset of illness among two groups of executives: those reporting high stress not followed by illness and those who became ill after stressful encounters. She found that the high stress-low illness executives, as compared with the high stress-high illness executives, were characterized by:

1. A clearer sense of values and goals and a belief in their personal importance (commitment rather than alienation).

2. A stronger tendency toward more active involvement with the environment (vigorousness rather than vegetativeness).

3. A general life plan and priorities (meaningfulness rather than meaninglessness).

4. A belief in personal, rather than external, control.

Kobasa (1982) contends that these components of what is called "hardiness" may be a buffer to stress because they are associated with the use of effective coping strategies.

Like the Type A behavior pattern, this individual difference approach has received not only a great deal of attention, but also a great deal of criticism. First, of the components of hardiness (often labeled challenge, control, and commitment), only the latter two are predictive of health (see Hull, Treuren, and Vernelli, 1987). In addition, the "nonhardy" person who reports experiencing no control and who has no commitments also scores high on neuroticism. It is known that neurotic individuals also report high levels of somatic complaints (see Allred and Smith, 1989). This suggests that hardiness is not a buffer to stress, but rather that the lack of both control and commitment associated with poor adjustment might themselves be considered stressful and therefore are associated with illness. In sum, the status of hardiness as a stress buffer is currently under question and, as is true for the Type A personality, its role in illness and health remains to be determined.

Social Support

Social support research has also been increasing at a rapid rate during the past decade. This research has been in vogue because it appears to buffer the effects of life stress on health and well-being (see Cohen and Wills, 1985) and because it suggests interventions for stressed individuals that will facilitate adjustment. However, again the conclusions that have been reached are not definitive. The fact that Type A personality, hardiness, and social support all are shrouded in uncertainty as far as their roles as determinants of adjustment to stress is an indicator of the complexity of this area of research.

One difficulty associated with the study of social support is the precise meaning of this term. Some investigators regard this as perceptions of support available to the person under stress. Others, however, define support as what actually is received. Still other investigators consider social network variables such as the number of living children and siblings, marital status, and so on, as the definition of social support. There is even further complexity, inasmuch as support provided by family, friends, confidants, etc. needs to be distinguished. And, as if this was not enough cause for scientific alarm, seeking social support is one form of coping and thus is a property of the person in addition to being a characteristic of the environment.

It is therefore not surprising that different investigators find different relations between social support and adverse health reactions to stress. One somewhat consistent finding is that perceived, as opposed to received, social support does serve as a buffer to stress. These two definitions of social support are not highly related to one another (Sarason, Shearin, Pierce, and Sarason, 1987). However, even this fact is clouded because perceiving that social support is available may indicate high self-esteem or a facilitative coping preference.

Self-Disclosure and Expression.   One of the major values of a social support network is that it may provide the opportunity for the expression of emotion and the sharing of traumatic experiences. It has long been held by both lay people and professional therapists that "confession is good for the soul." Individuals who come to therapy are encouraged to "get it out" and "get it off their chests." To what degree is the expression of one's emotions and the sharing of one's traumatic experiences helpful in coping with stress? Pennebaker (1990) has recently reported an extensive series of studies documenting the positive effects of "letting it out." Pennebaker reports that studies of those who suffer traumatic experiences in childhood have found that those who do not talk about their experiences have more health problems as adults than those who do talk about their experiences. Similarly those who have experienced recent traumas, such as the suicide or accidental death of a loved one, are more likely to have coped well with the loss if they have disclosed it than if they have not.

However, expression and disclosure need not be through discussion with another person. Pennebaker has found that even extensive writing about one's traumatic experiences is beneficial. In one study, Pennebaker and his colleagues had undergraduate subjects write about the most significant traumatic experience in their lives. Pennebaker discovered that those who were asked to write extensively about their thoughts and feelings showed a subsequent 50 percent reduction in visits to the student health center, compared to those who did not write about their thoughts and feelings.

A question concerning expression of traumatic experiences is whether the benefits of expression come primarily from the catharsis and discharge of the emotions involved or whether it is also important that some cognitive process of reworking the meaning in one's life also take place. In Pennebaker's study, those who were instructed to express only their emotions, as well as those instructed to express only their thoughts, showed less benefits than those who expressed both their emotions and thoughts. This is consistent with research on the expression of anger, in which Bohart (1980) concluded that sheer anger expression by itself does not appear to be beneficial, while anger expression accompanied by cognitive insight does.

Multicultural Aspects of Stress.   Several writers have pointed out that our dominant models of stress need to be modified to take into account the experience of diverse groups (Cervantes and Castro, 1985; Slavin, Ranier, McCreary, and Gowda, 1990). For instance, issues of acculturation (see Chapter 11) appear to be important as causes of stress for members of ethnic minority groups. Studies show that those who have not successfully resolved issues of acculturation experience more stress (Cervantes and Castro, 1985; Slavin, et al., 1990). Similarly, on the Holmes-Rahe scale it is events that occur to oneself or to one's spouse or children that are most influential sources of stress. However, in one study of Mexican subjects (Hough, McGarvey, Graham, and Timbers, 1982), it was found that illness symptoms were most associated with events that occurred to important *others* in one's environment (other than oneself, one's spouse, or one's children). This study illustrates how the meaning of *stressor* depends on how one's culture construes events. In a related manner, different cultural groups also rely on different strategies for coping with stress.

Conclusion

In conclusion, it seems reasonable to conclude that coping styles, other personality factors, multicultural factors, and objective characteristics in the environment are all germane to what is experienced as a stressor and to what buffers one from stress and its subsequent adverse health consequences. But stress research is still at a beginning stage and the complexities of stress are difficult to disentangle.

Summary

1. Emotions are "passions" as opposed to actions; their onset does not appear to be subject to volitional control.

2. Emotions have a number of distinguishing characteristics, including positive or negative quality, intensity, facial expressions and bodily postures, antecedent thoughts, and consequent actions. Not all emotions have all these characteristics.

3. Schachter and Singer contend that the process of emotion begins with a state of arousal. The individual then labels this arousal according to the cues in the social situation. This conception is now doubted.

4. Cognitive emotion theorists identify those characteristics of thought, such as increased or decreased likelihood of an event, perceived ideal vs. real self, and causal attributions, that give rise to specific emotions.

5. New models of emotion integrate cognitive, arousal, and other bodily aspects. Emotion is seen as resulting from a network of interrelationships. Further, emotion is seen as adaptive, mobilizing the organism for action.

6. People characteristically differ in their intensity of responding. This might be due to the tendency to personalize experience or the relative complexity of one's goals and thoughts.

7. Moods differ from emotions in that they are long-lasting and not tied to a specific object. Moods can be manipulated experimentally in a variety of ways, and influence memory retrieval.

8. Life event stress produces susceptibility to illness, as do daily hassles in living.

9. Type A behavioral pattern, which includes time urgency and hostility, has been linked with coronary heart disease, but that association is not definite.

10. A variety of coping mechanisms decrease the adverse effects of life stress. Both individual differences in "hardiness" and social support also may serve as buffers to adverse health reactions following stressors, although this remains to be established with certainty.

11. Self-disclosure seems to help individuals deal with stress and appears to reduce subsequent psychological and physical symptoms.

Thought Questions

1. Can you think of some situations where your emotions were determined by the rules and norms of the culture? Do you think your emotions were influenced or merely the outward expression of these emotions?

2. Recall some situations where you felt the emotions of anger, pity, and guilt. Did the concept of controllability and responsibility play a role in this experience?

3. Think about recent times in your life when you or someone else became physically ill. Were these times preceded by any stressful circumstances, and do you think that the stress might have brought about the illness?

4. How might a psychologist focusing on emotion and stress explain depression?

16 | Consciousness

At any given moment we are bombarded with a variety of external and internal stimulation. Although humans can process much information, there are limits to our capacities. It therefore follows that some information from the environment, or even from our own bodies, will be overlooked or will not attract our attention. Conversely, other information will be the focus of attention and we will be well aware of it. What is selected depends on our own biological receiving mechanisms, our needs, our past histories, and stimulus characteristics. For example, a number of voices are likely to be heard at any given moment at a party, but only one or two of them will be of concern and will be the focus of attention; other sounds will be ignored. These other inputs are likely to be registered, but they are not further processed or held in memory. Similarly, when we view a landscape, much will be "seen" or registered, but we will be aware of only a limited portion of the scene and only a small part of what meets the eye will be retained or recognized later. And on other occasions, as when auditioning for a part in a play or posing for a picture, we might be acutely aware of ourselves and even fewer external factors will be noticed. Thus, our personal consciousness represents only a small portion of reality.

When psychologists speak of *consciousness*, they are often referring to awareness, or what one knows about his or her experience and how reality is constructed. Consistent with this approach, John Locke defined consciousness as "the perception of what passes in a man's own mind" or, as Ornstein (1972) put it, "subjective life." As just indicated, we are frequently unaware of many aspects of our environment and, as Freud so clearly pointed out, individuals are also unaware of many of the important internal determinants of behavior. These inner causes are considered to be "unconscious," or "nonconscious." On other occasions, however, our consciousness may be "expanded"; that is, there is heightened sensitivity to external sounds and colors or increased awareness of our own feelings, past experiences, and thoughts. Repeated exposure to a new rock group may make us conscious of variations in the music of which we were not initially aware. Introspection about a problem in an important personal relationship can lead to the recognition of feelings toward the person that we never knew we had. One of the goals of psychoanalytic and Rogerian therapies (cf. Chapters 3 and 6) is to expand consciousness of our inner life. Eastern philosophies of Yoga and Zen Buddhism share this same goal and also place great emphasis on enhancing our experience of the physical world.

Instances of heightened inner awareness, as might be experienced when under the influence of a drug or during deep meditation, are examples of *altered states of consciousness*. Altered states are truly evident in physical objects, as when liquid water changes to solid (ice) or gas (steam). But whether the human mind can be "altered" to a state qualitatively different from the normal waking state is less clear. It is evident, however, that modifications in awareness are often accompanied by a number of profound physiological and psychological changes. For example, there are changes in the clarity and organization of thought, sense of control, and attention. It is also clear that individuals can readily pass from one level of consciousness to another, as from waking to daydreaming or reverie and then back to alert consciousness again. We thus move through different levels of consciousness during the normal course of our lives.

The issue of the nature of conscious and of its relationship to nonconscious functioning has been important to the study of personality since Freud's theory first postulated that many aspects of personality were based in the unconscious. In this chapter we first examine the relationship of consciousness to nonconscious functioning, and we look at their relationship to such behavioral phenomena as acting mindlessly, engaging in ruminative thought, and biases in how we perceive people. We also consider dissociative phenomena, the relationship of the self to consciousness, and whether nonconscious processes are "smart" (as Freud believed) or "dumb." From there we go on to consider other aspects of conscious and nonconscious functioning that are of relevance to personality, such as altered states of consciousness—including dreams, hypnosis, and drugs—the right brain-left brain dichotomy, and fantasy.

THE RELATIONSHIP OF CONSCIOUSNESS TO NONCONSCIOUS INFORMATION PROCESSING

In our discussion of the relation of consciousness to nonconsciousness, we adopt the term *nonconscious information processing* instead of the term *the unconscious* because when people see *the unconscious* they most often think of Freud's unconscious—full of primitive repressed thoughts, feelings, and motivations. Much modern work, while converging on a belief that *non*conscious processes — processes that lie outside of conscious awareness—can influence conscious functioning, still leaves unresolved the question of whether nonconscious processing has the motivational properties that Freud attributed to it. Therefore we have chosen to use the term *nonconscious* over the better-known term *unconscious.*

For a long time there was a split between clinical psychologists who do psychotherapy and academic psychologists who do research as to whether nonconscious processes existed. The opinion among most psychotherapists was that important nonconscious influences upon behavior can exist. These opinions ranged from those of Freud, who believed in a dynamic unconscious, to those of Rogers, who believed that we are often influenced by a feeling-experiencing process to which we do not consciously attend and of which we are not aware. In contrast, many academic psychologists, particularly those who held to radical behavioral or social learning perspectives, were skeptical about the existence of information processing processes that lay outside of awareness. However, their skepticism is rapidly diminishing, with many believing that the study of nonconscious processes has come of age (Bornstein and Pittman, 1992; Loftus, 1992; Uleman and Bargh, 1989).

If mental functioning can be conceived of as including both conscious and nonconscious elements, what is their relationship? First, we might ask "What is the purpose of consciousness?" A number of theoreticians and researchers have suggested that a major function of consciousness is to correct or reprogram behavior when behavior is not succeeding (Hofstader, 1979; Langer, 1989; Gilbert, 1989; Wegner, 1994; Carver and Scheier, 1981). Many theorists hold that there are two systems controlling behavior — a conscious, relatively voluntary or controlled system and a relatively more automatic system that usually functions outside of awareness. Many aspects of behavior are under relatively automatic control.

Control theories (Carver and Scheier, 1981; Powers, 1973) provide models that view behavior as a function of both conscious, or controlled, and relatively nonconscious, or automatic, processes. These theories view the human being as a *cybernetic system* — a system in which feedback from the environment is being continually monitored and then used to correct the behavior of the system. Individuals are seen as comparing their current states to their desired goal states and as assessing the progress they are making towards those desired goal states. If no difference is found, then individuals continue as they have been, or "exit the loop," and begin to pursue other goals. However, if a difference is noted (i.e., the individuals notice that there is a discrepancy between their desired goal state and the progress they are making towards it), then individuals alter their behavior in order to bring the current state closer to the one that is desired. It is when we are confronted with problems that we devote conscious attention to efforts of controlling various aspects of behavior. To quote Martin and Tesser (1989, p. 311), one major function of consciousness is that it is a "troubleshooting process."

Mindlessness

An example of the idea that consciousness is primarily utilized to alter automatic processes when necessary is provided by Langer's work on mindlessness. Consider the experiment by Langer, Blank, and Chanowitz (1978), in which a person about to use a copying machine was approached by an experimental confederate who asked for permission to use the machine first. The requestor stated that she had either a small or a large number of copies to make and made the request in one of three ways (Langer et al., 1978, p. 635):

1. Request only: *Excuse me, I have 5(20) pages. May I use the Xerox machine?*

2. Placebic information: *Excuse me, I have 5(20) pages. May I use the Xerox machine because I have to make copies?*

3. Real information: *Excuse me, I have 5(20) pages. May I use the Xerox machine because I'm in a rush?*

■ **Highlight 16.1** ▬▬▬▬▬▬▬▬▬▬▬

Learning Without Awareness

A controversy in psychology that generated much attention in the late 1950s and 1960s involved the examination of whether verbal behavior can be directly manipulated with reinforcement techniques. In a typical experiment, subjects were given a series of cards, each containing a verb and six personal pronouns (Taffel, 1955). The subjects were asked to make up a sentence using the verb and any pronoun. The experimenter then rewarded each sentence starting with *I* or *we* by saying "good" when the sentence was completed. It was found that during the reinforcement phase of this experiment the use of *I* and *we* greatly increased, but when reinforcement was later withheld, the use of these pronouns decreased. The subjects in the initial investigations reported that they were unaware of the contingency between their response and the reinforcement. It appeared that the learning took place because of the automatic strengthening property of the reinforcer. These research studies were interpreted as supporting both the Skinnerian position and, surprisingly, the Freudian notion of the unconscious.

　　Subsequent research, however, using more sophisticated, postexperimental interview techniques and indirect assessment procedures, found that only subjects who were aware of the contingency between the response and the reinforcement increased their rate of "correct" responding (see Spielberger, 1962). Subjects who remained unaware of the experimental linkage between *I* or *we* and *good* responded in a random manner. Cognitive psychologists contend that these findings refute the behaviorist belief in mechanical, stimulus-response connections.

Condition 2 is called "placebic information" because the reason offered is entirely redundant of the request. After all, "What else would one do with a copying machine except make copies of something?" (Langer et al., 1978, p. 48). The point is that condition 2 offers essentially the same information as condition 1. If subjects were really conscious of the information given, then the rate of compliance with the request should have been the same in the "placebic information" and "request only" conditions. The results of this investigation are shown in Table 16.1. The table shows that if the favor was small (few copies), then the rate of compliance was the same whether the information was placebic or real and in both cases was higher than compliance in the request only condition (Condition 1). That is, given relatively unimportant events, individuals may be unaware of the information provided by others. But if a favor is large, then they become

Table 16.1   The proportion of subjects who agreed to let the experimenter use the copier

	Reason		
	Request only	Placebic info.	Real info.
Small	.60	.93	.94
Big	.24	.24	.42

Source: Adapted from Langer, Blank, and Chanowitz, 1978, p. 637. Used by permission.

conscious of the phrasing of the request and comply more in real than in the placebic condition and request only conditions.

Many questions about this provocative research are now being raised (see Folkes, 1985). For example, it may be that people presume there is an adequate reason in the placebic condition. It also has been found that if people are provided with a poor reason (for example, "because I don't want to wait"), then compliance is weakened. In general, mindlessness is most evident when outcomes are not personally relevant, when no accountability is involved, and when the decision is unimportant (see review in Langer, 1989).

Automaticity

Langer's work suggests that we can alter some of our automatic processes when necessary. However, other researchers have argued that automatic scripts and schemas sometimes function outside of conscious control. Most of us have experienced unwanted thoughts or feelings (perhaps something so simple as a melody) that we can't get out of our minds no matter how hard we try. Many of us have had the experience of "choking" in a situation — of trying so hard to avoid making an error that the error occurs. And psychotherapy largely exists because simply having a conscious, intellectual conception of "how I should be" or "how I want to be" frequently does not affect or effect behavior (Todd and Bohart, 1994) — as many would-be dieters know. Finally, many individuals, especially after experiencing trauma or loss, have had ruminative thoughts, which they go over and over but cannot banish from their minds (Martin and Tesser, 1989; Tait and Silver, 1989).

In this regard, Wegner (1994) has described the "ironic" effects of some of our mental processes. In several studies, Wegner and his colleagues asked subjects to "NOT think of a white bear" (you can try this yourself). No matter how hard they tried, most subjects kept finding the image of a white bear reappearing in their thoughts even when it had temporarily been banished. Wegner notes that when we try to control ourselves not only do we not always succeed, but sometimes we end up doing the diametric opposite of what we want to do. The more we try to make ourselves go to sleep, the wider awake we become. The more we try to diet, the more we think about food.

Wegner holds that these ironic effects of efforts at mental control occur because there is a conscious, controlled process that is trying to achieve our goal, and an automatic, nonconsciously controlled process that is monitoring or keeping a look out for the very thing we don't want to happen. Sometimes, especially under stress, the conscious part of the process gets disrupted, and then what pops into awareness is the part of ourselves that is keeping an eye out for the thing we don't want to happen. The undesirable thing then floods into consciousness.

In one study, Wegner and Erber (1992) asked subjects to think or to not think about a target word (e.g., *house*) and then to give their associations to a variety of other words. Some of the other words they were given were related to the word they were to suppress (e.g., *home*) and some were unrelated (e.g., *adult*). Subjects who were to suppress a word and who were put under time pressure to respond frequently blurted out the very word they were supposed to not think about, more so than subjects who were not under time pressure to respond.

Priming

There are other ways nonconscious processes may influence our conscious activities. One of these can be demonstrated by the many studies of priming and accessibility. The idea of *priming* is based on the idea that we have many *schemas* —cognitive plans or structures for organizing our experience and guiding our actions—that are latent in the brain. If the schemas are primed, or stimulated, they become active and form the basis for how we interpret our experience in a given moment. In a typical priming study, a word or a phrase—say, the word *hostile*—is presented to the subject. Sometimes these words are presented subliminally, sometimes not. In another part of the study, which is presented to the subject as unrelated to the first part, the subject is asked to read an ambiguous description of a person and to give a characterization of that person's personality. Typically the subject "sees" the person in terms of the primed word. In our example, the subject would see the person as somewhat hostile. This effect appears to be stronger if the subject is unaware of having been primed (Higgins, 1989).

In an even more complex priming study, Lewicki (1986) had subjects respond to brief flashes on a screen by pressing a button. In actuality, the flashes were words presented so rapidly that subjects were unable to report seeing them. In one condition the words presented were *harm, rape, attack,* and *pain* (negative words). In another condition the words were neutral words, such as *chair* or *button*. In a second phase of the experiment, subjects were presented with a short essay describing a woman named Jane. The description was ambiguous, and subjects were asked to rate Jane on a series of traits, such as *resistant to threat, not fearful,* or *relaxed*. Men who had been exposed subliminally to the negative words saw Jane as feeling threatened and as vulnerable to threat. In contrast, women who had been exposed subliminally to the negative words saw Jane as not threatened and as resistant to threat. It is not clear why this occurred, but Lewicki speculates that nonconscious activation of a sense of physical threat in men influenced them to see Jane as a potential victim. In contrast, nonconscious activation of a sense of threat in women led them to perceive Jane as unlikely to be victimized. Lewicki believes this may be based on cultural stereotypes. Men may tend to underestimate threat and see it as something that pertains to others rather than to themselves, while women may see themselves as more likely to be victimized and therefore as needing to protect themselves from threat. The important point, however, is that whatever the mechanisms operating, they appear to have operated at a nonconscious level.

Some schemas may be *chronically accessible* (Higgins, 1989), guiding our experience but at a level of which we are unaware. For instance, many studies have suggested that negative schemas for construing experience are chronically accessible in depressives, who quickly perceive events in a negative fashion.

Dissociative Phenomena

Still other evidence of the relationship of consciousness to nonconsciousness comes from the study of pathology. In earlier chapters (see Chapters 3 and 15) the defense mechanisms, including repression, perceptual defense, and denial, were discussed. It was contended that such mechanisms prevent forbidden wishes, fears, and other feelings and thoughts from entering consciousness. But even more dramatic evidence concerning inhibited awareness is illustrated in what are called *dissociative phenomena*. These include:

1. *Somnambulism* — walking or carrying out acts while apparently in a sleeping state.

2. *Amnesia* — a loss of identity and/or recall of the past.

3. *Multiple personality* (now called *dissociative identity disorder*) — two or more seemingly well-organized identities functioning relatively independently of one another in the same person.

It seems inconceivable that multiple and independent personalities within the same person are possible. Yet, it is common that some limited aspects of ourselves, such as our "true" feelings toward others, are blocked out, particularly under conditions of great conflict. In cases of multiple personality, these mechanisms are carried to an extreme: it is as if the individual were an actor playing several different roles. The difference is that the multiple personality, unlike acting, is not within the individual's control. In addition, when the individual is in one role, he or she may have complete amnesia for the other roles.

Reported cases of multiple personality were once rare, however, in recent years there have been more and more. Perhaps the most famous split personality is Eve White, Eve Black, and Jane: the "three faces of Eve." Typically, the individual assumes two or three different personalities (although as many as sixteen or more have been reported), each personality with a distinct and stable pattern of cognitive and emotional behavior and different scores on tests of emotion. The separate personalities may or may not be aware of one another. In addition, a person may maintain one pattern of behavior for years, or change back and forth in a matter of minutes.

In earlier times, such multiple personalities were attributed to demonic possession by a distinct entity that could enter the body. Today the condition is most often interpreted as an attempt to escape from unbearable early trauma, with the expression of wishes through an alternative personality. It appears to develop most often in individuals who have a predisposition to experiencing dissociative states and who have been severely physically or sexually abused as children. Still, relatively little is known about the dynamics of multiple personality; and in the current edition of the Diagnostic and Statistical Manual of the American Psychiatric Association (DSM-IV, 1994), the name of this disorder is changed officially to *Dissociative Identity Disorder*. This disorder is clearly an example of the complex relationships that can exist between conscious and nonconscious processes.

The Relationship of the Self to Consciousness

Kihlstrom (1987, 1990) has recently speculated that the complex relationship between consciousness and nonconscious processes is mediated by the existence of the self. He has argued that consciousness requires that a mental representation of an event be linked to a mental representation of the self. Consciousness takes the form of "*I see* (or *hear, smell, taste,* etc.) *this, now*" (Kihlstrom, 1990, p. 458). In other words, there would be no conscious experience if there were no sense of self linked to that experience. This fits with our discussion of the development of the self in Chapter 10, in which we noted that the development of a self-concept appears to begin around the time that individuals develop self-awareness.

Kihlstrom goes on to suggest that amnesia and other instances in which individuals cannot consciously remember experiences they have had occur either because the experience was not associated with the self in the first place or because that association to the self was subsequently lost. This is congruent with many approaches to therapy, in which efforts are made to help clients integrate their experiences into their sense of self. For instance, helping someone to remember an abuse experience is in part helping them to recover that the experience happened "*to me*". If Kihlstrom's speculation is correct, then the nature of consciousness is intimately linked to the nature of the self, and disturbances in the association of self to experience leads to amnesia, dissociation, and other aspects of memory loss.

Are Nonconscious Processes "Smart" or "Dumb?"

While most psychologists now agree to the existence of nonconscious processes, there is still considerable controversy over their nature. Many of the great personality theorists, such as Freud, Rogers, and Jung, believed that processes that lay outside of awareness could involve the operation of complex mental pro-cesses. For instance, for Freud, the unconscious part of the individual's ego organized the defenses that protected the individual from conscious self-aware-ness of repressed material. In that sense the unconscious could operate in a "smart" fashion, although it consisted mainly of "primary process" material (see Chapter 3) and such processes were not necessarily "rational" in their operation. However, some modern psychologists (e.g., Greenwald, 1992) argue that there is no evidence for a "smart" unconscious that involves complex mental operations. Rather, nonconscious processes are seen as relatively simple and automatic, consisting of the automatic operation of simple well-learned routine procedures, such as that involved in driving.

Others, such as Erdelyi (1992) and Lewicki, Hill, and Czyzewska, (1992) disagree. They hold that information can be processed in complex and sophisti-cated ways at a nonconscious level. In other words, nonconscious processes involve more than simple routinized procedures, and in some sense they can be said to involve "thinking."

Complicating the resolution of this issue are methodological problems — it is difficult to assess whether or not an individual is really unaware of the informa-tion being processed (see Highlight 16.1 on p. 444). In studies demonstrating complex nonconscious information processing, questions have been raised as to the subjects' degree of lack of awareness. Clearly, this is an issue that awaits further research for resolution. However, its resolution will have important im-plications for some of our theories about personality.

ALTERED STATES OF CONSCIOUSNESS

Our normal waking state is but one form of consciousness. In this state, knowl-edge is communal, or consensual; that is, we share information with others and are mutually aware of the stimuli in the environment. In addition, the passage and constraints of time are recognized. Normal waking states are considered the primary condition of the mind; other types of consciousness are thought of as "unreal" or as "imaginary."

There are a number of states of mind that fall within the rubric of the "unreal." These include sleep and dream states, delirium, hypnotic trances, and drug and meditational experiences. In these conditions, new mental functions and capabilities are experienced that may not have counterparts in normal experi-ence. Time is distorted, illogical events are perceived as real or possible, and there may be a loss of self-awareness. These altered states may be externally induced, as in drug conditions, or part of our natural lives, as in sleep, dreaming, and day-dreaming. They may be of long or short duration. They may be passive experi-ences, with increased awareness of, openness/to, and preoccupation with the environment, or active and creative states with preoccupation with inner sensa-tions. They may give rise to positive or negative emotions. And they can be produced by under- or overstimulation. But in all such cases consciousness is perceived as somehow different.

Table 16.2   Sleep lengths among mammals

Animal	Length per 24 hours
Bat	19
Hamster	14
Cat	14
Chimpanzee	11
Jaguar	11
Mole	10
Man	7.4
Cow	7
Sheep	6
Bottle-nose dolphin	5
Elephant	4

Source: From *Foundations of Contemporary Psychology,* edited by Merle E. Meyer. Copyright © 1979 by Oxford University Press, Inc. Reprinted by permission.

Sleep

All mammals sleep, although there is great variety in the amount of sleeping activity (see Table 16.2). Among humans, there is also a wide range of individual differences in sleep habits, with the amount of sleep for college students averaging 7.4 hours during the week and 8.5 hours on the weekend (White, 1975). Contrary to popular belief, research has not substantiated the hypotheses that sleep is affected by viewing violent television programs or studying before bedtime. Indeed, there appears to be great stability in the sleeping process.

One of the main characteristics of sleep is that the sleeper is relatively unresponsive to the external world. However, there is not complete unawareness of environmental stimulation. For example, it has been found that important names are more likely to awaken the sleeper than irrelevant ones. A second characteristic of the sleeper is a great reduction in activity. The decreased behavior that accompanies sleep is thought by some to be the key to sleep's function (Webb, 1975). Such nonresponding could be instrumental to survival if it kept one protected from a hostile world and occurred when responding would be unlikely to result in goal attainment. Among humans, hunting was extremely hazardous at night because of our primary dependence on vision. Thus, it may

■ **Highlight 16.2** ■

If You Can't Sleep. . . .

Various suggestions have been offered to those experiencing difficulties in sleeping. They include:

1. Never oversleep because of a poor night's sleep. Get up at the same time each morning, for this establishes the body's internal sleep/wake mechanism.

2. Try to establish a relatively regular bedtime.

3. If you wake at night, relax in bed for a while. If that does not work, get out of bed and try some quiet activity until you are sleepy again.

4. Cut down on alcohol, smoking, chocolate, coffee, tea, and caffeinated soft drinks.

5. Schedule some time to write down worries or concerns about what you will do the next day.

6. Avoid heavy meals too close to bedtime.

7. Experiment with your bedroom's noise level and temperature until you find what is best for you.

8. Keep physically active, even after a bad night's sleep.

9. Try relaxation techniques such as visualizing peaceful scenes.

10. Find out if medical conditions or prescription drugs are keeping you awake.

In addition, sleep-disorder clinics are now located throughout the United States and are available for consultation.

have been survival relevant to "keep the curious quiet and the frightened still" (Webb and Bonnet, 1979, p. 465) until daylight. An alternative to this explanation of the function of sleep is that sleep enables the organism to restore body chemicals, a hypothesis that has received some substantiation. Furthermore, it takes as much energy to sleep as it does merely to lie quietly awake.

A number of sleep disorders have been identified (see Table 16.3). These disorders vary in intensity and frequency of occurrence for any given individual. Night terrors, the first disturbance indicated in Table 16.3, apparently do not originate in bad dreams, as is often thought, but result from abrupt awakening from deep sleep. Similarly, sleepwalking is also not dream related and is typically

Table 16.3   Sleep disturbances

	Age range primarily affected	Usually outgrown	Percentage of primary age range
Night terrors	3–5	Yes	2–5%
Enuresis	4–7 (bedwetting considered normal before bladder control learned)	Yes	15–25%
Sleepwalking (Somnambulism)	5–12	Yes	15%
Nightmares	Peak at 8–10	Lessen	95%
Narcolepsy	Onset 15–25	No	.05%
Sleep talking	All ages, primarily less than 25	Lessen	40–60%
Insomnia	All	No	14–20%

Source: From *Foundations of Contemporary Psychology,* edited by Merle E. Meyer. Copyright © 1979 by Oxford University Press, Inc. Reprinted by permission.

outgrown by adolescence; it is now considered a developmental disorder rather than a psychological disturbance. Table 16.3 also indicates that a small percentage of the population are victims of *narcolepsy,* or sudden "sleep attacks" that often occur without warning, particularly during times of heightened excitement, and last from a few to fifteen minutes. Narcolepsy is likely to be a genetic disorder; dogs bred from narcoleptic parents show exacerbation of this sleep tendency. Thus, it is not necessarily a sign of psychopathology. Finally, the table indicates that a large percentage of the population suffers from a perceived lack of sufficient sleep. However, this figure is probably inflated because the elderly seem to need less sleep and indeed do sleep less, yet are more likely to report sleep problems. Studies have been unable to uncover any personality differences between long- and short-duration sleepers.

Dreams

Sleep is also characterized by dream activity. Dreams exemplify primary process thinking (see Chapter 3): they may be illogical, are not bound by the constraints of time, there is fusion of objects into one, and they may include symbolic representations of thoughts and objects.

Freud contended that sleep is preserved by dreams. According to Freud, the antecedent for all fantasy behavior, including dreaming, is deprivation (unfulfilled wishes); the consequence of fantasy behavior is need reduction. By providing the opportunity for substitute or hallucinatory wish fulfillment, dreams "drain off" internal stimulation and preserve sleep. A simple illustration can clarify this idea. Assume that you go to bed without dinner. After some period of time, hunger cramps are felt that might cause awakening. During sleep, however, you dream about eating food. The content of the dream might be disguised with the food appearing in symbolic form (e.g., string rather than spaghetti). Such a wish-fulfilling dream produces a diminution in subjective hunger, thereby reducing stomach cramps and preserving sleep.

The Study of Dreams. As you might expect, it is extremely difficult to gather scientific evidence that dreams are wish fulfillments and that they preserve sleep by reducing internal stimulation. But advances in dream research have generated data that are pertinent to some of Freud's presumptions.

Useful scientific research on dreaming was initiated about forty years ago. One reason for this relatively recent start was that, prior to this time, only the dreamer had direct access to the dream. Therefore, it was not possible to assess the reliability of dream reports (that is, whether or not a dream had occurred, as opposed to the content of the dream). There was a need for a witness to the onset of the dream in addition to the dreamer.

An objective technique for the detection of dreams was discovered in the early 1950s (see Dement and Kleitman, 1957). During sleep, *rapid eye movements* (REM) were discovered, with the eyes exhibiting quick, side-to-side motions under the lids. Individuals awakened during these REM periods reported dreams more frequently than people awakened at other times. Some mental and cognitive activities do occur during non-REM (NREM) periods, but reports of visual and hallucinatory experiences occur only during REM sleep. NREM reports are more like thinking, being less visual and less unusual.

Research has also revealed that there are cyclical patterns of brain activity during the course of sleep (see Dement, 1965). This activity can be monitored with the recording of brain waves (EEG readings). Four different patterns of brain waves have been detected during sleep (see Fig. 16.1). Stage 1 sleep, in which there is a lack of long and narrow waves, as well as *delta,* or large, waves, is highly associated with REM periods and dream reports. It is now quite clear that REM observations and particular patterns of brain waves provide reliable, observable criteria for identifying internal dream processes.

During the course of an eight-hour sleep period, an individual has five or six dream episodes, or an average of about one dream every eighty to ninety minutes. In general, the longer one sleeps, the greater the total dream activity. The average dream lasts around fifteen minutes, with the length of the dream increasing as the night progresses. The initial episode lasts between five and ten minutes, while final dreams may continue for as long as fifty or sixty minutes. Individuals also progress through a regular nondream-dream sequence during the course of the evening. To enter a REM stage, there first is passage through stage 2 of the sleep cycle.

Figure 16.1   Sample EEG patterns for the waking state and the four stages of sleep. (From *New Directions in Psychology, Volume II,* by Frank Barron, William C. Dement, et al., copyright © 1965 by Holt, Rinehart and Winston, Inc., reprinted by permission of the publisher.)

The percentages of both sleep and dream time are systematically related to maturation (see Fig. 16.2). Figure 16.2 reveals that infants sleep more than half the time and that nearly half of this sleeping time, or around eight hours, is spent in REM activity. However, this percentage drops off rapidly; by early adolescence, the percentage of time spent dreaming begins to stabilize at around 20 percent. However, the total amount of sleep continues to decline very gradually. Foulkes (1990) has suggested that dreams mature along the same lines as does waking consciousness. As conscious mental processing expands in organization, range, and flexibility, so do dreams.

The Function of Dreams.   Freud believed that through dream analysis we could learn about unfulfilled wishes and desires, as well as about the symbolic manifestations of needs. Given an objective dream index, one might expect that the "royal road to the unconscious" (which is how Freud characterized dreams) would become a superhighway and that Freud's speculations would be either confirmed or discarded. Although this has not been the case, inferential data have been gathered that bear on some of the issues raised by Freud.

First, it appears that all individuals dream. The universality of the dream experience was anticipated by Freud. Indeed, many nonhuman species exhibit dream-state sleep (see Table 16.4 on p. 456). But if it is inferred from REM

Figure 16.2   Changes, with age, in total amounts of daily sleep. (From *Foundations of Contemporary Psychology*, edited by Merle E. Meyer. Copyright © 1979 by Oxford University Press, Inc. Reprinted by permission.)

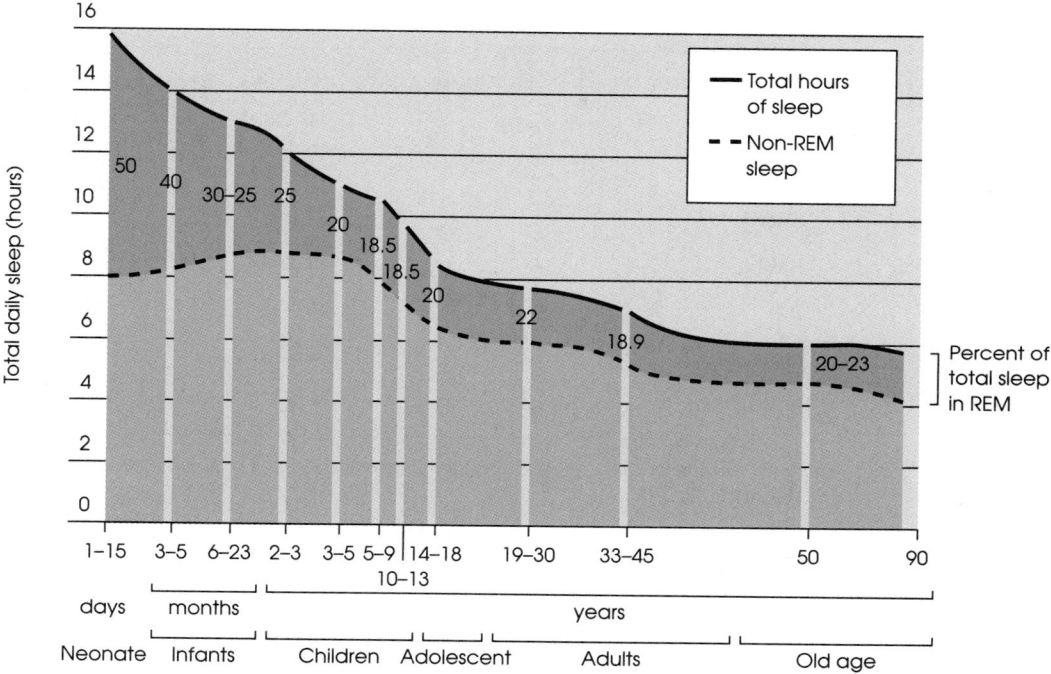

observations that lower organisms also dream, then it is difficult to contend that the function of dreams is to drain internal stimulation. It seems unlikely that dreams preserve sleep, but rather that the presence of sleep ensures dreams.

One finding in support of the Freudian conception of dreams is that there appears to be a need to dream (Dement, 1960). If the sleeper is awakened every time a REM period is entered, then the REM periods are more frequent on subsequent evenings, and it subsequently takes more vigor to awaken the sleeper. The organism seems to be making up for a REM deficit.

But if there is a need to dream, then dream deprivation should affect psychological functioning. At present it is uncertain whether this is the case. Some investigators do report that individuals become more emotional and less psychologically balanced after losing REM sleep, but other investigators find no such disturbing psychological effects. Furthermore, there are perfectly well-adjusted individuals who sleep less than one hour a night! Whether REM deprivation has adverse psychological effects may be dependent on the personality of the individual. A number of studies suggest that repressors (individuals prone to forget conflictual material) are more disturbed by REM interruption than nonrepressors (Cohen, 1977).

Table 16.4   Dream state in various mammalian species (young adult animals)

Species	Average length of dream period (min)	Average cycle length (min)	Dream time as percentage of total sleep
Humans	14	80–90	20–24
Monkey	4–10	40–60	11–20
Cat	10	20–40	20–60
Sheep	—	—	2–3
Rabbit	—	24	1–3
Rat	4–7	7–13	15–20
Mouse	—	3–4	—
Opossum	5	17	22–40

Source: E. Hartmann, 1965, p. 32. Reprinted by permission of *The New England Journal of Medicine, 273,* 32, 1965.

As already indicated, Freud stated that dreams preserve sleep by draining off internal stimulation. It is evident that what Freud labeled "day residues," or memory traces of experiences during the day, influence the content of dreams. In addition, stimulation during sleep, such as a flash of light or tactile input, is sometimes incorporated into dreams. But such stimulation does not instigate dreams. That is, the onset of stimulation that might awaken the sleeper does not initiate a REM episode. Furthermore, emotional upsets during the day, reported frustrations, and unfulfilled desires are unrelated to the amount of time spent in dream activity. Indeed, the vast majority of dreams involve commonplace activities in commonplace settings, and their emotional tone is often negative.

In sum, there is a cyclical course of sleep during the night which is relatively uniform across individuals. The question of the dream's psychological function remains moot. One must certainly question the notion of the dream as having substitute value and reducing internal stimulation. It seems more probable that dreams aid in thinking through problems and providing creative solutions that have escaped us during normal waking thought (see Singer, 1974). Some evidence has suggested that dream contents are similar to the daydream contents. A good deal of daydreaming is related to everyday concerns (Singer and Bonanno, 1990). That is, dreams may have a cognitive rather than a stimulus-reducing function. There is suggestive evidence from both animal and human studies that REM sleep may facilitate new learning and emotionally adaptive waking behavior (McGrath and Cohen, 1978). For example, a number of studies have demonstrated that groups deprived of REM sleep have poorer learning and retention than control groups deprived of an equal amount of sleep, but allowed to engage in REM (dream) sleep.

In addition, it appears that the dream state is not qualitatively different from waking thought, with factors such as sex, age, race, and social class all reflected in dream content. For example, women report more emotions in their dreams than do men, who report more aggressive content (Winget, Kramer, and Whitman, 1972). It seems that dream characteristics correctly reflect the concerns and styles of waking life (Webb and Cartwright, 1978; Hermans, 1987).

Hypnosis

Remember that Freud was led to the use of free association as a therapeutic technique after observing the curative effects of hypnosis. However, not all of his patients were able to be hypnotized, and he eventually found free association more suitable for his goals. In addition, in Chapter 3 it was revealed that a hypnotic demonstration was responsible for crystallizing Freud's idea that conscious beliefs may be quite inconsistent with unconscious desires.

The word *hypnos* is Greek for "sleep." For a long time hypnotic trances were thought to be akin to sleep, but this similarity is more apparent than real. Brain recordings and a variety of other indicators taken during hypnotic states are the same as those recorded in waking conditions, and both differ from the responses of a sleeping person. Furthermore, during hypnosis an individual can acquire and retain new information and be normally active or even hyperactive. Thus, the two main characteristics of sleep (nonresponsiveness to stimulation and lack of activity) do not describe the hypnotic subject.

Hypnotic trances have rather unique features:

1. The person ceases to make plans. There is a loss of initiative and the individual is generally passive, giving him- or herself over to the care of the hypnotist.

2. There is selective attention. Although this also is true in waking states, hypnotic subjects exhibit an even narrower range of focus.

3. Reality testing is reduced, and distortions and inconsistencies are accepted. This is sometimes called *trance logic*.

4. There is increased suggestibility and a compulsion to please and to follow the biddings of the hypnotist.

5. The subject readily enacts unusual roles, such as rowing a boat while in a room. Antisocial behavior may also be undertaken if it is not construed as antisocial by the person under hypnosis.

6. Subjective experience is altered in accordance with the hypnotist's suggestions.

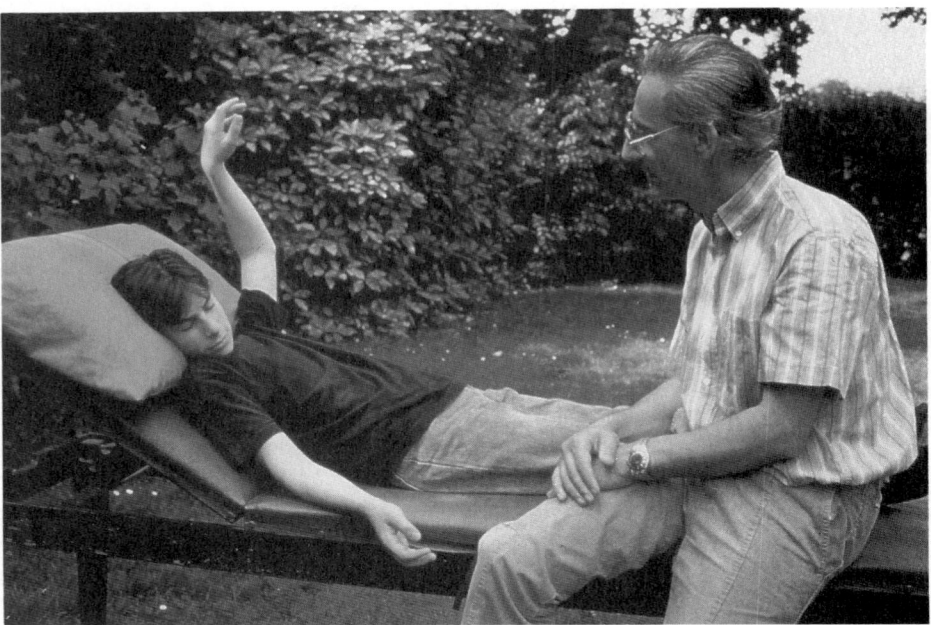

Hypnosis is a therapeutic technique sometimes used by psychologists — for example, for behavior modification. (Francoise Sauze/Science Photo Library/Photo Researchers)

7. There is increased control over bodily functions, such as the capacity to hear, see, and not feel pain. This will be elaborated on in the subsequent discussion.

8. There can be posthypnotic amnesia if suggested by the hypnotist. The extent of memory loss varies among individuals and according to the depth of the trance. This blockage is unique to hypnotic states.

There are differences in the extent to which these characteristics describe the state of any given individual during hypnosis. Around 10 percent of the population does not respond to hypnotic induction and, at the opposite pole, about 5 to 12 percent can enter deep trances in which even the commands of the hypnotist are no longer processed. A wide array of humans, including children and retardates, can be hypnotized. Furthermore, a single attempt is usually sufficient to determine if a person is susceptible to hypnosis and susceptibility has been found to be stable over a twenty-five year period (Piccione, Hilgard, and Zimbardo, 1989). Performance scales have been developed to indicate the susceptibility of an individual to hypnosis. Such scales require individuals to attempt experiences ranging, for example, from simple falling forward without stiffening to blockage of smells and voices (Weitzenhoffer and Hilgard, 1962).

One question that immediately comes to mind is whether there are traits that distinguish good hypnotic subjects from poor ones. J. R. Hilgard has suggested that a good subject must have the capacity to become deeply involved in imaginative experiences. For example, one highly susceptible subject described herself as follows (Hilgard, 1970, p. 24):

> When I get really involved in reading, I'm not aware of what is going on around me. I concentrate on the people in the book or the movie or in imagination as it is in hypnosis. Reading a book can hypnotize you.
> After each book, I'm completely washed out. After hypnosis, it was the same. I was completely washed out and couldn't keep my eyes open. I lacked the ability to communicate.

Although traits that clearly distinguish good from poor hypnotic subjects have not been convincingly demonstrated thus far, a capacity for total absorption and losing oneself does seem to correlate with level of hypnotic susceptibility (Nadon, Laurence, and Perry, 1987; Tellegen and Atkinson, 1974). In addition, there is increasing evidence that skill-training can enhance responsiveness to hypnotic induction (see Spanos, Lush, and Gwynn, 1989). The training procedures include instilling positive attitudes and motivation, exposure to videotaped models, and information about misconceptions regarding hypnosis (e.g., hypnosis does not involve total loss of personal control).

It is also interesting to speculate about child-rearing practices that might account for differences in hypnotic susceptibility. J. R. Hilgard has concluded that punitive upbringing might foster susceptibility because this type of child rearing promotes unquestioning obedience and escape through the use of imagination. Again, however, there is insufficient evidence to conclusively substantiate this hypothesis.

Control of Bodily Functions. The most dramatic reports concerning hypnosis involve control over basic sensory and cognitive functions. For example, in an experiment by Blum (1961), participants were instructed not to see a particular design on a card. This design, which had elicited great anxiety, gave rise to no physiological reactivity whatsoever after the hypnotic instructions.

However, hypnotic subjects do not become literally blind at the moment blindness is suggested; they will blink at a bright light. In a similar manner, apparent deafness can be easily induced in a hypnotic subject, but it can be demonstrated that the individual does process sound. In one such demonstration, individuals were tested in a delayed auditory feedback context, in which personal voice feedback is delayed by about one second, a delay that typically causes speech impairment. The adverse effects of auditory speech delay were not erased under hypnotic "deaf" instructions (Barber and Calverley, 1964).

As previously indicated, there is also apparent hypnotic influence on memory, for hypnosis is perhaps most often identified with amnesia for events during hypnosis. Yet even this aspect of hypnosis is not without ambiguity. For example, although participants are unable to consciously recall events during hypnosis that they have been instructed to forget, traditional measures of recognition and relearning are not affected by suggested amnesia (see Williamsen, Johnson, and

Eriksen, 1965). Further, other research has demonstrated that individuals *can* remember, under the right conditions, when not hypnotized (Spanos, 1986). Indeed, it has even been suggested that posthypnotic amnesia is not real, but is "pretended" by subjects (Coe, 1978). However, even if hypnotic amnesia is real, it is unclear whether the individual cannot retrieve the memories or whether the memories are not "stored" (Evans and Kihlstrom, 1973).

Most of the research on sensory blocking during hypnosis has examined pain reactions. In these experiments, subjects may be shocked or have their arms placed in very cold water. Control groups are hypnotized and either told nothing about pain or allowed to remain in a normal state. If normal, awake subjects are highly paid for this experience, they may tolerate a great deal of pain, like the hypnotic subjects. But, unlike the hypnotic subjects, they are aware of and remember the feeling. The hypnotic subjects appear neither to be consciously aware of nor to recall the pain. In one quite dramatic experiment, J. R. Hilgard (1970) told hypnotic subjects that they had lost their hands; when shock was administered to either hand, pain was not reported. However, in these experiments brain activity in response to pain was not altered.

Other research has demonstrated the positive effects of hypnosis on various other bodily functions. For instance, Klein and Spiegel (1989) have shown that hypnosis can be used to either stimulate or inhibit gastric acid secretion. For example, hypnotized subjects showed a 39 percent reduction in basal acid output. Other studies have found hypnosis beneficial in the treatment of duodenal ulcers (Colgan, Faragher, and Whorwell, 1988) and irritable bowel syndrome (Hammond, 1990).

Another attempt to demonstrate the apparently powerful effects of hypnosis concerns age regression. During hypnotic trance, subjects are told to return to an earlier period in their lives. This suggestion does produce experiential change, in that subjects might act and feel like children. But there are important differences between hypnotic regression and subjects' actual behavior as children. For example, age-regressed subjects' reports of what happened at particular birthday parties differ from reports by adults who attended those parties. Similarly, results of tests administered to age-regressed subjects and of actual tests taken at the earlier age do not correspond (see Orne, 1975).

What Is Hypnosis? Given this array of observation, it is now reasonable to ask, "What is hypnosis?" First of all, many aspects of the hypnotic state seem also to be part of the basic equipment of waking consciousness. These aspects include the capacity to become completely absorbed in an activity and to follow the suggestions of another. Second, it is evident that some role playing is involved in hypnosis. For example, in one investigation subjects were falsely told that the arms stiffen under hypnosis (Orne, 1959); more than half the subjects exhibited this reaction when hypnotized. In sum, hypnosis seems to be a complex phenomenon involving interpersonal relationships, the relinquishing of personal control, some role playing, and the ability to imagine and hallucinate.

Hilgard (1973) has further suggested a *neo-dissociative* theory of hypnosis

Figure 16.3   Reported pain during hypnosis (From *Introduction to Psychology*, 6th ed., by Ernest R. Hilgard, Richard C. Atkinson, and Rita L. Atkinson. Copyright © 1975 by Harcourt Brace Jovanovich, Inc.)

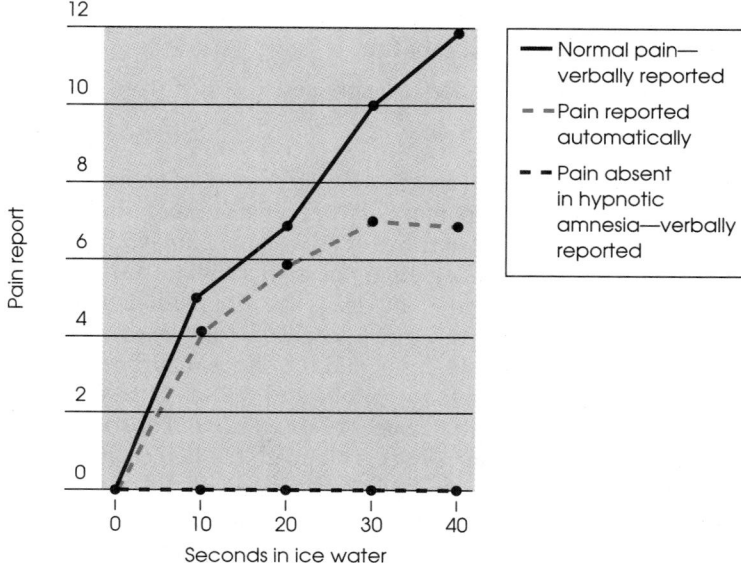

that calls attention to the similarities between hypnotic trances and such dissociative states as multiple personality and amnesia. In one demonstration, Hilgard placed one of the arms of hypnotized subjects in cold water following "no-pain" instructions. The subjects under hypnosis indeed did not report experiencing pain. But with the other hand they were told to report what they felt simultaneously, through automatic writing. These reports indicated feelings of pain (see Fig. 16.3).

Hilgard thus contended that there is a "hidden observer" during hypnosis, and that information is placed under some sort of barrier before entering consciousness. This implies, as Freud did much earlier, that there are multiple levels of awareness and that the levels may not be in communication with one another, a situation that is apparently not unique to hypnotic trances. In sum, it is still unclear whether hypnosis is or is not a "special" state.

Drugs

Consciousness may be changed by natural occurrences like sleep or by external sources like hypnotic induction. One frequent and controversial method of consciousness alteration through artificial induction is the ingestion of chemical substances. Any substance that affects the structure or function of the body can be considered a drug, including tobacco and caffeine. But here our attention is restricted to drugs that might alter consciousness by causing some combination of:

1. Change in thought.
2. Change in the sense of time.
3. Alteration of emotional responses.
4. Change in perception.

The effects of drugs on any particular person, of course, are dependent on many factors, including the personality of the drug taker, the amount of previous drug experience, the purity of the drug, the social climate during the drug experience, whether the drug is taken singly or in combination with other drugs, and so on.

The use of a number of drugs for nonmedicinal purposes has increased enormously over the past three decades. How drugs work, who takes them, the mechanisms behind addiction, and the effects of drugs on behavior have become topics of great interest to the public and the scientist alike. In terms of the major focus of this chapter, the aspect of drugs that is of special interest to us is their influence on consciousness. It is claimed that certain drugs "expand" consciousness; facilitate clearer, sharper perceptions of the physical world; help provide deeper insights into the psyche; expose hidden, repressed materials; and under some circumstances, enable the individual to achieve a more integrated self and sense of spiritual unity. These claims all require careful scientific scrutiny.

Not all drugs are alleged to have positive, consciousness-altering effects. Alcohol may produce a pleasant euphoric state and relax inhibitions, but it predominantly fosters inner confusion, perceptual distortions, and a narrowing rather than an expansion of consciousness. Narcotics like heroin also tend to produce changes in mood and self-confidence, with little else in the way of desirable psychological consequences. The class of drugs called the hallucinogens is most likely to give rise to unusual visual experiences and inner feelings. There is no doubt that the hallucinogens can dramatically alter consciousness. The problematic question is whether, in this alteration, any raising or expanding of consciousness takes place. The characters in the following story (Kukla, 1980, p. 520) illustrating some of the differences between the effects of LSD and marijuana hardly display psychological insight or perceptual acuity.

> The difference between being stoned and being spaced out is illustrated in a story about two men who arrive at the closed gates of a city at night. One has taken lysergic acid, which is the spacer-out *par excellence;* the other has smoked marijuana, which usually gets you stoned. "Let's sprout golden wings and fly over the gates into the city!" suggests the acid-head. The pothead, after a *very* long pause, replies, "Why don't we just sit down and wait till they open in the morning?"[1]

---

[1] Andre Kukla, "The Modern Language of Consciousness," in *The State of the Language,* L. Michaels and C. Ricks, © 1980; published by the University of California Press, Berkeley, CA.

Most hallucinogens have been known for many centuries, with the exception of lysergic acid diethylamide (LSD), which was first synthesized in 1938. The American Indians used peyote, whose active ingredient is mescaline, to induce states of ecstasy and mystical experience. In his book *The Doors of Perception,* Aldous Huxley (1954, pp. 16–18) helped popularize the consciousness-altering effects of mescaline.

> I took my pill at eleven. An hour and a half later, I was sitting in my study, looking intently at a small glass vase. The vase contained only three flowers. . . . I continued to look at the flowers, and in their living light I seemed to detect the qualitative equivalent of breathing—but of a breathing without return to a starting point, with no recurrent ebbs but only a repeated flow from beauty to heightened beauty, from deeper to even deeper meaning; words like "grace" and "transfiguration" came to my mind, and this, of course, was what, among other things, they stood for.

The possibility that hallucinogens could help individuals break through the ordinary barriers of consciousness and achieve a deeper level of self-understanding was explored by some psychotherapists (Caldwell, 1968). One patient, following a therapeutic session in which she had taken LSD, described her experience (Aaronson and Osmond, 1970, p. 330):

> After I had felt that hours must have gone by and then learned that it was only five minutes; after I had seen flowers open and close their petals and held in my hand a peeled grape that became, before my eyes, a tiny brain; and after I had closed my eyes and seen one beautiful vision right after another; well, then I decided that *anything* must be possible, including the transformations of character and personality I had heard about, and to some extent believed, but which only now I really felt confident could happen.

Although there were very occasional clinical reports of insights achieved through hallucinogenic drugs, there is no systematic evidence demonstrating their psychotherapeutic utility.

In addition, hallucinogens can produce very unpleasant experiences. "Bad trips" are not uncommon and experts (Caldwell, 1968) emphasize the necessity for careful supervision of the individual who takes hallucinogens, particularly LSD or mescaline. Huxley also stresses the need for monitoring, portraying mescaline as opening the door to either heaven or hell.

To evaluate the hallucinogens, their immediate effects on consciousness must be separated from their long-term effects. A vivid, dramatic, or ecstatic experience is not the equivalent of personality growth, of a new insight into oneself and the world. Thorough evaluation studies of the effects of LSD have not supported the hypothesis that taking LSD facilitates creativity, produces self-insight, or enhances one's perceptions of the surrounding environment (McGlothlin and Arnold, 1971; McGlothlin, Cohen, and McGlothlin, 1967). A similar conclusion applies to marijuana. The principal scientific uncertainty concerning the effects of repeated use of marijuana and other hallucinogens is over the likelihood of such

■ **Highlight 16.3** ■

Creativity and Madness

Just as hallucinogenic drugs have been thought by some to increase insight and creativity, some have argued that madness (another form of altered consciousness) increases creativity. As evidence in support of this belief, one study found that among thirty presently-established creative writers, twenty-four had been diagnosed with an affective disorder — a rate much greater than that for a matched group of other professionals. It also has been found that the families of writers are higher than normative in mental illness. Well-known creative artists such as Van Gogh, composers such as Schumann and Handel, and writers as diverse as Poe and Sylvia Plath are a few often-cited examples of an association between mental illness and artistic productivity.

Several reasons have been proposed for this connection. Manic states can heighten senses and accelerate the flow of ideas. In addition, depression might provide good material for creative work and may foster continued introspection. Conversely, others argue that the vast proportion of creative people are not and have never been psychotic. Even those with mental illness do their best work when in normal states. Most psychologists link productivity to psychological well-being and, in the long run, "bet on health."

Was Handel a great composer because of, or in spite of, his mental illness? (The Bettmann Archive)

negative personality effects as decreased energy and goal striving and subtle disturbances in thinking. Moreover, whatever the subjective experiences provided by marijuana, at the objective level marijuana intoxication interferes with motor coordination, visual perception, and reaction time (*Marijuana and Health,* 1977). In brief, aside from the temporary alterations in mood and perception that hallucinogens produce, their consciousness-expanding effects have yet to be scientifically demonstrated.

THE DIVIDED SELF: SPLIT-BRAIN EXPERIMENTS AND CONSCIOUSNESS

The human brain is divided into two halves. The left side (or *hemisphere*) controls the right side of the body, while the right hemisphere controls the left side of the body. In humans, these halves of the brain are functionally different, with the left side specialized in language functions such as speaking and writing, and the right half more limited in terms of language abilities. It has also been found by researchers that the right hemisphere is superior at visual-spatial tasks such as spatial orientation.

Under normal circumstances, information is relayed between the two halves of the brain. However, the connections can be severed experimentally, so that there is disruption of the knowledge flow and each half of the brain may be independently examined. Split-brain operations are typically performed on laboratory animals such as cats or monkeys. But very occasionally this operation is performed on humans, for it has been found that splitting the brain reduces the severity of epileptic seizures. Some individuals suffer such extreme forms of this illness, with as many as twelve seizures daily, that the operation is of great benefit in spite of negative side effects. In addition, through accidents some individuals have greatly damaged one side of their brains, thus permitting the experimental study of half the brain.

Split-brain experiments have revealed that each half of the brain can process information outside the realm of the other half's consciousness. For example, if a word is flashed to a split-brain patient's left (typically major) hemisphere, the patient is able to say the word and write it with his or her right hand. But if the right (typically minor) hemisphere receives this information, then the word cannot be verbalized or written with the left hand (see Sperry, 1968).

On the basis of these data, some individuals have argued that there are two independent spheres or modes of consciousness; that there is a duality in human consciousness, with the "conscious" left side of the brain specializing in verbalization capacities, and the "unconscious" right side not having this function. One might *experience* with the right hemisphere, but that experience would not be part of conscious (verbalizable) awareness. For example, in one experiment a patient was shown a picture of a nude. When the nude was presented to the left hemisphere, there was affect along with verbalization about the picture. But when it was viewed by the right hemisphere, there was affect without any apparent understanding of why. Indeed, the patient appeared to search for a reason to justify and make sense of his feelings.

These data led not only to speculation about the independent modes of consciousness, but also to the belief that there is a duality in human nature, with each aspect of a person having independent representation in the brain. Table 16.5 below characterizes the suggested duality in human consciousness and human nature. In a humorous but nevertheless thought-provoking extension of these controversial ideas, Kimble et al. (1974, p. 614) related the following scenario (based on Gazzaniga, 1970):

> Emotions can be different in the two hemispheres. One of these patients once got angry with his wife, grabbed her with the left hand, and shook her violently while the right hand tried to intercede and bring the other half under control. Suppose that the right hand had been unsuccessful and that the left hand had murdered the wife. Who would be guilty in such a case?

It now appears, however, that there has been an overdramatization of the uniqueness of the two sides of the brain (Gazzaniga and LeDoux, 1978). First of all, the hemispheres are typically intact and there is mental unity. If there really were two independent brains, where and how would they be integrated and synthesized? Furthermore, the right hemisphere can perform logical operations. For example, if the left hemisphere is damaged early in life, the right develops linguistic capabilities. In addition, although the right hemisphere cannot verbally label objects, if the left hand is allowed to feel an object, a correct match to an object flashed on a screen can be made. Thus, although response production

Table 16.5   The two dimensions of consciousness: A dichotomy

Left hemisphere	Right hemisphere
Intellectual	Sensuous
Masculine: yang	Feminine: yin
Day, light	Night, dark
Time, history	Eternity, timeless
Verbal	Spatial
Western culture	Eastern culture
Reason, logic	Passion, intuition

Source: Adapted from *The Psychology of Consciousness,*
Second Edition (p. 37), copyright © 1977 by Robert Ornstein.

through the linguistic mode is not possible by the right hemisphere, it is not without consciousness.

In sum, there are localized differences and specialization of brain functions, primarily due to linguistic development that is typically localized in the left hemisphere. But there is unity and integration in mental functioning, the two hemispheres do not oppose one another, and the differences between the hemispheres are quantitative rather than qualitative. The romance associated with split-brain research may be waning. For example, claims that the right brain is the seat of creativity and that artists are more oriented toward this hemisphere have not been substantiated. But it is evident from this research that there can be experience without verbalization, which is consistent with the theme presented throughout this chapter.

FANTASY AND CONSCIOUSNESS

Most of you have had the experience of finding yourself on the same page of a book after a half-hour supposedly spent studying. You wonder where the time went and what happened during the interval. You then realize that your mind has "wandered." Perhaps you were thinking about an upcoming date or a recent party, or imagined yourself reaching a goal or occupying a position of power and status. Our thought processes are engaged in this kind of fantasy activity a surprising amount of the time; our minds are rarely blank or idle. Engaging in such fantasies or daydreams does not entail as radical an alteration of consciousness as that produced by drugs or dreaming. However, there is a relation between these altered states of consciousness and fantasy activity. In all these experiences attention is directed toward or dominated by the inner, rather than the outer world. In reality-directed activity, we attend to real physical stimuli — sounds, odors, visual displays, and the like — while in fantasy or imaginary activity, we attend to internal representations of physical stimuli — thoughts and ideas. Hence, in fantasy our inner life plays the important role in determining the contents of consciousness.

One of the most common forms of inner fantasy is daydreaming. Research has found that most people are aware of daydreaming to some extent every day. The content of daydreaming varies considerably from individual to individual and from time to time. In general, research has identified three styles of daydreaming. One style is "positive-constructive" daydreaming, in which individuals use daydreaming to solve problems, both everyday concerns and long-range problems. A second style is "guilty-dysphoric" daydreaming, in which individuals tend to ruminate over failings and transgressions. The third style is a "poor attentional control" pattern, in which the individual is unable to focus on extended fantasy (Singer and Bonanno, 1990).

One important element of daydreams and related fantasy experience is the notion of *imagery,* or "pictures in the mind." Vivid imagery is readily induced by

hypnosis, is one of the consequences of hallucinogens, and is a common characteristic of dreams. Thinking in images has been shown to have different properties
than thinking in words. For example, images facilitate memory and appear to be
understood and stored differently than words (Paivio, 1971). There is also some
evidence that thinking in pictures is associated with right-brain activity, while
thinking in words is associated with left-brain activity (Robbins and McAdam,
1974). However, the evidence concerning the relationship between imagery and
brain hemisphere activity is not conclusive. One problem of interpretation is that
the right brain appears to be more responsive to emotions, primarily negative
emotions, than the left brain, and images frequently elicit strong emotional responses. Hence, it is difficult to disentangle whether the right brain is responding
to imagery or to the emotions produced by imagery (Ley, 1979).

There is evidence among both children and adults that individuals who
engage in fantasy experience are less impulsive and display more positive adjustment patterns than individuals who engage in very little fantasy activity (Singer,
1966, 1973). But the term *fantasy* is a broad construct embracing many different
kinds of activity such as imagery, constructing stories, engaging in play, and even
reading fiction and watching theatrical productions. It is not unlikely that the
effects of these disparate types of fantasy may be quite different.

In terms of the issues with which we have been concerned in this chapter, it is
of interest that the effects of an event portrayed on television differ dramatically,
depending on whether children viewing the event perceive it as real or as a
fantasy. In one experiment (Feshbach, 1972), children nine to eleven years old
were individually shown a six-minute segment of a campus riot, made up by
combining shots of a real campus riot with parts of a movie about a campus riot.
Before seeing the television program, children assigned to a reality-set condition
were told that the program was taken from a television newscast, while children
assigned to a fantasy-set condition were told that the program was part of a film
made in Hollywood. A control group was not shown a program. Each child was
then given the opportunity to aggress against the experimenter by administering
an aversive noise that varied in its loudness and severity. The data revealed that
children in the fantasy-set condition were less aggressive, while children in the
reality-set condition were more aggressive than the no-television control group.
The importance of this finding lies in its demonstration that the same event has a
different impact when experienced as a fantasy than when experienced as reality.

Summary

1. *Consciousness* refers to awareness, or what is known, about one's experiences. We are not consciously aware of all the internal and external sensa-
   tions that impinge upon us.

2. In this chapter, instead of the term the *unconscious,* we use the term *non-*

conscious to differentiate modern views of nonconscious information processing from Freud's view of the unconscious. Research generally supports the proposition that much information processing occurs at a nonconscious level.

3. *Automaticity* refers to the idea that many nonconscious properties operate automatically.

4. *Priming* refers to the idea that inactive nonconscious processes can be activated by a stimulus in the environment.

5. Trying not to think of something often increases the probability of thinking about it.

6. *Dissociative phenomena* include somnambulism, amnesia, and dissociative identity disorder. In these states there is dramatically diminished awareness of selected aspects of behavior.

7. There is much debate over whether nonconscious functioning is simply automatic or whether it is "smart."

8. Dreams are one of a number of *altered states of consciousness*. The presence of a dream is inferred by *rapid eye movements* (REM) and a particular pattern of brain activity. Humans and many nonhuman species pass through a typical dream cycle during the night.

9. Freud's speculations about dreams are not confirmed by dream research. Dream deprivation does not necessarily impede psychological functioning; the onset of external stimulation during sleep does not initiate a dream; and most dreams appear quite commonplace and somewhat unpleasant. Dreams may have a biological or problem-solving, rather than a wish-fulfilling, function.

10. Physiological activity during a hypnotic state corresponds to that in a normal waking condition. However, the individual is highly suggestible, reality testing is reduced, there may be heightened control over bodily functions, and there is posthypnotic amnesia. The hypnotic influence over seeing and hearing is not evident in subtle tasks related to these processes, such as delayed auditory feedback. The *neo-dissociative* theory of hypnosis accepts the notion of multiple layers of consciousness.

11. There are a variety of drugs. Hallucinogens have vivid and immediate effects on consciousness, but there is no evidence that they produce any long-term positive effects.

12. The brain has two hemispheres: the left specializing in language function and the right specializing in spatial orientation. Research has shown that presentation of visual material to the right side of the brain results in an experience that cannot be verbalized.

13. In fantasy, as in altered states of consciousness, attention is directed toward or dominated by the inner, rather than the outer, world.

Thought Questions

1. There are times, as during sporting events, when we are under great pain, but are able to "forget" that pain and continue striving. How might this be explained?

2. In what ways are dreams, hypnotically induced images, and daydreams similar? How do they differ?

3. What do you think of the proposition that we often act mindlessly?

COMPLEX PERSONALITY PROCESSES

C hapters 17 and 18 focus on complex personality processes and behaviors. In Chapter 17 we consider a set of topics that relate to an individual's being in charge of his or her life and being able to take effective, proactive action, especially in the face of failure experiences. In Chapter 18 we consider the theoretical and empirical literature on love and aggression. These topics are fundamental to human personality and represent active research areas. Other significant personality processes and behaviors, such as anxiety, have been considered at various other points in the text.

Chapters 17 and 18 also illustrate different aspects of personality research. Chapter 17 illustrates how concepts that are central to humanistic views of personality, such as feeling in control of oneself, taking responsibility for oneself, and feeling free, can be systematically investigated using objective, quantitative procedures. In addition, the study of achievement motivation illustrates how a personality construct can be used to investigate socioeconomic change and development in the larger culture. Chapter 18, on love and aggression, illustrates the multidetermined basis of personality and the interplay of diverse biological and social factors.

Attempts to explain complex personality processes and behaviors in terms of single causes are simplistic and misleading. There are many antecedents to major personality dimensions, and an adequate understanding of personal responsibility, achievement, and love and aggression requires analysis of the roles of each of them.

17 | Perceived Causality and Control

In Chapter 2 we discussed Western culture's emphasis on an individualistic self that must be able to direct and control its own activities. Further, this self must be responsible for itself, must be able to mobilize itself to take action to achieve its goals, and must be able to cope with adversity and failure. This emphasis appears in most of the major theories of personality. For Freud (see Chapter 3), the goal of psychotherapy was to put the ego in charge so that the individual could consciously make choices rather than be the victim of forces outside of his or her control. Kohut (see Chapter 4) believed that a fundamental component of a healthy self-structure was the ability to mobilize the self and work to achieve goals. Rogers (see Chapter 6) saw therapy as helping individuals grow towards autonomy, self-direction, and the ability to take responsibility for themselves. Finally, both cognitive and behavioral therapists (see Chapter 5) have devoted a great deal of effort to developing individuals' skills and perceptions related to effective self-management and self-control.

The belief in an individual self goes hand in hand with an emphasis on freedom and self-determination. Philosophically, there is much controversy in psychology concerning the degree to which individuals are "free" to direct their own behavior. While humanistic theorists such as Rogers have assumed freedom and self-direction, other theorists, such as Skinner, do not believe humans are free.

In his provocative book *Beyond Freedom and Dignity,* Skinner (1971) contended that we must give up the illusion of freedom and admit that behavior is controlled by reinforcements (see Chapter 5). According to the principles of operant reinforcement, *external* stimuli paired with rewards are responsible for behavior. For example, if food follows the pressing of a lever, then the appearance of that lever initiates a particular chain of behaviors. If we give up the illusion of freedom, Skinner argued, then our knowledge of behavioral engineering can be used to control human behavior for the betterment of society. But, Skinner went on to state, people refuse to give up this illusion and the false belief that we are autonomous actors, possessing free will and deserving credit for our actions. He concluded that, in order for society to survive, this conviction must be replaced with the acceptance of external control.

The issue of free will versus determinism is an old and persistent philosophical problem which neither philosophers nor psychologists have been able to solve satisfactorily. Consideration of the different ways with which this complex problem has been dealt would take us beyond the scope of this chapter. However, what is directly pertinent are the psychological effects of people's *perceptions* of their freedom of choice.

There is much research to suggest that the belief that one has some personal control over what happens is important to effective functioning. In this chapter we first consider the effects of perceiving oneself to have control in one's life and the opposite effects of feeling helpless. Next we consider efforts to preserve a belief that one has control over one's self and one's life. After this we consider some limitations to the belief that one has personal control.

Believing that one has some control over one's fate is related to how one perceives the causes of success and failure in one's life. In turn, how one perceives the causes of success and failure is related to how competently one copes with achievement situations and with failure experiences. So, we move from perceptions of control to a consideration of perceptions of causality and their relation to achievement motivation and competence. Following this we apply ideas from previous sections to perceptions of responsibility.

PERCEIVED CONTROL

A number of psychologists and philosophers have contended that personal control is integral to self-concept and self-esteem and constitutes a fundamental psychological need. Moreover, control appears to be especially important given stressful circumstances and helps reduce experiences of stress and aids with coping. For example, laboratory research has shown that when subjects are faced with shock, loud noise, a test, etc., and have no information about the timing or onset of those events and have no actions they can take to alter the events, then their reactions are especially negative. They experience "jitters," have reduced concentration, and report great discomfort (see, for example, Glass and Singer, 1972).

Locus of Control

In the field of personality, much of the current concern with the notions of freedom and self-responsibility grew from the concept of *locus of control* (Rotter, 1966) and a distinction between *internal* and *external* control (see Chapter 5). Locus of control refers to the perceived influence that one has on the attainment of reinforcement. This concept has its roots in social learning theory and is related to schedules of reinforcement. Reinforcement theorists have distinguished between two kinds of reinforcement schedules: ratio versus interval. Given a ratio schedule, the responder gets rewarded after a certain number of responses. That is, there is covariation between personal responding and the reward. On the other hand, given an interval schedule, the respondent receives a reward after a certain time interval. For the most part, the reward is independent of responding and is under the control of the experimenter. These types of schedules respectively capture the notions of internal versus external control.

There is a further distinction, in part generated by learning theorists, that also represents the difference between internal versus external control, namely, the differentiation between skill-determined versus luck-determined tasks. Given a skill-related activity, such as athletic games or general school performance, outcomes depend in part on effort and work input. These are under personal control. On the other hand, at luck-determined games, such as the toss of a coin, the outcome is not under personal control. Chance or fate is not subject to volitional change.

It has been postulated that internal versus external control is a dimension of personality; some persons perceive greater personal (internal) control, while others perceive the situation (external control) as more salient. Rotter (1966, p. 1) defined such internality and externality as follows:

> When a reinforcement is perceived . . . as . . . not being entirely contingent upon his action, then, in our culture, it is typically perceived as the result of luck, chance, fate, as under the control of powerful others, or as unpredictable because of the great complexity of forces surrounding him. When the event is interpreted in this way by an individual, we have labeled this a belief in *external control*. If the person perceives that the event is contingent upon his own behavior or his own relatively permanent characteristics, we have termed this a belief in *internal control*.

Similarly, Lefcourt (1976) cited a passage from an interview in Oscar Lewis's (1961, p. 171) classic book on Mexican culture to illustrate the thoughts of a person with an external locus of control:

> To me, one's destiny is controlled by a mysterious hand that moves all things. Only for the select, do things turn out as planned; to those of us who are born to be tamale eaters, heaven sends only tamales. We plan and plan and some little thing happens to wash it all away. Like once, I decided to try and save and I said to Paula, "Old girl, put away this money so that some day we'll have a little pile." When we have ninety pesos laid away, pum! my father got sick and I had to give all to him for doctors and medicine. It was the only time I had helped him and the only time I had tried to save! I said to Paula, "There you are! Why should we save if someone gets sick and we have to spend it all!" Sometimes I even think that savings bring on illness! That's why I firmly believe that some of us are born to be poor.

A number of psychologists have asked whether there are individual differences in beliefs about internal versus external control.

Assessment Procedure. There are many scales designed to assess the perception of events as internally versus externally controlled, for both children and adults. However, the most frequently used instrument is a 29-item self-report inventory (see Rotter, 1966). This test, called the *Internal-External Control Scale (I-E scale)*, has a forced-choice format with an internal belief pitted directly against an external belief for each item. The items on the scale are classified in six general subcategories on the basis of type of need portrayed and characteristics of described goals. The six categories are academic recognition, social recognition, love and affection, dominance, social-political beliefs, and life philosophy. Some sample items and their keyed responses (italic letters represent externality choices) are:

1. *a.* Many of the unhappy things in people's lives are partly due to bad luck.
   b. People's misfortunes result from the mistakes they make.
2. a. The idea that teachers are unfair to students is nonsense.
   b. Most students don't realize the extent to which grades are influenced by accidental happenings.

It is evident that the questions on the scale are very broad. As Rotter (1975, p. 62) indicated, "[The scale] was developed not as an instrument . . . to allow for a very high prediction of some specific situation, such as achievement or political behavior, but rather to allow for a low degree of prediction of behavior across a wide variety of potential situations." Typically, the situational cues in a setting most influence beliefs and behavior. However, generalized beliefs about control are also presumed, to a lesser extent, to influence a person's specific beliefs and actions.

Personality Correlates.   Phares (1976, p. 60) has stated that:

> The best single validity of the I-E scale would undoubtedly be evidence showing that internals are more active, alert, or directive in attempting to control and manipulate their environment than are externals. Since locus of control refers to expectancies for control over one's surroundings, a higher level of coping activity would be anticipated from internals.

There is some evidence supporting this position. In one early series of studies, Seeman and Evans (1962) and Seeman (1963) reported, respectively, on information seeking and retention of personally relevant information among institutionalized individuals. It was found that, among hospitalized tuberculosis patients, individuals classified as internals knew more about their illness and asked doctors more questions than patients who were external in locus of control. In addition, prisoners who were internals retained more information pertinent to parole than did externals. In sum, among both patients and prisoners, the behavior displayed by those high in internal control was instrumental to improving their life situations. On the other hand, it appeared that among those low in personal control, the acquisition of information was seen as less likely to serve any useful function.

Other investigators have studied the differential cognitive activity of internals and externals. For example, Wolk and DuCette (1974) presented subjects with protocols to be scanned for errors. It was found that internals were better at incidental learning (remembering the material that had been scanned) and at finding errors. In general, theorists in this area have contended that "the cognitive functioning of internals should enhance their personal effectiveness as compared to externals. And it apparently does" (Phares, 1976, p. 65). It is not at all clear, however, how these disparate dispositions come about, inasmuch as there is little pertinent developmental data.

One of the difficulties faced by researchers in this area is related to the trait-situation controversy examined in Chapter 9. It is quite evident that beliefs about personal control may vary from situation to situation. For example, one might perceive oneself to be personally responsible for positive outcomes in affiliative contexts, yet believe that success in academic affairs is a matter of good luck or help from others. These issues have been relatively neglected by researchers in locus of control (see Lefcourt, et al., 1979).

Learned Helplessness

The previous section has shown that perceiving oneself as having some control has psychological consequences. Perceiving oneself as not having control, i.e., as being helpless, may often be quite harmful. Two experimental investigations with rats as subjects dramatically illustrate some of these adverse effects. In fact, the procedures used and the consequences observed were so injurious in these particular investigations that lower organisms had to be the experimental subjects.

In one of the investigations, Mowrer and Viek (1948) gave hungry rats the opportunity to eat ten seconds before the onset of a shock. For half the animals, the shock could be terminated by jumping into the air. The second group of rats could not terminate the shock through their own actions. Rather, each was paired with a "controlling" rat and received the same amount of shock that the partner had received before the partner jumped to terminate its own shock.

Since it was known from prior experimental research that fear inhibits eating, the experimenters measured the eating behavior of both groups to examine the effects of the helplessness experience. The data revealed that the noncontrolling, or helpless, rats were inhibited in their eating, whereas the behavior of the controlling rats was not greatly affected. This difference existed even though the two groups received identical amounts of shock.

In the course of subsequent research, Richter (1958) observed cases of sudden death among rats during experimentation. For example, in a study of swimming endurance, many unexplained drownings occurred after the rats swam for only a short period of time. Richter speculated that (pp. 308–309) "the situation of these rats is not one that can be resolved by either fight or flight—it is rather one of hopelessness: Being restrained . . . in the swimming jar with no chance of escape is a situation against which the rat has no defense. . . . They seem literally to give up." In sum, a loss of control has dramatic and aversive effects on the well-being of an organism (see Lefcourt, 1973).

Further research investigations of helplessness were conducted with researchers administering inescapable shock to dogs for a period of time. The dogs were placed in a harness and shock was administered to one of their hind legs. Then these animals, as well as other dogs not given prior inescapable training, were placed in a two-compartment box. When a tone signaling that shock would follow was sounded, the dogs could move from the shock side to the no-shock side of the box. Seligman and Maier (1967) reported that many of the dogs given prior inescapable shocks did not attempt to escape in this situation. Rather, they passively accepted their supposed fate; they appeared to have "learned helplessness." The untrained dogs, on the other hand, engaged in a variety of responses until the escape response was learned. Similar differences in behavior have been reported in experiments using fish, rats, cats, and other nonhuman species. It must be noted, however, that not all animals exposed to inescapable shock exhibit helplessness, and deficits are displayed on some subsequent tasks but not on others. Furthermore, in some cases helplessness is exhibited if testing immediately follows training, while a waiting period erases helplessness effects (see critique by Levis, 1976). In sum, there are many questions yet unanswered about the existence of this psychological state.

The most systematic and influential analysis of loss of control is that reported by Seligman (1975), who contended that organisms are helpless when their actions are perceived as not influencing their outcomes. If a response does not increase the likelihood of receiving a reinforcement, then conditions for helplessness have been established. For example, assume that a baby goes to sleep after crying for one hour. The harried parents try to shorten this aversive period by rocking, feeding, or even playing music to the baby. Despite all these actions, however, the baby still doesn't fall asleep until an hour of crying has gone by. Thus, the reinforcer (the end of crying and the onset of sleep) is independent of the parents' behavior. The parents, therefore, are helpless in this situation.

To explain observations of learned helplessness, Seligman proposed a three-stage theory:

1. Information is gained about the contingency between outcomes and responding. In the case of helplessness training, this information reveals that there is no contingency or association between actions and reward.

2. This information results in the development of the expectation that responses and outcomes will remain independent in the future.

3. The low expectation causes deficits in future learning as well as motivational and emotional disturbance.

Learned-helplessness research then expanded to include human subjects. In one exemplary research investigation, Hiroto and Seligman (1975) exposed participants to either an escapable or an inescapable aversive tone. Subjects were then given a different task in which they could escape the noise by making a particular hand movement. It was found that individuals previously exposed to the inescapable tone performed poorly as compared to groups without prior inescapable-tone training.

Learned Helplessness and Depression.   The research of Seligman and others has called attention to a parallel between helplessness learning in the laboratory and human depression. Table 17.1 lists some of the similarities between the two phenomena. It certainly appears fruitful to think of some kinds of depression as akin to learned helplessness, but it must also be remembered that clinical depression is not a unitary illness; many kinds of depression have been identified, and there are many determinants of depression.

Table 17.1   Summary of features common to learned helplessness and depression

	Learned helplessness	Depression
Symptoms	Passivity	Passivity
	Difficulty learning that responses produce relief	Negative cognitive set
	Dissipates in time	Time course
	Lack of aggression	Introjected hostility (hostility turned inward)
	Weight loss, appetite loss, social and sexual deficits	Weight loss, appetite loss, social and sexual deficits
	Ulcers and stress	Ulcers (?) and stress
		Feelings of helplessness
Cause	Learning that responding and reinforcement are independent	Belief that responding is useless
Cure	Directive therapy: forced exposure to responses that produce reinforcement	Recovery of belief that responding produces reinforcement
	Electroconvulsive shock	Electroconvulsive shock
	Time	Time
Prevention	Immunization by mastery over reinforcement	(?)

Source: From *Helplessness: On Depression, Development, and Death*, p. 106, by Martin E.P. Seligman. W.H. Freeman and Company. Copyright © 1975.

More recently, attributional analyses of learned helplessness and depression have been formulated (Abramson, Seligman, and Teasdale, 1978; Miller and Norman, 1979). Recall from Chapter 9 that attribution theorists are concerned with the perceived causes of an event. It has been contended that how one perceives the causes of prior outcomes determines the type and course of depression. Specifically, if one experiences a negative event and attributes its cause to internal, stable, and global or relatively general factors, one is more likely to become depressed (Abramson, Metalsky, and Alloy, 1988). For example, one is more likely to become depressed after failing a test if one believes "I failed the test because I am stupid" rather than "I failed the test because I didn't study hard enough."

Abramson and her co-workers (1978) distinguished between personal helplessness and universal helplessness. *Universal helplessness* is experienced when responses and outcomes are not contingent for any person in that situation. For example, if a child develops leukemia, despite all efforts of the parents and doctors, the child's life may not be saved. The parents and doctors would probably not perceive themselves as personally responsible, although they would experience helplessness. Conversely, *personal helplessness* connotes a situation in which a person feels helpless but in which others might be able to attain the desired goal. For example, a person unable to receive passing grades in school in spite of effort will experience personal helplessness, for others obviously can receive passing grades. Although in both cases low expectancies and helplessness are experienced, low self-esteem is likely to be a consequence only of personal helplessness. Depressed patients may fail to make this distinction and may perceive situations of universal helplessness as indicative of personal helplessness and their own shortcomings.

Individual Differences. The merging of ideas about learned helplessness with perceptions of causality gave rise to a rich literature concerned with what has been called "attributional style," or the disposition to perceive or judge particular causes as most salient across a variety of situations. Some causal perceptions might be particularly dysfunctional and predispose one toward depression. Abramson et al. (1978) suggested that attributing failure to the self is particularly perilous because this would lower self-esteem. In addition, this might lead individuals to believe that change is not possible and that failure was out of their control. Hence, this attribution was anticipated to lead to the onset of depression; if combined with negative life events, this attribution makes individuals vulnerable to symptoms of helplessness (see Brewin, 1985).

This thinking resulted in the development of an Attributional Style questionnaire (Peterson et al., 1982). Scores on this measure were then related to depressive symptoms. The scale presents individuals with hypothetical positive or negative outcomes (e.g., "You go to a party and do not meet new friends."). The respondents then generate a causal explanation and rate that cause on the dimension of locus, stability, and cross-situational generality. This instrument has been marred by psychometric inadequacies (see Carver, 1989; Cutrona, Russell, and Jones, 1985), with the very typical problem related to a lack of cross-situational consistency. In discussing this issue, Anderson, Jennings, and Arnoult (1989) have concluded that Attributional Style has a "moderate level of specificity." That is, scores are:

> ". . . cross-situationally consistent only across situations that are similar in psychologically meaningful ways, but not across very divergent types of situations. This view maintains that within situation types (e.g., interpersonal failure) the relative standing of individuals will remain fairly constant from one situation to another, but that between different situation types (e.g., interpersonal failure vs. noninterpersonal success) there will be little correspondence" (p. 980).

And what about the relationship of helplessness to depression? There is a great deal of inconsistency in the literature, with some individual investigators and general reviews supporting the helplessness position, while others fail to find such support. The most recent summary articles present evidence that attributional style does weakly to moderately correlate with depression, and that scores on the locus subscale are particularly predictive (see Robbins, 1988). There is also some evidence that attributional style precedes depression onset (rather than depression causing alterations in perceived causality). However, the causation issue remains uncertain.

In sum, the issues are far from settled, and one can anticipate that research in this area will continue to flourish. For the present, the conclusions and advice of Anderson et al. (1988) seem very wise:

> "It was concluded that both the extreme pessimism of some recent researchers and the broad, sweepingly optimistic claims of some proponents are unwarranted, and that further work on specifying the appropriate level of assessment for attributional style would be useful" (p. 989).

Optimism

Recently Seligman (1990) has shifted his focus from helplessness to optimism. He argues that those who feel optimistic generally function more effectively and are both physically and psychologically more healthy. For Seligman an optimistic explanatory style is one in which individuals tend to attribute success to themselves, and failure to external circumstances. In a variety of research studies, Seligman and colleagues have developed a system to score public speeches, personal reports, and other verbal material for optimism. They have found, among other things, that baseball teams whose public statements contain more optimistic imagery are more likely to win, and presidential candidates whose speeches contain more optimism are more likely to win.

In a rather startling finding, Peterson, Seligman, and Vaillant (1988) report that explanatory style at age 25 (assessed by means of content analysis of available protocols of wartime experience) predicted health status at ages 45–60 (but not between the ages of 30–40). Seligman cites several studies suggesting that optimism is correlated with positive physical and mental health. In one study, individuals with cancer were trained to think in an optimistic manner. Compared to those who did not receive such training, the trained individuals showed an increase in immune system functioning.

Seligman paints an optimistic portrait of optimism. However, there is some evidence that pessimism is not always dysfunctional, depending on what kind of pessimism one is talking about. Norem (1989) has studied defensive pessimism. Defensive pessimists are individuals who predict catastrophe for themselves but then use that prediction to mobilize themselves for action. When they come to prepare for a midterm exam, they predict catastrophe, believing that they don't know the material well enough, they'll never pass, and so on. In effect, they scare themselves into studying harder and typically proceed to do well on their exam. Defensive pessimism, which leads to positive action, contrasts with dysfunctional pessimism, which leads to helplessness and inaction. Norem's research has suggested that defensive pessimism can be an adaptive style. She points out that there are roles — such as director of a nuclear power plant — in which most of us would prefer to have a defensive pessimist.

Efforts to Preserve a Sense of Personal Control

Because of the evidence that individuals who are optimistic and who perceive themselves to have an internal sense of control function better than those who feel helpless, it is no wonder that some researchers have found evidence that individuals strive to maintain a sense of personal freedom and control. In the following discussion, we consider three examples of this behavior. First, when individuals believe themselves to be intrinsically motivated to do something, they are more likely to continue to do it than when they believe that their motivation comes from external sources. Second, when individuals perceive their sense of freedom to be threatened, they react against this threat and act in ways to maintain that sense of freedom. Third, they strive to maintain an illusion that they have a sense of control over their fate.

Intrinsic Versus Extrinsic Motivation. Belief in an internal locus of control goes with the idea that when individuals perceive themselves to be the source of their actions there are different psychological effects than when they believe their actions are being controlled from without. This, in turn, relates to the issue of intrinsic versus extrinsic motivation. Teachers often feel that students study not because of *intrinsic* interest in the material, but rather because of the course grade, or the *extrinsic* motivator that is contingent on their efforts.

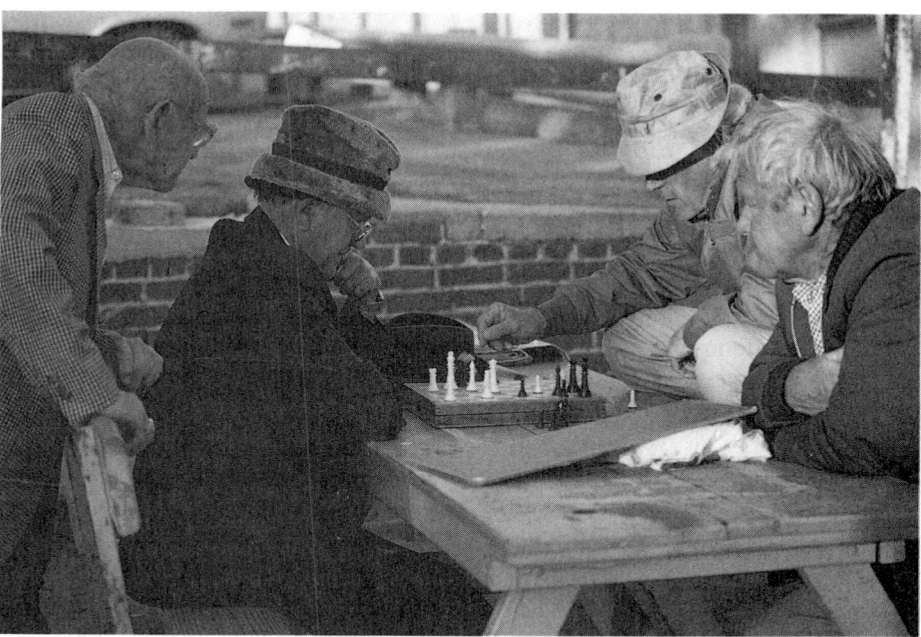

An intrinsically motivated activity. (Deborah Davis/PhotoEdit)

A fable reported by Ausubel (1948) provides an amusing illustration of the distinction between intrinsic and extrinsic motivation.

> In a little Southern town where the Klan was riding again, a Jewish tailor had the temerity to open his little shop on the main street. To drive him out of the town the Kleagle of the Klan sent a gang of little ragamuffins to annoy him. Day after day they stood at the entrance of his shop. "Jew! Jew!" they hooted at him. The situation looked serious for the tailor. He took the matter so much to heart that he began to brood and spent sleepless nights over it. Finally out of desperation he evolved a plan.
>
> The following day, when the little hoodlums came to jeer at him, he came to the door and said to them, "From today on anybody who calls me "Jew" will get a dime from me." Then he put his hand in his pocket and gave each boy a dime.
>
> Delighted with their booty, the boys came back the following day and began to shrill, "Jew! Jew!" The tailor came out smiling. He put his hand in his pocket and gave each of the boys a nickel, saying, "A dime is too much — I can only afford a nickel today." The boys went away satisfied because, after all, a nickel was money, too.
>
> However, when they returned the next day to hoot at him, the tailor gave them only a penny each.
>
> "Why do we get only a penny today?" they yelled.
>
> "That's all I can afford."
>
> "But two days ago you gave us a dime, and yesterday we got a nickel. It's not fair, mister."
>
> "Take it or leave it. That's all you're going to get!"
>
> "Do you think we're going to call you "Jew" for one lousy penny?"
>
> "So don't!"
>
> And they didn't.[1]

Anecdotes like the story of the tailor have been incorporated in a conception called *cognitive evaluation theory* (Deci, 1975). Deci contended that when someone receives extrinsic rewards for engaging in intrinsically motivating activities, there may be a change in beliefs about why one is engaging in the activity. Using the language of locus of control theory, perceived causation may change from internal (intrinsic interest) to external (the extrinsic reward initiates the activity).

An experiment by Lepper, Greene, and Nisbett (1973) demonstrated this phenomenon in the laboratory. In this study, nursery school children interested in a drawing task were selected as the subjects. The children were asked to perform the drawing task under one of three experimental conditions. In an *expected-reward* condition, the subjects were told beforehand that they would receive a Good Player Certificate if they played with the experimental materials. In an *unexpected-reward* condition, the subjects received the same reward, but had no knowledge that they were going to receive the certificate until the drawing activity was completed. Finally, in a control condition, the reward was neither expected nor received.

---

[1] Reprinted from *A Treasury of Jewish Folklore* by Nathan Ausubel. Copyright ©1948, 1976 by Crown Publishers, Inc. By permission of Crown Publishers, Inc.

Highlight 17.1

The Flow of Experience

Intrinsically-motivated activities are often associated with leisure time —one is doing what one wants for its own sake. On the other hand, extrinsically-motivated activities often are associated with work. One is engaged in the activity because of monetary reward and would not choose that activity as a way of spending time if there were no monetary rewards. In recent research, Csikszentmihalyi and his colleagues (e.g., Csikszentmihalyi and LeFevre, 1989) have examined differential reactions and affects when in work and leisure activities. They were especially concerned with the quality of those experiences and the notion of "flow," or optimal experiences of high challenge along with high skills that are associated with feeling active, alert, and creative. They used a method called experience sampling. In this procedure, the participants wear a "beeper" and at certain intervals are "buzzed" and asked to report on their activities as well as their feelings. Perhaps surprisingly, the vast majority of flow experiences are reported when working, not when in leisure activity. However, most intrinsic motivation was reported during leisure activity. But whether in leisure or in work activity, experience was most positive when demands were high in the face of high skills.

One or two weeks later the children were given the opportunity to perform the drawing task again during one of their regular classroom hours. The subjects were free to engage in the drawing activity or in other games that were available. No rewards were mentioned, and the teachers did not encourage play with any particular material. To assess the dependent variable (time spent with the drawing task), researchers secretly observed the children in their free-time activities through a one-way mirror. The data revealed that the children in the expected-reward condition exhibited less interest in the task during the free-time period than did the children in the other two conditions (see Condry, 1977).

It seems intuitively unreasonable to contend that reward always decreases interest. One useful distinction in this regard differentiates between the controlling and the informational aspects of a reward. Deci believed that every reward has both controlling and informational aspects. If the controlling aspect is made salient, then there will be a change in perceived locus of causality. But if the informational aspect is salient, then changes in feelings of competence and self-determination are initiated. Hence, rewards indicating that an individual is competent at a task often enhance, rather than undermine, intrinsic motivation. For example, a medal for the best performance, an indication of superiority, would not be expected to undermine interest. More generally speaking, when reward is not contingent on good performance, but is merely contingent on doing the task, then undermining is likely. In these latter instances the individual merely goes through the task as fast as possible in order to receive the reward.

The so-called "undermining" effect of extrinsic reward appears to be a robust and powerful phenomenon, given a tangible reward. The implication of such a finding for the practices of teachers in the classroom, or even for business managers, is enormous. But, in order for teachers, managers, and parents to effectively apply the principles of extrinsic versus intrinsic motivation, conditions must be specified in which undermining will occur as well as those in which reward will enhance intrinsic interest.

Reactance. Fights for political freedom have occurred throughout history, often involving acts of extreme heroism that dramatically illustrate the motivational effects of loss of freedom. Similarly, we may engage in daily battles to preserve our psychological freedom. Being confined to one's room as a child, being forced to accept a decision, hearing a message that one prefers not to listen to, being pressured by others, and having censorship imposed are some examples of loss of personal, psychological freedom.

According to Brehm (1966, 1972), when a person's freedom to engage in a behavior is threatened or taken away, the motivation to perform that behavior, and therefore to reinstate freedom, increases. As Brehm (1972, p. 1) stated, "A person is motivationally aroused any time he thinks one of his freedoms has been threatened or eliminated. This motivational arousal, or 'psychological reactance,' moves a person to try to restore his freedoms."

Many experimental investigations have demonstrated the motivational effects of *psychological reactance*. In the majority of these research studies, individuals find themselves unable to engage in behaviors that they thought were available. For example, an alternative is eliminated or an expected message is censored. The experimenter then typically measures the perceived attractiveness of the available and unavailable options. It is believed that a change in the desirability of the alternatives, so that the unavailable alternative gains in attractiveness, is one indication of an attempt to restore freedom.

In one of the first such experiments, children were asked to rank-order the desirability of nine different candy bars (Hammock and Brehm, 1966). As a reward for this task, some children were told that they would have a *choice* between two candy bars, while others in a control condition were told that they would be *given* one of two different kinds of candy bars. The children were then shown their third- and fourth-ranked candies, and all were given the more attractive of the two. Thus, reactance was created in the decision condition by telling the children who thought they would have a free choice that they were denied this opportunity. Following the giving of the candy (but before it was eaten), the experimenter had the children re-rate their candy preferences.

If the hypotheses about reactance and perceived attractiveness (attitude) are correct, then the preference for the denied (eliminated) alternative should increase in the choice condition. The data from this investigation are shown in Table 17.2. The findings indicated that the ranking of the eliminated alternative did

Table 17.2   Mean changes in ranking of the forced and eliminated candy bars

		Choice Alternative		
Conditions	N	Forced (rank 3)	Eliminated (rank 4)	Total reactance
Experimental	13	− 1.23*	.23	1.46
Control	14	.00	− .43	− .43

Source: T. Hammock and J.W. Brehm, "The Attractiveness of Choice Alternatives When Freedom to Choose Is Eliminated by a Social Agent," *Journal of Personality, 34,* 1966, p. 550. Copyright 1966, Duke University Press (Durham, N.C.).

* A minus indicates a decrease in attractiveness.

increase in the experimental or reactance condition. But even more dramatic was the decrease in the attractiveness of the candy bar that the children were forced to take.

Reactance notions have also been tested in field, rather than laboratory, settings. In Miami, Florida, an antipollution law was imposed that prohibited the use of cleaning materials containing phosphates. Reactance theory suggests that shoppers should have had an increased desire for these banned products. To test this idea, purchaser attitudes in Miami were compared with those in Tampa, where the antipollution law was not in effect (Mazis, 1975). The investigator had the experimental participants (housewives) rate the effectiveness of the various detergents they had used during the six months prior to the survey. Table 17.3 shows that the ratings of the phosphate detergents were significantly higher in Miami, where the products were unavailable, than in Tampa. In addition, in Miami there was a strong negative attitude toward the quality of the alternative detergents (for related research, see Brehm and Brehm, 1981).

The Illusion of Control.   Another way individuals have of maintaining a sense of control is to have an *illusion of control* in which individuals often perceive themselves as having control in situations when they do not. For instance, several studies have found that individuals believe they can influence the outcome of thrown dice if they throw the dice themselves (Fleming and Darley, 1990; Langer, 1975). However, Taylor and Brown (1988) report that depressed individuals do not exhibit this illusion. Paradoxically they are more realistic than nondepressed individuals in assessing how much control they have.

Issues of Personal Control.   While there is evidence that people strive to maintain a sense of control, a number of writers have raised some issues with the idea of personal control. The first issue comes from Bandura (1986), who has distinguished his conception of *self-efficacy* from personal control. Bandura notes that having a sense of efficacy, or a sense of "ableness" to do something, does not

Table 17.3   Means for effectiveness ratings of phosphate detergents

Characteristic	Miami (N = 76) M	Tampa (N = 45) M
Whiteness	8.68*	8.27
Freshness	8.77	7.87
Cleans in cold water	8.52	7.47
Brightness	8.31	7.84
Stain removal	8.00	6.96
Pours easily	9.45	9.07
Gentleness	8.81	8.71

Source: Adapted from Michael Mazis, "Antipollution Measures and Psychological Reactance Theory: A Field Experiment," *Journal of Personality and Social Psychology, 31,* 1975, p. 656. Copyright 1975 by the American Psychological Association. Adapted by permission of publisher and author.

* Based on an eleven-point scale with eleven labeled "absolutely perfect" and one labeled "poor."

necessarily mean one has control in that area. For instance, a baseball player may have a high sense of self-efficacy as a hitter yet succeed only one-third of the time. Clearly it would be dysfunctional for that person to believe that he or she has complete control over getting a hit. Yet it is functional to feel efficacious as a batter.

A second issue is whether it is always desirable to believe that one has control. There are instances in which trying to control things that are not controllable can cause problems. An example is sexual dysfunction. When an individual has problems getting aroused, trying to get aroused is counterproductive. Paradoxically, the way to get aroused is to stop trying to control one's arousal and to focus on other aspects of the situation. Mahoney (1985) has argued that Western culture's heavy emphasis on control may lead to certain kinds of psychiatric disorders. In contrast, in some Eastern cultures, acceptance of one's fate is more valued.

In recent formulations of models of effective control, the idea that active attempts at control are not always good has been included in the form of the idea of secondary control (Fiske and Taylor, 1984), that is, gaining some kind of control by giving up control in other areas. For example, an individual who is paralyzed in an auto accident may have to relinquish control over walking again and shift efforts to things he or she can control, such as activities that he or she will be able to engage in.

ACHIEVEMENT MOTIVATION

We have seen that believing oneself to have some control appears to be adaptive, at least in Western culture. The issue of control becomes most critical when we confront failure and adversity. Most important aspects of life — work, relationships, and family — involve periodic experiences with failure and adversity (Dweck and Leggett, 1988). How do we react to failure in a proactive, competent way? Do we simply give up or do we creatively and proactively strive to find new solutions? How we react to failure and adversity appears to have a great deal to do with how we perceive ourselves in relationship to the failure experience. If we see ourselves as able to cope, we will be more likely to persist and look for creative solutions. If we see ourselves as unable or helpless, we will be more likely to give up.

The study of achievement motivation was one of the first systematic efforts to look at how individuals cope with success and failure. We first consider this topic and then examine other research relevant to the topic of ways of coping with adversity.

Freud contended that there are two main avenues of satisfaction in life: *Arbeit und Liebe,* work and love. If the meanings of these terms are somewhat broadened to include what is called achievement and affiliation motivation, then Freud's statement seems to be correct. A count of our day's activities would reveal that, in general, most of the time is spent in accomplishing tasks and goals and in maintaining or expanding friendships or intimacy. Of course, humans also strive for power, seek entertainment, engage in acts of aggression, attempt to satisfy curiosity, and so on. But achievement and affiliation motivation appear to be dominant concerns within our culture. Thus, it is not surprising that the study of achievement strivings has played a major role in the psychology of personality.

The motivation to achieve takes many different forms. The college student working late into the night to "crack" the next day's examination, the teen-ager practicing each day in the schoolyard to perfect a basketball shot, the aspiring executive investing funds in a promising venture, and the scientist persisting in the effort to solve a difficult theoretical problem despite repeated frustration and failure are all displaying achievement motivation. What are the roots of achievement motivation? Why do some individuals strive to reach as high as their abilities will permit, while others are satisfied with much lower levels of accomplishment? What is the relationship between the culture or the economic structure of a society and achievement motivation? Why are some people so unrealistic in the goals they set for themselves? How do perceptions of the causes of success and failure alter our behavior?

The starting point for the systematic psychological study of achievement motivation was in the work of Henry Murray (1938), although other psychologists like Freud and Lewin also played significant roles. Murray was the head of the influential Harvard Clinic and one of the founders of the experimental approach to the study of personality. He devised a taxonomy that included twenty basic human needs. These needs were thought of as personality traits, or stable dispositions of the person. Individuals were assumed to vary along these personality dimensions, so that some persons had "more of" or stronger dispositions than others. One of these needs, called *achievement,* was conceived as the desire (Murray, 1938, p. 164):

> To accomplish something difficult. To master, manipulate or organize physical objects, human beings, or ideas. To do this as rapidly and as independently as possible. To overcome obstacles and attain a high standard. To excel one's self. To rival and surpass others. To increase self-regard by the successful exercise of talent.

These desires, Murray said, are accompanied by the following actions (p. 164):

> To make intense, prolonged and repeated efforts to accomplish something difficult. To work with singleness of purpose towards a high and distant goal. To have the determination to win. To try to do everything well. To be stimulated to excel by the presence of others, to enjoy competition.

The Measurement of Achievement Needs

For scientific progress, it is not sufficient merely to indicate that there is a predisposition to strive for achievement. Rather, a measure must be constructed to assess this characteristic accurately, so that individuals can be assigned a score indicating the *magnitude* of their need or motivation. Murray developed an instrument, called the Thematic Apperception Test (TAT), to assess need states (see Chapter 8); it was readily adapted for the assessment of achievement needs. One of the main reasons for its widespread use was that early influential investigators were guided by the Freudian belief that a good place to find indications of motivation is in the fantasy life of individuals. In free responses to ambiguous situations, like those portrayed in Rorschach cards or the TAT, just as in dreams and daydreams, it was believed that individuals revealed their underlying desires and true wishes.

The Procedure. The general TAT methodology used to assess achievement needs has remained virtually unchanged since its inception. Four to six pictures are projected on a screen, typically in a group setting, with subjects responding to four directing questions (What is happening? What led up to this situation? What is being thought? What will happen?) The pictures vary in content, portraying one or two individuals engaging in tasks, having an apparently serious or a casual discussion, and so forth. Four minutes of writing time are allowed for each story, and a total achievement need score is obtained for each person by summing the scores of the individual stories.

To score for achievement needs, it is decided whether a story contains achievement-related imagery. Examples of such story imagery include unique accomplishments, such as inventions or novels; long-term achievement concerns, such as wanting to be a success in life or a doctor; and competition with some standard of excellence, such as building the best model.

While the TAT has led to many useful results, it's methodology not without problems. First, a number of issues have been raised concerning internal consistency and test-retest reliability (see Chapter 7). Second, the test is cumbersome; there have been attempts to develop more easily scored objective measures of the need to achieve. A great deal of work is being done to demonstrate the usefulness of objective methods of measuring achievement motivation.

Achievement Needs as a Personality Structure

It has been indicated that Murray conceived of an achievement need as a trait or an enduring personality disposition. Therefore, two issues are of immediate relevance: (1) what is the generality (or extensiveness, or breadth) of the need for achievement? and (2) is this disposition stable, or at least relatively enduring? Unfortunately, neither question has been adequately answered. It is not known, for example, whether a person who strives for success in a particular occupation also exhibits such achievement drives on the tennis court, in night-school accounting class, or in other situations. It certainly seems reasonable to believe that there are circumscribed avenues or outlets for achievement expression in a given individual. For example, we might expect the driven athlete to exhibit competition on the playing field, but not in the classroom; on the football field, but not in a less central sport such as bowling or ping-pong. On the other hand, it is equally plausible that desires to achieve are expressed across a range of achievement-related situations. However, these questions have not been investigated and at present the generality or specificity of achievement as a trait is unknown. It may be, as Bem and Allen (see Chapter 9) have suggested, that there are individual differences in the generality of this disposition.

The stability of achievement needs has been the subject of more research than the issue of generality. This is perhaps surprising, inasmuch as longitudinal studies are difficult to conduct. An overview of this research suggests significant but weak correlations between scores on need achievement scales when the measures are taken as many as six years apart (Feld, 1967; Kagan and Moss, 1959; Moss and Kagan, 1961). Clearly, however, research of this type is hampered because of the uncertain test-retest reliability of the TAT. That is, it is impossible to determine if achievement needs are stable if the test-retest reliability of the measure employed is low. Note, therefore, how closely related the fields of personality structure, measurement, and development are. For example, the demonstration of stable structures and antecedents of development requires valid and reliable measurement instruments.

The question of motive stability is beset with other difficulties as well. For example, it has been found that some parents of low-achievement-orientation adolescents react to their children's lack of achievement concern by stressing independence and achievement. These reactions then influence subsequent achievement concerns and alter the stability of the need system, so that retesting will indicate low trait stability. Therefore, stability is in part dependent on the type and the consistency of socialization experiences.

The essential questions of generality and stability are unanswered. The next question is: what is known about people who are labeled as high in need for achievement, or high in the desire to achieve success? The clearest, most understandable correlates of achievement needs have been derived from the various theories of achievement motivation that are examined later in this chapter. However, there are several personality characteristics associated with achievement motivation that can be noted at this point. For example, there is some evidence that, given a choice among tasks of high, intermediate, or low difficulty, tasks of intermediate difficulty are more attractive to individuals highly motivated to succeed than to those lower in achievement needs. In a similar vein, individuals high in achievement needs have been characterized as realistic and have occupational goals that are congruent with their abilities (Mahone, 1960; Morris, 1966). The desire for intermediate risk may indicate a preference for personal feedback or knowledge about oneself. This informational explanation is consistent with the high achiever's reported preference for business occupations, where feedback (profit) is immediately evident (McClelland, 1961; Meyer, Walker, and Litwin, 1961). In addition, individuals high in need for achievement apparently are better able to delay gratification (Mischel, 1961) and get higher grades in school than individuals low in achievement needs, if the grades are instrumental to long-term success (Raynor, 1970). Furthermore, they are thought of as hope rather than fear oriented. For example, there is some evidence that they are especially optimistic about their chances of success (Feather, 1965). Finally, individuals high in achievement needs take personal responsibility for success and generally perceive themselves as high in ability (Kukla, 1972). This self-attribution for success increases their feelings of worth and may account, in part, for their high self-concept as reported by some investigators (Mukherjee and Sinha, 1970).

The Development of Achievement Needs

What, then, are the antecedents of the trait to strive for achievement? Questions of inheritability have not been addressed because it seems intuitively so unlikely that genetic factors could contribute to this need state. Thus neither monozygotic versus dyzygotic twin studies of the type reviewed in Chapter 1 nor investigations that trace family histories have been conducted.

On the other hand, maturational factors are believed to contribute to the growth of achievement strivings. There appear to be universal processes that are necessary precursors of the tendency to strive for success. For example, it has been contended that the development of achievement needs requires that the child be able to "direct the pleasure or the disappointment after success and failure . . . at the self, so that with success the child experiences pleasure about his competence and with failure experiences shame about his incompetence" (Heckhausen and Roelofsen, 1962, p. 378). This suggests that developing self-attribution is a necessary antecedent to achievement striving. A different cognitive analysis of achievement proposes three stages in the development of achieve-

A parent helping a child accomplish a task. It seems reasonable to believe that the amount of unsolicited help will influence later achievement strivings, but the empirical evidence is unclear in this regard. (Copyright © Susan Lapides, 1981)

ment strivings: (1) an intrapersonal competition, or autonomous, stage in which the child competes with itself; (2) an interpersonal competition, or social comparison, stage in which competition is with others rather than with the self; and (3) an integration of the two previous stages (Veroff, 1969). Passage from stage 1 to stage 2 typically takes place when the child enters school and acquires the ability to use social norm information in making comparative judgments.

The American research tradition in developmental psychology has been to search for the experiential (social) determinants of personality and to focus on early parental interactions as the prime influence of later behavior. However, any hypothesized relationships between child rearing and achievement needs remain to be clearly demonstrated. This search is obviously of great practical importance, for if antecedent experiences were identified, then, if one desired, achievement motivation could be promoted.

Atkinson's Theory of Achievement Motivation

A very prominent theory of achievement motivation was formulated by John Atkinson (1957, 1964). This theory was influenced by Miller's conflict model

◼ **Highlight 17.2** ◼

Age and Outstanding Achievements

For a long time there has been speculation about the association between a person's age and his or her accomplishments. A few facts are now known about this relation. First, productivity tends to rise fairly rapidly to a definite peak, and then declines gradually. The location of this peak depends in part on the domain of creative achievement. Some fields, including theoretical physics, pure mathematics, and lyric poetry show early peaks in the late twenties and early thirties. Creativity in other fields displays a leisurely rise and late peak, with the peak in the late forties or even early fifties. This holds for novel writing, history, and philosophy. Finally, other disciplines fall between these extremes, with maximum output rate around the age of forty. Psychology is among the fields exhibiting this productivity curve.

These curves have been shown to describe different cultures in distinct historical periods. For example, the gap in creativity between poets and prose authors has been found in every major literary tradition throughout the world. Poets exhibit a life expectancy across the globe and throughout history of about six years less than that of prose writers. In addition, precocious individuals also tend to live longer.

Finally, there is a relation between the quantity of one's work and the number of creations of outstanding quality. Those periods of a creator's life that produce the most masterpieces also produce the fewest masterpieces! That is, there is a "constant probability of success," with creativity related to total productivity (see Lehrman, 1953; Simonton, 1988a, 1988b).

Even in old age, Picasso remained productive and creative. (UPI/Bettmann)

(introduced in Chapter 14). Achievement-oriented behavior was viewed by Atkinson as a conflict between approach and avoidance tendencies. Associated with every achievement-related action is the possibility of success (with the consequent emotion of pride) and the possibility of failure (with the consequent emotion of shame). The strengths of these anticipated emotions determine whether an individual will approach or avoid achievement-oriented activities. That is, achievement behavior involves an emotional conflict between hopes for success and fears of failure. A significant feature of Atkinson's theory was that it could be stated in quantitative form. Because quantitative formulations in the personality area are rare, we shall not give the mathematical theory here.

Instead, we consider some hypotheses derived from Atkinson's conception and some empirical studies testing those hypotheses. Let us take the situation in which a person is confronted with a number of alternative choices varying in difficulty. For example, at an athletic event, a tennis player might choose to play against a competitor of equal skill, one who would be very difficult to beat, or one who should be fairly easy to beat. Or a student might have to decide among three sections of a course that vary in difficulty, such that the chances of getting an A or a B are very low in one section, intermediate in a second section, and almost a sure thing in the third section. Although some cynics might feel that most people would choose the easy section or the easy competitor, there are significant individual differences in the extent to which people select tasks of high, moderate, or low difficulty, that is, there are differences in their *level of aspiration* (Frank, 1935; Lewin, Dembo, Festinger, and Sears, 1944). The Atkinson model enables us to predict the choices that different people make.

Most importantly, according to the Atkinson model, attraction to a sure thing, to a long shot, or to a moderate challenge depends on the relationship between the levels of success motive and the difficulty of the task. Based on this model, motivation is highest for all individuals at tasks of intermediate difficulty. Thus, the intuitively reasonable observation is captured by the theory that athletic teams and spectators are most motivated when the score is even. However, this is more so for those with high achievement needs than for those with low achievement needs. The theory predicts that the higher the achievement needs, the greater the attraction toward tasks whose probability of success equals .50.

An Experimental Test of the Model. We have seen that the Atkinson model predicts that high-achievement individuals will prefer tasks of intermediate difficulty more than low-achievement individuals will. How do these predictions measure up when compared with empirical data? An experiment by Atkinson and Litwin (1960) bears directly on this question. In this investigation, subjects attempted to toss rings over a peg. They were allowed to stand at varying distances from the peg and could change position (increase or decrease aspirations) following each toss. It was assumed that a position close to the target corresponded to a high probability of success and that probability of success decreased as the distance from the peg increased. Thus, distance from the peg was the observable indicator of choice and of task difficulty. The subjects were classified into motive groups on the basis of individual differences measures, including the TAT. The data on choice behavior indicated that intermediate task preference was greatest for the high-motive group, least for subjects low in achievement needs, and neither high nor low for subjects at the middle in achievement needs.

An Alternative Explanation. Atkinson's prediction of disparate personality-group preferences is based on the belief that choice among achievement tasks follows the principle of maximization of positive affect. That is, anticipatory emotions and hedonistic concerns determine which tasks one will attempt to perform. As indicated in Chapter 14, most psychologists consider hedonism to be the main source of motivation and behavior.

An alternative interpretation of risk-preference appeals more to informational and self-concept principles than to hedonism, reflecting the trend toward cognitive explanations of action that is now prevalent in psychology. Research has demonstrated that outcomes at tasks of intermediate difficulty provide performers with the most information about their efforts and capabilities. There are logical reasons why this is the case. Selection of easy tasks typically results in success and the outcome is ascribed to the ease of the task. In a similar manner, selection of very difficult tasks generally results in failure, with blame placed on the characteristics of the task. Thus, selection of very easy or very difficult tasks usually confirms our knowledge about the external world. Success on tasks at which almost everyone succeeds and failure on tasks at which almost everyone does poorly tell very little about the skills of the individual engaged in those tasks. However, tasks of intermediate difficulty are just as likely to produce success as failure, and performance at such tasks provides information about the efforts and abilities of the person undertaking them. From this perspective, differential preference for tasks of varying difficulty between groups differing in achievement needs indicates disparate desires for personal feedback and self-evaluation. Of course, it is quite functional and adaptive to have a realistic view of oneself and one's capabilities. A research study by Trope (1975) supports the informational view that high achievers seek situations that are diagnostic of their relative level of ability.

Attribution Theory and Achievement Strivings

The discussion of choice behavior called attention to the informational or self-evaluative aspects of task selection. It is now apparent that other aspects of achievement motivation are also influenced by cognitive or inferential processes. Foremost among the mental events that affect achievement-related behaviors are causal attributions. This concept was examined earlier when perceived responsibility and helplessness were discussed.

Causal Attributions. *Causal attributions* in achievement-related contexts refer to beliefs about the reasons for one's success or failure. There are, of course, many possible reasons for a positive or a negative achievement outcome, but research has shown that a few factors are perceived as most responsible for success and failure. These factors include ability, effort, task ease or difficulty, luck, and help or hindrance from others. That is, if one succeeds, then the outcome is ascribed to high ability, hard work, the ease of the task, etc. In a similar manner, failure is generally ascribed to low ability, lack of effort, a difficult task, etc. Of these causes, ability and effort are particularly salient. That is, outcomes typically depend on what we *can* do and how hard we *try*. Other, less-used attributions for success and failure include the bias of a supervisor or teacher, mood, illness, fatigue, and home environment.

As revealed earlier, the perceived causes of success and failure have been incorporated within a few basic causal dimensions which describe the underlying properties of causes (Weiner, 1979, 1986). One dimension, which has been examined in some detail in the prior chapter, is labeled *locus of causality*. Causes are perceived as either internal (within the person) or external (in the environment). For example, ability and effort are person causes, whereas task difficulty, help from others, and luck are among the environmental determinants of an outcome. A second dimension of causality has been identified as the *stability* or constancy of a cause. Some causes, such as aptitude, the ease of a task, and conditions in the home, are typically perceived as relatively enduring or stable. On the other hand, causes such as effort expenditure, luck, mood, and illness are generally perceived as subject to momentary or periodic fluctuation. Still a third dimension of causality is the *controllability* of the cause. For example, how much effort we expend is subject to personal influence, whereas luck and illness generally are not. In sum, classifications of causes have been developed that allow each causal factor to be placed within a multidimensional framework.

The Consequences of Causal Attributions.   It has been demonstrated that causal attributions are linked to specific psychological consequences. The *locus* of a causal attribution influences affective reactions to success and failure. If, for example, one attributes success to such internal causes as ability or effort, then more pride and self-enhancement are experienced than if that success is attributed to external factors like task ease or good luck. The *stability* of a cause influences the subjective expectancy of success at the task, or how likely the person feels that future success is within reach. For example, if a previous failure is ascribed to lack of effort or bad luck, then future success might be anticipated. But if failure is attributed to a fixed cause such as "no mathematical aptitude," then future failure will be anticipated. The dimension of control is particularly important in interpersonal evaluations. For example, if you are a member of a team and you do poorly for reasons within your control, like lack of effort, then your teammates will be angry with you. On the other hand, poor performance due to an uncontrollable cause, like illness, often elicits sympathy from others. In addition, when one fails because of lack of effort, guilt is often experienced, whereas failure because of lack of ability tends to produce shame and humiliation.

Suppose, for example, that a student gets a low grade in a class and then decides to drop out of school (see Figure 17.1). How might an attribution theorist

Pride in accomplishment is one of the indicators of high achievement strivings. (August Gabriel/Photo Researchers)

explain this behavior? First, when the student receives this grade, he or she asks: "Why have I done so poorly?" If the student has failed in the past, while others have performed well, then the likely attribution for the current performance is to the self. The student might conclude: "I am dumb or unable." This attribution is internal to the student, so that self-esteem is decreased. In addition, the attribution is stable; ability is not anticipated to be changeable. Furthermore, attributions of failure to low ability produce humiliation, while others express pity. This feedback further enhances the belief that "I cannot" (see Highlight 17.3). Low

Figure 17.1   An attributional model of achievement strivings.

Causal ascriptions	Causal dimensions	Consequences	Behavior
Ability			
Effort	Locus →	Esteem-related affect	Choice
Task difficulty	Stability →	Expectancy	Intensity
Luck		Social affects	Persistence
Others	Control →	(guilt, shame, pity, anger)	

▦ **Highlight 17.3** ▦▦▦▦▦▦▦

Pity, Anger, and Achievement Performance

It is generally thought that pity and sympathy are "good" emotions and that anger is a "bad" emotion. However, attribution theorists have pointed out that the consequences of these emotional expressions are complex. In one investigation, Graham (1984) gave subjects (twelve-year-old children) false failure feedback during an achievement task. For some children, this was accompanied by the remark: "I feel sorry for you" as well as body postures and facial gestures that accompany sympathy (head down, hands folded, etc.). To other students, the experimenter said: "I am angry with you." Students receiving the pity feedback tended to blame the failure on themselves (low ability) and their performance declined. On the other hand, students receiving anger feedback attributed their failure to lack of effort and their performance subsequently increased. This is not to advocate that sympathy is always detrimental and anger always facilitative. Rather, the consequences of feedback depend on how that feedback is construed and what it means to the recipient of the communication. Other kinds of feedback, such as praise for success at an easy task and excessive and unsolicited helping, also tend to convey that the student is "unable" and therefore have some negative consequences.

self-esteem, humiliation, and low expectancy of success then result in the student's decision to drop out of school.

In sum, individuals who react to failure by attributing its cause to something fixed and uncontrollable about themselves are unlikely to be able to cope productively with challenges. They are more likely to be pessimistic about their chances of future success, and as we have previously noted, more likely to react in a helpless manner.

Explanatory Style and Achievement Strivings. Earlier in this chapter, we saw that individuals have biases or dispositions to attribute outcomes to particular causes. This attributional style has especially been related to depression. In addition, attributional or explanatory style has also been associated with achievement strivings. Peterson and Barrett (1987) reported that students who generally tend to explain bad academic events with stable causes internal to themselves, such as low aptitude, receive lower grades as freshman than students who tend to ascribe failure to external and unstable causes, such as bad luck. This pattern held even when ability was constant between the groups.

Attributional Training. If causal attributions for success and failure determine achievement strivings, then it logically follows that a change in these beliefs should produce a change in achievement behavior. A number of studies have been conducted examining this principle. The general approach in these studies has been to teach individuals with school problems that achievement outcomes are under their own control. More specifically, it has been the goal of these programs to lead subjects to attribute failure to a lack of effort rather than to the absence of ability. As previously indicated, because ability is a fixed and uncontrollable cause, ascriptions of failure to ability are particularly dysfunctional and debilitating.

One exemplary investigation in this area was conducted by Dweck (1975). Her subjects were eight- to thirteen-year-olds who had been independently identified by their teacher, school psychologist, and principal as having a high expectancy of failure and as displaying performance decrements in failure situations. Dweck's method was to verbalize to subjects that failure during a series of training sessions was due to lack of effort. During these training trials, 20 percent of the responses resulted in failure. The attributional training procedure was compared to the popular program of inducing 100 percent success (without any causal attributions) and, in so doing, supposedly increase self-confidence. Dweck's data, shown in Fig. 17.2, revealed the efficacy and value of attributional training

Figure 17.2   Mean percentage decrease in correct problems (Dweck, 1975, p. 82. Copyright 1975 by the American Psychological Association. Reprinted by permission.)

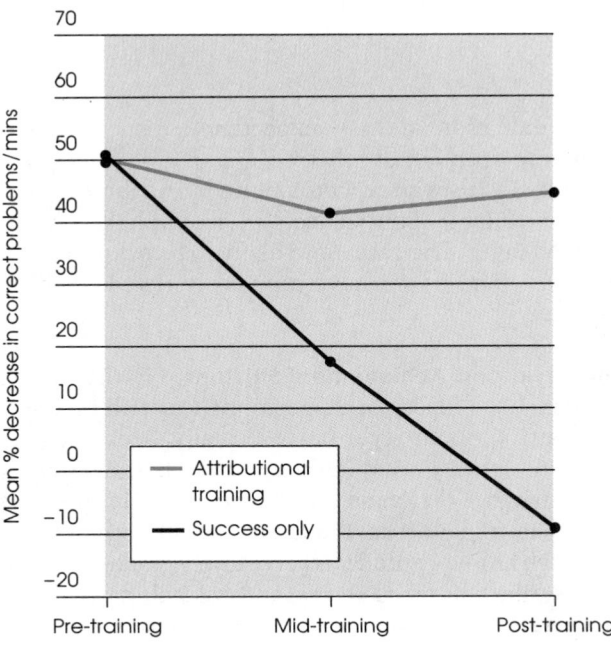

and its superiority over the success-only treatment. Following training, only the attributional treatment group did not show decrements in responding in the face of failure. However, the interpretation of these findings is somewhat complicated by the fact that the attributional group received partial reinforcement, which might have contributed to their relatively better performance (see Chapter 5).

Other change programs have been successful with less complex treatments. For example, Wilson and Linneville (1982, 1985) demonstrated that merely informing students that the policy of the university was to "ease up" on grading following the first year of study increased achievement strivings among students dissatisfied with their first-year performance. Information that the poor performance was due to an unstable cause (rather than, say, low ability) resulted in maintaining expectancy of future success and, in turn, increased motivation (see Foersterling, 1985).

Achievement Motivation and Economic Development

Numerous sociological and anthropological investigations of achievement motivation have gone on outside the laboratory. Foremost among these was an attempt by McClelland (1961) to relate achievement motivation to economic growth.

The initial influences on McClelland's analysis of economic growth were Winterbottom's (1953) data relating early independence training to the growth of achievement needs and the speculations of Max Weber (1904) concerning the Protestant reformation. Weber noted that the Protestant revolt emphasized the importance of self-reliance and productivity. Furthermore, because of religious beliefs, the results of one's labors could not be spent self-indulgently. Thus, profits were reinvested, resulting in further prosperity.

McClelland perceived a relationship between these notions and the work on achievement motivation. He suggested that Protestant values produced early independence training that, in turn, promoted need for achievement and economic development. This hypothesized sequence is shown in Fig. 17.3, which indicates four relationships: (1) Protestantism and early independence training; (2) early independence training and need for achievement; (3) need for achieve-

Figure 17.3   Hypothetical relationship between self-reliance values and economic development.

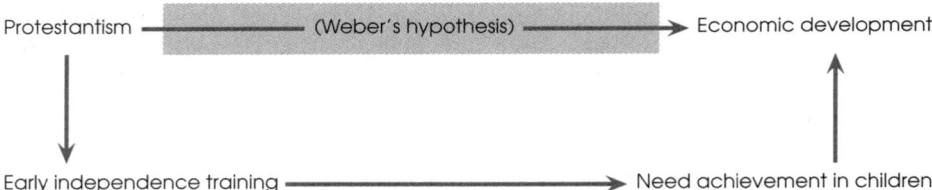

Figure 17.4

Mean frequency of achievement imagery in children's readers and the patent index in the United States, 1800–1950. (Adapted from de Charms and Moeller, 1962, p. 139. Used by permission.)

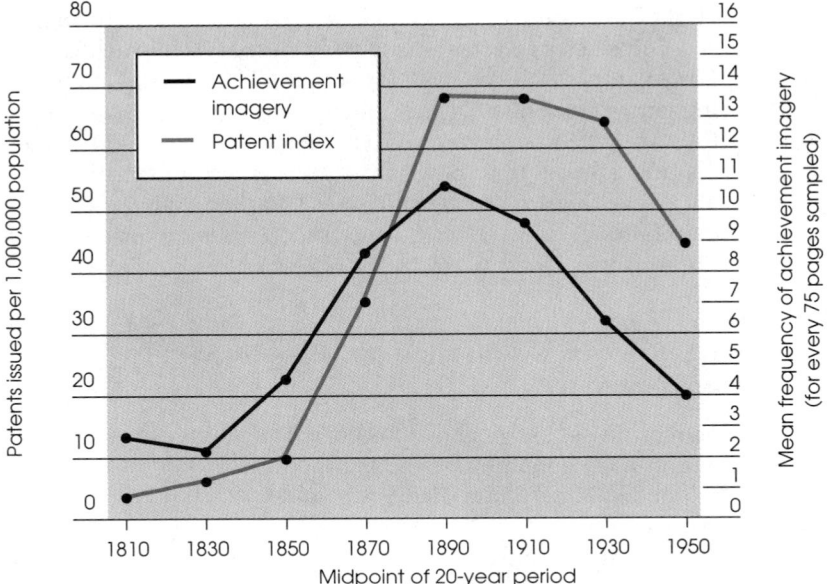

ment and economic development; and (4) Protestantism and economic development. Of these, the alleged relationship between achievement need and economic development has produced the most extensive, novel, and controversial findings.

The TAT assessment procedure originated by Murray has a unique advantage in that it is applicable to any prose material. Thus, to examine the relationship between achievement needs and economic growth, McClelland scored prose material, such as children's readers, speeches, folktales, and songs, for achievement needs. These scores were then related to available indexes of economic activity, such as consumption of electrical power, quantity of imports, and number of independent artisans within a society. Data from a wide array of cultures and times, including Tudor England and ancient Greece, provided evidence that increments in need for achievement, inferred from the scoring of the various prose material, precedes economic development, while decreases in need for achievement are predictive of economic decline.

You might be wondering, by this time, about the achievement motivation in U.S. culture. Figure 17.4 indicates that people's achievement needs in America, ascertained from children's readers, increased from 1800 to 1910. Since 1910 the indicators of achievement concerns have steadily decreased. Does this hint that our economy is also going to decline? Figure 17.4 also reveals that the patent index, one indicator of unique accomplishment and achievement needs, and an economic stimulant, is declining as well.

COMPETENCE

The study of achievement motivation has shown that high achievers approach tasks in such a way that they are more likely to achieve success because they are not paralyzed by attributing failure to stable, internal, uncontrollable causes. This finding is in keeping with other findings from the study of competence.

As we consider it here, *competence* is the ability to perform as capably as one can on a task, regardless of one's level of ability or skill. Primarily, competence has to do with how one perceives oneself, the task, and obstacles encountered as one works on the task. Findings from a wide variety of sources — such as research on Bandura's concept of self-efficacy (Bandura, 1986; see Chapter 5), Dweck and Leggett's (1988) research on a mastery-oriented versus helpless stance towards problems in children, and others (Sternberg and Kolligian, 1990) — converge on the following conclusions. First, a competent performance on a task involves keeping one's eye on the immediate aspects of the task itself rather than focusing on whether or not one is ultimately going to succeed. A good football team must take it "one play at a time" even if they are behind by twenty-one points. Second, one's attention must be focused outward on the task demands themselves rather than inward on what success or failure means about the self.

Consider as an example the work of Carol Dweck and her colleagues (Dweck and Leggett, 1988). Dweck's work has focused on the difference between children who adopt a "helpless" orientation towards tasks and those who take a "learning" or "mastery" orientation. In one study, children who had a helpless orientation (as measured by a particular scale) and those who had a mastery orientation were given a series of problems to solve. The study was arranged so that all children succeeded initially. When succeeding, helpless children performed as well as mastery-oriented children, showing as much effort, skill, and ability. However, differences between the two groups of children emerged when experimenters arranged for some individuals to begin to fail. The performance of children who perceived themselves as helpless deteriorated. These children tended to give up earlier in the face of failure, they failed to generate new and creative strategies, and they engaged in more defensive self-protective activities (talking about their talents in other areas). In essence, helpless children viewed the difficulties they encountered as signs of personal failure, which they took as indicative of low ability. In contrast, mastery-oriented children tended to persist when confronted with initial failure, trying out new and creative strategies. They remained focused on the task rather than on what the task meant about themselves, and therefore they did not engage in defensive self-protective behavior. Further research by Dweck and her colleagues also revealed that mastery-oriented and helpless children viewed obstacles differently. Helpless children assumed that one's inability to master something easily means that one has low ability in that area, while mastery-oriented children assumed the exact opposite, that one learns about one's ability only through struggling with difficult challenges.

The finding that competent performance involves a focus on the immediate demands of the task rather than on the self converges with Csikszentmihalyi's

(1990) research on the "flow" experience (which we looked at briefly in Highlight 17.1). Csikszentmihalyi has found that people are most likely to experience flow when they are absorbed in a challenging task. The implication is that effective functioning occurs when one loses sight of oneself as one works on something.

These findings also converge with researchers who argue that the competitive climate of the American school system is likely to foster an increase in a dysfunctional focus on the self and on performance rather than on mastery and learning (Ames, 1984; Covington and Beery, 1976; Covington and Omelich, 1979; Nicholls, 1984). These researchers suggest that individuals are more likely to be able to adopt a mastery orientation if learning becomes an end in itself in cooperative rather than competitive learning contexts.

Integrating Perceived Control with Achievement Motivation and Competence

There is a general trend underlying most of the topics considered in this chapter. Under the general umbrella of approaching life in an effective and proactive manner, we suggest that people who are more likely to approach challenges in a proactive, mastery-oriented manner are individuals: (1) who believe that they have some degree of control over the outcomes in their life, (2) who attribute success to themselves in such a way as to reward themselves for their efforts and who attribute failure to factors that do not cause them to paralyze themselves, (3) who feel optimistic and not helpless, (4) who believe that ability is changeable with effort, and (5) who, as they perform, focus on the immediate demands of the task rather than on the ultimate outcome of success or failure or on what success and failure mean about the self. Generally, people who are less likely to perform proactively are individuals: (1) who do not feel they have control, (2) who are pessimistic (especially if their pessimism leads them to believe they have no control), (3) who attribute success in such a manner that they get no reward for their efforts and who experience failure in such a manner that they feel hopeless to ever achieve success by their own efforts, (4) who believe their ability or its lack is fixed and unchangeable, and (5) who focus on success or failure rather than on immediate task mastery.

There may appear to be a contradiction between research suggesting that competent performance involves a focus on the task and *not* on the self and research suggesting that competence is enhanced by attributing success to oneself. This apparent contradiction can be resolved if we break task performance into two segments: the performance itself, and reflecting on the performance after it is over. While performing, it appears to be more functional to be not thinking about the self. (We have previously discussed the negative effects of excessive self-focused attention in Chapter 10.) However, after the performance is over and one reflects on why one has succeeded or failed, it appears to be effective to attribute success to oneself and failure to either oneself in the form of something controllable, such as a lack of effort, or to external factors, such as luck or task difficulty. Another implication of this is that not all kinds of internal attributions are beneficial. This becomes important as we shall see in the following discussion of attributions of responsibility.

ATTRIBUTIONS OF RESPONSIBILITY

When something positive or negative happens, we become concerned with the question of whether or not we can hold a person responsible for the outcome. Attribution of responsibility involves many of the same issues we have already considered in this chapter. Basically, in attributing responsibility for an outcome we ask ourselves: did this outcome arise or not arise from factors over which the person had control? Attributions of responsibility for the outcome of an event often determine how we subsequently respond to an individual.

Evaluation

As we have seen, achievement evaluation is affected by the responsibility that is assigned for success and failure. In one experimental demonstration (Weiner and Kukla, 1970), subjects were asked to pretend that they were teachers and were to provide evaluative feedback to their students. The pupils were described as having just completed an exam with one of five possible outcomes: excellent, fair, borderline, failure, and clear failure. In addition, the pupils were described jointly in terms of ability (high or low) and effort (high or low). For example, one pupil was characterized as high in ability, low in effort, and having a borderline test performance. Evaluation was indicated by giving each pupil a score from $+5$ (highest reward) to -5 (highest punishment).

The results are depicted in Fig. 17.5, which reveals that test outcome, a factor commonly known to affect evaluation, indeed influences feedback in the expected manner: the greater the success, the more favorable the feedback. But pupil characteristics and perceived personal responsibility also affect evaluation. First, high effort motivation results in a more positive evaluation than does low effort, at all outcome levels. And, perhaps surprisingly, low ability produces a higher evaluation than does high ability. This is because low ability coupled with high effort and success is especially rewarded. For example, the handicapped person who completes a marathon or the retarded child who persists in completing a task elicits great social approval because each is considered personally responsible for success. On the other hand, high ability coupled with low effort and failure is maximally punished. For example, the bright dropout or the gifted athlete who refuses to practice and performs poorly generates great social disapproval. Again this is because each is perceived as personally responsible for failure. These individuals did not *have* to fail; they had freedom of choice and could have chosen a different outcome. Because low ability coupled with high effort and success is so strongly rewarded, while high ability linked with low effort

Figure 17.5   Evaluation (reward and punishment) as a function of pupil ability, motivation, and examination outcome. (Weiner and Kukula, 1970, p. 3.)

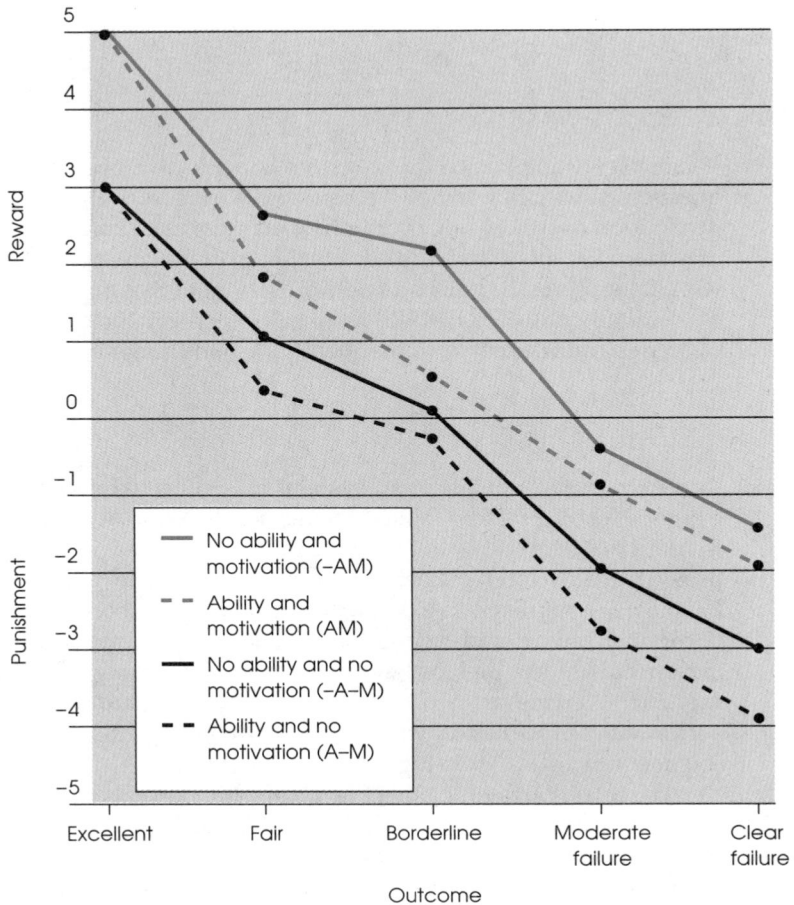

and failure is correspondingly punished, lack of ability emerges as a beneficial attribute in this particular kind of experiment.

Helping Behavior

It is also evident that whether we help others and the kind of aid we are willing to give are in part dependent on whether we perceive the person in need of aid as responsible for his or her plight. For example, it has been clearly demonstrated that people are more likely to help a disabled person than a drunk (Piliavin, Rodin, and Piliavin, 1969). In a similar manner, it is much easier for a charity to raise

A handicapped skier participating in the National Handicapped Ski Championships and Winterfestival, 1988, at Snowmass, Colorado. We exhibit great admiration toward those who overcome handicaps to accomplish difficult goals. What is your immediate reaction? (Brooks Dodge/Mountain Stock)

money for battered children or the blind than for the obese and alcoholics. This appears to be true because we perceive individuals as personally responsible for obesity and alcoholism; one should be able to control one's own eating and drinking behavior. On the other hand, this is not the case, for example, for blindness and other physical ailments (see Weiner, Perry, and Magnusson, 1988).

There is evidence that differential help giving is mediated by the feelings that are elicited by various persons in need of aid. We typically feel sympathy and pity toward the blind because they are not responsible, but anger and annoyance toward a drunk because she or he can be "blamed." These opposing emotional reactions guide approach and helping behavior versus avoidance and neglect (see Weiner, 1980). In a similar manner, you might be likely to help a classmate if he or she needed class notes because of illness or hospitalization. But if the same classmate cut class to go to the beach, or said that he or she merely "didn't feel like going to school," then the request for aid might elicit anger and neglect. In sum, our decision to help others and our feelings toward them are in good part determined by why the aid was needed and whether the needy are perceived as personally responsible for their plight. (see Schmidt and Weiner, 1988).

Attributions of Blame Following Traumatic Experience

As our feelings towards others are influenced by the degree to which we see them responsible for their plight, so our feelings towards ourselves may be equally influenced by whether or not we see ourselves responsible for our plight. There have been those who have argued that it is healthy for individuals to take responsibility for all outcomes in their lives, even for events such as illness or trauma, which most people typically think of as out of individual control. To what degree is it helpful for one to attribute responsibility to oneself for negative outcomes in one's life?

Janoff-Bulman (1988, 1989) has suggested that how we respond to a traumatic experience depends on whether we attribute responsibility to ourselves in the form of *characterological* self-blame or in the form of *behavioral* self-blame. From her studies with rape victims as well as with victims of other traumatic experiences, she has suggested that if we engage in characterological self-blame following a traumatic experience ("I'm a poor judge of character," "I never make the right decisions"), we are likely to feel helpless, guilty, or depressed. If we engage in behavioral self-blame ("I should have been more careful about the doors and windows"), we are less likely to respond with debilitating emotions because such attributions hold out hope for taking more proactive action in the future.

On the other hand, Frazier (1991) has argued that all kinds of self-blame are dysfunctional for rape victims. She summarizes the results of several research studies that she says do not support the distinction made by Janoff-Bulman. In one study (Frazier, 1990), it was found that both types of self-blame were associated with higher distress in rape victims. Clearly the issue of attributing responsibility to the self for certain kinds of negative outcomes is a complex one. What Frazier and Janoff-Bulman agree on is that after an experience such as rape, attributing some kind of responsibility to the self is dysfunctional. Whether more meaningful distinctions can be drawn between different kinds of self-blame so that some kinds of self-attributions of responsibility may be functional awaits further research.

CONCLUSION

How we perceive the causes of events in our lives influences whether or not we successfully respond to adversity, how we attribute responsibility, and the degree to which we have a sense of personal control. Having a sense of personal control appears to be related to positive coping in a variety of ways.

Summary

1. Skinner has contended that freedom is an illusion and that acceptance of this fact will lead to a better society.

2. *Locus of control* refers to beliefs regarding the perceived influence that one has on the attainment of a reinforcement. Questionnaires have been devised to classify individuals as *internal* versus *external* in locus of control. There is some evidence that persons labeled as internal function more effectively.

3. *Learned helplessness* develops when the likelihood of receiving a reward is unaffected by an organism's response. Learned helplessness impedes subsequent performance. There are some similarities between laboratory-induced helplessness and the state of depression.

4. An Attributional Style questionnaire has been developed to assess individual differences in causal perceptions. The disposition to attribute failure to the self may be a precursor for the onset of depression.

5. *Intrinsic* motivation indicates that behavior is undertaken for its own sake; *extrinsic* motivation connotes that the action is undertaken because of an extrinsic reward. Use of an extrinsic reward to motivate behavior may undermine or decrease intrinsic interest in the activity. Undermining occurs when the controlling, rather than the informational, aspects of the reward are salient.

6. Individuals attempt to restore freedom if it is taken away, a reaction termed *psychological reactance*. One manifestation of this attempt is demonstrated in attitudes: increased liking of a "forbidden" choice and decreased liking of available alternatives.

7. There is evidence that individuals maintain an illusion that they have control over their fates.

8. Henry Murray played an important role in the study of achievement needs by defining the achievement motive and specifying the actions that it instigates.

9. Need for achievement is typically assessed with a projective technique, the Thematic Apperception Test (TAT). However, this measure has a number of shortcomings, such as low internal consistency.

10. The generality of need for achievement as a trait remains uncertain, and there is only scattered evidence that the trait is relatively enduring.

11. Among the personality correlates of the need for achievement is the tendency for individuals high in achievement needs to (a) prefer intermediate-difficulty tasks, (b) be realistic in their aspirations, and (c) desire performance feedback.

12. Cognitive maturational factors, including self-attribution of success and integration of competitive stages, appear to be necessary precursors for the development of achievement strivings.

13. The effects of early socialization practices, such as early independence training and stress on good performance, have not been convincingly demonstrated as necessary antecedents for the development of high achievement needs.

14. Atkinson proposed a mathematical model of achievement motivation in which achievement tendencies are determined by the difference between hope for success and fear of failure. Atkinson's mathematical model leads to the prediction that individuals high in achievement needs prefer tasks of intermediate difficulty.

15. Studies on *diagnosticity,* or the information gained about one's ability following task performance, have shown that individuals highly motivated to succeed are especially desirous of feedback about their abilities.

16. *Causal attributions* for success or failure are important determinants of achievement striving. Three basic properties of causes — locus, stability, and controllability — influence, respectively, esteem-related affective reactions, expectancy of success, and social emotions.

17. There is some evidence that increments in need for achievement precede the positive economic growth of a society.

18. A variety of achievement-change programs focus attention on changing attributions for failure from lack of ability to insufficient effort.

19. Children who behave in a mastery-oriented manner keep attention focused on the task when they fail. They do not give up prematurely and they try new strategies. Helpless children when confronted with failure give up prematurely. Or, if they persist, they repeat the same dysfunctional strategy over and over. Further they focus their attention on what failure means about them rather than keeping attention focused on the task.

20. Evaluations of others are affected and the likelihood of help giving is minimized when others are perceived as personally responsible for their plight.

21. Following a traumatic experience, such as rape, it is dysfunctional to attribute blame to one's own *character.* There is controversy over whether or not it is helpful to take some responsibility for one's *actions.*

Thought Questions

1. What do you think of Skinner's position that we have only an illusion of control?

2. What situations in your present environment give rise to feelings of control and feelings of helplessness?

3. Can you recall a situation in which your freedom was restricted? What were your feelings and subsequent actions at the time? Did you make an attempt to restore freedom?

4. Do grades in school undermine your intrinsic interest in the subject matter? If grading were eliminated, would you have more or less interest in studying the material?

5. Do you think that achievement strivings tend to be expressed across a variety of situations or are specifically channeled into a few activities? Can you think of individuals who meet each of these descriptions?

6. When you do well on a test, what attributions do you generally make? How about when you do poorly? Do these influence your feelings and your expectations?

7. How might differences in male and female sex roles produce differences in achievement motivation?

18 | Love and Hate

The Bible, Shakespeare, contemporary literature, and clinical experiences all convey the presence and power of love and hate in human relationships. They are polar opposites — one fostering caretaking, giving, and growth, the other fostering discord, conflict, and destruction. However, they are often intimately connected. Love can give way to hate, as reflected in the number of homicides that take place between family members and lovers. In addition, some sexual behaviors have components of both love and hostility. Indeed, although mutually consenting sex is a loving act, there are some theorists who have suggested that hostility can nevertheless be a major source of sexual excitement (Stoller, 1979).

It is evident that love and hate are manifested in diverse ways and that they are complex terms. Each refers to a broad domain of feelings and behaviors. In this chapter, we shall distinguish between different meanings of love and caring and of hate and aggression. We shall also review the empirical exploration of these rather complex but fundamental dimensions of human experience. Aggression, in particular, has been extensively studied, whereas the empirical examination of love has been relatively recent. However, the research on love, like the research on aggression and hostility, demonstrates that despite the vagueness and ambiguity of the concept, a scientific approach can increase our understanding of the phenomenon.

Are humans fundamentally aggressive or loving? Is hatred learned? What is the relationship of the love of a parent for a child to the love between adult partners? What does it mean "to be in love"? Is it possible for society to control hatred and aggression effectively? Do sports and the entertainment media serve as outlets for aggression? Unfortunately, there are no simple answers to these questions and, in some instances, it is not yet possible to give *any* answer. However, theoretical analyses and empirical studies have at the very least provided a framework that enables us to discuss these issues sensibly and systematically.

LOVE'S INFINITE VARIETY

The ancients distinguished between at least three kinds of love. The *eros* of Plato, the *philia* of Aristotle and the *agape* of St. Paul and the Gospels are all types of love. They differ in their purpose, yet are often indistinguishable in their manifestations. Plato's eros, which Freud used as a label for libidinal strivings, has both a sexual and nonsexual connotation. In its earliest stage, eros, according to Plato,

■ **Highlight 18.1** ■■■■■■

The Varieties of Love

Elizabeth Barrett Browning's *Sonnets from the Portuguese* (1888) offers some extraordinarily beautiful and vivid descriptions of love. The following is a well-known sonnet from that volume:

> How do I love thee? Let me count the ways.
> I love thee to the depth and breadth and height
> My soul can reach, when feeling out of sight
> For the ends of Being and ideal Grace.
> I love thee to the level of everyday's
> Most quiet need, by sun and candlelight.
> I love thee freely, as men strive for Right;
> I love thee purely, as they turn from Praise.
> I love thee with the passion put to use
> In my old griefs, and with my childhood's faith.
> I love thee with a love I seemed to lose
> With my lost saints,—I love thee with the breath,
> Smiles, tears, of all my life!—and, if God choose,
> I shall but love thee better after death.

---

entails the love of the physical beauty of another's body. At later stages, eros becomes the love of virtue and knowledge. Thus Plato, in the *Symposium,* defines eros as the "desire for the perpetual possession of the good" (1972, p. 86).

Aristotle's *philia* refers to the reciprocal love in a friendship. This love is transitory when based upon the instrumental utility of the partners for each other—the economic help, the emotional support, the amusement, and so forth—that the partners may provide each other. As these qualities wane, the basis of the friendship is lost and the friendship fails. However, philia is enduring when it is based on "the friendship of men who are good and alike in virtue" (Aristotle, 1947, p. 475).

Whereas philia and eros are directly linked to and affected by the attributes of the beloved, agape is independent of the merits of the loved object. Agape is a more generalized feeling—a love of God and of all mankind. The Bible urges us to "Love the Lord your God with all your heart, with all your soul, with all your strength, and with all your mind; and your neighbors as yourself" (The New English Bible, 1971, p. 87).

These three categories—eros, philia, and agape—by no means exhaust the different meanings of the concept of love (for example, love of an activity such as music or sports, love of one's country, love of one's children). However, they convey important differences in the qualities of love, differences that are reflected in contemporary theoretical and empirical analyses of love. We have already reviewed in some detail one form of love, namely, the attachment of an infant to a caregiver (see Chapter 12). One might speculate that the formation of these early attachments is essential for the development of different forms of love manifested later in life. We do know from the data on early separation that disruption of these attachments in young children can produce emotional disturbances and persistent adjustment difficulties. However, these data, though indicating that early attachments are important to later development, do not tell us whether these early attachments provide the basis for subsequent love relationships. Psychoanalytic theory suggests that the individuals chosen as partners in a love relationship are very similar to individuals to whom one was attached as a child—not unlike the message of the opening lines of an old song, "I want a girl just like the girl that married dear old Dad." But songs and theory do not provide adequate support for the proposition that adult love relationships are rooted in early childhood love relationships.

RESEARCH ON LOVE

The many meanings of love and its elusive, almost mysterious quality posed difficult obstacles for psychological study, and for many years love remained a topic for psychological speculation rather than systematic research. A pioneering contribution was made by Z. Rubin (1970) who introduced a scale for measuring romantic love (see Table 18.1). By distinguishing between responses to an item when it referred to a partner with whom one was romantically involved as opposed to referring to a platonic friend, he was able to develop a Love Scale that

Table 18.1   Love and liking scales

Examples of Love Scale items	Examples of Liking Scale items
I feel that I can confide in _____ about virtually everything.	In my opinion, _____ is an exceptionally mature person.
If I could never be with _____, I would feel miserable.	I have great confidence in _____'s good judgment.
One of my primary concerns is _____'s welfare.	I think that _____ and I are quite similar to each other.
I would forgive _____ for practically anything.	_____ is one of the most likable people I know.

Source: Adapted from *Liking and Loving: An Invitation to Social Psychology* by Zick Rubin, copyright © 1973 by Holt, Rinehart and Winston, Inc., reprinted by permission of the publisher.

was factorially independent from a Liking Scale (see Chapter 7). Examples of items from the Love and Liking Scales are presented in Table 18.1. Rubin then administered the Love Scale to a sample of dating (but nonengaged) college-student couples who completed the instrument with respect to their dating partner and later with respect to a close friend of the same sex as the partner. As anticipated, the findings indicated that although loving and liking are related, they are only moderately correlated, though more for men than for women. Perhaps women are more able than men to recognize negative attributes in partners whom they love.

The construct validity of the Love Scale is supported by the finding that although both men and women loved their dating partner much more than their friend, there was very little difference in their liking of their dating partners and friends. Also, the love scores were more highly correlated with self-reports of being "in love" and with perception of the probability of marriage than the liking scores. In addition, observations of the couples in a laboratory situation revealed that couples who were strongly in love spent significantly more time gazing into one another's eyes than did couples who were only weakly in love.

An examination of the Love Scale items suggests that there are four different components contributing to the love score: needing, caring, trust, and tolerance (Kelley, 1983). Needing is the desire to be in the other's presence and to be cared for by that person. Caring entails a different set of attitudes and behaviors — the desire to help, to take care of the partner. Trust involves the exchange of confidences, of intimate, personal matters, whereas tolerance pertains to the willingness to accept another's faults. Are each of these components equivalent indicators of love? A study distinguishing care, needs, and trust indicates that this is not the case (Steck, Levitan, McLane, and Kelley, 1982). Hypothetical situations in which the care, need, and trust components were systematically varied were rated by college student samples for love, liking, attraction, and friendship. Situations depicting a high degree of caring for another were judged to display greater love than those depicting high need or high trust, although the latter did influence judgments of love. Although trust is more strongly related to ratings of friendship than to ratings of love, it is still a significant component of love. A study of self-disclosure between couples who were dating indicated that the amount of disclosure of personal intimacies between partners was significantly related to the measure of loving but unrelated to a measure of liking (Critelli and Dupre, 1978).

The finding that caring is more important to love than needing the other must be interpreted with caution. What these data say is that caring is a necessary component of romantic love. To indicate that you would be miserable without your partner but are not greatly concerned for their welfare implies a selfish need or attraction. However, caring without need, especially the needs entailed in strong attraction, implies love without great romance or passion. The Rubin Love Scale, which yields a single score, does not discriminate between these different combinations of care, need, and trust and the different types of love they might reflect. A multidimensional approach would better capture the variations of love.

A TRIANGULAR MODEL OF LOVE

The triangular model of love, proposed by Sternberg (1986), is a promising example of a multi-dimensional approach. Sternberg proposes that there are three essential components of love: intimacy, passion and decision/commitment. These components can be visualized as forming the vertices of a triangle as in Figure 18.1. Intimacy refers to the degree of closeness and warmth between two individuals. Sternberg and Grajek (1984) indicate that intimacy entails mutual understanding and communication, the desire to promote the welfare of the loved one, and feeling able to count on the loved one when in need. It also involves sharing, emotional support, and experiencing happiness when with the loved one.

To intimacy, Sternberg adds a passion component that connotes the romance and excitement that may be involved in a love relationship. While sexual feelings and needs usually constitute the principal contributors to passion, Sternberg suggests that other needs such as self-esteem, affiliation and dominance can also contribute to the experience of passion. Finally, to complete the model of love, Sternberg believes there is an important cognitive decision component that must be considered. He suggests that there is a short-term decision that one is in love and also a longer term commitment to maintain that love. The commitment dimension is clearly important. However, the significance of the short-term decision, independent of the feelings of love, remains unclear.

One of the properties of the triangular model is that it provides a framework or map for designating the components of different types of love, as in Figure 18.2 on p. 515. The vertices signify the type of love represented by each component alone. Thus intimacy, without passion or decision/commitment, is essentially liking, while passion without intimacy or decision/commitment constitutes

Figure 18.1   The Three Components of Love (From Sternberg, 1986, p. 119).

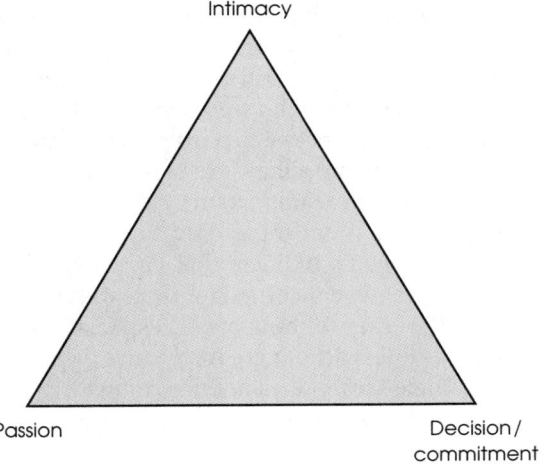

Figure 18.2 The Kinds of Loving as Different Combinations of the Three Components of Love. (From Sternberg, 1986, p. 123.)

Liking
(Intimacy alone)

Romantic love
(Intimacy +
Passion)

Companionate love
(Intimacy +
Commitment)

Consummate love
(Intimacy + Passion +
Commitment)

Infatuation
(Passion
alone)

Fatuous love
(Passion +
Commitment)

Empty love
(Decision/
Commitment
alone)

infatuation, and decision/commitment without intimacy or passion is merely hollow or Empty Love. Other forms of love are represented by different combinations of the components. Thus intimacy plus passion constitute Romantic Love, while intimacy plus decision/commitment make for Companionate Love in which the partners feel close and committed to each other but passion is absent. The presence of all three components constitutes Consummate Love, or the type of love that most individuals in this culture strive for in a marital relationship.

It may be noted that other relationships such as parental love for their children and closeness between friends can be mapped onto the triangular model of love, as well as sexually oriented romantic relationships.

PASSIONATE LOVE

Romantic love is clearly complex in nature, and its characteristics may change over time. More detailed analyses of one component of romantic love, *passionate love,* highlight the need component and the intensity of accompanying emotional responses. Passionate love is characterized by preoccupation with thoughts of the love object, with the desire to spend as much time as possible with him or her, with sharp variations in feeling—from the heights of elation to the depths of despair, and with strong sexual arousal (Hatfield, 1983; Hatfield and Walster, 1981). Why does one "fall in love"? What are the determinants of passionate love? Behavioral studies have not yet emerged with satisfactory, scientifically-based responses to these questions, which have preoccupied poets and youth for centuries. An influential theory of passionate love proposes three conditions as necessary (Berscheid and Walster, 1974; Hatfield and Walster, 1981):

1. *One must be raised in a culture that believes in the idea of romantic love, and reinforces that idea in young people.* Romantic love has been seen as largely a Western concept that arose in Europe in the Middle Ages. Only many centuries later did it become viewed as the appropriate basis for marriage. There is little doubt that cultural factors exert a strong influence on conceptions of love and on such practices as arranged marriages in contrast to marriages predicated on the partners being "in love." For instance, even in modern India 90 to 95 percent of the marriages are still arranged by families, a practice as common among educated professionals as among the less educated (Rosenbaum, 1992). Rosenbaum notes, "The general notion is that marriage is too important an economic and social arrangement to be left to the whim of personal impulse and attraction, and that love will grow from continued association and companionship" (p. 67). In cultures that believe in romantic love as a basis for marriage, cultural factors probably reinforce the idea of falling in love and increase its likelihood through expectancy. Moreover, cultures that reinforce the belief in love may also reduce inhibition and constraints that block passionate love and make available to the individual emotional relationships that are less accessible to someone in another culture. However, it should be noted that the idea that romantic love is only a Western concept has recently been challenged by several writers.

2. *The presence of an appropriate love object.* Here, the principal question is, What makes an appropriate love object? There is a good deal of evidence that physical attractiveness is an important variable (Folkes, 1982; Walster, et al., 1966). However, other factors are also important, particularly the degree to which the couple shares similar interests and the extent to which there is mutual reinforcement and gratification of needs (Berscheid and Walster, 1978).

3. Perhaps the most controversial is the requirement for *intense emotional arousal that is interpreted by the individual as love.* This condition is consonant with Schachter's (1964) theory of emotion, which maintains that specific emotional experiences are a consequence of one's cognitive interpretation of a nonspecific emotional arousal (see Chapter 15). Although there is evidence that different kinds of emotional processes, such as anxiety and anger (Driscoll, Davis and Lipetz, 1972), can increase feelings of attraction and love, these experiments are open to various interpretations and are subject to some of the same criticisms that have been offered of the Schachter theory of emotion.

   Passionate love is of sufficient interest in its own right that a scale has been developed to assess it specifically, thereby facilitating its investigation

(Hatfield and Sprecher, 1986). The following are examples of items on the Passionate Love scale:

Sometimes my body trembles with excitement at the sight of _____.

I would feel despair if _____ left me.

_____ always seems to be on my mind. I eagerly look for signs indicating _____'s desire for me.

Although there is some overlap in the content of the Passionate Love Scale and the Rubin Love Scale, the items on the Passionate Love Scale generally reflect more intense feeling. Nevertheless, the two scales are very highly correlated, Hatfield and Sprecher (1986) finding correlations greater than .80. These data reflect a very close relationship between the emotional excitement and romantic passion associated with "being in love," and the attitudes and feelings of needing, caring, trust, and tolerance for one's partner. Whether these attitudes and feelings are simply consequences or manifestations of passionate love or whether they exist prior to and contribute to "falling in love" remains an open question. Probably both processes occur.

These data also pose an interesting issue for Sternberg's triangular model. We generally recognize a difference between infatuation and a romantic love relationship. People can become infatuated with individuals whom they have only seen and to whom they have never spoken; in some instances, to individuals whom they have seen only by photograph. Surely, elements of intimacy — of mutual understanding, sharing and closeness — are absent from this relationship. But does the person who is infatuated feel this difference? Clearly, important research issues remain to be addressed.

COMPANIONATE LOVE

Although there is disagreement about the conditions that are essential to the manifestation of passionate love, the evidence is clear that passionate love typically declines in intensity the longer a couple has been together (Hatfield and Walster, 1981). What becomes essential in long-term relationships between partners are the factors that contribute to *companionate love,* which is defined as "the affection we feel for those with whom our lives are deeply intertwined" (Berscheid and Walster, 1978). Here, the caring component (Steck, et al., 1982) becomes more salient and critical. Shared experiences and interests and mutual trust contribute to the relationship. In addition, although sexual gratification may remain important, even if the intensity of the passion has declined, gratification of other needs that the relationship provides becomes more central. The factor of commitment is of particular importance.

The factors that foster commitment to a relationship overlap with those that foster love. However, there can be love without commitment, as in the case of the

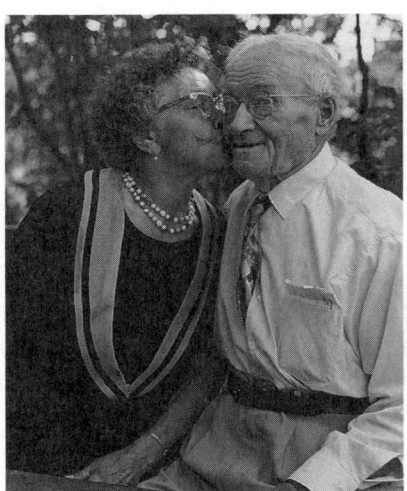

An example of companionate love. (© Frank Siteman MCMLXXX/The Picture Cube)

partner who refuses to make a commitment to a relationship because of personality, economic issues, or other reasons, despite his or her feelings of love. There can also be commitment without love as exemplified by couples who no longer love each other but remain married "because of the children," for fear of social rejection, or for financial or religious reasons. An analysis of the relationship between love and commitment is presented in Figure 18.3 (Kelley, 1983, p. 266). The distinction between stable and unstable factors is helpful here (see Chapter 17). Examples of positive stable factors that might promote an interaction (close relationship) between two individuals are shared interests and attitudes and personality attributes such as intelligence, warmth, and assertiveness. Physical attractiveness, although relatively stable, may well change during the course of the relationship. Examples of unstable positive factors are sexual arousal and a fun evening together.

According to this model, although both unstable and stable positive factors contribute to love, only stable factors are assumed to promote commitment. Examples of nonpositive stable factors that foster commitment, but not love, are feelings of obligation to a contract and shared economic interests that make termination of the relationship costly. In terms of this analysis, the most enduring and satisfying relationships are ones based on positive stable factors that foster both love and commitment.

INTIMACY

As we know, even relationships that appear to begin with stable positive factors of shared interests and attitudes may end in conflict and dissolution. One problem area is difficulty in maintaining intimacy. The study of intimacy and close rela-

Figure 18.3   The conceptual relation between love and commitment. Among all the causal conditions that promote interaction, love refers to a major subset of the positive conditions and commitment refers to all of the stable conditions. (Adapted from *Close Relationships*, p. 266, by Harold H. Kelley, et al. W. H. Freeman and Company. Copyright © 1983.)

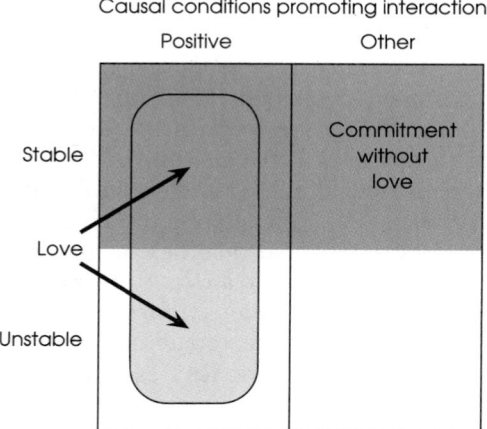

tionships has emerged as a major research area for psychologists (Hendrick, 1989; Perlman and Duck, 1987). Research on intimacy indicates that the establishment of intimacy will vary with situation and partners, but there is also evidence of personality differences in the ease or difficulty with which an individual establishes intimate relationships.

One such personality difference influencing the maintenance of intimacy is in the degree of self-monitoring (cf. Chapter 10). It will be recalled that the high self-monitoring individual is predominantly situationally oriented, whereas the low self-monitoring person tends to be more directed by inner attitudes and dispositions. One might conjecture that an intimate relationship requires some consistency of behavior and of interest in the partner in different situations. "Out of sight, out of mind" is unlikely to foster a close, intimate relationship. Thus, one would expect high self-monitoring individuals to form more superficial relationships than the low self-monitors. And there are data to support this expectation (Snyder and Simpson, 1987). High self-monitors were found to be more willing than low self-monitors to change their current dating partner, to take longer to develop an intimate relationship, and to tend to prefer less close, less exclusive romantic relationships.

Another factor that discriminates individuals who have difficulty in maintaining intimacy is communication skills. Training programs have been developed to improve communication skills in partners who experience conflict and lack of intimacy in their relationship (Hatfield, 1988). The partners are encouraged to express their feelings, even where some risk may be involved. At the same time, they learn skills in how best to convey their feelings and how best to respond to the reactions of their partners.

Attachment Styles

Still another variable shown to be related to the establishment of intimate relationships are individual differences in modes of attachment (Hazan and Shaver, 1987). Shaver and his co-workers have proposed that a critical component of romantic love is the attachment process that is first manifested by the infant in the interaction with his/her caretaker (Shaver, Hazan, and Bradshaw, 1988). They point out there are striking parallels between features of adult love and characteristics of infant attachment. Some of these parallels are enumerated in Table 18.2 (Shaver and Hazen, 1988, p. 481). To explore more specifically the relationship between variations in attachment and qualities of the love experience, brief one-paragraph versions appropriate for adults were prepared of Ainsworth's descriptions of Secure, Insecure (or Anxious, Ambivalent) and Avoidant attachment types (cf. Chapter 12). The Secure paragraph states that the individual finds it relatively easy to get close to others and isn't especially worried about being abandoned by the partner; the Insecure description focuses on concern about the love and commitment of the partner; and the Avoidant paragraph reflects discomfort at getting too close to others. Adult respondents chose which of the three descriptions best fit them and were categorized accordingly.

Significant differences in features of the love experience were found for several samples of adult respondents, depending upon their attachment style (Hazan and Shaver, 1987). Those in the Secure attached group were more likely to describe love as especially happy, friendly, and trusting, and they were able to accept the partner despite the partner's faults. Moreover, the mean duration of their relationships was impressively longer than those reported by the other two groups — 10.0 years in comparison to 4.9 years for the Insecure and 6.0 years for the Avoidant groups. The Insecure respondents were more likely to describe love as involving obsession, emotional highs and lows, and extreme sexual attraction and jealousy. The Avoidant group descriptions also tended to convey emotional highs and lows and jealousy, plus a fear of intimacy.

Although the primary research focus has been on the role of the attachment system in adult love, it has been proposed that biologically-bound behavioral systems are also involved in varying degrees in adult love — caregiving and sexuality (Shaver, Hazan, and Bradshaw, 1988). Caregiving is especially evident in parental love, but it is also believed to be an important element in maintaining enduring romantic relationships.

LOVE AND SEX

What is the relationship between sexual desire and love? We have already indicated that with the passage of time, the erotic or passionate component of love

Table 18.2   Some features of attachment and adult romantic love

Attachment	Romantic love
Formation and quality of the attachment bond depend on the attachment figure's perceived sensitivity and responsiveness.	Romantic love includes an intense desire for the partner's (real or imagined) interest and reciprocation.
Infant's feelings of joy and distress depend on the attachment figure's perceived availability and responsiveness.	Adult lover's moods depend on his or her current perceptions of the partner's reciprocation or rejection.
When the infant's attachment relationship is secure, she or he is happier, has a higher threshold for distress, is more willing to explore unfamiliar environments and interact with strangers.	When adults are in love, they often report feeling more relaxed, less worried, less defensive, more creative and spontaneous and more courageous.
Attachment behaviors include: maintenance of proximity and contact—holding, touching, caressing, kissing, rocking, smiling, making eye-contact, following, etc.	Adult romantic love is indicated by: holding, touching, caressing, kissing, rocking, smiling, making eye contact, following, etc.
Separation from the attachment figure causes intense distress, initiates vigorous, attention-consuming reunion efforts, and results in despair if reunion proves impossible.	Unchosen separation from the partner causes intense distress, initiates attention-consuming reunion efforts, and results in grief if reunion is impossible.
Intense desire to share discoveries and reactions with the attachment figure.	Intense desire to share discoveries, feelings, opinions, etc., and to give gifts to one's love partner.
Infants coo, 'sing', talk baby talk, etc., and attachment figures talk baby talk.	Adult lovers coo, sing, talk baby talk, use affectionate baby-like names for each other.

Taken from Shaver and Hazen, 1988, p. 48.

tends to decline, while other elements become more significant. Does it mean that the sexual element is irrelevant to the experience of love in later phases of the relationship? Although sexual intimacy may not be necessary to a loving relationship between partners, it probably is the case that sexual contact helps maintain and enhance the partners' love for each other.

However, clinical evidence and theory are not consistent on this point. Most clinicians, including psychoanalysts, feel that given physically healthy partners, continuing sexual contact is both an expression of and helps maintain the love relationship. Yet, according to psychoanalytic theory "love is aim-inhibited sexuality" (Sigmund Freud, 1955, p. 142), suggesting that love is a form of modified sexual feeling. It would then follow that given a fixed level of sexual energy, the more energy that is invested in sex, the less energy that is available for love! The solution to this paradox is suggested by the high level of sexual passion that the partners direct to each other in the initial phases of a romantic relationship. Given this initial level, even if sexual energies are diverted, or "converted," as it were, into love, there still would be sufficient libido available for sexual intimacy. At the same time, Freud's conjecture implies that a close, caring, loving relationship will not develop if the couple attempts to maintain sexual passion at the high level of intensity that characterized their early relationship.

Sexual feelings can be a significant component of love. However, a relationship based on sexual attraction alone is a very different from one based on love. According to Erich Fromm (1956),

> Sexual desire can be stimulated by the anxiety of aloneness, by the wish to conquer, or be conquered, by vanity, by the wish to hurt and even to destroy, as much as it can be stimulated by love. . . Sexual attraction creates, for the moment, the illusion of union, yet without love this "union" leaves strangers as far apart as they were before — sometimes it makes them feel ashamed of each other, or even makes them hate each other, because when the illusion has gone they feel their estrangement even more markedly than before (pp. 54–55).

Yet sex without love does not necessarily lead to the kinds of negative feelings between partners described by Fromm. For some individuals and couples, love is a prerequisite for sex, whereas others are quite clear that their sexual intimacy has no implications beyond physical attraction and sexual satisfaction. In a two-year longitudinal study bearing on this issue (Peplau, Rubin and Hill, 1977), college-age dating couples were divided into three groups:

1. *Sexually traditional* couples who felt that the commitment of marriage as well as love is a necessary prerequisite for sexual intercourse.

2. *Sexually moderate* couples for whom sex is permissible if the partners love each other.

3. *Sexually liberal* couples who may feel that sex with love is desirable, but do not view love as a prerequisite for sexual intercourse.

These three orientations were, as to be expected, related to the timing of the first intercourse — abstention characterizing the first group, later sex the second group, and early sex describing the third group. Most germane to the question of the influence of sex on the relationship was the finding that couples in all three groups reported similar satisfaction with their relationship. Moreover, there was no difference two years later in the dating status of each group. About 46 percent of the couples had broken up, 34 percent were still dating, and 20 percent had gotten married. These percentages were similar, regardless of the amount of sexual intimacy. Apparently, neither early or late sex nor abstention had a consistent effect on the development of a lasting commitment.

Nor does sexual exclusiveness have a clear impact on a love relationship. In a study comparing gay male couples who had agreed on sexually-open relationships with gay male couples who had agreed on a closed relationship of sexual exclusivity, no differences were found between the groups in degree of love and liking for partner, and degree of satisfaction with and commitment to the relationship (Blasband and Peplau, 1985). Whether a similar finding would obtain for heterosexual couples with sexually-open and sexually-exclusive relationships would be of interest to determine. In this regard, it may be noted that a number of similarities have been observed in heterosexual and gay or lesbian relationships (Peplau, 1988). Homosexuals, like heterosexuals, typically desire enduring relationships and frequently are able to achieve them. The same models of love — the triangular model, the attachment model, passionate and companionate love, in all likelihood apply with equal cogency to both homosexual and heterosexual relationships.

LOVE AND HATE

Love and hate are typically conceived of as polar opposites and, indeed, for the most part they are. They pertain to fundamentally different ways in which organisms can interact. A key question is the extent to which interactions are dominated by love-related tendencies, such as cooperation, mutual assistance, and self-sacrifice, versus hate-related tendencies, such as threats, attack, and killing (Eibl-Eibesfeldt, 1974).

At the human level, scholars over centuries have argued about whether humans are fundamentally governed by love-based impulses or hostile, aggressive urges (compare the views of the different theorists discussed in Chapters 3–6). For Freud, Eros (love) and Thanatos (hostility, anger, aggression) constituted two basic, biologically rooted drives from which all other significant human motivations emerged. Eros and Thanatos are not necessarily in conflict, as in the case of sadistic and masochistic behaviors, which are characterized by erotic pleasure being associated with aggressive acts — whether inflicting pain or being the recipient of pain.

Also, as noted earlier, there is evidence that anger can enhance sexual arousal (Barclay, 1969) and romantic love (Driscoll, et al., 1972). It has been suggested that the uncertainty associated with someone about whom one feels ambivalent may heighten one's attraction to them, and that jealousy, frustration, and anger as well as reward, intimacy, and joy may enhance one's passion (Hatfield and Walster, 1981). Nevertheless, although there are circumstances in which the love-passion motivational system and the hate-anger-aggression motivational system may be mutually facilitating, on the whole they lead to incompatible behaviors and attitudes. Love diminishes the likelihood of hostile, aggressive acts toward the love object, and hate diminishes caring, loving acts toward the individual eliciting hostile feelings.

Love and hate may be connected to each other in another way. One of the sad ironies of close relationships is that the love on which they were based frequently gives way to hostility. In addition, in many instances, the more intense the love when the relationship was harmonious, the more intense the hostility when the relationship becomes discordant. Why should a relationship in which loving feelings initially are predominant become vulnerable to negative, hostile interaction? There appear to be three basic reasons for this:

1. *In any relationship in which there is close, frequent interactions over an extended period of time* — between husband and wife, parent and child, sisters and brothers, or roommates — *conflicts are likely to arise.* Each individual in the pair has his or her own needs, interests, and habits, and these have to be coordinated and sometimes reconciled. Studies of young heterosexual couples reflect an extremely wide variety of issues over which conflict may arise (Gottman, 1979; Peterson, 1983). Conflicts arise over money, household chores, in-laws, personal habits, frequency of sexual intercourse, jealousies, child-rearing, and a host of other issues. More harmonious couples deal with conflicts more effectively by focusing on issues that they perceive differently and by keeping the boundary of the discussion specific to the issues in question (Raush, et al., 1974). The more distressed couples tend to extend the discussion beyond the behaviors or views at issue, and attack the partner in general terms with negative aspersions about their personality. An example of the difference between harmonious and discordant couples in their approach to conflicts would be discussing a conflict over expenditure of money in terms of each partner's views regarding freedom of choice and economic priorities versus discussing the partner's stinginess, selfishness, immature, spendthrift nature, or other personality aspersions.

2. *The risk and vulnerability entailed in love itself.* If one does not love, one cannot feel rejected. The greater the love, the greater the pain of rejection, and the greater the pain, the greater the likelihood of anger and hostility. Individuals who feel inadequate and whose self-concept is very much dependent upon the approval of the partner are particularly prone to react to possible rejection with anger. Because they tend to be readily threatened, such individuals can be beset by feelings of jealousy, with its attendant problems of conflict and hostility (White, 1981).

3. *The unrealistic perceptions that one typically has of one's partner* (Hatfield and Walster, 1981). Romantic love, as the popular saying goes, is blind. One tends to idealize the partner's virtues and to be oblivious to failings; but as relationships continue, reality begins to intrude, and the unrealistic perceptions culminate in profound disappointment. One might feel frustrated, misled, or even bitter, attributing the initial erroneous impression of the partner to his or her deceptiveness rather than to one's own love-clouded vision.

Love need not be as fragile as suggested by these problems of conflict, jealousy, and misperceptions with which it is often associated. Love is also associated with understanding, acceptance, forgiveness, and compromise. Although some relationships that begin in romantic love end in discord and hostility, others develop into deeply intimate, supportive, and caring partnerships. Some of the reasons love may turn into hostility rather than a companionate relationship have been suggested. A more thorough and systematic understanding requires an examination of the dynamics of aggression.

WHAT IS AGGRESSION?

The term *aggression,* as used by both layperson and scientist, covers many different behaviors. It includes murder, physical attack, verbal insults, and outbursts of rage. To these we might add destruction of property, menacing gestures, social humiliation, prejudice, playful jostling, and violent dreams and fantasies. And the listing is still far from exhaustive (see Highlight 18.2). While the behaviors embraced by the term *aggression* may have important elements in common, their diversity makes it difficult to establish general laws or principles that apply to all forms of aggression. It also leads to confusion in communication, so that different investigators might mean different things when they refer to aggressive behavior. In addition, people may differ in their perceptions of what is aggressive so that the same act may be viewed as non-aggressive by one person and aggressive by another (Tedeschi, 1983). Biologists, in fact, prefer to use the term *agonistic behavior* as an alternative to aggression. Agonistic behavior includes offensive and defensive fighting, competitive behaviors, and even sounds and gestures that function as threats and may serve to avert more serious conflicts. While these definitions are useful, the ultimate answer to the question of what aggression is will have to depend on research that tells us which kinds of aggressive behaviors go together and which ones have different properties.

There are certain theoretical distinctions that are helpful in understanding some of the controversies and experimental findings concerning the causes and functions of aggression. First, it is important to distinguish between the response or behavior and the motive or reason for that response. For example, an attack by a mugger is a clear instance of an aggressive act. However, there may be important psychological differences in the reasons for such an attack. The mugger's primary motive might be to steal the victim's wallet. If the wallet falls or can be successfully picked out of the victim's pocket, the mugger will be equally satisfied. In this instance, the aggressive attack is one of a number of possible *instrumental* behaviors that may or may not involve aggression for achieving a basically nonaggressive goal. Suppose, however, that the mugger is angry at his victim and that his primary goal is to humiliate and physically hurt the victim, with theft being incidental. Here, the aggressive behavior is no longer instrumental to a nonaggressive goal (i.e., money) but is motivated by *aggressive drive,* or *drive-instigated* hostility. What is critical to the mugger is that the victim be injured or publicly disgraced. He would be equally satisfied if he witnessed someone else carrying out

■ **Highlight 18.2** ■

Some Examples of Aggressive Behavior

1. A boy swats at a hornet and gets stung.
2. A cat kills a mouse, parades around with it, and then discards it.
3. A wolf kills and devours a stray sheep.
4. A farmer beheads a chicken and prepares it for Sunday dinner.
5. A hunter kills an animal and mounts it as a trophy.
6. A dog snarls at the mailman, but never bites him.
7. A tennis player smashes his racket after missing a volley.
8. A boxer gives his opponent a bloody nose.
9. A small boy daydreams of beating up the neighborhood bully.
10. A woman nags and criticizes her husband, and he ignores her in return.
11. A firing squad executes a prisoner.
12. A bombardier presses a button and hundreds below are killed.
13. A bank robber is shot in the back while attempting to escape.
14. A politician evades legislation that might help clear up a crime-ridden slum.
15. A man commits suicide.
16. An assassin misses his target.
17. A man dislikes all blacks, Jews, and long-haired college students.
18. Two friends get into a heated quarrel after drinking too much.

Source: From *Aggression: In Man and Animals* by Roger N. Johnson, pp. 4–5. Copyright ©1972 by W.B. Saunders Company.

the attack or if a member of the victim's family were injured. Other factors also influence the nature of the aggressive action, and sometimes instrumental aggression and aggressive drive-motivated behavior may overlap (e.g., the mugger may both hate his victim and want his money). But, as we will try to show, the distinction between instrumental and drive-instigated aggression helps clarify some of the theoretical confusion and debate concerning the causes of human aggression. For example, social learning theorists have been largely concerned with the acquisition and performance of *instrumental* aggression (cf. discussion of Bandura, Chapter 5), while psychoanalytic theorists have focused on the dynamics of aggressive *drive*. In addition, not all aggressive acts are necessarily instrumental or motivated by aggressive drive. Some aggressive acts may be responses that are innately or through conditioning elicited by aggressive *cues*. For example, the perception of a weapon might stimulate aggressive thoughts and other aggressive responses.

Two young boys engaging in aggressive behavior, which may not be motivated by aggressive drives if they are only "playing." (© Elizabeth Crews)

BIOLOGICAL ASPECTS OF AGGRESSION

Do humans have an innate propensity to use instrumental aggressive responses? Do they have an innate aggressive drive that, like hunger and thirst, must somehow be satisfied? There are three areas of biological study that relate to these questions:

1. Ethology, which entails systematic observations of animals in their natural settings.

2. Physiological research on hormones, brain structures, and brain chemistry involved in aggression.

3. Genetic research, with both animals and humans, on the inheritance of aggression.

Ethological Research

The investigation of the bases for aggression in animals has been and continues to be of major interest to ethologists. A substantial part of the research for which two pioneering ethologists, Konrad Lorenz (1966) and Nikita Tinbergen (1953, 1968), received Nobel prizes involved contributions to our knowledge of aggression. Among these contributions was the discovery that there are stimuli that act as innate *releasers* of aggressive responses. For example, male robins, on perceiving the red patch on the breast of a rival, will respond by attacking him. Removal of the red patch eliminates the aggressive response (Lack, 1943). Another well-known instance is the aggressive response of a male stickleback fish to the red belly of another stickleback who enters his territory (Tinbergen, 1951), although subsequent research has shown this releasing effect to be strongly influenced by other variables (Peeke, Wyers, and Herz, 1969). In some cases, like that of the famous tropical fighting fish (*Betta splendens*), there appears to be no specific releasing stimulus. All it takes for a male fighting fish to put on an aggressive display and begin an attack is the perception of another male *Betta,* or even of his own image in a mirror.

However, ethologists have also discovered that, in most species, fighting between members of the same species rarely escalates to killing or even to severe injury. Much of the fighting is ritualistic and, in many cases, involves only threat displays, with little or no physical contact. For example, a study of aggression among elephant seals indicated that for every actual fight, there were sixty-seven aggressive encounters that consisted solely of aggressive threat displays (LeBoeuf and Peterson, 1969). These displays vary according to the species under study. In a cat, the back arches, the hackles rise, the teeth bare, and the claws extend, all of which serve to make the cat appear larger. Birds commonly fluff their feathers and spread their wings for the same effect. And wild chimpanzees engage in a variety of rituals, including staring an opponent into submission, stomping the ground, and hooting and screaming (Van Lawick-Goodall, 1968*b*).

These aggressive displays commonly serve to inhibit the behavior of the target animal that provoked the aggressive display. Such provoking behaviors include intrusion on territory, approach to another's female partner or cache of food, and efforts at dominance. If threat gestures do not suffice and an actual fight takes place, in many species ritualized behaviors come into play that act as *inhibitory* rather than releasing stimuli, so that a victorious animal will cease its aggressive attack before the vanquished animal is seriously injured. For example, a dog who is the loser of a fight may present its unprotected neck to the mouth of the victor or roll over on its back exposing its vulnerable underside (Lorenz, 1966). Thus, for most animal species a sequence of interactions has evolved to act as a brake on intraspecies fighting and killing. Severe fighting does occur and intraspecies killing does take place; lions of one group have been observed to attack and kill lions of another group (Eibl-Eibesfeldt, 1977, p. 130).

Also, occurrences of infanticide by adult males have been observed in a number of mammalian species, including primates (Struhsaker and Leland, 1987). In addition, contrary to earlier impressions of the great apes, extensive observations of chimpanzees in their natural settings have revealed instances of invasions by groups of males of the territory of a branch community of chimpanzees and the killing of several members of that community (Goodall, 1986). However, these incidents are infrequent, and the behaviors of the chimpanzee groups can hardly be characterized as "warlike" (Huntingford, 1987). Ethological studies of aggression in nonhuman species do not support the notion that it is biologically "natural" for people to kill each other or, as some maintain (Ardrey, 1967), that we humans have an inborn killer instinct.

Two German shepherds and a husky in combat. Within-species nonhuman aggression rarely results in death. (Julie O'Neil/The Picture Cube)

What these studies do suggest is that it is possible that some instrumental aggressive responses are innately "wired into" our neuromuscular system. Observations of children born deaf and blind indicate that a number of patterns of aggressive behavior, such as stamping the feet, clenching the teeth, and making fists are present in these children despite lack of opportunity to observe these behaviors (cf. Eibl-Eibesfeldt, 1977, p. 135). It is also possible that these aggressive reactions are wired to releasing stimuli. However, there are no good examples in humans of simple stimuli that automatically release an aggressive response. The possible counterparts of releasing stimuli—restraint of infant movement, intense discomfort, exposure to deliberate frustration, or malicious attack on a loved family member—are complex affective-cognitive situations rather than relatively simple physical stimuli. And, if there are innate aggression inhibitors in humans—for example, tears, pleading, and submissive gestures— they are unfortunately quite weak and all too frequently do not work. The human capacity to experience empathy, the sharing of another's perspective and feelings (cf. Chapter 12), may be one mechanism that helps restrain an aggressor from continuing an attack, but empathy is not automatic and requires experience and training (N. Feshbach, 1979).

Anger and Aggressive Drive.   Several of the innate aggressive reactions that have been described resemble the emotions of anger or rage. Anger, like other emotions, has an important adaptive value: the organism becomes fiercer and more capable of defending itself when angry. Anger adds to one's strength and to the intensity of one's behaviors, as the following comment from a nineteenth-century California preacher conveys: "Although I weigh a hundred and twenty pounds, when I'm mad I weigh a ton!" (cf. Stratton, 1923). Anger, like the other emotions, is also a form of social communication; the facial expressions, sounds, and postures displayed by an angry organism tell another animal or individual to stay away or desist from whatever it is doing. This threat property, noted by Charles Darwin (1872), has probably evolved to ensure adequate territorial spacing of the species, with distributed access to food, and, in primates, to foster the maintenance of a socially stable group with an effective dominance hierarchy (Bernstein and Gordon, 1974).

Darwin, in his above-cited book on emotions, also commented on the possible functions of emotional expression as a means of discharging excess tension. When an emotion is very strong or blocked, the organism is motivated to express that feeling. In the case of rage, the motivation to discharge angry feelings would seem to be related to the notion of aggressive drive. However, it is not aggressive drive in the sense that Freud and others use this concept; namely, as a drive to inflict injury. Rather, the drive is to discharge the feeling through expressing it or getting rid of the tension in some other way. It is the angry, aggressive movements—the snarling, the shouting, the clawing, and the biting—that are critical, rather than seriously hurting the rival. These expressions of anger can lead to serious injury and sometimes killing, but that is the *consequence,* not the purpose, of the action. However, the idea that anger expression *discharges* anger has been questioned (see the section on catharsis later in this chapter).

Intrinsic Aggression.   There is evidence that some animals will seek opportunities for aggression. We will call this motivation toward aggressive response *intrinsic aggression* (Reykowski, 1979) to distinguish it from aggressive *drive,* which traditionally implies the motive to inflict injury. Intrinsic aggression refers to the motivation to perform an aggressive act: to fight, rather than to hurt or inflict damage. When intrinsic aggression is observed, it is usually the result of blocking an aggressive response after exposure to an aggression-releasing stimulus or after interruption of a fight sequence. It is as if the organism has to complete the aggressive sequence (Berkowitz, 1965a), just as there appears to be a need to express emotions once they are aroused.

Although the great majority of aggressive behaviors observed in nonhumans are instrumental in character, it also appears that some animals, under some circumstances, seek aggression for its own sake. Mice have been observed to cross an electric grid to resume fighting that had been interrupted (Lagerspetz, 1979). For the male fighting cock, the simple lapse of time without an opportunity for fighting increases the likelihood of aggressive acts (Kruijt, 1964). Fighting cocks raised in complete isolation display periods of agitated aggressive-like behaviors in which they attempt to attack their own tails and even their own shadows with their spurs and beaks.

A word of caution is necessary at this point. In reviewing the animal literature, the focus has been on innate mechanisms that influence the occurrence and inhibition of aggression. However, it must be emphasized that these patterns of aggressive behavior are strongly affected by learning and social experience. The role of learning becomes more powerful as one ascends the evolutionary ladder. While it can be shown that genetic, physiological, and other biological factors influence aggression in mammals, even within nonhumans patterns of aggression are sharply affected by learning experiences. For example, victory and defeat are naturally occurring experiences that have a major effect on aggressive response tendencies. In rodents or in primates, these outcomes determine dominance hierarchies and patterns of aggression in social groups. An experimental mouse, rewarded by his apparent success, substantially increases the frequency of attack on other mice, including mice with which he would not ordinarily fight (Scott, 1958). On the other hand, punishment decreases the frequency of attack. If learning experiences are important in influencing the aggressive behavior of mice, how much more significant their influence is likely to be on human aggression!

Physiological Influences

Alcohol, Drugs, and Aggression. In a famous novel by Robert Louis Stevenson, the hero, a friendly, gracious, civil English doctor, becomes transformed into a hostile, cruel, sadistic monster by simply swallowing a potion. We are all familiar with the Jekyll-and-Hyde story. While there are no chemicals that have this dramatic an effect, a number of chemicals have been identified that significantly influence aggressive behavior. The relationship between alcohol and aggression is one obvious example. Drinking is a major contributor to violent incidents.

The mechanism by which alcohol influences aggression is complex and involves more than internal physiological effects. Although the occurrence of aggression is related to the amount of alcohol that is consumed (Taylor and Gammon, 1975), it is also strongly influenced by features of the social context in which the drinking takes place. Intoxicated individuals are not automatically aggressive. It depends upon whether there are frustrating events or other aggression-instigating cues in the situation. In addition, because alcohol appears to affect judgment and attention (Hull and VanTreuren, 1986; Steele and Josephs, 1988), alcoholics may be quite responsive to clear "messages" but miss less obvious but no less important cues.

The process of alcohol facilitating aggression through disruption of attention to less obvious or more complex cues is nicely demonstrated in an experiment in which male undergraduates were randomly assigned to an alcohol condition or to a control condition with no alcohol (Leonard, 1989). Each subject was placed in a competitive situation with an opponent where electric shocks of varying degrees of intensity could be received and administered. Half the subjects in each group heard the opponent express an intention to set the shock at the highest possible level (aggressive cue), with the other half hearing the opponent's intention to set the lowest shock. After the subjects were given an opportunity to shock their opponent (Trial 1), they were able to see that their alleged opponent had actually set the shock at the lowest level. And for all subsequent trials, the opponent continued to set shocks at the lowest level. It can be seen from Figure 18.4 that while the no-alcohol group, which had been exposed to the explicit aggressive intention cue, sharply reduced the level of shock on Trial 2 after the non-aggressive behavior of their opponent, the alcohol-intoxicated subjects, who had been exposed to aggressive intent of the opponent, did not modify their aggressive reaction. They maintained their high shock levels over the remaining five trials of the experiment. Note that there were no significant differences in level of aggression between the alcohol and no-alcohol groups under non-aggressive cue conditions and in the initial explicit aggressive cue trial. In addition, this theoretical model of the effects of alcohol suggests that if the opponent had set high shock levels after the explicit non-aggressive statement of intent, the alcohol group should display *less* aggression on Trial 2 and subsequent trials than the no-alcohol group. That is an important and non-intuitive prediction that should be tested.

There are a number of drugs that appear to decrease rather than enhance aggression. Violent, assaultive behaviors in mental patients have been shown to be markedly reduced by the use of phenylthiazines, a group of powerful tranquilizing drugs that have made the once-familiar straitjacket obsolete. A novel index

Figure 18.4   Mean shock setting as a function of alcohol condition, cue condition, and trial. (From K. E. Leonard, *Personality and Social Psychology Bulletin*, 1989, *15*, p. 396. Copyright © 1989, reprinted by permission of Sage Publications, Inc.)

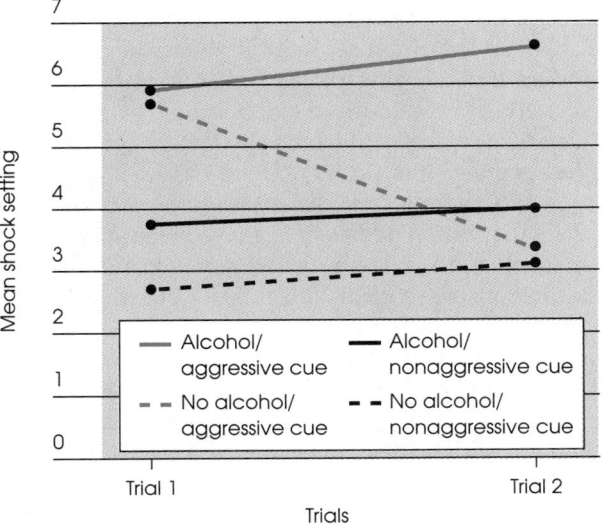

of tranquilizers' reduction of aggression is provided by the following statistical comparison. In 1955, before the staff of New York's Rockland State Hospital began to use tranquilizers for their seriously emotionally disturbed patients, 8,000 windowpanes were broken in that one year. Three full-time glaziers were kept busy keeping the windows in repair. By 1960, when phenylthiazines were in widespread use, the level of breakage was down to 1,900 windowpanes (Kline, 1962)! Although the impact of these drugs is quite dramatic, it must be emphasized that their effects are also quite complex. They influence other behaviors and processes besides aggression; for example, they reduce response to pain (Valzelli, 1976). Some tranquilizers affect the motor system and act as muscle relaxants. And, as one might expect, situational factors and individual differences among patients influence the response to tranquilizers.

Sex Hormones and Aggression. Still other well-known chemical influences on aggression, familiar even in ancient times, are the male sex hormones, the androgens. The symbol of violence, the bull, is rendered a docile ox through castration. In general, removal of androgens tends to lower aggression, whereas the administration of androgens tends to increase it. Also female hormones, the estrogens, tend to reduce aggressivity (Moyer, 1971). However, the relationships among hormones, sexuality, and aggression are quite complex for both lower animals and humans (Herbert, 1970).

The species and the age at which administration or removal of the hormone takes place are particularly critical variables. Hormonal manipulation during the very early stages of development is believed to have a critical influence upon the organization of the brain and is generally more effective than at later periods. Nevertheless, the relationship between sex hormones and level of aggression in humans has not been well established and remains a matter of debate. In a recent study, Dabbs and Morris (1990) studied testosterone levels in 4,462 men and found that high levels tended to correlate with a variety of antisocial behaviors such as adult delinquency and substance abuse. This relationship, however, was moderated by socioeconomic status — the relationship was weaker among men higher in socioeconomic status. Another study of young male prisoners indicated higher levels of testosterone in prisoners who had engaged in more aggressive crimes such as armed robbery, assault, and murder during adolescence. The testosterone levels in prisoners whose offenses had been restricted to more routine offenses of burglary and larceny were, on the other hand, relatively low (Kreuz and Rose, 1972). However, the meaning of this finding is unclear since there was no relationship between testosterone levels and the amount of fighting and other aggressive behaviors displayed in prison. A study of male adolescents, carried out in Sweden, indicated a significant positive relationship between the boys' aggressive responses to frustration or threat and their testosterone levels. But, complicating the interpretation of this finding, testosterone level was not associated with unprovoked aggressive behavior (Olweus, 1986).

Although the connection, if any, between the sexual biological system and the aggressive biological system has not yet been resolved in humans, there has been some medical interest in hormonal treatment of male sex offenders who commit aggressive acts. In most modern societies, castration of sex offenders is not permissible either as a punishment or as a treatment. However, voluntary castration of prisoners convicted of certain violent crimes and who wish to have their sentences reduced has been permissible in some European countries. Follow-up studies of these individuals do not provide clear support for a direct relationship between testosterone level and aggressive behavior. Similarly, the effects of a form of "chemical castration" through administering a female sex hormone to the offender are unclear (Rubin, 1987). Also, the mechanisms by which a female sex hormone such as estrogen affect the aggressive behavior of sexual offenders are not understood. Estrogen has been shown to reduce the sexual drive and virility of the young males in these studies. Consequently, when estrogen was administered, child molestation by these males was reduced since their aggressive behavior was in service of a sexual goal that was no longer desired. Whether such hormonal treatment would affect the behaviors of rapists whose primary goal is the humiliation and injury of their victim is, at best, uncertain. Quite apart from our ignorance of how these hormones work and their possible side effects, these treatments raise serious ethical issues. Questions of irreversibility of the effects and of the informed and free consent of the prisoner are involved. These same ethical questions arise when other biological treatments for aggression are considered.

When Should Drugs Be Used?.   Should tranquilizers or other drugs affecting aggression be used in prisons as they are in mental hospitals? Should they be used for all difficult prisoners? Only for prisoners with a diagnosed psychiatric problem? Who is to determine when the aggressive behavior in a prison is the prisoner's problem and when the behavior is a legitimate response to an abusive prison regimen? As the following extract from an investigator (Moyer, 1976, p. 263) working with one of the mild tranquilizers indicates, the ethical issues extend beyond prisons and mental hospitals.

> In my laboratory at Carnegie-Mellon we have squirrel monkeys which are vicious
> and untameable. A hand put in the cage to touch or pet them will be savagely and
> repeatedly bitten. . . . it is possible to put a few thousandths of a gram of
> diazepam in the milk that we give them; they evidently cannot taste it, nor could
> I. When the drug begins to take effect, they lose their hostility and can be handled
> with bare hands. As others have reported, the drug does not sedate them, it
> simply makes them more friendly. Most of the milk available today is pasteurized
> and homogenized and has vitamin D added. Will the milk available tomorrow
> have an anti-hostility drug added, or will such a drug be added to the water
> supply? Will this make for a peaceful population, and if so, will it be worth it?

Genetics and Aggression

Infants display striking differences in temperament (see Chapter 1). Longitudinal studies suggest that these temperamental differences interact in time with environmental experiences to form the child's personality (Thomas and Chess, 1976). Some of these temperamental traits appear closely related to aggression. For example, the pattern of unpleasant moods, unfriendly social responses, and intense motor reactions may be a precursor to aggressiveness. There are a number of possible prenatal factors that may be the principal causes of these aggression-related temperamental differences: mother's diet, activity level, smoking, and ingestion of alcohol or other drugs. But perhaps the most likely places to look for the cause of temperamental differences are genetic disparities.

At the nonhuman level, the genetic influence on aggression is evident to any dog breeder. To demonstrate the aggressivity of terriers, litters of fox terriers and beagles were raised together. The terriers, although smaller, dominated access to food and male terriers had primary access to females (James, 1951). In addition to studying aggressive differences between existent breeds, it is also possible to create strains of aggressive and nonaggressive animals through selective breeding for aggression (see Chapter 1). Again, it must be emphasized that genetically-based temperamental differences in aggression can be strongly influenced by environmental factors. For example, when mice are reared together, genetic influences on aggression are less evident than when they are reared in isolation. Victory and defeat also affect aggressivity (Lagerspetz, 1969).

It has been more difficult to conclusively demonstrate genetic influences on aggression at the human level. In the late 1960s, there was a flurry of excitement over a presumed connection between male criminality and a certain genetic abnormality: an extra Y chromosome added to the normal male XY sex chromosome. Since the X chromosome comes from the female and the Y chromosome from the male, the added Y factor suggested to some scientists the notion of more maleness and therefore more aggressiveness. But systematic studies failed to substantiate earlier claims concerning the XYY connection to aggression. A large-scale survey carried out in Denmark did reveal a marginal tendency for XYY males to be overrepresented in the criminal population as compared to XY males. However, there was no evidence of any tendency on the part of XYY males to commit aggressive, violent offenses (Witkin et al., 1976).

There have been many efforts to determine whether there is a genetic basis for criminality. The most systematic and extensive of these have been a series of studies carried out in Denmark, where the excellence of national records of social deviance, psychopathology, identical and fraternal twins, adoption, and divorce permit systematic, detailed analyses of the role of genetics and environment in various behavioral disorders and social problems (Mednick and Christiansen, 1977). These data provide us with some evidence for a genetic factor in criminality: the concordance rate for identical twins is about twice that for dyzygotic or fraternal twins (cf. Chapter 1). In addition, a study of adoptees indicated that sons whose biological fathers were criminals were twice as likely to have criminal records as sons whose biological fathers were not criminals (see Table 18.3).

Although not as strong in this instance as the biological factor, environmental factors also exert an influence; the adopted son is more likely to have a criminal record when both the adopted father and the biological father are criminals known to the police (Hutchings and Mednick, 1977). However, using a larger

Table 18.3   "Cross-fostering" analysis: Percentage of adoptive sons who are registered criminals

		Is biological father criminal?	
		Yes	**No**
Is adoptive father criminal?	Yes	36.2 (of 58)	11.5 (of 52)
	No	22.0 (of 219)	10.5 (of 333)

Source: Hutchings and Mednick, 1977, p. 137. Reprinted by permission.

sample of adoptees, it was possible to separate property offenders from violent offenders (Mednick, Brennan and Kandel, 1988). As Figure 18.5 indicates, a strong relationship held between biological parent criminality and property offenses, while that between biological parent criminality and violent offenses was small and statistically nonsignificant.

In view of the animal literature demonstrating the genetic contribution to aggression, it seems plausible that genetic factors also influence aggression in humans. The differences in aggression manifested by males and females, which appear to be related to genetically-linked differences between the sexes in such factors as physique and hormones, also support the genetic position concerning the innate determinants of aggression. But, given the evidence and given the fact that this genetic influence may reflect factors other than aggression, such as low IQ and various mental disorders, the literature on criminality fails to provide definitive support for the proposition that aggressive tendencies are genetically

Figure 18.5   Percent male adoptee property offenders and violent offenders by biological parent convictions. (From S. A. Mednick, P. Brennan, and E. Kandel. *Aggressive Behavior,* 1988, *14*, p. 29.)

transmitted. Greater support for the role of genetic factors in aggression is provided by studies comparing identical twins with fraternal twins and employing self-report questionnaire measures of aggression (Rushton et al., 1986; Tellegen et al., 1988). Given the questionable contribution of genetic factors to aggressive criminal offenses and given the possibility that the genetic influence revealed by twin studies may reflect factors other than aggression (such as variations in intelligence, emotionality, fearfulness, to cite but a few possibilities), the specific role of genetic factors in aggressive behavior remains to be established.

CULTURAL INFLUENCES

Many critics now argue that the United States is a violent culture. For instance, they can point to the fact that 73 percent of Chicago's eighth graders have seen someone shot, stabbed, robbed, or killed, and that violent injuries seen at Children's National Medical Center in Washington, D.C. have gone up 1,740 percent since 1986 (DeAngelis, 1993). But is the United States unique in this, or are all cultures violent? In fact, it appears that some cultural groups are peaceful; others are warlike. In some cultures, violent solutions to conflict are common; in others, they are rare. For some groups, killing is a sin; for others, it is a virtue. The enormous variations in the level of violence between societies underline the importance of social influences on human aggression. Biological factors, as we have seen, exert a significant influence on aggressive behavior. But the influence of biological factors is very much dependent on the social context and the organism's past experiences.

The importance of cultural influences on aggressive behavior is readily illustrated by a simple inspection of national differences in homicide rates. In Table 18.4, homicide rates for selected countries are presented for 1974 to 1976 and 1990. Suicide rates are also included for comparison purposes. It is noteworthy that the United States was consistently among those countries with the highest homicide rates. When the United States is compared with other English-speaking nations, it can be seen to have had about ten times the homicide rate of Ireland or England, and four to six times that of Australia, Canada, or Scotland. Very little change has occurred in this pattern since that time. Of this English-language group, only Northern Ireland, beset by civil war, has a higher rate of killings than the United States. It has been argued by some theorists that the amount of violence in any culture is a constant, so that if violence is not expressed outwardly, as in homicides, then it will be expressed inwardly in the form of suicides. From this perspective, the amount of violence is largely biologically determined, while the role of culture is to shape the form or direction in which the violence is expressed. However, homicide and suicide are not inversely related; in Table 18.4 one can find every combination of high, middle, and low homicide and suicide rates among these nations. The amount as well as the form of violence varies with the culture.

Since homicide and suicide are but two of the many ways in which aggression can be expressed, it is possible that if other manifestations of aggression were

Table 18.4

Homicide and suicide rates, selected countries: 1974 to 1976 and 1990 (homicide rates per 100,000 people of all ages, suicide rates per 100,000 people 15 years and older)

Country	Homicides			Suicides			
	1974	1975	1976	1974	1975	1976	1990
United States	10.2	10.0	9.1	12.1	16.9	16.4	12.2
Australia	1.8	1.6	1.3	11.7	15.2	14.8	13.3
Austria	1.5	1.6	1.3	23.7	31.3	29.2	21.7
Belgium	1.0	.9	.9	15.6	20.8	21.2	21.0
Canada	2.5	2.7	(NA)	12.9	16.8	(NA)	13.1
Denmark	.7	.6	.7	26.0	31.1	30.7	22.4
Finland	2.6	3.6	(NA)	25.1	31.9	(NA)	27.5
France	.9	1.0	.9	15.6	20.5	20.4	19.6
Germany, Fed. Rep.	1.2	1.2	1.3	21.0	26.4	27.2	14.5
Greece	.6	.8	.7	3.4	3.6	3.6	(NA)
Ireland	.7	1.0	(NA)	3.8	6.9	(NA)	(NA)
Israel[1]	1.0	1.3	1.4	5.5	11.9	11.8	(NA)
Japan	1.3	1.3	1.3	17.5	23.6	23.1	15.4
Netherlands	.8	.7	.8	9.2	11.9	12.5	10.0
Norway	.6	.7	.7	10.4	12.8	14.1	15.3
Philippines	1.3	1.4	(NA)	1.2	1.5	(NA)	(NA)
Poland	.9	1.0	1.2	11.3	14.7	15.7	13.8
Portugal	1.3	1.9	(NA)	8.5	11.6	(NA)	8.5
Puerto Rico	17.7	16.1	(NA)	7.7	11.8	(NA)	(NA)
Spain	.4	.6	(NA)	4.0	5.3	(NA)	7.1
Sweden	1.2	1.1	1.3	20.1	24.4	23.8	17.8
Switzerland	1.0	.9	.9	20.6	28.8	28.1	20.1
United Kingdom:							
England[2]	1.0	1.0	1.1	7.9	9.7	10.0	7.5
Northern Ireland	13.6	11.4	13.7	4.0	5.1	6.2	(NA)
Scotland	1.2	1.5	1.9	8.4	10.8	10.8	10.1

Sources: U.S. Bureau of the Census, *Statistical Abstract of the United States* (Washington, D.C.: U.S. Government Printing Office, 1979), p. 182; U.S. Bureau of the Census, *Statistical Abstract of the United States* (Washington, D.C.: U.S. Government Printing Office, 1993, p. 848).

NA = not available.
[1] Jewish population.
[2] Includes Wales.

taken into account, much smaller cultural differences in total aggression would be observed. But the fact remains that there is little evidence for such a position. Studies of preliterate cultures reflect similar variations in aggression; some seem to be permeated with violence and aggressive ideation; some have mixed patterns; and there are a few where very little aggression is evident. An example of the latter are the Senoi, an isolated tribe found on the Malay Peninsula. Because neighboring tribes fear the presumed magical powers of the Senoi, they never attack them. At the same time, the Senoi have no interest in initiating attacks on others. This pattern of peace has apparently endured for over a century. More significant is the absence of violence between members of the Senoi tribe. They are described as psychologically integrated, emotionally mature, and socially constructive. "In the realms of family, economics, and politics, their society operates smoothly on the principle of contract, agreement and democratic consensus, with no need of police force [or] jail . . . to reinforce the agreements or to confine those who are not willing or able to reach consensus" (Stewart, 1969, p. 160).

While this image of the Senoi may be idealized (and some writers have criticized Stewart's conclusions), profound differences appear to remain between this peaceful and relatively conflict-free society and the violence and social conflict that characterize so many other cultures. The challenge for the psychologist is to determine those features of the culture that are primarily responsible for the observed cultural differences in aggression. Is it the child-rearing practices? the type of social organization? economic resources? the type of living arrangements? In the ensuing sections, we will examine various factors contributing to aggression that could account for cultural and individual differences in aggressive behavior.

THE PHYSICAL ENVIRONMENT

As we saw in Chapter 2, the physical environment in which people live may exert a significant impact on their personality and social behavior. Aggressiveness is commonly cited as an example of a significant personality component that is strongly affected by features of the physical environment — for example, by heat, crowded living conditions, urban noise, and so on. However, research indicates that many factors influence the effects of these environmental stimuli. For example, in one study of crowding, males in a crowded room displayed more aggression than males in a room less densely populated, whereas an opposite effect was observed for females (Freedman, Levy, Buchanan, and Price, 1972). Males do not consistently show a crowding effect; for example, four- to five-year-olds were found to display significantly *less* aggression when they played in a small area than when they played in a much larger one (Loo, 1972). A theoretical interpretation accounting for these discrepant findings proposes that crowding serves to intensify whatever behavior is prepotent at the time (Freedman, 1975). If a nonaggressive response is stronger, as appears to be most often the case for females and possibly for the preschool boys who knew each other quite well, then crowding will enhance nonaggressive responding. On the other hand, when aggressive responses are stronger, crowding should then increase the level of aggression.

The intensification interpretation just suggested has its roots in Hullian, Dollard-Miller learning theory (cf. Chapter 5), which asserts that generalized tension or arousal has an enhancing effect on whatever responses are prepotent at the time. One advantage of the arousal interpretation is that it helps predict when noise and other arousers will facilitate aggression. Consider the following experiment by Donnerstein and Wilson (1976). Male college students were either angered or treated positively by an experimental confederate. They were subsequently given the opportunity to administer electric shocks of varying intensities to the confederate while wearing earphones through which low-intensity or high-intensity noise was transmitted. From Fig. 18.6, it can be seen that noise enhanced aggression only for the subjects who had been angered, that is, for whom aggressive responses were more dominant. The same effect occurs when physical exercise rather than noise is the source of physiological arousal. Two and one-half minutes of strenuous physical exercise significantly heightened the level of aggression toward a confederate among those subjects who had previously been angered by the confederate, while having no effect on the nonangered subjects (Zillman, Katcher, and Milarsky, 1972).

Of course, the experimental effects of noise manipulation may differ from those of real noise. Real-life noises can be either more or less grating, annoying, louder, and painful than those used in experimental investigations. In addition, the effects of persistent, long-lasting noise may be different from those of the sporadic, short-duration noise used in most research. All of these effects must be

Figure 18.6   Effects of low-intensity (65 db) and high-intensity (95 db) noise on aggression. (Based on data from Donnerstein and Wilson, 1976.)

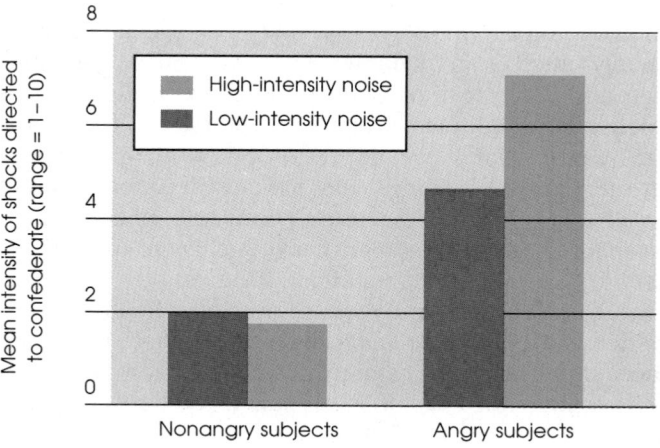

evaluated in order to determine whether noise pollution in our urban environments is a significant contributor to urban violence.

PERSONALITY THEORIES AND THE ANTECEDENTS OF AGGRESSION

We have seen that human aggression is influenced by biological and social variables, neurological mechanisms, cultural differences, individual learning experiences, and the physical and social environment. How do the facts on aggression relate to theories of personality? We will find that the personality theories that have given special attention to the problem of aggression differ in the relative emphasis placed on biological versus social variables, and in the particular social influences believed to be of primary importance. A discussion of theoretical views and research on the principal mechanisms causing aggression provides a basis for integrating the diverse data on aggression with other personality issues and for understanding the controversies concerning the development of aggression and its control.

Psychoanalytic Theory

Freud's views on aggression, like his views on other issues, underwent substantial modification during the course of his long career. In his early writings, Freud believed aggression to be primarily an innate reaction to frustration and pain: "the ego hates, abhors and pursues with intent to destroy all objects which are for it a source of painful feelings" (Freud, 1925, p. 81). This view persisted but was made subordinate to a subsequent formulation of aggression as arising from a biological drive. He proposed a new dichotomy in which the libidinal instinct, Eros, was enlarged to embrace all of the positive, constructive, life-enhancing tendencies and was contrasted with the death instinct, Thanatos, which encompassed the organism's tendencies toward aggression, self-destruction, and ultimately death (Freud, 1920). By the late 1920s, partly in response to the destruction of World War I, Freud had elevated aggression urges to a status equivalent to that of libidinal urges.

The death instinct is one of Freud's more speculative concepts and is not an integral part of psychoanalytic theory (see Chapter 3). However, while the concept of a death instinct has gained little acceptance, many psychologists support the assumption of an innate, biologically-rooted aggressive drive. This view of aggression has important social consequences. It leads one to emphasize social controls and power as a means of checking human aggression rather than to modify social conditions and relationships that might foster aggression. Concerning the necessity of strong social controls, Freud stated: "Civilized society is perpetually mirrored with disintegration through this primary hostility of men toward one another. . . . Culture has to call up every possible reinforcement in order to erect barriers against the aggressive instincts of men" (Freud, 1930, p. 86).

Broad assumptions about human behavior, such as the view that humans have innate aggressive urges, are difficult to test or disprove. The work of ethologists like Lorenz and Tinbergen is sometimes cited as support for the innate aggressive drive hypothesis. However, as has been noted earlier, there are fundamental differences between the observations of ethologists and the psychoanalysts' conception of innate aggression. These differences may be summarized as follows:

1. Nonhuman aggression is primarily reactive rather than internally generated. Aggression is elicited by specific stimuli, referred to as *releasers*.

2. Innate aggressive responses by animals are primarily instrumental. If the object of aggression ceases the aggression-eliciting behaviors (e.g., intruding on territory, competing for food), then the aggressive attack usually ceases.

3. Withdrawal by or a submissive signal (an inhibitor) from the opponent is usually sufficient to terminate a conflict. Injury to a same-species opponent is not required for an animal to terminate aggression.

4. Consistent with the psychoanalytic hypothesis, aggressive displacement has been observed in some animals. There is also evidence that some animals are motivated to continue or initiate a fight and will cross an electrified grid to do so. However, an animal's drive to complete an aggressive response, to express anger, or even to initiate a fight must be distinguished from the psychoanalytic conception of an innate drive to inflict injury.

5. The desire to hurt, to inflict injury, and to seek revenge is observed primarily in humans, not in animals. It seems quite likely that an aggressive drive in this sense is an acquired or learned motivation (Feshbach, 1974).

We have noted that, in psychoanalytic theory, the theme of reactive aggression coexists but is theoretically subordinate to the theme of innate aggressive drive. Nevertheless, in their writings, and especially in their practice, psychoanalysts also make extensive use of the idea that aggression is a reaction to particular experiences. Thus, in exploring the basis for a particular patient's anger and hostility, the analyst will look for situations in early childhood that might be responsible for the patient's aggression; for example, rivalry with a sibling may be exacerbated by parental favoritism toward that sibling. Psychoanalysts have also believed that frustration of biologically based oral or anal impulses (cf. Chapter 3) is a significant cause of aggression. However, studies investigating the relationship of aggression to the severity of weaning or toilet training have yielded negative or inconsistent findings (Feshbach, 1970). Modern psychoanalytic theory, with its emphasis on object relations and ego development, is more likely to look for the causes of aggression in the child's relationship with its parents and in the factors that promote the ineffective development of self-control, rather than to focus on the biology of the organism.

Learning Theory Models of Aggression

Learning theory models of aggression have in common the effort to establish systematic relationships between antecedent events and aggressive behavior. They differ in the particular antecedents or mechanisms thought to be most important. Adherents of Hullian and the Dollard-Miller theory have focused on frustration as an antecedent to aggressive drive. The elaboration of the relationship between frustration and aggression eventually led to a reformulation of the frustration-aggression hypothesis through the incorporation of significant elements from cognitive theory. In contrast, adherents of Bandura's learning theory have addressed their attention to the acquisition of instrumental aggressive responses and to the role of imitation in the development of aggression. Investigators favoring a Skinnerian model of learning have stressed the role of direct and subtle reinforcements in the acquisition of instrumental aggressive behaviors. In addition, several other theoretical positions will be considered that have incorporated aspects of learning theories but also have some unique features and emphases (Berkowitz, 1989, Feshbach, 1974).

The Frustration-Aggression Hypothesis. The formulation of the frustration-aggression hypothesis and the publication in 1939 of the Dollard et al. volume *Frustration and Aggression* marked the first systematic treatment by psychologists of aggressive behaviors. In addition, it provided a significant link between psychoanalytic theory and experimental psychology. And finally, the frustration-aggression hypothesis helped integrate a very diverse set of observations, ranging from violent dreams reported during psychotherapy to the frequency of lynchings, by linking these events to frustrations experienced by the individual and by members of a group. Although psychologists have significantly revised the hypothesis, it is still extensively used by social scientists and considered to be a landmark theoretical proposition.

The frustration-aggression hypothesis asserts very simply that the frustration (interference, blocking) of an ongoing activity produces an instigation (drive, motivation) whose goal response is injury to some person or object. No assumption is made regarding how the connection between frustration and aggression comes about, whether it is innate or learned, although it is acknowledged that reactions to frustration can be altered through learning. The initial statement of the hypothesis, namely that "aggression is *always* a consequence of frustration" has two implications: (1) aggression is always due to frustration and (2) frustration always leads to aggression. These statements are not equivalent; one can be false and the other true. For example, it might be that frustration always produces an impetus to aggression but that there are other factors besides frustration that also instigate aggression. It was immediately recognized by critics and also by the authors that, in using such exclusive terms as *always,* these propositions were too strongly phrased. The authors then acknowledged that there are other causes of aggression besides frustration and maintained that frustration produces a tendency to aggress as well as other response tendencies (Miller 1941). Consequently, overt aggression, while likely, is not an inevitable response to frustration, and the relationship between frustration and aggression can be modified through learning. But the hypothesis, even if less strongly stated, still had a number of important properties. The amount of aggression was hypothesized to be quantitatively related to the amount of frustration experienced by the organism. In addition, the authors also proposed that when the instigation to aggression was blocked through, for example, fear of punishment, there would still remain an instigation to aggress toward available targets. Thus, the formulation provided a model for the analysis of the displacement of aggression.

The frustration-aggression hypothesis has stimulated a good deal of research. A very early study, which reflects its potential utility as an explanatory tool, used as the measure of aggression the number of lynchings that took place yearly in the United States, largely in fourteen southern states, during the period from 1882 to 1930. Since cotton was the basic commodity in these states, the value of the cotton yield each year during this period was also determined. It was hypothesized that the lower the cotton yield, the greater the economic frustration experienced by the community, and the greater the likelihood of displaced aggression toward an available target (in this case, primarily blacks). An analysis of the data revealed a sizable and significant negative correlation consistent with the hypothesis: the lower the yearly cotton yield, the higher the frequency of lynchings that year. Recent reanalyses of these data, using more sophisticated statistical procedures, have confirmed the original results, although the negative correlation is not as high as initially reported (Hepworth and West, 1988).

A more direct test of the effects of the magnitude of frustration employed a simple but clever experimental procedure in a natural setting (Harris, 1974). The experimenter had a confederate cut into a line of individuals who were waiting their turn at places like ticket windows, restaurants, and grocery stores. The critical dependent variable was the amount of aggression displayed by the individual whose place in line the confederate had displaced. Hypothesizing that the amount of frustration would be greater the closer that individual was to the beginning of the line, the confederate cut in front of either the second or the twelfth person in line. The person who had been closer indeed displayed much more aggression (fortunately, mostly verbal) toward the confederate than the person who had been farther along in line.

While these findings point to the usefulness of the frustration-aggression hypothesis, it is also the case that many investigators have failed to find an increase in aggression following frustration (Feshbach, 1970). The difficulty in evaluating these negative findings is that the level of frustration experimentally induced in the laboratory may often be too weak to evoke aggression. However, apart from the question of the adequacy of experimental tests, it is clear that the frustration-aggression hypothesis has serious limitations. First, the concept of frustration is vague. Insults and physical pain have been shown to be powerful elicitors of aggression. But are they frustrations? Failure would seem to be an obvious frustration, yet the frustrating effects of failure are dependent on expectancy. Your reaction to failing an examination would greatly depend on whether you had expected to pass. Second, in addition to the need to establish explicit criteria for what constitutes a frustration, the particular motivations that are frustrated must also be taken into account. Experiences that threaten an individual's self-esteem and sense of security appear to be much more likely to elicit hostility than experiences that interfere with satisfactions of a physiological drive like hunger (Maslow, 1941). It is not surprising, then, that parental rejection of a child or separation of the child from the parents results in more aggressive children than a severe weaning experience (Feshbach, 1970).

Although the frustration-aggression hypothesis has some validity, then, it is too broadly stated. What is required is a determination of the particular properties of interfering events that tend to foster aggressive reactions. Cognitive theories have proved to be very helpful in this regard. Cognitive attributes both determine the meaning of the frustration and strongly influence the likelihood of an aggressive response to the frustration. At least four cognitive attributes of frustration can be specified. While these are related to one another, it is helpful to separate them.

1. *Expectancy.* As has been noted, the degree to which a negative experience is frustrating depends on the degree of expectation of that experience. We expect some amount of discomfort in a crowded subway car and consequently react with less anger to jostling than if the car were half-empty. Expectancy also has significant implications for predicting the response to economic deprivation. Individuals from middle-class backgrounds who are unable to attain the standard of living they experienced when living in their parents' home are likely to feel more frustrated than individuals at the same income level but from poorer backgrounds. The aggression that sometimes accompanies small improvements in economic level in economically disadvantaged groups is also understandable in terms of expectancy, in that the small economic advance may have led to increased expectancies for substantial economic improvement that are subsequently frustrated.

2. *Arbitrariness or inequity.* A frustration is more likely to evoke aggression if it is perceived as arbitrary rather than justified. You are much more likely to get angry at a poor grade if you feel the instructor assigned the grade at random or was otherwise unfair than if you feel the grade was deserved. The roles of both arbitrariness and expectancy are nicely illustrated in an experiment in which subjects were promised a prize and given their first, second, or third choice under one of three anticipatory conditions: (a) they might or might not receive their first choice (no-expectancy); (b) they would receive their first choice (expectancy); or (c) they would be able to select any prize they wished (choice). The subjects were not given a reason when they did not receive their expected choice. This lack of explanation increased the likelihood that they would perceive the frustration as arbitrary. It is evident from Fig. 18.7 that not receiving a desired prize is not, in itself, sufficiently frustrating to provoke verbal aggression (no-expectancy group). It is only when expectancies are violated and the frustration is arbitrary that aggression is evoked.

Figure 18.7   Reactions to expected and unexpected frustration. (Adapted from "The Effect of Three Types of Arbitrary Thwarting on Instigation to Aggression," by Stephen Worchel. *Journal of Personality* 1974, 42, 300–331. Copyright 1974, Duke University Press, Durham, N. C.)

3. *Intentionality.*   We are much less likely to be angered by the same frustrating or painful event (e.g., being tripped while walking down an aisle) if we perceive it as accidental rather than intentional. This effect is clearly demonstrated in an experiment in which subjects received either strong or weak electric shocks administered at the presumed option of a confederate (Nickel, 1974). Half the subjects in each of these two groups were then informed that a switch had been placed in the wrong position and that the shock level actually intended was directly opposite to the one received. The amount of aggression subsequently expressed by the subjects toward the confederate was much more closely linked to the confederate's intended shock than to the actual level of shock inflicted. Intentionality also has been shown to contribute to individual differences in aggressive tendencies: Aggressive boys display a consistent tendency to overattribute hostile intentions to their peers as compared to nonaggressive boys (Dodge, 1980; Dodge and Frame, 1982).

4. *Responsibility.*   Related to intentionality is the attribution of responsibility. The greater the perceived responsibility of the frustrating agent, the greater the likelihood of an aggressive response. Given the same frustration, one does

not react with equal aggression or punishment when the agent is a two-year-old as when the agent is a twelve-year-old. The role of responsibility is explicitly recognized in our legal code. If a person is forced to commit a criminal aggressive act, then he or she is not held "responsible" and the penalty is much less severe (see Chapter 17).

A full understanding of the relationship between frustration and aggression must consider the cognitive attributes or meaning of the frustration. There is naturalistic and experimental evidence that sometimes people become angry and aggressive even when a frustration is perceived as accidental or justified (Averill, 1982; Berkowitz, 1989). However, cognitive attributes are important determinants of the amount of aggression that is elicited by frustration (Averill, 1982; Ferguson and Rule, 1983; Weiner, 1985). Learning also influences the response to frustration. Children can, for instance, be trained to respond less aggressively to frustrating events (Davitz, 1952). As we will see, learning is a powerful determinant of aggressive behavior.

A further change has been introduced in the frustration-aggression hypothesis by Berkowitz (1989) who proposes that frustrations elicit aggression only to the extent that they produce negative affect. The hypothesis would then be broadened to read "negative affect–frustration." This formulation integrates findings demonstrating that physical pain (Monteith, Berkowitz, Kruglanski, and Blair, 1989), disgust (Zillmann, Bryant, Comiskey, and Medoff, 1981), unpleasantly high room temperatures (Rule, Taylor and Dobbs, 1987), and depressed affect (Berkowitz, 1983) as well as frustrating, goal-interfering events can evoke angry feelings and aggression.

The Influence of Modeling on Aggression. Several of the basic experiments by Bandura and his coworkers, which provided the foundation for his theory of observational learning, involved the modeling of aggression (Bandura, 1962; Bandura, Ross, and Ross, 1963a; cf. Chapter 5). Preschool children who had observed an adult model carry out a series of discrete aggressive responses toward a Bobo doll (an inflated plastic clown) subsequently displayed a striking degree of imitation of the adult aggressive behavior in interacting with the Bobo doll. As Fig. 18.8 indicates, the children imitated the adult whether the model was live, on film, or dressed as a cartoon cat. The finding that children imitated filmed adult aggression and cartoon aggression suggested that similar effects might occur as a result of children observing televised aggression and has stimulated research and theorizing on the possible modeling influence of television on the aggressive behavior of child and adult viewers.

Although imitation is undoubtedly one process by which children acquire aggressive and other social behaviors, children obviously do not imitate every aggressive act they observe. We need to know the conditions under which they are likely to imitate an aggressive model. There have been a number of studies addressed to this issue. For example, verbalization of aggressive actions increases the amount and persistence of imitation (Bandura, Grusec, and Menlove, 1966). In addition, children are more likely to imitate an aggressive model if they have

Figure 18.8   Mean imitative aggressive responses performed by children. (Plotted from data by Bandura, Ross, and Ross, 1963a, pp. 3–11.)

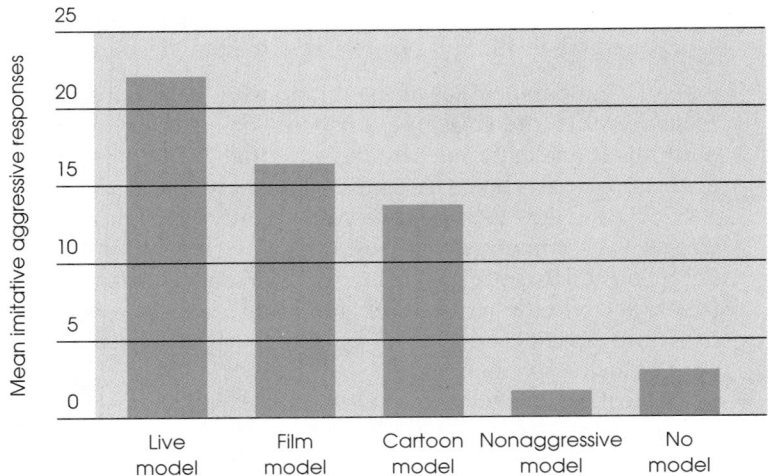

had a prior frustrating experience as, for example, when losing in competitive play (Nelson, Gelfand, and Hartmann, 1969). And witnessing a model being rewarded for aggression tends to increase imitation, while punishment of the model's behavior tends to reduce imitation. However, there is some evidence that children learn the punished response and will perform it when inhibitory factors in the situation are lessened (Hicks, 1968).

The concept of modeling has been applied to the spread of violent actions. An event can be modeled through verbal description, without visual representation, as in a newspaper report. It has been argued that media publicity given to airline hijackings, random shootings on highways, suicide, and other violent acts has increased the frequency of such acts through the process of modeling. However, in view of the enormous variability in imitation of observed behaviors, we need to know much more about the situational and individual factors that determine when a model is imitated.

Reinforcement. Why have some people learned to be aggressive? One reason may be that they have been exposed to models of aggressive parents, peers, and perhaps favorite television characters. Another, probably more potent, reason is that they have found that aggression "pays off," that it gets them the rewards of money, sex, status, and power over others that they seek. There is a good deal of evidence that aggressive behavior is governed by the same principles that govern other instrumental responses. Aggression increases when reinforced and declines when not rewarded or when punished (Brown and Elliot, 1965; Walters and Brown, 1963). We have seen, in our discussion of nonhuman aggression, that victory and defeat play a powerful role in determining the level of aggressive behavior. A naturalistic study in which preschool children were observed over a nine-month period indicated that similar effects are at work at the human level (Patterson, Littman, and Bricker, 1967). The effects of reinforcement and punishment were especially noticeable in passive children who entered nursery school with weak aggressive tendencies. The passive children who were attacked by other children and whose counterattacks were unsuccessful remained submissive in their behaviors. However, the initially passive children whose counterattacks were successful showed a significant increase in aggressive tendencies.

There has been a great deal of interest in the use of reinforcement procedures for the modification of aggression in highly aggressive youngsters. These reinforcement programs have been carried out in institutional settings, in classrooms, and in the home. The programs are characterized by the careful monitoring of the child's behavior, the administration of positive rewards (e.g., prizes and privileges) for prosocial behaviors, and either ignoring of or mild punishment (e.g., brief isolation periods, loss of privileges) for aggression and related negative behaviors. Patterson and his colleagues have pioneered in the development of methods for training parents to cope more effectively with aggressive problem children through the appropriate utilization of reinforcement procedures (Patterson, 1979, Patterson and Bank, 1989). Their findings indicate that after twenty-five to thirty treatment hours with parents and children, over a period of several months, significant reductions occur in the level of the children's aggression and other aversive behaviors (e.g., whining). In addition, positive and negative changes in parental behaviors, such as monitoring of the child, are significantly related to decreases and increases in antisocial behaviors.

One of the contributions of the behavioral method developed by Patterson and others on the basis of Skinnerian principles is that it requires close attention to the behavior that is to be discouraged or rewarded. The parent, teacher, and other authority figures thus become more conscious of the subtle ways in which they may be reinforcing an undesired behavior: for example, they may reinforce aggression by paying attention to a child whenever he is difficult or by finally yielding to demands after an escalating sequence of aggression and punishment. In addition, aggression may be rewarded quite directly. Bandura and Walters (1959) found that fathers of aggressive adolescent boys tended to urge their sons to fight their peers even though they discouraged aggression in the home; the attitude of these fathers is not very far from the ambivalent attitude toward male aggression that prevails in American culture. Aggression is, to be sure, discouraged, but it is also admired. The "he-man," virile cowboy image remains a significant component of the American conception of what it is to be a man (*New York Times*, 1980).

Aggressive Cues. When individuals are frustrated, have strong aggressive tendencies due to reinforcement, or are otherwise aggressively disposed, they are not aggressive all the time. An *aggressive cue* is usually required in order for the aggressive tendency to be expressed in behavior. Leonard Berkowitz (1978)

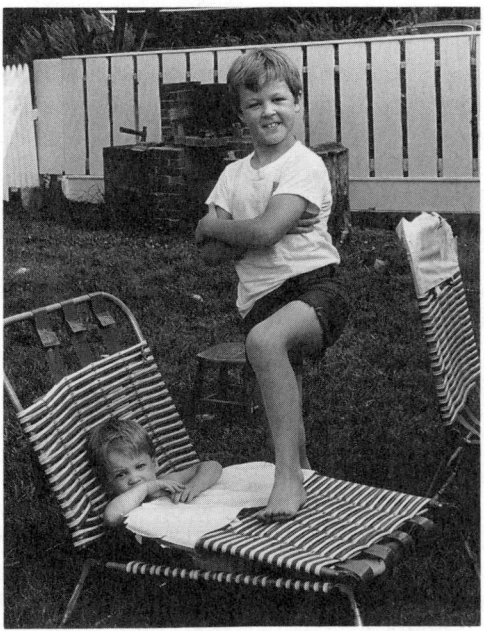

Aggression can be reinforcing! (Joseph Szabo/Photo Researchers, Inc.)

proposed that these aggressive cues have acquired the property of eliciting aggression through the learning mechanism of classical conditioning. It is assumed that aggressive words and aggressive instruments have accompanied frustration and other stimulus events that evoke aggressive responses and, through this pairing, become conditioned stimuli or cues for aggression. Berkowitz and his students have carried out an extensive series of ingenious experiments demonstrating the importance of such cues in the regulation of aggressive behavior (Berkowitz, 1965b; Berkowitz and Geen, 1966). For example, subjects who had seen a film depicting a brutal prize fight and who had previously been angered by a confederate administered a greater number of shocks to the confederate when he was described as a college boxer than when he was described as a speech major. Several control conditions that were included indicated that this difference in cue labeling was not effective unless the subject had seen the fight film and was also angry. A similar effect was obtained when the confederate was introduced to the subject merely with the same first name as the major character in the boxing film (Berkowitz and Geen, 1966).

In another provocative demonstration of the role of aggressive cues, angered or nonangered subjects were given the opportunity to shock a confederate either while observing a .38-caliber revolver and a 12-gauge shotgun placed in the vicinity of the shock button or with these objects absent (Berkowitz and LePage,

1967). The amount of shock delivered by the subjects who had been angered was significantly greater when the weapon cues were present than with the weapons absent. These findings, if confirmed, would suggest another reason why the reduction of available firearms in the community should result in a reduction in the amount of violence, particularly on the part of angry individuals. But subsequent efforts to repeat these findings have yielded mixed results. Some investigators have obtained the "weapons effect," while others have not. Nevertheless, there is little doubt concerning the role of aggressive cues in the facilitation of aggressive behavior.

Social Influence.   Social norms and social influences can be considered aggressive cues that may directly encourage aggressive behavior. Even non-aggressive individuals may participate in aggressive actions because of conformity to social expectations and social pressure. A dramatic demonstration of the power of an authority figure to elicit conformity and obedience to rather extreme demands and expectations is provided in a famous experiment by Stanley Milgram (1963). Adult volunteers were requested and then commanded to use increasing levels of shock whenever a confederate made an error on a learning task. The switches controlling shock levels were clearly labeled, with the indicator ranging from 15 to 450 volts. Protesting subjects augmented the shock levels under pressure from the experimenter, even when the presumed "victim" pounded on the wall that separated himself from the subject, as if in great pain. Whenever the subject wanted to stop the proceedings, the experimenter would exert additional pressure. Under these circumstances, 65 percent of the subjects proceeded to the final 450-volt shock. Perhaps because of the experimental situation and the belief that a university professor would not encourage a violent act that was truly painful or destructive, the 65 percent compliance figure is inflated. Nevertheless, the Milgram study suggests that conformity pressures can induce individuals to carry out extreme aggressive acts. Many individuals who participated in implementing the atrocities ordered by the Nazis were probably doing so out of such obedience and fear.

It is evident from this review of the diverse explanations that have been offered for human aggression that there are many different processes mediating aggressive behavior. There is no single mechanism that one can point to as *the* cause of aggression. The various personality theories have tended to focus on different processes rather than offering rival interpretations of aggression. Thus, frustration, particularly when perceived as intentional or arbitrary; rewards and punishments; modeling; the presence of aggressive cues; and conformity to social norms are all determinants of aggression. The least satisfactory hypothesis is the psychoanalytic assumption of an instinctive aggressive drive, or innate hostility. However, there are undoubtedly biological factors involved in some forms of aggression. In other respects, as in its focus on the family's role in the development of aggression, the psychoanalytic contribution to our understanding of aggression has been substantial.

DEVELOPMENTAL INFLUENCES

Child-Rearing Practices

On the basis of the antecedents of aggression that have been discussed, we might expect that a history of frustration and parental rejection, or of parental permissiveness and reinforcement of aggression, would be associated with the development of aggression in offspring. This is indeed the case (Feshbach, 1970; Parke and Slaby, 1983). Parents who are permissive about aggression or, like the fathers cited earlier, encourage some forms of aggression; parents who make few demands of their children with regard to positive social behaviors and who are lax in their supervision; and parents who essentially reject the child through their coldness or actual hostility are likely to have highly aggressive children. What about the effects of parental punitiveness, particularly the use of physical punishment? There is some disagreement among investigators on this issue. From a theoretical standpoint, physical punishment can affect aggression in several different ways. First, because of its aversive features, it has an inhibitory function for the disapproved behavior. However, physical punishment is painful, frustrating, and frequently humiliating—all of which are likely to stimulate aggression. In addition, the parent, while physically punishing the child, is serving as a model to the child. Imitation of the parent's behavior would enhance aggression. And, in this connection, the parent may be teaching the child a social norm that essentially states that if you are injured or frustrated by someone, you respond by physically punishing them.

With few exceptions, studies of child-rearing practices have indicated that the frequency of parental use of physical punishment is one of the best predictors of aggression in children (Feshbach, 1970; Olweus, 1980). Differences arise in the interpretation of this relationship since these studies as a rule do not clearly distinguish between physical punishment that is limited and restrained and punishment that is brutal. In addition, it may be that more aggressive children elicit more severe and more frequent punishment from their parents. The previously cited studies by Patterson and his colleagues indicate that there is an interaction between problems posed by the child and limitations in parental child-rearing skills.

The report of a major ten-year longitudinal study of the development of aggression (Eron, Walder, and Lefkowitz, 1971; Lefkowitz, Eron, Walder, and Huesmann, 1977), indicated that "moderate punishment by parents in the long run produced less aggressive children than either no punishment or harsh punishment" (p. 192). Thus, permissiveness of aggression and severe punishment had the same consequence: highly aggressive children. There are also cross-cultural data supporting this relationship between physical punishment and aggression, including a substantial correlation that was obtained in a study carried out in several Japanese and Indonesian communities between parental use of physical punishment and a projective TAT-type measure of aggression (Kornadt, 1983).

Child Abuse

Other evidence of the relationship between physical punishment and aggression pertains to the commonly cited observation that parents who physically abuse their children have often been themselves physically abused as children (cf. Gerbner, Ross, and Zigler, 1980). Child abuse is a form of aggression that is particularly distressing in that young children are the objects of physical abuse and adults, most often parents, are the abusers. It is a problem that unfortunately is not rare; estimates of the number of children in the United States who are physically abused each year range in the hundreds of thousands (Kempe and Kempe, 1978). Moreover, the parents cannot be considered psychotic or suffering from serious psychopathology. Personality studies of child abusers have reported some differences between this group and nonabusing parents, but the differences are not great and are outnumbered by the similarities (Parke and Collmer, 1975).

There is some evidence that the same factors associated with aggression in general also are involved in child abuse. Observations of child-abusing parents reveal that they are more irritable and engage more frequently in other negative interactions with their children than nonabusing parents (Reid, 1986). Frustrations, such as job dissatisfaction, are also more common among abusive parents (McKinley, 1964). In addition, abusive parents tend to expect more of their children than is age appropriate. They are more likely to see the child as a fully responsible agent and perceive the child's failure to conform to parental requests as intentionally motivated. In addition, one of the personality characteristics of abusive parents that does distinguish them from other parents is low self-esteem; threats to self-esteem are generally considered to be among the most powerful instigators of anger and hostility.

However, it should be pointed out that those who have been abused as children are not doomed to become abusers. While being abused increases the likelihood of becoming an abuser, only about 30 percent of those who were abused go on to become abusers (Widom, 1989). Also it is interesting to note that the majority of adults who abuse children were *not* abused as children (Widom, 1989). Therefore, while child abuse certainly contributes to an increased likelihood of being aggressive, many other factors are involved in whether an adult, abused as a child or not, will be an abuser.

AGGRESSION AS A PERSONALITY TRAIT

The literature that has been reviewed provides substantial evidence of situational factors influencing aggression. But data have also been cited reflecting individual differences in aggressivity. For instance, some recent research has shown that children who exhibit antisocial aggressive behavior exhibit some characteristic differences in how they process information compared to children who are not aggressive (Dodge and Crick, 1990). First, they interpret the behavior of others in ways that make them feel more hostile towards those others. For instance, they are more likely to attribute hostile intentions to others when others act in ways that provoke them. Second, they seem to have access to fewer alternative strategies when they are provoked; they tend to think only of aggressive options. Third, they evaluate the usefulness and effectiveness of aggressive behavior differently than do nonaggressive children. For instance, they are more likely to believe that aggressive behavior will lead to more favorable interpersonal outcomes (e.g., peer approval).

Other evidence for the stability of aggressive behavior over long periods of time provides strong support for viewing aggression as a personality dimension in which individuals differ. In a detailed review of sixteen studies on the stability of aggressive behavior patterns, an impressive degree of consistency in aggressive characteristics was observed over periods ranging from six months to as much as twenty-one years (Olweus, 1979). In a very ambitious longitudinal study, aggression at age eight proved to be predictive of antisocial behavior at age thirty, including criminal behavior and spouse abuse (Huesmann, et al., 1984).

Data from these and other studies indicate that aggression is not only relatively stable over time but that there are also consistencies among different indicators of aggression. Self-report questionnaires have been shown to be related to peer ratings of aggression, while these measures in turn are related to aggressive choices and to aggressive behaviors (Carlson, Marcus-Newhall, and Miller, 1989; Lefkowitz, et al., 1977; Olweus, 1978). Although there is evidence for the consistency of aggressive behavior, the role of situational factors should not be minimized. A very aggressive person at home and among peers may be unaggressive in a work situation because the job is particularly satisfying or because of fear of losing the job.

Fear of punishment and guilt or anxiety over aggression complicate the findings on the consistency of aggressive behavior. Aggression-anxious persons would appear, at a superficial level, to be inconsistent in their aggressive behavior, displaying very little aggression in some situations and exaggerated aggression in other contexts (Eron, et al., 1971; Feshbach, Stiles, and Bitter, 1967). But by taking into account both their conflict over aggressive impulses and the presence of situational cues that elicit anxiety, one can find order and consistency in their behavior (cf. Miller's conflict model, Chapter 14). Thus, a more indirect, subtle indicator of aggression — withholding rewards — was shown in one study to be more discriminating of aggressive attitudes than the administration of electric shock (Caprara, et al., 1986).

Other data bearing on the question of aggression as a trait address the question of the personality of aggressive individuals. Are they fearful? bored? suspicious? impulsive? With regard to the personality correlates of aggression, conflicting findings are reported by different investigators and it is likely that there is more than one "aggressive personality."

Studies of criminally assaultive individuals provide additional examples of personality varying with type of aggression. Megargee (1966) found that the moderately aggressive criminal has weak inhibitions against aggression, a low threshold for aggression, and a history of aggressive behavior: an *undercontrolled aggressive* type. In contrast, an extremely assaultive person whose criminal aggressive act was of homicidal intensity is more likely to fall into the *chronically overcontrolled* category (Megargee and Mendelsohn, 1962).

> The extremely assaultive person is often a fairly mild-mannered long-suffering individual who buries his resentment under rigid but brittle controls. Under certain circumstances he may lash out and release all his aggression in one, often disastrous, act. Afterwards he reverts to his usual overcontrolled defenses. Thus he may be more of a menace than the verbally aggressive "chip-on-the-shoulder" type who releases his aggression in small doses.

The Megargee findings and those reported by other investigators provide a picture of extreme violence that is in greater accord with a psychodynamic model and with concepts of frustration-produced aggressive drive and repression than with the learning models of Bandura and Skinner which focus on the imitation or reinforcement of instrumental aggression.

Megargee's image of the overcontrolled assaultive type also is an interesting contrast to Toch's (1969) personality description of prisoners and parolees with a history of violent encounters. Toch arranged for other prisoners and parolees to conduct extensive interviews with this sample of undercontrolled aggressive persons. A large subgroup consisted of individuals whose violence stemmed from basic insecurity and low self-esteem. Some expressed this insecurity in their excessive sensitivity to any sign of a slight, while others tried to convey an exaggerated image of fearlessness. Other subgroups were characterized by infantile expectations of indulgence, by a sense of being in danger and becoming a victim, and by a need to defend their status as tough and powerful. Still another subgroup fell into the category of bullies or sadists who seemed to enjoy inflicting pain on helpless victims.

In summary, the response to the question of the personality characteristics of aggressive individuals depends on the degree and type of aggression. Instrumental aggression, reactive aggression, aggressive drive, and repressed hostility are interwoven in various combinations and shades; each pattern of aggression seems to have a different constellation of personality factors.

THE INFLUENCE OF THE MASS MEDIA

Up to this point, in examining the role of social factors in the development of aggression, we have considered such child-rearing factors as the reinforcement of aggressive behaviors, the use of extreme punishment, lax demands, hostility, and rejection. However, the family is only one of the many socializing influences on a child's development. Another socialization influence that has received a great deal of attention as a potential antecedent of aggression and crime is the mass media, particularly the depiction of violence on television.

Television Violence

Observation of television violence can foster aggression in the viewer through a number of possible mechanisms including:

1. Imitation of aggressive television character models.
2. Disinhibition of aggression; sending a "message" that violence is "okay."
3. Providing aggressive cues.
4. Adaptation to and acceptance of violence after constant exposure.

There is experimental evidence, some of which has been cited earlier, for each of these potential aggression-facilitating mechanisms.

On the other hand, exposure to violence in the mass media could conceivably have the opposite effect of reducing aggression through:

1. Serving as a substitute for direct aggression by providing an opportunity for the vicarious expression of angry feelings, or *catharsis.*
2. Reinforcing fantasy behavior by providing entertainment and associating pleasurable feelings with television viewing.
3. Providing recognition of and insights into aggressive feelings.
4. Associating punishment with antisocial aggressive behaviors.

There is some experimental evidence consistent with the first and second of these potential aggression-reducing influences. But if one compares the amount of empirical support for mechanisms that result in the augmentation of aggression with those that might reduce aggressive behavior, there is clearly much more support for aggression-enhancing effects of television viewing. Bandura's findings on the imitation of an aggressive film model and Berkowitz's investigations of exposure to the fight film in conjunction with aggressive cues are examples of studies indicating that violence on television and in films can facilitate and augment aggressive behavior. However, one must still distinguish between these potential effects of television violence as determined in the laboratory and the actual effects of observing television violence in the complex natural context in which most viewing takes place.

Although many, if not most, behavioral scientists believe that the depiction of violence on television is a significant contributor to violence in the society, the evidence from more naturalistic field studies is quite mixed and not nearly as persuasive as the data based on laboratory experiments (Freedman, 1984). The primary field method used has been correlational. These studies have found that the frequency with which aggressive television programs are viewed is positively correlated with the degree of aggressive behavior. One of the limitations of these studies is the difficulty of determining the direction of cause and effect. Do aggressive children prefer and select aggressive programs to view or does the observation of aggressive programs cause the viewer to be aggressive? Some investigations have made use of longitudinal methods that permitted the analysis

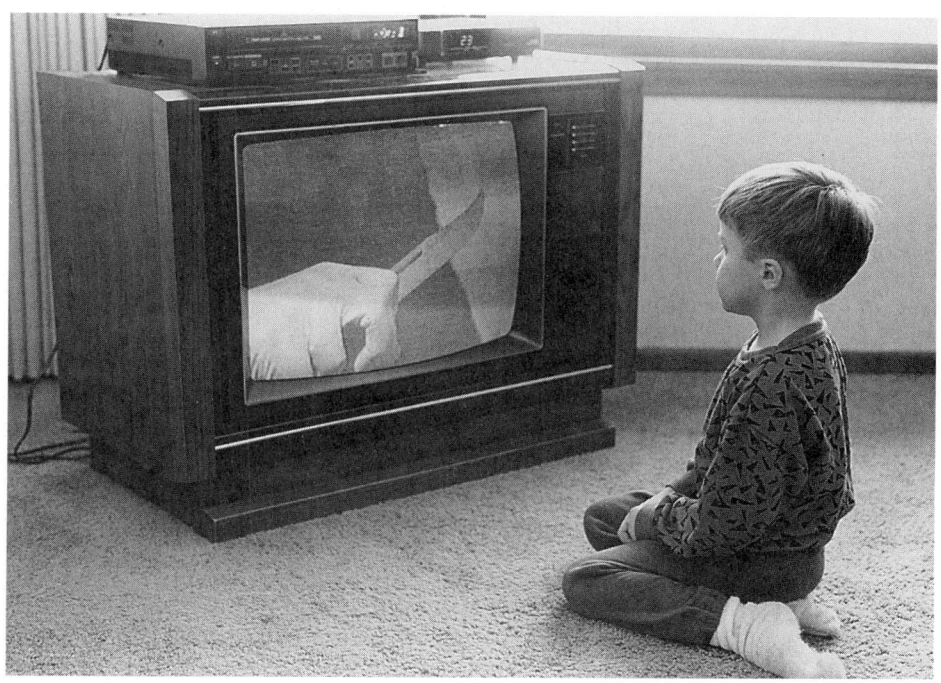

A child watching violence depicted on television. This could increase violence if it leads to modeling and imitation. But the effects of watching television violence on actual behavior are complex and uncertain. (© Michael Siluk/The Image Works)

of changes in behavior over time and concluded that viewing violence on television was a significant cause of aggressive behavior (Huesmann and Eron, 1986; Singer and Singer, 1986). However, other correlational studies, equally well controlled, have found a negligible relationship between television viewing and aggression or find that the relationship disappears when relevant variables are controlled (Hartnagel, Teevan, and McIntyre, 1975; Jessor and Jessor, 1977). Data from a longitudinal study carried out in several European countries and in the United States suggest that the relationship between aggressive behavior and television violence is bidirectional, in that aggressive children tend to view television violence, and television violence, in turn, engenders aggression (Huesmann, Lagerspetz, and Eron, 1986).

In an experimental effort to control television viewing in a natural setting, Feshbach and Singer (1971) arranged for preadolescents and adolescents living in private schools or boys' homes to be exposed to a predominantly aggressive or nonaggressive television diet for a six-week period. The private school students were unaffected by the television manipulation but the boys' home sample actually displayed a significant decline in aggression relative to controls. Still another well-known and ambitious series of field experiments by Milgram and Shotland

(1973) failed to provide any evidence for modeling a television theft of money from a charity box or the use of obscene language in a telephone call. Each of these field experiments has methodological limitations, as do the few field studies that report an increase in aggression following television viewing (Leyens, Camino, Parke, and Berkowitz, 1975; Stein and Friedrich, 1971).

Rather than trying to decide whether television violence causes aggression, we might address the more properly phrased question of the conditions under which television violence facilitates aggression, decreases aggression, or is likely to have no effect on aggressive behavior. The experiment described earlier, contrasting the effects of a reality set versus a fantasy set in responding to an aggressive television sequence (cf., Chapter 16), suggests that a reality orientation enhances the aggression-stimulating effect while a fantasy orientation is more conducive to a reduction in aggression, or catharsis. Sometimes it is difficult to establish the reality-fantasy status of television programming, as in the case of sports events, which are "games" that may involve real aggression. These events typically are publicized through several media, including television, radio, and newspapers. One ingenious study compared the frequency of homicides in the United States for 1973 to 1979 during the week before and after a heavyweight championship prizefight (Phillips, 1983; Phillips and Hensley, 1984); the study found a 12 percent increase in the frequency of homicides following heavyweight championship fights! While methodological criticisms have been raised regarding these findings (Barm and Reiss, 1985), this approach to the naturalistic analysis of the effects of different kinds of TV violence remains a promising one.

Another problem for those who argue that media violence is a major cause of violence in the United States is that Japan, where violent movies, books, and television shows are more common than they are in the United States, is one of the least violent societies in terms of behavior. It is unclear why this is so, but possible reasons include the homogeneous nature of Japanese society and the country's gun control laws. Nevertheless, we can see that violence in the media does not inevitably cause violent behavior. Like most other influences on human behavior, media violence is probably only one factor that interacts with a variety of others to influence violent behavior. A related question that has barely been addressed but which has at last begun to be examined is why children and adults are attracted at all to violence in the mass media. The response to this question will undoubtedly be related to the deeper issue of why people watch drama at all.

Erotica

Violence in the mass media is not the only type of content that may influence the viewer's level of aggression. There has also been some interest in the effects of erotic themes on viewers' aggressive behavior. This interest stems in part from the social relevance of determining the effects of erotic stimuli and in part from its relevance to the broader personality question of the relationship between the sexual and the aggressive behavior systems. There are a number of experiments indicating that watching an erotic film or reading a highly erotic story, in comparison to exposure to neutral stimuli, results in elevated levels of aggression (Jaffe, et al., 1974; Zillman, 1971). However, other studies have also reported a decrement in aggression following exposure to sexual materials (Baron, 1974; Frodi, 1977; Malamuth, Haber, and Feshbach, 1980). Erotic stimuli that are intertwined with aggressive components, such as sado-masochism and rape, are especially likely to stimulate aggression, and have been shown to result in more accepting attitudes of social violence directed toward females (Donnerstein, 1980; Malamuth, 1983). In one experiment (cited in Linz, et al., 1986) male college students who had watched five feature-length films depicting sexual violence, one every other day, became less sympathetic to rape victims and seemed to have been desensitized to the negative aspects of the film content.

Several mechanisms have been proposed to account for these relationships. Some studies have obtained evidence consistent with the hypothesis that when sexual arousal is accompanies by anxiety, aggression is inhibited; without anxiety, aggression is facilitated (Jaffe, 1975; Malamuth, Feshbach, and Jaffe, 1977). Furthermore, it is proposed that this interaction between sex and aggression occurs principally in cultures and individuals whose training and experience have linked these two systems of behavior. Other investigators have emphasized the role of physiological arousal, whether produced by erotic or other stimuli, in augmenting aggressive responses (Donnerstein, 1980; Zillman, 1984). These processes are not mutually exclusive and are further moderated by cognitive mechanisms, such as the cues in a situation that influence how an individual labels his or her aroused feelings. Violent erotica may also modify interpretation of situational cues; for example, the depiction of a woman suffering pain, which would ordinarily function as an inhibitor of sexual feelings, may be reinterpreted as a result of exposure to violent erotica as an indicator of female sexual arousal.

CATHARSIS AND THE REGULATION OF AGGRESSION

At various points in this chapter reference has been made to factors relevant to the control and reduction of aggression. There are a number of methods for modifying anger and the response to aggressive provocation. It would be misleading if the presentation of these alternatives suggested that it is a relatively simple matter to modify aggression. The methods are intended only as guides. They offer a basis for designing procedures to cope with and hopefully mitigate destructive social behaviors.

Catharsis

Originally, the term *catharsis* referred to the discharge of feelings resulting from witnessing a dramatic play. Currently, it is used to refer to the reduction of aggression through any aggressive activity, whether shouting epithets, witnessing the depiction of violence on the stage or in film, inflicting injury on an innocent target, or directly aggressing against the instigating source. There are a number of studies indicating that, in order for a reduction in aggression to occur, the individual must be angry at the time of the aggressive act (Doob and Wood, 1972; Feshbach, 1964; Konecni, 1975). Hitting a punching bag will not reduce aggression toward an irritating supervisor unless one is angry at the supervisor while punching the bag. The evidence for catharsis is also stronger when fantasy aggression is expressed directly toward the instigating target rather than toward a displaced target. While there are several studies indicating that the expression of aggression in fantasy or imagination can be cathartic (Feshbach, 1956; Manning and Taylor, 1975), there are others that question this effect and suggest that only direct, overt expressions of aggression are cathartic (Hokanson and Burgess, 1962).

It is significant that an aggressive act in which too much or too little pain is inflicted will not provide drive reduction (Fromkin, Goldstein, and Brock, 1977). This finding is in keeping with the proposition that aggressive drive is based on social norms or rules that regulate retaliation; these rules state essentially that if you have been injured by someone, you are supposed to reciprocate by inflicting an equivalent injury on that person (Feshbach, 1974).

Finally, it is widely believed that expressing anger will reduce the anger, that feelings are discharged through expression. However, a good deal of research has suggested that while expressing anger can be beneficial and can lead to anger reduction, it does not always do so (Bohart, 1980). Furthermore, the idea that anger — or any emotion, for that matter — can be discharged simply through expression appears to be at least partially wrong because emotional discharge alone is not always helpful (Bohart, 1980; Nichols and Efran, 1985). Other factors that appear to be important in determining whether expression relieves one's feelings include gaining new understanding through the expression (Bohart, 1980), sharing one's feelings with an empathic other (Bohart, 1980), gaining a sense of acceptance of the emotion (Greenberg and Safran, 1987), restructuring one's dysfunctional cognitions as a result of emotional expression (Greenberg, Rice, and Elliott, 1993), or dealing with the frustrating events that instigated the feeling (Lewis and Bucher, 1992).

Incompatible Responses

The second mode of reducing aggression is through training a response that is incompatible with anger; for example, "turning the other cheek" or walking away when provoked. A very promising program for the training of mediating cognitive responses that are incompatible with anger has been developed by Novaco (1985). An essential feature of that program is the training of angry individuals to relax when provoked and to rehearse nonaggressive statements.

Cognitive Control Mediators and Prosocial Expression of Anger

Experienced anger can be controlled through the subject's empathy with the frustrating agent and through the capacity to delay expression of anger and contemplate alternatives. If one can take the perspective of those with whom one is in conflict and understand their feelings, their behavior is less likely to seem frustrating and arbitrary and therefore is less likely to evoke aggression. The ability to think before acting, to consider a range of possible responses to a provocative situation, is also likely to increase the probability of nonaggressive, prosocial alternatives. Several promising programs designed to enhance prosocial behavior and reduce aggression through empathy training (N. Feshbach, 1979), social understanding (Pitkänen-Pulkkinen, 1979), and problem-solving skills (Goldstein, 1981; Spivack and Shure, 1974) have been developed.

Altering Stimulus Meaning

Aggression and anger can also be modified by changing the meaning of a stimulus. For example, an individual may be perceived as not being responsible for or not having intended some injurious act. An example of this procedure is provided by a study in which an experimenter acted in a rude and obnoxious manner. The subjects were informed that the experimenter was very "uptight" about a forthcoming midterm examination. This information resulted in a sharp reduction in subjects' verbal aggression and blood pressure. The latter finding suggests that the subjects were not simply inhibiting their anger (Zillman and Cantor, 1976).

Punishment

The last of the methods for modifying aggression is punishment, which may inhibit the aggressive response but leave the underlying anger unaffected. Mild punishment or punishment that is meaningfully related to the aggressive infraction, such as having someone do something positive for the injured person, coupled with one of the other procedures, could prove to be a very effective method for reducing aggression.

Summary

1. The concept of love has many different connotations. Two connotations that have been distinguished and measured are romantic love and liking.

2. There are data indicating that caring is a more critical component of love than need. This is especially likely to be the case for companionate love, as compared to passionate love.

3. The triangular model of love asserts that there are different types of love in accordance with different combinations of Passion, Intimacy, and Decision/Commitment.

4. It has been proposed that passionate love is a function of cultural beliefs, the presence of an appropriate love object, and the labeling of aroused emotion.

5. There are striking similarities between patterns of adult love and patterns of early attachment, suggesting that the attachment process may be basic to love.

6. Studies indicate that the degree of sexual intimacy prior to marriage is unrelated to the development of a lasting commitment.

7. Love is linked to hate and anger through the generalization of arousal, the pain of rejection, and the overidealization of the loved object.

8. The term *aggression* includes a great many behaviors that may have different functions and causes. Distinctions should be made between the emotion of anger and the motivation to inflict injury, or *aggressive drive,* and the *instrumental* use of aggression to obtain nonaggressive goals.

9. For many nonhuman species, intraspecies aggression is regulated by stimuli called releasers that elicit innate aggressive responses and inhibitory stimuli that serve to terminate an aggressive interaction.

10. Although there is evidence that male sex hormones will, under certain conditions, increase aggressive behavior for several nonhuman species, no clear relationship between male sex hormones and aggression has been established for humans.

11. There is some evidence that genetic factors influence criminality and aggressive behavior. However, in either case environmental factors have been shown to exert powerful effects.

12. Crowding and noise have been shown to both increase and decrease aggressive behavior. These factors apparently intensify whatever behavior, aggressive or nonaggressive, is prepotent at the time.

13. The extent to which frustration elicits aggression depends on the nature of the motivation that is frustrated and on such cognitive factors as expectancy of frustration and whether the frustration is perceived as arbitrary, intentional, and caused by a responsible agent.

14. Violent, extremely assaultive behaviors are associated with a history of strong punishment for and extreme inhibition of aggression.

15. The majority of laboratory studies indicate that observation of aggression in films and on television tends to stimulate and facilitate aggressive behavior. The results of field studies reflect a more complex relationship between aggression and exposure to violence in the mass media.

16. Exposure to erotic stimuli has been shown to both enhance and decrease aggressive behavior. A critical variable appears to be the degree of anxiety and related inhibitory reactions elicited by the erotic situation.

Thought Questions

1. Why should marriages be based on romantic love rather than on friendship?

2. Is love an innate biological motive, need, or emotion? What influence, if any, does learning have on love?

3. To what extent is modern warfare a result of biologically based aggressive tendencies?

4. If a drug were discovered that practically eliminated violent behavior through chemical action on brain sites, would you favor its administration to violent criminals?

5. Some people maintain that rock music, especially when played to large audiences, is a significant source of violence in adolescents and young adults. What studies bear on this contention? What is your own opinion on this issue?

19 | Summing Up

As we noted in our introduction, we have adopted an integrative philosophy in writing this text. For instance, rather than favoring any one of the major theoretical perspectives (see Chapters 3 through 6), we have attempted to show the contribution that each makes to the understanding of various topics such as personality continuity or change, aggression, or consciousness. In this chapter we consider some broadly integrative themes in the current study of human personality that have recurred throughout the text. Four major themes recur: interactionism, the multidimensionality of the person, the self, and personality as a science. After identifying these recurrent themes and reaching some general conclusions about them, we look to the future. Using a combination of a crystal ball and our own sense of current trends, we will suggest the directions in which the field of personality is moving and which problems we think should be addressed in the years to come.

INTERACTIONISM

Human behavior and personality are a function of the interaction between the person and the environment. The important theme of interaction is present throughout this text. It appears in the early chapters on the biological versus the physical, social, and cultural determinants of personality. These chapters make it evident that both nature and nurture exert significant influences on personality. For example, how can one possibly argue that all the determinants of behavior reside in the environment, given the similarities between the traits of monozygotic twins, or given the differential concordance rates for schizophrenia among monozygotic versus dizygotic twins? On the other hand, how can one logically believe that genetic determinants of behavior account for cultural and social class differences? Individuals strictly committed to either an environmental or a genetic approach cannot give satisfactory answers to these questions.

But the concept of interaction implies even more; it indicates that the influences of nature and nurture do not work in isolation, but rather are interdependent. For example, both nonhuman and human data indicate that a predisposition to alcoholism can be inherited. But the genetic predisposition alone cannot produce alcoholism. An environment in which alcohol is available is also necessary. In certain cultures, such as Moslem communities where alcohol consumption is forbidden, an inherited vulnerability to alcoholism is not likely to emerge.

Aside from the availability of alcohol, the development of alcoholism may also depend on the interaction of a genetic predisposition with other environmental factors such as repeated situational stress.

Another example of the interaction between biological and environmental factors is the relationship between physique and personality. A child's physique is influenced by environmental as well as genetic factors. He or she must have the appropriate diet and exercise if a genetic predisposition toward athletic (mesomorphic) body build is to be manifested. Because of muscularity, there may in turn be increased likelihood of the child's experiencing success in aggressive encounters or sports. The culture may also share certain stereotypes about mesomorphic individuals, like the belief that they are dominant, courageous, and aggressive. The child may then acquire these behaviors in the process of living up to stereotyped expectations. Thus, it would be just as wrong to say that a child's assertiveness is due to his or her inherited physique as to view the attribute as solely determined by environmental experiences. Both biological and environmental factors contribute to personality traits. In this example, the interaction between the child's body structure and subsequent experiences is critical.

The theme of interaction extends beyond the nature-nurture controversy. It is also intrinsic to the dynamics of behavior. For example, different periods of life pose special problems for adaptation and development. By knowing that someone is an adolescent or in midlife, we glean some information about the kinds of problem situations that person will confront. Clearly, the situations encountered by a teenager are very different from those of an adult in midlife crisis. But there are also significant individual differences between and among adolescents and adults in approaching problem situations, in the intensity of developmental crises, and in how the situations are resolved.

Numerous other instances of the person-situation interaction can be found in the text. Many reactions to frustration have been identified. For example, frustration may increase the probability of aggression. But this effect is more marked in children who are "undercontrolled" than in children who are labeled as "overcontrolled" (Block and Martin, 1955). In addition, while some individuals react to frustration with hostility, childishness, and disruptiveness, others may withdraw and become apathetic, while still others respond with increased problem-solving activity that can lead to new, creative solutions for overcoming the source of frustration. You are encouraged to look for other experimental examples of person-situation interactions that are cited or implicit in the text.

At one level, it may appear that the interaction notion is so obvious that it hardly requires special emphasis. However, it is all too easy to view behavior as determined by either situational or person factors. Indeed, the procedures used in investigating personality frequently lend themselves to a one-sided perspective. To simplify their studies, researchers may concentrate on the effects of the situation and ignore differences in personal attributes or, conversely, they may focus on individual differences while ignoring the properties of the situation that are relevant to those individual differences. For example, consider the following experiments which have demonstrated a situational focus: exposure to a television episode depicting altruism or to a nurturant caretaker increases prosocial behavior in young children; the visual presence of a prospective reward reduces delay of gratification; frustration decreases the constructiveness of play; and precise instructions for completing a task lead to decreased satisfaction. In these and many more studies, the investigators manipulated some situational property and determined its effects on behavior, but the attributes of the person that were essential to these situational effects were ignored. Because subjects are not equally affected by experimental manipulations, psychologists conduct experiments with many subjects, rather than simply generalizing from the responses of one particular individual. A few subjects, in fact, may respond in a manner opposite to the general trend. For some, very precise instructions and a high degree of structure may result in heightened, rather than decreased, satisfaction. This does not mean that the experiments are flawed or uninformative, or that the experimenters were unaware of the importance and possible interactions of subject attributes. Rather, it is easy to forget that one is really dealing with interactions even when an investigation has focused on situational variables.

A comparable problem arises when experimenters center on person variables. In these instances, the situational component of the interaction is neglected. You may recall that there is a tendency to overestimate the importance of personal traits and to underestimate the importance of the situation as a determinant of others' behavior. We tend to characterize people in trait terms that are independent of situations, such as introversion-extroversion or high achievement need-low achievement need. The situations in which introversion or high achievement strivings are evoked are typically unspecified. This is also the case in experimental studies. For example, reports that high achievement-oriented persons are more realistic than those low in achievement needs ignore the fact that this finding was obtained under particular circumstances, in a specific situation.

Although traits are often considered properties of the person, they may be better conceptualized as predispositions to respond to particular classes of situations in certain ways. Thus, when an individual is labeled high in anxiety, this should not be taken to mean that that person is always anxious; rather, he or she is predisposed to become anxious in certain situations. The range of situations can be quite broad, such as becoming anxious whenever competing, or more narrow, such as becoming anxious whenever taking a test in a classroom. But whether the range of situations in which a trait is manifested is broad or narrow, trait effects, like situational effects, always imply an interaction.

In phenomenological theory, the interaction between person and situation is exhibited in the subjective perceptions and meanings that individuals impose. Theorists in the phenomenological tradition tend not to be concerned with traits or with external physical events, but assume instead that the individual's subjective experience is of fundamental interest. This experience reflects an interaction between the objective stimulus situation, or what is "out there," and the attributes of the person that filter the external environment and provide meaning to the world. Thus, phenomenological theorists are concerned with interactions at the level of subjective perception and personal understanding.

THE MULTIDIMENSIONALITY OF THE PERSON

Human beings are thinking, feeling, motivated, behaving organisms. Some theoretical approaches, notably the learning theories, have placed primary emphasis on overt behavioral responses, largely because these are observable and subject to direct verification. Psychoanalytic theorists, on the other hand, stress the feelings and motivations of the organism, while the phenomenological, cognitive theorists are particularly interested in the individual's thoughts and perceptions. In the approach to personality that has been followed in this text, all these dimensions of human functioning are considered significant.

Some theorists might argue that, while all components — thoughts, feelings, desires, and response tendencies — are necessary to understanding human personality, one is primary and the others are secondary. For example, it could be argued that cognitions determine feelings, motivations, and behavior. Thus, if you believe that someone deliberately humiliated you (cognition), then you are likely to become angry (emotion) and wish to retaliate (desire). If you believe that you have a good chance of retaliating without punishment (cognition), then you might act aggressively toward the person who injured you (behavior). In this example, cognitions are primary, producing certain feelings, motivations, and behaviors. But motivations are sometimes primary. For example, an extremely ambitious person might perceive other people as obstacles and threats, in which case motivations determine cognitions. And overt responses or behaviors can also be primary: a boy may act aggressively because he has been repeatedly reinforced for aggressive acts. When acting aggressively, he may rationalize his behavior, perceiving other children as initiators of the hostile exchange.

Under certain circumstances, then, each component might be of central importance and determine the other processes. At a more fundamental level, the cognitive, affective, motivational, and behavioral aspects of human personality are interrelated. For example, a highly aggressive person not only has a low threshold for responding with aggressive behaviors, but also tends to perceive others as threatening. Thus, the disparate aspects of personality form an organized whole; each aspect has a significant role and none can be considered sufficient to account for the complexity of human action.

There is an apparent contradiction in human behavior that also highlights the necessity of being willing to draw on insights from each of the major approaches. On the one hand, humans are quite rational. They can consciously employ coping strategies to handle threat and anxiety; goal expectancies are calculated and logical decisions are made; information is sought out and processed; causal inferences are made; and self-insight can be attained. On the other hand, it is also evident that we are sometimes irrational. Motivations are unconscious and we defend ourselves in ways unknown to us; in times of stress and frustration, distinctions may be blurred and fixated behavior is displayed; overgeneralizations are made when there have been prior unfavorable outcomes and perceived lack of control; information is not properly processed; illogical decisions are reached; and there is personal delusion.

A list of the contradictions in human behavior could go on and on. Because logical and rational or illogical and irrational behavior might be exhibited in any given situation, the creation of a general theory of personality is indeed a difficult undertaking. And, given this diversity, one must accept that many equally important components or processes play an active role in human personality and behavior.

THE SELF

The self and related ideas of self-concept and self-esteem were discussed in some depth in Chapter 10. However, research and theories about the self are by no means restricted to the contents of that chapter; in virtually all the other chapters of this text, issues involving some aspect of the self have been addressed.

Consider first the place of the self in the various theories of personality. Clearly, the self is a central construct for phenomenological theorists, with their concentration on self-worth, self-perception, the ego ideal, and self-actualization. But the other theoretical approaches also place considerable importance on the self. Psychoanalytic defenses such as regression, reaction formation, and projection are mechanisms for maintaining self-esteem and preventing the individual from awareness of painful attributes of the self (Hilgard, 1949). And social learning theory gives considerable attention to self-monitoring processes. Another attribute of the self that has assumed central importance in social learning theory is the sense of self-competence or self-efficacy.

In a very general way, phenomenological theorists have focused on the cognitive, experiential aspects of the self (who am I?); psychoanalytic theorists have been oriented toward the motivational properties of the self (how can I protect myself?); and the social learning theorists have stressed the response properties of the self (what are the response consequences of high or low self-efficacy?). Remember, though, that these differences are a matter of emphasis, inasmuch as all the theoretical approaches recognize the cognitive, motivational, and behavioral components of the self.

The various aspects of the self have assumed a significant role in personality research. For example, we have reviewed studies in this text that concern self-control, self-esteem, self-focus, discrepancies between perceived and ideal self, and the relations between self-attributions and affect. Furthermore, how we believe we appear to others and the avoidance of guilt and shame are among the most powerful of human motivations and determinants of human striving. But the importance of the concept of the self has perhaps been best revealed in the discussion of perceived freedom and personal responsibility. An impressive amount of data indicates that self-determination and the perception that one has choice and control over life events have profound behavioral consequences.

In addition, the very nature of what a self is has become a focal point for the increasingly important discussion of how factors of cultural and other kinds of diversity need to be included in a truly comprehensive view of personality. The fact that many cultures view the self in sociocentric, inclusive terms rather than in egocentric, exclusive terms (as most influential Western theories have done) may significantly challenge much of the research and many of the views of the self heretofore held. Similarly, increased awareness of ethnicity, gender, sexual orientation, and other factors have led us to an awareness that development of a coherent self and identity may intimately involve sociocultural and group factors and may not be just a matter of individual achievement.

The role of the self in the analysis of personality often goes unrecognized. But close inspection reveals that it is one of the unifying themes in the study of personality. It stands alongside interactionism and the multidimensionality of the person as a strong motif in this text.

PERSONALITY AS A SCIENCE

At the outset, we indicated that the study of personality must be guided by experimental procedures and empirical evidence. Certainly, many of the complex issues in personality are difficult to investigate. Manipulation of antecedent conditions thought to influence personality development, such as parental warmth, are neither feasible nor ethical, and precise measurement of constructs such as parental warmth are exceedingly difficult. Nonetheless, the study of personality is not exempt from the scientific method.

Throughout this book we have asked if assumptions or conclusions are supported by appropriate evidence. For example:

1. Psychoanalytic theory postulates a death instinct and conceptualizes humans as closed energy systems. It was pointed out that these presumptions are not supported by empirical evidence, but rather are theoretical assumptions not subject to proof or disproof. On the other hand, there is some empirical support for the existence and function of psychoanalytic defenses, such as repression, denial, and intellectualization.

2. Social learning theorists hypothesize that exposure to a model influences learning and behavior. This has been well established. In addition, other social learning theorists accept the belief that rewards and punishments alter behavior. This is certainly true, but there are exceptions or contradictions to this fundamental principle. For example, rewards and punishments do not appear to influence frustration-induced fixation, and an extrinsic reward might actually undermine an intrinsic interest.

3. The humanistic principle of self-actualization has not been subject to scientific proof or disproof, although studies of the resiliency of human beings are compatible with some aspects of the self-actualization hypothesis. Similarly, in support of humanistic hypotheses, there is evidence that the discrepancy between the ideal self and the perceived self does change during the course of psychotherapy.

The number of known and established facts about personality is truly enormous. At the same time, our ignorance is all too apparent. We have tried to indicate what the facts are and when we are ignorant, what is speculation and what is established. One must constantly try to remain aware of this distinction. A major theme of this book is that appropriate data should always be brought to bear on statements concerning personality.

THE FUTURE

The field of personality is constantly changing. New theoretical approaches are being developed, new content areas are being explored, new methodologies are evolving, and new empirical findings are being reported every year. It is extremely difficult to predict future developments in the field, given this constant ferment and change. What we can do, however, is suggest some future directions that the study of personality may take, as well as indicate the topics that we would like to see pursued.

It is evident from the text that many issues remain to be resolved. Some broad and fundamental empirical questions still at issue include the role of nature and nurture and their interaction in determining human personality; the degree of trait consistency and generality; the extent to which personality is crystallized in childhood; and the modifiability of basic personality attributes in later life. There is also disagreement on many quite specific issues. Psychologists are not in agreement on the extent of sex differences in personality, the validity of self-report personality scales, the major antecedents of aggression, and the effects of factors such as anxiety, stress, meditation, and self-esteem on performance quality and intensity. Clearly, many more disagreements can be added to this short list of examples.

The fact that so many issues remain unresolved does not mean that there has not been significant progress in the investigation and understanding of personality. In the study of personality, it is true that similar questions have been examined again and again. But when the questions do reappear, they are in improved forms that make more meaningful answers possible. As one looks at the history of inquiry into personality issues, it can be seen that there have been profound changes in the sophistication of the questions asked and the methods of research employed.

These positive trends are illustrated in the study of aggressive instincts. Questions regarding the instinctiveness of aggressive behavior have been addressed for many years by philosophers and early psychologists. In previous eras it was believed that aggression was a product of an aggressive instinct and that one either had or did not have such an instinctive tendency. Research first revealed that aggressive behavior is not an either-or matter, but involves degrees or amounts of aggression; that is, there is variability in the extent of aggressive actions. It was later determined that environmental variables, such as aggressive models, frustration, and the presence of weapons in the environment, may contribute to aggressive actions. The investigation of the contribution of learning and situational factors to aggressive behavior caused still further revision of thought on the matter. It became clear that, for a genetic predisposition to be manifested, particular environmental conditions were required. Thus, regardless of the relative contributions of personal and situational determinants of hostility, aggression is always determined by both innate qualities and the environment. In addition, more precise analyses of aggressive phenomena revealed that the phrase *aggressive instinct* is far too vague and undifferentiated. The internal determinants of aggressive responses that appear to be instinctive, like those studied by ethologists, must be distinguished from aggressive drives, and these drives must, in turn, be distinguished from simple expressions of anger.

There is no fully satisfactory answer to the question of the instinctive nature of human aggression. But the systematic study of personality has enabled us to provide a more sophisticated answer than was possible in the prescientific era. A similar statement can be made about virtually any of the topics reviewed in this text. In accordance with this analysis, we do not expect that developments in the immediate future of personality will provide final answers to the difficult and unresolved issues. However, we do believe that they will help provide better, more sophisticated answers.

Personality Structure

A *structure* refers to something made up of interdependent elements or parts, with a fixed pattern of organization. Thus, when we discuss the structure of personality, we mean the relatively fixed and interdependent components of the person. There have been many references in this text to various aspects of personality structure. *Introversion, need for achievement,* and *aggressive inclination* are structural terms; id, ego, and superego are also structural concepts, as is the self, including the "split" within the self. In some cases, the meaning of these terms is clear and procedures are available for measuring and studying them. However, in other instances the concepts are unclear and difficult to assess, as is the case for the concepts of ego and split personality.

But an even greater shortcoming is the absence of a coherent system that specifies the interrelationships among the many structural terms. Part of the difficulty here is that psychological structure is analogous to physical structure; it is easy to equate and confuse the two. But a psychological split is not the same as a physical split, and psychological distance cannot be measured in physical dimensions of inches or feet. Indeed, psychological direction may be opposite to physical direction, as when one runs toward a fire in order to escape from it. Furthermore, passing an examination or getting married involves psychological movement, even though there may be no change in physical location.

In spite of these difficulties, there is some utility in thinking of personality in terms of structural concepts derived from the physical sciences. The chapters on the development of the self, traits, and consciousness all have to do with the structure and organization of personality. The issue, then, is not one of establishing that there is a structure to personality. Rather, the task is to formulate a logical set of constructs relating to personality and to develop a clear set of procedures for measuring and making inferences about these constructs.

Individual Differences and Their Development

Psychologists have devoted a great deal of attention to the study of individual differences in personality. Measures have been developed for traits like introversion, aggression, achievement, and the belief in internal versus external control, to cite a few. After establishing a trait category or dimension of individual difference, a logical next step is to identify the antecedents of a trait. There have been some investigations of the effects of differences in socialization practices on personality development. And, especially in recent years, there has been considerable interest in the role of biological variables in personality development. But, in general, insufficient attention has been paid to the causes of individual differences, and much more research has been directed toward establishing trait categories and trait measures than toward sources of individual differences.

We can anticipate that there will be more extensive and coordinated efforts in this area. In particular, what is needed in addition to more research on social and biological variables is an integration of these two research traditions. Much of the biologically oriented research has been devoted to the demonstration that there are genetic and physiological factors influencing personality. In a similar manner, socialization research has focused on demonstrating the role of child rearing and cultural variables. But more attention must be given to the interplay of both sets of variables. We anticipate that there will be an increasing number of investigations tracing the interaction over time between a child's biologically based inclinations and the behaviors encouraged by parents, peers, and other socializing agents.

An additional source of personality influence that contributes to this interaction is the character of the physical environment, both natural and artificial, in which the child is reared. Because of the complexity of the interactions among these influences, we can expect new research methods to be formulated to facilitate investigations of personality development.

New directions in the study of individual differences are being developed by those interested in variables such as identity, life tasks, personal strivings, and personal projects (see Chapter 11). The study of these kinds of variables represents a new trend in personality research in that these variables can be studied both by looking at differences between individuals (i.e., we can study the unique organization of how a given individual's personal projects affect his or her life) and by looking at general trends across all individuals (i.e., we can study the general kinds of personal projects people typically set for themselves).

Personality Dynamics

A close inspection of the studies in Chapter 14 concerned with psychodynamics will reveal that they were conducted earlier than the experiments discussed in other chapters of this text. The investigations of substitution undertaken by Kurt Lewin and his students took place, for the most part, in the 1920s and 1930s; and studies of conflict were conducted primarily in the 1940s and 1950s. We find it unfortunate that the experimental study of these topics is only weakly represented in contemporary psychology, inasmuch as behavioral dynamics encompasses extremely important and interesting issues for the field of personality.

There are many understandable reasons why investigators do not continue to pursue a particular phenomenon. First, there are diminishing payoffs for the study of any given problem or theory. Second, there are many other interesting ideas and issues competing for attention. Third, scientists quite naturally want to establish their own reputations in uncharted areas. Finally, the problems of psychodynamics are especially difficult to solve, discouraging investigators who then seek more fruitful fields elsewhere. These are valid reasons and the goals of the investigators are laudable. But as a result of premature diminution of research in an area, problems are left behind before sufficient scientific progress has been made.

We believe that there should and will be a return to the study of basic psychodynamic phenomena, such as substitution and displacement, in the future. Lewin and Freud both pointed out the importance of the interrelationships of need systems and the fact that attainment of one goal can serve to satisfy other unfulfilled needs. This and related problems in psychodynamics are key issues for the field of personality and are in need of systematic investigation. Such a return is already under way in the study of emotions.

An Integrated Theory of Personality

The current state of personality theory is unsatisfactory. Chapters 3 through 6 presented a number of alternative conceptions of human behavior. In some reviews of personality, as many as twenty-five different theories are presented, one chapter after the other, with little or no theoretical integration or connection. Inasmuch as one of the tasks of science is to provide a general theory with as few constructs as possible, one hopes that in the next decade there will be a significant reduction in the number of theories of personality that are offered. Of course, for this to be true there must first be an increase in the availability of pertinent data that permit one to reject certain theories and accept others.

There are some who argue that we shouldn't be spending as much time as we do teaching the old "grand theories of personality" (e.g., Freud, Rogers, Kelly). Mendelsohn (1993) argues that these are not even theories in the scientific sense because many aspects of them are untestable. Further, he notes that these theories were largely developed in the early 1900s and are of questionable contemporary relevance. Mendelsohn's critique is in accord with those who believe that personality theory has largely been shaped by "dead white males" and that modern sensibility demands a greater attention to the experience of diverse people and groups in formulating a truly comprehensive view of personality.

At the same time, most of the major research questions explored by personality psychologists have been derived, in one way or the other, from these grand theories. Therefore, while they may not be proper scientific theories, they have been fruitful sources of ideas concerning human behavior.

As we have already indicated, these grand theories have some aspects that are primarily philosophical. If they are not proper scientific theories, they are general philosophical perspectives on the nature of human beings, from which more testable theories can be derived. Therefore, while we agree with Mendelsohn that too much emphasis is sometimes placed on these grand theories, we nonetheless believe that they still have a role to play in the study of personality.

There are several possible directions theory development in personality may take. First, many personality researchers are developing theories that are specific to some aspect of functioning rather than attempting to develop a grand theory that would explain all of human personality. Throughout this text, we have considered a number of examples of this approach such as the use of attribution theory to help understand achievement behavior, personal control, and competence. One advantage of starting with the development of a solid theory in a specific area of study, such as achievement motivation, is that such theory, after having been solidly tested in one domain, can sometimes be extended into new domains. Ideas based on attribution theory in the study of achievement behavior, for instance, are now being generalized to help us understand stigma and perceptions of responsibility in general (e.g., Weiner, 1993).

A second direction that theory development may take is towards integration. We have previously noted that personality is multidimensional and that aspects emphasized by each of the major theories are important. This suggests the possibility of building an integrative theory to take all of these aspects into account. For instance, there could be a theory developed that somehow balanced both conscious and unconscious factors and cognition and feeling, viewed humans as both exhibiting continuity and change, and took into account both internal psychological factors as well as environmental and reinforcement factors. It would seem that this will ultimately be what will evolve. However, at the present time this will not be easy to achieve because, as we have discussed earlier, different theories consider different aspects to be primary.

In a field related to personality theory, the area of psychotherapy, there have been numerous attempts to integrate psychoanalytic, cognitive, behavioral, and humanistic perspectives (see Arkowitz, 1992, for an overview of the field of psychotherapy integration). Each attempt, however, has tended to consider as primary one or the other of the major orientations and, for that reason, none have been successful at capturing the allegience of those who hold a different primary orientation.

Therefore, for the forseeable future, it is unrealistic to expect that the field of personality will be able to settle on one theory that is acceptable to all. Although one can anticipate that competing theories will be with us for a long time, it is both possible and valuable to begin to formulate a comprehensive theory of personality based on an integration of compatible elements drawn from extant theories. Each theory — Freudian, Jungian, Rogerian, social learning, and so on — has important statements to make that are consistent with the available data about personality. These propositions about personality can begin to be incorporated within a common framework and a common terminology.

The matter of language is not a simple obstacle to overcome, since the theories employ such different concepts. However, for a number of reasons we feel that a common theoretical language can now be formulated. Contemporary psychological thinking is more flexible and broader than was the case a decade or two ago; cognitive psychology has achieved respectability; there is a general interest in affects and their relation to motivation and behavior; the concept of self is widely used; and both the mind and the emotions have been readmitted to formal, scientific psychology. With increasing agreement about the appropriateness of structural, cognitive, emotional, motivational, and behavioral terms, it may well be possible to start the task of a more integrated and comprehensive theory of personality.

Summary

Four themes that are represented throughout this text have been pointed out: interactionism, multidimensionality, the self, and personality as a science. In addition, future directions in the areas of structure, development, dynamics, and theory have been suggested. The field of personality is vital and growing; this growth is evident in the increasing sophistication of the questions asked and in the increasing refinement of the answers provided.

Thought Questions

1. Which personality areas do you feel are most in need of study?
2. In which personality areas do you feel that the most progress has been made and the most knowledge has been generated?
3. Which personality areas discussed in the text most interested you and motivated you to find out more about them? Why?
4. Do you think that any one of the personality theories discussed in the text will be dominant in the future? Defend your answer.

Glossary

adolescence   The transitional period of human development between childhood and adulthood, from the onset of puberty to the early twenties.

aggression   Hostile, injurious, or destructive behavior.

agonistic behavior   Offensive and defensive fighting and competitive activity; a term used by biologists to define aggression.

altered states of consciousness   Instances of heightened inner awareness, as might be experienced when under the influence of a drug or during deep meditation.

altruism   Concern for the welfare of another without regard for oneself.

ambivalent behavior   Behavior that oscillates from approach to withdrawal.

amnesia   A loss of both identity and recall of the past.

analytic psychology   Jung's personality theory that deviates from psychoanalysis in its emphasis on the collective unconscious and on the human striving toward self-fulfillment.

anxiety   A state of unrealistic fear.

approach-approach conflict   Lewin's classification for conflict in which there are two or more positive alternatives to choose from.

approach-avoidance conflict   Lewin's classification for conflict that occurs when both positive and negative consequences are associated with the same action.

archetypes   In Jungian theory, the primeval contents of the collective unconscious.

arousal   The intensity, state of activation, or drive characterizing an individual.

associationist learning theory   A learning theory that views humans in terms of stimulus-response variables and as essentially creatures of habit.

attribution theory   A theoretical approach based on the view that people attempt to explain and understand behavioral events through attributing the causes of those events to characteristics of the person or to factors in the environment; these causal ascriptions significantly influence goal expectancies and behavioral responses.

autism   A severe mental illness of early childhood, characterized by absorption in fantasy, isolation, and extremely defective thinking and language abilities.

automaticity   A cognitive version of the "unconscious." It is assumed that many of the schemas that guide our behavior operate automatically outside of awareness.

autonomy   The ability to act for and by oneself.

avoidance-avoidance conflict   Lewin's classification for conflict in which a choice is confined to two or more unattractive alternatives.

behavior   Any activity, covert or overt, of an organism.

behavior modification   Therapeutic techniques that use Skinnerian methods of changing behavior to modify disturbed behaviors.

behavior therapy   Psychotherapeutic techniques based on learning principles.

the "Big Five"   Many personality researchers now believe there are five basic personality traits. One popular classification system identifies them as: neuroticism versus emotional stability, extraversion, openness to experience, conscientiousness, and agreeableness.

biofeedback   The process of monitoring and providing information to the person about involuntary body functioning, usually as a therapeutic method for learning how to control maladaptive physiological responses.

body image   The organized perception of one's physical structure.

bonding (attachment behavior)   The formation of stable attachments to particular caregivers.

catharsis   The reduction of emotional tension through expressive release activity; sometimes restricted to release through vicarious activity, such as watching a play or film.

cathexis The psychic energy that has been invested in a desired object.

causal attributions A term used in achievement-related contexts to connote beliefs about the reasons for one's success or failure—for example, ability, effort, task ease or difficulty, or luck.

client-centered therapy The psychotherapeutic approach used by Rogers, which employs trust, acceptance, and empathy to help clients realize their goals.

cognitive behavior modification A modified Skinnerian approach to human behavior, derived from modified Skinnerian principles, that stresses the role of cognitive factors in mediating behavior and attempts to bring about change through alteration of these cognitions.

cognitive conceit A defensive belief in one's own greater intelligence and insight.

cognitive style A person's consistent ways of perceiving in relation to himself or herself and the surrounding world.

cognitive theory The theory of personality that focuses on human thought processes and levels of understanding as a major determinant of behavior.

collective unconscious In Jungian theory, the site of inherited primitive, universal attitudes and ideals (archetypes) of which we are not conscious.

complex In Jung's theory, a group of feelings, ideas, memories, and behaviors organized around a significant object.

concrete reciprocal hedonism The view that if one person does something for another, it is right for the other to do something in return.

conditions of worth The conditional positive regard—the "do's" or "don'ts," "shoulds" and "shouldn'ts"—that people live by in order to feel appreciated and accepted by others.

conflict A psychological state in which two or more varying forces or alternatives are present simultaneously.

consciousness Awareness, or self-knowledge, of one's experiences.

construct validity The degree to which a test represents the meaning of the construct it is designed to measure.

constructive alternativism Kelly's basic tenet

that "meaning" and "reality" are dependent on the person's interpretation and therefore are subject to change.

content validity The degree to which a test adequately represents the content it is designed to assess.

convergent validity The degree to which a test measures the same construct as that assessed by other tests.

correlation A mathematical index used to express the degree of association between two variables.

criterion validity The degree to which a test predicts, or correlates with, a subsequent factor (*predictive validity*), as well as the degree to which it is associated with other indexes that exist at the same point in time (*concurrent validity*).

cue Any stimulus, often a subtle one, that directs behavior.

decentration The cognitive capacity to assume the point of view of another.

defense mechanisms In psychoanalytic theory, unconscious strategies that enable a person to avoid awareness of unpleasant or anxiety-arousing experiences.

depression A disturbing condition involving feelings of sadness, lowered initiative, and an attitude of self-blame.

diagnosticity The information gained about one's ability following task performance.

discriminant validity The degree to which a test measures a different construct than that assessed by other tests.

discriminative conflict As noted in Pavlov's studies, a conflict in which similar stimuli are associated with different consequences so that it is difficult to distinguish whether the outcome of a choice will be favorable or unfavorable.

displacement A defense mechanism in which a person shifts a reaction from an original target person or situation to some other person or situation.

dissociation An altered state of consciousness in which a person lacks awareness of significant segments of his or her behavior or identity.

drive Any motive or need that impels action.

drive reduction A decrease in the intensity of a motive or need force, which, according to associationist learning theory, also strengthens the stimulus-response connection.

ectomorph A person with a tall, thin physique, whom Sheldon observed as also tending to have an introverted temperament.

ego In Freudian theory, the part of the personality that mediates between the demands of id impulses, superego, and external reality.

ego ideal In Freudian theory, standards that guide behavior because they are believed to constitute worthy goals to strive toward.

egocentricity A self-centered frame of reference in which one assumes that others perceive the world from the same perspective as oneself.

emotion A subjective feeling state, with cognitive, physiological, and/or behavioral components.

empathy The ability to discriminate and label feelings in others, to assume the perspective and role of another person, and to experience and respond with feelings similar to another.

endomorph A person with a rounded physique, whom Sheldon observed as also tending to have a relaxed and gregarious temperament.

enviromental psychology The study of the role of environment in regulating behavior.

existential humanism A personality theory that views the individual as responsible for his or her own actions and as having to cope with guilt and anxiety.

expectancy-value theory A motivational theory emphasizing that behavior depends on the probability that an act will lead to a goal and upon the value of that goal.

extrinsic motivation The undertaking of an activity for an expected external reward.

extroversion From Jung, the tendency to be strongly oriented toward other people and social stituations.

face validity The degree to which the items on a test appear to sample the content domain.

factor analysis A statistical method of reducing a large amount of data from tests, rating scales, or behavioral observations to a smaller and presumably more basic number of dimensions of personality factors.

fixation The persistence of responses that apparently result in repeated failure and nonreward.

frustration A state of arousal that occurs when a person is unable to reach his or her goal and produces behaviors as disparate as aggression, fixation, regression, and enhanced goal striving.

genotype A person's set of inherited characteristics, as determined by genetic makeup.

gerontology The study of the phenomena of aging in humans.

hallucination Perception of visual images or audible sounds that are not actually present in the environment.

hallucinogen Any drug that produces hallucinations.

homeostasis Equilibrium or balance among internal processes.

humanistic psychology The system of psychology that focuses not only on what a person is, but also on what a person has the potential to become.

hypnosis A trancelike state in which the cooperative subject is highly responsive to suggestions made by the hypnotist.

hysteria A psychological reaction state (for example, dissociation) characterized by high excitability and anxiety, incapacitating bodily symptoms, and altered states of consciousness.

id In Freudian theory, the most primitive and inaccessible part of the personality, made up of sexual and aggressive instincts, which strive continually for gratification.

idealism A dissatisfaction with the state of the world, a desire to improve it and to make life more fulfilling.

identification The process by which the child imitates and subsequently internalizes the perceived attitudes and values of the parent while still maintaining a distinction between its own and the parent's identities.

identity The sense of being a physical and psychological self separate from the environment.

imagery Pictures one visualizes or imagines, which can facilitate memory and alter feelings and behaviors.

implicit psychology The perceived laws of behavior held by naive observers, or the personality theories of individuals who are untrained psychologists.

imprinting The process of establishing an attachment of first exposure to an object (noted in Lorenz's studies of newborn nonhumans).

instinct An innate, biologically based mode of response to certain stimuli.

interactionism The personality theory that views behavior as governed by both the properties of the person and the situation in which the person is acting.

internal consistency A measure of test reliability; the degree of consistency within a test during any given time period.

intrinsic aggression Aggressive behavior motivated by the satisfaction of engaging in aggressive activity, as contrasted with behavior motivated by the desire to inflict injury.

intrinsic motivation The undertaking of an activity for its own sake without expectation of external reward.

introversion In Jung's theory, the tendency to be attentive and interested in one's own thoughts and feelings.

isolation paradigm The experimental procedure used to study innate behaviors in which infant nonhumans are isolated so that they cannot observe others' responses and hence exhibit only innate responses.

learned helplessness The acquired expectation that one's actions will exert little control over outcomes.

learning theory As applied to the area of personality, a set of assumptions that the development and functioning of the personality is based on experimentally derived principles of learning.

libido Freud's term of psychic energy, derived primarily from the sexual, pleasure-seeking instincts of the id.

life structure Levinson's term for the basic pattern governing a peron's adult life stages.

measurement error The degree to which the observed score on a measuring instrument deviates from the true score.

mediated generalization An unobservable association process by which dissimilar situations elicit the same mediating response.

mediating response Any unobservable internal response that intervenes between the observable stimulus and the overt response.

meditation Any attempt to alter consciousness by means of systematic concentration and sustained self-regulation of attention.

mesomorph A person with an athletic physique, whom Sheldon observed as also tending to have an energetic and assertive temperament.

midlife crisis In Levinson's theory, a transitional period in adult development (the forties) during which one assesses his or her basic life structure.

modeling (imitation) (observational learning) The process of acquiring new behaviors through observation of another person performing them.

narcolepsy Sudden "sleep attacks" that often occur without warning, particularly during times of heightened excitement, lasting from a few to fifteen minutes.

natural behavior Patterns of behavior that one has the potential for developing and that will develop under normal environmental circumstances.

neurosis An emotional, nonpsychotic disorder characterized by anxiety and other symptoms and resulting in partial impairment of functioning.

nonshared environment effect Findings from genetic research have indicated that siblings growing up in the same family appear to share little in common in terms of their personalities. This suggests that while individuals are growing up in the same general family environment, they do not share the same "subenvironments" within the family.

object relations theory In psychoanalytic ego psychology, the theory that ego development and subsequent interpersonal relationships are based on the infant's attachment to the mother and other figures.

object representation A person's internalized image of a significant object.

oedipal conflict (Oedipus complex for boys; Electra complex for girls) In Freud's psychosexual theory of development, sexual attraction to the opposite-sex parent, and jealousy and hostility toward and fear of punishment from the rival, same-sex parent.

operant conditioning (operant reinforcement) A manipulation of behavior in which the response is controlled by the reinforcement following it.

operants Behaviors that "operate" on and change the environment—for example, releasing a latch that opens a door.

organismic humanism Maslow's theory of personality and human motivation describing a hierarchical human needs system, from strong physiological needs to self-actualization needs.

partial reinforcement An intermittent reward schedule that strengthens a response.

peak experience A moment of great ecstasy or

awe that is experienced without the use of drugs or other stimulants.

personal construct theory Kelly's personality theory that focuses on how a person, as perceiver, organizes his or her world and interprets, or construes, events.

personal space A small, invisible area surrounding a person, within which an intrusion by another person causes discomfort and annoyance.

personality Relatively enduring behavior patterns and traits that distinguish people, groups, and cultures; the overall organization and structure of these enduring patterns and traits; and the interactions among these patterns and the interactions of these patterns with fluctuations in the internal state and with changing external stimuli.

personality continuity The stability of personality traits and behavior over time.

personality measurement A system of assessing the extent of specific personality traits and other characteristics.

personality structure The organization of the basic components of the personality.

personification The image of oneself or another based on one's personal feelings and attitudes.

phenomenology The study of subjective experience, or the "meaning" that a person gives to events.

phenotype The totality of observed characteristics or behaviors of an organism that result from the interaction between genotype and environmental influences.

polygraph An instrument used to monitor various physiological indicators.

pride A sense of self-satisfaction typically arising from the attribution of success to one's own efforts and abilities.

primary drive An innate, biologically based motivational force, such as hunger or thirst.

projection In Freud's theory, a defense mechanism involving the unconscious attribution of one's own unacceptable feelings or motives to others.

projective test A test consisting of ambiguous stimuli, to which an individual produces spontaneous responses; scoring is often subjective.

prosocial behavior Positive social behavior, often socially prescribed and viewed as moral action, that is enacted to help others.

psychoanalysis A system of psychology and psychotherapy, founded on Freud's theory of conflict in relation to unconscious libidinal impulses.

psychodynamics (personality dynamics) The psychological "motion" of the personality produced by forces acting on the individual: the expression and inhibition of needs, the entering or leaving of a particular state of consciousness, and the functions or goals of behavior.

psychological reactance A motivational arousal state in which a person increases behavior to secure that which is threatened or has been experienced but made unavailable.

psychopathology The science of the study of mental disorders.

psychosis Severe mental disorder involving personality disorganization and impairment of contact with reality.

psychosocial stages In Erikson's theory of personality, the periods from birth to maturity posing particular developmental tasks and providing the basis for specific personality characteristics.

puberty The period of maturation of the sex organs and other sexual characteristics.

Q-sort A rating technique in which a set of adjectives or statements is categorized into piles according to the degree to which they are descriptive of an individual.

radical behaviorism The approach to psychology that views human behavior as controlled by external stimulus situations.

reaction formation In Freud's theory, a defense mechanism in which a person behaves in a way directly opposite from some underlying anxiety-provoking impulse.

regression In Freudian theory, a return to some earlier stage of psychosexual development in the face of some current frustration.

reinforcement Stimulation following a response, which increases the probability that the same response will occur again in the same situation.

reliability The consistency, or degree of accuracy, of a measuring instrument.

repression A defense mechanism in which an anxiety-arousing memory or impulse is prevented from becoming conscious.

repression-sensitization continuum An approach-avoidance stylistic dimension of individual differences in defense reactions.

response bias The tendency to respond to a test

item in a particular way regardless of item content.

schizophrenia   A severe psychosis characterized by major disturbances in thought, emotion and behavior, often reflected in withdrawal and a fantasy life of delusions and hallucinations.

self   A person's fundamental sense of identity.

self-actualization   A principle of human behavior stating that individuals strive to develop their capacities and talents to the fullest—that is, growing and enhancing the basic self.

self-concept   The organized set of perceptions and ideas that the individual has of himself or herself.

self-consistency   The relationship between one's concept of oneself and one's behavior.

self-efficacy   A person's expectation that he or she can effectively cope with and master situations and bring about desired outcomes through personal efforts.

self-esteem   The value, respect, and honor one has for oneself.

self-ideal discrepancy   The difference between how one perceives oneself and how one would like to be.

self-insight   Increased awareness of one's feelings, drives, and attitudes.

sex role   The pattern of behavior expected of a male or female by society.

shame   A sense of devaluation, dishonor, or loss of respect based on the attribution of misbehavior to the self.

shaping   The process of establishing a behavior by rewarding successively closer approximations of that behavior.

situational theory   The personality theory that emphasizes the impact of situations over the impact of personality characteristics in determining behavior.

social desirability   A factor, to be considered on personality tests, that connotes a person's tendency to respond in a socially approved or favorable manner.

social deviance   Nonconforming, socially unapproved behavior(s).

social learning theory   Several related personality approaches that emphasize an individual's expectancy that certain behaviors will be rewarded by parents and society.

social stratification   The ranking of individuals into groups within a culture.

socialization   The process of developing the motivations and behaviors that are appropriate in one's culture.

somnambulism   Walking or carrying out acts while apparently in a sleeping state.

source traits   In Cattell's factor analyses of personality traits, basic organizing structures that underlie and determine surface traits.

state anxiety   Temporary anxiety that varies in intensity, fluctuates over time, and is strongly influenced by situational factors.

states of mind   Mardi Horowitz's modern psychodynamic idea that individuals at different moments experience different states of mind in which they see themselves differently, have different emotional experiences, and see others differently.

stress   Any force acting on a person that produces psychological or physiological strain.

sublimation   In Freudian theory, a defense mechanism in which libidinal (sexual) energy is redirected from an unacceptable to a socially approved mode of expression.

substitution   The gratification provided by goals attained in place of one's original goal.

superego   In Freudian theory, the part of the personality representing the morals, values, and ideals of one's society.

surface traits   In Cattell's factor analyses of personality traits, clusters of responses or overt behaviors that are related or fit together.

symbiosis   A state of a rewarding attachment and interdependence between two organisms.

temperament   Behavioral characteristics that are present at an early age and that are believed to have some basis in biological processes partly determined by heredity.

template-matching technique   Bem and Funder's measurement of personality that matches individuals with ideal types (those that are most likely to behave in a given manner in a given situation) to predict specific behaviors.

test-retest reliability   The correlation between scores obtained by administering a test on two occasions to the same group of individuals.

time-binding   A process that helps delay the immediate gratification of a need.

trait A distinguishing personal characteristic that is relatively stable and enduring.

trait anxiety An enduring tendency to be anxious.

trait psychology The system of psychology based on the study of personality characteristics that are believed to be general over situations and enduring over time.

transactional model An approach to human development that views the interaction between the child and its environment as a reciprocal and continuous process.

unconditional positive regard Rogers' term for the accepting and valuing of a person per se, regardless of the degree to which he or she exhibits specific behaviors that are approved or disapproved.

validity The degree to which a test actually measures what it is intended to measure.

variability In personality testing, individual differences reflecting both true differences and error.

variable In personality testing, an individual characteristic that can be measured.

References ━━━━━━━━━━

Aaronson, B., and Osmond, H. *Psychedelics: The use and implications of hallucinogenic drugs.* Garden City, N.Y.: Anchor Books/Doubleday, 1970.

Abramson, L. Y., Metalsky, G. I., and Alloy, L. B. The hopeless theory of depression: Does the research test the theory? In L. Y. Abramson (Ed.), *Social cognition and clinical psychology.* New York: Guilford, 1988, 33–65.

Abramson, L. Y., Seligman, M. E. P., and Teasdale, J. D. Learned helplessness in humans: Critique and reformulation. *Journal of Abnormal Psychology,* 1978, 87, 49–74.

Adams, G. R., Gullota, T. P., and Markstrom-Adams, C. *Adolescent life experiences.* Pacific Grove, CA: Brooks/Cole, 1994.

Adams, G. R., and Montemayer, R. *Patterns of identity development during late adolescence: A descriptive study of stability, progression, and regression,* 1988. Manuscript submitted for publication, as referenced in Adams, G. R., Gullota, T.P., and Markstrom-Adams, C. *Adolescent life experiences.* Pacific Grove, CA: Brooks/Cole, 1992.

Adler, A. *Practice and theory of individual psychology.* New York: Harcourt, Brace & World, 1927.

Adorno, I. W., Frenkel-Brunswick, E., Levinson, D. J., and Sanford, R. N. *The authoritarian personality.* New York: Harper & Row, 1950.

Agros, W. S., Schneider, J. A., Arnow, B., Rachurn, S. D., and Telch, C. F. Cognitive-Behavioral and response-prevention treatments for Bulimia Nervosa. *Journal of Consulting and Clinical Psychology,* 1989, 57, 215–221.

Ahadi, S., and Diener, E. Multiple determinants and effect size. *Journal of Personality and Social Psychology,* 1989, 56, 398–406.

Ainsworth, M. D. S. *Infancy in Uganda.* Baltimore: Johns Hopkins, 1967.

——— . Attachments beyond infancy. *American Psychologist,* 1989, 709–716.

——— , and Stayton, D. Individual differences in strange situation behavior of one-year-olds. In H. R. Schaffer (Ed.), *The origins of human social relations.* London: Academic Press, 1971.

——— , Blehar, M. C., Waters, E., and Wall, S. *Patterns of attachment.* Hillsdale, N.J.: Lawrence Erlbaum, 1978.

Alden, L. E. Behavioral Self-management Controlled-Drinking strategies in a context of secondary prevention. *Journal of Consulting and Clinical Psychology,* 1988, 56, 280–286.

Aldis, O. *Play fighting.* New York: Academic Press, 1975.

Alexander, I. E. The Freud-Jung relationship — The other side of Oedipus and countertransference. *American Psychologist,* 1982, 37, 1009–1018.

——— . Personality, psychological assessment, and psychobiography. *Journal of Personality,* 1988, 56, 265–294.

Allen, K. E., and Harris, F. R. Elimination of a child's excessive scratching by training the mother in reinforcement procedures. *Behavior Research and Therapy,* 1966, 4, 79–84.

Allen, M. J., and Yen, W. M. *Introduction to measurement theory.* Belmont, CA: Brooks/Cole, 1979.

Allport, G. W. *Personality: A psychological interpretation.* New York: Henry Holt, 1937.

——— . *Becoming: Basic consideration for a psychology of personality.* New Haven, CT: Yale University Press, 1955.

——— . *Pattern and growth in personality.* New York: Holt, 1961.

——— , and Odbert, H. S. Trait-names: A psycholexical study. *Psychological Monographs,* 1936, 47(1, Whole No. 211).

——— , and Vernon, P. E. *Studies in expressive movement.* New York: Macmillan, 1933.

Allred, K. D., and Smith, T. W. The hardy personality: Cognitive and physiological responses to evaluative threat. *Journal of Personality and Social Psychology,* 1989, 56, 257–266.

Altman, I. *The environment and social behavior.* Belmont, CA: Brooks/Cole, 1975.

————. Environmental psychology and social psychology. *Personality and Social Psychology Bulletin,* 1976, *2,* 96–113.

American Psychiatric Association. *Diagnostic and statistical manual of mental disorders.* Washington, DC: American Psychiatric Association, 1994.

American Psychologist, 1965, *20,* 990.

Ames, C. Competitive, cooperative, and individualistic goal structures: A cognitive-motivational analysis. In Ames, R. E., and Ames, C. (Eds.), *Motivation in education, Vol. 1.* San Francisco: Academic Press, 1984, 177–207.

Ames, L. B. The sense of self of nursery school children as manifested by their verbal behavior. *Journal of Genetic Psychology,* 1952, *81,* 193–232.

Amsterdam, B. Mirror self-image reactions before age two. *Developmental Psychobiology,* 1972, *5,* 297–305.

Anastasi, A. *Psychological testing* (4th ed.). New York: Macmillan, 1976.

Anderson, C. A. Temperature and aggression: Effects on quarterly, yearly, and city rates of violent and nonviolent crime. *Journal of Personality and Social Psychology,* 1987, *52,* 1161–1173.

————. Temperature and aggression: The ubiquitous effect of heat on the occurrence of human violence. *Psychological Bulletin,* 1989, *106,* 74–96.

————, Jennings, D. L., and Arnoult, L. H. Validity and utility of the atributional style construct at a moderate level of specificity. *Journal of Personality and Social Psychology,* 1988, *55,* 979–990.

Ansbacher, H. L., and Ansbacher, R. R. (Eds.). *The individual psychology of Alfred Adler.* New York: Basic Books, 1956.

———— (Eds.). *Superiority and social interest by Alfred Adler.* Evanston, Ill.: Northwestern University Press, 1964.

Anspach, M. S. Is a change in the theory of the person necessary? *Theoretical and Philosophical Psychology,* 1991, *11,* 111–115.

Antill, J. K. Parents' beliefs and values about sex roles, sex differences and sexuality: Their sources and implications. In P. Shaver and C. Hendrick (Eds.), *Sex and gender: Review of personality and Social Psychology:* Vol. 7. Beverly Hills, CA: Sage, 1987, 294–328.

Archer, J. Effects of population density on behavior in rodents. In J. H. Croobe (Ed.), *Social behaviors in birds and mammals.* New York: Academic Press, 1970.

————. The sociobiology of bereavement: A reply to Littlefield and Rushton. *Journal of Personality and Social Psychology,* 1988, *55,* 272–278.

Archer, S. L. A feminist's approach to identity research. In G. R. Adams, T. P. Gullotta, and R. Montemayer (Eds.), *Adolescent identity formation.* Newbury Park: Sage, 25–49, 1992.

Ardrey, R. *African genesis.* New York: Dell, 1967.

Aristotle. *Introduction to Aristotle, Nicomachean Ethics,* Richard McBeon (Ed.). New York: Random House, 1947.

Arkes, H. R., and Garske, J. P. *Psychological theories of motivation.* Belmont, CA: Brooks/Cole, 1977.

Arkoff, A. Resolution of approach-approach and avoidance-avoidance conflicts. *Journal of Abnormal and Social Psychology,* 1957, *55,* 402–404.

Arkowitz, H. Integrative theories of therapy. In D. Freedheim (Ed.), *History of psychotherapy: A century of change.* Washington, DC: American Psychological Association, 1992.

Aronfreed, J. The origins of self-criticism. *Psychological Review,* 1964, *71,* 193–218.

Ashmore, R. D. Sex, gender, and the individual. In L. A. Pervin (Ed.), *Handbook of personality.* New York: Guilford, 486–526, 1990.

Astin, A. N., Green, K. C., and Korn, W. S. *The American freshman: Twenty year trends.* Los Angeles, CA: University of California at Los Angeles, Higher Education Research Institute, 1987.

Atkinson, J. W. Motivational determinants of risk-taking behavior. *Psychological Review,* 1957, *64,* 359–372.

————. *An introduction to motivation.* Princeton, NJ: Van Nostrand, 1964.

————, and Litwin, G. H. Achievement motive and test anxiety conceived as motive to approach success and motive to avoid failure. *Journal of Abnormal and Social Psychology,* 1960, *60,* 52–63.

————, and Raynor, J. O. (Eds.). *Motivation and achievement.* Washington, DC: V. H. Winston, 1974.

Ausubel, N. (Ed.). Applied psychology. In *A treasury of Jewish folklore.* New York: Crown, 1948.

Averill, J. R. *Anger and aggression: An essay on emotion.* New York: Springer-Verlag, 1982.

Ayllon, T., and Azrin, N. H. The measurement and

reinforcement of behavior of psychotics. *Journal of Experimental Analysis of Behavior,* 1965, *8,* 357–383.

Balay, J., and Shevrin, H. The Subliminal Psychodynamic Activation method, A critical review. *American Psychologist,* 1988, *43,* 161–174.

Baldwin, A. L. The effect of home environment on nursery school behavior. *Child Development,* 1949, *20,* 49–62.

Baltes, P. B., and Schaie, K. W. *Life-span developmental psychology: Personality and socialization.* New York: Academic Press, 1973.

Bandura, A. Social learning through imitation. In M. R. Jones (Ed.), *Nebraska Symposium on Motivation.* Lincoln: University of Nebraska Press, 1962.

——— . Influence of models' reinforcement contingencies on the acquisition of imitative responses. *Journal of Personality and Social Psychology,* 1965, *1,* 589–595.

——— . *Principles of behavior modification.* New York: Holt, 1969.

——— . Psychotherapy based upon modeling principles. In A. E. Bergin and S. L. Garfield (Eds.), *Handbook of psychotherapy and behavior change.* New York: Wiley, 1971.

——— . *Aggression: A social learning analysis.* Englewood Cliffs, NJ: Prentice-Hall, 1973.

——— . *Social learning theory.* Morristown, NJ: General Learning Press, 1976.

——— . Self-efficacy: Toward a unifying theory of behavioral change. *Psychological Review,* 1977a, *84,* 191–215.

——— . *Social learning theory.* Englewood Cliffs, NJ: Prentice-Hall, 1977b.

——— . The self system in reciprocal determinism. *American Psychologist,* 1978, *33,* 344–358.

——— . *Social foundations of thought and action: A social cognitive theory.* Englewood Cliffs, NJ: Prentice-Hall, 1986.

——— . Human agency in social cognitive theory. *American Psychologist,* 1989, *44,* 1175–1184.

——— et al. *Journal of Consulting and Clinical Psychology,* 1985, *53,* 406–414.

——— , Adams, N. E., and Beyer, J. Cognitive processes mediating behavioral changes. *Journal of Personality and Social Psychology,* 1977, *35,* 125–139.

Bandura, A., Grusec, J. E., and Menlove, F. L. Observational learning as a function of symbolization and incentive set. *Child Development,* 1966, *37,* 499–506.

——— . Vicarious extinction of avoidance behavior. *Journal of Personality and Social Psychology,* 1967, *5,* 16–23.

Bandura, A., and Huston, A. Identification as a process of incidental learning. *Journal of Abnormal and Social Psychology,* 1961, *63,* 311–318.

Bandura, A., and Jeffrey, R. W. Role of symbolic coding and rehearsal processes in observational learning. *Journal of Personality and Social Psychology,* 1973, *26,* 122–130.

Bandura, A., and McDonald, F. J. Influence of social reinforcement and the behavior of models in shaping children's moral judgments. *Journal of Abnormal and Social Psychology,* 1963, *67,* 274–281.

Bandura, A., and Mischel, W. Modification of self-imposed delay of reward through exposure to live and symbolic models. *Journal of Personality and Social Psychology,* 1965, *2,* 698–705.

Bandura, A., O'Leary, A., Taylor, C. B., Gauthier, J., and Gossard, D. Perceived self-efficacy and pain control: Opioid and non-opioid mechanism. *Journal of Personality and Social Psychology,* 1987, *53,* 563–571.

Bandura, A., Reese, L., and Adams, N. E. Microanalysis of action and fear arousal as a function of differential levels of perceived self-efficacy. *Journal of Personality and Social Psychology,* 1982, *43,* 5–21.

Bandura, A., Ross, D., and Ross, S. A. Transmission of aggression through imitation of aggressive models. *Journal of Abnormal Social Psychology,* 1961, *63,* 575–582.

——— . Imitation of film-mediated aggressive models. *Journal of Abnormal and Social Psychology,* 1963, *66,* 3–11.

——— . Vicarious reinforcement and imitative learning. *Journal of Abnormal and Social Psychology,* 1963b, *67,* 601–607.

Bandura, A., and Walters, R. H. *Adolescent aggression.* New York: Ronald, 1959.

——— . *Social learning and personality development.* New York: Holt, 1963.

Bandura, A., and Wood, R. Effect of Perceived Controllability and performance standards on self-regulation of complex decision making. *Journal of*

Personality and Social Psychology, 1989, *56,* 805–814.

Bannister, D., and Fransella, F. *Inquiring man.* Baltimore: Penguin, 1971.

Barber, T. X., and Calverley, D. S. Experimental studies in "hypnotic" behavior: Suggested deafness evaluated by delayed auditory feedback. *British Journal of Psychology,* 1964, *55,* 439–446.

Barclay, A. M. The effect of hostility on physiological fantasy responses. *Journal of Personality,* 1969, *37,* 651–667.

Barglow, P., Vaughn, B. E., and Molitor, N. Effects of maternal absence due to employment on the quality of infant-mother attachment in a low-risk sample. *Child Development,* 1987, *58,* 945–954.

Barlow, D. H. *Anxiety and its disorders.* New York: Guilford, 1988.

Barlow, D. H., Abel, G. G., and Blanchard, E. G. Gender identity change in a transsexual: An exorcism. *Archives of Sexual Behavior,* 1977, *6,* 387–395.

Barker, R. G. Ecology and motivation. In M. R. Jones (Ed.), *Nebraska Symposium on Motivation* (Vol. 8). Lincoln: University of Nebraska Press, 1960.

———. Explorations in ecological psychology. *American Psychologist,* 1965, *20,* 1–13.

———. *Ecological psychology.* Stanford, CA: Stanford University Press, 1968.

———, Dembo, T., and Lewin, K. Frustration and regression. In R. G. Barker, J. S. Kounin, and H. F. Wright (Eds.), *Child behavior and development.* New York: McGraw-Hill, 1943.

Barnett, M. A., Matthews, K. A., and Howard, J. A. Relationships between competitiveness and empathy in 6- and 7-year-olds. *Developmental Psychology,* 1979, *15,* 221–222.

Baron, J. N., and Reiss, P. C. Same time, next year: Aggregate analyses of the mass media on violent behavior. *American Sociological Review,* 1985, *50,* 347–363.

Baron, R. A. The aggression-inhibiting influence of heightened sexual arousal. *Journal of Personality and Social Psychology,* 1974, *30,* 318–322.

———. *Human aggression.* New York: Plenum, 1977.

———. Effects of negative ions on interpersonal attraction: Evidence for intensification. *Journal of Personality and Social Psychology,* 1987, *52,* 547–553.

———, Russell, G. W., and Arms, R. L. Negative ions and behavior: Impact on mood, memory, and aggression among Type A and Type B persons. *Journal of Personality and Social Psychology,* 1985, *48,* 746–754.

Barry, H., Child, I., and Bacon, M. Relation of child training to subsistence economy. *American Anthropologist,* 1959, *61,* 51–63.

Barzun, J. *God's country and mine.* Boston: Atlantic Monthly, 1954.

Bateson, C., Jackson, D. D., Haley, J., and Weakland, J. H. Toward a theory of schizophrenia. *Behavioral Science,* 1956, *1,* 251–264.

Baumeister, R. F. How the self became a problem: A psychological review of historical research. *Journal of Personality and Social Psychology,* 1987, *52,* 163–176.

———. *Identity: Cultural change and the struggle for self.* New York: Oxford University Press, 1986.

———. Suicide as escape from self. *Psychological Review,* 1990, *97,* 90–113.

———. Conceptions of self and identity: A modern retrospective on Allport's view. In K. H. Craik, R. Hogan, and R. N. Wolfe (Eds.), *Fifty years of personality psychology.* New York: Plenum, 177–186, 1993.

Baumrind, D. Parental disciplinary patterns and social competence in children. *Youth and Society,* 1978, *9,* 239–276.

———. Sex differences in moral reasoning: Response to Walker's (1984) conclusion that there are none. *Child Development,* 1986, *57,* 511–521.

———. Current patterns of parental authority. *Developmental Psychology Monographs,* 1971, *1,* 1–103.

———. Socialization and instrumental competence in young children. In W. W. Hartup (Ed.), *The young child: Reviews of research* (Vol. 2). Washington, DC: National Association for the Education of Young Children, 1972.

Beach, F. The descent of instinct. *Psychological Review,* 1955, *62,* 401–410.

Beck, A. T. *Depression. Clinical, experimental, and theoretical aspects.* New York: Hoeber, 1967.

———. *Cognitive therapy and the emotional disorders.* New York: International Universities Press, 1976.

———. Cognitive approaches to stress. In R.

Woolfold and P. Lehrer (Eds.), *Principles and practice of stress management.* New York: Guilford Press, 1984.

————, Rush, A. J., Shaw, B. F., and Emery, G. *Cognitive therapy of depression.* New York: Guilford, 1979.

Becker, W. C. Consequences of different kinds of parental discipline. In M. L. Hoffman and L. W. Hoffman (Eds.), *Review of child development research* (Vol. 1). New York: Russell Sage, 1964.

Bell, P. A., and Byrne, D. Repression-sensitization. In H. London and J. E. Exner, Jr. (Eds.), *Dimensions of personality.* New York: Wiley, 1978.

Bell, R. Q. Developmental psychology. *Annual Review of Psychology,* 1965, *16,* 1–38.

Belsky, J. Early human experience: A family perspective. *Developmental Psychology,* 1981, *17,* 3–23.

————, Garduque, L., and Hrncir, E. Assuming performance, competence and executive capacity in infant play: Relations to home environment and security of attachment. *Developmental Psychology,* 1984, *20,* 406–417.

Belsky, J., and Rovine, M. Temperament and attachment security in the strange situation: An empirical rapprochement. *Child Development,* 1937, *58,* 787–795.

Belsky, J., Sternberg, L. D., and Walker, A. The ecology of day-care. In M. Lamb (Ed.), *Childrearing in nontraditional families.* Hillsdale, NJ: Erlbaum, 1982, 71–116.

Belson, W. A. *Television violence and the adolescent boy.* Teakfied Limited, England: Saxon House, 1978.

Bem, D. J., and Allen, A. On predicting some of the people some of the time: The search for cross-situational consistencies in behavior. *Psychological Review,* 1974, *81,* 505–520.

Bem, D. J., and Funder, D. C. Predicting more of the people more of the time: Assessing the personality of situations. *Psychological Review,* 1978, *85,* 485–501.

Bem, S. L. The measurement of psychological androgyny. *Journal of Consulting and Clinical Psychology,* 1974, *42,* 165–172.

————. Sex-role adaptability: One consequence of psychological androgyny. *Journal of Personality and Social Psychology,* 1975, *31,* 634–653.

Benn, R. K. Factors promoting secure attachment relationships between employed mothers and their sons. *Child Development,* 1986, *57,* 1224–1231.

Bentham, J. (1779) *An introduction to the principles of morals and legislation.* Oxford: Blackwell, 1948.

Berglas, S., and Jones, E. E. Drug choice as a self-handicapping strategy in response to noncontingent success. *Journal of Personality and Social Psychology,* 1978, *36,* 405–417.

Berkowitz, L. The concept of aggressive drive: Some additional considerations. In L. Berkowitz (Ed.), *Advances in experimental social psychology* (Vol. 2). New York: Academic Press, 1965.

————. Some aspects of observed aggression. *Journal of Personality and Social Psychology,* 1965b, *2,* 359–369.

————. External determinants of impulsive aggression. In W. W. Hartup and J. de Wit (Eds.), *Origins of aggression.* The Hague: Mouton, 1978.

————. Aversively stimulated aggression: Some parallels and differences in research with animals and humans. *American Psychologist,* 1983, *38,* 1135–1144.

————. Frustration aggression hypothesis: Examination and reformulation. *Psychological Bulletin,* 1989, *106,* 59–72.

————, and Geen, R. G. Film violence and the cue properties of available targets. *Journal of Personality and Social Psychology,* 1966, *3,* 525–530.

Berkowitz, L., and Le Page, A. Weapons as aggression-eliciting stimuli. *Journal of Personality and Social Psychology,* 1967, *7,* 202–207.

Berlyne, D. *Conflict, arousal, and curiosity.* New York: McGraw-Hill, 1960.

Bernstein, B. Elaborated and restricted codes: Their social origins and some consequences. In J. Gumpery, and D. Hymes (Eds.), *The ethnography of communication* (American Anthropologist Special Publication), 1964, *66,* 55–69.

Bernstein, I. S., and Gordon, T. P. The function of aggression in primate societies. *American Scientist,* 1974, *62,* 304–311.

Berry, D. S., and McArthur, L. Z. Perceiving character in faces: The impact of age-related craniofacial changes in social perception. *Psychological Bulletin,* 1986, *100,* 3–18.

Berry, J., Kim, U., Power, S., Young, M., and

Bujaki, J. Acculturation attitudes in plural societies. *Applied Psychology*, 1989, *38*, 185–205.

Berry, J. W. Independence and conformity in sub-
sistence-level societies. *Journal of Personality and
Social Psychology*, 1967, *7*, 415–418.

———. *Human ecology and cognitive style*. New
York: Russell Sage, 1976.

Berscheid, E., and Walster, E. H. *Interpersonal attraction*. Reading, MA: Addison-Wesley, 1978.

Bettelheim, B. Individual and mass behavior in extreme situations, *Journal of Abnormal and Social
Psychology*, 1943, *38*(4), 417–452.

Bickman, L. The effect of another bystander's ability to help on bystander intervention in an emergency. *Journal of Experimental Social Psychology*,
1971, *7*, 367–379.

Binet, A., and Henri, V. La psychologie individuelle.
Année psychologique, 1895, *2*, 411–463.

Binswanger, L. *Being-in-the-world: Selected papers of
Ludwig Binswanger*. J. Needleman, trans. New
York: Basic Books, 1963.

Birren, J. E., Butler, R. N., Greenhouse, S. W., So-
bolofe, C., and Yarrow, M. R. *Human aging: A
biological and behavioral study*. Bethesda, Md.:
U.S. Public Health Service, 1963.

Blasband, D., and Peplau, L. A. Sexual exclusivity
versus openness in gay male couples. *Archives of
Sexual Behavior*, 1985, *14*(5), 395–412.

Blasi, A. Bridging moral cognition and moral action:
A critical review of the literature. *Psychological
Bulletin*, 1980, *88*, 593–637.

Block, J. *The Q-sort method in personality assessment
and psychiatric research*. Springfield, Ill.: Charles
C Thomas, 1961.

———. *The challenge of response sets: Unconfound-
ing meaning, acquiescence, and social desirability
in the MMPI*. New York: Appleton-Century-
Crofts, 1965.

———. Advancing the psychology of personality:
Paradigmatic shift or improving the quality of re-
search. In D. Magnussen and N. S. Endler (Eds.),
*Personality at the crossroads: Current issues in in-
teractional psychology*. Hillsdale, NJ: Lawrence
Erlbaum, 1977.

———. *A contrarian view of the five-factor approach to personality description*. Unpublished
manuscript, University of California, Berkeley,
1993.

———. Studying personality the long way. In
D. C. Funder, R. D. Peake, C. Tomlinson-Keasey,
and K. Widaman (Eds.), *Studying lives through
time*. Washington, DC: American Psychological
Association, 9–44, 1993.

———, Block, J. H., and Harrington, D. M. Some
misgivings about the matching familiar figures
test as a measure of reflection-impulsivity. *Developmental Psychology*, 1974, *10*, 611–632.

Block, J., Block, J. H., and Keyes, S. Longitudinal
foretelling drug usage in adolescence: Early childhood personality and environmental precursors.
Child Development, 1988, *59*, 336–355.

Block, J. H. Conceptions of sex role: Some cross-cultural and longitudinal perspectives. *American Psychologist*, 1973, *28*, 512–529.

———. Issues, problems and pitfalls in assessing
sex differences. *Merrill-Palmer Quarterly*, 1976,
22, 283–308.

———. Personality development in males and females: The influence of differential socialization.
Paper presented as part of the Master Lecture
Series at the meeting of the American Psychological Association. New York, September, 1979.

———, and Block, J. The role of ego-control and
ego-resiliency in the organization of behavior. In
W. A. Collins (Ed.), *Minnesota Symposium on
Child Development* (Vol. 13). Hillsdale, NJ:
Lawrence Erlbaum, 1980.

Block, J. H., and Martin, B. Predicting the behavior
of children under frustration. *Journal of Abnormal
Social Psychology*, 1955, *51*, 281–285.

Blum, G. S. *A model of the mind*. New York: Wiley,
1961.

Blyth, D. A., Simmons, R. G., Bucraft, R., Felt, D.,
Vancleave, E. F., and Bush, D. M. The effects of
physical development on self-image and satisfaction with body-image for early adolescent males.
In R. G. Simmons (Ed.), *Research in community
and mental health*, *2*, 43–73. Greenwich, Conn.:
JAI Press, 1981.

Booth-Kewley, S., and Friedman, H. S. Psychological predictors of heart disease: A quantitative
review. *Psychological Bulletin*, 1987, *101*, 343–
362.

Borgida, E., and Nisbett, R. The differential impact
of abstract vs. concrete information on decisions.
Journal of Applied Social Psychology, 1977, *7*,
258–271.

Bohart, A. Toward a cognitive theory of catharsis.

Psychotherapy: Theory. Research and Practice, 1980, *17,* 192–201.

Bohart, A. The person-centered therapies. In A. Gurman and S. Messer (Eds.), *Modern psychotherapies.* New York: Guilford, In press.

Bohart, A. Experiencing: The basis of psychotherapy. *Journal of Psychotherapy Integration,* 1993, *3,* 51–67.

Bornstein, M. H. Sensitive periods in development: Structural characteristics and causal interpretations. *Psychological Bulletin,* 1989, *105,* 179–197.

Bornstein, R. F., and Pittman, T. S. (Eds.), *Perception without awareness.* New York: Guilford.

Boss, M. *Psychoanalysis and daseinanalysis.* L. B. Lefebre, trans. New York: Basic Books, 1963.

Botwin, M. D., and Buss, D. M. Structure of act-reported data: Is the five-factor model of personality recaptured? *Journal of Personality and Social Psychology,* 1989, *56,* 988–1001.

Bouchard, T. J., Jr., Lykken, D. T., McGue, M., Segal, N. L., and Tellegen, A. Sources of human psychological differences: The Minnesota Study of Twins Reared Apart. *Science,* 1990, *250,* 223–228

Bowers, K. S. Situationalism in psychology: An analysis and critique. *Psychological Review,* 1973, *80,* 307–336.

Bowlby, J. The nature of the child's tie to his mother. *International Journal of Psycho-Analysis,* 1958, *39,* 350–373.

———. *Attachment and love: Attachment* (Vol. 1). New York: Basic Books, 1969.

Bowman, M. L. Testing individual differences in ancient China. *American Psychologist,* 1989, *44,* 576–578.

Brackbill, Y. *Research and clinical work with children.* Washington, DC: American Psychological Association, 1962.

Bradburn, N. M. Achievement and father dominance in Turkey. *Journal of Abnormal and Social Psychology,* 1963, *67,* 464–468.

Brandstader, J., and Greve, W. The aging self: Stabilizing and protective processes. *Developmental Review,* *14,* 52–80.

Breger, L. *From instinct to identity.* Englewood Cliffs, NJ: Prentice-Hall, 1974.

Brehm, J. W. (Ed.). *A theory of psychological reactance.* New York: Academic Press, 1966.

———. *Responses to loss of freedom: A theory of psychological reactance.* Morristown, NJ: General Learning Press, 1972.

Brehm, S. S., and Brehm, J. W. *Psychological reactance: A theory of freedom and control.* New York: Academic Press, 1981.

Breland, K., and Breland, M. The misbehavior of organisms. *American Psychologist,* 1961, *16,* 681–684.

Brewin, C. R. Depression and causal attributions: What is their relation? *Psychological Bulletin,* 1985, *98,* 297–309.

Briere, J., and Conte, J. Self-reported amnesia for abuse in adults molested as children. *Journal of Traumatic Stress,* 1993, *6,* 21–31.

Briggs, S. P., and Cheek, J. M. On the nature of self-monitoring: Problems with assessment, problems with validity. *Journal of Personality and Social Psychology,* 1988, *54,* 663–678.

Broadhurst, P. L. Analysis of maternal effects in the inheritance of behaviour. *Animal Behaviour,* 1961, *9,* 129–141.

Brodie, F. *Richard Nixon: The shaping of his character.* New York: Norton, 1981.

Brody, N. .5 + or − .5: continuity and change in personal dispositions. In T. F. Heatherton and J. L. Weinberger (Eds.), *Can personality change?* Washington, DC: American Psychological Association, 1994, 59–82.

Bronfenbrenner, U., and Ceci, S. J. Heredity, environment, and the question "how?"—A first approximation. In R. Plomin and G. E. McClearn (Eds.), *Nature, nurture and psychology,* Washington, DC: American Psychological Association, 1993, 313–324.

Brown, J. S. Gradients of approach and avoidance responses and their relation to level of motivation. *Journal of Comparative and Physiological Psychology,* 1948, *41,* 450–465.

———. Principles of intrapersonal conflict. *Journal of Conflict Resolution,* 1957, *1,* 135–154.

Brown, L. M., and Gilligan, C. *Meeting at the crossroads.* Cambridge, MA: Harvard University Press. 1992.

Brown, P., and Elliott, R. Control of aggression in a nursery school class. *Journal of Experimental Child Psychology,* 1965, *2,* 103–107.

Browning, E. B. *A selection from the poetry of Elizabeth Barrett Browning.* London: Smith, Elder & Co, 1888.

Brunner, J. S. A cognitive theory of personality. *Contemporary Psychology,* 1956, *1,* 355–357.

————, and **Tagiuri, R.** The perception of people. In G. Lindzey (Ed.), *Handbook of social psychology.* Reading, MA: Addison-Wesley, 1954.

Bryan, J. H., and Test, M. A. Models and helping: Naturalistic studies in aiding behavior. *Journal of Personality and Social Psychology,* 1967, *6,* 400–407.

Bryan, J. H., and Walbek, N. Preaching and practicing generosity: Children's actions and reactions. *Child Development,* 1970, *41,* 329–353.

Bühler, C. Genetic aspects of the self. *Annals of the New York Academy of Science,* 1962, *96,* 730–764.

Burchinal, M., Lee, M., and Ramey, C. Type of day care and pre-school intellectual development in disadvantaged children. *Child Development,* 1989, *60,* 128–137.

Burns, M. O., and Seligman, M. E. P. Explanatory style across the life span: Evidence for stability over 52 years. *Journal of Personality and Social Psychology,* 1989, *56,* 471–477.

Burton, R. V. Generality of honesty reconsidered. *Psychological Review,* 1963, *70,* 481–499.

Buss, A. H., Plomin, R., and Willerman, L. The inheritance of temperaments. *Journal of Personality,* 1973, *41,* 513–524.

Buss, D. M., and Barnes, M. Preferences in human mate selection. *Journal of Personality and Social Psychology,* 1986, *50,* 559–570.

Butcher, J. N. (Ed.) *New developments in the use of the MMPI.* Minneapolis: University of Minnesota Press, 1979.

————, and **Tellegen, A.** Common methodological problems in MMPI research. *Journal of Consulting and Clinical Psychology,* 1978, *46,* 620–628.

Butler, J. M., and Haigh, G. V. Changes in the relation between self-concepts and ideal concepts consequent upon client-centered counseling. In C. R. Rogers and R. F. Dymond (Eds.), *Psychotherapy and personality change.* Chicago: University of Chicago Press, 1954.

Byrne, D. The repression-sensitization scale: Rationale, reliability, and validity. *Journal of Personality,* 1961, *29,* 334–349.

Cairns, R. B. *Antecedents of social reinforcer effectiveness.* Unpublished manuscript, Indiana University, 1962.

————. Attachment and dependency: A psychobiological and social learning synthesis. In J. Gewirtz (Ed.), *Attachment and dependency.* New York: Winston, 1972.

————. Social international methods: An introduction. In R. B. Cairns (Ed.), *The analysis of social interaction: Methods, issues and illustrations.* Hillsdale, NJ: Erlbaum, 1979.

Caldwell, W. V. *LSD psychotherapy: An exploration of psychedelic and psycholytic therapy.* New York: Grove, 1968.

Cameron, P. Stereotypes about generational fun and happiness versus self-appraised fun and happiness. *The Gerontologist,* 1972, *12,* 120–123.

Campbell, D. E., and Beets, J. L. Lunacy and the moon. *Psychological Bulletin,* 1978, *85,* 1123–1129.

Campbell, J. (Ed.). *The portable Jung* (R. F. C. Hull, trans.). New York: Viking, 1971. (Other editions Baltimore: Penguin, 1976, 1978.)

Campbell, J. D. *Clarity of the self-concept.* Invited address at the American Psychological Association Convention, Toronto, Canada. August 1993.

Campbell, J. P. *Handbook for the Strong-Campbell Interest Inventory.* Stanford, CA: Stanford University Press, 1974.

————. Psychometric theory. In M. D. Dunnette (Ed.), *Handbook of industrial and organizational psychology.* Chicago: Rand McNally, 1976.

Cann, D. R., and Donderi, D. C. Jungian personality typology and the recall of everyday and archetypal dreams. *Journal of Personality and Social Psychology,* 1986, *50,* 1021–1030.

Cantor, N. From thought to behavior: "Having" and "doing" in the study of personality and cognition. *American Psychologist,* 1990, *45,* 735–750.

Cantor, N. Life task problem solving: Situational affordances and personal needs. *Personality and Social Psychology Bulletin,* 1994, *20,* 235–243.

————, and **Kihlstrom, J.** *Personality and social intelligence.* Englewood Cliffs, NJ: Prentice-Hall, 1986.

Cantor, N., and Zirkel, S. Personality, cognition, and purposive behavior. In L. A. Pervin (Ed.), *Handbook of personality.* New York: Guilford, 135–164, 1990.

Caprara, G. V., Passerini, S., Pastorelli, C., Renzi, P., and Zelli, A. Instigating and measuring interpersonal aggression and hostility: A methodological contribution. *Aggressive Behavior*, 1986, *12*, 237–248.

Carey, G., Goldsmith, H. H., Tellegen, A., and Gottesman, I. I. Genetics and personality inventories: The limits of replication with twin data. *Behavior Genetics*, 1978, *8*, 299–313.

Carkhuff, R. R. *Helping and human relations. Vol. 1: Selection and training. Vol. 11: Practice and research.* New York: Holt, 1969.

———, and Berenson, B. G. *Beyond counseling and therapy.* New York: Holt, 1967.

Carlsmith, L. Effect of early father-absence on scholastic aptitude. *Harvard Educational Review*, 1964, *34*, 3–21.

Carlson, L., and Carlson, A. Affect and psychological magnification: Derivations from Tomkins' script theory. *Journal of Personality*, 1984, *52*, 36–45.

Carlson, M., Marcus-Newhall, A., and Miller, N. Evidence for a general construct of aggression. *Personality and Social Psychology Bulletin*, 1989, *15*, 377–389.

Carter, J. E., and Heath, B. Somatotype methodology and kinesiology research. *Kinesiology Review*, 1971, *2*, 10.

Carver, C. S. How should multifaceted personality constructs be tested? Issues illustrated by self-monitoring, attributional style, and hardiness. *Journal of Personality and Social Psychology*, 1989, *56*, 577–585.

———, Blaney, P. H., and Scheier, M. F. Focus of attention, chronic expectancy and response to a feared stimulus. *Journal of Personality and Social Psychology*, 1979, *37*, 1186–1195 (a).

———. Reassertion and giving up: The interactive role of self-directed attention and outcome expectancy. *Journal of Personality and Social Psychology*, 1979, *37*, 1859–1870 (b).

Carver, C. S., and Scheier, M. F. *Attention and self-regulation: A control theory approach to human behavior.* New York: Springer–Verlag, 1981.

———. Control theory: A useful conceptual framework for personality — social, clinical, and health psychology. *Psychological Bulletin*, 1982, *92*, 111–135.

Caspi, A. Why maladaptive behaviors persist: Sources of continuity and change across the life course. In D. C. Funder, R. D. Peake, C. Tomlinson-Keasey, and K. Widaman (Eds.), *Studying*

lives through time. Washington, DC: American Psychological Association, 343–376, 1993.

———, and Bem, D. J. Personality continuity and change across the life course. In L. Pervin (Ed.), *Handbook of personality.* New York: Guilford, 549–575, 1990.

———, and Elder, G. H., Jr. Continuities and consequences of interactional styles across the life course. *Journal of Personality*, 1989, *57*, 375–406.

Cattell, R. B. *Manual for forms A and B: Sixteen Personality Factor Questionnaire.* Champaign, Ill.: Institute for Personality and Ability Testing, 1949.

———. *Personality and motivation, structure and measurement.* Yonkers, NY: World Book, 1957.

———. *The scientific analysis of personality.* Baltimore: Penguin, 1965.

———, Eber, H. W., and Tatsuoka, M. M. *Handbook for the Sixteen Personality Factor Questionnaire (16 PF).* Champaign, Ill.: Institute for Personality and Ability Testing, 1970.

Cervantes, R. C., and Castro, F. G. Stress, coping, and Mexican American mental health: A systematic review. *Hispanic Journal of Behavioral Sciences*, 1985, *7*, 1–73.

Chaplin, W. F., and Goldberg, L. R. A failure to replicate the Bem and Allen study of individual differences in cross-situational consistency. *Journal of Personality and Social Psychology*, 1985, *47*, 1074–1090.

———, John, D. P., and Goldberg, L. R. Conceptions of traits and states: Dimensional attributes with ideals as prototypes. *Journal of Personality and Social Psychology*, 1988, *54*, 541–557.

Charry, J. M., and Hawkinshire, F. B. W. Effects of atmospheric electricity on some substrates of disordered social behavior. *Journal of Personality and Social Psychology*, 1981, *41*, 185–197.

Chase-Lansdale, P. L., and Owen, M. T. Maternal employment in a family context: Effects on infant-mother and infant-father attachments. *Child Development*, 1987, *58*, 1505–1512.

Chatz, T. L. Recognizing and treating dangerous sex offenders. *Journal of Offender Therapy*, 1972, *16*, 109–115.

Chazan, S. E. Development of object permanence as a correlate of dimensions of maternal care. *Developmental Psychology*, 1981, *17(1)*, 79–81.

Cheek, J. M. Aggregation, moderator variables, and the validity of personality tests: A peer-rating study. *Journal of Personality and Social Psychology,* 1982, *43,* 1254–1269.

Chess, S., Thomas, A., and Birch, H. G. *Your child is a person.* New York: Viking, 1965.

Chess, S., and Thomas, A. *Origins and evolution of behavior disorders.* New York: Brunner/Mazel, 1984.

Child, I. L. Personality in culture. In E. F. Borgatta and W. W. Lambert (Eds.), *Handbook of personality theory and research.* Chicago: Rand McNally, 1968.

———, and Waterhouse, I. K. Frustration and the quality of performance: III. An experimental study. *Journal of Personality,* 1953, *21,* 298–311.

Chipuer, H. M., Plomin, R., Pederson, N. L., McClearn, G. E., and Nesselrode, J. R. Genetic influence on family environment: The role of personality. *Developmental Psychology,* 1993, *29,* 110–118.

Christophersen, E. R. Injury control. *American Psychologist,* 1989, *44,* 237–241.

Chwalisz, K., Diener, E., and Gallagher, D. Autonomic arousal feedback and emotional experience: Evidence from the spinal cord injured. *Journal of Personality and Social Psychology,* 1988, *54,* 820–828.

Clarke-Stewart, A. *Daycare.* Cambridge, MA: Harvard University Press, 1982.

Clemes, S. R. Repression and hypnotic amnesia. *Journal of Abnormal and Social Psychology,* 1964, *69,* 62–69.

Clore, G. L., Ortony, A., and Foss, M. A. The psychological foundations of the affective lexicon. *Journal of Personality and Social Psychology,* 1987, *53,* 751–766.

Coe, W. C. The credibility of posthypnotic amnesia: A contextualist's view. *International Journal of Classical and Experimental Hypnosis,* 1978, *26,* 673–681.

Cofer, C. N., and Appley, M. H. *Motivation: Theory and research.* New York: Wiley, 1964.

Cohen, D. B. Neuroticism and dreaming sleep: A case for interactionism in personality of research. *British Journal of Social and Clinical Psychology,* 1977, *16,* 153–163.

Cohen, K. N., and Clark, J. A. Transitional object attachments in early childhood and personality characteristics in later life. *Personality and Social Psychology,* 1984, *46,* 106–111.

Cohen, S., and Wills, T. A. Stress, social support, and the buffering hypothesis. *Psychological Bulletin,* 1985, *98,* 310–357.

Colgan, S. M., Faragher, E. B., and Whorwell, P. J. Controlled trial of hypnotherapy in relapse prevention of duodenal ulceration. *Lancet,* 1988, *11,* 1299–1300.

Condry, J. Enemies of exploration: Self-initiated versus other-initiated learning. *Journal of Personality and Social Psychology,* 1977, *35,* 459–477.

Conger, J. J. Hostages to Fortune: Youth, values and the public interest. *American Psychologist,* 1988, *43,* 291–300.

Cooper, L. M. Hypnotic amnesia. In E. Fromm and R. E. Shor (Eds.), *Hypnosis: Research developments and perspectives.* Chicago: Aldine-Atherton, 1972.

Cooper, R. M., and Zubek, J. P. Effects of enriched and restricted early environments on the learning ability of bright and dull rats. *Canadian Journal of Psychology,* 1958, *12,* 159–164.

Coopersmith, H. S. *The antecedents of self-esteem.* San Francisco: Freeman, 1967.

Condon, T. J., and Allen, G. J. Role of psychoanalytic merging fantasies in systematic desensitization: A rigorous methodological examination. *Journal of Abnormal Psychology,* 1980, *89,* 437–443.

Costa, P. T., and McCrae, R. R. Age differences in personality structures revisited: Studies in validity, stability and change. *International Journal of Aging and Human Development,* 1977, *8,* 261–276.

Costa, P. T., and Widiger, T. A. Introduction. In P. T. Costa and T. A. Widiger (Eds.), *Personality Disorders and the five-factor model of personality.* Washington, D.C.: American Psychological Association, 1–12, 1994.

Covington, M., and Omelich, C. Effort: The double-edged sword in school achievement. *Journal of Educational Psychology,* 1979, *71,* 169–182.

Covington, M. V., and Beery, R. G. *Self-worth and school learning.* New York: Holt, 1976.

Cowan, G., and Avants, S. K. Children's influence strategies: Structure, sex differences, and bilateral mother-child influences. *Child Development,* 1988, *59,* 1303–1313.

Cowan, P. A. *Piaget: With feeling.* New York: Holt, Rinehart, & Winston, 1978.

Crandall, J. E. Adler's concept of social interest:

Theory, measurement, and implications for adjustment. *Journal of Personality and Social Psychology,* 1980, *39,* 481–495.

Crawford, C., Smith, M., and Krebs, D. (Eds.) *Sociobiology and psychology: Ideas, issues and applications.* Hillsdale, NJ: Erlbaum, 1987.

Critelli, J. W., and Dupre, K. M. Self-disclosure and romantic attraction. *Journal of Social Psychology,* 1978, *106*(1), 127–128.

Crits-Christoph, P., and Singer, J. L. An experimental investigation of the use of positive imagery in the treatment of phobias. *Imagination, Cognition, and Personality,* 1983–84, *3,* 305–323.

Cronbach, L. J. Beyond the two disciplines of scientific psychology. *American Psychologist,* 1975, *30,* 116–127.

Csikszentmihalyi, M. *Flow.* New York: Harper & Row, 1990.

Csikszentmihalyi, M., and LeFevre, J. Optimal experience in work and leisure. *Journal of Personality and Social Psychology,* 1989, *56,* 815–822.

Cumming, E., and Henry, W. H. *Growing old.* New York: Basic Books, 1961.

Cunningham, M. R. What do you do when you're happy and blue? *Motivation and Emotion,* 1988, *12,* 309–331.

Cutrona, C. E., Russell, D., and Jones, R. D. Cross-situational consistency in causal attributions: Does attributional style exist? *Journal of Personality and Social Psychology,* 1985, *47,* 1043–1058.

Dabbs, J. M., and Morris, R. Testosterone, social class, and antisocial behavior in a sample of 4,462 men. *Psychological Science,* 1990, *1,* 209–211.

Dahlstrom, W. G. Recurrent issues in the development of the MMPI. In J. N. Butcher (Ed.), *MMPI: Research developments and clinical applications.* New York: McGraw-Hill, 1969.

———, and Welsh, G. S. *An MMPI handbook: A guide to use in clinical practice and research.* Minneapolis: University of Minnesota Press, 1960.

———, and Dahlstrom, L. E. *An MMPI handbook: Clinical interpretation* (Vol. I) (Rev. ed.). Minneapolis: University of Minnesota Press, 1972.

———. *An MMPI handbook: Research applications* (Vol. II) (Rev. ed.). Minneapolis: University of Minnesota Press, 1975.

Darwin, C. *On the origin of species by means of natural selection or the preservation of favoured races in the struggle for life.* New York: Appleton, 1869.

———. (1872) *The expression of the emotions in man and animals.* Chicago: University of Chicago Press, 1965.

———. *The descent of man, and selection in relation to sex.* New York: Appleton, 1873.

Datan, N., Rodeheaver, D., and Hughes, F. Adult development and aging. *Annual Review of Psychology,* 1987, *38,* 1, 53–80.

Davis, P. J., and Schwartz, G. Repression and the inaccessibility of affective memories. *Journal of Personality and Social Psychology,* 1987, *52,* 155–162.

Davison, G. C. Elimination of a sadistic fantasy by a client-controlled counter-conditioning technique: A case study. *Journal of Abnormal Psychology,* 1968, *73,* 84–89.

Davitz, J. The effects of previous training on post-frustration behavior. *Journal of Abnormal Social Psychology,* 1952, *47,* 309–315.

DeAngelis, T. Despite rise of violence by youth, solutions exist. *APA Monitor,* October 1993, *24,* 40.

de Charms, R. *Personal causation.* New York: Academic Press, 1968.

———. Personal causation training in the schools. *Journal of Applied Social Psychology,* 1972, *2,* 95–113.

———. *Enhancing motivation: Change in the classroom.* New York: Irvington, 1976.

———, and Moeller, G. H. Values expressed in American children's readers: 1800–1950. *Journal of Abnormal and Social Psychology,* 1962, *64,* 136–142.

Deci, E. L. *Intrinsic motivation.* New York: Plenum, 1975.

DeLongis, A., Folkman, S., and Lazarus, R. S. The impact of daily stress on health and mood: Psychological and social resources as mediators. *Journal of Personality and Social Psychology,* 1988, *54,* 486–495.

Dement, W. C. The effect of dream deprivation. *Science,* 1960, *131,* 1705–1707.

———. An essay on dreams: The role of physiology in understanding their nature. In F. Barron (Ed.), *New directions in psychology* (Vol. 2). New York: Holt, 1965.

———, and Kleitman, N. The relation of eye movements during sleep to dream activity: An objective method for the study of dreaming. *Journal of Experimental Psychology,* 1957, *53,* 339–346.

Dengerink, H. A., O'Leary, M. R., and Kasner, K. H. Individual differences in aggression responses to attack: Internal-external locus of control and field dependence-independence. *Journal of Research in Personality,* 1975, *9,* 191–199.

DeVore, I. (Ed.). *Primate behavior: Field studies of monkeys and apes.* New York: Holt, 1965.

DiCaprio, N. S. *Personality theories: Guides to living.* Philadelphia: Saunders, 1974.

DiCara, L. V. Learning in the autonomic nervous system. *Scientific American,* January 1970, 30–39.

Dicks-Mireaux, M. J. Extraversion-introversion in experimental psychology: Examples of experimental evidence and their theoretical implications. *Journal of Analytical Psychology.* 1964, *9,* 117–128.

Digman, J. M., and Inouye, J. Further specification of the five robust factors of personality. *Journal of Personality and Social Psychology,* 1986, *50,* 116–123.

Dixon, L. K., and Johnson, R. C. *The roots of individuality: A survey of human behavior genetics.* Monterey, CA: Brooks/Cole, 1980.

Dixon, N. F. *Subliminal perception: The nature of a controversy.* London: McGraw-Hill, 1971.

Dodge, K. A. Social cognition and children's aggressive behavior. *Child Development,* 1980, *51,* 162–170.

————, **and Coie, J. D.** Social-Information processing factors in reactive and proactive aggression in children's peer groups. *Journal of Personality and Social Psychology,* 1987, *53,* 1146–1158.

Dodge, K. A., and Crick, N. R. Social information-processing bases of aggressive behavior in children. *Personality and Social Psychology Bulletin,* 1990, *16,* 8–22.

Dodge, K. A., and Frame, C. L. Social cognitive biases and deficits in aggressive boys. *Child Development,* 1982, *53,* 620–635.

Dollard, J., Doob, L. W., Miller, N. E., Mowrer, O. H., and Sears, R. R. *Frustration and aggression.* New Haven: Yale University Press, 1939.

Dollard, J., and Miller, N. E. *Personality and psychotherapy.* New York: McGraw-Hill, 1950.

Donnerstein, E. Aggressive erotica and violence toward women. *Journal of Personality and Social Psychology,* 1980, *39,* 269–277.

————, **and Wilson, D. W.** The effects of noise and perceived control upon ongoing and subsequent aggressive behavior. *Journal of Personality and Social Psychology,* 1976, *34,* 774–781.

Doob, A. N., and Wood, L. Catharsis and aggression: The effects of annoyance and retaliation on aggressive behavior. *Journal of Personality and Social Psychology,* 1972, *22,* 156–162.

Dornbusch, S., Ritter, P., Liederman, P., Roberts, D., and Fraleight, M. The relation of parenting style to adolescent school performance. *Child Development,* 1987, *58,* 1244–1257.

Driscoll, R., Davis, K. E., and Lipetz, M. E. Parental interference and romantic love: The Romeo and Juliet effect. *Journal of Personality and Social Psychology,* 1972, *24,* 1–10.

Dudek, S. Z., and Hall, W. B. Personality consistency: Eminent architects 25 years later. *Creativity Research Journal,* 1991, *4,* 213–232.

Dulany, D. E., Jr. Avoidance learning of perceptual defense and vigilance. *Journal of Abnormal and Social Psychology,* 1957, *55,* 333–338.

Dunnette, M. D. Aptitudes, abilities, and skills. In M. D. Dunnette (Ed.), *Handbook of industrial and organizational psychology.* Chicago: Rand McNally, 1976.

————, **and Borman, W. C.** Personnel selection and classification systems. *Annual Review of Psychology,* 1979, *30,* 477–525.

Dutton, D. G., and Aron, A. P. Some evidence for heightened sexual attraction under conditions of high anxiety. *Journal of Personality and Social Psychology,* 1974, *30,* 510–517.

Duval, S., and Wicklund, R. A. *A theory of objective self-awareness.* New York: Academic Press, 1972.

————. Effects of objective self-awareness on attribution of causality. *Journal of Personality and Social Psychology,* 1973, *9,* 17–31.

Dweck, C. S. The role of expectation and attribution in the alleviation of learned helplessness. *Journal of Personality and Social Psychology,* 1975, *31,* 674–685.

Dweck, C. S., and Leggett, E. L. A social-cognitive approach to motivation and personality. *Psychological Review,* 1988, *95,* 256–273.

Eagle, M. N. *Recent developments in psychoanalysis: A critical evaluation.* New York: McGraw-Hill, 1984.

Earley, P. C. Social loafing and collectivism: A comparison of the United States and the People's Republic of China. *Administrative Science Quarterly*, 1989, *34*, 565–581.

Eaton, W. O., and Enns, L. R. Sex differences in human motor activity level. *Psychological Bulletin*, 1986, *100*, 19–28.

Eaton, W. O., and Yu, A. P. Are sex differences in child motor activity level a function of sex differences in maturational status? *Child Development*, 1989, *60*, 1005–1011.

Ebel, R. L. Comments on some problems of employment testing. *Personnel Psychology*, 1977, *30*, 55–63.

Eckerman, C. O., and Rheingold, H. L. Infants' exploratory responses to toys and people. *Developmental Psychology*, 1974, *10*, 255–259.

Edney, J. J. Territoriality and control: A field experiment. *Journal of Personality and Social Psychology*, 1975, *31*, 1108–1115.

Edwards, A. L. *Manual for the Edwards Personal Preference Schedule*. New York: Psychological Corporation, 1954.

——— . *The social desirability variable in personality research*. New York: Dryden, 1957.

——— . *Edwards Personal Preference Schedule*. New York: Psychological Corporation, 1959.

——— . The social desirability hypothesis: Theoretical implications for personality measurement. In S. Messick and J. Ross (Eds.), *Measurement in personality and cognition*. New York: Wiley, 1962.

——— . Social desirability and performance on the MMPI. *Psychometrika*, 1964, *29*, 295–308.

Egeland, J. A., Gerhard, D. S., Pauls, D. L., Sussex, J. N., Kidd, K. K., Allen, C. R., Hostetter, A. M., and Housman, D. E. Bipolar affective disorders linked to DNA markers on chromosome 11. *Nature*, 1987, *325*, 783–787.

Eibl-Eibesfeldt, I. *Ethology: The biology of behavior*. New York: Holt, 1970.

——— . *Love and Hate*. New York: Schocken, 1974.

——— . Evolution of destructive aggression. *Aggressive Behavior*, 1977, *3*, 127–144.

Eisenberg, N., and Lennon, R. Sex differences in empathy and related capacities. *Psychological Bulletin*, 1983, *94*, 100–131.

Eisenberg, N., Shell, R., Pasternak, J., Lennon, R., Beller, R., and Mathy, R. M. Prosocial development in middle childhood: A longitudinal study. *Developmental Psychology*, 1987, *23*, 712–718.

Eisenberg, W., and Miller, P. A. The relation of empathy to prosocial and related behaviors. *Psychological Bulletin*, 1987, *101*, 91–119.

Eisenberg-Berg, N., and Geisheker, E. Content of preachings and power of the model preacher: The effect on children's generosity. *Developmental Psychology*, 1979, *15*, 168–175.

Ekman, P. Facial expression and emotion. *American Psychologist*, 1993, *48*, 384–392.

Ekman, P., and Friesen, W. V. *Unmasking the face*. Englewood Cliffs, NJ: Prentice-Hall, 1975.

——— , O'Sullivan, M., Chan, A., Tarlatzis, I. D., Heider, K., Krause, R., LeCompte, W. A., Pitcairn, T., Ricci-Bitti, P. E., Scherer, K., Tomita, M., and Tzavaras, A. Universals and cultural differences in the judgments of facial expressions of emotion. *Journal of Personality and Social Psychology*, 1987, *53*, 712–717.

Elder, G. Jr. Military times and turning points in men's lives. *Developmental Psychology*, 1986, *22*, 233–245.

Elkind, D. *Children and adolescents: Interpretive essay on Jean Piaget*. New York: Oxford University Press, 1970.

——— . *The child and society*. New York: Oxford University Press, 1979.

Ellis, A. The validity of personality questionnaires. *Psychological Bulletin*, 1946, *43*, 385–440.

——— . *Reason and emotion in psychotherapy*. New York: Lyle Stuart, 1967.

Emmerich, W., Cocking, R. R., and Sigel, I. E. Relationships between cognitive and social functioning in preschool children. *Developmental Psychology*, 1979, *15*, 495–504.

Emmons, R. A. The personal striving approach to personality. In L. A. Pervin (Ed.), *Goal concepts in personality and social psychology*. Hillsdale, NJ: Lawrence Erlbaum, 87–121, 1989.

——— , and King, L. A. Conflict among personal strivings: Immediate and long-term implications for psychological and physical well-being. *Journal of Personality and Social Psychology*, 1988, *54*, 1040–1048.

Endler, N. S. The person versus the situation—a pseudo issue? A response to Alker. *Journal of Personality*, 1973, *41*, 287–303.

——— , and Hunt, J. McV. S-R inventories of hostility and comparisons of the proportions of variance from persons, responses, and situations for hostility and anxiousness. *Journal of Personality and Social Psychology,* 1968, *9,* 309–315.

Endler, N. S., and Magnussen, D. *Interactional psychology and personality.* Washington, DC: Hemisphere, 1976.

Entwisle, D. R. To dispel fantasies about fantasy-based measures of achievement motivation. *Psychological Bulletin,* 1972, *77,* 377–391.

Epstein, L. Psychophysiological measurement in assessment. In M. Hersen and A. S. Bellack (Eds.), *Behavioral Assessment.* New York: Pergamon, 1976.

Epstein, S. The self-concept revisited or a theory of a theory. *American Psychologist,* 1973, *28,* 405–416.

————. Traits are alive and well. In D. Magnusson and N. S. Endler (Eds.), *Personality at the crossroads.* New York: Wiley, 1977.

————. The stability of behavior: I. On predicting most of the people much of the time. *Journal of Personality and Social Psychology,* 1979, *37,* 1097–1126.

————. The self-concept: A review and the proposal of an integrated theory of personality. In E. Staub (Ed.), *Personality: Basic issues and current research.* Englewood Cliffs, NJ: Prentice-Hall, 1980.

————. The stability of behavior: II. Implications for psychological research. *American Psychologist,* 1980, *35,* 790–866.

Erdelyi, M. H. A new look at the new look: Perceptual defense and vigilance. *Psychological Review,* 1974, *81,* 1–25.

————. Psychodynamics and the unconscious. *American Psychologist,* 1992, *47,* 784–787.

Erhardt, A. A. A Transactional perspective on the development of gender differences. In J. M. Reinisch, L. A. Rosenbaum, and S. A. Sanders (Eds.), *Masculinity/Femininity: Basic Perspectives.* New York: Oxford University Press, 1987.

Ericksen, C. W. Unconscious processes. In M. R. Jones (Ed.), *Nebraska Symposium on Motivation.* Lincoln: University of Nebraska Press, 1958.

————. Discrimination and learning without awareness: A methodological survey and evaluation. *Psychological Review,* 1960, *67,* 279–300.

Erikson, E. H. *Childhood and society.* New York: Norton, 1950.

————. *Young man Luther.* New York: W. W. Norton, 1958.

————. *Identity and the life cycle.* (Psychological Issues Monograph 1, Vol. 1, No. 1). New York: International Universities Press, 1959.

————. *Insight and responsibility.* New York: Norton, 1964.

————. The concept of identity in race relations: Notes and queries. *Daedalus,* 1966, *95,* 145–171.

————. *Identity: Youth and crisis.* New York: Norton, 1968.

————. *Ghandi's truth on the origins of militant nonviolence.* New York: W. W. Norton, 1969.

————. *Toys and reasons.* New York: Norton, 1976.

Escalona, S. K. *The roots of individuals: Normal patterns of development in infancy.* Chicago: Aldine, 1968.

Evans, F. J., and Kihlstrom, J. F. Posthypnotic amnesia as disrupted retrieval. *Journal of Abnormal Psychology,* 1973, *82,* 317–332.

Evans, R. B., and Koelseh, W. A. Psychoanalysis arrives in America. The 1909 Psychology Conference at Clark University. *American Psychologist,* 1985, *40,* 942–948.

Exner, J. E. *The Rorschach: A comprehensive system.* New York: Wiley, 1974.

————. Projective techniques. In I. B. Weiner (Ed.), *Clinical methods in psychology.* New York: Wiley, 1976.

Eysenck, H. J. *Dimensions of personality.* London: Routledge, 1947.

————. *The structure of human personality.* London: Methuen, 1952.

————. Cortical inhibition, figured after effect and theory of personality. *Journal of Abnormal and Social Psychology,* 1955, *51,* 94–106.

————. *The biological basis of personality.* Springfield, Ill.: Charles C Thomas, 1967.

————, and Eysenck, S. B. G. *The manual of the Eysenck personality inventory.* San Diego: Educational and Industrial Testing Service, 1964.

————, and Rachman, S. *The causes and cures of neurosis: An introduction to modern behavior therapy based on learning theory and the principles of conditioning.* San Diego: Knapp, 1965.

Fagot, B. I., and Leinbach, M. D. The young child's gender schema: Environmental input, internal organization. *Child Development,* 1989, *60(3),* 663–672.

Fagot, B. I., Leinbach, M. D., and Hagan, R. Gender

labeling and the adoption of sex-typed behaviors. *Developmental Psychology,* 1986, *22,* 440–443.

Fairbairn, W. R. D. *Psycho-analytic studies of the personality.* New York: Basic Books, 1952.

Faraone, S. V., and Tsuang, M. T. Quantitative models of the genetic transmission of schizophrenia. *Psychological Bulletin,* 1985, *98,* 41–66.

Feather, N. T. The relationship of expectation of success to *n* Achievement and test anxiety. *Journal of Personality and Social Psychology,* 1965, *1,* 118–126.

Feingold, A. Cognitive gender differences are disappearing. *American Psychologist,* 1988, *43,* 95–103.

Feld, S. Longitudinal study of the origins of achievement strivings. *Journal of Personality and Social Psychology,* 1967, *7,* 408–414.

Feningstein, A. On the nature of public and private self-consciousness. *Journal of Personality,* 1987, *55,* 543–554.

Ferguson, T. J., and Rule, B. G. An attributional perspective on anger and aggression. In R. G. Geen and E. I. Donnerstein (Eds.), *Aggression: Theoretical and Empirical Reviews. Vol. 1.* New York: Academic Press, 1983, 41–74.

Feshbach, N. D. Sex differences in children's modes of aggressive responses toward outsiders. *Merrill-Palmer Quarterly,* 1969, *15,* 249–258.

————. The relationship of child rearing factors to children's aggression, empathy, and related positive and negative social behaviors. In J. de Wit and W. W. Hartup (Eds.), *Determinants and origins of aggressive behavior.* The Hague: Mouton, 1975.

————. Studies on empathic behavior in children. In B. A. Maher (Ed.), *Progress in experimental personality research.* New York: Academic Press, 1978.

Feshbach, N. D. Cross-cultural studies of teaching styles in four-year-olds and their mothers. In Pick, A. D. (Ed.), *Minnesota Symposia on Child Psychology: VII.* Minneapolis, MN: U. Minnesota Press, 1973.

————. Empathy training: A field study in affective education. In S. Feshbach and A. Fraczek (Eds.), *Aggression and behavior change: Biological and social processes.* New York: Praeger, 1979.

————, and Feshbach, S. The relationship between empathy and aggression in two age groups. *Developmental Psychology,* 1969, *1*(2), 102–107.

————, Feshback, S., Fauvre, M., and Ballard-Campbell, M. *Learning to care.* Glenview: Scott, Foresman, 1983.

Feshbach, N. D., and Roe, L. Empathy in six- and seven-year-olds. *Child Development,* 1968, *39,* 133–145.

Feshbach, S. The catharsis hypothesis and some consequences of interaction with aggressive and neutral play objects. *Journal of Personality,* 1956, *24,* 449–462.

————. The function of aggression and the regulation of aggressive drive. *Psychological Review,* 1964, *71,* 257–272.

————. Aggression. In P. H. Mussen (Ed.), *Carmichael's manual of child psychology.* New York: Wiley, 1970.

————. Effects of reality versus fantasy in filmed violence. In J. P. Murray, E. A. Rubinstein, and G. A. Comstock (Eds.), *Television and social behavior: Television and social learning* (Vol. II). Washington, DC: U.S. Government Printing Office, 1972.

————. The development and regulation of aggression: Some research gaps and a proposed cognitive approach. In W. W. Hartup and J. de Wit (Eds.), *Determinants and origins of aggressive behavior.* The Hague: Mouton, 1974.

————. The environment of personality. *American Psychologist,* 1978, *33,* 447–455.

————. Child abuse and the dynamics of human aggression on violence. In G. Gerbner, E. Zigler, and C. Ross (Eds.), *Child abuse.* New York: Oxford University Press, 1980.

————, Adelman, H., and Fuller, W. The prediction of reading and related academic problems. *Journal of Educational Psychology,* 1977, *69,* 299–308.

Feshbach, S., and Feshbach, N. D. The influence of the stimulus object upon the complementary and supplementary projection of fear. *Journal of Abnormal and Social Psychology,* 1963, *66,* 498–502.

Feshbach, S., and Singer, R. *Television and aggression.* San Francisco: Jossey-Bass, 1971.

Feshbach, S., Stiles, W., and Bitter, E. The reinforcing effect of witnessing aggression. *Journal of Experimental Research in Personality,* 1967, *2,* 133–139.

Festinger, L. *A Theory of cognitive dissonance.* Stanford, CA: Stanford University Press, 1957.

Field, L. H., and Williams, M. The hormonal treatment of sexual offenders. *Medicine, Science, and the Law,* 1970, 27–34.

Fillenbaum, G. B. An examination of the vulnerability hypothesis. *International Journal of Aging and Human Development, 1977, 8,* 155–160.

Fisher, S. Projective methodologies. *Annual Review of Psychology,* 1967, *18,* 165–190.

———, and Cleveland, S. E. *Body image and personality.* (Rev. ed.) New York: Dover Publications, 1968.

Fiske, S. T., and Taylor, S. E. *Social cognition.* Reading, MA: Addison-Wesley, 1984.

Flavell, J. H., Bothin, P. T., Fry, C. L., Wright, J. W., and Jarvis, P. E. *The development of role-taking and communication skills in children.* New York: Wiley, 1968.

Fleming, J., and Darley, J. M. The purposeful-action sequence and the "illusion of control": The effects of foreknowledge and target involvement on Observers' judgments of others' control over random events. *Personality and Social Psychology Bulletin,* 1990, *16,* 346–357.

Foersterling, F. Attributional retraining: A review. *Psychological Bulletin,* 1985, *98,* 495–512.

Folkes, V. S. Communicating the causes of social rejection. *Journal of Experimental Social Psychology,* 1982, *18,* 235–252.

———. Forming relationships and the matching hypothesis. *Personality and Social Psychology Bulletin,* 1982, *8,* 631–636.

———. Mindlessness in social interaction, fact or fiction? *Journal of Personality and Social Psychology,* 1985, *48,* 600–604.

Folkman, S., and Lazarus, R. S. Coping as a mediator of emotion. *Journal of Personality and Social Psychology,* 1988, *54,* 466–475.

———, Dunkel-Schetter, C., DeLongis, A., and Gruen, R. The dynamics of a stressful encounter: Cognitive appraisal, coping, and encounter outcomes. *Journal of Personality and Social Psychology,* 1986, *50,* 992–1003.

Forgas, J. P., and Bower, G. H. Mood effects on person-perception judgments. *Journal of Personality and Social Psychology,* 1987, *53,* 53–60.

Foulkes, D. Dreaming and consciousness. *European Journal of Cognitive Psychology,* 1990, 2, 39–55.

Frank, J. D. Individual differences in certain aspects of the level of aspiration. *American Journal of Psychology,* 1935, *47,* 119–128.

Frank, L. K. Projective methods for the study of personality. *Journal of Psychology,* 1939, *8,* 343–389.

Frankl, V. E. *Man's search of meaning: An introduction to logotherapy.* I. Lasch, trans. New York: Washington Square Press, 1963.

Fransella, F., and Adams, B. An illustration of the use of repertory grid technique in a clinical setting. *British Journal of Social and Clinical Psychology,* 1966, *5,* 51–62.

Franz, C. E. Does thought content change as individuals age? A longitudinal study of midlife adults. In T. F. Heatherton and J. L. Weinberger (Eds.), *Can personality change.* Washington, DC: American Psychological Association, 227–250, 1994.

Frazier, P. A. Victim attributions and postrape trauma. *Journal of Personality and Social Psychology,* 1990, *59.*

———. Self-blame as a mediator of postrape depressive symptoms. *Journal of Social and Clinical Psychology,* 1991, *10,* 47–57.

Freedman, D. G. Smiling in blind infants and the issue of innate vs. acquired. *Journal of Child Psychology and Psychiatry.* 1964, *5,* 171–184.

Freedman, J. L. *Crowding and behavior.* San Francisco: Freeman, 1975.

———. Reconciling apparent differences between the responses of humans and other animals to crowding. *Psychological Review,* 1979, *86,* 80–85.

———. Effect of television violence on aggressiveness, *Psychological Bulletin,* 1984, *96,* 227–246.

———, Levy, A. S., Buchanan, R. W., and Price, J. Crowding and human aggression. *Journal of Experimental Social Psychology,* 1972, *8,* 528–548.

Freedman, J. L., Sears, D. O., and Carlsmith, J. M. *Social psychology* (2nd ed.). Englewood Cliffs, NJ: Prentice-Hall, 1978.

Freud, A. *The ego and the mechanisms of defense.* New York: International Universities Press, 1946.

———. Adolescence. *The Psychoanalytic Study of the Child,* 1958, *13,* 255–278.

———, and Dann, S. An experiment in group upbringing. *Psychoanalytic Study of the Child,* 1951, *6,* 127–168.

Freud, S. (1911) Formulations regarding the two principles of mental functioning. In *Collected Papers* (Vol. IV). New York: Basic Books, 1959.

———. (1915) *A general introduction to psycho-*

analysis. New York: Washington Square Press, 1934.

———. (1920) *Beyond the pleasure principle. The standard edition* (Vol. 18). London: Hogarth, 1955.

———. *Collected papers*. London: Hogarth, 1925.

———. *An autobiographical study*. James Strachey (Trans.). New York: W. W. Norton and Company, 1935.

———. (1926) *The problem of anxiety*. New York: W. W. Norton, 1935.

———. (1930) *Civilization and its discontents*. London: Hogarth, 1961.

———. (1933) *New introductory lectures on psychoanalysis*. New York: Norton, 1961.

Freundl, P. C. *When is assertion aggressive?* Unpublished doctoral dissertation, University of California, Los Angeles, 1977.

Friedman, H. S., and Booth-Kewley, S. Validity of the Type A construct: A reprise. *Psychological Bulletin*, 1988, *104*, 381–384.

Frijda, N. H., and Swagerman, J. Can computers feel? Theory and design of an emotional system. *Cognition and Emotion*, 1987, *1*, 35–258.

Frodi, A. Sexual arousal, situational restrictiveness, and aggressive behavior. *Journal of Research in Personality*, 1977, *11*, 48–58.

Fromkin, H. L., Goldstein, I. H., and Brock, T. C. The role of "irrelevant" derogation in hostility catharsis: A field experiment. *Journal of Experimental Social Psychology*, 1977, *13*, 239–252.

Fromm, E. *Escape from freedom*. New York: Rinehart, 1941.

———. *The sane society*. New York: Rinehart, 1955.

———. *The art of loving*. New York: Harper & Row, 1956.

———. *The heart of man*. New York: Harper & Row, 1964.

———. *Man for himself*. New York: Rinehart, 1974.

Fuhrmann, B. S. *Adolescence. Adolescents*. Boston: Little, Brown, 1986.

Funder, D. C. Accuracy in personality judgment and the dancing bear. In D. M. Buss and N. Cantor (Eds.), *Personality psychology: Recent trends and emerging directions*. New York: Springer-Verlag, 210–223, 1989.

———. Global traits: A neo-Allportian approach to personality. *Psychological Science*, 1991, *2*, 31–39.

———, and Colvin, C. R. Explorations in behavioral consistency: Properties of persons, situations, and behaviors. *Journal of Personality and Social Psychology*, 1991, *60*, 773–794.

Furstenberg, F. F., Jr., Brooks-Gunn, J., and Morgan, S. P. *Adolescent mothers in later life*. Cambridge, MA: Cambridge University Press, 1987.

Gabrenya, W. K., Wang, Y. E., and Latane, B. Social loafing on an optimizing task: cross-cultural differences among Chinese and Americans. *Journal of Cross-Cultural Psychology*, 1985, *16*, 223–242.

Gallup, G. G., Jr. Chimpanzees: Self-recognition. *Science*, 1970, *167*, 86–87.

———. Towards an operational definition of self-awareness. In R. H. Tuttle (Ed.), *Socioecology and psychology of primates*. The Hague: Mouton, 1975.

———. Self-awareness in primates. *American Scientist*, 1979, *67*, 417–421.

———, McClure, M. K., Hill, S. D., and Bundy, R. Capacity for self-recognition in differentially reared chimpanzees. *Psychological Record*, 1971, *21*, 69–74.

Gamble, T. J., and Zigler, E. Effects of infant day care: Another look at the evidence. *American Journal of Orthopediatry*, 1986, *56*, 26–41.

Gangestad, S., and Snyder, M. On the nature of self-monitoring: An examination of latent causal structure. In P. Shaker (Ed.), *Review of Personality and Social Psychology* (Vol. 6). Beverly Hills, CA: Sage, 1985, 65–85.

Garcia, J., and Koelling, R. A. Relation of cue to consequences in avoidance learning. *Psychonomic Science*, 1966, *4*, 123–124.

Gardner, R. W., Holtzman, P. S., Klein, G. S., Linton, H. B., and Spence, D. P. *Cognitive control: A study of individual consistencies in cognitive behavior* (Psychological Issues Monograph 4). New York: International Universities Press, 1959.

Garmezy, N. Current status of a sample of other high-risk research programs. In L. C. Wyne, R. C. Cromwell, and S. Mattlynke (Eds.), *The nature of schizophrenia: New approaches to research and treatment*. New York: Wiley, 1978.

Gay, Peter. *Freud. A life for our time*. New York: W. W. Norton and Co., 1988.

Gaylord-Ross, R. J., Haring, T. G., Brun, C., and

Pitts-Conway, V. The training and generalization of social interaction skills with autistic youths. *Journal of Applied Behavior Analysis,* 1984, *17,* 229–247.

Gazzaniga, M. S. *The bisected brain.* New York: Appleton-Century-Crofts, 1970.

———, and LeDoux, J. R. *The integrated mind.* New York: Plenum, 1978.

Geisler, C. The use of subliminal psychodynamic activation in the study of regression. *Journal of Personality and Social Psychology,* 1986, *5,* 844–851.

George, A. L., and George, J. L. *Woodrow Wilson and Colonel House: A personality study.* New York: Dover, 1964.

Gerardo, C. J., and Bohan, J. B. Development of a sense of self-identity in children. *Child Development,* 1971, *42,* 1909–1921.

Gerbner, G., Ross, C. J., and Zigler, E. *Child abuse: An agenda for action.* New York: Oxford University Press, 1980.

Gerwirtz, J. L. A learning analysis of the effects of normal stimulation, privation, and deprivation on the acquisition of social motivation and attachment. In B. M. Foss (Ed.), *Determinants of infant behavior* (Vol. 1). New York: Wiley, 1961.

Gewirtz, J. L. *Attachment and dependency.* Washington, DC: V.H. Winston and Sons, 1972.

Gibbon, F. X. Social comparison and depression: Company's effect on misery. *Journal of Personality and Social Psychology,* 1986, *51,* 140–148.

Gil, D. G. *Violence against children: Physical child abuse in the United States.* Cambridge, MA: Harvard University Press, 1970.

Gilbert, D. T. Thinking lightly about others: Automatic components of the social inference process. In J. S. Uleman and J. A. Bargh (Eds.), *Unintended thought.* New York: Guilford, 189–211, 1989.

———, Pelham, B. W., and Krull, D. S. On cognitive busyness: When person perceivers meet persons perceived. *Journal of Personality and Social Psychology,* 1988, *54,* 733–740.

Gilligan, C. *In a different voice: Psychological theory and women's development.* Cambridge, MA: Harvard University Press, 1982.

———, Brown, L., and Rogers, A. Psyche embedded: A place for body, relationships, and culture in personality theory. In A. I. Rabin, R. A. Zucker, R. A. Emmons, and S. Frank (Eds.), *Studying persons and lives.* New York: Springer, 86–147, 1990.

Ginsberg, H. J., and Miller, S. M. Sex differences in children's risk-taking behavior. *Child Development,* 1982, *53,* 426–428.

Glass, D. C., and Singer, J. E. *Urban stress.* New York: Academic Press, 1972.

Gleason, J. B. Code switching in children's language. In T. E. Moore (Ed.), *Cognitive development and the acquisition of language.* New York: Academic Press, 1973.

Goffman, E. *Asylums.* Garden City, N.Y.: Doubleday, 1961.

Goldfarb, W. Psychological privation in infancy and subsequent adjustment. *American Journal of Orthopsychiatry,* 1945, *15,* 247–255.

Goldfried, M. R. Behavioral assessment. In I. B. Weiner (Ed.), *Clinical methods in psychology.* New York: Interscience-Wiley, 1976.

Goldstein, A. P. Problem-solving training. In A. P. Goldstein, E. G. Carr, W. S. Davidson II, and Paul Weber (Eds.), *In response to aggression: Methods of control and personal alternatives.* Elmford, NY: Pergamon Press, 1982.

———, and Michaels, G. Y. *Empathy: Developmental training and consequences.* Hillsdale, NJ: Erlbaum, 1985.

Goodall, J. *The chimpanzees of Gambe: Patterns of behavior.* Cambridge: Harvard University Press, 1986.

Goodwin, D. W., Schulsinger. F., Hermansen, L., Guze, S. B., and Winokur, G. Alcohol problems in adoptees raised apart from alcoholic biological parents. *Archives of General Psychiatry,* 1973, *28,* 238–243.

Gottesman, I. I., and Shields, J. Contributions of twin studies to perspectives on schizophrenia. In B. Maher (Ed.), *Progress in experimental personality research* (Vol. 3). New York: Academic Press, 1966.

———. *Schizophrenia and genetics: A twin study vantage point.* New York: Academic Press, 1972.

Gottesman, I. I. Origins of schizophrenia: Past as prologue. In R. Plomin and G. E. McClearn (Eds.), *Nature, nurture and psychology.* Washington, DC: American Psychological Association, 231–244, 1993.

Gottman, J. M. *Marital interaction: Experimental investigations.* New York: Academic Press, 1979.

Gough, H. G. The Adjective Checklist as a personality assessment research technique. *Psychological Reports,* 1960, *6,* 107–122.

―――. Conceptual analysis of psychological test scores and other diagnostic variables. *Journal of Abnormal Psychology,* 1965, *70,* 294–302.

Gould, K. L. The phases of adult life: A study in developmental psychology. *American Journal of Psychiatry,* 1972, *129,* 521–531.

―――. *Transformation.* New York: Simon and Schuster, 1978.

Gould, R. Adult life stages: Growth toward self-tolerance. *Psychology Today,* 1975, *8,* 74–78.

Graham, J. R. *The MMPI: A practical guide.* New York: Oxford University Press, 1977.

Graham, S. Communicated sympathy and anger to black and white children: The cognitive (attributional) consequences of affective cues. *Journal of Personality and Social Psychology,* 1984, *47,* 40–54.

Granick, S., and Patterson, R. D. *Human aging. II: An eleven-year follow-up biomedical and behavioral study.* Bethesda, MD: U.S. Public Health Service, 1972.

Gray, H., and Wheelwright, J. Jung's psychological types, their frequency and occurrence. *Journal of General Psychology,* 1964, *34,* 3–17.

Greenberg, L. S., and Safran, J. D. *Emotion in psychotherapy.* New York: Guilford, 1987.

Greenberg, L. S., Rice, L. N., and Elliott, R. *Facilitating emotional change: The moment-by-moment process.* New York: Guilford, 1993.

Greenspoon, J. Verbal conditioning and clincial psychology. In A. J. Bachrach (Ed.), *Experimental foundations of clinical psychology.* New York: Basic Books, 1962.

Greenwald, A. G. New look 3: Unconscious cognition reclaimed. *American Psychologist,* 1992, *47,* 766–779.

Grosskurth, P. *Melanie Klein: Her World and Her Work.* New York: Alfred A. Knopf, 1986.

Grotevant, H. D., and Adams, G. R. Development of an object measure to assess ego identity in adolescence: Validation and replication. *Journal of Youth and Adolescence,* 1984, *13,* 419–438.

Guardo, C. J., and Bohan, J. B. Development of a sense of self-identity in children. *Child Development,* 1971, *42,* 1909–1921.

Guilford, J. P. *An inventory of factors STDCR.* Beverly Hills, CA: Sheridan Supply, 1940.

―――, and Martin, H. G. *The Guilford-Martin inventory of factors GAMIN: Manual of directions and norms.* Beverly Hills, CA: Sheridan Supply, 1943.

Guilford, J. P., and Zimmerman, W. S. Fourteen dimensions of temperament. *Psychological Monographs,* 1956, *70* (No. 10).

Gur, R. C., and Sackheim, H. A. Self-deception: A concept in search of a phenomenon. *Journal of Personality and Social Psychology,* 1979, *37,* 147–169.

Guttman, D. The cross-cultural perspective: Notes toward a comparative psychology of aging. In J. E. Birren and K. W. Schaie (Eds.), *Handbook of the psychology of aging.* Princeton, NJ: Van Nostrand, 1977.

Hahlweg, K. and Markman, H. J. Effectiveness of behavioral marital therapy. Empirical status of behavioral techniques in preventing and alleviating marital distress. *Journal of Consulting and Clinical Psychology,* 1988, *56,* 440–447.

Haley, G. A. Eye movement responses of repressors and sensitizers to a stressful film. *Journal of Research in Personality,* 1974, *8,* 88–94.

Halfall, S. E., and Lieberman, J. R. Personality and social resources in immediate and continued stress resistance among women. *Journal of Personality and Psychology,* 1987, *52,* 18–26.

Hall, C. S., and Lindzey, G. *Theories of Personality* (2nd ed.). New York: Wiley, 1970.

Hall, W. B., and MacKinnon, D. W. Personality inventories as predictors of creativity among architects. *Journal of Applied Pscyhology,* 1969, *53,* 322–326.

Hamachek, D. E. Development of dynamics of the self. In James F. Adams (Ed.), *Understanding adolescence: Current developments in adolescent psychology.* Boston: Allyn and Bacon, 1976.

Hamilton, J. C., Greenberg, J., Pyszczynski, T., and Cather, C. A self-regulatory perspective on psychopathology and psychotherapy. *Journal of Psychotherapy Integration,* 1993, *3,* 205–249.

Hammock, T., and Brehm, J. W. The attractiveness of choice alternatives when freedom to choose is eliminated by a social agent. *Journal of Personality,* 1966, *34,* 546–554.

Hammond, D. C. (Ed.). *Handbook of hypnotic suggestions and metaphors.* New York: Norton, 1990.

Hampson, J. L. Determinants of psychosexual orientation. In F. A. Beach (Ed.), *Sex and behavior.* New York: Wiley, 1965.

Harari, H., and Kaplan, R. M. *Psychology: Personal and social adjustment.* New York: Harper & Row, 1977.

Harlow, H. F. Motivation as a factor in the acquisition of new responses. In M. R. Jones (Ed.), *Nebraska Symposium on Motivation.* Lincoln: University of Nebraska Press, 1953.

——— . The nature of love. *American Psychologist,* 1958, *13,* 673–685.

——— . *Learning to love.* San Francisco: Albion, 1971.

——— , and Suomi, S. J. Social recovery by isolation-reared monkeys. *Proceedings of the National Academy of Sciences,* 1971, *68,* 1534–1558.

Harman, H. H. *Modern factor analysis* (2nd ed.). Chicago: University of Chicago Press, 1967.

Harris, M. B. Mediators between frustration and aggression in a field experiment. *Journal of Experimental Social Psychology,* 1974, *10,* 561–571.

Harris, R. L., Ellicott, A. M., and Holmes, D. S. The timing of psychosocial transitions and changes in women's lives: An examination of women aged 45 to 60. *Journal of Personality and Social Psychology,* 1986, *51,* 409–416.

Harter, S. The perceived competence scale for children. *Child Development,* 1982, *53,* 87–97.

——— . Developmental perspectives on the self-system. In P. H. Mussen (Ed.), *Handbook of child psychology:* E. M. Hetherington (Ed.), *Volume IV: Socialization, personality, and social development.* New York: Wiley, 1983.

——— . Developmental perspectives on the self system. In P. H. Mussen (Ed.), *Revised Carmichael manual of child development,* Volume IV. New York: Harper, 1983.

Harter, S. Processes underlying adolescent self-concept formation. In R. Montemayor, G. R. Adams, and T. P. Gullotta (Eds) *From childhood to adolescence.* Newbury Park: Sage, 205–239, 1990.

Hartmann, D. P. Considerations in the choice of interobserver reliability estimates. *Journal of Applied Behavioral Analysis,* 1977, *10,* 103–116.

Hartmann, E. The D-State: A review and discussion of studies on the physiological state concomitant with dreaming. *New England Journal of Medicine,* 1965, *273,* 30–35.

Hartmann, H. *Ego psychology and the problem of adaptation.* New York: International Universities Press, 1958.

——— . *Essays on ego psychology: Selected problems in psychoanalytic theory.* New York: International Universities Press, 1964.

——— , Kris, E., and Loewenstein, R. M. Comments on the formation of psychic structure. *Psychoanalytic study of the child,* 1946, 11–18.

Hartnagel, T. F., Teevan, J. J., and McIntyre, J. J. Television violence and violent behavior. *Social Forces,* 1979, *54,* 341–351.

Hartshorne, H., and May, M. A. *Studies in the nature of character. Vol. 1. Studies in deceit.* New York: Macmillan, 1928.

——— , and Maller, J. B. *Studies in service and self control.* New York: Macmillan, 1929.

Hartshorne, H., May, M. A., and Shuttleworth, F. H. *Studies in the nature of character. Vol. 3. Studies in the organization of character.* New York: Macmillan, 1930.

Harvey, J. H., Orbuch, T. L., Chwalisz, K. D., and Garwood, G. Coping with sexual assault: The roles of account-making and confiding. *Journal of Traumatic Stress,* 1991, *4,* 515–531.

Harvey, J. H., Orbuch, T. L., and Weber, A. L. *Restoring identity and control by account-making after major trauma.* Paper presented as part of a symposium on "Narrative Self-Interpretation," American Psychological Association Convention, Toronto, Canada, August 1993.

Hatfield, E. What do women and men want from love and sex? In E. R. Allgeier and N. B. McCormick (Eds.), *Changing boundaries: Gender roles and sexual behavior.* Palo Alto, CA: Mayfield, 1983.

——— . Passionate and compassionate love. In Robert J. Sternberg and Michael L. Barma (Eds.), *The psychology of love.* New Haven: Yale University Press, 1988.

——— , and Sprecher, S. Measuring passionate love in intimate love. *Journal of Adolescence,* 1986, *9,* 383–410.

Hatfield, E., and Walster, G. W. *A new look at love.* Reading, MA: Addison-Wesley, 1981.

Hauser, S. T., and Kasendorf, E. *Black and White identity formation.* Florida: Robert E. Krieger Publishing Co., 1983.

Havighurst, R. J., Neugarten, B. L., and Tobin, S. S. Disengagement and patterns of aging. In B. L. Neugarten (Ed.), *Middle age and aging.* Chicago: University of Chicago Press, 1968.

Hawkins, R. P., Peterson, R. F., Schweid, E., and Bijou, S. W. Behavior therapy in the home: Amelioration of parent-child relations with the parent in a therapeutic role. *Journal of Experimental Child Psychology,* 1966, *4,* 99–107.

Hay, D. F. Cooperative interactions and sharing between very young children and their parents. *Developmental Psychology,* 1979, *15,* 647–653.

Hazan, C. and Shaver, P. Romantic love conceptualized as an attachment process. *Journal of Personality and Social Psychology,* 1987, *52,* 511–524.

Heatherton, T. F., and Nichols, P. A. Conceptual issues in assessing whether personality can change. In T. F. Heatherton and J. L. Weinberger (Eds.), *Can personality change?* Washington, DC: American Psychological Association, 3–18, 1994.

Heckhausen, H., and Roelofsen, I. Anfange und Entwicklung der Leistungsmotivation: (I) Im Wetteifer des Kleinkindes. *Psychologisches Forschungen,* 1962, *26,* 313–397.

Heckhausen, J., Dixon, R. A., and Baltes, P. B. Gains and losses in development throughout adulthood as perceived by different adult age groups. *Developmental Psychology,* 1989, *25,* 109–121.

Heider, F. Social perception and phenomenal causation. *Psychological Review,* 1944, *51,* 358–374.

———. *The Psychology of interpersonal relations.* New York: Wiley, 1958.

Heimberg, R. G. *Cognitive and behavioral treatments for social phobia: A critical analysis,* 1989, *9,* 187–188.

Heller, K., Davis, J. D., and Myers, R. A. The effects of interviewer style in a standardized interview. *Journal of Consulting Psychology,* 1966, *30,* 501–508.

Helmreich, R. L., and Spence, J. T. The work and family orientation questionnaire: An objective instrument to assess components of achievement motivation and attitudes toward family and career. *JSAS catalog of selected documents in psychology,* 1978, *8,* 35.

Helson, R. Critics and their texts: An approach to Jung's theory of cognition and personality. *Journal of Personality and Social Psychology,* 1982, *43,* 409–418.

———. Comparing longitudinal studies of adult development: Toward a paradigm of tension between stability and change. In D. C. Funder, R. D. Parke, C. Tomlinson-Keasey, and K. Widaman (Eds.), *Studying lives through time.* Washington, DC: American Psychological Association, 93–120, 1993.

Helson, R., Mitchell, V., and Moane, G. Personality and patterns of adherence and nonadherence to the social clock. *Journal of Personality and Social Psychology,* 1984, *46,* 1079–1096.

Helson, R., and Stewart, A. Personality change in adulthood. In T. F. Heatherton and J. Weinberger (Eds.), *Can personality change?* Washington, DC: American Psychological Association, 201–226, 1994.

Henderson, N. D. Human behavior genetics. *Annual Review of Psychology,* 1982, *33,* 403–440.

Hendrick, C. (Ed.) *Close relationships: Review of Personality and Social Psychology,* 1989, *10.* Newbury Park, CA: Sage Publications.

Hepworth, J. T., and West, S. G. Lynchings and the economy: A time-series reanalysis of Hovland and Sears (1940). *Journal of Personality and Social Psychology,* 1988, *55,* 239–247.

Herbert, J. Hormones and reproductive behaviors in Rhesus and Talapoin monkeys. *Journal of Reproduction and Fertility* (supplement), 1970, *11,* 119–140.

Hermans, H. J. M. The dream in the process of valuation: A method of interpretation. *Journal of Personality and Social Psychology,* 1987, *53,* 163–175.

Hess, E. H. Attitude and pupil size. *Scientific American,* 1965, *212,* 46–54.

Hicks, D. J. Effects of co-observer's sanctions and adult presence on imitative aggression. *Child Development,* 1968, *39,* 303–309.

Hicks, L. H., and Birren, J. E. Aging, brain damage, and psychomotor slowing. *Psychological Bulletin,* 1970, *74,* 377–396.

Higgins, E. T. Self-discrepancy: A theory relating

self and affect. *Psychological Review,* 1987, *94,* 319–340.

Higgins, E. T. Knowledge accessibility and activation: Subjectivity and suffering from unconscious sources. In J. S. Uleman and J. A. Bargh (Eds.), *Unintended thought.* New York: Guilford, 75–123, 1989.

———, Strauman, T., and Klein, R. Standards and the process of self-evaluation. In Sorrentino, R. M., and Higgins, E. T. (Eds.), *Handbook of motivation and cognition.* New York: Guilford Press, 1986, 23–63.

Hilgard, E. R. Human motives and the concept of the self. *American Psychologist,* 1949, *4,* 374–382.

———. A neodissociation interpretation of pain reduction in hypnosis. *Psychological Review,* 1973, *80,* 396–411.

———, Atkinson, R. C., and Atkinson, R. L. *Introduction to psychology* (6th ed.). New York: Harcourt, Brace, Jovanovich, 1975.

Hilgard, J. R. *Personality and hypnosis.* Chicago: University of Chicago Press, 1970.

Hinde, R. A. Energy models of motiviation. *Symposium of the Society of Experimental Biology,* 1960, *14,* 199–213.

Hineline, P. N. The language of behavior analysis: Its community, its functions, and its limitations. *Behaviorism,* 1980, *8,* 67–86.

Hirai, T. *Psychophysiology of Zen.* Tokyo: Igaku Shoin, 1974.

Hiroto, D. S., and Seligman, M. E. P. Generality of learned helplessness in man. *Journal of Personality of Social Psychology,* 1975, *31,* 311–327.

Hoare, C. H. Psychosocial identity development and cultural others. *Journal of Counseling and Development,* 1990, *70,* 45–53.

Hobfoll, S. E., and Lieberman, J. R. Personality and social resources in immediate and continued stress resistance among women. *Journal of Personality and Social Psychology,* 1987, *52,* 18–26.

Hochchild, A. *The managed heart: The commercialization of human feeling.* Berkeley, CA: University of California Press, 1983.

Hoffman, M. L. Conscience, personality, and socialization techniques. *Human Development,* 1970, *13,* 90–126.

———. Altruistic behavior and the parent-child relationship. *Journal of Personality and Social Psychology,* 1975, *31,* 937–943.

Hofstader, D. *Godel, Escher, & Bach.* New York: Vintage, 1979.

Hogan, R. *Personality theory.* Englewood Cliffs, NJ: Prentice-Hall, 1976.

———, DeSoto, C. B., and Solano, C. Traits, tests, and personality research. *American Psychologist,* 1977, *32,* 255–264.

Hogan, R., and Hogan, J. *Hogan Personality Inventory manual.* Tulsa, Oklahoma: Hogan Assessment Systems, 1992.

Hokanson, J. E., and Burgess, M. The effects of three types of aggression on vascular processes. *Journal of Abnormal and Social Psychology,* 1962, *64,* 446–449.

Hollingworth, H. L. *Psychology of the functional neurotic.* New York: Appleton-Century, 1920.

Holmes, T. H., and Rahe, R. H. The social readjustment rating scale. *Journal of Psychosomatiç Research,* 1967, *11,* 213–218.

Holt, E. B. *Animal drive and the learning process, an essay toward radical empiricism* (Vol. 1). New York: Holt, 1931.

Hong, K. The transitional phenomena: A theoretical integration. *Psychoanalytic Study of the Child,* 1978, *33,* 47–79.

Horney, K. *Neurotic personality of our times.* New York: Norton, 1937.

———. *Our inner conflicts.* New York: Norton, 1945.

Horowitz, M. J. *Introduction to psychodynamics.* New York: Basic Books, 1988.

Horrocks, J. E. *The psychology of adolescence.* Boston: Houghton Mifflin, 1969.

———. Development and dynamics of the self. In J. F. Adams (Ed.), *Understanding adolescence.* Boston: Allyn and Bacon, 1976.

Hough, R. L., McGarvey, W., Graham, J., and Timbers, D. Cultural variations in the modeling of life change—illness relationships. Unpublished 1982 manuscript cited in Cervantes, R. C., and Castro, F. G. Stress, coping, and Mexican American Mental Health: A systematic review. *Hispanic Journal of Behavioral Sciences,* 1985, *7,* 1–73.

Houston, B. K. Cardiovascular and neuroendocrine reactivity, global Type A and components of Type A behavior. In B. K. Houston and C. R. Snyder (Eds.), *Type A behavior pattern: Research, theory, and intervention.* New York: Wiley, 1988, 212–253.

Howard, A., and Bray, D. *Managerial lives in transition: Advancing age and changing times.* New York: Guilford, 1988.

Howard, G. S. Culture tales: A narrative approach to thinking, cross-cultural psychology, and psychotherapy. *American Psychologist*, 1991, *46*, 187–197.

Howes, D. H., and Solomon, R. L. Visual duration threshold as a function of word-probability. *Journal of Experimental Psychology*, 1951, *41*, 401–410.

Huesmann, L. R. and Eron, L. D. *Television and the aggressive child: A cross-national comparison,* Hillsdale, NJ: Erlbaum, 1986.

Huesmann, L. R., Eron, L. D., Lefkowitz, M. M., and Walder, L. O. The stability of aggression over time and generations. *Developmental Psychology, 1984, 20,* 1120–1134.

Huesmann, L. R., Lagerspetz, K., and Eron, L. D. Intervening variables in the television violence-aggression relation: Evidence from the two countries. *Developmental Psychology*, 1983, *19*, 71–77.

Hull, C. L. *Principles of behavior.* New York: Appleton-Century-Crofts, 1943.

——— . *Essentials of behavior.* New Haven: Yale University Press, 1951.

——— . *A behavior system: An introduction to behavior theory concerning the individual organism.* New Haven: Yale University Press, 1952.

Hull, J. G., and VanTreuren, R. R. Experimental social psychology, and the causes and effects of alcohol consumption. In H. D. Cappell (Ed.), *Research advances in alcohol and drug problems.* New York: Plenum Press, 1986.

——— , and Vernelli, S. Hardiness and health: A critique and alternative approach. *Journal of Personality and Social Psychology, 53,* 1987, 518–530.

Hunter, E. J. The prisoner of war: Coping with the stress of isolation. In R. H. Moos (Ed.), *Human adaptation: Coping with life crises.* Lexington, MA: Heath, 1976.

Huntingford, F. A. Animals fight, but do not make war. In J. Groebel and R. A. Hinde (Eds.), *Aggression and war.* Cambridge: Cambridge University Press, 1987.

Huston, A. C. Sex-typing. In P. H. Mussen (Ed.), *Handbook of child psychology;* E. M. Hetherington (Ed.), *Volume IV: Socialization, personality, and social development.* New York: John Wiley & Sons, 1983.

Hutchings, B., and Mednick, S. A. Criminality in adoptees and their adoptive and biological parents: A pilot study. In S. Mednick and K. O. Christiansen (Eds.), *Biosocial bases of criminal behavior.* New York: Gardner, 1977.

Huxley, A. *The doors of perception.* New York: Harper & Row, 1954.

Hyde, J. S. How large are sex differences in aggression? A developmental meta-analysis. *Developmental Psychology*, 1984, *20*, 722–736.

——— , and Linn, M. C. Gender differences in verbal ability: A meta-analysis. *Psychological Bulletin*, 1988, *104*, 53–69.

Hyde, J. S., Fennema, E., and Lamon, S. J. Gender differences in mathematics performance: A meta-analysis. *Psychological Bulletin*, 1990, *107*, 139–155.

Inkeles, A. Society, social structure, and child socialization. In J. A. Clausen (Ed.), *Socialization and society.* Boston: Little, Brown, 1968.

——— , and Rossi, P. H. National comparisons of occupational prestige. *American Journal of Sociology,* 1966, *61*, 329–339.

Isabella, R. A., Belsky, J. and von Eye, A. Origin of infant-mother attachment: an examination of interactional synchrony during the infant's first year. *Developmental Psychology*, 1989, *25*, 12–21.

Isen, A. M., Nygren, T. E., and Ashby, F. G. Influence of positive affect on the subjective utility of gains and losses: It is just not worth the risk. *Journal of Personality and Social Psychology*, 1988, *55*, 710–717.

Ittelson, W. H., Proshansky, H. M., Rivlin, L. G., and Winkel, G. H. *An introduction to environmental psychology.* New York: Holt, 1974.

Izard, C. E. *Human emotions.* New York: Plenum, 1977.

——— . Basic emotions, relations among emotions, and emotion-cognition relations. *Psychological Review*, 1992, *99*, 561–565.

Jacklin, C. N. Female and male: Issues of gender. *American Psychologist*, 1989, *44*, 127–133.

Jackson, D. H., and Messick, S. Response styles and the assessment of psychopathology. In S. Messick and J. Ross (Eds.), *Measurement of personality and cognition.* New York: Wiley, 1962.

Jacobsen, T., Edelstein, W., and Hoffman, V. A longitudinal study of the relation between representations of attachment in childhood and cognitive functioning in childhood and adolescence. *Developmental Psychology*, 1994, *30*, 112–124.

Jaffe, Y. *Sex and aggression: An intimate relationship*. Unpublished doctoral dissertation, University of California, Los Angeles, 1975.

———, Malamuth, N., Feingold, J., and Feshbach, S. Sexual arousal and behavioral aggression. *Journal of Personality and Social Psychology*, 1974, *30*, 759–764.

James, W. T. Social organization among dogs of different temperaments: Terriers and beagles reared together. *Journal of Comparative Physiological Psychology*, 1951, *44*, 71–77.

Janoff-Bulman, R. *Shattered assumptions*. New York: Free Press, 1992.

Janoff-Bulman, R. Assumptive worlds and the stress of traumatic events: Applications of the schema construct. *Social Cognition*, 1989, *7*, 113–138.

Jenkins, A. H. *The psychology of the Afro-American*. New York: Pergamon, 1982.

Jensen, G. D., and Tolman, C. W. Activity level of the mother monkey, *Macaca nemestrina*, as affected by various conditions of sensory access to the infant following separation. *Animal Behaviour*, 1962, *10*, 228–230.

———. Mother-infant relationship in the monkey, *Macaca nemestrina*: The effect of brief separation and mother-infant specificity. *Journal of Comparative and Physiological Psychology*, 1962, *55*, 131–136.

Jerremalm, A., Jannson, L. and Ost, L. G. Cognitive and physiological reactivity and the effects of different behavioral methods in the treatment of social phobia. *Behavior Research and Therapy*, 1986, *24*, 171–180.

Jessor, R., Graves, T. D., Hanson, R. C., and Jessor, S. L. *Society, personality, and deviant behavior*. New York: Holt, 1968.

John, O. P. The "big five" factor taxonomy: Dimensions of personality in the natural language and in questionnaires. In L. A. Pervin (Ed.), *Handbook of personality*, 66–100, 1990.

Johnson, D. W., and Norem-Hebeisen, A. Attitudes toward interdependence among persons and psychological health. *Psychological Reports*, 1977, *40*, 843–850.

Johnson, R. C., McClearn, G. E., Yuen, S., Nagoshi, C. T., Ahern, F. M., and Cole, R. E. Galton's data a century later. *American Psychologist*, 1985, *40*, 875–892.

Johnson, R. N. *Aggression in man and animals*. Philadelphia: Saunders, 1972.

Jones, E. *The life and work of Sigmund Freud* (Vols. I-III). New York: Basic Books, 1953–1957.

Jones, E. E. The rocky road from acts to dispositions. *American Psychologist*, 1979, *34*, 107–117.

———, and Davis, K. E. From acts to dispositions: The attribution process in person perception. In L. Berkowitz (Ed.), *Advances in experimental social psychology* (Vol. 2). New York: Academic Press, 1965.

Jones, E. E., and Nisbett, R. E. *The actor and observer: Divergent perceptions of the causes of behavior*. Morristown, N.J.: General Learning Press, 1971.

Jones, R. M. Ego identity and adolescent problem behavior. In G. R. Adams, T. P. Gullotta, and R. Montemayer (Eds.), *Adolescent identity formation*. Newbury Park: Sage, 216–233, 1992.

Jordan, J. V., Kaplan, A. G., Miller, J. B., Stiver, I. P., and Surrey, J. L. *Women's growth in connection*. New York: Guilford, 1991.

Josselson, R. L. *Finding herself: Pathways of identity development in women*. New York: Jossey-Bass, 1988.

Jung, C. (1904) Studies in word association. In *Experimental researches, collected works* (Vol. 2). Princeton, NJ: Princeton University Press, 1973.

———. *Analytical psychology*. New York: Moffat, Yard, 1916.

———. (1936) *The concept of the collective unconscious*. In *Collected work* (Vol. 9, Part I). NJ: Princeton University Press, 1959.

———. *The basic writings of C. G. Jung* (V. de Laszlo, Ed.). New York: Random House, 1959.

Kabasa, L. C., Maddi, L. R., Puccetti, M., and Zola, J. Relative effectiveness of hardiness, exercise and social support as resources against illness, *Journal of Psychosomatic Research*, 1986, *29*, 525–533.

Kadushin, A. *Adopting older children*. New York: Columbia University Press, 1970.

Kagan, J. Developmental studies in reflection and analysis. In A. H. Kidd and J. L. Rivoire (Eds.), *Perceptual development in children*. New York: International Universities Press, 1966.

Kagan, J. Temperamental contributions to social behavior. *American Psychologist,* 1989, *44,* 668–674.

Kagan, J., Klein, R. E., Finley, G. E., Rogoff, B., Nolan, E., and Kogan, N. Individual variation in cognitive processes. In P. H. Mussen (Ed.), *Carmichael's manual of child psychology* (Vol. 1). New York: Wiley, 1970.

Kagan, J., and Moss, H. A. Stability and validity of achievement fantasy. *Journal of Abnormal and Social Psychology,* 1959, *58,* 357–364.

———. *Birth to maturity.* New York: Wiley, 1962.

Kagan, J., and Snidman, N. Infant predictors of inhibited and uninhibited profiles. *Psychological Science,* 1991, 2, 40–44.

Kagan, J., Arcus, D., and Snidman, N. The idea of temperament: Where do we go from here? In R. Plomin and G.E. McClearn (Eds.), *Nature, nurture and psychology.* Washington, DC: American Psychological Association, 197–212, 1993.

Kagan, S., and Madsen, M. C. Cooperation and competition of Mexican, Mexican-American, and Anglo children of two ages. *Developmental Psychology,* 1971, 5, 32–39.

Kagitcibasi, E., and Berry, J. W. Cross-cultural psychology: current research and trends. *Annual Review of Psychology,* 1989, *46,* 493–531.

Kallman, W. M., and Feuerstein, M. Psychophysiological procedures. In A. R. Ciminero, K. S. Calhoun, and H. E. Adams (Eds.), *Handbook of behavioral assessment.* New York: Interscience-Wiley, 1977.

Kamiya, J. Operant control of the EEG and some of its reported effects on consciousness. In C. T. Tart (Ed.), *Altered states of consciousness.* New York: Wiley, 1969.

Kanfer, F. H. Self-regulation: Research, issues and speculations. In C. Neuringer, J. L. Michael (Eds.), *Behavior modification in clinical psychology.* New York: Appleton-Century-Crofts, 1970.

———, and Marston, A. R. Determinants of self-reinforcement in human learning. *Journal of Experimental Psychology,* 1963, *66,* 245–254.

Kanfer, F. H., and Saslow, G. Behavioral diagnosis. In C. M. Franks (Ed.), *Behavior therapy: Appraisal and status.* New York: McGraw-Hill, 1969.

Kaplan, R. M., and Saccuzzo, D. S. *Psychological testing: Principles and applications.* Belmont, CA: Brooks/Cole, 1981.

Kardiner, A. *The psychological frontier of society.* New York: Columbia University Press, 1945.

Kastenbaum, R., Derbin, V., Sabatini, P., and Artt, S. "The age of me": Towards personal and interpersonal definitions of functional aging. *International Journal of Aging and Human Development,* 1972, 3, 197–211.

Kaufman, H., and Feshbach, S. Displaced aggression and its modification through exposure to antiaggressive communications. *Journal of Abnormal and Social Psychology,* 1963, *67,* 79–83.

Kazdin, A. E. Artifact, bias, and complexity of assessment: The ABCs of reliability. *Journal of Applied Behavior Analysis,* 1977, *10,* 141–150.

———, Bass, D., Siegal, T., and Thomas, C. Cognitive-Behavioral therapy and relationship therapy in the treatment of children referred for antisocial behavior. *Journal of Consulting and Clinical Psychology,* 1989, *57,* 522–535.

Keiner, J. Klexographien, Part VI. In R. Pissin (Ed.), *Keiners Werke.* Berlin: Bong & Co., 1857.

Kelley, C. K., and King, G. D. Behavioral correlates of the 2-7-8 MMPI profile type in students at a university mental health center. *Journal of Consulting and Clinical Psychology,* 1979, *47,* 679–685.

Kelley, H. H. Attribution theory in social psychology. In D. Levine (Ed.), *Nebraska symposium on motivation.* Lincoln: University of Nebraska Press, 1967.

———, Love and commitment. In H. H. Kelley, E. Berscheid, A. Christensen, J. H. Harvey, T. L. Huston, G. Luimger, E. McClintock, L. A. Peplau, D. R. Peterson (Eds.), *Close relationships.* New York: W. H. Freeman & Co, 1983.

Kelly, G. A. *The psychology of personal constructs.* New York: Norton, 1955.

———. Man's construction of his alternatives. In G. Lindzey (Ed.), *Assessment of human motives.* New York: Grove, 1958.

———. (1966) A summary statement of cognitive-oriented comprehensive theory of behavior. In J. C. Mancuso (Ed.), *Readings for a cognitive theory of personality.* New York: Holt, 1970.

Kempe, R. S., and Kempe, C. H. *Child abuse.* Cambridge: Harvard University Press, 1978.

Keniston, K. The sources of student dissent. *Journal of Social Issues,* 1967, *22,* 108–137.

Kernberg, O. F. *Borderline conditions and pathological narcissism*. New York: Jason Aronson, 1975.

Kihlstrom, J. F. The cognitive unconscious. *Science*, 1987, *237*, 1445–1452.

Kihlstrom, J. F. The psychological unconscious. In L. A. Pervin (Ed.), *Handbook of personality*. New York: Guilford, 445–464, 1990.

Kimble, G. A., Garmezy, N., and Zigler, E. *Principles of general psychology* (4th ed.) New York: Ronald, 1974.

King, L. F., Armitage, S. G., and Tilton, J. A therapeutic approach to schizophrenia of extreme pathology. *Journal of Abnormal and Social Psychology*, 1960, *61*, 276–286.

Kinsey, A. C., Pomeroy, W. B., and Martin, C. E. *Sexual behavior in the human male*. Philadelphia: Saunders, 1948.

——— , and Gebhard, P. H. *Sexual behavior in the human female*. Philadelphia: Saunders, 1953.

Kirsch, I. Self-efficacy and expectancy: Old wine with new labels. *Journal of Personality and Social Psychology*, 1985, *49*, 824–830.

Klein, G. S. Peremptory ideation: Structure and force in motivated ideas. In R. Jessor and S. Feshbach (Eds.)., *Cognition, personality and clinical psychology*. San Francisco: Jossey-Bass, 1967.

——— . Freud's two theories of sexuality. In L. Breger (Ed.), *Clinical-cognitive psychology*. Englewood Cliffs, NJ: Prentice-Hall, 1969.

——— . *Perception, motives and personality*. New York: Knopf, 1970.

Klein, K. B., and Spiegel, D. Modulation of gastric acid secretion by hypnosis. *Gastroenterology*, 1989, *96*, 1383–1387.

Klein, M. *The psycho-analysis of children* (2nd ed.). London: Hogarth, 1937.

——— . *Contributions to psychoanalysis, 1921–45*. London: Hogarth, 1948.

Klein, R. *Some factors influencing empathy in six and seven year old children varying in ethnic background*. Unpublished doctoral dissertation, University of California, Los Angeles, 1970.

Kleinmuntz, A., and Szucko, J. J. A field study of the fallibility of polygraphic lie detection. *Nature*, 1984a, *308*, 449–450.

——— . Lie detection in ancient and modern times. *American Psychologist*, 1984b, *39*, 766–776.

Kline, N. Drugs are the greatest practical advance in the history of psychiatry. *New Medical Material*, 1962, *4*, 49.

Kline, P. *Fact and fancy in Freudian theory*. London: Methuen, 1972.

Klineberg, O. *Race differences*. New York: Harper & Brothers, 1935.

Klinger, E. Fantasy need achievement as a motivational construct. *Psychological Bulletin*, 1966, *66*, 291–303.

——— . Current concerns and disengagement from incentives. In F. Halisch and J. Kuhl (Eds.), *Motivation, intention, and volition*. New York: Springer-Verlag, 337–347, 1987.

Klopfer, B. (Ed.), *Developments in the Rorschach technique*. Yonkers, NY: World Book, 1954–1970.

Klopfer, W. G., and Taulbee, E. S. Projective tests. *Annual Review of Psychology*, 1976, *26*, 543–568.

Knight, G. P., and Kagan, S. Development of prosocial and competitive behaviors in Anglo-American and Mexican-American children. *Child Development*, 1977, *48*, 1385–1394.

Knott, P. D., Lasater, L., and Shuman, R. Aggression: Guilt and conditionability for aggressiveness. *Journal of Personality*, 1974, *42*, 332–344.

Kobasa, S. C. Stressful life events, personality, and health: An inquiry into hardiness. *Journal of Personality and Social Psychology*, 1979, *37*, 1–11.

——— . The hardy personality: Toward a social psychology of stress and health. In G. Sanders and J. Suls (Eds.), *Social psychology of health and illness*. Hillsdale, NI: Erlbaum, 1982, 3–32.

Kobasa, S. C., and Maddi, S. R. Existential personality theory. In R. J. Corsini (Ed.), *Current personality theory*, Itasca, IL: F. E. Peacock, 243–276, 1977.

Kohlberg, L. *The development of modes of moral thinking and choice in the years ten to sixteen*. Unpublished doctoral dissertation, University of Chicago, 1958.

——— . A cognitive-developmental analysis of children's sex-role concepts and attitudes. In E. Maccoby (Ed.), *The development of sex differences*. Stanford, CA: Stanford University Press, 1966.

——— . Stage and sequence: The cognitive-developmental approach to socialization. In D. Goslin

(Ed.), *Handbook of socialization theory and research*. Chicago: Rand McNally, 1969a.

———. *Stages in the development of moral thought and action*. New York: Holt, 1969b.

———. Moral stages and moralization: The cognitive-developmental approach. In T. Lickona (Ed.), *Moral development and behavior: Theory, research and social issues*. New York: Holt, 1976.

Kohut, H. *The analysis of the self: A systematic approach to the psychoanalytic treatment of narcissistic personality disorders* (Monograph Series of the Psychoanalytic Study of the Child, No. 41). New York: International Universities Press, 1971.

———. *The restoration of the self*. New York: International Universities Press, 1977.

Kohut, Heinz. *How does analysis work?* Arnold Goldberg (Ed.), Paul Stepansky (Collaborator). Chicago: University of Chicago Press, 1984.

———. *How does analysis cure?* Chicago: University of Chicago Press, 1984.

Kopp, C. B. The growth of self-regulation. Caregivers and children. In N. Eisenberg (Ed.), *New directions in developmental psychology*. New York: Wiley, 1987.

Kornadt, H. J. A cross-cultural analysis of the development of aggression. In J. B. Derigowski, S. Dzinvawiec and R. C. Annis (Eds.), *Expiscations in Cross-Cultural Psychology*. Selected papers from the Sixth International Conference of the International Association for Cross-Cultural Psychology. Lisse: Swets and Zeitlinger B. V., 1983, 285–297.

Krasner, L., and Ullman, L. P. *Behavior influence and personality*. New York: Holt, 1973.

Kretschmer, E. *Physique and character*. New York: Harcourt, Brace, 1925.

Kreuz, L. E., and Rose, R. M. Assessment of aggressive behaviors and plasma testosterone in a young criminal population. *Psychosomatic Medicine*, 1972, *34*, 321–332.

Kroger, J. Intrapsychic dimensions of identity during late adolescence. In G. R. Adams, T. P. Gullotta, and R. Montemayer (Eds.), *Adolescent identity formation*. Newbury Park: Sage, 122–144, 1992.

Kruijt, J. *Ontogeny of social behavior in Burmese red jungle fowl* (Gallus gallus spodiceus) (Behavior Supp. 12). Leiden: Brill, 1964.

Kuder, G. F., and Richardson, M. W. The theory of the estimation of reliability, *Psychometrika*, 1937, *2*, 151–160.

Kuiper, N. A., MacDonald, M. R., and Derry, P. A. Parameters of a depressive self-schema. In J. Suls and A. G. Greenwald (Eds.), *Psychological perspectives on the self*. Hillsdale, NJ: Erlbaum, 1983.

Kukla, A. Attributional determinants of achievement-related behavior. *Journal of Personality and Social Psychology*, 1972, *21*, 166–174.

———. The modern language of consciousness. In L. Michaels and C. Ricks (Eds.), *The state of the language*. Berkeley: University of California Press, 1980.

Kurtines, W., and Greif, E. B. The development of moral thought: Review and evaluation of Kohlberg's approach. *Psychological Bulletin*, 1974, *81*, 453–470.

Lack, D. L. *The life of the robin*. Cambridge: Cambridge University Press, 1943.

La Freniere, P., Strayer, F. F., and Gauthier, R. The emergence of same sex affiliative preferences among preschool peers: A developmental ethological perspective. *Child Development*, 1984, *55*, 1958–1965.

La Fromboise, T., Coleman, H. L. K., and Gerton, J. Psychological impact of biculturalism: Evidence and theory. *Psychological Bulletin*, 1993, *114*, 395–412.

Lagerspetz, K. Aggression and aggressiveness in laboratory mice. In S. Garattini and E. B. Sigg (Eds.), *Aggressive behavior*. Amsterdam: Excerpta Medica, 1969.

———. Modification of aggressiveness in mice. In S. Feshbach and A. Fraczek (Eds.), *Aggression and behavior change: Biological and social processes*. New York: Praeger, 1979.

Lagerspetz, K. M., Bjorkgvist, K., and Peltoren, T. Is indirect aggression typical of females? Gender differences in aggressiveness in 11 to 12 year old children. *Aggressive Behavior*, 1988, *14*, 403–414.

Laing, R. D. *The divided self: An existential study in sanity and madness*. Baltimore: Penguin, 1965.

Lamb, D. Anxiety. In H. London and J. E. Exner (Eds.), *Dimensions of personality*. New York: John Wiley, 1978.

Lamb, M. E. Father-infant and mother-infant interaction in the first year of life. *Child Development*, 1977, *48*, 167–181.

——— (Ed.) *Social and personality development.* New York: Holt, Rinehart, & Winston, 1978.

———. Maternal employment and child development: A review. In M. E. Lamb (Ed.), *Nontraditional families: Parenting and child development.* Hillsdale, NJ: Erlbaum, 1982, 43–69.

Landrine, H. Clinical implications of cultural differences: The referential versus indexical self. *Clinical Psychology Review,* 1992, *12,* 401–415.

Lang, P. J. The application of psychophysiological methods to the study of psychotherapy and behavior modification. In A. E. Bergin and S. L. Garfield (Eds.), *Handbook of psychotherapy and behavior change.* New York: Wiley, 1971.

Langer, E. J. The illusion of control. *Journal of Personality and Social Psychology,* 1975, *32,* 311–328.

Langer, E. J. Minding matters: The consequences of mindlessness-mindfulness. In Berkowitz, L. (Ed.), *Advances in Experimental Social Psychology,* Vol. 22. San Diego: Academic Press, 1989, 137–173.

Langer, E. J. *Mindfulness.* Reading, MA: Addison-Wesley, 1989.

———, Blank, A., and Chanowitz, B. The mindlessness of ostensibly thoughtful action: The role of "placebic" information in interpersonal interaction. *Journal of Personality and Social Psychology,* 1978, *36,* 635–642.

Langer, E. J., and Rodin, J. The effects of choice and enhanced personal responsibility for the aged: A field experiment in an institutional setting. *Journal of Personality and Social Psychology,* 1976, *34,* 191–98.

Larson, R. J., and Diener, E. A multitrait–multimethod examination of affect structure: Hedonic level and emotional intensity. *Personality and Individual Differences,* 1985, *6,* 631–636.

———. Affect intensity as an individual difference characteristic: A review. *Journal of Research in Personality,* 1987, *21,* 1–39.

———, and Cropanzano, R. S. Cognitive operations associated with individual differences in affect intensity. *Journal of Personality and Social Psychology,* 1987, *53,* 767–774.

Lashley, K. S. The mechanism of vision: I. A method for rapid analysis of pattern-vision in the rat. *Pedagogical Seminary and Journal of Genetic Psychology,* 1930, *37,* 453–460.

Last, U. *Motives, styles, contents and products of identification in the authority figure.* Unpublished doctoral dissertation, Hebrew University, 1975.

Lawson, R. *Frustration: The development of a scientific concept.* New York: Macmillan, 1965.

Lazarus, A. A. *Behavior therapy and beyond.* New York: McGraw-Hill, 1971.

Lazarus, R. S. *Psychological stress and the coping process.* New York: McGraw-Hill, 1966.

———. Thoughts on the relation between emotion and cognition. *American Psychologist,* 1982, *37,* 1019–1024.

———. Puzzles in the study of daily hassles. *Journal of Behavioral Medicine,* 1985, *7,* 375–389.

———, and Alfert, E. The short circuiting of threat by experimentally altering cognitive appraisal. *Journal of Abnormal and Social Psychology,* 1964, *69,* 195–205.

Lazarus, R. S., and Averill, J. R. Emotion and cognition: With special reference to anxiety. In C. D. Spielberger (Ed.), *Anxiety: Current trends in theory and research.* New York: Academic Press, 1972.

Lazarus, R. S., and Smith, C. A. Knowledge and appraisal in the cognition–emotion relationship. *Cognition and Emotion,* 1988, *2,* 281–300.

LeBoeuf, B. J. and Peterson, R. S. Social status and mating activity in elephant seals. *Science,* 1969, *163,* 91–93.

Lecky, P. *Self-consistency: A theory of personality.* New York: Island Press Co-operative, 1945.

Lefcourt, H. M. The function of illusions of control and freedom. *American Psychologist,* 1973, *28,* 417–425.

———. *Locus of control.* Hillsdale, NJ: Lawrence Erlbaum, 1976.

———, Von Baeyer, C. L., Ware, E. E., and Cox, C. J. The multidimensional-multiattributional causality scale: The development of a goal specific locus of control scale. *Canadian Journal of Behavioral Science,* 1979, *11,* 286–304.

Lefkowitz, M. M., Eron, L. D., Walder, L. O., and Huesmann, L. R. *Growing up to be violent.* New York: Pergamon, 1977.

Lehman, C. H., and Witty, P. A. Faculty psychology and personality traits. *American Journal of Psychology,* 1934, *44,* 486–500.

Lehman, D. R., Wortman, C. B., and Williams, A. F. Long–term effects of losing a spouse or child in a motor vehicle crash. *Journal of Personality and Social Psychology,* 1987, *52,* 218–231.

Lehrman, D. S. A critique of Konrad Lorenz's theory of instinctive behavior. *Quarterly Review of Biology,* 1953, *28,* 337–363.

———. Semantic and conceptual issues in the nature-nurture problem. In L. R. Aronson, E. Tobach, D. S. Lehrman, and J. S. Rosenblatt (Eds.), *Development and evolution of behavior.* San Francisco: Freeman, 1970.

Lehrman, H. C. *Age and achievement.* Princeton, NJ: Princeton Univ. Press, 1953.

Lennenberg, E. H. *Biological foundations of language.* New York: Wiley, 1967.

Leonard, K. E. The impact of explicit aggressive and implicit nonaggressive cues on aggression in intoxicated and sober males. *Personality and Social Psychology Bulletin,* 1989, *15,* 390–400.

Lepper, M. R., Greene, D., and Nisbett, R. E. Undermining children's intrinsic interest with extrinsic reward: A test of the overjustification hypothesis. *Journal of Personality and Social Psychology,* 1973, *28,* 129–137.

Levant, R. F., and Schlien, J. M. *Client-centered therapy and the person-centered approach.* New York: Praeger, 1984.

Leventhal, H. A perceptual-motor theory of emotion. In L. Berkowitz (Ed.), *Advances in experimental social psychology.* New York: Academic Press, 1984.

Levinson, D. J. *The seasons of a man's life.* New York: Ballantine, 1978.

———. A conception of adult development. *American Psychologist,* 1986, *41,* 3–13.

Levis, D. J. Learned helplessness: A reply and an alternative S-R interpretation. *Journal of Experimental Psychology: General,* 1976, *105,* 47–65.

Levy, S. M. The aging woman: Developmental issues and mental health needs. *Professional Psychology,* 1981, *12,* 92–101.

Lewicki, P. *Nonconscious social information processing.* New York: Academic Press, 1986.

Lewicki, P., Hill, T., and Czyzewska, M. Nonconscious acquisition of information. *American Psychologist,* 1992, *47,* 788–791.

Lewin, K. *A dynamic theory of personality.* New York: McGraw-Hill, 1935.

———, Dembo, T., Festlinger, L., and Sears, P. S. Level of aspiration. In J. McV. Hunt (Ed.), *Personality and the behavioral disorders* (Vol. 1). New York: Ronald, 1944.

Lewinsohn, P. M., Mischel, W., Chaplin, W., and Barton, R. Social competence and depression: The role of illusory self-perception. *Journal of Abnormal Psychology,* 1980, *89,* 203–212.

Lewis, M. Early sex role behavior and school adjustment. In J. M. Reinisch, L. A. Rosenbaum and S. A. Sanders (Eds.), *Masculinity/Femininity: Basic Perspectives.* New York: Oxford University Press, 1987.

———, and Brooks-Gunn, J. *Social cognition and the acquisition of self.* New York: Plenum, 1979.

Lewis, M. and Feisking, C. Infant, mother, and mother-infant interaction behavior and subsequent attachment. *Child Development,* 1989, *60,* 831–837.

Lewis, M., Sullivan, M. W., Stanger, C., and Weiss, M. Self-development and self conscious emotions. *Child Development,* 1989, *60,* 146–156.

Lewis, M. J. Self-knowledge and social development in early life. In L. A. Pervin (Ed.), *Handbook of personality.* New York: Guilford, 277–300, 1990.

Lewis, O. *Children of Sanchez.* New York: Random House, 1961.

Lewis, W. A., and Bucher, A. M. Anger, catharsis, the reformulated frustration-aggression hypothesis, and health consequences. *Psychotherapy,* 1992, *29,* 385–392.

Ley, R. G. Cerebral asymmetries, emotional experience, and imagery: Implications for psychotherapy. In A. A. Sheilah and J. T. Shaffer (Eds.), *The potential of fantasy and imagination.* New York: Brandon House, 1979.

Leyens, J. P., Camino, L., Parke, R. D., and Berkowitz, L. Effects of movie violence on aggression in a field setting as a function of group dominance and cohesion. *Journal of Personality and Social Psychology,* 1975, *32,* 346–360.

Liebert, R. M., and Allen, K. M. *The effects of rule structure and reward magnitude on the acquisition and adoption of self-reward criteria.* Unpublished manuscript, Vanderbilt University, 1967.

Liebert, R. M., and Spiegler, M. D. *Personality: Strategies for the study of man.* (Rev. ed.) Homewood, Ill.: Dorsey Press, 1974.

Lindzey, G. The Thematic Apperception Test: Interpretive assumptions and related empirical evidence. *Psychological Bulletin,* 1952, *49,* 1–25.

———. Some remarks concerning incest, the incest taboo, and psychoanalytic theory. *American Psychologist,* 1967a, *22,* 1051–1059.

———. Behavior and morphological variation. In J. N. Spuhler (Ed.), *Genetic diversity and human behavior.* Chicago: Aldine, 1967b.

Linville, P. W. Affective consequences of complexity regarding self and others. In M. S. Clark and S. T. Fiske (Eds.), *Affect and cognition: The 17th Annual Carnegie Symposium on Cognition.* Hillsdale, NJ: Erlbaum, 1982.

———. Self-complexity and affective extremity: Don't put all your eggs in one cognitive basket. *Social Cognition,* 1985, *3,* 94–120.

Linz, D., Donnerstein, E., Bross, M., and Chapin, M. Mitigating the influence of violence on television and sexual violence in the media. In R. J. Blanchard and D. C. Blanchard (Eds.), *Advances in the study of aggression, Volume 2.* Orlando: Academic Press, 1986.

Lissner, K. Die Entspannung von Bedürfnissen durch Ersatzhandlungen. *Psychologische Forschung,* 1933, *18,* 218–250.

Little, B. R. Personal projects analysis: Trivial pursuits, magnificent obsessions, and the search for coherence. In D. M. Buss and N. Cantor (Eds.), *Personality Psychology: Recent trends and emerging directions.* New York: Springer-Verlag, 15–31, 1989.

Littlefield, C. H., and Rushton, J. P. When a child dies: The sociobiology of bereavement. *Journal of Personality and Social Psychology,* 1986, *51,* 797–802.

Livson, N., and Peskin, H. Perspectives on adolescence from longitudinal research. In J. Adelson (Ed.), *Handbook of adolescent psychology.* New York: Wiley, 47–98, 1980.

Loeb, A., Beck, A. T., Diggory, J. C., and Tuthill, R. Expectancy, level of aspiration, performance, and self-evaluation in depression. *Proceedings of the 75th Annual Convention of the American Psychological Association,* 1967, *2,* 193–194.

Loehlin, J. C. Partitioning environmental and genetic contributions to behavioral development. *American Psychologist,* 1989, *44,* 1285–1292.

Loehlin, J. C., and Nicholls, R. C. *Heredity, environment, and personality.* Austin, TX: University of Texas Press, 1976.

Loevinger, J. *Ego development.* San Francisco: Jossey-Bass, 1976.

Loftus, E. F. (Ed.). Science watch. *American Psychologist,* 1992, *47,* 761–809.

Loftus, E. F. The reality of repressed memories. *American Psychologist,* 1993, *48,* 518–537.

Lomangino, L. *The depiction of subliminally and supraliminally presented aggressive stimuli and its effect on the cognitive functioning of schizophrenics.* Unpublished doctoral dissertation, Fordham University, 1969.

London, P. The rescuers: Motivational hypotheses about Christians who saved Jews from the Nazis. In J. R. McCaulay & L. Berkowitz (Eds.), *Altruism and helping behavior.* New York: Academic Press, 1970.

Loo, C. M. The effects of spatial density on the social behavior of children. *Journal of Applied Social Psychology,* 1972, *2,* 372–381.

Lorenz, K. Der Kumpan in der umwelt des vogels. *Journal für Ornithologie,* 1935, *83,* 137–213, 289–413.

———. The comparative method in studying innate behaviour patterns. *Symposium of the Society of Experimental Biology,* 1950, *4,* 221–268.

——— *On aggression.* New York: Bantam, 1966.

Lovaas, O. I. Some studies on the treatment of childhood schizophrenia. In J. M. Shlien (Ed.), *Research in psychotherapy.* Washington, DC: American Psychological Association, 1968.

———. Behavioral treatment and normal education and intellectual functioning in young autistic children. *Journal of Consulting and Clinical Psychology,* 1987, *55,* 3–9.

———, Freitag, G., Gold, V. J., and Kassorla, I. C. Experimental studies in childhood schizophrenia: 1. Analysis of self-destructive behavior. *Journal of Experimental Child Psychology,* 1965, *2,* 67–84.

Lowenthal, M. F., Thurnher, M., and Chiriboga, D. *Four stages of life-span.* San Francisco: Jossey-Bass, 1975.

Lubin, B., Wallis, R. R., and Paine, C. Patterns of psychological test usage in the United States, 1935–1969. *Professional Psychology,* 1971, *2,* 70–74.

Luborsky, L. Momentary forgetting during psychotherapy and psychoanalysis: A theory and research method. In R. R. Holt (Ed.), *Motives and thought: Psychoanalytic essays in honor of David Rappaport* (Psychological Issues Monograph

18/19). New York: International Universities Press, 1967.

———, and Crits-Christoph, P. *Understanding transference: The CCRT method.* New York: Basic Books, 1990.

Luck, P. W., and Heiss, J. Social determinants of self-esteem in adult males. *Sociology and Social Research,* 1972, *57,* 69–84.

Lykken, D. T., McGue, M., Tellegen, A., and Bouchard, T. J., Jr. Emergenesis: Genetic traits that may not run in families. *American Psychologist,* 1992, *47,* 1565–1577.

Maccoby, E. E. Gender as a social category. *Developmental Psychology,* 1988, *24,* 755–765.

———, and Feldman, S. S. Mother attachment and stranger reactions in the third year of life. *Monographs of the Society for Research in Child Development,* 1972, 37(1).

Maccoby, E. E., and Jacklin, C. N. *The psychology of sex differences.* Stanford, CA: Stanford University Press, 1974.

———. Sex differences in aggression: A rejoinder and reprise. *Child Development,* 1980, *51,* 964–980.

Macfarlane, J. W., Allen, L., and Honzik, M. P. A development study of the behavior problems of normal children between 20 months and 14 years. *University of California Publications in Child Development,* 1954, *2.*

MacKay, D. G. *The organization of perception and action: A theory for language and other cognitive skills.* Berlin, Heidelberg, London, Paris, New York, Tokyo: Springer-Verlag, 1987.

MacKinnon, D. W. The nature and nurture of creative talent. *American Psychologist,* 1962, *17,* 484–495.

Maddi, S. R. On the problem of accepting facticity and pursuing possibility. In S. B. Messer, L. A. Sass, and R. L. Woolfolk (Eds.), *Hermeneutics and psychological theory: Interpretative perspectives on personality, psychotherapy and psychopathology.* New Brunswick, NJ: Rutgers University Press, 1988.

Maddi, S. R. *Personality theories: A comparative analysis* (3rd ed.). Homewood, Ill.: Dorsey, 1976.

———, Bartone, P. T., and Puccetti, M. C. Stressful events are indeed a factor in physical illness: Reply to Schroeder and Costa (1984). *Journal of Personality and Social Psychology,* 1987, *52,* 833–843.

Maddox, G. L. Fact and artifact: Evidence bearing on disengagement theory. In E. Palmore (Ed.), *Normal aging.* Durham, NC: Duke University Press, 1970.

Maddux, J. E., Norton, L. W., and Stoltenberg, C. D. Self-efficacy expectancy, outcome expectancy, and outcome value: Relative effects on behavioral intentions. *Journal of Personality on Social Psychology,* 1986, *51,* 783–789.

Madsen, M. C., and Shapira, A. Cooperative and competitive behavior of urban Afro-American, Anglo-American, Mexican-American, and Mexican village children. *Developmental Psychology,* 1970, *3,* 16–20.

Maduro, R. J., and Wheelwright, J. B. Analytical psychology. In R. J. Corsini (Ed.), *Current personality theories.* Itasca, Illinois: F. E. Peacock, 1977.

Magnussen, D., and Endler, N. S. Interactional psychology: Present status and future prospects. In D. Magnussen and N. S. Endler (Eds.), *Personality at the crossroads: Current issues in interactional psychology.* Hillsdale, NJ: Lawrence Erlbaum, 1977, 99–111.

Magnussen, D. Personality development from an interactional perspective. In L. A. Pervin (Ed.), *Handbook of personality.* New York: Guilford, 193–224, 1990.

Mahler, M. S. *On human symbiosis and the vicissitudes of individuation.* New York: International Universities Press, 1968.

Mahler, V. Ersatzhandlungen verschiedenen Realitätsgrade. *Psychologische Forschung,* 1933, *18,* 26–89.

Mahone, C. H. Fear of failure and unrealistic vocational aspiration. *Journal of Abnormal and Social Psychology,* 1960, *60,* 253–261.

Mahoney, M. J. *Cognition and behavior modification.* Cambridge, MA: Ballinger, 1974.

Mahoney, M. *Human change processes.* New York: Basic Books, 1991.

Mahoney, M. Psychotherapy and human change processes. In M. J. Mahoney and A. Freeman (Eds.), *Cognition and psychotherapy.* New York: Plenum, 3–48, 1985.

Mahrer, A. R. The role of expectancy in delayed reinforcement. *Journal of Experimental Psychology,* 1956, *52,* 101–105.

Maier, N. R. F. *Frustration: The study of behavior without a goal.* New York: McGraw-Hill, 1949.

Main, M. and Cassidy, J. Categories of responses to

reunion with the parent at age 6: Predictable from infant attachment classification and stable over a one month period. *Developmental Psychology,* 1988, *24,* 415–426.

Main, M., Kaplan, K., and Cassidy, J. Security in infancy, childhood and adulthood: A move to the level of representation. In I. Bretherton and E. Waters (Eds.), *Growing points of attachment theory and research. Monographs of The Society for Research in Child Development,* 1985, *50,* Serial No. 209 (1–2), 66–104.

Mair, M. *Between psychology and psychotherapy.* New York: Routledge, 1988.

Malamuth, N. M. Factors associated with rape as predictors of laboratory aggression against women. *Journal of Personality and Social Psychology,* 1983, *45,* 433–442.

———, Feshbach, S., and Jaffe, Y. Sexual arousal and aggression: Recent experiments and theoretical issues. In A. Peplau and C. Hammen (Eds.), *Journal of Social Issues,* 1977, *33,* 110–133.

———, Haber, S. F., and Feshbach, S. Testing hypotheses regarding rape: Exposure to sexual violence, sex differences, and the "normality" of rapists. *Journal of Research in Personality,* 1980, *14,* 121–137.

Maltzman, I. Awareness: Cognitive psychology vs. behaviorism. *Journal of Experimental Research in Personality,* 1966, *1,* 161–165.

Manning, M. M., and Wright, T. L. Self-efficacy expectancies, and the persistence of pain control in childbirth. *Journal of Personality and Social Psychology,* 1983, *45,* 421–431.

Manning, S. A., and Taylor, D. A. Effects of viewed violence and aggression: Stimulation and catharsis. *Journal of Personality and Social Psychology,* 1975, *31,* 180–188.

Marcia. J. E. Identity in adolescence. In J. Adelson (Ed.), *Handbook of adolescent psychology.* New York: Wiley, 1980.

Marcus, R. F., Telleen, S., and Poke, E. J. Relation between cooperation and empathy in young children. *Developmental Psychology,* 1979, *15,* 346–347.

Marijuana and Health: Seventh Annual Report to the United States Congress from the Secretary of Health, Education, and Welfare. Washington, DC: U.S. Government Printing Office, 1977.

Marin, G. V., Marin, G., Otero-Sabogal, R., Sabogal, F., and Perez-Stable, E. *Cultural differences in*

attitudes toward smoking: Developing messages using the theory of reasoned action (Tech. Rep.), 1987. (Available from Box 0320, 400 Parnassus Ave., San Francisco, CA 94117).

Markstrom-Adams, C. A consideration of intervening factors in adolescent identity formation. In G. R. Adams, T. P. Gullotta, and R. Montemayer (Eds.), *Adolescent identity formation.* Newbury Park: Sage, 173–192, 1992.

Markstrom-Adams, C., and Berman, R. *Identity formation among Canadian Jewish adolescents in minority and majority community contexts.* Paper presented as part of a symposium on "Cultural Contexts of Identity Formation: Some International Perspectives," American Psychological Association Convention, Toronto, Canada, August, 1993.

Markstrom-Adams, C., Berman, R. C., and Brusch, G. *Identity formation among Jewish adolescents in dissonant and consonant community contexts.* Paper submitted for publication, 1993.

Markus, H. Self-schemata and processing information about the self. *Journal of Personality and Social Psychology,* 1977, *35,* 63–78.

———, Crane, M., Bernstein, S., and Siladi, M. Self-schemas and gender. *Journal of Personality and Social Psychology,* 1982, *42,* 38–50.

Markus, H., and Kitayama, S. Culture and the self: Implications for cognition, emotion, and motivation. *Psychological Review,* 1991, *98,* 224–253.

Markus, H., and Kunda, Z. Stability and malleability of the self-concept. *Journal of Personality and Social Psychology,* 1986, *51,* 858–866.

Markus, H., and Nurius, P. Possible selves. *American Psychologist,* 1988, *41,* 954–969.

Markus, H., and Wurf, E. The dynamic self-concept: A social psychological perspective. *Annual Review of Psychology,* 1987, *38,* 299–337.

Marsden, G. Content analysis studies of psychotherapy: 1954 through 1968. In A. E. Bergin and S. L. Garfield (Eds.), *Handbook of psychotherapy and behavior change.* New York: Wiley, 1971.

Marsh, K. L., and Weary, G. Depression and attributional complexity. *Personality and Social Psychology Bulletin,* 1989, *15,* 325–336.

Marshall, G. D., and Zimbardo, P. G. Affective consequences of inadequately explained physiological arousal. *Journal of Personality and Social Psychology,* 1979, *37,* 970–988.

Martin, C. L., and Halverson, C. F., Jr. A schematic

processing model of sex-typing and stereotyping in young children. *Child Development*, 1981, *52*, 1119–1134.

———. The roles of cognition in sex-roles and sex-typing. In D. B. Carter (Ed.), *Current conceptions of sex roles and sex-typing: Theory and research.* New York: Praeger, 1987.

Martin, L. L., and Tesser, A. Toward a motivational and structural theory of ruminative thought. In J. S. Uleman and J. A. Bargh (Eds.), *Unintended thought.* New York: Guilford, 306–326, 1989.

Martindale, A., E., and Martindale, C. Metaphorical equivalence of elements and temperaments: Empirical studies of Bachelard's theory of imagination. *Journal of Personality and Social Psychology,* 1988, *55*, 836–848.

Martindale, D. A. Territorial dominance behavior in dyadic verbal interactions. *Proceedings of the 79th Annual Convention of the American Psychological Association,* 1971, *6*, 305–306.

Maslach, C. Negative emotional biasing of unexplained arousal. *Journal of Personality and Social Psychology,* 1979, *37*, 953–969.

Maslow, A. H. Deprivation, threat and frustration. *Psychological Review,* 1941, *48*, 364–366.

———. A theory of human motivation. *Psychological Review,* 1943, *50*, 370–396.

———. *The farther reaches of human nature.* New York: Viking, 1971.

Masson, J. M. *The assault on truth: Freud's suppression of the seduction theory.* New York: Penguin, 1985.

Masten, A. S., Best, K. M., and Garmezy, N. Resilience and development: Contributions from the study of children who overcome adversity. *Development and Psychopathology,* 1990, *2*, 425–444.

Masters, W., and Johnson, V. *Human sexual response.* Boston: Little, Brown, 1966.

Matarazzo, J. D., and Wiens, A. N. *The interview: Research on its anatomy and structure.* Chicago: Aldino-Atherton, 1972.

———, Matarazzo, R. G., and Saslow, G. Speech and silence behavior in clinical psychotherapy and its laboratory correlates. In J. Shlien, H. Hunt, J. D. Matarazzo, and C. Savage (Eds.), *Research in psychotherapy* (Vol. 3). Washington, DC: American Psychological Association, 1968.

Matas, L., Arend, R. A., and Sroufe, L. A. Continuity of adaptation in the second year: The relationship between quality of attachment and later competence. *Child Development,* 1978, *49*, 483–494.

Matheny, Jr., A., Wilson, R. S., and Thaben, A. S. Home and mother: Relations with infant temperament. *Developmental Psychology,* 1987, *23*, 323–331.

Matthews, K. Å. Coronary heart disease and Type A behaviors: Update and alternative to the Booth-Kewley and Friedman (1987) quantitative review. *Psychological Bulletin,* 1988, *104*, 373–380.

———, Batson, C. D., Horn, J., and Rosenman, R. H. "Principles in his nature which interest him in the fortune of others . . ." The heritability of empathic concern for others. *Journal of Personality,* 1981, *49*, 237–247.

Mazis, M. B. Antipollution measures and psychological reactance theory: A field experiment. *Journal of Personality and Social Psychology,* 1975, *31*, 546–660.

McAdams, D. P. *Power, intimacy, and the life story.* New York: Guilford, 1988.

McAdams, D. P. The development of a narrative identity. In D. M. Buss and N. Cantor (Eds.), *Personality psychology: Recent trends and emerging directions.* New York: Springer-Verlag, 160–176, 1989.

McAdams, D. P. Unity and purpose in human lives: The emergence of identity as a life story. In A. I. Rabin, R. A. Zucker, R. A. Emmons, and S. Frank (Eds.), *Studying persons and lives.* New York: Springer, 148–200, 1990.

McAdams, D. P. *Generative lives: Suffering, redemption, and personal destiny.* Paper presented at the American Psychological Association Convention, Toronto, Canada, August 1993.

McAdams, D. P., de St. Aubin, E., and Logan, R. L. Generativity among young, midlife, and older adults, *Psychology and Aging,* 1993, *8*, 221–230.

McAdams, D. P. Can personality change? Levels of stability and growth in personality across the life span. In T. F. Heatherton and J. L. Weinberger (Eds.), *Can personality change?* Washington, DC: American Psychological Association, 299–314, 1994.

McClearn, G. E. The inheritance of behavior. In L. Postman (Ed.), *Psychology in the making.* New York: Knopf, 1962.

McClelland, D. C. Methods of measuring human motivation. In J. W. Atkinson (Ed.), *Motives in fantasy, action, and society.* Princeton, NJ: Van Nostrand, 1958.

———. *The achieving society.* Princeton, NJ: Van Nostrand, 1961.

———, **and Atkinson, J. W.** The projective expression of needs: I. The effect of different intensities of the hunger drive on perception. *Journal of Psychology,* 1948, *25,* 205–222.

McClelland, D. C., Davis, W. N., Kalin, R., and Wanner, E. *The drinking man.* New York: Free Press, 1972.

McClelland, D. C., and Pilon, D. A. Sources of adult motives in patterns of parent behavior in early childhood. *Journal of Personality and Social Psychology,* 1983, *44,* 564–574.

McCrae, R. R., and Costa, P. T. Jr. *Emerging lives, enduring disposition: Personality in adulthood.* Boston: Little, Brown, 1984.

———. Validation of the five-factor model of personality across instruments and raters. *Journal of Personality and Social Psychology,* 1987, *1,* 81–90.

McCrae, R. R., and Costa, P. T., Jr. *Personality in adulthood.* New York: Guilford, 1990.

McCrae, R. R., and John, O. P. An introduction to the five factor model and its applications. *Journal of Personality,* 1992, *60,* 175–215.

McGinnies, E. Emotionality and perceptual defense. *Psychological Review,* 1949, *56,* 244–251.

McGlothlin, W. H., and Arnold, D. D. LSD revisited. *Archives of General Psychiatry,* 1971, *24,* 35–49.

McGlothlin, W. H., Cohen, S., and McGlothlin, M. S. Long lasting effects of LSD on normals. *Archives of General Psychiatry,* 1967, *17,* 521–532.

McGrath, M. J., and Cohen, D. B. REM sleep facilitation of adaptive waking behaviors: A review of the literature. *Psychological Bulletin,* 1978, *85,* 24–57.

McGue, M., and Lykken, D. T. Genetic influence on risk of divorce. *Psychological Science,* 1992, *3,* 368–373.

McGuire, W. J., and Padawer-Singer, A. Trait salience in the spontaneous self-concept. *Journal of Personality and Social Psychology,* 1976, *33,* 743–754.

McKinley, D. G. *Social class and family life.* New York: Free Press, 1964.

Mednick, S., and Christiansen, K. O. *Biosocial bases of criminal behavior.* New York: Gardner, 1977.

Mednick, S. A., Brennan, P., and Kandel, E. Predis-

position to violence. *Aggressive Behavior,* 1988, *14,* 25–33.

Mednick, S. A., Moffitt, T. E., and Stack, S. *The causes of crime: New biological approaches.* New York: Cambridge University Press, 1987.

Meehl, P. E. *Clinical versus statistical prediction.* Minneapolis: University of Minnesota Press, 1954.

———. Schizotaxia, schizotypy, schizophrenia. *American Psychologist,* 1962, *17,* 827–838.

Megargee, E. I. Undercontrolled and overcontrolled personality types in extreme antisocial aggression. *Psychological Monographs,* 1966, *80* (Whole No. 611).

———, **and Mendelsohn, G. A.** A cross validation of twelve MMPI indices of hostility and control. *Journal of Abnormal and Social Psychology,* 1962, *65,* 431–438.

Meiselman, K. *Incest: A psychological study of causes and effects with treatment recommendations.* San Francisco: Jossey-Bass, 1979.

Mendelsohn, G. A. It's time to put theories of personality in their place, or, Allport and Stagner got it right, why can't we? In K. H. Craik, R. Hogan, and R. N. Wolfe (Eds.), *Fifty years of personality psychology.* New York: Plenum, 103–118, 1993.

Menzies, E. S. *Preference in television content among violent prisoners* (FCI Research Reports). Tallahassee: Federal Correctional Institution, 1974.

Merton, R. K. *Social theory and social structure.* Glencoe, Ill.: Free Press, 1957.

Messick, S. The standard problem: Meaning and values in measurement and evaluation. *American Psychologist,* 1975, *30,* 955–966.

———, **and Jackson, D. N.** Acquiescence and the factorial interpretation of the MMPI. *Psychological Bulletin,* 1961, *58,* 299–304.

Meyer, H. H., Walker, W. B., and Litwin, G. H. Motive patterns and risk preferences associated with entrepreneurship. *Journal of Abnormal and Social Psychology,* 1961, *63,* 570–574.

Midlarsky, E., and Bryan, J. H. Affect expressions and children's imitative altruism. *Journal of Experimental Research in Personality,* 1972, *6,* 195–203.

Milgram, S. Behavioral study of obedience. *Journal of Abnormal and Social Psychology,* 1963, *67,* 371–378.

———. *Obedience to authority.* New York: Harper & Row, 1974.

———, **and Shotland, R. L.** *Television and antiso-*

cial behavior: Field experiments. New York: Academic Press, 1973.

Miller, D. R., and Swanson, G. E. Inner conflict and defense. New York: Holt, 1960.

Miller, I. W., III, and Norman, W. H. Learned helplessness: A review and attribution-theory model. Psychological Bulletin, 1979, 86, 93–118.

Miller M. M. Treatment of chronic alcoholism by hypnotic aversion. Journal of the American Medical Association, 1959, 171, 1492–1495.

Miller, N. E. The frustration-aggression hypothesis. Psychological Review, 1941, 48, 337–342.

———. Experimental studies in conflict. In J. McV. Hunt (Ed.), Personality and the behavioral disorders (Vol. 1). New York: Ronald, 1944.

———. Liberalization of basic S-R concepts: Extensions to conflict, motivation, and social learning. In S. Koch (Ed.), Psychology: A study of a science (Vol. 2). New York: McGraw-Hill, 1959.

———, and Banuazizi, A. Instrumental learning by curarized rats of a specific visceral response, intestinal or cardiac. Journal of Comparative and Physiological Psychology, 1968, 65, 1–17.

Miller, N. E., and Bugelski, R. Minor studies in aggression. II. The influence of frustration imposed by the in-group attitudes expressed toward out-groups. Journal of Psychology, 1948, 25, 437–442.

Miller, N. E., and Dollard, J. Social learning and imitation. New Haven: Yale University Press, 1941.

Miller, P. A., and Eisenberg, N. The relation of empathy to aggressive and externalizing/antisocial behavior. Psychological Bulletin, 1988, 103, 324–344.

Miller, W. R., and C'deBaca, J. Quantum change: Toward a psychology of transformation. In T. F. Heatherton and J. L. Weinberger (Eds.), Can personality change? Washington, DC: American Psychological Association, 253–280, 1994.

Millett, R. A. Measures of learning and conditioning. In H. J. Eysenck (Ed.), Experiments in personality (Vol. II). London: Routledge, 1960.

Mischel, W. Delay of gratification, need for achievement, and acquiescence in another culture. Journal of Abnormal and Social Psychology, 1961, 62, 543–552.

———. A social learning theory view of sex differences in behavior. In E. E. Maccoby (Ed.), The

development of sex differences. Stanford, CA: Stanford University Press, 1966.

———. Personality and assessment. New York: Wiley, 1968.

———. Introduction to personality. New York: Holt, 1971.

———. Toward a cognitive social learning reconceptualization of personality. Psychological Review, 1973, 80, 252–283.

———. Cognitive appraisals and transformations in self-control. In B. Weiner (Ed.), Cognitive views of human motivation. New York: Academic Press, 1974a.

———. Process in delay of gratification. In L. Berkowitz (Ed.), Advances in experimental social psychology (Vol. 7). New York: Academic Press, 1974b.

———. On the future of personality measurement. American Psychologist, 1977, 32, 246–254.

———. On the interface of cognition and personality: Beyond the person-situation debate. American Psychologist, 1979, 34, 740–754.

———. Convergences and challenges in the search for consistency. American Psychologist, 1984, 39, 351–364.

———, and Ebbesen, E. B. Attention in delay of gratification. Journal of Personality and Social Psychology, 1970, 16, 329–337.

Mischel, W., Ebbeson, E. B., and Zeiss, A. R. Cognitive and attentional mechanisms in delay of gratification. Journal of Personality and Social Psychology, 1972, 21, 204–218.

Mischel, W., and Mischel, H. N. A cognitive social learning approach to morality and self-regulation. In T. Lickona (Ed.), Moral development and behavior: Theory, research and social issues. New York: Holt, 1976.

Mischel, W., and Mischel, H. N. Self-control and the self. In T. Mischel (Ed.), The Self: Psychological and philosophical issues. Totowa, New Jersey: Rowan and Littlefield, 1977.

Mischel, W., and Peake, P. K. Beyond déjà vu in the search for cross-situational consistency. Psychological Review, 1982, 89, 730–755.

Mischel, W., Shoda, Y., and Peake, P. K. The nature of adolescent competencies predicted by preschool delay of gratification. Journal of Personality and Social Psychology, 1988, 54, 687–696.

Mischel, W., Peake, P. K., and Zeiss, A. Cognitive and attentional mechanisms in delay of gratification. *Journal of Personality and Social Psychology,* 1972, *21,* 204–218.

Mitchell, C., and Stuart, R. B. Effects of self-efficacy on dropout from obesity treatment. *Journal of Consulting and Clinical Psychology, 1984, 52,* 1100–1101.

Mitchell, J. E., Baker, L. A., and Jacklin, C. N. Masculinity and femininity in twin children: genetic and environmental factors. *Child Development,* 1989, *60,* 1475–1485.

Money, J. (Ed.). *Sex research, new developments.* New York: Holt, 1965.

Monte, C. F. *Beneath the mask.* New York: Praeger, 1977.

Monteith, M., Berkowitz, L., Kruglanski, A., and Blair, C. The influence of physical discomfort on experienced anger and anger related ideas, judgments, & memories. Manuscript in preparation, 1990.

Montemayer, R., and Eisen, M. The development of self-conceptions from childhood to adolescence. *Developmental Psychology,* 1977, *13,* 314–319.

Moos, R. H. Conceptualizations of human environment. *American Psychologist,* 1973, *28,* 652–665.

Morash, M. A. Working class membership and the adolescent identity crisis. *Adolescence,* 1980, *15,* 313–320.

Morokoff, P. J. Effects of sex guilt, repression, sexual "arousibility," and sexual experience on female sexual arousal during erotica and fantasy. *Journal of Personality and Social Psychology,* 1985, *49,* 177–187.

Morris, J. L. Propensity for risk taking as a determinant of vocational choice: An extension of the theory of achievement motivation. *Journal of Personality and Social Psychology,* 1966, *3,* 328–335.

Moss, H. A., and Kagan, J. Stability of achievement and recognition seeking behaviors from early childhood through adulthood. *Journal of Abnormal and Social Psychology,* 1961, *62,* 504–513.

Mowrer, O. H. *Learning theory and behavior.* New York: Wiley, 1960.

————, and Viek, P. An experimental analogue of fear from a sense of helplessness. *Journal of Abnormal and Social Psychology,* 1948, *43,* 193–200.

Moyer, K. E. The physiology of aggression and the implications for aggression control. In J. L. Singer (Ed.), *The control of aggression and violence.* New York: Academic Press, 1971.

Mukherjee, B. N., and Sinha, R. Achievement values and self-ideal discrepancies in college students, *Personality: An International Journal,* 1970, *1,* 275–301.

Munroe, R. H., Shimmin, H. S., and Munroe, R. L. Gender understanding and sex-role preferences in four cultures. *Developmental Psychology,* 1984, *20,* 673–682.

Murray, H. A. The effect of fear upon estimates of the maliciousness of other personalities. *Journal of Social Psychology,* 1933, *4,* 310–329.

————. *Explorations in personality: A clinical and experimental study of fifty men of college age.* New York: Oxford University Press, 1938.

Murstein, B. I. *Theory and research in projective techniques.* New York: Wiley, 1963.

Mussen, P. H. The development of personality and social behavior. In P. Mussen and M. R. Rosenzweig (Eds.), *Psychology: An introduction.* Lexington: D. C. Heath, 1977.

————, and Eisenberg-Berg, N. *Roots of caring, sharing, and helping. The development of prosocial behavior in children.* San Francisco: Freeman, 1977.

Myers, I. *The Myers-Briggs Type Indicator.* Princeton, NJ: Educational Testing Service, 1962.

Myers, L. J., Speight, S. L., Highlen, P. S., Cox, C. I., Reynolds, A. L., Adams, E. M., and Hanley, C. P. Identity development and worldview: Toward an optimal conceptualization. *Journal of Counseling and Development,* 1990, *70,* 64–71.

Nadon, R., Laurence, J. R., and Perry, C. Multiple predictors of hypnotic susceptibility. *Journal of Personality and Social Psychology,* 1987, *53,* 948–960.

Nation, J. R., Cooney, J. B., and Gartrell, K. E. Durability and generalizability of persistence training. *Journal of Abnormal Psychology,* 1979, *88*(2), 121–136.

Neisser, U. Five kinds of self-knowledge. *Philosophical Psychology,* 1988, *1,* 35–59 .

Nelson, J. D., Gelfand, D. M., and Hartmann, D. P. Children's aggression following competition and exposure to an aggressive model. *Child Development,* 1969, *40,* 1085–1097.

Neugarten, B. L. Personality and aging. In J. E. Birren and K. W. Schaie (Eds.), *Handbook of the psy-*

chology of aging. New York: Van Nostrand Reinhold, 1977.

Newcomb, T. *Personality and social change.* New York: Dryden, 1943.

Newson, J., and Newson, E. *Four years old in an urban community.* Chicago: Aldine, 1968.

————. Cultural aspects of child rearing in the English-speaking world. In A. Skolnick (Ed.), *Rethinking childhood.* Boston: Little, Brown, 1976. *The New York Times,* Sunday, June 8, 1980, Section 2, p. 15.

Nicholls, J. G. Conceptions of ability and achievement motivation. In Ames, R. E., and Ames, C. (Eds.), *Motivation in education, Vol. 1.* San Francisco: Academic Press, 1984, 39–73.

Nichols, M. P., and Efran, J. S. Catharsis in psychotherapy: A new perspective. *Psychotherapy,* 1985, 22, 46–58.

Nickel, T. W. The attribution of intention as a critical factor in the relation between frustration and aggression. *Journal of Personality,* 1974, 42, 482–492.

Nisan, M., and Kohlberg, L. Universality and variation in moral judgment: A longitudinal and cross-sectional study in Turkey. *Child Development,* 1982, 53, 865–876.

Nisbett, R. E., and Borgida, E. Attribution and the psychology of prediction. *Journal of Personality and Social Psychology,* 1975, 32, 932–943.

Nisbett, R. E., and Schachter, S. Cognitive manipulation of pain. *Journal of Experimental Social Psychology,* 1966, 2, 227–236.

Nobles, W. Psychological nigrescence: An Afrocentric view. *The Counseling Psychologist,* 1989, 17, 253–257.

Norem, J. K. Cognitive strategies as personality: Effectiveness, specificity, flexibility, and change. In D. M. Buss and N. Cantor (Eds.), *Personality psychology: Recent trends and emerging directions.* New York: SpringerVerlag, 45–60, 1989.

Norem-Hebeisen, A. A., and Johnson, D. W. The relationship between cooperative, competitive, and individualistic attitudes and differentiated aspects of self-esteem. *Journal of Personality,* 1981, 49, 415–426.

Norman, W. T. Toward an adequate taxonomy of personality attributes: Replicated factor structure in peer nomination personality ratings. *Journal of*

Abnormal and Social Psychology, 1963, 66, 574–583.

————. On estimating psychological relationships: Social desirability and self-report. *Psychological Bulletin,* 1967, 67, 273–293.

Novaco, R. W. *Anger control: The development and evaluation of an experimental treatment.* Lexington, MA: Lexington Books, 1975.

————. Anger and its therapeutic regulations. In M. A. Chesney and R. Rosenman (Eds.), *Anger and hostility in cardiovascular and behavioral disorders.* New York: Hemisphere, 1985.

Nunnally, J. C. *Psychometric theory* (2nd ed.). New York: McGraw-Hill, 1978.

Nuttin, J. M. Jr. Narcissism beyond Gestalt and awareness: The name-letter effect. *European Journal of Social Psychology,* 1985, 15, 353–361.

Ochse, R., and Plug, C. Cross-cultural investigation of the validity of Erikson's theory of personality development. *Journal of Personality and Social Psychology,* 1986, 50, 1240–1252.

Offer, D. *The psychological world of the teenager.* New York: Basic Books, 1969.

————, and Offer, J. B. *From teenage to young manhood.* New York: Basic Books, 1975.

Oliner, S. P., and Oliner, P. M. *The altruistic personality: Rescuers of Jews in Nazi Europe.* New York: The Free Press, 1988.

Olowse, A. A. A cross-cultural study of adolescent self-concept. *Journal of Adolescence,* 1984, 6, 263–274.

Olweus, D. Familial and temperamental determinants of aggressive behavior in adolescent boys: A causal analysis. *Developmental Psychology,* 1980, 16, 644–666.

————. Aggression and hormones: Behavioral relationship with testosterone and adrenaline. In D. Olweus, J. Block, and M. Radke-Yarrow (Eds.), *Development of antisocial and prosocial behavior: Research, theories, and issues.* Orlando, FL: Academic Press, 1986.

————, Mattisson, A., Schalling, D., and Lam, H. Testosterone, aggression, physical, and personality dimensions in normal adolescent males. *Psychosomatic Medicine,* 1980, 42, 253–269.

Olweus, D. Personality and aggression. In J. K. Cole and D. D. Jensen (Eds.), *Nebraska Symposium on Motivation* (Vol. 21). Lincoln: University of Nebraska Press, 1973.

———. Personality factors and aggression: With special reference to violence within the peer group. In J. de Wit and W. W. Hartup (Eds.), *Determinants and origins of aggressive behavior*. The Hague: Mouton, 1974.

———. *Aggression in the schools: Bullies and whipping boys*. Washington, DC: Hemisphere, 1976.

———. A critical analysis of the "modern" interactionist position. In D. Magnussen and N. S. Endler (Eds.), *Personality at the crossroads: Current issues in interactional psychology*. Hillsdale, NJ: Lawrence Erlbaum, 1977. (a)

———. Aggression and peer acceptance in preadolescent boys. Two short-term longitudinal studies of ratings. *Child Development*, 1977, *48*, 1301–1313. (b)

———. Stability of aggressive reaction patterns in males: A review. *Psychological Bulletin*, 1979, *86*, 852–875.

Opler, M. K. (Ed.). *Culture and mental health*. New York: Macmillan, 1959.

———. *Culture and social psychiatry*. New York: Atherton, 1967.

Orlinsky, D., and Howard, B. The good hour. *Archives of General Psychiatry*, 1967, *16*, 621–632.

Orne, M. T. The nature of hypnosis: Artifact and essence. *Journal of Abnormal and Social Psychology*, 1959, *58*, 277–299.

———. On the social psychology of the psychological experiment. *American Psychologist*, 1962, *17*, 776–783.

———. Hypnosis. In G. Lindzey, C. Hall, and R. F. Thompson, *Psychology*. New York: Worth, 1975.

Ornstein, R. E. *The psychology of consciousness*. San Francisco: Freeman, 1972.

Ortony, A., and Turner, T. J. What's basic about basic emotions? *Psychological Review*, 1990, *97*, 315–331.

Orvis, B. R., Cunningham, J. D., and Kelley, H. H. A closer examination of causal inference: The role of consensus, distinctiveness, and consistency information. *Journal of Personality and Social Psychology*, 1975, *32*, 605–616.

Ostwald, P., and Bittner, E. Life adjustment after severe persecution. *American Journal of Psychiatry*, 1968, *124*, 87–94.

Ozer, D. J., and Gjerde, P. F. Patterns of personality consistency and change from childhood through adolescence. *Journal of Personality*, 1989, *57*, 483–507 .

Paivio, A. *Imagery and verbal processes*. New York: Holt, 1971.

Parke, R. D. The role of punishment in the socialization process. In R. A. Hoppe, G. A. Milton, and E. C. Simmel (Eds.), *Early experiences and the processes of socialization*. New York: Academic Press, 1970.

———, and Colmer, C. W. Child abuse: An interdisciplinary analysis. In E. M. Hetherington (Ed.), *Child Development Research, 5*, 1975.

Parke, R. D., and Slaby, R. G. The development of aggression. In P. H. Mussen (Gen. Ed.) and E. M. Hetherington (Vol. Ed.), *Handbook of child psychology: Vol. 4, Socialization, personality, and social development* (4th ed.). New York: Wiley, 1983, 547–641.

Parke, R. D., and Suomi, S. J. Adult male-infant relationships: Human and nonprimate evidence. In K. Immelmann, G. Barlow, M. Main, and L. Petrinovitch (Eds.), *Behavioral development: The Bielefeld interdisciplinary project*. New York: Cambridge University Press, 1980.

Parke, R. D., and Walters, R. H. Some factors influencing the efficacy of punishment training for inducing response inhibitions. *Monographs of the Society for Research in Child Development*, 1967, *32* (1, Serial No. 109).

Parker, G., Tupling, H., and Brown, L. B. A parental bonding instrument. *British Journal of Medical Psychology*, 1979, *52*, 1–10.

Passini, F. T., and Norman, W. T. A universal conception of personality structure? *Journal of Personality and Social Psychology*, 1966, *4*, 44–49.

Passman, R., and Weisberg, P. Mothers and blankets as agents for promoting play and exploration by young children in a novel environment. *Developmental Psychology*, 1975, *11*, 170–177.

Patterson, C. J. Self-control and self-regulation in childhood. In T. Field and A. Huston-Stein (Eds.), *Review of human development*. New York: Wiley, 1982.

———, and Mischel, W. Effects of temptation-inhibiting and task-facilitating plans on self-control. *Journal of Personality and Social Psychology*, 1976, *33*, 209–217.

Patterson, G. R. *Coercive family process*. Eugene, Oregon: Castalia Press, 1982.

———, and Bank, L. Some amplifying mechanisms for pathological processes in families. In

M. Gunner (Ed.), *Minnesota symposium on child psychology*. Hillsdale, NJ: Lawrence Erlbaum Associates, 1989.

Patterson, G. R., Chamberlain, P., and Reid, J. B. A comparative evaluation of a parent training program. *Behavior Therapy*, 1982, *13*, 638–650.

Patterson, G. R., Cobb, J. A., and Ray, R. S. A social engineering technology for retraining the families of aggressive boys. In H. E. Adams and I. P. Unibel (Eds.), *Issues and trends in behavior therapy*. Springfield, Ill.: Charles C Thomas, 1973.

Patterson, G. R., Littman, R. A., and Bricker, W. Assertive behavior in children: A step toward a theory of aggression. *Monographs of the Society for Research in Child Development*, 1967, *32*(5, Serial No. 113).

Patterson, S. J., Sochting, I., and Marcia, J. E. The inner space and beyond: Women and identity. In G. R. Adams, T. P. Gullotta, and R. Montemayer (Eds.), *Adolescent identity formation*. Newbury Park: Sage, 9–24, 1992.

Paul, G. L. *Insight vs. desensitization in psychotherapy*. Stanford, CA: Stanford University Press, 1966.

Paunonen, S. V., and Jackson, D. N. Idiographic measurement strategies for personality and prediction: Some unredeemed promissory notes. *Psychological Review*, 1985, *92*, 486–511.

Peeke, H. R. S., Wyers, E. J., and Herz, M. J. Waning of the aggressive response to male models in the three spined stickleback (*Gasterosteus aculeatus L.*). *Animal Behavior*, 1969, *17*, 224–228.

Pelto, P. The difference between tight and loose societies. *Transaction*, April 1968, 37–40.

Penk, W. E., Carpenter, J. C., and Rylee, K. E. MMPI correlates of social and physical anhedonia. *Journal of Consulting and Clinical Psychology*, 1979, *47*, 1046–1052.

Pennebaker, J. W. Stream of consciousness and stress: Levels of thinking. In J. S. Uleman and J. A. Bargh (Eds.), *Unintended thought*. New York: Guilford, 327–350, 1989.

Pennebaker, J. W. *Opening up*. New York: William Morrow, 1990.

Peplau, L. A. *Research on lesbian and gay relationships. A decade review*. Paper presented at the 4th International Congress on Personal Relationships held at the University of British Columbia in Vancouver, Canada, July 3–8, 1988.

———, Rubin, A., and Hill, C. T. Sexual intimacy in dating relationships. *Journal of Social Issues*, 1977, *33*, 86–109.

Perlman, D., and Duck, S. *Intimate relationships: Development, dynamics, deterioration*. Newbury Park, CA: Sage Publications, 1987.

Pervin, L. A. (Ed.). *Goal concepts in personality and social psychology*. Hillsdale, NJ: Lawrence Erlbaum, 1989.

Petersen, A. C. Adolescent development. *Annual Review of Psychology*, 1988, *39*, 583–607.

Peterson, C., and Barrett, L. C. Explanatory style and academic performance among university freshmen. *Journal of Personality and Social Psychology*, 1987, *53*, 603–607.

Peterson, C., Seligman, M. E. P., and Vaillant, G. Pessimistic explanatory style is a risk factor for physical illness: A thirty-five year longitudinal study. *Journal of Personality and Social Psychology*, 1988, *55*, 23–27.

Peterson, C., Semmel, A., von Baeyer, C., Abramson, L. Y., Metalsky, G. I., and Seligman, M. E. P. The Attributional Style Questionnaire. *Cognitive Therapy and Research*, 1982, *6*, 287–299.

Peterson, D. R. Conflict. In H. H. Kelley, E. Berscheid, A. Christenson, J. H. Harvey, T. L. Huston, G. Levinger, E. McClintock, L. A. Peplau, and D. R. Peterson (Eds.), *Close relationships*. New York: W. H. Freeman, 1983.

Phares, E. J. *Locus of control in personality*. Morristown, NJ: Generaly Learning Press, 1976.

Phillips, D., McCartney, K., and Scarr, S. Child-care quality and children's social development. *Developmental Psychology*, 1987, *23*, 537–543.

Phillips, D. J. The impact of mass media violence on U.S. homicides. *American Sociological Review*, 1983, *48*, 560–568.

Phillips, D. J., and Hensley, J. E. When violence is rewarded or punished: The impact of mass media stories on homicide. *Journal of Communication*, 1984, *34*, (3), 101–116.

Phinney, J. S. Ethnic identity and self-esteem: A review and integration. *Hispanic Journal of Behavioral Sciences*, 1991, *13*, 193–208.

Phinney, J. S., and Chavira, V. Ethnic identity and self-esteem: An exploratory longitudinal study. *Journal of Adolescence*, in press.

Phinney, J. S., and Rosenthal, D. A. Ethnic identity in adolescence: Process, context, and outcome. In G. R. Adams, T. P. Gullotta, and R. Montemayer

(Eds.), *Adolescent identity formation.* Newbury Park: Sage, 145–172, 1992.

Pianka, E. R. On r- and K-selection. *American Naturalist,* 1970, *104,* 592–597.

Piccione, C., Hilgard, E. R., and Zimbardo, P. G. On the degree of stability of measured hypnotizability over a 25-year period. *Journal of Personality and Social Psychology,* 1989, *56,* 289–295.

Piliavin, I. M., Rodin, J., and Piliavin, J. A. Good Samaritanism: An underground phenomenon? *Journal of Personality and Social Psychology,* 1969, *13,* 289–299.

Pilleri, G., and Knuckey, J. Behaviour patterns of some delphinidae observed in the western Mediterranean. *Zeitschrift fur Tierpsychologie,* 1969, *26*(1), 48–72.

Pitkänen-Pulkkinen, L. Self-control as a prerequisite for constructive behavior. In S. Feshbach and A. Fraczek (Eds.), *Aggression and behavior change: Biological and social processes.* New York: Praeger, 1979.

———. Self-control and continuity from childhood to adolescence. In P. B. Baltes and O. G. Brim (Eds.), *Life-span development and behavior (Vol. 4).* New York: Academic Press, 1982.

Plato. *The Symposium.* Translated by W. Hamilton. London: Penguin Books Ltd, 1972.

Plomin, R. *Development, genetics, and psychology.* Hillsdale, NJ: Erlbaum, 1986.

———. Environment and genes. *American Psychologist,* 1989, *44,* 105–111.

Plomin, R., Chipuer, H. M., and Loehlin, J. C. Behavioral genetics and personality. In L. A. Pervin (Ed.), *Handbook of personality.* New York: Guilford, 225–243, 1990.

Plomin, R., Corely, R., DeFries, J. C., and Fulker, D. W. Individual differences in television viewing in early childhood: Nature as well as nurture. *Psychological Science,* 1990, *1,* 371–377.

Polansky, N., Freeman, W., Horowitz, M., Irwin, L., Papanis, N., Rappaport, D., and Whaley, F. Problems of interpersonal relations in research on groups. *Human Relations,* 1949, *2,* 281–291.

Posner, M. I., and Rothbart, M. K. Intentional chapters on unintended thoughts. In J. S. Uleman and J. A. Bargh (Eds.), *Unintended thought.* New York: Guilford, 450–470, 1989.

Powers, W. T. *Behavior: The control of perception.* Chicago: Aldine, 1973.

Pratt, M. W., Kerig, P., Cowan, P. A., and Cowan, C. P. Mothers and fathers teaching three year olds: Authoritative parenting and adult scaffolding of young children's learning. *Developmental Psychology,* 1988, *24,* 832–839.

Proshansky, H., and Newton, P. Colour: The nature and meaning of Negro self-identity. In P. Watson (Ed.), *Psychology and Race.* Chicago, Ill.: Aldine, 1973, 176–212.

Provence, S., and Lipton, R. C. *Infants in institutions.* New York: International Universities Press, 1962.

Rabkin, J. G., and Streuning, E. L. Life events, stress, and illness. *Science,* 1976, *194,* 1013–1020.

Rabkin, L. Y., and Rabkin, K. Children of the kibutz. *Readings in Psychology Today* (3rd ed.). Del Mar, CA: CRM, 1974.

Radke-Yarrow, M., Zahn-Waxler, C., and Chapman, M. Children's prosocial dispositions and behavior. In P. H. Mussen (Ed.), *Handbook of child psychology;* E. M. Hetherington (Ed.), *Volume IV: Socialization, personality, and social development.* New York: Wiley, 1983.

Rahe, R. H. The pathway between subjects' recent life change and their near-future illness reports: Representative results and methodological issues. In B. S. Dohrenwend and B. P. Dohrenwend (Eds.), *Stressful life events: Their nature and effects.* New York: Wiley, 1974.

Rainwater, L. Crucible of identity. The Negro lower-class family. *Daedalus,* 1966, *95,* 172–216.

Ramirez, M. *Psychology of the Americas: Mestizo perspectives on personality and mental health.* New York: Pergamon, 1983.

Ramirez, M. *Psychotherapy and counseling with minorities.* New York: Pergamon, 1991.

Rapaport, D. *Emotions and memory.* Baltimore: Williams & Wilkins, 1942.

———. The structure of psychoanalytic theory. In S. Koch (Ed.), *Psychology: A study of a science* (Vol. 3). New York: McGraw-Hill, 1959.

———. *The structure of psychoanalytic theory: A systematizing attempt* (Psychological Issues Monograph 6). New York: International Universities Press, 1960.

Rathbun, C., McLaughlin, H., Bennett, O., and Garland, J. A. Later adjustment of children following radical separation from family and culture. *Ameri-*

can *Journal of Orthopsychiatry,* 1965, *35,* 604–609.

Raush, H. L., Barry, W. A., Hertel, R. K., and Swain, M. A. *Communication, conflict and marriage.* San Francisco: Jossey-Bass, 1974.

Raynor, J. O. Relationships between achievement-related motives, future orientation, and academic performance. *Journal of Personality and Social Psychology,* 1970, *15,* 28–33.

Read, D., Adams, G. R., and Dobson, W. R. Ego-identity, status, personality and social influence style. *Journal of Personality and Social Psychology,* 1984, *46,* 169–177.

Reid, J. B. Social-interactional patterns in families of abused and nonabused children. In C. Zahn-Waxler, E. M. Cummings, and R. Iannotti (Eds.), *Altruism and aggression.* New York: Cambridge University Press, 1986.

Reisenzein, R. The Schachter theory of emotion: Two decades later. *Psychological Bulletin,* 1983, *94,* 239–264.

Reiss, D. Genes and the environment: Siblings and synthesis. In R. Plomin and G. E. McClearn (Eds.), *Nature, nurture and psychology.* Washington, DC: American Psychological Association, 417–432, 1993.

Remmers, H. H., and Radler, D. H. *The American teenager.* Indianapolis: Bobbs-Merrill, 1957.

Reyker, J. Hypnosis in research on psychopathology. In J. E. Gordon (Ed.), *Handbook of clinical and experimental hypnosis.* New York: Macmillan, 1967.

Reykowski, J. Intrinsic motivation and intrinsic inhibition of aggressive behavior. In S. Feshbach and A. Fraczek (Eds.), *Aggression and behavior change: Biological and social processes.* New York: Praeger, 1979.

Rheingold, H. L. The modification of social responsiveness in institutional babies. *Monographs of the Society for Research in Child Development,* 1956, *21* (2, Whole No. 63).

Ribble, M. *The rights of infants.* New York: Columbia University Press, 1943.

Richter, C. P. The phenomenon of unexplained sudden death in animals and man. In W. H. Gant (Ed.), *Physiological basis of psychiatry.* Springfield, Ill.: Charles C Thomas, 1958.

Ricoeur, P. Narrative and hermeneutics. In J. Fisher (Ed.), *Perspective on the work of Monroe C. Beards-*

ley. Philadelphia: Temple University Press, 149–162, 1983.

Riegel, K. Adult life-crises: A diabetic interpretation of development. In M. Dutan and L. H. Ginsberg (Eds.), *Life span developmental psychology: Normative life crises.* New York: Academic Press, 1975.

Ritu, K., and Sukhdeep, G. Relations between acceptance-rejection and self-esteem. *Indian Psychology Review,* 1986, *30,* 15–21.

Robbins, C. J. Attributions and depression: Why is the literature so inconsistent? *Journal of Personality and Social Psychology,* 1988, *54,* 880–889.

Robbins, K., and McAdam, D. Interhemispheric alpha symmetry and imagery mode. *Brain and Language,* 1974, *1,* 189–193.

Rodgers, D. A. Factors underlying differences in alcohol preference among inbred strains of mice. *Psychosomatic Medicine,* 1966, *28,* 498–513.

——, and McClearn, G. E. Alcohol preference of mice. In E. L. Bliss (Ed.), *Roots of behavior.* New York: Harper & Row, 1962.

Rodin, J., Elias, M., Silberstein, L. R., and Wagner, A. Combined behavioral and pharmacological treatment for obesity: Predictors of successful weight maintenance. *Journal of Consulting and Clinical Psychology,* 1988, *56,* 399–404.

Rodin, J., and Langer, E. J. Long-term effects of a control-relevant intervention with the institutionalized aged. *Journal of Personality and Social Psychology,* 1977, *35,* 897–902.

——. Aging labels: The decline of control and the fall of self-esteem. *The Journal of Social Issues,* 1980, *36,* 12–29.

Rogers, C. R. A theory of therapy, personality, and interpersonal relationships, as developed in the client-centered framework. In S. Koch (Ed.), *Psychology: A study of a science* (Vol. 3). New York: McGraw-Hill, 1959.

——. *On becoming a person.* Boston: Houghton Mifflin, 1961.

——. Actualizing tendency in relation to "motives" and to consciousness. In M. R. Jones (Ed.), *Nebraska symposium on motivation.* Lincoln: University of Nebraska Press, 1963.

——. *A way of being.* Boston: Houghton Mifflin, 1980.

——. *Freedom to learn for the '80's.* Columbus, OH: Charles E. Merrill, 1983.

——, and Dymond, R. F. (Eds.). *Psychotherapy*

and personality change. Chicago: University of Chicago Press, 1954.

Rogers, C. R., Gendlin, E. T., Kiesler, D. J., and Truax, C. B. *The therapeutic relationship and its impact.* Madison: University of Wisconsin Press, 1967.

Rohner, R. P. *The warmth dimension.* Beverly Hills: Sage, 1986.

Rorer, L. G., and Goldberg, L. R. Acquiescence in the MMPI? *Educational and Psychological Measurement,* 1965, *25,* 801–817.

Rorschach, H. *Psychodiagnostik.* Bern: Bircher, 1921. (Trans. Hans Huber Verlag, 1942).

Rose, R. J., Koskenvuo, M., Kaprio, J., Sarna, S., and Langinvainio, H. Shared genes, shared experiences, and similarity of personality: Data from 14,288 adult Finnish co-twins. *Journal of Personality and Social Psychology,* 1988, *54,* 161–171.

Rosenbaum, R. Psychotherapy and integration in India. *Journal of Psychotherapy Integration,* 1992, *2,* 65–70.

Rosenberg, M. Self-concept and psychological well-being in adolescence. In R. L. Leahy (Ed.), *The development of the self.* New York: Academic Press, 205–246, 1985.

Rosenberg, M. *Society and the adolescent self-image.* Princeton, NJ: Princeton University Press, 1965.

——— . *Conceiving the self.* New York: Basic Books, 1979.

——— , and Pearlin, L. I. Social class and self-esteem among children and adults. *American Journal of Sociology,* 1978, *84,* 53–77.

Rosenthal, D. *Genetic theory and abnormal behavior.* New York: McGraw-Hill, 1970.

Rosenthal, R., and Jacobson, L. *Pygmalion in the classroom: Teacher expectation and pupils' intellectual development.* New York: Holt, 1968.

Ross, H. S., and Goldman, B. D. Establishing new social relations in infancy. In T. Alloway, P. Pliner, and L. Krames (Eds.), *Attachment behavior: Advances in the study of communication and affect* (Vol. 3). New York: Plenum, 1977.

Ross, L. The intuitive psychologist and his shortcomings. Distortions in the attribution process. In L. Berkowitz (Ed.), *Advances in experimental social psychology* (Vol. 10). New York: Academic Press, 1977.

Rotter, J. B. *Social learning and clinical psychology.* Englewood Cliffs, NJ: Prentice-Hall, 1954.

——— . Generalized expectancies for internal versus external control of reinforcements. *Psychological Monographs,* 1966, *80*(1, Whole No. 609).

——— . *Applications of a social learning theory of personality.* New York: Holt, 1972.

——— . Some problems and misconceptions related to the construct of internal versus external control of reinforcement. *Journal of Consulting and Clinical Psychology,* 1975, *43,* 55–67.

——— . Interpersonal trust, trustworthiness, and gullibility. *American Psychologist,* 1980, *35,* 1–7.

——— , Chance, J. E., and Phares, E. J. An introduction to social learning theory. In J. B. Rotter, J. E. Chance, and E. J. Phares (Eds.), *Applications of a social learning theory of personality.* New York: Holt, 1972.

Rotton, J., and Frey, J. Air pollution, weather, and violent crimes: Concomitant time-series analysis of archival data. *Journal of Personality and Social Psychology,* 1985, *49,* 1207–1220.

Rowe, D. C. Genetic perspectives on personality. In R. Plomin and G.E. McClearn (Eds.), *Nature, nurture, and psychology.* Washington, DC: American Psychological Association, 179–196, 1993.

Rowe, D. C. *The limits of family influence.* New York: Guilford, 1994.

Rozin, P., and Fallon, A. E. A perspective on disgust. *Psychological Review,* 1987, *94,* 23–41.

Rubin, R. T. The neuroendocrinology and neurochemistry of antisocial behavior. In S. A. Mednick, T. E. Moffitt, and S. A. Stack (Eds.), *The causes of crime.* Cambridge: Cambridge University Press, 1987, pp. 239–262.

Rubin, Z. Measurement of romantic love. *Journal of Personality and Social Psychology,* 1970, *16,* 265–273.

——— . *Liking and loving: an invitation to social psychology.* New York: Holt, 1973.

Ruble, D. N., Brooks-Gunn, J. The experience of menarche. *Child Development,* 1982, *53,* 1557–1566.

Ruble, D. N., Parsons, J. E., and Ross, J. Self-evaluative responses of children in an achievement setting. *Child Development,* 1976, *47,* 990–997.

Rule, B. G., and Neasdale, A. R. Emotional arousal and aggressive behavior. *Psychological Bulletin,* 1976, *83,* 851–863.

Rule, B. G., Taylor, B., and Dobbs, A. R. Priming

effects of heat on aggressive thoughts. *Social Cognition,* 1987, *5,* 131–144.

Runyan, W. M. *Life histories and psychobiography.* New York: Oxford University Press, 1982.

Runyan, W. M. Progress in psychobiography. *Journal of Personality,* 1988, *56,* 295–321.

Rushton, J. P. Socialization and the altruistic behavior of children. *Psychological Bulletin,* 1976, *83,* 898–913.

———, Brainerd, D. J., and Pressley, M. Behavioral development and construct validity: The principle of aggregation. *Psychological Bulletin,* 1983, *94,* 18–38.

Rushton, J. P., Fulker, D. W., Neale, M. C., Nias, D. K. B. and Eysenck, H. J. Altruism and aggression: The heritability of individual differences. *Journal of Personality and Social Psychology,* 1986, *50,* 1192–1198.

Russell, J. A. A circumplex model of affect. *Journal of Personality and Social Psychology,* 1980, *39,* 1161–1178.

———. Pancultural aspects of the human conceptual organization of emotions. *Journal of Personality and Social Psychology,* 1983, *45,* 1281–1288.

Rutter, M. Maternal deprivation, 1972–1978: New findings, new concepts, new approaches. *Child Development,* 1979, *50,* 283–305.

———. *Changing youth in a changing society. Patterns of adolescent development and disorder.* Cambridge, MA: Harvard University Press, 1980.

———, and Garmezy, N. Developmental psychopathology. In P. H. Mussen (Ed.), *Handbook of child psychology;* E. M. Hetherington (Ed.), *Volume IV: Socialization, personality, and social development.* New York: Wiley, 1983.

Ryan, R. M., and Lynch, J. H. Emotional autonomy versus detachment: Revisiting the vicissitudes of adolescence and young adulthood. *Child Development,* 1989, *60,* 340–356.

Ryff, D. C. Self-perceived personality change in adulthood and aging. *Journal of Personality and Social Psychology,* 1982, *42,* 108–115.

Saccuzzo, D. P. Canonical correlation as a method of assessing the correlates of good and bad therapy hours. *Psychotherapy: Theory, research, and practice.* Menasha, Wisconsin: American Psychological Association, 1975.

Sagi, A., and Hoffman, M. L. Empathic distress in newborns. *Developmental Psychology,* 1976, *12,* 175–176.

Sameroff, A. J. Early influences in development: Fact or fancy? *Merrill-Palmer Quarterly,* 1975, *21,* No. 4, 267–294.

———. *Theoretical and empirical issues in the operationalization of transactional research.* Paper presented at the biennial meeting of the Society for Research in Child Development, San Francisco, March, 1979.

———, and Chandler, M. J. Reproductive right and the continuum of caretaking casualty. In F. D. Horowitz (Ed.), *Review of child development research: Vol. 4.* Chicago: University of Chicago Press, 1975.

Sampson, R. J., and Laub, J. H. Crime and deviance over the life course: The salience of adult social bonds. *American Sociological Review,* 1990, *55,* 609–627.

Sarason, B. R., Shearing, E. N., Pierce, G. R., and Sarason, I. G. Interrelations of social support measures: Theoretical and practical implications. *Journal of Personality and Social Psychology,* 1987, *52,* 813–832.

Sarason, I. G. The test anxiety scale: Concept and research. In C. D. Spielberger and I. G. Sarason (Eds.), *Stress and anxiety* (Vol. 5). Washington, DC: Hemisphere, 1978.

———, Smith, R. E., and Diener, E. Personality research: Components of variance attributable to the person and the situation. *Journal of Personality and Social Psychology,* 1975, *3,* 199–204.

Sarason, S. B., Davidson, K. S., Lightchal, F., Waite, R. R., and Ruebush, B. K. *Anxiety in elementary school children.* New York: Wiley, 1960.

Sarbin, T. R. A contribution to the study of actuarial and individual method of predictions. *American Journal of Sociology,* 1942, *48,* 593–602.

Scarr, S., and Carter-Saltzman, L. Twin method: Defense of a critical assumption. *Behavior Genetics,* 1979, *9,* 527–542.

———. Behavior genetics and intelligence. In R. J. Sternberg (Ed.), *Handbook of human intelligence.* New York: Cambridge University Press, 1985.

Schachter, S. *The psychology of affiliation.* Stanford, CA: Stanford University Press, 1959.

———. The interaction of cognitive and physiological determinants of emotional state. In L. Berkowitz (Ed.), *Advances in experimental social psychology* (Vol. 1). New York: Academic Press, 1964.

———, and **Singer, J. E.** Cognitive, social, and physiological determinants of emotional state. *Psychological Review,* 1962, *69,* 379–399.

Schafer, R. The loving and beloved super ego in Freud's structural theory. In O. Fenichel et al. (Eds.), *Psychoanalytic study of the child* (Vol. 15). New York: International Universities Press, 1960.

———. *A new language for psychoanalysis.* New Haven: Yale University Press, 1976.

———. *Retelling a life.* New York: Basic Books, 1992.

Schanberg, S. M., and Kuhn, C. M. Maternal deprivation: An animal model of psychosocial dwarfism. In E. Vadin, T. L. Sourkes, and M. E. Youdin (Eds.), *Enzymes and neurotransmitters.* New York: Wiley, 1980.

Schlosberg, H. Three dimensions of emotion. *Psychological Review,* 1954, *61,* 81–88.

Schludermann, S. M. and Schludermann, E. H. Sociocultural change and adolescents' perceptions of parent behavior. *Developmental Psychology,* 1983, *19*(5), 674–685.

Schmidt, G., and Weiner, B. An attribution-affect-action theory of behavior: Replications of judgments of help giving. *Personality and Social Psychology Bulletin,* 1988, *14,* 610–621.

Schneider, D. J. Implicit theory: A review. *Psychological Bulletin,* 1973, *79,* 294–309.

Schuckit, M. A. Biological vulnerability to alcoholism. *Journal of Consulting and Clinical Psychology,* 1987, *55,* 301–309.

Schuerger, J. M., Zarrella, K. L., and Hotz, A. S. Factors that influence the temporal stability of personality by questionnaire. *Journal of Personality and Social Psychology,* 1989, *56,* 777–783.

Schultz, D. *Theories of personality.* Belmont, CA: Brooks/Cole, 1976.

Schweder, R. A., and Bourne, D. J. Does the concept of the person vary cross-culturally? In R. A. Schweder and R. A. LeVine (Eds.), *Culture Theory; Essays in mind, self, and emotion.* Cambridge, England: Cambridge University Press, 1984, 158–199.

Scott, J. P. *Aggression.* Chicago: University of Chicago Press, 1958.

Sears, R. R., Rau, L., and Alpert, R. *Identification and child rearing.* Stanford, CA: Stanford University Press, 1965.

Seeman, M. Alienation and social learning in a reformatory. *American Journal of Sociology,* 1963, *69,* 270–284.

———, and **Evans, J. W.** Alienation and learning in a hospital setting. *American Sociological Review,* 1962, *27,* 772–783.

Segal, H. *Introduction to the work of Melanie Klein.* New York: Basic Books, 1973.

Seligman, M. E. P. *Helplessness: On depression, development, and death.* San Francisco: Freeman, 1975.

———, and **Maier, S. F.** Failure to escape traumatic shock. *Journal of Experimental Psychology,* 1967, *74,* 1–9.

Seligman, M. E. P. *Learned optimism.* New York: Knopf, 1990.

Service, E. R. *The hunters.* Englewood Cliffs, NJ: Prentice-Hall, 1966.

Shakow, D., and Rapaport, D. The influence of Freud on American psychology. *Psychological Issues,* 1964, No. 13.

Shapira, A., and Madsen, M. C. Between and within group cooperation and competitive behavior among kibbutz and non-kibbutz children. *Developmental Psychology,* 1974, *10,* 140–145.

Shapiro, D., and Giber, D. Meditation and psychotherapeutic effects. *Archives of General Psychiatry,* 1978, *35,* 294–302.

Shapiro, D., and Surwit, R. S. Learned control of physiological functions and disease. In H. Leitenberg (Ed.), *Handbook of behavior modification and behavior therapy.* Englewood Cliffs, NJ: Prentice-Hall, 1976.

Shapiro, D. J., and Alexander, I. E. Extroversion-introversion: Affiliation and anxiety. *Journal of Personality,* 1969, *37,* 387–406.

Shaver, P., and Hazan, C. A biased overview of the study of love. *Journal of Social and Personal Relationships,* 1988, *5,* 473–501.

———, and **Bradshaw, D.** Love as attachment. In Robert J. Sternberg and Michael L. Barma (Eds.), *The psychology of love.* Yale University Press, 1988.

Shaver, P., Schwartz, J., Kirson, D., and O'Connor, C. Emotion knowledge: Further exploration of a prototype approach. *Journal of Personality and Social Psychology,* 1987, *52,* 1061–1086.

Shedler, J., Mayman, M., and Manis, M. The illusion of mental health. *American Psychologist,* 1993, *48,* 1117–1131.

Sheehan, G. *Running and being*. New York: Warner, 1978.

Sheehy, G. *Passages*. New York: Dutton, 1976.

Sheldon, W. H. *Atlas of men*. New York: Harper & Brothers, 1954.

————, and Stevens, S. S. *The varieties of temperament: A psychology of constitutional differences*. New York: Harper, 1942.

————, and Tucker, W. B. *The varieties of human physique: An introduction to constitutional psychology*. New York: Harper, 1940.

Sherif, M., Harvey, O. J., White, B. J., Hood, W. R., and Sherif, C. *Intergroup conflict and cooperation: The robber's cave experiment*. Norman: University of Oklahoma Book Exchange, 1961.

Shevrin, H. Brain wave correlates of subliminal stimulation, unconscious attention, primary and secondary process thinking and repressiveness. In *Psychoanalytic research: Three approaches to the experimental study of subliminal processes* (Psychological Issues Monograph 30). New York: International Universities Press, 1974.

————, and Dickman, S. The psychological unconscious: A necessary assumption for all psychological theory. *American Psychologist*, 1980, *35*, 421–434.

Shields, J. Heredity and environment. In H. J. Eysenck and G. D. Wilson (Eds.), *A textbook of human psychology*. Baltimore: University Park Press, 1976.

Showers, C. Evaluatively integrative thinking about characteristics of the self. *Personality and Social Psychology Bulletin*, 1992, *18*, 719–729.

Shure, M., and Spivack, G. Means-ends thinking, adjustment and social class among elementary school-aged children. *Journal of Consulting and Clinical Psychology*, 1972, *38*, 348–353.

Signorella, M. L., Jamison, W., and Krupa, M. H. Predicting spatial performance from gender stereotyping in activity preferences and in self-concept. *Developmental Psychology*, 1989, *25*, 89–95.

Silverman, L. H. Psychoanalytic theory: "The reports of my death are greatly exaggerated." *American Psychologist*, 1976, *31*, 621–637.

————. The subliminal psychodynamic activation method: Overview and comprehensive listing of studies. In J. Masling (Ed.), *Empirical studies of psychoanalytic theories* (Vol. 1, pp. 69–100). Hillsboro, NJ: Erlbaum, 1983.

————. Research on psychoanalytic psychodynamic propositions. *Clinical Psychology Review*, 1985, *5*, 247–257.

————, Bronstein, A., and Mendelsohn, E. The further use of the subliminal psychodynamic activation method for the experimental study of the clinical theory of psychoanalysis: On the specificity of relationships between manifest psychopathology and unconscious conflict. *Psychotherapy: Theory, Research and Practice*, 1976, *13*, 2–16.

Simmons, R. G., and Blyth, D. A. *Moving into adolescence: The impact of pubertal change and school contact*. New York: Aldine, 1987.

Simonds, P. F. Peers, parents and primates: The developing network of attachments. In T. Alloway, P. Pliner, and L. Krames (Eds.), *Attachment behavior: Advances in the study of communication and affect*. New York: Plenum, 1977.

Simonton, D. K. *Scientific genius: A psychology of science*. Cambridge, England: Cambridge University Press, 1988a.

————. Age and outstanding achievement: What do we know after a century of research? *Psychological Bulletin*, *104*, 1988b, 251–267.

Singer, J. L. *Daydreaming*. New York: Random House, 1966.

————. *The child's world of make believe*. New York: Academic Press, 1973.

————. *Imagery and daydream methods in psychotherapy and behavior modification*. New York: Academic Press, 1974.

————, and Kolligian, Jr. Personality: Developments in the study of private experience. In M. R. Rosenzweig and L. M. Porter (Eds.), *Annual Review of Psychology*, 1987, *38*, 533–574.

Singer, J. L., and Singer, D. G. Family experience and television viewing as predictive of children's imagination, restlessness, and aggression. *Journal of Social Issues*, 1986, *42*, 107–124.

Singer, J. L., and Bonanno, G. A. Personality and private experience: Individual variations in consciousness and in attention to subjective phenomena. In L. A. Pervin (Ed.), *Handbook of personality*. New York: Guilford, 419–444, 1990.

Skinner, B. F. *The behavior of organisms*. New York: Appleton-Century-Crofts, 1938.

————. *Walden two*. New York: Macmillan, 1948.

————. *Science and human behavior*. New York: Macmillan, 1953.

————. Operant behavior. *American Psychologist,* 1963, *18,* 503–515.

————. *Beyond freedom and dignity.* New York: Knopf, 1971.

Slade, A. Quality of attachment and early symbolic play. *Developmental Psychology,* 1987, *23,* 78–85.

Slavin, L. A., Rainer, K. L., McCreary, M. L., and Gowda, K. K. Toward a multicultural model of the stress process. *Journal of Counseling and Development,* 1990, *70,* 156–163.

Smith, C. A., and Ellsworth, C. Patterns of cognitive appraisal in emotion. *Journal of Personality and Social Psychology,* 1985, *48,* 813–838.

————. Patterns of appraisal and emotion related to taking an exam. *Journal of Personality and Social Psychology,* 1987, *52,* 475–488.

Smith, D. L. Psychotherapy and narration: The contribution of Paul Ricoeur. *The Humanistic Psychologist,* 1988, *16,* 323–331.

Smith, P. B., and Bond, M. H. *Social psychology across cultures.* Boston: Allyn & Bacon, 1993.

Smith, P. B., and Pederson, D. R. Maternal sensitivity and patterns of infant-mother attachment. *Child Development,* 1988, *59,* 1097–1101.

Smith, P. K., and Daglish, L. Sex differences in parent and infant behavior in the home. *Child Development,* 1977, *48,* 1250–1254 .

Smith, R., Smythe, L., and Lien, D. Inhibition of helping behavior by a similar or dissimilar nonreactive fellow bystander. *Journal of Personality and Social Psychology,* 1972, *23,* 414–419.

Smith, R. T. A comparison of socioenvironmental factors in monozygotic and dizygotic twins: Testing an assumption. In S. G. Vandenberg (Ed.), *Methods and goals in human behavior genetics.* New York: Academic Press, 1963.

Smollar, J., and Youniss, J. Adolescent self-concept development. In R. L. Leahy (Ed.), *The development of the self.* New York: Academic Press, 247–266, 1985.

Snow, C. Relevance of the notion of a critical period to language acquisition. In M. H. Bernstein (Ed.), *Sensitive periods in development: Interdisciplinary perspectives.* Hillsdale, NJ: Erlbaum, 1987, 183–209.

Snyder, M. Self-monitoring of expressive behavior. *Journal of Personality and Social Psychology,* 1974, *30,* 526–537.

————. *Public appearances/ private realities: The psychology of self-monitoring.* New York: W. H. Freeman, 1987.

————, and Gangestad, S. The nature of self-monitoring. *Journal of Personality and Social Psychology,* 1986, *51,* 125–139.

Snyder, M., and Simpson, J. A. Orientation toward romantic relationships. In Daniel Perlman and Steve Duck (Eds.)., *Intimate relationships: Development, dynamics, deterioration.* Newbury Park, CA: Sage Publications, 1987.

Sommer, R., and Ross, H. Social interaction on a geriatric ward. *International Journal of Social Psychiatry,* 1958, *4,* 128–133.

Sommershield, H., and Reyker, J. Posthypnotic conflict, repression and psychopathology. *Journal of Abnormal Psychology,* 1973, *82,* 278–290.

Sorenson, R. C. *Adolescent sexuality in contemporary America: Personal values and sexual behavior ages 13–19.* New York: Abrams, 1973.

Spanos, N. P. Hypnosis and the modification of hypnotic susceptibility: A social psychological perspective. In P. L. N. Naish (Ed.), *What is hypnosis: Current theories and research.* Philadelphia: Open University Press, 85–120, 1986.

Spanos, N. P., Lush, N. I., and Gwynn, M. I. Cognitive skill-training enhancement of hypnotizability: Generalization effects and trance logic responding. *Journal of Personality and Social Psychology,* 1989, *56,* 795–804.

Spence, D. P. *Narrative truth and historical truth.* New York: Norton, 1982.

Spence, J. T., and Helmrich, R. L. *Masculinity and femininity: Their psychological dimensions, correlates, and antecedents.* Austin: University of Texas Press, 1978.

Sperry, R. W. The great cerebral commissure. *Scientific American,* 1964, *210,* 42–52.

————. Hemisphere deconnection and unity in conscious awareness. *American Psychologist,* 1968, *23,* 723–733.

Spielberger, C. D. The role of awareness in verbal conditioning. In C. W. Eriksen (Ed.), *Behavior and awareness.* Durham, NC: Duke University Press, 1962.

————. Anxiety as an emotional state. In C. D. Spielberger (Ed.), *Anxiety: Current trends in theory and research,* Vol. 1. New York: Academic Press, 1971a.

———— (Ed.). *Anxiety: Current trends in theory and research, Vol. II.* New York: Academic Press, 1971b.

————, Gorsuch, R. L., and Lushene, R. E. *Manual for the state-trait anxiety inventory.* Palo Alto, CA: Consulting Psychologists Press, 1970.

Spinetta, J. J., and Rigler, D. The child-abusing parent: A psychological review. *Psychological Bulletin,* 1972, *77,* 296–304.

Spitz, R. A. Hospitalism. An inquiry into the genesis of psychiatric conditions in early childhood. In O. Fenichel et al. (Eds.), *The psychoanalytic study of the child* (Vol. 1). New York: International Universities Press, 1945.

Spivack, G., and Levine, M. *Self-regulation in acting-out and normal adolescents* (Report M-4351). Washington, DC: National Institute of Health, 1963.

Spivack, G., and Shure, M. B. *Social adjustment of young children: A cognitive approach to solving real-life problems.* San Francisco: Jossey-Bass, 1974.

Sroufe, A., Fox, N., and Pancake, V. Attachment and dependency in developmental perspective. *Child Development,* 1983, *54,* 1615–1627.

Sroufe, L. A., Carlson, E., and Shulman, S. Individuals in relationships: Development from infancy through adolescence. In D. C. Funder, R. D. Parke, C. Tomlinson-Keasey, and K. Widaman (Eds.), *Studying lives through time* (pp. 315–342). Washington, DC: American Psychological Association, 1993.

Sroufe, L. A., and Waters, E. Attachment as an organizational construct. *Child Development,* 1977, *48,* 1184–1199.

————. Heart rate as a convergent measure in clinical and developmental research. *American Behavioral Scientist,* 1977, *20*(3), 295–318.

Stangor, C., and Ruble, D. N. Differential influences of gender schemata and gender constancy on children's information processing and behavior. *Social Cognition,* 1989, *7,* 353–372.

Staub, E. Instigation to goodness: The role of social norms and interpersonal influence. *Journal of Social Issues,* 1972, *28,* 131–150.

————. Helping a distressed person: Social, personality, and stimulus determinants. In L. Berkowitz (Ed.), *Advances in Experimental Social Psy-*

chology (Vol. 7). New York: Academic Press, 1974.

Steck, L., Levitan, D., MacLane, D., and Kelley, H. H. Care, need and conceptions of love. *Journal of Personality and Social Psychology,* 1982, *43,* 481–491.

Steele, C. M., and Josephs, R. A. Drinking your troubles away. II: An attention-allocation model of alcohol's effect on psychological stress. *Journal of Abnormal Psychology,* 1988, *97*(2), 196–205.

Stein, A., and Friedrich, L. K. Television content and young children's behavior. In J. P. Murray, E. A. Rubinstein, and G. A. Comstock (Eds.), *Television and social behavior: Television and social learning* (Vol. 2). Washington, DC: U.S. Government Printing Office, 1971.

Steinberg, L., Elman, J. D., and Mounts, Nina S. Authoritative parenting, psychosocial maturity, and academic success among adolescents. *Child Development,* 1989, *60,* 1424–1436.

Steinberg, L., and Silverberg, L. The vicissitudes of autonomy in adolescence. *Child Development,* 1986, *57,* 841–851.

Stephenson, W. *The study of behavior.* Chicago: University of Chicago Press, 1953.

Stern, D. N. *The interpersonal world of the infant.* New York: Basic Books, 1985.

Sternberg, R. J. *Human intelligence: Perspectives on its theory and measurement.* Norwood, New Jersey: Ablex Publishing Corporation, 1979.

————. A triangular theory of love. *Psychological Review,* 1986, *93,* 119–135.

————, and Grajek, S. The nature of love. *Journal of Personality and Social Psychology,* 1984, *47,* 312–329.

Sternberg, R. J., and Kolligian, J. (Eds.). *Competence considered.* New Haven: Yale University Press, 1990.

Stevenson, H. C., Jr. *New theoretical considerations in assessing racial socialization attitudes in African American youth: Getting an Eye's view of the "WE".* Paper presented as part of an invited symposium on 'Cultural Contexts of Identity Formation—Some International Perspectives,' American Psychological Association Convention, Toronto, Canada, August, 1993.

Stewart, A. J., and Gold-Steinberg, S. Midlife Women's Political Consciousness: Case studies of psychosocial development and political commitment. *Psychology of Women Quarterly,* 1990, *14, 4.*

Stewart, A. J., and Healy, J. M. Jr. Linking individual development and social changes. *American Psychologist,* 1989, *44,* 30–42.

Stewart, K. Dream theory in Malaya. In C. T. Tart (Ed.), *Altered states of consciousness.* New York: Wiley, 1969.

Stipek, D., Weiner, B., and Li, K. Testing some attribution-emotion relations in the People's Republic of China. *Journal of Personality and Social Psychology,* 1989, *56,* 109–116.

Stokols, D. Enviromnental psychology. In L. W. Porter and M. R. Rosenweig (Eds.), *Annual review of psychology* (Vol. 29). Palo Alto, CA: Annual Reviews, 1978.

Stoller, R. J. *Sexual excitement: Dynamics of erotic life.* New York: Pantheon Books, 1979.

Storms, M. D. Videotape and the attribution process: Reversion actors' and observers' points of view. *Journal of Personality and Social Psychology,* 1973, *27,* 165–175.

Stotland, E., and Dunn, R. E. Identification, authoritarian defensiveness, self-esteem, and birth order. *Psychological Monographs,* 1962, *76,* (No. 528).

Stratton, G. M. *Anger: Its religious and moral significance.* New York: Macmillan, 1923.

Straus, M. A. Communication, creativity and problem solving ability of middle and working class families in three societies. *American Journal of Sociology,* 1968, *73,* 417–431.

Strong, E. K. *Vocational interests of men and women.* Stanford, CA: Stanford University Press, 1943.

Struhsaker, T., and Leland, L. Columbines: Infanticide by adult males. In B. B. Smith, D. L. Cheney, R. M. Seyfarth, R. W. Wranghaus and T. T. Struhsaker, *Primate societies.* Chicago: University of Chicago Press, 1987.

Sullivan, H. S. *The interpersonal theory of psychiatry.* New York: Norton, 1953.

Suomi, S. J. Development of attachment and other social behaviors in Rhesus monkeys. In T. Alloway, P. Pliner, and L. Krames (Eds.), *Attachment behavior: Advances in the study of communication and affect.* New York: Plenum, 1977.

———, Harlow, H. F., and Kimball, S. D. Behavioral effects of prolonged partial social isolation in the rhesus monkey. *Psychological Reports,* 1971, *29,* 1171–1177.

Susman, E. J., Inoff-Germain, G., Nottelmann, E. D., Loriaux, D. L., Cutler, G. B., Jr., and Chrauses, G. P. Hormones, emotional dispositions and aggressive attributes in young adolescents. *Child Development,* 1987, *58,* 1114–1134.

Swann, W. B., Griffin, J. J., Predmore, A. C., and Gaines, B. Cognitive-affective crossfire: When self-consistency meets self-enhancement. *Journal of Personality and Social Psychology,* **1987**, *52,* 881–889.

Swann, W. B., and Hill, C. A. When our identities are mistaken: Reaffirming self-conceptions through social interaction. *Journal of Personality and Social Psychology,* 1982, *43,* 59–66.

Swann, W. B., and Read, S. J. Self-verification processes: How we sustain our self-conception. *Journal of Experimental Social Psychology,* 1981, *17,* 351–372.

Taffel, C. Anxiety and conditioning in verbal learning. *Journal of Abnormal and Social Psychology,* 1955, *51,* 496–501.

Tagiuri, R. Person perception. In G. Lindzey and E. Aronson (Eds.), *Handbook of social psychology.* Vol. 3. Reading, MA: Addison-Wesley, 1969.

Tait, R., and Silver, R. C. Coming to terms with major negative life events. In J. S. Uleman and J. A. Bargh (Eds.), *Unintended thought* (pp. 351–382). New York: Guilford, 1989.

Taylor, J. A. A personality scale of manifest anxiety. *Journal of Abnormal and Social Psychology,* 1953, *48,* 285–290.

Taylor, R. B., and Lanni, J. C. Territorial dominance: The influence of the resident advantage in triadic decision making. *Journal of Personality and Social Psychology,* 1981, *41,* 900–915.

Taylor, S., and Gammon, C. Effects of type and dose of alcohol on human physical aggression. *Journal of Personality and Social Psychology,* 1975, *32,* 169–175.

Taylor, S. E., and Brown, J. D. Illusion and well-being: A social psychological perspective on mental health. *Psychological Bulletin,* 1988, *103,* 193–210.

Tedeschi, J. T. Social influence theory and aggression. In R. G. Geen and E. I. Donnerstein (Eds.), *Aggression: Theoretical and empirical reviews.* Volume 1. New York: Academic Press, 1983, pp. 135–162.

Teleki, G. *The predatory behavior of wild chimpanzees.* Lewisburg, PA: Bucknell University Press, 1973.

Tellegen, A., and Atkinson, G. Openness to absorbing and self-altering experiences ("absorption"), a trait related to hypnotic susceptibility. *Journal of Abnormal Psychology,* 1974, *83,* 268–277.

Tellegen, A., Lykken, T., Bouchard, T. J., Jr., Wilcox, K. J., Segal, N. L., Rich, S. Personality similarity in twins reared apart and together. *Journal of Personality and Social Psychology,* 1988, *54,* 1031–1039.

Tempone, V. J. Extension of the repression-sensitization hypothesis to success and failure experience. *Psychological Reports,* 1964, *15,* 39–45.

Tenopyr, M. L. Content-construct confusion. *Personnel Psychology,* 1977, *30,* 47–54.

Tesser, A. The importance of heritability in psychological research: The case of attitudes. *Psychological Review,* 1993, *100,* 129–142.

Thomas, A., and Chess, S. Behavioral individuality in childhood. In L. Aronson, E. Tabach, D. Lehrmon, and J. Rosenblatt (Eds.), *Development and evolution of behavior.* San Francisco: Freeman, 1976.

———, Birch, H. G., Hertzig, M. L., and Korn, S. J. *Behavioral individuality in early childhood.* New York: New York University Press, 1963.

———. *Temperament and behavior disorders in children.* New York: New York University, 1968.

Thompson, R. A. Socioemotional development: Enduring issues and new challenges. *Developmental Review,* 1993, *13,* 372–402.

Thompson, R. A., Connell, J. P., and Bridger, L. J. Temperament, emotion, and social interactive behavior in the strange situation: A component process analysis of attachment system functioning. *Child Development,* 1988, *59,* 1102–1110.

Thompson, W. R. The inheritance and development of intelligence. *Association for Research in Nervous and Mental Diseases: Research Pub.,* 1954, *33,* 209–231.

Thorndike, E. L. *Principles of teaching.* New York: Seiler, 1906.

Thorne, A. The press of personality: A study of conversations between introverts and extroverts. *Journal of Personality and Social Psychology,* 1987, *53,* 718–726.

Tieger, T. On the biological basis of sex differences in aggression. *Child Development,* 1980, *51,* 943–963.

Tinbergen, N. *The study of instinct.* London: Oxford University Press, 1951.

———. Fighting and threat in animals. *New Biology,* 1953, *14,* 9–24.

———. On war and peace in animals and man. *Science,* 1968, *160,* 1411–1418.

Tizard, B. *Adoption: A second change.* London: Open Books, 1977.

———, and Hodges, J. The effect of early institutional rearing on the development of eight-year-old children. *Journal of Child Psychology and Psychiatry,* 1978, *19,* 99–118.

Tizard, B., and Rees, J. The effect of early institutional rearing on the behavior problems and affectional relationships of four-year-old children. *Journal of Child Psychology and Psychiatry,* 1975, *16,* 61–74.

Todd, J. T., and Bohart, A. C. *Foundations of clinical and counseling psychology* (2nd ed.). New York: Harpercollins, 1994.

Toch, H. *Violent men.* Chicago: Aldine, 1969.

Tolman, A. E., Diekmann, K. A., and McCartney, K. Social connectedness and mothering: Effects of maternal employment and maternal absence. *Journal of Personality and Social Psychology,* 1989, *56,* 942–949.

Tomkins, S. S. *The Thematic Apperception Test: The theory and technique of interpretation.* New York: Grune & Stratton, 1947.

———. Affect as the primary motivational system. In M. B. Arnold (Ed.), *Feelings and emotions.* New York: Academic Press, 1970.

Tongas, P. N. The Kaiser-Permanente smoking control program: Its purpose and implications for an HMO. *Professional Psychology,* 1979, *10,* 409–418.

Trevarthen, C. Emotions in infancy: regulators of contacts and relationships with persons. In K. Scherer and P. Ekman, (Eds.), *Approaches to emotion.* Hillsdale, NJ: Erlbaum, 1983.

Triandis, H. C. The self and social behavior in different cultural contexts. *Psychological Review,* 1989, *96,* 506–520.

Troll, L. E., Neugarten, B. L., and Kraines, R. J. Similarities in values and other personality characteristics in college students and their parents. *Merrill-Palmer Quarterly,* 1969, *15,* 323–326.

Trope, Y. Seeking information about one's own ability as a determinant of choice among tasks. *Journal of Personality and Social Psychology,* 1975, *32,* 1004–1013.

Truax, C. B., and Carkhuff, R. R. *Toward effective counseling and psychotherapy: Training and practice.* Chicago: Aldine, 1967.

Truax, C. B., and Mitchell, K. M. Research on certain therapist interpersonal skills in relation to process and outcome. In A. E. Bergin and S. L. Garfield (Eds.), *Handbook of psychotherapy and behavior change.* New York: Wiley, 1971.

Truax, C. B., Wargo, D. G., Frank, J. D., Imber, S. D., Battle, C. C., Hoehn-Saric, R., Nash, E. H., and Stone, A. R. Therapist empathy, genuineness and warmth and patient therapeutic outcome. *Journal of Consulting Psychology,* 1966, *30,* 395–401.

Turiel, E. An experimental test of the sequentiality of developmental states in the child's moral judgments. *Journal of Personality and Social Psychology,* 1966, *3,* 611–618.

Turner, J. A., and Clancy, L. Comparison of operant behavioral and cognitive-behavioral group treatment for chronic low back pain. *Journal of Consulting and Clinical Psychology,* 1988, *56,* 261–266.

Tversky, A., and Kahneman, D. Belief in the law of small numbers. *Psychological Bulletin,* 1971, *76,* 105–110.

————. Causal schemas in judgments under uncertainty. In M. Fishbein (Ed.), *Progress in social psychology.* Hillsdale, NJ: Lawrence Erlbaum, 1980.

Tyler, L. E. *The work of the counselor* (3rd. ed.). New York: Appleton-Century-Crofts, 1969.

————. *Tests and measurements* (2nd ed.). Englewood Cliffs, NJ: Prentice-Hall, 1971.

Uleman, J. S., and Bargh, J. A. (Eds.). *Unintended thought.* New York: Guilford, 1989.

U.S. Bureau of the Census. *Fertility of American women* (Current Population Reports, Series P-20, No. 406). Washington, DC: U.S. Government Printing Office, 1986.

————. *Statistical abstract of the United States.* Washington, DC: U.S. Government Printing Office, 1993.

Vaillant, G. E. *The wisdom of the ego.* Cambridge, MA: Harvard University Press, 1993.

Valins, S. Cognitive effects of false heart-rate feedback. *Journal of Personality and Social Psychology,* 1966, *4,* 400–408.

Valzelli, L. Drugs and aggressiveness. In K. Moyer (Ed.), *Physiology of aggression and implications for control.* New York: Raven, 1976.

Vandell, P. L., Henderson, V. K., and Wilson, K. S. A longitudinal study of children with daycare experiences of varying quality. *Child Development,* 1988, *59,* 1286–1292.

Van Hook, E., and Higgins, E. T. Self-related problems beyond the self-concept: Motivational consequences of discrepant self-guides. *Journal of Personality and Social Psychology,* 1988, *55,* 625–633.

Van Ijzendoorn, M. H., and Kroonenberg, P. M. Trans-cultural patterns of attachment: A meta-analysis of the strange situation. *Child Development,* 1988, *59,* 147–156.

Van Lawick-Goodall, J. Tool-using bird: The Egyptian vulture. *National Geographic,* 1968, *133,* 631–641. (a)

————. The behavior of free-living chimpanzees in the Gombe Stream Reserve. *Animal Behavior Monographs,* 1968(I, Part III). (b)

Vaughn, B. E., Lefever, G., Sefier, R., and Barglow, P. Attachment behavior, attachment security and temperament during infancy. *Child Development,* 1989, *60,* 728–737.

Veroff, J. Social comparison and the development of achievement motivation. In C. P. Smith (Ed.), *Achievement-related motives in children.* New York: Russell Sage, 1969.

————, Atkinson, J. W., Feld, S. C., and Gurin, G. The use of thematic apperception to assess motivation in a nationwide interview study. *Psychological Monographs,* 1960, *74* (No. 12).

Volosinov, V. N. *Freudianism: A Marxist critique.* New York: Academic Press, 1976.

Walker, L. J. Sex differences in the development of word reasoning: A critical review. *Child Development,* 1984, *55,* 677–691.

————. A longitudinal study of moral reasoning. *Child Development,* 1989, *60,* 157–166.

Walster, E., Hatfield, E., Aronson, V., Abrahams, D., and Rottman, L. Importance of physical attractiveness in dating behavior. *Journal of Personality and Social Psychology,* 1966, *4,* 508–516.

Walters, R. H., and Brown, M. Studies of reinforcement of aggression: III. Transfer of responses to an interpersonal situation. *Child Development,* 1963, *34,* 536–571.

Wapner, S., and Hiatt, F. L. *The holistic, de-*

velopmental, systems-oriented approach. Paper presented as part of a symposium on "Psychology's 'World Views': General Approaches to Understanding Human Behavior," American Psychological Association Convention, Toronto, Canada, August, 1993.

Wapner, S. Commentary: Process and context in the conception of cognitive style. In S. Messick (Ed.), *Individuality in learning: Implications of cognitive styles and creativity for human development*. San Francisco: Jossey-Bass, 73–78, 1976.

Washburn, S. L. Human behavior and the behavior of other animals. *American Psychologist, 1978, 33,* 405–418.

Waterman, A. S. Identity development from adolescence to adulthood: An extension of theory and a review of research. *Developmental Psychology, 1982, 18,* 341–358.

——— . Identity as an aspect of optimal psychological functioning. In G. R. Adams, T. P. Gullotta, and R. Montemayer (Eds.), *Adolescent identity formation*. Newbury Park: Sage, 5072, 1992.

Waterman, A. S. Individualism and interdependence. *American Psychologist, 1981, 36,* 762–773.

Waters, E. The reliability and stability of individual differences in infant-mother attachment. *Child Development, 1978, 49,* 483–494.

——— , and Crandall, V. J. Social class and obscured maternal behaviors from 1940 to 1960. *Child Development, 1964, 35,* 1021–1032.

Watkins, R. P., Peterson, R. F., Schweid, E., and Bijou, S. W. Behavior therapy in the home: Amelioration of problem parent-child relations with the parent in a therapeutic role. *Journal of Experimental Child Psychology, 1966, 4,* 99–107.

Watson, G. A. Some personality differences in children related to strict or permissive parental discipline. *Journal of Psychology, 1957, 44,* 227–249.

Watson, J. B. *Behaviorism* (Rev. ed.). New York: Norton, 1930.

Weary, G. B. Self-serving biases in the attribution process: A re-examination of the fact or fiction question. *Journal of Personality and Social Psychology, 1978, 36,* 56–71.

Webb, J. T. *The relation of MMPI two-point codes to age, sex, and education level in a representative nationwide sample of psychiatric outpatients*. Paper presented at Southeastern Psychological Association meetings, Louisville, KY, April 1970.

Webb, W. B. *Sleep, the gentle tyrant*. Englewood Cliffs, NJ: Prentice-Hall, 1975.

——— , and Bonnet, M. H. Sleep and dreams. In M. E. Meyer (Ed.), *Foundations of contemporary psychology*. New York: Oxford University Press, 1979.

Webb, W. B., and Cartwright, R. D. Sleep and dreams. *Annual Review of Psychology, 1978, 29,* 223–252.

Weber, M. (1904) *The Protestant ethic and the spirit of capitalism*. New York: Scribner's, 1958.

Wegner, D. M. Ironic processes of mental control. *Psychological Review, 1994, 101,* 34–52.

Wegner, D. M., and Erber, R. The hyperaccessibility of suppressed thought. *Journal of Personality and Social Psychology, 1992, 63,* 903–912.

Wegner, D. M., and Vallacher, R. R. *Implicit psychology*. New York: Oxford University Press, 1977.

Weinberger, D. A., Schwartz, G., and Davidson, R. Low-anxious, high-anxious and repressive coping styles: Psychometric patterns and behavioral and physiological responses to stress. *Journal of Abnormal Psychology, 1979, 88,* 369–380.

Weinberger, J. L. Can personality change? In T. F. Heatherton and J. L. Weinberger (Eds.), *Can personality change?* Washington, DC: American Psychological Association, 33–350, 1994.

Weiner, B. Effects of motivation on the availability and retrieval of memory traces. *Psychological Bulletin, 1966, 65,* 24–37.

——— . Achievement strivings. In H. London and J. Exner (Eds.), *Dimensions of personality*. New York: Wiley, 1978.

——— . A theory of motivation for some classroom experiences. *Journal of Educational Psychology, 1979, 71,* 3–25.

——— . A cognitive (attribution)–emotion-action model of motivated behavior: An analysis of judgments of help-giving. *Journal of Personality and Social Psychology, 1980, 39,* 186–200.

——— . An attributional theory of achievement motivations and emotion. *Psychological Review, 1985, 92,* 548–573.

——— . *An attributional theory of motivation and emotion*. New York: Springer-Verlag, 1986.

——— . On sin versus sickness: A theory of perceived responsibility and social motivation. *American Psychologist, 1993, 48,* 957–965.

————, and Kukla, A. An attributional analysis of achievement motivation. *Journal of Personality and Social Psychology,* 1970, *15,* 1–20.

Weiner, B., Perry, R. P., and Magnusson, J. An attributional analysis of reactions to stigmas. *Journal of Personality and Social Psychology,* 1988, *55,* 738–748.

Weiner, B., Russell, D., and Lerman, D. Affective consequences of causal ascriptions. In J. H. Harvey, W. J. Ickes, and R. F. Kidd (Eds.), *New directions in attribution research* (Vol. 2). Hillsdale, NJ: Lawrence Erlbaum, 1978.

————. The cognition-emotion process in achievement-related contexts. *Journal of Personality and Social Psychology,* 1979, *37,* 1211–1220.

Weinraub, M., Brooks, J., and Lewis, M. The social network: A reconsideration of the concept of attachment. *Human Development,* 1977, *20,* 31–47.

Weisman, A. D. Coping with untimely death. *Psychiatry,* 1973, *36,* 366–378.

Weisz, J. R., Suwanlert, S., Chaiyasit, W. C., and Walter, B. R. Over- and uncontrolled referral problems among children and adolescents from Thailand and the United States: The Wat and Wai of cultural differences. *Journal of Consulting and Clinical Psychology,* 1987, *55,* 719–726.

Weitzenhoffer, A. M., and Hilgard, E. R. *Stanford hypnotic susceptibility scale.* Stanford, CA: Stanford University Press, 1962.

Wells, B. W. P. The psycho-social influence of building environment: Sociometric findings in large and small office spaces. In R. Gutman (Ed.), *People and buildings.* New York: Basic Books, 1972.

Wells, W. D. Television and aggression: Replication of an experimental field study. Unpublished manuscript, University of Chicago, 1971.

Werner, C. M., Brown, B. B., and Damron, G. Territorial marking in a game arcade. *Journal of Personality and Social Psychology,* 1981, *41,* 1094–1104.

Werner, E. E., and Smith, R. S. *Vulnerable but invincible: A study of resilient children.* New York: McGraw-Hill, 1982.

Westen, D., Ludolph, P., Lerner, H., Ruffins, S., and Wiss, F. C. Object relations in borderline adolescents. *Journal of the American Academy of Child and Adolescent Psychiatry,* 1990, *29,* 338–348.

White, G. L. Some correlates of romantic jealousy. *Journal of Personality,* 1981, *49,* 129–146.

————, and La Barba, R. C. The effects of tactile and kinesthetic stimulation on neonatal development in the premature infant. *Journal of Developmental Psychobiology,* 1976, *9,* 569–577.

White, R. M. *Sleep length and variability: Measurement and interrelationships.* Unpublished doctoral dissertation, University of Florida, 1975.

White, R. W. (Ed.) *The study of lives.* New York: Atherton, 1966.

Whiteman, M. Children's conceptions of psychological causality. *Child Development,* 1967, *38,* 143–155.

Whiting, B. B. *Six cultures: Studies of child rearing.* New York: Wiley, 1966.

———— (Ed.). *Six cultures series* (Vol. I–VII). New York: Wiley, 1966.

————, and Whiting, J. W. M. *Children of six cultures.* Cambridge, MA: Harvard University Press, 1975.

Whiting, J. W. M. The cross-cultural method. In G. Lindzey (Ed.), *Handbook of social psychology.* Reading, MA: Addison-Wesley, 1954.

————. Methods and problems in cross-cultural research. In G. Lindzey and E. Aronson (Eds.), *Handbook of social psychology* (Vol. 2). Reading, MA: Addison-Wesley, 1968.

————, and Child, I. L. *Child training and personality.* New Haven: Yale University Press, 1953.

Whiting, J. W. M., Kluckhohn, R., and Anthony, A. The function of male initiation ceremonies at puberty. In E. E. Maccoby, T. M. Newcomb, and E. L. Hartley (Eds.), *Readings in social psychology* (3rd ed.). New York: Holt, 1958.

Wicker, A. W. Undermanning, performances, and students' subjective experiences in behavioral settings of large and small high schools. *Journal of Personality and Social Psychology,* 1968, *10,* 255–261.

————, and Kirmeyer, S. From church to laboratory to national park: A program of research on excess and insufficient populations in behavior settings. In D. Stokols (Ed.), *Perspectives on environment and behavior.* New York: Plenum, 1977.

Widiger, T. A., and Frances, A. J. Toward a dimensional model for the personality disorders. In P. T. Costa and T. A. Widiger (Eds.), *Personality disor-*

ders and the five-factor model of personality. Washington, DC: American Psychological Association, 19–40, 1994.

Widom, C. S. Does violence beget violence? A critical examination of the literature. *Psychological Bulletin,* 1989, *106,* 3–28.

Wiens, A. H. The assessment interview. In I. B. Weiner (Ed.), *Clinical methods in psychology.* New York: Wiley, 1976.

Wiggins, J. S. Interrelationships among MMPI measures of dissimulation under standard and social desirability instructions. *Journal of Consulting Psychology,* 1959, *23,* 419–427.

——— . Strategic, method, and stylistic variance in the MMPI. *Psychological Bulletin,* 1962, *59,* 224–242.

——— . *Personality and prediction: Principles of personality assessment.* Reading, Mass.: Addison-Wesley, 1973.

——— , Renner, K. E., Clore, G. L., and Rose, R. J. *The psychology of personality.* Reading, MA: Addison-Wesley, 1971.

Williams, L. M. Adult memories of childhood abuse: Preliminary findings from a longitudinal study. *The Advisor: American Professional Society on the Abuse of Children,* 1992, *5(3),* 19–21.

Williamsen, J. A., Johnson, H. J., and Eriksen, C. W. Some characteristics of posthypnotic amnesia. *Journal of Abnormal Psychology,* 1965, *70,* 123–131.

Wilson, E. O. *Sociobiology: The new synthesis.* Cambridge, MA: Harvard University Press, 1975.

——— . Biology and the social sciences. *Daedalus,* 1977, *11,* 127–140.

Wilson, G. Introversion/extraversion. In H. London and J. E. Exner, Jr. (Eds.), *Dimensions of personality.* New York: Wiley, 1978.

Wilson, J. Q., and Herrnstein, R. J. *Crime and human nature.* New York: Simon & Schuster, 1985.

Wilson, T. D., and Linville, P. W. Improving the performance of college freshmen with attributional techniques. *Journal of Personality and Social Psychology,* 1985, *49,* 287–293.

——— . Improving the academic performance of college freshmen: Attribution theory revisited. *Journal of Personality and Social Psychology,* 1982, *42,* 367–376.

Wine, J. D. Test anxiety and direction of attention. *Psychological Bulletin,* 1971, *76,* 92–104.

Winget, C., Kramer, M., and Whitman, R. Dreams and demography. *Canadian Psychiatric Association Journal,* 1972, *17,* 203–208.

Winnicott, D. W. Transitional objects and transitional phenomena. *International Journal of Psychoanalysis,* 1953, *34,* 89–97.

Winston, H. D., and Lindzey, G. Albinism and water escape performance in the mouse. *Science,* 1964, *144,* 189–191.

Winter, D. L., and Carlson, L. A. Using motive scores in the psychobiographical study of an individual. The case of Richard Nixon. *Journal of Personality,* 1988, *56,* 75–104.

Winterbottom, M. R. The relation of childhood training in independence to achievement motivation. Unpublished doctoral dissertation, University of Michigan, 1953.

Witkin, H. A., Dyk, R. B., Faterson, H. F., Goodenough, D. R., and Karp, S. A. *Psychological differentiation.* New York: Wiley, 1962.

Witkin, H. A., Mednick, S. A., Schulsinger, F., Bakkestrom, E., Christianses, K. O., Goodenough, D. R., Hirschhorn, K., Lundsteen, C., Owen, D. R., Phillip, J., Rubin, D. B., and Stocking, M. Criminality in XYY and XXY men. *Science,* 1976, *196,* 547–555.

Witkin, H. A., and Goodenough, D. *Cognitive styles: Essences and origins.* New York: International Universities Press, 1981.

Wolf, T. M. Effects of live modeled sex-inappropriate play behavior in a naturalistic setting. *Developmental Psychology,* 1973, *9,* 120–124.

Wolk, S., and DuCette, J. Intentional performance and incidental learning as a function of personality and task dimensions. *Journal of Personality and Social Psychology,* 1974, *29,* 90–101.

Wolpe, J. *Psychotherapy by reciprocal inhibition.* Stanford, CA: Stanford University Press, 1958.

——— . *The practice of behavior therapy.* New York: Pergamon, 1969.

Woodworth, R. S. *Personal data sheet.* Chicago: Stoelting, 1920.

Worchel, S. The effect of three types of arbitrary thwarting on the instigation to aggression. *Journal of Personality,* 1974, *42,* 300–318.

Wortman, C. B., and Brehm, J. W. Responses to

uncontrollable outcomes: An integration of reactance theory and the learned helplessness model. In L. Berkowitz (Ed.), *Advances in experimental social psychology* (Vol. 8). New York: Academic Press, 1975.

Wortman, C. B., and Silver, R. C. The myths of coping with loss. *Journal of Consulting and Clinical Psychology,* 1989, *57,* 349–357.

Wrightsman, L. *Social psychology* (2nd ed.). Belmont, CA: Brooks/Cole, 1977.

Wylie, R. G. *The self-concept: A review of methodological considerations and measuring instruments* (Rev. ed.) (Vol. 1). Lincoln: University of Nebraska Press, 1974.

————. *The self-concept: Theory and research on selected topics* (Vol. 2). Lincoln: University of Nebraska Press, 1979.

Yando, R. M., and Kagan, J. The effect of task complexity on reflection-impulsivity. *Cognitive Psychology,* 1970, *1(2),* 192–200.

Yates, A. B. *Frustration and conflict.* London: Methuen, 1962.

Yee, B. W. K. Adaptation in old age: Japanese and Vietnamese elderly women. *The Asian American Psychological Association Journal,* 1987, *12,* 38–50.

Young, P. T. *Emotion in man and animal.* New York: Wiley, 1943.

Zahn–Waxler, C., and Radke-Yarrow, M. The development of altrusion: Alternative research strategies. In N. Eisenberg-Berg (Ed.), *The development of prosocial behavior.* New York: Academic Press, 1982.

Zajonc, R. B. Feeling and thinking: Preferences need no inferences. *American Psychologist,* 1980, *39,* 151–175.

Zigler, E., and Yospe, L. Perceptual defense and the problem of response suppression. *Journal of Personality,* 1960, *28,* 220–239.

Zillman, D. Excitation transfer in communication-mediated aggressive behavior. *Journal of Experimental Social Psychology,* 1971, *7,* 419–434.

————. Attribution and misattribution of excitatory reactions. In J. H. Harvey, W. J. Ickes, and R. F. Kidd (Eds.), *New directions in attribution research* (Vol. 2). Hillsdale, NJ: Lawrence Erlbaum, 1978.

————. *Connections between sex and aggression.* Hillsdale, NJ: Lawrence Erlbaum, 1984.

————, **Bryant, J., Comiskey, P., and Medoff, N.** Excitation and hedonic valence in the effect of erotica on motivated intermale aggression. *European Journal of Social Psychology,* 1981, *11,* 233–252.

Zillman, D., and Cantor, J. R. Effect of timing of information about mitigating circumstances on emotional responses to provocation and retaliatory behavior. *Journal of Experimental Social Psychology,* 1976, *12,* 38–55.

Zillman, D., Katcher, A. H., and Milarsky, B. Exitation transfer from physical exercise to subsequent aggressive behavior. *Journal of Experimental Social Psychology,* 1972, *8,* 247–259.

Zinberg, N. E. (Ed.). *Alternate states of consciousness.* New York: Free Press, 1977.

Zubin, J., Eron, L. D., and Schumer, F. *An experimental approach to projective techniques.* New York: Wiley, 1965.

Zuckerman, M., Koestner, R., DeBoy, T., Garcia, T., Maresca, B. C., and Sartoris, J. M. To predict some of the people some of the time: A reexamination of the moderator variable approach in personality theory. *Journal of Personality and Social Psychology,* 1988, *54,* 1006–1019.

Index of Names

Index of Concepts